TESTING PROBLEMS
IN PERSPECTIVE

TESTING PROBLEMS
IN PERSPECTIVE

TWENTY-FIFTH ANNIVERSARY VOLUME
OF TOPICAL READINGS FROM THE INVITATIONAL
CONFERENCE ON TESTING PROBLEMS

EDITED BY ANNE ANASTASI
Professor of Psychology, Graduate School, Fordham University

AMERICAN COUNCIL ON EDUCATION

PREFACE

This book has been prepared under the auspices of Educational Testing Service to memorialize the twenty-fifth anniversary of its Invitational Conference on Testing Problems. The conference originated in 1936 as the Conference of State Testing Leaders, sponsored by the American Council on Education. Following a change in name, new sponsorship, a broadening of scope, a phenomenal growth in size, and a four-year interruption during World War II, the conference held its twenty-fifth meeting in 1964. During each of these years, the conference met at the Hotel Roosevelt, in New York City, on the last Saturday in October. While ETS handles all meeting arrangements and administrative matters for the conference, the selection of topics and speakers is the responsibility of a Conference Chairman elected each year from nationally recognized leaders in psychometrics.

The nature, origins, and development of the Invitational Conference itself are briefly surveyed in Chapter 1. Papers presented at the early conferences, prior to the annual publication of *Proceedings,* are cited in that chapter chiefly because of their historical interest. In the rest of the book, however, the orientation is predominantly substantive rather than historical. Chapters 2 to 12 contain 58 papers presented by 47 different authors at Invitational Conferences held from 1947 to 1964. These papers have been selected and organized in terms of their specific contributions to significant topics in educational and psychological measurement. That some are also historically noteworthy, because of the time at which they were given, is incidental. The editor's introduction to each chapter is designed to integrate the papers on each topic and point up their special significance. The book has been so organized as to be maximally useful to the professional worker in tests and measurement who wishes to keep abreast of developments in the field, as well as to the student in courses on psychological testing, test construction, multivariate analysis, and the educational use of tests.

Since all papers at the Invitational Conference are given by invitation only, they are characteristically of high quality and each can be expected to make a significant contribution at the time it is presented. For this reason, the complete list of conference papers has been reproduced by title and author in the Appendix. Those papers given from 1946 on have been published in the annual *Proceedings,* although their availability in this form is limited.

With a few exceptions, papers presented prior to 1946 are unavailable and could not be considered for inclusion in this book. Other papers were eliminated because they represented an earlier treatment of a topic discussed more fully at a later conference, sometimes by the same author. Still others were timely when presented but soon became outdated because of developments in the field. The papers dealing with automation and machine methods provide a good example of this basis for exclusion. Some papers were omitted because they constituted interim reports of ongoing projects which were more fully reported in later publications. On the other hand, a paper was likely to be included if it provided a succinct and readable summary of a complete research project, technique, or topic treated elsewhere at much greater length or at a more highly technical level. Such papers serve a useful function for the nonspecialist who may find a reading of the more comprehensive source impracticable. For the sake of well-balanced topical coverage, final selection of papers was also influenced by the relative number available on different topics. Thus a larger proportion of papers is likely to have been retained on those topics covered more sparsely at the Invitational Conference. It is also understandable that the more recent conferences are more fully represented in this collection than are the earlier conferences.

Because of the variety and complexity of selection criteria, it must be stressed that exclusion of any one paper from the collection is no indication that it is intrinsically less meritorious than those included. It should also be noted that since 1951 the conferences have included a luncheon address by a distinguished speaker, and although these luncheon addresses have been included in the complete listing in the Appendix, for various reasons it was decided not to reproduce any in the book. A few were unavailable, several would have required condensation because of length, and most dealt with topics of current interest at the time but not directly relevant to testing.

The procedures followed in the selection of individual papers fell into three major steps and involved independent evaluation by many judges. First, all papers published in the *Proceedings,* covering the period from 1946 to 1964, were classified into major specialties; the papers within each specialty were submitted to the appropriate ETS staff member for rating on a five-point scale with regard to suitability for this collection. Then the papers presented at each conference, regardless of topical specialty, were submitted to the Chairman of that conference for rating on the same scale. All papers receiving a rating of 3 or higher by either rater were re-evaluated by the editor, who made the final selection.

In all stages in the preparation of this book, the editor has received invaluable assistance from the ETS staff and has relied heavily on its resources. The project was initiated by William W. Turnbull, who also served as Chairman of the Selection Committee and who provided continuing advice and encouragement. Anna Dragositz performed such diversified and numerous functions, that her role can only be described as that of executive director of the project. John A. Connolly was responsible for the initial topical classification of the papers for rating purposes and for the tabulation of all ratings. Thanks are extended to the following ETS staff members who participated in the rating procedure: Miriam M. Bryan, William E. Coffman, John E. Dobbin, Henry S. Dyer, John S. Helmick, John K. Hemphill, Frederic M. Lord, S. Donald Melville, Samuel Messick, William B. Schrader, and Wesley W. Walton. Grateful acknowledgment is made to Louise R. Ritenour and Estelle Spremulli for their thorough and expert editing of the final papers and for their assistance in proofreading, preparation of author index, and other editorial functions. Finally, the editor wishes to express her appreciation to the Conference Chairmen, whose names are listed in the Appendix, for finding time in their busy schedules to rate the papers presented at the conferences they had organized. In addition, Ben D. Wood and Herschel T. Manuel graciously provided unpublished material and information concerning the early conferences, which helped to fill out the historical background of the Invitational Conference.

ANNE ANASTASI

TABLE OF CONTENTS

PART II: PSYCHOMETRIC THEORY AND METHOD

1 · THE INVITATIONAL CONFERENCE ON TESTING PROBLEMS

THE PHENOMENAL GROWTH of educational and psychological testing during the second quarter of the twentieth century, as well as the broadening utilization of mass testing programs as aids to important practical decisions, called for an increasing sense of professional responsibility on the part of psychometricians. With the development of group intelligence tests and personality inventories, which are easy to administer and score, relatively untrained persons began to use tests too widely and too soon. Interpretations of test scores in individual cases were often of questionable value. Moreover, the communication of test results to laymen—such as administrators, parents, or examinees themselves—presented a host of professional problems, even when tests were employed by appropriately trained professional persons.

Aware of these serious professional problems, psychometricians began to take steps to curb the misuse of tests, to raise standards of test construction, and to improve the interpretation of test results. An outstanding example of such steps was the initiation in 1938 of the series of *Mental Measurements Yearbooks,* under the editorship of Oscar K. Buros (6). Particularly through their critical test reviews, prepared by experts in each area, these yearbooks stimulate test authors and publishers to meet higher standards of test development and help the test user in evaluating and choosing tests. Another major step was the publication in 1954 of the *Technical Recommendations for Psychological Tests and Diagnostic Techniques* (2), prepared by a joint committee of the American Psychological Association, the American Educational Research Association, and the National Council on Measurements Used in Education. A companion statement, entitled *Technical Recommendations for Achievement Tests* (1), was prepared by the committees on test standards of the two latter groups and published in 1955 by the National Education Association. A revised edition, combining both sets of recommendations, was published in 1966 by the American Psychological Association under the title of *Standards for Educational and Psychological Tests and Manuals* (3).

It was in the same spirit of professional responsibility and concern about the proper use of tests that the Invitational Conference on Testing Problems originated. In 1936 a small group of psychometricians, composed primarily of leaders of state-wide educational testing programs, met informally to discuss their common problems on the day following a two-day educational conference. This meeting became immediately established as an annual affair and soon evolved into the much broader Invitational Conference on Testing Problems now held under the auspices of Educational Testing Service.

History of the Invitational Conference

The Invitational Conference on Testing Problems began as an offshoot of the Educational Conference. The latter was first convened in 1932 under the joint auspices of the American Council on Education and the Educational Records Bureau.[1] Commonly known as the "ERB Conference," it has met annually in New York City, except for the war years (1942–45).

Immediately following the 1936 Educational Conference, the Committee on Measurement and Guidance of the American Council on Education called a short meeting of leaders of state testing programs who had been attending the Educational Conference. Thirteen state testing programs were represented at this meeting, together with the sponsoring committee. Similar meetings were convened in 1937, 1938, and 1939 under the same auspices and conditions. Brief references to the first three meetings (4, pp. 17–18; 8; 13, p. 12; 18, p. 300) and a fuller account of the 1939 meeting (14) were published in *The Educational Record,* the official organ of the American Council on Education. In the reports of these four meetings, the title employed was "Conference of State Testing Leaders." The fifth conference, held in 1940, was described under the title of "Conference of Testing Leaders" (15). At this point, the participants modestly objected to being designated as "testing leaders," a label which seems to have taken on a different and broader connotation from that originally intended! Accordingly, the name was changed to "Invitational Conference on Testing Problems," the name employed by all subsequent conferences beginning in 1941 (16).

---

[1] Reports of these conferences were published in *Educational Record Supplements* in the year following each conference.

Since no meetings of either the Educational Conference or its offshoot were held between 1942 and 1945, the seventh Invitational Conference was held in 1946 and the eighth in 1947, both under the original auspices. Beginning in 1948, sponsorship of the Invitational Conference was assumed by the newly formed Educational Testing Service. The year 1964 marked the twenty-fifth consecutive session of the Invitational Conference under its present or earlier names. At that time it was deemed appropriate to memorialize the occasion with an overview of the conference and a set of representative conference papers, included in this book.

Over the years, the Invitational Conference has expanded in size, in coverage of topics, and in heterogeneity of participants. Beginning with a small group of leaders of state educational testing programs, the conference gradually came to include educators and psychologists concerned with all types of tests in a variety of contexts and from both theoretical and practical viewpoints. The range of topics discussed was correspondingly broadened, as will be seen in the next section. It is interesting to note that that the second postwar conference, held in 1947, was the first meeting containing no direct discussion of state or regional testing programs. It was also the first to include papers on personality testing—and projective techniques, at that—to which the entire morning session was devoted. By this time, the metamorphosis was complete, in both name and content.

The most dramatic change undoubtedly occurred in sheer size. At the first conference, in 1936, there were a total of 19 participants.[2] The report of the 1939 meeting, attended by 33 persons, contained the following statement: "Although the conference has been an invitational affair, the only restriction on guests has been designed to keep the group small enough to gather around one table" (14, p. 184). This objective quickly proved unrealistic. In 1940 and 1941, the number of participants rose to 50 (15) and 71 (16). At the first postwar conference, it was 109 (17). In 1964, although attendance was still by invitation, the number of persons registered was 935 (12).

Lest it appear that the directors of state testing programs—who started it all—were lost in this metamorphosis, it should be added that they not only continued to participate in the expanded Invitational Conference, but in 1951 they also reconstituted themselves into a new group that meets informally at Princeton on the two days following the Invitational Conference. It is to be hoped that this rebirth will permit them to pursue their problems without further metamorphoses!

[2] Unpublished minutes of 1936 conference, provided by courtesy of Herschel T. Manuel.

CONTENT OF EARLY CONFERENCES

At the initial meeting in 1936, discussion focused sharply on the need for preventing the misuse of tests in educational contexts. Following reports by the participants on the status of their individual testing programs and the principal difficulties they were facing, a memorandum was prepared which still sounds quite timely after 25 years. It is obvious that the particular problems to which it was addressed have not yet been satisfactorily solved and that they underlie some of the current public unrest regarding test use. The memorandum contained three principal recommendations, which were extensively discussed and strongly endorsed at the following year's meeting (4, p. 18). Because of its broad interest, the first of these recommendations is reproduced in detail below.

Those conducting state testing programs must recognize that it is their major responsibility to educate teachers and school administrators to a wiser and more effective use of test materials in dealing with the individual pupil. This is a responsibility which transcends that of insuring high quality in the technical materials and services required in the testing program, since the techniques of testing have already been developed to a point far beyond the ability of the schools to make the most of the possibilities now presented. In any attempt to educate the test users, major emphasis must be placed on the use of test results for the guidance of the individual pupil, while the use of tests in the evaluation of formal group instruction, and the values derived from testing programs by any single cooperating institution, must be deliberately minimized. The following are suggestive of approaches that might be employed in an adequate educative program:

a) Group conferences should be arranged in various strategic points throughout the state to acquaint teachers and administrators with the possibility of guidance through testing. Such conferences might well be organized in cooperation with state departments of education, teacher training institutions, teachers' associations, etc.

b) Demonstration centers should be selected for the practical application of the best that is known about test usage. Without doubt, demonstration centers can be the best single method of bringing to teachers and administrators the value of systematical test use.

c) Teacher training institutions should be encouraged to vitalize and to give greater prominence to courses in testing and guidance. What is needed is a type of course in which major stress is placed upon the significance of individual differences, upon the underlying principles of good test construction (rather than upon the characteristics of special tests), upon the nature and function of achievement tests (with emphasis upon limitations of existing instruments), and upon the case-study approach in guidance. Only the minimum of statistics needed for an appreciation of the magnitude of individual differences and for the interpretation of norms should be included.

d) Literature regarding test usage should be prepared and distributed widely with the administrator and classroom teacher in mind. Such literature should avoid technical statistical material as much as possible. It should draw attention to, and attempt to correct, the many prevalent misconceptions concerning tests. It should draw specific attention to the many abuses of test results in the hands of administrators and should contain concrete and practicable suggestions for the use of test results in the classroom situation. Above all, it should strive to develop in the teacher's mind the broad principles of individual guidance through concrete case-study types of illustrations. It was recognized that the programs in many states were now limited by the absence of clear interpretations of their purpose and activities.[3]

The second major recommendation was that leaders of state testing programs assume the responsibility for coordinating the activities of all agencies concerned in a state testing and guidance program. Finally, the conference agreed that there definitely was a need for a national coordinating agency on testing problems, and drew up a long list of services that might be rendered by such an agency to improve both the construction and the use of tests.

During the period when these conferences were getting under way, several educational innovations were germinating; these innovations occupied a prominent place in the informal and unscheduled discussions of the early conferences. Ideas that are now generally accepted were presented at these sessions by some of the pioneers, often arousing vigorous protests from other participants. Reminiscing about the first three conferences, Ben D. Wood writes, "Technological equipment [such as classroom films and automated teaching devices], like objective tests, was roundly denounced as mechanizing education by some of the conferees who insisted on using only essay examinations and who also identified education as teaching by the teachers instead of independent, self-propelled learning by the individual pupils. . . . One other important idea that came in early in our discussions was . . . that our tests should involve more problems and fewer rote memory facts and thus would influence both teachers and students to deal with ideas and reasoning instead of memorized facts."[4] These ideas were shortly

[3] Unpublished minutes of 1936 conference, provided by courtesy of Herschel T. Manuel.
[4] Personal communication from Ben D. Wood, June 3, 1965.

implemented in the development of the now-familiar types of achievement tests that combine objective item forms with problems requiring the application of knowledge, critical thinking, and other complex intellectual processes.

The need for disseminating information about tests and improving the use of test results was repeatedly recognized in these conferences. The previously cited memorandum prepared at the initial meeting in 1936 included several relevant recommendations, with particular reference to teachers and school administrators. At the 1938 conference, W. V. Bingham again observed that "the making of tests has outstripped the research without which test results have but vague meaning for guidance" (5, p. 142). Calling attention to the lack of comparability of scores obtained on different tests, he recommended the preparation of a "counselor's handbook for ready reference" that would provide information on equivalent scores on different tests, predictive validity, and other interpretive aids. With regard to the use of tests in guidance, which was the major theme of his paper, Bingham emphasized that the primary goal of testing is to help the student to know himself. In a paper entitled "The Use of Test Results," also presented at the 1938 conference, H. T. Manuel focused on the potential uses of tests in individualizing instruction. Once more it was brought out that teachers need to be educated in the use of test results as an important source of information on individual differences. After noting several misuses of tests in education, Manuel added, "I sometimes wish that at least a few tests could be patented so that they could not be used at all except to understand and assist individual children" (11, p. 161). In the light of some of the current concerns about misuses of tests, this statement appears quite timely.

At the first postwar meeting in 1946, E. F. Lindquist gave a progress report on "The Measurement Book Project of the American Council on Education" (17). The entire project called for the preparation of two distinctly different volumes: an elementary manual for classroom teachers, concerned primarily with the preparation of informal classroom examinations; and a handbook for advanced students and measurement workers, concerned primarily with the theory and technique of test construction. The elementary manual was published in 1936 (9). The second, more advanced volume, subsequently published under the title of *Educational Measurement* (10), was the subject of Lindquist's progress report. In addition, three of the co-authors engaged in the preparation of the book presented papers at the same session, dealing with units and norms, validity, and reliability. They thus provided short samples of the type of material to be covered in the projected book. Following its publication in 1951, this book served for many years as a comprehensive and authoritative source of information on the theory and technique of educational measurement; plans for a revised edition were initiated in 1965.

No account of conference discussions on the dissemination of test information would be complete without mention of Buros' reports on the *Mental Measurements Yearbooks.* In 1938, the conference was first told about the forthcoming 1938 *Yearbook,* which launched the series. And in the published summary of the 1941 conference we learn that "Oscar K. Buros, editor of *Mental Measurements Yearbook,* presented an informal but delightful account of the difficulties and pleasures which characterized the monumental task of compiling, publishing, and selling the *Yearbooks"* (16, p. 140).

Automation and computer technology in education represent a continuing interest of the Invitational Conference over the years. At the earliest meetings, this interest centered on the newly developed IBM test-scoring machine. A major item on the agenda of the 1937, 1938, and 1939 conferences was a report by IBM representatives on the current status of this machine and its availability at centers throughout the country. These reports were followed by detailed discussions of such questions as the development of an item-analysis unit, the design and improvement of answer sheets, and the desirability of uniform rates for scoring services. A special committee was appointed to study these problems further.

Another topic receiving considerable attention at the conferences is the need for improving norms and derived scores. In 1938 and 1939, the agenda included reports by J. C. Flanagan on the Scaled Scores developed for use with the achievement tests of the Cooperative Test Service. These scores, subsequently described in a printed bulletin (7), were standard scores so adjusted that a score of 50 represented the average score expected if an unselected group of students of a given age and in a given grade took a standard course in the particular subject; the unit was one-tenth of the standard deviation of such a group. In the development of these scores, students of "average ability" were chosen on the basis of grade placement for age, as well as performance on an intelligence test and a general achievement battery. These Scaled Scores represent one of the first attempts to meet a common difficulty in the normative interpretation of achievement test scores. Since students who study different subjects differ in academic aptitude, they do not provide comparable samples for normative purposes. The individual taking a "difficult" subject would thus be handicapped and the one taking an "easy" subject favored by the use of unadjusted norms.

Uniformity of units and norms was again a focus of interest at the 1939 conference. H. T. Manuel urged the development of "universal units that will form a continuous scale or succession of scales each articulated to the preceding and reaching from the abilities of the new-born to those of superior adults" (14, p. 186). He proposed further that basic tests could then be prepared and calibrated in terms of these units, and all test authors and publishers could translate their scores into the units of these basic tests. At the same meeting, H. A. Toops presented a paper on the use of a "standard million" in compiling test norms. Utilizing the actuarial concept of "standard million," Toops went on to describe seven criteria for choosing a representative, standard sample on which adequate norms might be based.

At the 1940 conference, E. E. Cureton recommended the development of an "anchor test," as contrasted with Toops's "standard million" technique. In this connection, he again referred to the possible establishment of a central agency for the coordination of test research and the dissemination of information about tests—a recurrent consideration first proposed, it will be recalled, in the 1936 Memorandum. Maintaining that such an agency should do more than investigate and report upon tests, Cureton concluded with the following list of its recommended functions:

1) This agency should survey existing factorial analyses of the major school subjects, and make or encourage others to make additional investigations if necessary.

2) It should itself construct a basic anchor test which should be an improvement on existing group intelligence scales.

3) It should undertake to find a genuine representative sample of the general population, and to derive accurate age norms for the anchor test.

4) It should investigate the curve of growth of mental ability carefully, as well as the distribution of ability at each age level. These studies should lead to the derivation of a system of equal-unit scores for the test, and to the determination of the true zero-point in terms of these scores.

5) It should make a special study of the score-levels of young adults in order to determine the location of the 100-point. The equal-unit scale could then be transformed into the maturity scale of final level scores. The age norms could also be transformed into the same units.

6) It should equate the raw scores of acceptable intelligence tests and achievement tests of all publishers to this common scale.

7) Finally, it should publish a test manual giving all of this information. The date of publication of such a manual would be the date of maturity of educational and mental measurements as a science, and of educational guidance and counseling as a profession (15, pp. 135–136).

In addition to units and norms, other technical characteristics of tests have been a frequent subject of conference papers. In the early conferences, examples include a discussion of test reliability by M. W. Richardson in 1940, containing references to the newly derived Kuder-Richardson techniques, and a re-examination of the concept of reliability in 1941 by Paul Horst. Both papers stressed the many unsolved problems that face research workers in determining the reliability of measuring instruments. Validity received considerably less attention at these early conferences, the first scheduled paper on this topic being P. J. Rulon's discussion at the 1946 conference. Undoubtedly one reason for the relatively late consideration of this test characteristic is the primary focus of the participants on achievement tests, in which the problem is less central than in aptitude and other predictive or diagnostic tests. Some implications for the concept of validity, however, can be found in J. M. Stalnaker's 1939 paper entitled "Factor Analysis from the Point of View of the Practical Test Man," which contained an incisive critique of the Thurstone Tests of Primary Mental Abilities. Unfortunately, the shortcomings described by Stalnaker were not corrected in later editions of these tests.

Another area of interest reflected the increasing use of tests in the selection and classification of personnel, with particular reference to occupational specialties. Business occupations are represented by W. J. E. Crissy's 1939 paper outlining the testing program of a joint committee of the National Office Managers Association and the Business Council of the Business Education Association, designed to measure proficiency and certify candidates in such fields as typing, stenography, machine transcription, calculating machine operation, bookkeeping, and filing. The 1946 conference included a paper by A. E. Traxler describing a project on the selection of personnel for public accounting, as well as K. W. Vaughn's report on various projects of the Graduate Record Office, including one on the development of tests for engineering school applicants. The use of tests for military purposes was discussed—with commendable foresight—at the 1940 and 1941 conferences by W. V. Bingham and by T. W. Harrell and H. W. Bues, Jr. In view of the extensive and effective utilization of tests in all branches of the armed services during World War II, it is of some historical interest to note that, as late as 1941, the speakers felt it necessary to report in their concluding statement that "In general, the use of psychological tests for classification within the Army is well accepted by Army authorities" (16, p. 139).

Finally, certain papers highlight the interest in strictly educational problems characterizing many of the early conference participants. Apart from the continuing discussions of state, regional, and national testing programs at the elementary and high school levels, with which the conferences began, this educational orientation is illustrated at the 1940 conference by P. J. Rulon's progress report on the American Council on Education study of educational evaluation, which he directed, and by J. U. Yarborough's discussion of guidance in education, based on the experiences of the Texas Commission on Coordination in Education; and at the 1941 conference, by R. W. Tyler's paper on the influence of tests on teaching and by A. E. Traxler's paper on problems of measurement in reading.

It is also interesting to note that in the general discussion at the end of the 1946 conference, one of the participants remarked that "for a long time, this group has regarded itself as test technicians. The group is beginning to show a little more interest in the whole science of education" (17, p. 74). Subsequent conferences, however, did not actually follow this trend. Although topical coverage has broadened and papers dealing with strictly educational problems are certainly still included, the greatest increase has been in the number of papers on testing problems, and especially on their more technical aspects.

ORGANIZATION OF SELECTED PAPERS

All the papers presented at the 25 Invitational Conferences between 1936 and 1964 have been listed by title and author in the Appendix. The papers reproduced in their entirety in Chapters 2 to 11 have been grouped according to major topics, without regard to chronology. Since no *Proceedings* were published prior to 1946, the earlier papers have been cited only in the historical survey of the preceding section. It might be noted that, while chronology was not a factor in the selection of papers to be reproduced, the papers actually chosen cover the conference years from 1947 to 1964, each of these years being represented by at least one paper. The entire postwar period is thus fairly well sampled.

In both selecting and organizing papers for this book, we were guided in part by the topics that are of primary interest today. In this connection, however, we were impressed with the viability of many of the topics discussed during the early conferences. Several recurrent themes can be identified throughout the 25-year period.

The book comprises three major parts, in addition to the present chapter which provides a short historical orientation. Part I, *Test Development and Use,* contains papers of relatively broad interest to educators and test users, grouped under the following topics: goals and functions of testing, the educational context in which tests are used, methods for improving the construction and use of educational tests, and the utilization of tests in the selection and evaluation of professional personnel. Part II, *Psychometric Theory and Method,* is concerned with the more technical aspects of test construction, measurement theory, and the interpretation of test results within the context of relevant psychological research. The specific topics covered are: norms, units, and scales; reliability, validity, and homogeneity; multivariate procedures in test construction; and nature and development of intellectual traits. Part III, *Special Problems in the Assessment of Individual Differences,* deals with certain methodological and interpretive problems of measurement encountered in special situations. The papers in this section fall under three headings: cultural differentials in test performance, personality testing, and judgmental assessment procedures.

REFERENCES

1. American Educational Research Association & National Council on Measurements Used in Education. *Technical recommendations for achievement tests.* Washington, D.C.: National Education Association, 1955.
2. American Psychological Association. *Technical recommendations for psychological tests and diagnostic techniques.* Washington, D.C.: American Psychological Association, 1954. (Also in *Psychological Bulletin,* 1954, 51, No. 2, Part 2.)
3. American Psychological Association. *Standards for educational and psychological tests and manuals.* Washington, D.C.: American Psychological Association, 1966.
4. Atkins, J. K. The 1937 Educational Conference: a review. *The Educational Record,* 1938, 19 (Suppl. No. 11), 5–18.
5. Bingham, W. V. A national perspective on testing and guidance. *The Educational Record,* 1939, 20 (Suppl. No. 12), 137–150.
6. Buros, O. K. (Ed.) *The nineteen thirty-eight mental measurements yearbook.* New Brunswick, N.J.: Rutgers Univer. Press, 1938.
7. *The Cooperative Achievement Tests: a bulletin reporting the basic principles and procedures used in the development of their system of scaled scores.* New York: Cooperative Test Service, American Council on Education, 1939.
8. Conference of State Testing Leaders. *The Educational Record,* 1937, 18, 139–140.
9. Hawkes, H. E., Lindquist, E. F., & Mann, C. R. (Eds.) *The construction and use of achievement examinations.* Boston: Houghton Mifflin, 1936.

10. Lindquist, E. F. (Ed.) *Educational measurement.* Washington, D.C.: American Council on Education, 1951.
11. Manuel, H. T. The use of test results. *The Educational Record,* 1939, 20 (Suppl. No. 12), 151–162.
12. *Proceedings of the 1964 Invitational Conference on Testing Problems.* Princeton, N.J.: Educational Testing Service, 1965.
13. Seder, Margaret, & Shanner, W. M. The 1938 Educational Conference: a review. *The Educational Record,* 1939, 20 (Suppl. No. 12), 5–13.
14. Shank, D. J. The State Testing Leaders meet again. *The Educational Record,* 1940, 21 (Suppl. No. 13), 184–189.
15. Shank, D. J. The Testing Leaders Conference. *The Educational Record,* 1941, 22 (Suppl. No. 14), 131–136.
16. Shank, D. J. The Invitational Conference on Testing Problems. *The Educational Record,* 1942, 23 (Suppl. No. 15), 135–140.
17. Vaughn, K. W. (Ed.) National projects in educational measurement: a report of the 1946 Invitational Conference on Testing Problems. *American Council on Education Studies, Series I—Reports of Committees and Conferences,* 11, No. 28, 1947.
18. Zook, G. F. The President's annual report (ACE). *The Educational Record,* 1937, 18, 290–326.

PART I

TEST DEVELOPMENT AND USE

2 · GOALS AND FUNCTIONS OF TESTING

THE TWENTY-FIFTH ANNIVERSARY of the Invitational Conference comes at a time when testing is the target for public attack from several angles. Despite the cautions and reservations of psychometricians, the rapid expansion of testing in many practical contexts has led to certain difficulties. In this period of over-popularization, tests have been widely misunderstood, misused, and misinterpreted. As a result, the public has come to have misgivings about testing in general. Exploitation of these feelings by sensational writers has in turn aroused more vigorous public protests, as illustrated by legislative proposals to curb testing. Against such a background, it seems appropriate to introduce this collection of papers with a sober and considered examination of some of the principal popular criticisms of testing. Ebel's paper provides an incisive analysis of major issues, with special reference to the use of tests in education. After identifying four harmful consequences that critics have attributed to tests, he shows how the proper use of tests can not only prevent these potential dangers but also achieve desirable goals.

Among the potential social dangers of testing discussed by Ebel is that the extensive use of tests as a basis for decision making may lead to a society dominated by the testers. Some test critics have created the impression that such domination by testers is especially characteristic of modern American society, with its proclivities for mass-production, super-efficiency, and automation, in the most pejorative sense of these terms. Ebel points out that such domination is not nearly so serious in contemporary American society as in some other countries, both ancient and modern. Examples of greater test domination can easily be found in older cultures than ours, where life proceeded at a more leisurely pace—and where essay tests had not yet been replaced by multiple-choice items! A case in point is the traditional British "11-plus system," also followed in many other countries, whereby performance on examinations taken at the age of 11 determined

15

rather rigidly the individual's subsequent educational career. An example from a still older culture is the theme of the provocative and entertaining paper by DuBois, who describes the system of Civil Service Examinations prevailing in the Chinese empire for some three thousand years.

This system proved successful as long as the tests remained relevant to their objectives, i.e., as long as they provided valid measures of the criterion behavior they were designed to predict. When the job requirements changed, however, the tests did not change to keep pace with such developments. In his concluding paragraphs, DuBois notes that while there were increasing demands for technological skills in government service, the examinations remained predominantly literary. The result was the eventual abandonment of the system. These events highlight the need for repeated "job analyses," "criterion analyses," or "task analyses," to keep tests valid and consistent with changing educational, occupational, and social conditions.

Any constructive discussion of criticisms and misuses of tests perforce includes a consideration of some of the positive functions served by testing. As already noted, Ebel's paper devotes considerable attention to some of the goals of effective testing. More specific discussions of three major applications of testing can be found in the papers by Gustad, Tyler, and Cronbach. Since these three papers cover the use of tests in quite different contexts, they also provide some notion of the wide diversity of roles that tests can play.

Gustad's paper is concerned with the utilization of tests in counseling. In contrast to the early view of vocational guidance, from which modern counseling evolved, Gustad emphasizes the use of test results by the client himself, to promote self-understanding and aid in decision making. He presents test-taking experience as an integral part of the counseling process, rather than as a source of information for the counselor. He also discusses the nondirective or client-centered counseling technique of introducing tests when the client perceives a need for them and of having the client participate in the selection of tests.

A recurrent concern in education pertains to the influence that standardized achievement tests may exert upon what teachers teach and what students learn. It is these potential influences—both desirable and undesirable—that Tyler analyzes in his paper. He begins by citing evidence that inappropriate or poorly constructed tests, which ignore the major objectives of a course or other educational program, encourage trivial or irrelevant learning. He then goes on to show that, when tests are properly designed and judiciously introduced, they can serve important functions in the educational process. They can facilitate learning by providing motivation, self-evaluation, and feedback. Moreover, the test-taking process itself can serve a teaching function. In fact, test-taking as a form of learning is the basic process in the so-called teaching machines.

In the last paper of the chapter, Cronbach considers some of the contributions that decision theory can make to the evaluation of tests and the utilization of test results. Basically, the decision-theory model is appropriate to the use of tests in any context, including counseling, clinical psychology, and education. It will probably find its major application, however, in large-scale selection and classification of personnel in military and industrial settings, and in the admission of students to colleges and professional schools. Without going into the mathematical operations required for the detailed application of decision theory, Cronbach discusses some of the concepts most relevant to the use of tests in personnel decisions. The paper illustrates ways in which the questions we ask about tests can be reformulated in terms of decision theory so as to provide fuller and more realistic evaluations of the effectiveness of tests in specific situations.

The Social Consequences of Educational Testing

ROBERT L. EBEL

1963

I have an uneasy feeling that some of the things that will be said in this talk on the social consequences of educational testing may be regarded as somewhat controversial. Let me try to begin, therefore, with some statements on which we may all be able to agree.

POPULARITY AND CRITICISM

Tests have been used increasingly in recent years to make educational assessments. The reasons for this are not hard to discover. Educational tests of aptitude and achievement greatly improve the precision, objectivity, and efficiency of the observations on which educational assessments rest. Tests are not alternatives to observations. At best they represent no more than refined and systematized processes of observation.

But the increasing use of tests has been accompanied by an increasing flow of critical comment. Again, the reasons are easy to see. Tests vary in quality. None is perfect and some may be quite imperfect. Test scores are sometimes misued. And even if they were flawless and used with the greatest skill, they would probably still be unpopular among those who have reason to fear an impartial assessment of some of their competencies.

Many of the popular articles critical of educational testing that have appeared in recent years do not reflect a very adequate understanding of educational testing, or a very thoughtful, unbiased consideration of its social consequences. Most of them are obvious potboilers for their authors, and sensational reader-bait in the eyes of the editors of the journals in which they appear. The writers of some of these articles have paid courteous visits to our offices. They have listened respectfully to our recitals of fact and opinion. They have drunk coffee with us and then taken their leave, presumably to reflect on what they have been told, but in any event, to write.

18

What appears in print often seems to be only an elaboration and documentation of their initial prejudices and preconceptions, supported by atypical anecdotes and purposefully selected quotations. Educational testing has not fared very well in their hands.

Among the charges of malfeasance and misfeasance that these critics have leveled against the test makers there is one of nonfeasance. Specifically, we are charged with having shown lack of proper concern for the social consequences of our educational testing. These harmful consequences, they have suggested, may be numerous and serious. The more radical among them imply that, because of what they suspect about the serious social consequences of educational testing, the whole testing movement ought to be suppressed. The more moderate critics claim that they do not know much about these social consequences. But they also suggest that the test makers don't either, and that it is the test makers who ought to be doing substantial research to find out.

THE ROLE OF RESEARCH

If we were forced to choose between the two alternatives offered by the critics, either the suppression of educational testing or extensive research on its social consequences, we probably would choose the latter without much hesitation. But it is by no means clear that what testing needs most at this point is a large program of research on its social consequences. Let me elaborate.

Research can be extremely useful, but it is far from being a sure-fire process for finding the answers to any kind of a question, particularly a social question, that perplexes us. Nor is research the only source of reliable knowledge. In the social sciences, at least, most of what we know for sure has not come out of formal research projects. It has come instead from the integration of a very large number of more or less incidental observations and accounts of human behavior in natural, rather than experimental, situations. There are good reasons why research on human behavior tends to be difficult, and often unproductive, but that is a story we cannot go into now.

For present purposes, only two points need to be mentioned. The first is that the scarcity of formal research on the social consequences of educational testing should not be taken to mean that there is no reliable knowledge about those consequences, or that those engaged in educational testing have been callously indifferent to its social consequences. The second is that scientific research on human behavior may require commitment to values that are in basic conflict with our democratic concerns for individual welfare. If boys and girls are used as carefully controlled experimental subjects in tough-minded research on social issues that really matter, not all of them will benefit, and some may be disadvantaged seriously. Our society is not yet ready, and perhaps should never become ready, to acquiesce in that kind of scientific research.

HARMFUL CONSEQUENCES

Before proceeding further, let us mention specifically a few of the harmful things that critics have suggested educational testing may do:

1) It may place an indelible stamp of intellectual status—superior, medio-cre, or inferior—on a child, and thus predetermine his social status as an adult, and possibly also do irreparable harm to his self-esteem and his educational motivation.

2) It may lead to a narrow conception of ability, encourage pursuit of this single goal, and thus tend to reduce the diversity of talent available to society.

3) It may place the testers in a position to control education and determine the destinies of individual human beings, while, incidentally, making the testers themselves rich in the process.

4) It may encourage impersonal, inflexible, mechanistic processes of evaluation and determination, so that essential human freedoms are limited or lost altogether.

These are four of the most frequent and serious tentative indictments. There have been, of course, many other suggestions of possible harmful social consequences of educational testing. It may emphasize individual competition and success rather than social cooperation, and thus conflict with the cultivation of democratic ideals of human equality. It may foster conformity rather than creativity. It may involve cultural bias. It may neglect important intangibles. It may, particularly in the case of personality testing, involve unwarranted and offensive invasions of privacy. It may do serious injustice in particular individual cases. It may reward specious test-taking skill, or penalize the lack of it.

If time and our supply of ideas permitted, it would be well for us to consider all of these possibilities. But since they do not, perhaps the demands of the topic may be reasonably well met if we limit attention to the first four items mentioned as possibly harmful consequences of educational testing, namely: permanent status determination, limited conceptions of ability, domination by the testers, and mechanistic decision making.

At this point in the presentation, a major choice must be made. Shall we explore the foundations for these apprehensions and attempt to dispel them? Shall we, in other words, attempt to refute the allegations of harmful social consequences of educational testing? Clearly, most of these social dangers can be, and probably have been, exaggerated. Little solid evidence exists to justify the fears that have been expressed with such apparent concern.

Or shall we assume that the concerns which have been expressed are not wholly fanciful? Shall we, therefore, set as our task the discovery and delineation of things that might be done by those who make and use tests to limit the causes for concern? On reflection, it seemed that for one speaking to a group of specialists in educational testing, the second course of action was clearly the more reasonable, and would be likely to be the more useful. So that is the course that has been chosen.

Permanent Status Determination

Consider first, then, the danger that educational testing may place an indelible stamp of inferiority on a child, ruin his self-esteem and educational motivation, and determine his social status as an adult. The kind of educational testing most likely to have these consequences would involve tests purporting to measure a person's permanent general capacity for learning. These are the intelligence tests, and the presumed measures of general capacity for learning they provide are popularly known as IQ's.

Most of us here assembled are well aware of the fact that there is no direct, unequivocal means for measuring permanent general capacity for learning. It is not even clear to many of us that, in the state of our current understanding of mental functions and the learning process, any precise and useful meaning can be given to the concept of "permanent general capacity for learning." We know that all intelligence tests now available are direct measures only of achievement in learning, including learning how to learn, and that inferences from scores on those tests to some native capacity for learning are fraught with many hazards and uncertainties.

But many people who are interested in education do not know this. Many of them believe that native intelligence has been clearly indentified and is well understood by expert psychologists. They believe that a person's IQ is one of his basic, permanent attributes, and that any good intelligence test will measure it with a high degree of precision. They do not regard an IQ simply as another test score, a score that may vary considerably depending on the particular test used and the particular time when the person was tested.

Whether or not a person's learning is significantly influenced by his predetermined capacity for learning, there is no denying the obvious fact that individual achievements in learning exhibit considerable consistency over time and across tasks. The superior elementary school pupil may become a mediocre secondary school pupil and an inferior college student, but the odds are against it. Early promise is not always fulfilled, but it is more often than not. The A student in mathematics is a better bet than the C student to be an A student in English literature as well, or in social psychology.

On the other hand, early promise is not always followed by late fulfillment. Ordinary students do blossom sometimes into outstanding scholars. And special talents can be cultivated. There is enough variety in the work of the world so that almost anyone can discover some line of endeavor in which he can develop more skill than most of his fellow men.

In a free society that claims to recognize the dignity and worth of every individual, it is better to emphasize the opportunity for choice and the importance of effort than to stress genetic determinism of status and success. It is better to emphasize the diversity of talents and tasks than to stress general excellence or inferiority. It is important to recognize and to reinforce what John Gardner has called "the principle of multiple chances," not only across time but also across tasks.

The concept of fixed general intelligence, or capacity for learning, is a hypothetical concept. At this stage in the development of our understanding of human learning, it is not a necessary hypothesis. Socially, it is not now a useful hypothesis. One of the important things test specialists can do to improve the social consequences of educational testing is to discredit the popular conception of the IQ. Wilhelm Stern, the German psychologist who suggested the concept originally, saw how it was being overgeneralized and charged one of his students coming to America to "kill the IQ." Perhaps we would be well advised, even at this late date, to renew our efforts to carry out his wishes.

Recent emphasis on the early identification of academic talent involves similar risks of oversimplifying the concept of talent and overemphasizing its predetermined components. If we think of talent mainly as something that is genetically given, we will run our schools quite differently than if we think of it mainly as something that can be educationally developed.

If human experience, or that specialized branch of human experience we call scientific research, should ever make it quite clear that differences among men in achievement are largely due to genetically determined differences in talent, then we ought to accept the finding and restructure our society and social customs in accord with it. But that is by no means clear yet, and the structure and customs of our society are not consistent with such a basic assumption. For the present, it will be more consistent with the facts as we know them, and more constructive for the society in which we live, to think of talent not as a natural resource like gold or uranium to be discovered, extracted, and refined, but as a synthetic product like fiberglass or DDT—something that, with skill, effort, and luck, can be created and produced out of generally available raw materials to suit our particular needs or fancies.

This means, among other things, that we should judge the value of the tests we use not in terms of how accurately they enable us to *predict* later achievement, but rather in terms of how much help they give us to *increase* achievement by motivating and directing the efforts of students and teachers. From this point of view, those concerned with professional education who have resisted schemes for very long-range predictions of aptitude for, or success in, their professions have acted wisely. Not only is there likely to be much more of dangerous error than of useful truth in such long-range predictions, but also there is implicit in the whole enterprise a deterministic conception of achievement that is not wholly consistent with the educational facts as we know them, and with the basic assumptions of a democratic, free society.

Whenever I try to point out that prediction is not the exclusive, nor even the principal, purpose of educational measurement, some of my best and most intelligent friends demur firmly, or smile politely to communicate that they will never accept such heretical nonsense. When I imply that they use the term "prediction" too loosely, they reply that I conceive it too narrowly. Let me try once more to achieve a meeting of the minds.

I agree that prediction has to do with the future, and that the future ought to be of greater concern to us than the past. I agree, too, that a measurement must be related to some other measurements in order to be useful, and that these relationships provide the basis for, and are tested by, predictions. But these relationships also provide a basis, in many educational endeavors, for managing outcomes—for making happen what we want to happen. And I cannot agree that precision in language or clarity of thought is well served by referring to this process of controlling outcomes as just another instance of prediction. The etymology and common usage of the word "prediction" imply to me the process of foretelling, not of controlling.

The direct, exclusive, immediate purpose of measurement is always description, not either prediction or control. If we know with reasonable accuracy how things now stand (descriptions), and if we also know with reasonable accuracy what leads to what (functional relations), we are in a position to foretell what will happen if we keep hands off (prediction) or to manipulate the variables we can get our hands on to make happen what we want to happen (control). Of course, our powers of control are often limited and uncertain, just as our powers of prediction are. But I have not been able to see what useful purpose is served by referring to both the hands-off and the hands-on operations as prediction, as if there were no important difference between them. It is in the light of these semantic considerations that I suggest that tests should be used less as bases for prediction of achievement, and more as means to increase achievement. I think there is a difference, and that it is important educationally.

Limited Conceptions of Ability

Consider next the danger that a single widely used test or test battery for selective admission or scholarship awards may foster an undesirably narrow conception of ability and thus tend to reduce diversity in the talents available to a school or to society.

Here again, it seems, the danger is not wholly imaginary. Basic as verbal and quantitative skills are to many phases of educational achievement, they do not encompass all phases of achievement. The application of a common yardstick of aptitude or achievement to all pupils is operationally much simpler than the use of a diversity of yardsticks designed to measure different aspects of achievement. But overemphasis on a common test could lead educators to neglect those students whose special talents lie outside the common core.

Those who manage programs for the testing of scholastic aptitude always insist, and properly so, that scores on these tests should not be the sole consideration when decisions are made on admission or the award of scholarships. But the question of whether the testing itself should not be varied from person to person remains. The use of optional tests of achievement permits some variation. Perhaps the range of available options should be made much wider than it is at present to accommodate greater diversity of talents.

The problem of encouraging the development of various kinds of ability is, of course, much broader than the problem of testing. Widespread commitment to general education, with the requirement that all students study identical courses for a substantial part of their programs, may be a much greater deterrent to specialized diversity in the educational product. Perhaps these requirements should be restudied too.

Domination by the Testers

What of the concern that the growth of educational testing may increase the influence of the test makers until they are in a position to control educational curricula and determine the destinies of students?

Those who know well how tests are made and used in American education know that the tests more often lag than lead curricular change, and that while tests may affect particular episodes in a student's experience, they can hardly ever be said to determine a student's destiny. American education is, after all, a manifold, decentralized, loosely organized enterprise. Whether it restricts student freedom too much or too little is a subject for lively debate. But it does not even come close to determining any student's destiny, not nearly so close as the examination systems in some other countries, ancient and modern.

But test makers have, I fear, sometimes given the general public reason to fear that we may be up to no good. I refer to our sometime reluctance to take the layman fully into our confidence, to share fully with him all our information about his test scores, the tests from which they were derived, and our interpretations of what they mean.

Secrecy concerning educational tests and test scores has been justified on several grounds. One is that the information is simply too complex for untrained minds to grasp. Now it is true that some pretty elaborate theories can be built around our testing processes. It is also true that we can perform some very fancy statistical manipulations with the scores they yield. But the essential information revealed by the scores on most educational tests is not particularly complex. If we understand it ourselves, we can communicate it clearly to most laymen without serious difficulty. To be quite candid, we are not all that much brighter than they are, much as we may sometimes need the reassurance of thinking so.

Another justification for secrecy is that laymen will misuse test scores. Mothers may compare scores over the back fences. The one whose child scores high spreads the word around. The one whose child scores low may keep the secret, but seek other grounds for urging changes in the teaching staff or in the educational program. Scores of limited meaning may be treated with undue respect and used to repair or to injure the student's self-esteem rather than to contribute to his learning.

Again it is true that test scores can be misued. They have been in the past and they will be in the future. But does this justify secrecy? Can we minimize abuses due to ignorance by withholding knowledge? We do not flatter our fellow citizens when we tell them, in effect, that they are too ignorant, or too lacking in character to be trusted with the knowledge of their children, or of themselves, that we possess.

Seldom acknowledged, but very persuasive as a practical reason for secrecy regarding test scores, is that it spares those who use the scores from having to explain and justify the decisions they make. Preference is not, and should not, always be given to the person whose test score is the higher. But if score information is withheld, the disappointed applicant will assume that it was because of his low score, not because of some other factor. He will not trouble officials with demands for justification of a decision that, in some cases, might be hard to justify. But all things considered, more is likely to be gained in the long run by revealing the objective evidence used in reaching a decision. Should the other, subjective considerations prove too difficult to justify, perhaps they ought not to be used as part of the basis for decision.

If specialists in educational measurement want to be properly understood and trusted by the public they serve, they will do well to shun secrecy and to share with the public as much as it is interested in knowing about the methods they use, the knowledge they gain, and the interpretations they make. This is clearly the trend of opinion in examining boards and public education authorities. Let us do what we can to reinforce the trend. Whatever mental measurements are so esoteric or so dangerous socially that they must be shrouded in secrecy probably should not be made in the first place.

The testers do not control education or the destinies of individual students. By the avoidance of mystery and secrecy, they can help to create better public understanding and support.

Mechanistic Decision Making

Finally, let us consider briefly the possibility that testing may encourage mechanical decision making, at the expense of essential human freedoms of choice and action.

Those who work with mental tests often say that the purpose of all measurement is prediction. They use regression equations to predict grade point averages, or contingency tables to predict the chances of various degrees of success. Their procedures may seem to imply not only that human behavior is part of a deterministic system in which the number of relevant variables is manageably small, but also that the proper goals of human behavior are clearly known and universally accepted.

In these circumstances, there is some danger that we may forget our own inadequacies and attempt to play God with the lives of other human beings. We may find it convenient to overlook the gross inaccuracies that plague our measurements, and the great uncertainties that bedevil our predictions. Betrayed by over-confidence in our own wisdom and virtue, we may project our particular value systems into a pattern of ideal behavior for all men.

If these limitations on our ability to mold human behavior and to direct its development did not exist, we would need to face the issue debated by B. F. Skinner and Carl Rogers before the American Psychological Association some years ago. Shall our knowledge of human behavior be used to design an ideal culture and to condition individuals to live happily in it at whatever necessary cost to their own freedom of choice and action?

But the aforementioned limitations do exist. If we ignore them and undertake to manage the lives of others so that those others will qualify as worthy citizens in our own particular vision of utopia, we do justify the concern that one harmful social consequence of educational testing may be mechanistic decision making and the loss of essential human freedoms.

A large proportion of the decisions affecting the welfare and destiny of a person must be made in the midst of overwhelming uncertainties concerning the outcomes to be desired and the best means of achieving such outcomes. That many mistakes will be made seems inevitable. One of the cornerstones of a free society is the belief that in most cases it is better for the person most concerned to make the decision, right or wrong, and to take the responsibility for its consequences, good or bad.

The implications of this for educational testing are clear. Tests should be used as little as possible to *impose* decisions and courses of action on others. They should be used as much as possible to provide a sounder basis of *choice* in individual decision making. Tests can be used and ought to be used to support rather than to limit human freedom and responsibility.

CONCLUSION

In summary, we have suggested here today that those who make and use educational tests might do four things to alleviate public concerns over their possibly adverse social consequences:

1) They could emphasize the use of tests to improve status, and de-emphasize their use to determine status.

2) They could broaden the base of achievements tested to recognize and develop the wide variety of talents needed in our society.

3) They could share openly with the persons most directly concerned all that tests have revealed about their abilities and prospects.

4) They could decrease the use of tests to impose decisions on others, and instead increase their use as a basis for better personal decision making.

When Paul Dressel read a draft of this paper, he chided me gently on what he considered to be a serious omission. I had failed to discuss the social consequences of *not* testing. What are some of these consequences?

If the use of educational tests were abandoned, the distinctions between competence and incompetence would become more difficult to discern. Nathan Womack, former president of the National Board of Medical Examiners, has pointed out that only to the degree to which educational institutions can define what they mean by competence, and determine the extent to which it has been achieved, can they discharge their obligation to deliver competence to the society they serve.

If the use of educational tests were abandoned, the encouragement and reward of individual efforts to learn would be made more difficult. Excellence in programs of education would become less tangible as a goal and less demonstrable as an attainment. Educational opportunities would be extended less on the basis of aptitude and merit and more on the basis of ancestry and influence; social class barriers would become less permeable. Decisions on important issues of curriculum and method would be made less on the basis of solid evidence and more on the basis of prejudice or caprice.

These are some of the social consequences of *not* testing. In our judgment, they are potentially far more harmful than any possible adverse consequences of testing. But it is also our judgment, and has been the theme of this paper, that we can do much to minimize even these possibilities of harmful consequences. Let us, then, use educational tests for the powerful tools they are with energy and skill, but also with wisdom and care.

A Test-Dominated Society:
China, 1115 B.C.–1905 A.D.

PHILIP H. DuBois

1964

Our negative enthusiasm for the present government in Peking should not lead us to a lack of appreciation for great Chinese achievements of the past. They have been many.

It is often said that the Chinese invented gunpowder and, quite humanely, used it to frighten, rather than to kill, their enemies.

Certainly they solved the problem of diverse languages with the remarkable invention of a common written language—a code by which peoples who could not communicate with one another orally were able to communicate freely by means of writing. This invention was so successful that the Chinese came to regard themselves as a single people.

They invented paper, which the West did not know how to make until some Chinese papermakers were captured by Arabs at Samarkand in 751 A.D. They invented printing. They developed the arts. But, more importantly for our purposes this morning, they invented the psychological test, applying it to government, the very framework of their society, in such a manner that the test-makers, in effect, determined over many centuries much of the format of Chinese society.

The prolonged and intensive Chinese experience with testing seems to have been completely ignored by contemporary psychometricians. In none of the writings on psychometrics with which I am familiar is there any mention of some 3,000 years of examinations in the Chinese empire. This is rather surprising because in civil service procedures it is easy to trace the continuity of Eastern and Western methods. Continuity between Western educational and psychological examining methods on the one hand and Chinese civil service testing on the other is more difficult to demonstrate, but some influence is probable.

Even if Western psychometrics had been completely independent of Chinese testing, the Eastern experience would have been of great interest to us. It affords the one historical example of a society in which examining methods introduced to attain certain restricted objectives actually began to determine many characteristics of the society itself.

It should be noted that through the ages the Chinese empire, unlike the West, did not have a numerous hereditary aristocracy to constitute its governing class. The chief way to a political career was through passing a series of examinations in which competition was very severe. Moreover, China lacked another invention of the West: the university. The learned Chinese was one who had been successful in passing competitive examinations, and whose success brought changes in his attire and in his title as well as public recognition of his abilities, and employment in government service.

For long periods of time the system worked very well indeed. Only occasionally were examinations suspended, one notable period being the time in which the Mongol emperors ruled in Peking. (The accounts of Marco Polo, who spent a number of years in China during their rule, make no reference to the Chinese civil service examining procedures.)

The Chinese scholar seems to have been a reasonably successful public administrator. Public office was often distributed by lot among the mandarins who had passed three successive sets of examinations.

Millions of men prepared for the tests, often for decades, and relatively few achieved final success. The selection ratio was so small that the tests themselves would not have had to be very valid in order to be useful. That they were useful is perhaps indicated by their long history and by the fact that for many centuries, with relatively few interruptions, the government of the Chinese empire preserved internal peace, provided security from many would-be invaders, and permitted a flowering of civilization that in many respects was far more advanced than that prevailing contemporaneously in the West.

The earliest development seems to have been a rudimentary form of proficiency testing. About the year 2200 B.C., the emperor of China is said to have examined his officials every third year. After three examinations, he either promoted or dismissed them from the service. There seems to be no record of the exact content nor of the methods of testing, but the precedent of periodic examinations was to continue for many generations.

A thousand years later in 1115 B.C., at the beginning of the Chan dynasty, formal examining procedures of candidates for office were established. Here the record is clear. Job sample tests were used requiring proficiency in the five basic arts: music, archery, horsemanship, writing, and arithmetic. Of the five, at least two, writing and arithmetic, still have validity for public office. Knowledge of a sixth art was also required—skill in the rites and ceremonies of public and social life.

It should be pointed out that this examining system, which was later to be centered upon the Confucian classics, was actually in existence long before the time of Confucius (551–478 B.C.).

While the procedures changed from time to time, and the sources to which I have had access are somewhat contradictory, a few dates seem to be clear. In 165 B.C., by which time Confucian ethics had become current, moral standards were introduced in the selection of competitors. District magistrates were required to send to the capital candidates who had acquired a reputation for filial piety and integrity. Those whose moral character had been sufficiently attested were then examined with respect to their intellectual qualifications. At this time, the test included not only measures of the six arts, but also familiarity with the geography of the empire, civil law, military matters, agriculture, and the administration of revenue.

After 622 A.D., open, competitive examinations took place at more or less regular intervals. By 1370 A.D., three levels of examinations were well established. The candidate who passed the examination in his district became eligible to take a test at the provincial capital, and those successful at the provincial capital were eligible for final examinations in Peking. For about 500 years the system was stable and a description by William A. P. Martin (6) in 1870 is pertinent:

. . . The candidates for office,—those who are acknowledged as such, in consequence of sustaining the initial trial,—are divided into the three grades of *siu-ts'ai, chu-jin,* and *tsin-shi,*—"Budding Geniuses," "Promoted Scholars," and those who are "Ready for Office." The trials for the first are held in the chief city of each district . . . . They are conducted by a chancellor, whose jurisdiction extends over an entire province, containing, it may be, sixty or seventy such districts, each of which he is required to visit once a year, and each of which is provided with a resident sub-chancellor, whose duty it is to examine the scholars in the interval, and to have them in readiness on the chancellor's arrival.

About two thousand competitors enter the lists, ranging in age from the precocious youth just entering his teens up to the venerable grandsire of seventy winters. Shut up for a night and a day, each in his narrow cell, they produce each a poem and one or two essays on themes assigned by the chancellor, and then return to their homes to await the bulletin announcing their place in the scale of merit. The chancellor, assisted by his clerks, occupies several days in sifting the heap of manuscripts, from which he picks out some twenty or more that are distinguished by beauty of penmanship and grace of diction. The authors of these are honored with the degree of "Budding Genius," and are entitled to wear the decorations of the lowest grade in the corporation of mandarins. The successful student wins no purse of gold and obtains no office, but he has gained a prize, which he deems a sufficient compensation for years of patient toil. He is the best of a hundred scholars, exempted from liability to corporal punishment, and raised above the vulgar herd . . . .

Once in three years these "Budding Geniuses," these picked men of the districts, repair to the provincial capital to engage in competition for the second degree,—that of *chu-jin,* or "Promoted Scholar." The number of competitors amounts to ten thousand, more or less, and of these only one in every hundred can be admitted to the coveted degree. The trial is conducted by special examiners sent down from Peking and this examination takes a wider range than the preceding. No fewer than three sessions of nearly three days each are occupied instead of the single day for the first degree. Compositions in prose and verse are required, and themes are assigned with a special view to testing the extent of reading and depth of scholarship of the candidates. Penmanship is left out of the account,—each production, marked with a cipher, being copied by an official scribe, that the examiners may have no clew to its author and no temptation to render a biased judgment.

The victor still receives neither office nor emolument; but the honor he achieves is scarcely less than that which was won by the victors in the Olympic games. Again, he is one of a hundred, each of whom was a picked man; and as a result of this second victory he goes forth an acknowledged superior among ten thousand contending scholars. He adorns his cap with the gilded button of a higher grade, erects a pair of lofty flag-staffs before the gate of his family residence, and places a tablet over his door to inform those who pass by that this is the abode of a literary prize-man. But our "Promoted Scholar" is not yet a mandarin, in the proper sense of the term. The distinction already attained only stimulates his desire for higher honors,—honors which bring at last the solid recompense of an income.

In the spring of the following year he proceeds to Peking to seek the next higher degree, the attainment of which will prove a passport to office. This contest is still with his peers, that is, with other "Promoted Scholars," who like himself have come up from all the provinces of the empire. But the chances are this time more in his favor, as the number of prizes is now tripled, and if the gods are propitious his fortune is made . . . . If his name appears among the favored few, he not only wins himself a place in the front ranks of the lettered, but he plants his foot securely on the rounds of the official ladder by which, without the prestige of birth or the support of friends, it is possible to rise to a seat in the grand council of state or a place in the Imperial Cabinet. All this advancement presents itself in the distant prospect, while the office upon which he immediately enters is one of respectability, and it may be of profit. It is generally that of mayor or sub-mayor of a district city, or sub-chancellor in the district examinations,—the vacant posts being distributed by lot, and therefore impartially, among those who have proved themselves to be "ready for office."

Before the drawing of lots, however, for the post of a magistrate among the people, our ambitious student has a chance of winning the more distinguished honor of a place in the Imperial Academy. With this view, the two or three hundred survivors of so many contests appear in the palace, where themes are assigned them by the Emperor himself, and the highest honor is paid to the pursuit of letters by the exercises being presided over by his Majesty in person. Penmanship reappears as an element in determining the result, and a score or more of those whose style is the most finished, whose scholarship the ripest, and whose handwriting the most elegant, are drafted into the college of Hanlin, the "forest of pencils," a kind of Imperial Institute, the members of which are recognized as standing at the head of the literary profession. These are constituted poets and historians to the Celestial Court, or deputed to act as chancellors and examiners in the several provinces.

But the diminishing series in this ascending scale has not yet reached its final term. The long succession of contests culminates in the designation by the Emperor of some individual whom he regards as the Chuang-Yuen or model scholar of the empire . . . . Provinces contend for the shining prize, and the town that gives the victor birth becomes noted forever. Swift heralds bear the tidings of his triumph, and the hearts of the people leap at their approach. We have seen them enter a humble cottage, and amid the flaunting of banners and the blare of trumpets announced to its startled inmates that one of their relations had been crowned by the Emperor as the laureate of the year. And so high was the estimation in which the people held the success of their fellow-townsman, that his wife was requested to visit the six gates of the city, and to scatter before each a handful of rice, that the whole population might share in the good fortune of her household . . . .

It is obvious that which excites so profoundly the interest of a whole nation must be productive of very decided results. That it leads to the selection of the best talents for the service of the public we have already seen; but beyond this— its primary object—it exercises a profound influence upon the education of the people and the stability of the government. It is all, in fact, that China has to show in the way of an educational system. She has no colleges or universities,— if we except one that is yet in embryo,—and no national system of common schools; yet it may be confidently asserted that China gives to learning a more effective patronage than she could have done if each of her emperors were an Augustus and every premier a Maecenas. She says to all her sons, "Prosecute your studies by such means as you may be able to command, whether in public or in private, and when you are prepared, present yourselves in the examination hall. The government will judge of your proficiency and reward your attainments."

Nothing can exceed the ardor which this standing offer infuses into the minds of all who have the remotest prospect of sharing in the prizes. They study not merely while they have teachers to incite them to diligence, but continue their studies with unabated zeal long after they have left the schools; they study in solitude and poverty; they study amidst the cares of a family and the turmoil of business; and the shining goal is kept steadily in view until the eye grows dim.

Some of the aspirants impose on themselves the task of writing a fresh essay every day; and they do not hestitate to enter the lists as often as the public examinations recur, resolved, if they fail, to continue trying, believing that perseverance has power to command success and encouraged by the legend of the man who, needing a sewing-needle, made one by grinding a crowbar on a piece of granite.

This quotation from Martin, describing and praising the Chinese testing system, is by no means unique. The use of competitive examinations for the selection of state officials was praised by many Western observers and writers, including Voltaire. In fact, it is clear that initially all civil service examining in Europe and in the United States used the Chinese system, directly or indirectly, as a model. Civil service testing was introduced in France as a 1791 reform, only to be abolished by Napoleon. In England the first competitive examinations in connection with public office were instituted for the selection of trainees for the civil service in India by men familiar with the Chinese system. Later, when the question of civil service examinations for Great Britain as a whole was debated in Parliament, the Chinese model was discussed with both favorable and unfavorable comments. As a part of an extensive study, Congressman Thomas A. Jenckes, one of the fathers of the United States Civil Service, wrote 12 pages on the civil service of China (4).

Westerners seem to have been particularly impressed with the fact that competition was open, that distinction came from merit, and that a highly literate and urbane group of public officials resulted from the examination system.

The great crisis in Chinese affairs came, of course, when the Chinese realized that they were militarily inferior to the West. They quickly discovered that equality in military power could not be achieved without modern science and technology. Accordingly, technological schools and universities were set up, but as long as the civil service examinations, which were largely literary in character, continued to be the way for an ambitious man to have a career, modern education was not sufficiently attractive. Consequently, in 1905, the Chinese examination system was abolished as a reform measure.

So much for a description and a bit of the history of an ancient Chinese venture in psychological examining as a tool of government. What can be said about their testing techniques from the point of view of the modern psychometrician? In the first place, I find no evidence to indicate that they invented either the multiple-choice format, the test-scoring machine, or item analysis. They did, however, recognize that a relatively short performance under carefully controlled conditions could yield an estimate of the ability to perform under less rigorously controlled conditions and for a longer period of time. I think there is no doubt that the procedure selected capable public servants.

They recognized the problem of objectivity, concealing candidates' names, and sometimes using a bureau of copyists to copy examination material before it was graded. In some cases, tests were read by two independent examiners who handed their sealed evaluations to a third examiner who reconciled any differences. Scores seem to have been in terms of rank order.

The need for uniformity in testing conditions was well recognized. Considerable attention was given to proctoring the examination halls, which were large and permanent installations consisting of hundreds of small cells. Sometimes candidates died during the rigors of the examinations, which went on day and night.

In this year 1964, when psychological tests are being used more and more extensively at critical points in the careers of all our citizens, we will do well to consider their effects on individuals, on specific institutions, and on society. The long Chinese experience is a pertinent case history. It is a plausible hypothesis that much of the great strength of the Chinese empire came from the intellectual vigor of men who were bright enough to compete in examinations requiring the writing of poems and "eight-legged essays."

Certainly the opportunities that were opened up by success in the examinations stimulated millions of individuals to long years of scholarship. Perhaps the greatest drawback was that the scholarship was not always pertinent. In the nineteenth century, China suddenly found herself surpassed in technology by the West. While Chinese civilization had been relatively static, Westerners invented the steam engine, the power loom, and the ironclad. It was then that the Chinese, in order to preserve their country and their institutions, began to desire progress according to the Western model. At that time the age-old examining system was discovered to be a hindrance.

So far, with 60 years of experience, we Westerners have not found our psychological examining a hindrance. But it is becoming increasingly apparent that our test-makers, like those of ancient China, establish goals for individuals and influence the shape of social institutions. Item writers as well as song writers mold the patterns of a culture.

REFERENCES[1]

1. Franke, W. *The reform and abolition of the traditional Chinese examination system.* Cambridge: Harvard Univer. Press, 1961.
2. Hsin, T'ang shu. *Le traité des examens.* Paris: Librairie Ernest Leroux, 1932.
3. Hsü, E. *Pratique des examens littéraires en Chine.* Chang-Hai: Imprimerie de la Mission Catholique, 1894.
4. Jenckes, T. A. Civil service of the United States. Report No. 47, 40th Congress, 2nd Session, May 25, 1868.
5. Kracke, E. A., Jr. *Civil service in early Sung China, 960–1067.* Cambridge: Harvard Univer. Press, 1953.
6. Martin, W. A. P. Competitive examinations in China. *North American Review,* 1870, 111, 62–77.
7. Têng, Ssŭ-yü. Chinese influence on the western examination system. *Harvard Journal of Asiatic Studies,* 1943, 7, 267–312.
8. Têng, Ssŭ-yü, & Fairbank, J. K. *China's response to the west.* Cambridge: Harvard Univer. Press, 1954.

[1] Stanley E. Spector, chairman of the Department of Chinese and Japanese at Washington University, suggested certain of these references. His helpfulness is gratefully acknowledged.

Helping Students Understand
Test Information

JOHN W. GUSTAD

1955

The past fifteen years have seen developments in most branches of science and technology that even their greatest apologists would have felt to be impossible. Psychology in general and testing in particular have been in the van of these developments. Testing is quite a bit bigger business than it was when Wolfle (21) rendered an accounting just under ten years ago. While comparatively few Americans will, in their lifetimes, encounter psychologists directly, vast numbers will encounter tests. This will occur in school or college, in the military, in industry, in hospitals, clinics, or prisons. The chances of an individual's avoiding testing are rapidly approaching his chances of avoiding fingerprinting, having chest X-rays, or paying income taxes.

There are numerous highly verbal critics who see, or profess to see, in this movement portents of the brave new world or of 1984. Zealous advocates are equally sure that God's in His heaven and all will be right with the world as soon as testing is applied to all human relations enterprises. As usual, the truth probably lies between these poles. Many psychologists are deeply concerned that test construction has lagged behind the rapidly developing science, and that a technical product that does not represent the best thinking available is being marketed in the name of psychology. There are undoubtedly good reasons for these and other concerns. Growth spurts often bring with them some loss of coordination.

One group from which we have heard comparatively little but whose reactions should concern us greatly is made up of the rapidly growing pool of people who have been tested. These consumers have opinions; they also have money and votes. Since we professionals do most of the writing, the ideas of the consumers have not been well represented in the literature. The situation is especially critical in counseling and clinical psychology, for here much of the process rests on the assumption that the client will be

37

willing to make use of information about himself derived in part from tests.

The vision that Parsons (15) incorporated in his book nearly half a century ago is becoming dim. There are good reasons for this, because his simple, three-step scheme was somewhat too simple. Nevertheless, the general notion that one should analyze the individual, analyze the job, and match the individual and the job can still serve a useful purpose. When Parsons wrote his book, methods for individual analysis were few in number and crude in character. Today, a glance at Buros' latest volume (5) might be taken by some as prima facie evidence that there were more than enough analytic methods available. I doubt that many of us would accept this verdict wholeheartedly. Still, among the thousands of tests available, there are some whose validities and reliabilities are respectable enough to make them useful.

When tests are used administratively, as in the military establishment or in industry, administrators must consider public relations. Most will recall the furor associated with the introduction of the Selective Service Qualification Test. In the counseling situation, where client rapport is even more critical, where the usefulness of tests is measured—or should be measured—in terms of the adequacy of the decisions made by the client, we encounter problems striking at the very core of our operation. The opinions of clients are not known with any degree of accuracy; among counselors and clinicians, the dissatisfaction, the *malaise,* the gnawing uncertainty, are acute.

Why, one might ask, can one not interview a client with a vocational choice problem, assign a battery of tests, give him the scores, and then expect that he will act as appropriately as the situation allows? This *modus-operandi* was—and perhaps still is in some quarters—in effect for a long time with, it should be noted, not entirely bad effects. Yet most of us share some of the acute dissatisfaction with this approach.

Our colleagues with the well-thumbed volumes of Freud's collected works on their shelves have pointed out that such procedures ignore the facts of life regarding motivation, conscious and unconscious. People, even college sophomores, have motives. Worse, these motives are dynamic, whatever that means. Sometimes, clients will not do their best on our tests. Most tests presume the presence of the old college try. On personality and interest tests, clients will sometimes lie to us, to themselves, or to both. Even if they do not lie very much and if they do try to answer the items to the best of their abilities, they will often refuse to believe or to act on the results of the tests they have taken. Anyone who has ever tried to convince an aspiring pre-medic that he just does not have the ability to make it, especially if a favorite uncle once patted him on the head and told him he was a real smart boy, will know what I mean. Most perverse of all, many will finally acquiesce on the surface but will, once outside of the counselor's office, go on doing the same old maladaptive things, be that trying to get into medical school with a tenth percentile ACE score or trying to get through engineering school with an equally low score on the Engineering and Physical Science Aptitude Test.

It seems to me that the problem may be considered from two major points of view. First, we might well examine the client and especially the task that our tests have set for him. Second, we might consider the techniques used by counselors and clinicians in trying to help the client complete his task successfully. The client's task is, to a considerable extent, determined by the psychologist, and I would like to turn first of all to this aspect of the problem. As scientists in more or less good standing, we share a passion for precision and accuracy. We sometimes share the feeling of Samuel Butler who said, "I do not mind lying, but I hate inaccuracy." The language of numbers is rather natural for us, and sometimes it is productive. Moreover, we have a passion for speaking scientifically, which often means that we cover our tracks with qualifications so extensive and intricate that even we are sometimes in doubt about what our colleagues really are saying. Useful and proper as the language of numbers and standard errors is, it is not the language of the clients with whom we deal. Yet the process goes inexorably on with us following the currents in our science and drifting farther and farther away from the consumers of our technology.

Binet set out to measure intelligence. Most people think they know what intelligence is. Before he got very far on the way, Binet had introduced a strange new concept: mental age. Stern, searching for a metric by means of which to express this characteristic, put mental age into a ratio with chronological age, multiplied the whole *mélange* by 100, and came up with the IQ. This has become after forty years a household term, but by now most of us doubt its value and for the most part leave it out of our test development enterprises. Yet notice how far from the client's universe of discourse the first widely used test got and in how short a time.

The same pattern may be seen in the development of personality tests. Woodworth set out to accomplish a fairly straightforward task: to sort out neurotics. Most people have some idea about neurosis. At least, they think it is a bad thing that has something to do with the personality. Perhaps this is enough. But what has happened in the past thirty-five years? Introversion-extraversion tests were developed. By the time these terms were becoming dimly understood, dominance and submission tests were the thing. Current tests locate the client on continua such as psychasthenia, *FC* and *CF, D* and *Dd, W,* rhathymia, *K, F,* anxiety, and repression. How productive these particular traits are is not at issue here. The point is that we have, in groping toward a better understanding of personality, departed a great distance from the language of the client. It is, of course, true that some of these tests are not meant for the client's perusal, but only for the counselor's edification. Nevertheless, the problem remains in many instances.

Some years back, Paterson and his colleagues in the Employment Stabilization Research Institute attempted to extend the psychograph principle. The occupational ability profile, while something of a misnomer, nevertheless represented an attempt to make test scores meaningful to counselors and clients, to come to terms with the dictum about a picture and a thousand words. The usefulness of occupational ability profiles for the personnel man has been fairly well demonstrated. Considerably less has been said about the client's problem of trying to learn about himself from the inspection of such profiles. One of the few thorough treatments is that of Bennett, Seashore, and Wesman (1). Profiles are still very much with us, but the more expert the counselor or clinician, the more he sees or professes to see in the relationships among the points in the profile. Clearly, profile analysis as it is usually practiced is not for the college sophomore. Parenthetically, I am somewhat intrigued by the different treatment afforded to profiles of ability scores and those of personality or interest scores. In the latter case, the interpretations often border on the mystifying. The MMPI, Strong, and Rorschach seem especially vulnerable. Except for some attempts with the Wechsler, I know of few instances where people have become particularly "dynamic" with profiles of ability scores. This leads me to wonder whether we are missing the boat in interpreting ability profiles or whether the interpretations of personality and interest profiles represent rather stupefying metaphysical leaps. Only time—and good criteria—will tell.

There is another line of development that has perforce contributed to the present difficulties. Binet worked hard to measure a global trait, intelligence. Other test constructors followed suit with tests of neuroticism, adjustment, mechanical aptitude, etc. Increasingly, there has been a tendency to try to measure pure traits. This tendency has arisen largely as a result of the developments in factor analysis. I happen to be among those who believe that this line of endeavor will in the long run pay off with better tests and better descriptions of human behavior. The problem with which I am concerned here, however, is the intelligibility of tests scores to the client. I would like to repeat here a notion I first expressed several years ago (12); namely, that the difficulty of test interpretation is inversely related to the counselor's understanding of the trait measured and to its predictive significance. It seems unlikely that we should try to give all of our clients a short course in psychometric and factor theory so that they will understand our tests. This task is hard enough with graduate students.

It would be possible to go on at considerable length documenting the difficulties that a developing test technology and theory present to clients and counselors, but I hope that the point has been made adequately. We are in somewhat the same situation as the physicist who, when asked to describe a chair, quite accurately states that it is largely made up of empty space crisscrossed by wandering atoms. Such an answer is of comparatively little use to a person who wishes to know whether or not he should sit down and, if so, what the consequences will be. I am certainly not proposing that we return to the measurement of the old, complex, global traits like mechanical aptitude and general intelligence. I am, however, suggesting that we have created a considerable gap between the client and his language and our tests and their language. Parenthetically, and related to this same area, we might do well to consider the problem of validity. I sometimes wonder how much rapport we lose when a client, trying to decide between medicine and engineering, takes an inventory that asks him whether he would rather be a motorman or a conductor. We are all aware of the predictive validity of such items, but clients are not. Perhaps something more might be done following Gulliksen's distinction (11) between intrinsic and correlational validity.

Turning now to the other issue, the counselor's methods, there has been growing for the past several years the feeling that our methods of introducing testing in the first place and of interpreting tests in the second have something to do with the problems we face in getting tests and test results accepted and acted upon. The general tenor of the arguments presented by Rogers (16) is too well known to need repeating. Among those happier with the use of tests in counseling, Bordin and Bixler (4) proposed that the process of test selection be considered an integral part of counseling, not an intruding element. They went on to suggest that the identification with the process achieved by encouraging the client to participate was worth any difficulties it might create.

The subsequent work of Seeman (18) provided some substantiation for the ideas expressed by Bordin and Bixler. Seeman was interested in whether, in a permissive situation, clients would select appropriate tests in sufficient number. He concluded that they tended to do so. A study recently completed at Maryland bears on the same point; discussion of it will be postponed until later.

With respect to client participation in test interpretation, much the same situation obtains. Bixler and Bixler (3) proposed that such participation would have salutory effects on counseling. Several studies provide partial substantiation. Dressel and Matteson (7) concluded that students who participated most gained correspondingly in self-understanding, in security with respect to the choice made, and in satisfaction with counseling. Kamm and Wrenn (14) concluded that client acceptance of test information was best when several conditions were met: first, when the client and counselor were completely at ease; second, when the client took a positive attitude throughout counseling; third, when the client was ready to respond on the basis of the new information; fourth, when the information presented was directly related to the client's problem; and fifth, when the information presented was not in conflict with the client's self concept. Kamm and Wrenn seem to be describing nondefensive clients. These are certainly desirable, but the techniques for reducing defensiveness are somewhat difficult to isolate.

Taking a slightly different tack, Rogers (17) compared two methods of counseling, one of which encouraged client participation, the other of which did not. He found no differences between the groups handled by the two methods, but he did find that higher level intelligence and more active client participation in counseling were related to better outcomes.

Intrigued by some of the same problems, we recently completed a study (13) at Maryland, conducted under a contract with the Office of Naval Research, dealing with different methods of test introduction and test interpretation and their effects on client learning as a dependent variable. Very briefly, we selected three methods of introducing and selecting tests, four methods of interpreting test results. The dependent variable was a discrepancy index employing differences between self-ratings and tested positions. The discrepancy index was adjusted for initial accuracy so that clients who showed high accuracy on pre-counseling ratings would not thereby be penalized in post-counseling ratings. Test introduction methods varied from extremely permissive to quite directive. Test interpretation methods included the use of profiles, verbal descriptions without visual aids, and two methods in which the clients' initial ratings were compared with test scores.

Neither the rows nor the columns, introduction and interpretation methods, were related differentially to the dependent variable. Equal changes were observed for all groups. Moreover, the interaction term between interpretation and introduction was not significant. These results are in close agreement with those reported by Singer and Stefflre (19).

In connection with the same research project, Tuma (20) undertook to study certain personality characteristics of pairs of clients and counselors as these might be related to the dependent variable. His research followed the general line laid down by Fiedler (8, 9, 10). He found some relationships existing which suggested that methods as such, taken apart from the personalities involved, are perhaps not the most fruitful variables for study. He found, for instance, significant differences in average gains among clients seen by different counselors and significant correlations between client-counselor similarity indices on selected personality traits and the dependent variable. These correlations were significant only for the ability variables. Dominance, social participation, and social presence were the variables with the highest correlations.

A point to be kept in mind in the above studies concerns the different kinds of dependent variables employed. Singer and Stefflre, Tuma, and I employed adjusted discrepancy indices. Correlations between initial and final self-ratings and test scores have been used (2) as well as unadjusted discrepancy indices. All of these, it must be remembered, are only intermediate criteria, not ultimate ones. Dependent variables seem in general to vary in availability inversely with their importance. Dressel (6, p. 71) has summed up the case very well in the following:

... our real concern ... is only in part with the here and now; the ultimate concern is with the years after completion of school. Lacking the means for expensive follow-ups, recognizing the difficulty in attribution to counseling its exact contribution, and having a natural impatience for immediate action, we turn to criteria such as grades, graduation, stay in school, stability, or satisfaction with choice of major. Such criteria are not always applicable to all individuals in the same way and their relation to ultimate goals is not clear.

If I may summarize and perhaps oversimplify in doing so, it appears that the solution to the problem of how to make test scores meaningful to clients lies imbedded in the interpersonal relationships obtaining in the counseling interview. Moreover, techniques as such are probably not the final question; rather, we must seek to find those techniques that can be applied by selected counselors to appropriate clients. This is a large order.

In the meantime, I would like to reiterate my earlier point, namely, that we turn some attention to bridging the gap between our tests and our clients. I am certainly not proposing any abandonment of the search for better and more meaningful traits, but tests used in counseling are to a considerable extent useful in direct proportion to their intelligibility and acceptability to the client. Both for this kind of enterprise, as well as for the work to be done on devising and revising techniques, we need criteria that are closer to the life situations in which decisions are made and acted on. Until we get these, our research must remain under the cloud of suspicion that clients simply learn how, during the process of counseling, to say things that will make the counselor happy.

Since I have spent my time talking about problems and areas of ignorance rather than laying down nice clean, simple, guaranteed rules for making test information meaningful, I am afraid that this may have sounded like that most pedestrian of all prose productions, the doctoral dissertation. Rather than closing, then, with a plea for further research, I will read a couplet of Alexander Pope's that seems to sum up as well as anything the job we have to do:

> Men must be taught as if you taught them not,
> And things unknown proposed as things forgot.

REFERENCES

1. Bennett, G., Seashore, H., & Wesman, A. *Counseling from profiles.* New York: Psychological Corporation, 1951.
2. Berdie R. Changes in self-ratings as a method of evaluating counseling. *Journal of Counseling Psychology,* 1954, 1, 49–54.
3. Bixler, R., & Bixler, Virginia. Test interpretation in vocational counseling. *Educational and Psychological Measurement,* 1946, 6, 145–155.
4. Bordin, E., & Bixler, R. Test selection: a process of counseling. *Educational and Psychological Measurement,* 1946, 6, 361–373.
5. Buros, O. (Ed.) *The fourth mental measurements yearbook.* Highland Park, N.J.: Gryphon Press, 1953.
6. Dressel, P. Evaluation of counseling. In Berdie, R. (Ed.), *Concepts and programs of counseling.* Minneapolis: Univer. of Minnesota Press, 1951.
7. Dressel, P., & Matteson, R. The effect of client participation in test interpretation. *Educational and Psychological Measurement,* 1950, 10, 693–706.
8. Fiedler, F. A comparison of therapeutic relationships in psychoanalytic, nondirective, and Adlerian theory. *Journal of Consulting Psychology,* 1950, 14, 436–445.
9. Fiedler, F. The concept of an ideal therapeutic relationship. *Journal of Counsulting Psychology,* 1950, 14, 239–245.
10. Fiedler, F. Factor analyses of psychoanalytic, nondirective, and Adlerian therapeutic relationships. *Journal of Consulting Psychology,* 1951, 15, 32–38.
11. Gulliksen, H. Intrinsic validity. *American Psychologist,* 1950, 5, 511–517.

12. Gustad, J. Test information and learning in the counseling process. *Educational and Psychological Measurement,* 1951, 11, 788–795.

13. Gustad, J. The effects of differing methods of test selection and interpretation on learning in the interview. Final report, Office of Naval Research Contract Nonr 1225 (00), 1955. Mimeographed.

14. Kamm, R., & Wrenn, C. Client acceptance of self-information in counseling. *Educational and Psychological Measurement,* 1950, 10, 32–42.

15. Parsons, F. *Choosing a vocation.* New York: Houghton Mifflin, 1909.

16. Rogers, C. Psychometric tests and client-centered counseling. *Educational and Psychological Measurement,* 1946, 6, 139–144.

17. Rogers, L. B. A comparison of two kinds of test interpretation interview. *Journal of Counseling Psychology,* 1954, 1, 224–231.

18. Seeman, J. A study of client self-selection of tests in vocational counseling. *Educational and Psychological Measurement,* 1948, 8, 327–346.

19. Singer, S., & Stefflre, B. Analysis of the self-estimate in the evaluation of counseling. *Journal of Counseling Psychology,* 1954, 1, 252–255.

20. Tuma, A. An exploration of certain methodological and client-counselor personality characteristics as determinants of learning in the counseling of college students. Unpublished doctoral dissertation, Univer. of Maryland, 1955.

21. Wolfle, D. Testing is big business. *American Psychologist,* 1947, 2, 26.

What Testing Does to Teachers and Students

RALPH W. TYLER

1959

The use of testing to influence students is a long-established practice. Teachers have often been classified by their pupils as "tough" or "soft" in terms of the frequency and searching character of their examinations. Well-motivated students have commonly put extra time and effort into study when they thought they were soon to be tested. Quite probably, too, pupils having great difficulty in their school work felt even more incompetent when confronted with a test and, because it seemed too difficult, were not stimulated to study more effectively thereby. These differential effects of testing on students have been mentioned in the literature of teaching since the earliest years of publication.

With the advent of the "new type" of test following World War I, questions began to be raised about the effects of short answer forms of tests in contrast to essay tests upon the motivation and study practices of pupils. A number of investigators sought through interviews and questionnaires addressed to high school and college students to find out whether the form of test used made any difference in their study practices. The results of these investigations, as typified by the reports of Douglass and Tallmadge (1) in 1934 and George Meyer (2, 3) in 1934 and 1935, showed that a considerable majority of students reporting both in high school and college followed clearly different study procedures when they anticipated being given a "new-type" test from those followed when they expected an essay examination.

For a "new-type" test, the majority went over and over assigned material seeking to memorize every point, including specific details. For an essay test, the majority gave much less attention to specific details in the assignment and more attention to identifying a few major points around which they could write brief descriptive or expository paragraphs. These studies made it clear that students were strongly influenced in preparing for tests by their

46

perceptions of what the tests measured, that is, what behavior they would need to exhibit and with what content.

The Regents' Inquiry into the Character and Cost of Public Education in New York State, begun in 1936, provided objective evidence regarding the influence of testing on teachers as well as students. An intensive study was made of 61 school districts within the state, examining their curriculum guides and testing their high school students for several of the objectives specified in the curriculum guides. It was found that the achievement of the students paralleled more closely the objectives tested by the Regents' examinations than the objectives given major emphasis in the local curricula. Interviews with a sample of teachers in these communities revealed the fact that most of them were conscious of the objectives being tested in the Regents' examinations and sought to emphasize these kinds of learning in their classes rather than to follow the objectives recommended in the local curriculum guides.

My own experience in the Eight-Year Study corroborated these findings. When new ideas regarding the secondary school curriculum were advanced, we always found teachers raising the question of the relationship of these new proposals to the achievements which were being appraised by the College Entrance Examination Board tests. Only through the arrangement worked out with colleges which permitted high school graduates to be considered for admission on the basis of scholastic aptitude tests and test data submitted by the schools in the Eight-Year Study were we able to get thoughtful consideration by the teachers of new curriculum proposals. Many were then able to shift from their previous practice of planning their teaching to correspond with their view of what would be required of their students on college entrance tests to planning based on judgments of the educational values of various kinds of learning.

A third kind of illustration of the influence of testing on students and teachers is the prevalence of coaching for tests. Some schools turn the junior and senior classes in the college preparation curriculum into coaching sessions several weeks before external tests are to be given. Some schools do not modify the teaching in the regular classes, but arrange for special coaching for students planning to take these tests. In some communities, where no provisions for coaching are made in schools, some parents arrange for special coaching classes or for tutoring in the belief that this will aid their children to perform better on the tests. A quick examination of book stores and of advertisements also provides an indication of demand for coaching. Books and pamphlets purporting to help students pass important tests are widely sold.

Before concluding this brief review of the current influence of testing, mention should be made of the criticisms that are periodically raised regarding the effect of testing in intensifying the motivation of some students to an undesirable degree or attaching the motivation to undesirable objects. It is sometimes claimed that testing creates undue anxiety on the part of pupils who anticipate difficulties or inadequacies of test performance in comparison with their aspirations. This emotional tension, it is charged, not only interferes with successful performance on the test but increases the pupil's preoccupation with self-criticisms and distracts his attention from school work generally, thus lowering the effectiveness of his learning. A related criticism is that test scores are often seen by parents and children as ends in themselves in the competition to do better than their neighbors and to rise in the scale of social esteem. This obsession with getting high test scores attaches motivation to an external criterion rather than aiding the student to find satisfactions in learning and to become motivated to continue study and inquiry under his own steam.

The extent to which these criticisms are valid has not been established by comprehensive empirical studies, but there is enough case material to justify the conclusion that for some undetermined number of children, the anticipation of taking a test sets off an anxiety mechanism and that some parents use the results of tests as a means for rewarding or punishing children beyond the limits of common practice of teachers. It also seems clear from available cases that for many pupils and teachers, test performance is viewed as the major end of school instruction, rather than being a useful but not infallible indicator of student achievement.

I believe it is a fair summary of the current situation to say that tests have marked effects on many students and teachers. For pupils who have some confidence in their ability to perform on the tests, the knowledge that tests are to be given serves as a strong stimulation to study and the later report of their test performance provides a powerful reinforcement mechanism of reward or punishment that helps to maintain the motivation for learning. Not only does testing afford forceful motivation, but it also directs the efforts of many students and teachers toward learning activities that they believe are most relevant to what they think the test calls for. In many cases, this may focus the attention on goals different from those purportedly emphasized by the school, and in some cases, this results in "coaching" rather than long-term, systematic instruction. Furthermore, testing can be a source of anxiety to some pupils and parents and can become for some the ends of education rather than a device for appraisal. Testing is a powerful instrument with potentialities for both good and bad.

When faced with this generalization, we who are concerned with the improvement of education and the effectiveness of learning must consider together how to achieve the maximum good potential in testing and to minimize or eliminate the bad. The problem cannot be met by denying the existence of the double-edged sword and by claiming that tests are "neutral" and are not in themselves agents for good or bad. Too much evidence of these varied effects of testing is available to disregard them, and so many teachers and school administrators have become concerned that steps of some sort will be taken. Wise action rather than no action should be sought. The problem cannot be met by advising schools to reduce sharply or eliminate testing. The need for more objective appraisals of pupil abilities and achievements for guidance and for curriculum evaluation as well as for instruction is even more widely recognized, and the use of tests is on a very sharp increase. Testing will continue, and the problem to be faced is how to conduct testing programs to derive the greatest benefits from them.

Since tests have a powerful directive influence on teaching and the study of pupils, a major policy to follow is to establish a testing program that faithfully reflects the objectives sought by the school. In this way, the influence of testing is to reinforce the other efforts of teaching. For a testing program to reflect faithfully the school's educational objectives, the tests used should not focus on behavior or content irrelevant to the school's purposes, but rather there should be included in the total testing program some appraisal of student achievement of all of the major objectives. This, of course, places a joint responsibility both upon the school and upon the producers of tests. The school in its selection of tests and in making clear its needs creates a demand for tests that appraise important educational objectives, while the thought, ingenuity, and effort of test producers are required to develop and distribute the kind of testing instruments needed.

There is more to this policy than may be apparent at first glance. For a test or other form of evaluative instrument to be appropriate for a given educational objective, it must evoke from the student the kind of behavior implied by the objective, and it must also deal with the content the objective implies. Thus, if one of the objectives of a social studies course is to develop an understanding of the concepts useful in analyzing the social structure of an American community, an appropriate test will require the student to show his understanding; that is, not merely to give or recognize a memorized statement of the concepts, but to state them in his own words, to recognize examples, to give illustrations of the concepts, and to compare and contrast related concepts. These kinds of behavior are commonly considered to be involved in understanding something. Furthermore, the appropriate test will deal with the concepts useful in analyzing the structure of an American community. A test of this sort can focus the attention of the student and teacher upon one of the objectives actually sought in the course rather than directing their efforts at some achievement irrelevant to it.

Or, as another example, if one of the objectives of a physics course in the school is to develop the ability of the students to apply basic principles of physics in explaining common physical phenomena and predicting the probable consequences of particular physical forces in action, then an appropriate test for this objective will require the student to explain various common physical phenomena using basic principles of physics in the explanation, and it will also involve exercises in which the student is expected to predict on the basis of his understanding of these basic principles what the probable consequences will be in various situations involving physical forces. If every major objective of the school is appraised by tests and other devices that are appropriate to evoke the desired behavior in connection with the specified content, then the testing reinforces the school's efforts to attain its objectives rather than interfering with the learning desired.

However, it is not enough for the testing to reflect faithfully the educational objectives of the school. The pupils and teachers are directed by their perceptions of what the tests call for. When, at the Ohio State University, we began to use tests in biology that required students to apply biological principles in the solution of biological problems, the students looked at the tests and saw that the concrete situations described were not the ones outlined in the lectures, explained in the text, or worked on in the laboratory. Because they thought of achievement tests as measuring their memory of material dealt with in the course, they threw up their hands. These were questions that had not been answered previously in the course. So we spent some time explaining the purpose of each test and showing the kind of behavior required. This clarified the nature of the examinations used and also served to direct the students' subsequent study.

If the perceptions of students and teachers of the requirements of particular tests are to be accurate, more must be done than to give appropriate names to the tests. Manuals explaining what the tests involve are useful, and examples of test items with an explanation of the way each item is attacked help still more in clarifying perceptions, but demonstration testing sessions with explanations are also likely to be necessary.

In this connection, most people have only a vague notion of the concept of sampling as it applies to the content and the situations included in a test. Hence, some teachers having seen one form of a test attempt to coach students on the particular items in this form. They fail to understand that comparable forms of a test will all require the same kind of behavior, but each will draw its content and the particular test situations from the total universe defined by the objective the test seeks to appraise. Thus, one form of a test will help to clarify the kind of behavior involved in all forms, but the learning and practice should be distributed over the total content and the variety of situations implied by the objective. The explanation and demonstration of this is an important part of the test manual, the sample exercises, and the discussion that takes place in the demonstration of the procedure for attacking the exercises in a test. This also serves to make the test as perceived by students and teachers a more accurate reflection of the educational objectives emphasized by the school.

Another policy that can increase the positive values of testing is to use similar tests periodically throughout the instructional program and to review with the students their performance on each test. This serves several purposes. It provides another means of explaining the nature of the tests and thus clarifying the educational objectives of the school. It reduces markedly the likelihood that the novelty of the test will affect the pupil's performance on it. This practice also reduces the emotional tension surrounding testing. Testing becomes a natural part of the total learning process, rather than an infrequent and traumatic experience. Teaching machines, which are in essence self-testing, self-scoring devices, are widely interesting, even absorbing, to elementary and secondary school pupils. Much of the attraction of teaching machines lies in the immediate opportunity to tests one's performance and to see how adequate it is. Tests properly selected so that the pupils who take them are able to demonstrate what they have learned, as well as what they have still to master, can help to build confidence in taking tests rather than to arouse anxiety.

Tests are here to stay and their uses will increase. They can be an obstacle to an effective educational program, distracting attention from the school's basic purposes and arousing undue excitement and fear. On the other hand, because testing can increase motivation and provide an additional source of reinforcement to learning, and because it can help to clarify the objectives of the school and focus effort on them, testing should be used as a positive factor in the educational program. To do so, the tests used should faithfully reflect the school's objectives, pupils and teachers should clearly perceive what behaviors the tests call for and what content they involve, and they should have continuing experience with appropriate tests to gain confidence in their ability to learn and to perform and to utilize the reinforcement potential of the tests as an important dynamic factor in learning.

REFERENCES

1. Douglass, H. R., & Tallmadge, Margaret. How university students prepare for new types of examinations. *School and Society,* 1934, 39, 318–320.
2. Meyer, G. An experimental study of the old and new types of examinations: I. the effect of the examination set on memory. *Journal of Educational Psychology,* 1934, 25, 641–661.
3. Meyer, G. An experimental study of the old and new types of examinations: II. methods of study. *Journal of Educational Psychology,* 1935, 26, 30–40.

New Light on Test Strategy from Decision Theory[1]

LEE J. CRONBACH

1954

In every practical use of tests, our aim is to make decisions. This is obvious in personnel selection, but it is also true of testing in the classroom and in the clinic. The teacher uses tests because he has to make decisions about appropriate instructional methods. The clinician uses tests as an aid in deciding on therapeutic tactics. Sometimes, as in vocational guidance, the decisions are made not by the tester but by the person tested. Test theory should indicate how to reach the best possible decision in any of these situations.

In decision theory, the word *strategy* refers to the process by which an individual arrives at a decision. A strategy may be very simple: "I shall examine the applicant's grade average, and if it is B or better I shall accept him." The strategy may instead be complex, stating what tests, if any, will be given, what decision will be made for any particular pattern of results, and what further steps will be taken to decide on borderline cases. Choosing among alternative strategies is the essential problem of test theory.

There are two questions in choosing a strategy. First, with any given procedure for gathering information, what is the best procedure for translating this information into final decisions? The second, but logically prior, question is: among several alternative procedures for gathering information, which is most profitable?

In order to compare two strategies, we have to determine how much benefit we gain from either one. Most of the problems of decision theory therefore reduce to determining just how much benefit is gained from a particular decision-making procedure.

Since this morning's program is intended to deal primarily with insights

[1] Based on work conducted under Contract N6ori-07146 with the Office of Naval Research. The extensive developments in this field since 1954 are reported in Cronbach and Gleser (6).

from some of these newer points of view, I shall not dwell on the mathematics of decision problems. There is available a large amount of relevant theory in the work of economists on utility, in the theory of games (2), and in the statistical decision theory of Abraham Wald (11). Decision problems can be attacked in many ways, but we have confined ourselves to strategies that maximize expected utility. This is reasonable only if we are dealing with a stable and familiar situation.[2]

The decision model requires us to specify three aspects of any decision. One is the proposed strategy or decision rule. For example, the strategy might be to give two tests, combine scores by a regression formula, and accept everyone above a given cutoff. Second, we consider the adequacy of the information to be used. The usual contingency matrix or scatter diagram relating test scores and criterion scores deals with this question. The third necessary element is an evaluation matrix. This, sometimes called a payoff matrix, states specifically just what benefit or detriment accompanies each possible decision. Once these three aspects of a problem have been described, we are ready to compute the payoff a person can expect if he bases decisions upon this information and this strategy.

It is difficult and at times impossible to write the evaluation matrix for a particular situation. To let this difficulty deter us from using decision theory, however, would be to deny the possibility of sound test theory. Test effectiveness simply *cannot* be evaluated without an evaluation matrix. Even the conventional procedures of test analysis assume certain payoffs covertly, and the reasonableness of some of these hidden assumptions is open to question. In the future, testers may wish to determine utilities by a sort of cost accounting in any specific practical situation, in order to arrive at the best decisions (3, 8). Our project is proceeding along different lines. We are working with hypothetical (but we hope realistic) decision problems. By assuming that the evaluation matrix has some characteristic form, we are able to judge the utility of different types of tests and strategies. Such an approach can be no better than our assumptions. We hope, nonetheless, to arrive at general principles of testing that will illuminate many real situations.

Let me turn to some of the concepts a decision approach brings to our attention. I shall cover four such points.

1) Our model suggests that the value of test information should be judged by how much it improves decisions over the best possible decisions made without the test, whereas the conventional validity coefficient reports how much better test decisions are than *chance* decisions. In the majority of

[2] Further introductory discussions of decision theory can be found in 4, 7, 10.

situations where tests could be used, a substantial amount of information is already available, and if no test were given, the decision would still be considerably better than chance.

Our most valid tests are essentially work samples of their criteria. Where such a work sample might be used, evidence of past performance is also a valid basis for decisions, and such evidence is often readily available. In predicting school marks, for example, a scholastic aptitude test is not greatly more valid than past school records. The contribution of this test to decision making is much smaller than its zero-order validity coefficient would indicate, because better-than-chance decisions could be made without it.

A similar conception applies to classroom testing. The basic knowledge and skill objectives can be assessed with considerable accuracy from day-to-day assignments; a test can add only a small increment to the soundness of decisions. On the other hand, a teacher has rather little basis for judging which pupils have problems of adjustment. The teacher may, therefore, gain more useful knowledge from a test of adjustment which has limited validity, than from an achievement test which largely duplicates data already available. There are serious weaknesses in our tests for such educational outcomes as creativity, reasoning habits, attitudes, and application of knowledge to problem situations. They are markedly inferior in validity to tests of general intelligence or factual knowledge. But the factors that make testing difficult also prevent valid nontest decisions about these objectives. It may therefore be wiser to use imperfect tests of important objectives that are hard to measure, than to use highly valid tests that merely supplement nontest data.

2) Utility analysis leads us to examine the value of adapting to individual differences in either selection or placement. This can best be considered in terms of a placement problem, such as assigning students to sections of freshman English according to their initial ability. We might think of the various levels as predetermined, and of the test as assigning persons to each category using fixed cutting scores. It is sounder to see the test, the curricula, and the cutting scores as interlocked. We can increase or decrease the demands instruction in any section makes, to fit it to the ability of the persons assigned. Under this procedure, we benefit more from testing than when we leave the treatment fixed.

Certain simple assumptions lead to interesting conclusions. If a sample is divided into groups, using fixed cutting scores, the extent to which treatment for the groups should be differentiated depends on the validity of the placement test. If the information has zero validity, utility is maximized when we teach all sections in the manner suited to the average of the population. As validity increases, the treatments given the sections may differ more; but no matter how valid the test, there is an optimum degree of differentiation of treatment. If treatment is differentiated beyond this point, the benefit from sectioning declines. Indeed, it is possible to differentiate treatments so radically that a *loss* in utility results from sectioning, even though the test used has considerable validity.

This analysis raises a serious question as to whether we are right when we urge teachers to adapt to individual differences. If the teacher has a standard plan, well fitted to the average of the group, he should hesitate to depart from it. Marked alteration of the plan to fit individuals appears to be advisable only when individual differences are validly assessed and their implications for treatment clear.

3) We turn, now, to another suggestion encountered in decision theory. It is customary to look at a test as a unit, and to use it just for one terminal decision. At any point in testing, however, we can make a terminal decision or can continue to gather information. New frontiers open for us when we view testing as a multi-stage, or sequential, operation.

Suppose, in a simple selection problem, we have several short aptitude tests, which together might constitute a selection battery. We give the first short test; some men can be rejected or accepted at once, but less clear-cut cases are retained for further testing. After the second test is given to these men, we can make more final decisions, and only a borderline group goes on to the third test. This process terminates when the benefit from information to be gained at any stage is outweighed by the cost of testing. Considering cost of testing, the sequential method is more profitable than giving the same test to everyone. If testing is expensive, one reaches the final decision for a surprisingly large proportion of men after only the first short test. One paper on this line of attack has been published by Arbous and Sichel (1), but our detailed results will differ from theirs in important respects.

A sequential plan would require new ways of organizing testing. I shall discuss one procedure for possible use in vocational guidance, clinical diagnosis, or evaluation of classroom learning. Here it can be described in terms of the job assignment problem. For different jobs, so many abilities are relevant that we cannot hope to measure them all accurately in a reasonable period. With brief tests, however, one could crudely measure as many as 50 variables in a half day. Such a survey will indicate some jobs for which the man is an unlikely prospect, and a second group of jobs for which the tests show possible high aptitude. For the man's second test session, perhaps only an hour after the first test, we would assemble a set of booklets to test him more thoroughly on those promising aptitudes. This progressive narrowing would be continued. When the final job assignment is made, we would have a highly reliable measure of the man's aptitude for that job, and also a good measure for the other jobs seriously considered as alternatives. But we would have wasted little time in getting an accurate measure of his space ability or his dexterity if these areas were not among his better aptitudes on the first survey.

We might actually develop different sorts of tests for the earlier and later screens. The Strong Vocational Interest Blank might be replaced by a brief questionnaire, perhaps one page long. This seems likely to identify the important interest groups for a given man. There might then be a separate, longer interest blank for each of these interest groups, to provide more precise differentiation between related occupations than is now possible.

4) Perhaps our most far-reaching conclusion is that we should take a more favorable view of tests with low validity. Traditionally, if a score has low validity, we conclude that it should not be used. But such tests become valuable when selection ratios are low—as Taylor and Russell (9) noted; when they give even a little new evidence on an important decision; and particularly when they are used as a preliminary survey.

The survey is especially important when many decisions are to be made. Sometimes, as in vocational choice, the decisions are interrelated and lead to one final course of action. The decisions may, on the other hand, be quite independent, as when one diagnoses many persons. The problem in testing is ordinarily to select information-getting devices that will yield greatest benefit for the time available. If we spend a lot of time to get an accurate answer to one question, we must answer other questions without added information. In this situation, it may be much wiser to use several tests of limited validity, so that every decision is made with some wisdom, than to get highly accurate information for just one of the decisions.

The difference between validity and utility is clear when we compare group and individual tests. An individual mental test measures one person with essentially the same expenditure of effort by the tester as the group test measuring one hundred. If the two tests have the same validity, the group test gives us 100 times as much information and bears on 100 decisions while the individual test bears on one. Hence, the improvement of decisions is vastly greater when the group test is used. If the individual test has much higher validity than the group test, which is best to use would depend on the specific decision problem.

This conception permits a favorable view of interviews and other clinical procedures that cover many aspects of the personality (5). These methods, though undependable, are well suited to a wide-casting survey, gathering a little information on each of hundreds of questions. Such a preliminary scanning draws attention to the critical areas where further information should be gathered prior to any decision. The traditional, narrowly focused measuring device is ideal when we know in advance exactly what question needs to be answered. But in deciding whether a man will make a good executive, or in locating a patient's chief conflict areas, no such focus is possible. The first task of the assessor is to discover which critical variables will dictate the proper decision about the individual; in different cases, different variables will be critical.

Personnel workers regard the interview as indispensable, and clinicians have considerable faith in projective methods and qualitative analysis of intelligence test protocols. In my opinion, this faith has developed largely because of rewarding experience with these techniques in their survey function, i.e., as the first stage in a sequential assessment. If it is true that these multidimensional techniques have a unique place in assessment, we should judge how well they do that job, and should not demand that they be good measuring instruments—which they are not. On the other side of the picture, if their proper function is to make preliminary surveys so that more intensive examination can follow, one should not rest final judgments on these fallible instruments.

Taken as a whole, decision theory is a mathematical system that permits us to examine the problems we face in developing tests, choosing between tests, and interpreting tests. Whenever we can specify any particular decision problem in detail, then decision theory can tell us just what to do. By studying common type-problems, decision theory can also offer general recommendations regarding testing strategy.

Conventional test theory assumes that we use tests to obtain numerical measures on an interval scale, as in the physical sciences. That is rarely or never true. The function of psychological and educational tests is to aid in making discrete decisions. The greatest contribution of decision theory is to help testers see this function more clearly.

REFERENCES

1. Arbous, A. G., & Sichel, H. S. On the economies of a pre-screening technique for aptitude test batteries. *Psychometrika,* 1952, 17, 331–346.
2. Blackwell, D., & Girshick, M. A. *Theory of games and statistical decisions.* New York: Wiley, 1954.

3. Brogden, H. E., & Taylor, E. K. The dollar criterion—applying the cost accounting concept to criterion construction. *Personnel Psychology,* 1950, 3, 133–154.
4. Bross, I. D. J. *Design for decision.* New York: Macmillan, 1953.
5. Cronbach, L. J. The counselor's problems from the perspective of communication theory. In Vivian H. Hewer (Ed.), *New perspectives in counseling.* Minnesota Studies in Personnel Work, No. 7. Minneapolis: Univer. of Minnesota Press, 1955.
6. Cronbach, L. J., & Gleser, Goldine C. *Psychological tests and personnel decisions.* (2nd ed.) Urbana: Univer. of Illinois Press, 1965.
7. Edwards, W. The theory of decision making. *Psychological Bulletin,* 1954, 51, 380–417.
8. Goodman, L. A. The use and validity of a prediction instrument. *American Journal of Sociology,* 1953, 58, 503–510.
9. Taylor, H. C., & Russell, J. T. The relationship of validity coefficients to the practical effectiveness of tests in selection: discussion and tables. *Journal of Applied Psychology,* 1939, 23, 565–578.
10. Thrall, R. M., Coombs, C. H., & Davis, R. L. (Eds.) *Decision processes.* New York: Wiley, 1954.
11. Wald, A. *Statistical decision functions,* New York: Wiley, 1950.

3 · THE EDUCATIONAL CONTEXT

WHILE THE RANGE of topics covered at Invitational Conferences has expanded conspicuously over the years, educational testing remains a major focus of interest. To provide a better orientation for such test uses, several sessions have been devoted to the educational context within which testing occurs. Periodic reconsideration of educational conditions and problems by psychometricians should help to keep tests relevant to current educational objectives.

In the opening paper of this chapter, Tyler provides an overview of curriculum theory over a fifty-year period. Implicit in this survey is a three-way relationship among educational curriculum, societal demands, and test construction. To maintain its vitality, the curriculum must keep step with changes in the society for which students are being educated; and to remain relevant and valid, tests must reflect both curricular and broader societal developments. The need for recurrent "task analysis" in the construction of both tests and curriculum is clearly apparent. It should be noted that Tyler's paper was presented in 1956. It thus provides a background against which we can view the rapid expansion and major innovations that characterized American education during the subsequent ten years.

Among these educational innovations, one that has aroused widespread interest and lively controversy is automation. Beginning with its earliest meetings, the Invitational Conference has given considerable attention to the utilization of "machine techniques" and automation in testing as well as in education. In Chapter 1, reference has already been made to the discussions of the newly developed IBM test-scoring machine, held at the 1937, 1938, and 1939 conferences. In 1953, conference participants were given an impressive view of the rapid progress that had occurred in test-scoring machines as well as in the application of computers to the processing of test results. A session of the 1959 conference was devoted to teaching machines and programmed learning. By 1962, the discussion of "machine techniques" had expanded into a comprehensive session on computer technology, covering not only machine scoring and computerized teaching machines, but also the use of computers in information storage and retrieval, in the processing of research data, in institutional record keeping, and in administrative decision making.

The paper by Holland, presented at the 1959 session on teaching machines, explains and illustrates the technique of "linear programming," derived from Skinner's learning theory. The major educational contributions of teaching machines stem, not from the "hardware" employed to present stimuli and record responses, but from their utilization of programmed learning. Programming involves essentially the preparation of a series of steps through which the learner is guided in a systematically established sequence. In this respect, it will be recognized as a specific application of sound principles of curriculum building. Typically, teaching machines also provide for active learner participation, immediate feedback, and individual pacing.

In the next paper, Pressey—himself a pioneer in the development of teaching machines—discusses another topic of concern to contemporary educators, namely, the educational acceleration of superior students. Although educators are divided in their opinions about acceleration, psychologists who have worked with gifted children are generally agreed about its advantages. One argument in its favor is that acceleration is a means of allowing for the wide individual differences found in learning rate. Another is that acceleration helps to reduce the ever-lengthening period of preparation required for high-level work in science and other professional specialties. It might be noted that educational acceleration creates a number of new testing needs, as illustrated by the advanced placement tests of the College Entrance Examination Board.

Stuit's paper approaches the educational scene from still another angle. The question Stuit poses is: how can we measure the quality of a college or university? Recognizing the difficulties of evaluating institutional products directly, he singles out four factors for special consideration: objectives, faculty, students, and institutional climate. An important source of student data is provided by test results, including not only scholastic aptitude and achievement tests, but also tests of attitudes and other nonintellectual traits. Recently developed techniques for the objective measurement of institutional climate are also cited as a potential tool for institutional evaluation. To aid in all aspects of such evaluation, Stuit emphasizes the need for normative or comparative data on institutional characteristics.

The Curriculum—Then and Now

RALPH W. TYLER

1956

Any effort to review the development during the past fifty years of the school curriculum of the United States encounters a confusing complexity. This condition is not due alone, or even primarily, to the fact that we have no centralized control of education in this country, although it is true that the variations among the 48 states are easily marked. These local variations are less pronounced than are the differences of another sort.

One may analyze the development of curriculum theory, that is, the statements of rationale for the curriculum and the related discussions which seek to explain it and to make it more coherent and systematic. One may examine the work of the persons and groups who have designed courses of study and prepared curriculum guides. One may assemble reports of the curriculum in operation in certain schools to obtain a picture of what teachers are actually teaching at a given time in the few schools on which this kind of report is available. These three reviews will give quite different content, yet each is a significant aspect of the American school curriculum.

Another factor in the complexity of this topic arises from the unusually comprehensive definition of the term "curriculum" which is currently employed in American educational circles. The term is not limited in this country, as it commonly is abroad, to refer to the outline of the content to be taught, but is used to include all of the learning of students which is planned by and directed by the school to attain its educational goals. This inclusive definition covers the formulation of educational objectives, the planning, use, and organization of learning experiences, and the appraisal of student learning. It also includes not only the learning activities carried on in the classroom and laboratory but also those at home or in extracurricular situations insofar as these are planned and directed by the school to attain its aims. The line drawn between the curriculum and other activities of the students is that which separates activities designed by the school to contribute to educational ends from those which are provided for recreation or for other purposes, or are not part of the school's plan. It is true that the current definition of the curriculum is a more adequate one for thinking about, for planning, and for conducting an educational program, but it does mean that a review of the curriculum must include a larger range of matters than would be required if the definition were limited to the outline of content to be taught.

To bring my task into manageable size, I have chosen to focus attention on the development of curriculum theory over the past fifty years with occasional comments on the ways in which courses of study and curriculum guides diverge from the accepted rationale and with still fewer occasional comments on the discrepancies between teaching practices and curriculum theory. To simplify this complex review still further, we shall examine each of three major aspects of the curriculum in turn, treating the formulation of educational objectives, the selection of learning experiences, and the organization of learning experiences.

THE FORMULATION OF EDUCATIONAL OBJECTIVES

A major step in most theories of curriculum development is the formulation of the educational objectives of the school, that is, the goals to be attained by its educational program. To be sure, this is not an appropriate step in John Dewey's educational philosophy in which the direction of learning is guided by careful consideration of the quality of the learning experiences. Insofar as the learning experiences provide for continuity and interaction, in Dewey's terms the program is effective. His philosophy does not involve a distinction between ends and means. But the other chief leaders of American curriculum thought emphasize the importance of clear objectives as the basis for planning the learning experiences and appraising the results.

Since the turn of the century, there have been several marked changes connected with the formulation of the objectives of the school. One of the most obvious has been the changed conception of the nature of educational objectives. The dominant educational psychology in 1900 was based on the theory of formal discipline and expressed in terms of "faculty psychology." The mind had certain faculties such as memory and reason which could be trained or disciplined by proper exercise. The objectives of the school were stated in terms of the faculties to be trained, and the learning experiences were those exercises in which these faculties were engaged on content particularly rich in opportunities for memorization, reasoning, and the like. Certain subjects by the very nature of their form and content were superior means for cultivation of these faculties. Language, particularly Latin, for example, was a superior subject because the learning of it required the exercise of memory, while its grammatical structure provided exercise in orderly reasoning.

With the decreasing acceptance of the theory of formal discipline and the elimination of faculty psychology, the prevailing view became increasingly behavioral. Learning was then conceived as the acquisition of patterns of behavior which the student had not previously followed. Human behavior was defined quite generally to include all the reactions of an individual—his thinking, feeling, acting.

Educational objectives are now couched in behavioral terms. An objective is a statement of a kind of behavior pattern which the school seeks to have the student develop. In the first flush of behavioral concepts, roughly from 1918 to 1925, the objectives were commonly stated in highly specific terms, such as ability to add 2 plus 3, ability to use the indefinite article "an," ability to spell "believe," ability to recall the atomic weight of sulphur. This was a natural corollary to the prevailing associationist theory in the psychology of learning. Every number combination, for example, was viewed as a different stimulus to which the student was to learn an appropriate response. This extreme view led to the listing of nearly three thousand specific objectives for arithmetic, and nearly two thousand for English. A student had attained the goals of the curriculum when he had learned to make the appropriate responses to all of the specific stimuli, that is, when all of these innumerable objectives had been reached.

By 1925, this view of objectives had largely fallen of its own weight. On the side of the teacher it required keeping in mind far too many goals to be remembered, and on the side of the student, it denied the development of generalized behavior patterns which quite obviously were developing. The formulation of other theories of learning which took into account the phenomenon of generalized behavior provided terms in which educational objectives have commonly been stated since 1930. For example, in 1936, the Department of Superintendence of the National Education Association published a yearbook on "The Social Studies Curriculum" (2). Among the objectives suggested were:

1) Acquisition of important information
2) Familiarity with technical vocabulary
3) Familiarity with dependable sources of information on current social issues
4) Immunity to malicious propaganda
5) Facility in interpreting social science data

6) Facility in applying significant facts and principles to social problems of daily life
7) Skill in investigating social science problems
8) Interest in reading about social problems and in discussing them
9) Sensitivity to current social problems
10) Interest in human welfare
11) The habit of working cooperatively with others
12) The habit of collecting and considering appropriate evidence before making important social decisions
13) Attitudes favorable to social improvement

These obviously present a conception of generalized behavior. However, although they avoid the piecemeal aims of highly specific objectives, they may be as limited in their value for guiding teaching as the earlier statements of objectives in terms of faculties to be developed, unless each of these 13 objectives is clearly enough defined to have meaning for the teacher so that he can easily think of concrete illustrations of the general aims. The developments since 1935 in the conception of the nature of educational objectives have largely focused on defining in concrete terms aims which are expressed at a similar level of generality as those above. These efforts have been applied to defining the kind of behavior implied by such general terms as "understanding," "applying principles to concrete problems," "ability to interpret reading material," and to indicating the range of content to which each kind of behavior is to be applied. Thus, the objective "to develop understanding of the basic concepts of physiology" has been defined from the standpoint of behavior and of content. The behavior "understanding" is defined as "the ability to recall the concepts, to state them in one's own words, to give illustrations of them, to recognize illustrations given by others, and to compare and contrast related concepts." The content termed "the basic concepts of physiology" is defined by listing some two score concepts which these curriculum makers have selected as basic to this science. This kind of definition helps greatly to clarify the aims of the curriculum so that they can actually be utilized in planning and conducting an educational program in terms of the prevailing conception of the psychology of learning.

A second marked change in the objectives of the American school curriculum has been in the sources used to derive the aims. To some extent all of the five major sources have been used in every period of American history but at a given time certain sources are dominant in their influence while others are given only minor attention. Between 1900 and 1918, the judgments of subject specialists and the prevailing conception of the psychology of learning were dominant in formulating objectives. At the high school level, the Committee of Ten used subcommittees of mathematicians, historians, language scholars, and the like to outline the objectives of secondary school instruction in these fields. Although the prevailing educational philosophy had already emphasized knowledge and skill for the layman as a major aim of the American high school, this source was given little attention in deciding on objectives. No studies were made of the needs of society nor of the needs of students to help in identifying appropriate objectives.

As a result of the success of job analysis in building vocational curricula during World War I, the process of formulating objectives from 1918 to 1933 leaned heavily upon job analyses, activity analyses, word counts and other techniques for identifying the demands made on the individual by contemporary social life. At this time, curriculum makers also gave attention to the notions of educational psychologists as to what behaviors could be taught. However, during this period, little attention was given to the prevailing social and educational philosophy regarding the characteristics of the good man and the good society. The opinions of subject specialists were given much less weight than in the previous period.

From 1933 to 1945, studies of children and youth served as a major source of suggestions for objectives. With an emphasis upon the responsibility of the school for meeting the needs of children and youth, curriculum commissions drew upon child-study data and reports of adolescent studies to derive objectives. This approach largely coincided with the prevailing emphasis in educational philosophy and to some extent the work of educational psychologists was used. But the use of studies of social demands was notably less than in the decade previous, while the opinions of subject specialists played a very minor role.

Since the Second World War, the shift in emphasis among the five kinds of sources has been marked. Primary attention is currently given to the opinions of subject specialists, particularly in mathematics and science. Very little weight is currently given to studies of the learner, but the specialists are asked to outline what they believe to be important potential contributions of their fields which will be of value to laymen as well as persons planning to specialize in the field. In this respect, the emphasis is different from that in 1900. Today, some attention is also being given to an examination of social demands, and to a lesser extent to the current conception of the psychology of learning. Much less use is made today of studies of the learner than was true 15 years ago. In general, the shifts which have taken place in the primary sources used to derive educational objectives most closely parallel the changes which can easily be seen in the statements of objectives appearing in courses of study and in curriculum guides. Because the actual practice of teaching depends so largely on the habits and outlooks of the thousands of American school teachers, the shifts in practice are not so easily discerned.

A third marked change has been in the range of objectives which the American schools have not only accepted for themselves but have actively championed. At the turn of the century, there was a sharp difference between the claims made regarding the schools' general contribution in promoting citizenship and character and the working objectives of the curriculum which were focused on knowledge and skills and intellectual discipline. The development of many basic attitudes, values, interests, and habits was recognized as a primary function of the home and church, and for those habits, attitudes, and skills relevant to work the employer was expected to play a strong role. The school today commonly lists the whole range of educational goals required for the induction of young people into effective adulthood. It includes objectives relating to home life, personal-social relations, civic life, occupations, and the like. It includes not only knowledge and intellectual abilities but also interests, attitudes, and social and recreational skills. Frequently, too, there is no indication of relative weighting. Developing social skills and a cooperative attitude appear to be viewed as jobs as important for the school as developing understanding of basic concepts of science and the social studies or the acquisition of the skills involved in reading.

Since the level of learning required of people today is a high one, a major problem in education is to select wisely among all the possible goals the important tasks which the school can do well and to concentrate its energies effectively. Since the total educational job is very great, the home, the church, the employer, and the other potential educative agencies of the community need to be encouraged and strengthened to take their share while the school concentrates on the things it can do best, and in many cases the things that only the school can do. Hence, the present shift in school objectives is toward a more discriminating selection, toward the kinds of learning that involve intellectual skills, that require sequential experiences to reach the necessary level of competence, that involve concepts and principles that are not apparent on the surface and for this reason are not likely to be learned through the guidance of laymen. This shift is likely to reduce the great range of objectives, and to diminish the emphasis upon social adjustment and similar goals that fail to recognize the importance of individuality and individual creativity in responding to experiences and in solving problems. The increasing emphasis upon understanding and thinking as kinds of objectives, with lessened stress upon attitudes and habits as primary goals, may help to revive the conception of the individual who controls his feelings and actions in terms of his knowledge and thought rather than one who simply seeks to express "acceptable" attitudes and feelings and to do the "proper" thing. This is a shift in objectives which will be interesting to observe.

THE SELECTION OF LEARNING EXPERIENCES

Among the changes taking place in the learning experiences provided by the American schools, those in the prevailing notions of the nature of learning experiences are particularly significant. At the beginning of this century, the term was not used. "Exercises," "assignments," "examples," "problems" were the words commonly employed to designate the learning tasks set for students outside of the class session, while the term "recitation" was used to refer to the oral responses expected of the student in the class. No mention was made of the student's mental reactions in the class, although it was clear that he was expected to pay attention, that is, to watch and listen to the teacher's presentations. When I began to teach more than thirty-five years ago, we had to file lesson plans for each week in advance. These plans outlined the content to be covered, what the teacher expected to do and the out-of-class assignments to be made. The focus of planning was on the teacher.

John Dewey and other educational leaders gave wide publicity to the increasing psychological evidence that learning could be most readily interpreted in terms of what the learner was doing. It was his reactions that he learned—not the teacher's. The teacher's role was to stimulate, guide, and reward the learner as he carried on the behavior which the school sought to teach him. This view placed attention upon the activity of the learner as the basic factor in attaining educational goals. By 1925, both writings of theorists and curriculum guides were commonly using the term "learning activities" to refer to the basic elements of the teaching-learning situation. Courses of study were listing reading activities, listening activities, study activities, and laboratory activities in outlining the day-by-day program of the school.

By 1935 curriculum writers were pointing out certain limitations in the concept of learning activity. For example, two students might both be reading an historic account of the California "Gold Rush," yet each might be carrying on quite different mental reactions and making different emotional responses. One might be thinking of the excitement and challenge involved in the long wagon haul the pioneers made in crossing the country, thrilling himself as he imagined the Indian encounters. The other might be thinking of the rough, lawless life of the early mining community, wondering why people would leave the comforts of civilization to live in such trying conditions. In terms of the course of study, both were engaged in the same learning activity but each was having a different experience and to that extent was learning something different. This kind of analysis led to the adoption of the term "learning experience" to refer to the reactions of the student in the situation. In 1938, Dewey's book, *Experience and Education* (1), clarified this concept further by emphasizing the notion that "experience" involves the interaction of the individual with the situation. This interaction involves some mutual effects—the individual modifying his reactions in terms of the demands of the situation, and also modifying the situation through his reaction to it. Today, almost all curriculum writers use the term "learning experience," and they seek to plan the learning situation so as to give direction to the experience the student has, that is, to his internal perception of the situation and his own interaction with it. This requires consideration of what the learner brings to the situation, what it will mean to him, how he is likely to respond to it mentally, emotionally, and in action.

Beginning with James and Thorndike, and exercising increasing influence in recent years, is the conception of the learning situation as one which should provide for certain essential conditions of learning. Thorndike's earlier work emphasized two conditions—exercise and affect. Current curriculum guides mention such conditions as motivation, opportunity for practice, guidance of desired behavior, provision of satisfaction when desired behavior is elicited, and the like. Hence, some of the current courses of study are pointing out the need to consider these conditions in selecting the learning experiences for a particular class group from a larger list of suggested ones.

A second marked change in learning experiences can be found in their range. Although the sloyd movement had influenced forward-looking American schools in the late 1800's to introduce manual training, not as vocational training but as a means of "learning through the hands," most of the learning exercises employed at the turn of the century were verbal ones. Listening and reciting, reading and writing represented the ways of learning the "academic subjects," except for the laboratory periods in high school science. Even the laboratory exercises were heavily verbal, with detailed instructions in the manual and a formal plan for writing up each "experiment." Map work in geography and field work in biology were strongly recommended by the writers of the period from 1905–15. Most courses of study advised having children make maps and locate points of geographic interest on them. At this time, too, high school botany courses typically required the student to collect and identify fifty or more plants.

By 1910, high school agriculture was widely offered in rural areas. These were first courses to introduce the project, or "student initiated" enterprise, which, it was hoped, would help him to understand and to apply the knowledge he was gaining in the course. The use of projects spread to other fields and to the elementary school, thus providing a much wider range of learning experiences than schools had commonly used. The writers who urged the introduction of projects conceived of them as involving a range of experiences as broad as life itself, but in the actual use of projects in the schools, activities involving the construction of objects have been predominant. Many teachers think of a project as making, growing, or producing some physical object. The extended inquiry which Dewey thought had largest potentialities as an educational project is rarely found. The intellectual learning experiences are frequently quite minor to the physical manipulations required to complete a "construction project."

During the depression, with its great reduction in opportunities for remunerative work for youth, many secondary school leaders recommended the addition of work experience to the high school program. Although only a small minority of high schools introduced work experience as part of the curriculum, some developed well-planned programs which involved using a wide variety of work activities as means for attaining educational objectives related to science, social studies, mathematics, and English as well as vocational fields.

The greatest impetus to extending the range of learning experiences has been the technological developments in communication. Lantern slides were in use at the turn of the century, but were not found in many schools. At best, they served only to extend the number of pictures which could be employed, to add concreteness, or to give variety to the teacher's presentation. The perfection of the motion picture, however, made it possible to analyze movements, to show time and space relationships much more graphically, and to increase the sense of reality in dealing with many subjects which require vicarious treatment. The addition of the sound track heightened the sense of reality and added another dimension of analysis. The sound-slide film gave some of the features of the sound motion picture in a more economical form, but it lacked the distinctive assets of motion. The television set made possible instantaneous viewing of events in a fashion much like the motion picture but with a further sense of the reality of the event, because the viewer realizes that it is taking place at the same time he is seeing it. These technological developments have gone far in removing the physical limitations to providing as wide a range of learning experiences in the school as those of life outside. But much of the comprehensive, effective development of these potentialities lies ahead. They still represent a small percentage of the learning experiences provided by American schools.

The selection of learning experiences so as to provide for individual differences among students is another respect in which changes have taken place in the last fifty years. Attention to individual differences has been accentuated by two factors: the psychological studies which have identified the extent of differences among schools, among classes and among students in the same class; and the increased visibility of individual differences brought about by the enrollment in the school of children from heterogeneous ethnic groups and social classes. There are few teachers now who fail to recognize a variety of differences among the students in their classes —differences which affect interests, meanings, efforts, and outcomes in school work.

Typical devices to provide for differences among students have involved adaptations in the time given for completing learning exercises, or variations in the exercises themselves, or both. The first type of adaptation requires a plan for students to work at varying rates. Among the early developments were the San Francisco, Dalton, and Winnetka plans, all of which involved organizing the school day into two parts, one for group activity and the other for individual work. These plans also required the development of a series of assignments with full directions on paper so that the students could work as individuals on different assignments at the same time. As a student took an assignment, it became his "contract" which he undertook to finish before he went on with another assignment in the same field. He might, therefore, complete his assignment much earlier or much later than the average.

Adaptations of the learning experiences themselves were first found in courses of study which marked some of the exercises as those to be required of all students and others as optional for the better students. By 1915, this was common among American schools. By 1925, a number of cities had introduced "ability grouping" in which the course of study was differentiated in such fields as reading and arithmetic into three levels—the superior, the average, and the slow sections. These three courses of study differed in the time provided for learning exercises and to a lesser extent in the nature of the exercises. In reading, the amount of material dealing with personal and social activities of children was greater in the slow sections, while the adult material was greater in the superior sections. In arithmetic, more concrete objects were counted and compared in the slow sections than in the others.

The use of individual projects was also a means of adapting to the individual student's interest and ability. This was recommended in courses of study as early as 1915. Learning exercises carried out by small groups (two to ten students) were first employed in the late 1800's to compensate for inadequate laboratory equipment. The apparatus was insufficient to provide opportunity for every student working individually to carry out the assignment. By 1930, small-group projects were being used by many schools as a manageable means of providing for individual differences. The projects themselves could differ in the rigor of their intellectual demands, and the division of labor among the students in the small group could adapt further to the abilities and interests of the individual. Unfortunately, all too often the slowest learner was given some handwork which involved little if any new learning. By 1950, with the publication of research on the psychology of small groups, educational writers were recommending the use of small-group projects as a means of heightening motivation and increasing the amount of meaningful learning activity. Since 1948, the attention of educational leaders has focused increasingly on the "education of the gifted student." This has led to emphasizing learning experiences that require greater understanding, or skill, or effort than those usually provided in the course of study. It has also stimulated some schools to develop learning experiences that can be carried on as independent work.

The most typical development in the past twenty years found in courses of study to provide for individual differences has been the listing of a large number of suggested learning experiences from which a given teacher may select ones particularly appropriate for his class as a whole or for groups or individuals within the class. The uniform lesson plan so common when I started to teach is almost unknown now. Most curriculum guides include a discussion of how to select from among the large number of learning experiences suggested in the course of study those which are likely to be most effective for students with varying backgrounds and abilities.

THE ORGANIZATION OF LEARNING EXPERIENCES

Important educational objectives involve patterns of behavior of such complexity that they can be developed only gradually over considerable periods of time. For example, the ability to read critically and to make comprehensive interpretations of what one reads is not acquired in a few brief lessons. To understand the basic principles of science and to use these principles in explaining the biological and physical phenomena round about us require a variety of related experiences extending over many hours. If the development of such complex behavior patterns as these is left to isolated or unrelated periods of learning, adequate achievement is impossible. Hence, a major phase in building a curriculum is to work out an organization of the many, many learning experiences required so that the student develops these complex behavior patterns gradually, day by day, and relates them to others so as to have an increasingly unified understanding, and a well-integrated command of essential skills.

The purpose of organizing learning experiences is to maximize the cumulative effect of the large number of learning experiences required to develop complex behavior patterns. Three criteria are commonly considered as standards to be met by a well-organized curriculum, namely, continuity, sequence, and integration. Continuity refers to the reiteration of the desired behavior through the many learning experiences used. Sequence refers to the gradation of the learning so that each subsequent experience not only builds on previous ones but goes beyond in order to require a higher level of skill, or a broader or deeper degree of understanding. Integration refers to the relation of what the student is learning in one field to what he is learning at about the same time in other fields. A broader and deeper understanding is facilitated by comprehending the relation among the various concepts, facts, and principles being studied, and a more adequate command of basic skills is achieved as the relation of these skills to one another is seen.

One surprising fact about curriculum development in the last fifty years has been the limited attention given to the theory of curriculum organization. Other than the common-sense notions of these criteria and of such rule-of-thumb principles as "learning experiences should proceed from that which is known to that which is unknown, from the simple to the complex, from the easy to the difficult," no new formulations have been made since the time of Herbart and of James. This is an area crying for substantial theory to be tested in practice and to provide a guide for practice.

At the more specific level, developments in reading and in the foreign languages have been most marked. In reading, continuity and sequence are commonly achieved through carefully controlled vocabulary development, adding new words gradually and systematically, and through the control of sentence structure in the reading materials, beginning with simple declarative sentences and moving gradually to compound and complex ones. Integration is sought both by relating the reading material to the common activities of the children and by introducing work-type reading in the other subjects on a gradual basis. A similar scheme of organization is commonly followed in the foreign languages.

In arithmetic, the development of skills is usually facilitated through an organization which begins with learning experiences involving addition and subtraction, then multiplication and division, then common fractions and decimal fractions. No explicit scheme of organization for concept development in arithmetic can be found in the current courses of study. The content of arithmetic problems has changed greatly since 1900. Beginning about 1920, studies were made of the kinds of problems commonly encountered by children and adults. Typically, arithmetic courses now order the problem content in terms of frequency of occurrence of the problems outside of school and in terms of the age level at which this kind of problem is commonly encountered by children.

The typical high school curriculum in mathematics has changed little in the past fifty years so far as organization is concerned. Tenth-grade geometry builds little, if at all, upon algebra. Advanced algebra and solid geometry in the eleventh grade have little sequential relationship to tenth-grade geometry, and trigonometry in the twelfth grade does not provide a clear sequence for the eleventh-grade work. The so-called modern mathematics program which is now getting under way with the sponsorship of the mathematical organizations should provide a much better organized curriculum for high school mathematics.

In organizing the so-called content fields, like the sciences and the social studies, major attention has been given to the ordering of content rather than behavior. At the beginning of this century, science was not commonly taught in the elementary school, while in the high school, botany was most frequently offered in the tenth grade, physics in the eleventh, and chemistry in the twelfth. By 1920, general science was offered as the introductory science course in more than one-fourth of the high schools, and now it is taught in almost all schools in the eighth or ninth grade, with biology in the tenth, and physics and chemistry, where offered, being placed in the eleventh or twelfth grades. The content of general science is usually selected to relate to the scientific phenomena most commonly observed by children. The content of biology is usually chosen to explain the human body, the maintenance of health, and the conservation of natural resources. The organizing notion here is to begin with phenomena which are common in the student's environment and in which he is likely to be interested. The advanced science courses, physics and chemistry, deal with the more abstract principles, which are thought to be less common and more difficult. The organization of these two courses has not greatly changed in the past fifty years. These illustrations in the field of science indicate the attention given to organizing the content dealt with in the learning experiences, but no similar effort has been made to organize the behavior, that is, the skills and abilities to be developed.

This is also true for the social studies. The changes taking place in their organization have been changes in the ordering of content. The most common sequence of content in the social studies is to begin with the community, then the state, then the nation, and finally the world. There is little evidence to indicate that this is sequential in terms of difficulty in learning.

Thus far, we have been reviewing the continuity and sequence of learning experiences in the content fields. The problem of integration, that is, how to relate learning experiences so as to aid the student in seeing the relations between what he is learning in one field with what he is learning in another, has been attacked most commonly through changes in the structure of the curriculum. In 1900, the elementary school curriculum was composed of ten or more specific subjects like reading, writing, spelling, arithmetic, geography, history, nature study, hygiene, music, drawing. Now, the typical course of study includes reading and the language arts, arithmetic, science, fine arts, health. This reduction in the number of subjects has been accomplished by building a more closely related series of learning experiences in language, in which reading, writing, and spelling are involved; in social studies, where geography and history are interrelated; and in the fine arts, where music, drawing, and painting are brought together.

In the high school, the broad fields of English, mathematics, science, social studies, foreign language, and fine arts have frequently replaced more specific subjects, and in some cases, the core curriculum has been developed which provides a large structure for learning experiences that occupy from one-third to one-half of the high school student's day. Since these larger structures are usually planned as courses rather than several separate subcourses, there is opportunity for better integration. Typically, however, the only principle of integration thus far explored is to bring together the content and skills needed to deal with each of the student "problems" which provide basic units of the course. This principle does not always provide for the necessary continuity and sequence nor for all of the more helpful relationships among the fields involved. In many cases, a particular problem involves knowledge or skills from certain fields in only a minor degree and does not suggest the more significant ways in which these fields are related.

It is clear after reading the works of curriculum theorists and examining courses of study that the past fifty years have not been a time of great development in the organization of learning experiences. In this respect, curriculum changes have been relatively few. The careful, systematic work done in the field of reading is a shining exception. The arousal of interest and stimulation of thought among secondary school teachers who have worked on the construction of core curricula suggest the great intellectual resources available under effective leadership to attack fundamentally and systematically the problem of developing a better organized curriculum.

SUMMARY

This review of changes in the curriculum of the American schools during the past fifty years has touched several high spots, but it has not presented possible explanations for the kinds of changes noted. It is probable that many of these developments can be understood in terms of the tasks which the American schools were facing at these different periods and the ideas prevailing in the field of psychology which school leaders found when they sought from scholars assistance in attacking critical school problems.

In the period prior to World War I, the elementary school was steadily growing to include a larger percentage of the children of age 6 to 14. The critical task was to teach the 3 R's to children of immigrant parents and those from the working classes. This required a re-examination of the psychology of reading and arithmetic, for the usual background of interest in and experience with language and children's stories could not be taken for granted, nor could early experiences with number concepts in the home be assumed for all children. It is not surprising that in this period long lists of specific objectives for these subjects were worked out, and that special attention was given to children's interests and abilities in devising learning experiences.

World War I ushered in a fifteen-year period when the economy developed rapidly and workers were in demand. No wonder that job analyses and other forms of analyses of social life were used to identify more definitely the demands which the individual would be expected to meet and to use this source in setting objectives. From 1930 until World War II, the great depression increased rather than decreased the number of youth in school because of the limited opportunities for employment. But the same limitations in jobs made the analysis of social demands a less relevant source for educational objectives than a study of youth themselves to find needs and potentialities that might justify educational effort when no great social demand was apparent. This period also was a difficult time for many secondary schools because youth saw no future and had no interest in deferred educational values. In their eyes, school work had to be justified immediately in terms of its interest and meaning to them. Hence, the devising of learning experiences of immediate interest and relevance to students and their organization around student problems helped to meet this pressing problem.

Since World War II, the insatiable demand for technically trained people has focused attention on the opinions of subject experts as a source of objectives and has given greater emphasis to knowledge and skills. The current demand for highly competent professionals and technicians has increased the interest of the schools in the education of gifted children and in devising a better organized curriculum to reach high levels of achievement. The shortage of teachers has furthered the demand for technological devices that increase the range of learning experiences, such as television and the sound motion picture.

Throughout the fifty years, the schools have been pressed by continuing conditions that create critical problems which cannot be solved without further curriculum developments. The first of these is the rapid change in technological development and social life which requires a continually increasing level of education on the part of our people. The second is the increasing proportion of children and youth who are sent to the schools for education. The third is the dislocation in other educational institutions— the home, the church, the neighborhood—which rapid social change has engendered. The educational needs of today and the immediate future are greater than even before. American education has done an amazing job in getting almost all children and youth in school and providing schools for this immense number. The schools have been astoundingly successful in building confidence on the part of the public in the capabilities of education in building our civilization. The time has come, however, to recognize realistically the magnitude of the job, to identify the objectives which the schools can best attain, to encourage the home, the church and other institutions to undertake the tasks appropriate to them, to devise learning experiences clearly relevant to the school's proper objectives, and to work out an organization of the curriculum that aids the students in attaining a high level of educational competence. These steps still lie ahead of us.

REFERENCES

1. Dewey, J. *Experience and education.* New York: Macmillan, 1938.
2. National Education Association Department of Superintendence. *Social studies curriculum: fourteenth yearbook.* Washington, D.C.: National Education Association of the United States, 1938.

Teaching Machines: An Application of Principles from the Laboratory[1]

James G. Holland

1959

Much has been said of teaching machines recently—but the emphasis has tended to be on the gadgets rather than on the much more significant development of a new technology of education initiated by B. F. Skinner (15, 17). The technology does use a device called a teaching machine which presents a finely graded series of problems and provides immediate "reward" or reinforcement for the student's correct answers. But emphasis on machines has tended to obscure the more important facets of the new technology based on application of principles from the laboratory. The machines of today are not necessarily better than those of yesterday. Indeed, adequate machines could have been built hundreds of years ago. The movement today is not simply the mechanization of teaching, but instead the development of a new technology—a behavioral engineering of teaching procedures.

The history of unsuccessful teaching machines illustrates the relatively greater importance of the technique as opposed to the gadgets. The first teaching machine was patented in 1866. There have since been a series of patents and a promising burst of activity by Sidney Pressey and his associates (13) in the 1920's. None of these early efforts really caught hold. But during this period in which the idea of mechanized teaching has been latent, the science of behavior has developed principles which permit extremely precise control of behavior. This new technology is not only the so-called automation of teaching but is an attempt to obtain the kind of behavioral control shown possible in the laboratory.

We have, of course, seen other practical applications of scientific psychology. We are all familiar with the development of a technology of

[1] The work discussed in this paper has been supported by grants from the Carnegie Corporation and the Ford Foundation.

80

testing which permits placing an individual in situations suited to his abilities. We are also familiar with another technology called human engineering, which fits machines and jobs to the capacities of man. One places a man in a job that suits him; the other alters the job to suit the man; *neither* attempts to alter or control man's behavior.

For years, in the laboratory, we *have* controlled the behavior of experimental subjects—both animal and human—by a widening array of principles and techniques. The new technology of education is the application of behavioral laws in modifying or controlling behavior. Such a technology became possible with the realization that we are actually referring to a verbal repertoire (16) controlled by the same laws as other behavior. The old, defunct, explanatory concepts of knowledge, meaning, mind, or symbolic processes have never offered the possibility of manipulation or control; but behavior, verbal or otherwise, can be controlled with ease and precision.

While machines are not the essential or defining aspect of this technology, they do play an important role in providing some of this fine control the technology requires. We will now examine several machines and notice the advantages they offer.

At Harvard, there is a self-instruction room with ten booths, each containing a machine like the one shown in Figure 1. The student gets one set of material from the attendant and places it in the machine. He closes the machine and begins his studies.

This machine presents one item of material at a time. The subject reads the statement which has one or more words missing and he completes the statement by writing in the answer space. He then raises the lever and a small shutter opens revealing the correct answer, and simultaneously, his answer is moved under glass where it can be read and compared with the now-exposed correct answer. After comparing his answer with the correct answer, the student indicates to the machine, with an appropriate movement of the lever, whether his answer was correct or incorrect, and the next item appears in the window. All items answered wrong are repeated after he completes the set of items. Correctly answered items are not repeated.

A critical feature of the machine is that it provides immediate reinforcement for correct answers. Being correct is known to be a reinforcer for humans (12). In machine teaching, reinforcement is immediate. We know from laboratory work that a delay between a response and its reinforcement of a few seconds will greatly reduce the effectiveness of the reinforcement. Adult humans have developed behavior which serves to mediate small delays; nevertheless, any delay makes reinforcement less effective.

Although other techniques such as programmed workbooks (8), "self-correcting" homework (3), and flashcards are sometimes used in this new behavioral technology, they offer less control. Teaching machines eliminate undesirable forms of responses which would also be successful in obtaining the right answer. For example, the teaching machine insures that the student answer before peeking at the indicated answer. There is a strong temptation to glance ahead with only a poorly formulated, unwritten answer when flashcards are used.

This write-in machine is a prototype of the most common machine. There is another machine used for teaching young children material which consistently has a single possible answer. In the machine, the constructed answer is automatically compared with the true answer. The child is presented a problem, perhaps a statement such as $2 + 2 = $ _____, and he must provide the "4." By moving a slider appropriately, he can insert the 4 into the answer space. He then turns the crank, and the next item appears immediately, and therefore, immediate reinforcement is provided.

Both of the machines described thus far require the student to compose the answer. Figure 2 shows a machine for a less mature organism who cannot yet compose an answer. This machine can be used for teaching preschool children (4). There is a large top window and three small windows. In the large window, there is some sort of problem, and in the three smaller windows, there are three alternative choices. For example, in the machine as seen in the picture, the subject chooses one of the three alternatives which has the same form as the sample, independent, in this case, of color or size. When the correct choice is made, the next frame is presented.

A teaching machine for a still lower organism is shown in Figure 3. The pigeon in the picture, with the aid of a teaching machine, has learned to hit the name plaque appropriate for a color projected above him. The principal difference between this and the other machines is that food reinforcement is used. With humans, simply being correct is sufficient reinforcement—pigeons will not work for such meager gains.

Enough of machines. They should not be allowed to obscure the truly important feature of the new technology, namely, the application of methods for behavioral control in developing programs for teaching. We need to say no more about the well-known principle of immediate reinforcement. Our second principle is also well known. Behavior is learned only when it is *emitted* and reinforced. But in the classroom, the student performs very little, verbally. However, while working with a machine, the student necessarily emits appropriate behavior and this behavior is usually reinforced since the material is designed so that the student is usually correct. Not only is reinforcement needed for learning; a high density of cor-

FIG. 1. *College student using a teaching machine.*

FIG. 2. *Preschool child using a teaching machine.*

Fig. 3. *Pigeon using a teaching machine.*

rect items is necessary because material which generates errors is punishing. Laboratory experiments (1) have shown that punishment lowers the rate of the punished behavior. In our experience with teaching machines we have also observed that students stop work when the material is so difficult that they make many errors. Furthermore, they become irritated, almost aggressive, when errors are made.

The third important principle is that of gradual progression to establish complex repertoires. A visitor once asked if Skinner had realized that pigeons were so smart before he began using them as subjects. The answer given by a helpful graduate student was that they weren't so smart before Skinner began using them. And indeed they weren't. The behavior developed in many experiments is like that developed in the classroom. Both are complex operants. Both require a careful program of gradual progression. We cannot wait for a student to describe the content of a psychology course and then reinforce the performance; nor can we wait for a pigeon to emit such an improbable bit of behavior as turning a circle, facing a disk on the wall, pecking the disk if it is lit, and then bending down to a new exposed food tray and eating.

When developing a complex performance in a pigeon, we may first reinforce simply the behavior of approaching the food tray when the tray is presented with a loud click. Later, the pigeon learns to peck a key which produces the click and the food tray. Still later, he may learn to peck this key only when it is lit, the peck being followed by the loud click and approach to the food tray. In the next step, he may learn to raise his head or hop from one foot to another, or walk a figure eight, in order to produce the lighted key which he then pecks; the click follows; and he approaches the food tray.

This principle of gradual progression runs through many of the teaching-machine techniques. Both human and avian scholars deserve the same careful tutorage. The teaching-machine program moves in very finely graded steps, working from simple to an ever higher level of complexity. Such a gradual development is illustrated in Table 1 by a few items taken from a psychology program (7).

The principle of gradual progression serves not simply to make the student correct as often as possible, but it is also the fastest way to develop a complex repertoire. In fact, a new complex operant may never appear except through separately reinforcing members of a graded series (11). Only this way can we quickly create a *new pattern* of behavior. The pigeon would not have learned the complex sequence necessary to receive the food if he had not learned each step in its proper order. Obviously, a child can't

TABLE 1

Items from the Psychology Program Illustrating the
Gradual Development of a New Concept
(Items selected from Holland and Skinner, 7)

Item	Correct Answer	Percentage of Students Giving the Answer
1. Performing animals are sometimes trained with "rewards." The behavior of a hungry animal can be "rewarded" with _____.	Food	96
2. A technical term for "reward" is reinforcement. To "reward" an organism with food is to _____ it with food.	Reinforce	100
3. *Technically* speaking, a thirsty organism can be _____ with water.	Reinforced	100
- - - - - - - - - -		
50. A school teacher is likely, whenever possible, to dismiss a class when her students are rowdy because she has been _____ by elimination of the stimuli arising from a rowdy class.	Reinforced	92
51. The teacher who dismisses a class when it is rowdy causes the frequency of future rowdy behavior to (1) _____, since dismissal from class is probably a(n) (2) _____ for rowdy children.	(1) Increase (2) Reinforcement	86
- - - - - - - - -		
54. If an airplane spotter never sees the kind of plane he is to spot, his frequency of scanning the sky (1) _____. In other words his "looking" behavior is (2) _____.	(1) Decreases (2) Extinguished (or: Not Reinforced)	94

begin with advanced mathematics, but neither can he begin with 2 + 2 = 4;
even this problem is too complex and requires a gradual progression.

Our fourth principle is, in a sense, another form of gradual progression—
one which involves the gradual withdrawal of stimulus support. This we

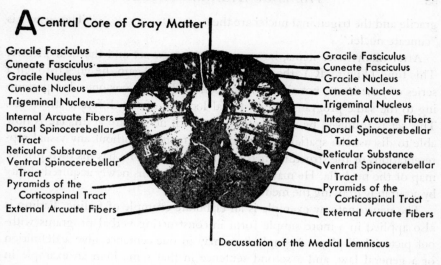

A **Central Core of Gray Matter**

Gracile Fasciculus
Cuneate Fasciculus
Gracile Nucleus
Cuneate Nucleus
Trigeminal Nucleus
Internal Arcuate Fibers
Dorsal Spinocerebellar Tract
Reticular Substance
Ventral Spinocerebellar Tract
Pyramids of the Corticospinal Tract
External Arcuate Fibers

Gracile Fasciculus
Cuneate Fasciculus
Gracile Nucleus
Cuneate Nucleus
Trigeminal Nucleus
Internal Arcuate Fibers
Dorsal Spinocerebellar Tract
Reticular Substance
Ventral Spinocerebellar Tract
Pyramids of the Corticospinal Tract
External Arcuate Fibers

Decussation of the Medial Lemniscus

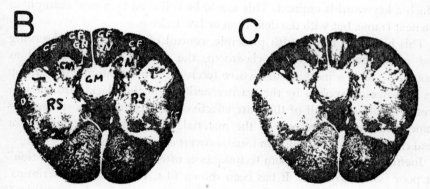

B **C**

FIG. 4. *Diagrams illustrating the technique of fading. Figure 4A is in front of the student as he works on the earliest items of a neuroanatomy program; 4B is in front of him for later items; 4C for still later items.*

shall call fading. This method will be illustrated with some neuroanatomy material (2). In Figure 4A is a fully labeled cross section of the medulla oblongata. This is placed before the student while he works with a large set of items pertaining to the spatial arrangement of the various structures. For example, "posterior to the cuneate nuclei are the _____." The answer is: "cuneate fasciculi."

After many such items, he begins another set and has another picture (Figure 4B) before him, but now the structures are only labeled with initials. A new set of items again asks a long series of questions pertaining to the spatial position of the various structures. For example, "between the gracile and the trigeminal nuclei are the _____.'' The answer is "cuneate nuclei."

After many more items, he proceeds to a new set and the next picture. This time (Figure 4C), the picture is unlabeled. Again, he goes through a series of new items, not simple repetition of the previous ones, but pertaining to the same program of the spatial location of the different structures. This set is followed by still another, but with no picture at all. He is now able to discuss the spatial position of the structures without any visual representations of the structures before him. In a sense, he has his own private map of the medulla. He may further demonstrate his newly acquired ability by accurately drawing the medulla.

The neuroanatomy example is an elaborate example of fading. Fading is also applied in a more simple form in constructing verbal programs without pictorial displays. A single item may in one sentence give a definition or a general law, and a second sentence in that same item an example in which a key word is omitted. This would be followed by a new example in the next frame, but with the definition or law lacking.

This brings us to our fifth principle, control of the student's observing and echoic behavior. In the classroom, the student is often treated as though he were some kind of passive receiver of information who can sop up information spoken by the teacher, written on the blackboard, or presented by films. But all of these are effective only insofar as the student has some behavior with respect to the material. He must listen carefully, or read carefully, thus engaging in usually covert echoic behavior.

Ineffectiveness of classroom techniques is often credited to "inattention" or poor "concentration." It has been shown (14, 19) that if a discrimination is to be learned, adequate observing behavior must first be established. We have further found (5) that observing behavior, or, speaking loosely, "attention" is subject to the same forms of control as other behavior. This control of observing behavior is of prime importance. When the student becomes very "inattentive" in the classroom, the teaching material flows on; but with a machine, he moves ahead only as he finishes an item. Lapses in active participation result in nothing more than the machine sitting idle until the student continues.

There is, however, a more subtle aspect to the control of observing behavior than this obvious mechanical one. In many of the examples we have seen, success in answering the problem only depends on the student's careful observation of the material in front of him at the moment. This may be illustrated by more material from the psychology program. A graph showing stimulus generalization data is in front of the student while he works on the machine. In the program he may complete a statement like the following: "As the wave length changes in either direction from the wave length present during reinforcement, the number of responses _____." The answer is "decreases." The item serves only to control the behavior of observing the data. Of course, many more such items are used to discuss the same data.

This principle of controlled observation extends to the details of writing a single item. For example, "Two events may have a common effect. An operant reinforced with two reinforcers appropriate to different deprivations will vary with _____ deprivations." The answer is "two" or "both." Here the programmer's choice of the omission serves to insure a careful reading of the item. *Only* those parts of an item which must be read to correctly complete a blank can safely be assumed to be learned.

Our sixth principle deals with discrimination training. In learning spoken languages, for example, it is necessary to be able to identify the speech sounds. A student may listen to a pair of words on a special phonograph which repeats the passage as many times as he desires. The visual write-in machine instructs him to listen to a specific passage. For example, the student may hear two words such as: "sit, set." He listens as many times as he needs, then writes the phonetic symbols in the write-in machine and operates the machine, thereby exposing the true answer and providing immediate reinforcement for his correct discrimination.

However, little academic education is *simple* discrimination. More often, it is abstraction or concept formation. An abstraction is a response to a single isolated property of a stimulus. Such a property cannot exist alone. Redness is an abstraction. Anything that is red has other properties as well —size, shape, position in space, to name a few. There are red balls, red cars, red walls. The term "red" applies to all of them, but not to green balls, blue cars, or yellow walls. To establish an abstraction (9, 10), we must provide many examples; each must have the common property, but among the various examples there must be a wide range of other properties. This is best illustrated by examples from the preverbal machine shown in Figure 5.

These are from a program (18) that teaches a child to respond to the abstract property of form. In each item, the upper figure is the sample and the lower three are the alternatives. While developing a program for establishing an abstraction, we remember our earlier principles, and move through a gradual progression. The first several items would be like the first one; here there is a sample and a single match, the other two being blank. The sample and its match are exactly alike at this stage.

After many such items, we would begin to have others like the next one in which the sample and its match again correspond in size, color and form, but an additional incorrect alternative has been added which differs from the sample in all these aspects. Later, we move on to frames with three choices, again the sample and its match corresponding exactly. Next, the sample and the match may differ in some property such as color, in the case of the next item shown, or size in the next. It is essential that the program contain many items among which the sample and correct match differ in all

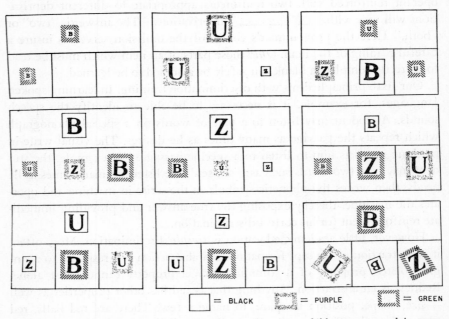

Fig. 5. *Selected items from a program that teaches young children to respond in terms of the abstract property of form. The upper rectangle in each frame is the sample. The child must choose the alternative that corresponds to the sample in form. The color of each letter, as it would appear in the actual program, is indicated here by various shaded areas.*

properties except the one providing the basis for the abstraction. Otherwise, the abstraction will be incomplete because the extraneous property will share some of the control over the abstract response.

As we move on with additional examples, the sample and the correct match differ both in color and in size, and the incorrect alternatives are beginning to share some of the extraneous properties with the sample. The student continues with many such problems in which the only common property between the sample and the correct match is the shape, regardless of size and color. Even now, our abstraction may be incomplete. We have kept the figures in only one orientation. Therefore, we also have a series in which the samples are rotated as in the next item.

A great deal of academic education consists of trying to teach abstractions. Concepts such as force, reinforcement, supply-and-demand, freedom, and many, many other possible examples are all abstractions. Furthermore, in the academic setting, the student seldom adequately forms abstractions. The trigonometry student commonly uses triangles with the right angle as one of the two lower angles. If the triangle is rotated 90°, so that the right angle is upward, the student often does not recognize it as a right triangle. Neither is an abstraction developed simply by learning a definition. The psychology student who learns the definition of reinforcement in formal terms and is acquainted with a laboratory example of food reinforcement,

Fig. 6. *"Boy, do we have this guy conditioned! Every time I press the bar down, he drops a pellet in."* (By permission of Columbia University *Jester*.)

may not realize the horrible consequences of sending his girl friend flowers to end an argument. Thus, in the psychology program, to develop a new concept, we follow the pattern in the preverbal example. A wide range of examples are analyzed which differ in as many aspects as possible, each still having the common property which characterizes the concept.

The last principle I shall discuss is really a question of methodology which has served so well in the laboratory. This principle is to let the student write the program. A few years ago, the cartoon shown in Figure 6 was published in the Columbia *Jester*. The rat leaning on the bar is saying to the other rat: "Boy, do we have this guy conditioned! Every time I press the bar down, he drops a pellet in."

Although said in jest, it is true that the rat controls the experimenter's behavior. When interesting things are observed about the rat's behavior the control circuits are rewired to investigate the interesting new facet of behavior. In a sense, the rat is wiring the control circuit. Similarly, the behavioral engineer who prepares good teaching-machine material must be under the control of the student's responses. When the student has trouble with part of a program, the programmer must correct this. The student's answers reveal ambiguities in items; they reveal gaps in the program and erroneous assumptions as to the student's background. The answers will show when the program is progressing too rapidly, when additional prompts are necessary, or when the programmer should try new techniques. When unexpected errors are made, they indicate deficiencies *not* in the student but in the program.

The most extensive experience with this principle of modifying the program to fit the student has been at Harvard (6) with the psychology program. In 1958, we had a program consisting of 48 disks or lessons of 29 frames each. After using the program and making a detailed, item-by-item analysis of the students' answers, we diagnosed the particular deficiencies in the program and revised it accordingly. The program was also extended to cover a larger amount of subject matter and, in 1959, it consisted of 60 disks. You have already seen a few items from the course. After using the revised material in 1959, we evaluated the extent of its improvement. Table 2 shows the percentage of errors on the first 20 disks for each of the two years.

TABLE 2

A Comparison of the Students' Errors in Using the Revised (1959) and Unrevised (1958) Program in Psychology

Program	Percentage of Errors	Percentage of Items Improperly Scored by Students
1958	20.1	3.6
1959	11.0	1.4

The revision eliminated about half the errors. The last column of the table gives percentage of improper self-scoring by the students. Revision also cut these scoring errors approximately in half. Furthermore, the revision decreased the time required to complete the material. Although the second year's material had more disks—60 as opposed to 48—it actually required the average student about one hour less to complete the work than it had required for the shorter first version. Frequency distributions on the median times in minutes for completion of the various disks are shown in

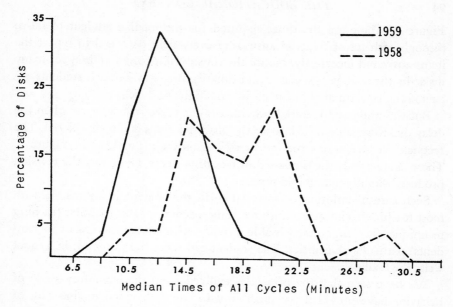

FIG. 7. *Frequency distributions for the median times to complete disks or "lessons" for the revised and unrevised psychology program. Raw frequencies were converted to percentages to equate the area under the curves.*

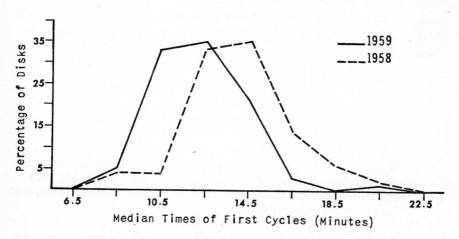

FIG. 8. *Frequency distributions for the median times to complete only the first cycles for the revised and unrevised psychology program. Raw frequencies were converted to percentages to equate area under the curves.*

Figure 7. These are the times required for the median student to move through each set of material answering every item once and to repeat the items answered incorrectly. Notice the considerable time required for many disks in the first year's material. Primarily this was because students repeated the larger number of items missed in the first cycle.

But the improved material provided faster performance, even when the delay due to repetition of incorrectly answered items is not considered. The frequency distributions for the first cycle only are provided in Figure 8. These data exclude the time used in repeating items. Here, too, the revision produced slightly more rapid progress.

Such careful tailoring of material to fit the student is impossible with most teaching techniques. With teaching machines, as in no other teaching technique, the programmer is able to revise his material in view of the students' particular difficulties. The student can write the program; he cannot write the textbook.

We have seen that the principles evolved from the laboratory study of behavior have provided the possibility for the behavioral engineering of teaching. This new technology is thoroughly grounded in some of the better established facts of behavioral control. The future of education is bright if persons who prepare teaching-machine programs appreciate this, and appropriately educate themselves in a special, but truly *not* esoteric, discipline. But it is vital that we continue to apply these techniques in preparing programs. The ill-advised efforts of some of our friends, who automatize their courses without adopting the new technology, have an extremely good chance of burying the whole movement in an avalanche of teaching-machine tapes.

REFERENCES

1. Azrin, N. H. Some effects of two intermittent schedules of immediate and non-immediate punishment. *Journal of Psychology,* 1956, 42, 3–21.
2. Brethower, D. M., & Holland, J. G. Unpublished material used at Harvard Univer. for research purposes.
3. Diederich, P. B. Self-correcting homework in English. *Proceedings of the 1959 Invitational Conference on Testing Problems.* Princeton, N.J.: Educational Testing Service, 1960. Pp. 70–79.
4. Hively, W. A multiple-choice visual discrimination apparatus. *Journal of the Experimental Analysis of Behavior,* 1964, 7, 387–389.

5. Holland, J. G. Human vigilance. *Science,* 1958, 128, 61–67.
6. Holland, J. G. Teaching psychology by a teaching-machine program. Paper presented at American Psychological Association, Cincinnati, September, 1959.
7. Holland, J. G., & Skinner, B. F. *The analysis of behavior: a program for self-instruction.* New York: McGraw-Hill, 1961.
8. Homme, L. E., & Glaser, R. Relationships between the programmed textbook and teaching machines. In E. Galanter (Ed.), *Automatic teaching: the state of the art.* New York: Wiley, 1959. Pp. 103–107.
9. Hovland, C. I. A "communication analysis" of concept learning. *Psychological Review,* 1952, 59, 461–472.
10. Hovland, C. I. A set of flower designs for experiments in concept formation. *American Journal of Psychology,* 1953, 66, 140–142.
11. Keller, F. S., & Schoenfeld, W. N. *Principles of psychology.* New York: Appleton-Century-Crofts, 1950.
12. Perin, C. T. The effect of delayed reinforcement upon the differentiation of bar responses in white rats. *Journal of Experimental Psychology,* 1943, 32, 95–109.
13. Pressey, S. L. A simple apparatus which gives tests and scores—and teaches. *School and Society,* 1926, 23, 373–376.
14. Reid, L. S. The development of noncontinuity behavior through continuity learning. *Journal of Experimental Psychology,* 1953, 46, 107–112.
15. Skinner, B. F. The science of learning and the art of teaching. *Harvard Educational Review,* 1954, 24, 86–97.
16. Skinner, B. F. *Verbal behavior.* New York: Appleton-Century-Crofts, 1957.
17. Skinner, B. F. Teaching machines. *Science,* 1958, 128, 969–977.
18. Skinner, B. F. Unpublished program used at Harvard Univer. for research purposes.
19. Wyckoff, L. B. The role of observing responses in discrimination learning. *Psychological Review,* 1952, 59, 431–442.

Acceleration: Basic Principles and Recent Research

SIDNEY L. PRESSEY

1954

Sometimes a topic becomes so involved with situations emotionally charged that dispassionate consideration of it seems almost impossible. Occasionally an unfortunate label leads thinking astray. Educational acceleration is a subject which has suffered greatly from these handicaps—and more. It was closely associated with the war and two clumsy expedients then: college entrance without completion of secondary school, which aroused bitter antagonism in public school people; and lengthened college year, which burdened and antagonized college faculties. "Acceleration" implies hurry with probable superficiality. And every experienced educator has known bright youngsters double-promoted into an older group who felt miserably out of place there—perhaps he had been such a case.

In contrast, this paper will beg your open-minded consideration of the possibility that for abler students to progress through school at faster-than-average pace is normal *for them,* not hurrying; that there are ways of facilitating their progress which help rather than hinder good social adjustment; and that such steps can lessen the load and facilitate the work of our over-crowded schools. An additional gain should be very timely. Russian universities and technical schools appear now to be graduating about three times as many engineers and twice as many scientists a year as American institutions (3). Multiple evidence indicates that facilitating the progress of able students leads more of them to complete collegiate and professional training; also probably the occasional notable genius (the Edisons or Einsteins) will thus be more likely to reach full fruition.

Two Major Neglected Facts of Human Development

Of basic importance are two conclusions from recent developmental studies regarding the gifted—in childhood and youth, *and* in adult career.

First, gifted children tend to develop more rapidly than the average young-ster, not only intellectually and educationally but also physically and in per-sonality. The bright six-year-old is likely to be not only in intelligence, but also in reading and physique and social assurance, more like a second- than a first-grade child. The bright sixteen-year-old is probably not only in ability and in general knowledge up with the general run of eighteen-year-old high school seniors or even nineteen-year-old college freshmen; he proba-bly reached puberty earlier than average and is in physique, interests, and social adjustment more mature than the average for his age. To have him in the eleventh or twelfth rather than the tenth grade, or to start the bright six-year-old in the second grade, is not to hurry him but rather to have him progress according to his real growth rate. Terman remarks that, "The ex-ceptionally bright student who is kept with his age group finds little to challenge his intelligence and too often develops habits of laziness that later wreck his college career. I could give you some choice examples of this in my gifted group" (5, 6). There is also evidence that holding a bright youngster back with his age group is less favorable to good social adjustment than carefully advancing him into a group more like him in ability and maturity of personality.

A second major question of educational policy regarding the able student is usually not faced squarely: if he is to be most productive in career and most adequate as a citizen, at about what age should he be through with full-time school and really begin his adult life? Vital statistics show the late teens and early twenties to be the healthiest years; physical tests and athletic records show them to be physically the most vigorous. And Lehman's very extensive findings regarding ages of most brilliant scientific discoveries, most important inventions, best writing, most remarkable paintings, all in-dicate that the most outstanding creative work is done early in the adult years—often in the twenties, sometimes even in the teens (2). The total of such evidence is impressive. Nevertheless, American educational programs for our most able young people are being more and more lengthened; such students must have not only college but also graduate or professional train-ing, perhaps an "intern" experience—possibly even some post-doctoral work. Before the second world war, the median age of receiving the Ph.D. degree in this country was 30; now, it tends to be a little later. By the age of 25, Edison and Einstein were doing important creative work. If they were of that age in this country now, they should instead probably be worrying about their language requirements! However, Edison might have been spared such difficulties; he would probably not have been admitted to an American university, not having even been to high school!

The argument thus is that *able students should progress more rapidly than at the lockstep rate through school and college, because they develop more rapidly than the average young person, and should get into their productive careers earlier than they can with the lockstep.* But what about possible social maladjustment, gaps in training, or damage to health?

MEANS OF "ACCELERATION"

By a historical perversity, the worst means for rapid progress—grade-skipping in school and the lengthened school year in college—have been so much more used than better methods that, to many people, these worst ways are synonymous with "acceleration." The boy who is skipped from fourth grade to sixth (obviously a half-grade skip is less risky) may suffer at least briefly from ignorance of some arithmetic process taken up in the fifth grade. If he is a conspicuous only one thus to be advanced into a close-knit little sixth-grade social unit, he may initially meet hostility—and parents may talk. But even this clumsy method—grade-skipping—need not cause much trouble. Bright children are usually ahead of their age in their reading and other subjects; a little help from a teacher or parent usually takes care of any omissions. If grade-skipping of bright pupils is made fairly common and if (as is common nowadays) changes in the membership of a grade group are frequent for other reasons, social difficulties are usually minimal. Trouble is likely only if the "accelerated" child is not really of superior ability but is pushed ahead because of parental pressure, or because of school work neurotically superior in compensation for a social maladjustment already existing. Grade-skipping is the easiest method of advancing a pupil, especially in a small school; and if "skippers" are selected carefully on the basis of adequate measurement (and a little help is given in adjusting for the skipped work and to the new group), outcomes are usually good—as will be seen shortly.

However, there need be no skipping over possibly needed school content, or moving an occasional child into a strange group. Children may be admitted to the first grade (or transferred from kindergarten) on the basis of mental age and reading readiness rather than chronological age; and some half-dozen investigations have all shown bright five-year-olds, so admitted, thereafter excellent in school work and in relations with other children. Or bright six-year-olds with some initial skill in reading may be started in the second grade. Or, a "primary pool" may throw together all children usually in the first three grades, and move each on into the fourth grade when he is ready. Large junior high schools may have rapid-progress sections, made up of bright youngsters with excellent school records to date and good social adjustment, which do the usual three years' work in two. And several careful investigations have shown these rapid-progress pupils doing as well in senior high school, academically *and* in relations with other students, as pupils of the same general ability and total record at the beginning of junior high but who spent the usual three years there. Similar rapid-progress sections (three years in two) in senior high have shown similar success in college.

A few college students may be really fatigued by a lengthened school year, though a total of six weeks or more of vacation usually still remains; both fatigue and protest seem greater in the faculty. A few students who need the earnings or the experience of summer employment may miss these benefits. But the questionableness of a double assumption in the method must be stressed: that bright students can learn only in college courses, and that they must spend as much time in these courses as average students. A substantial number of studies have shown that students who obtained credit for a course by passing a comprehensive examination in it instead of going to class (preparation having been obtained from superior or extra work in secondary school, from independent study, travel, or otherwise), do excellently in later courses in that subject and also in total college record. Streamlined sections of college courses, with methods adapted to the superior student and with reduced hours in class to facilitate acceleration, have been reported as successful, also honors programs combining or replacing several courses, and guided independent study. *In short, the progress of superior youngsters may be facilitated in a variety of ways; most of them are better than grade-skipping or lengthened school year.* It need hardly be mentioned that wise use of each requires initial testing to assure superiority, and continuing measurement thereafter to guide progress and determine outcome.

Whatever the methods for rapid progress, modifications should be attempted of the present powerful social pressures for the lockstep. Thus, from the day of entrance, the college student is designated a member of the class which is to graduate *four* years later; the entrant in '54 is a member of the class of '58 (English universities are wiser—there, an entrant in '54 is a member of the class of '54). Each of the four years is given a distinctive name and status; special opportunities (as for presidencies of student organizations) are open only to students in their fourth year. A student who finishes college in three years soon becomes a social anomaly who belongs nowhere. Instead, the feeling should be fostered of belonging to the school, not the class; associations and friendships should be freely formed within the total student body without class distinction. And status should be determined by academic progress and other accomplishments, not time served. That would be the democractic way; and it would benefit not only the gifted but also those who for some reason take longer than the usual time to finish an academic program.

OUTCOMES OF "ACCELERATION"—AND "THE COLD WAR"

As already indicated in passing, the evidence is that most able students do not suffer from acceleration. But much evidence goes further. *They actually seem to gain!* When Terman compared those in his gifted group who graduated from high school young (under 15½) with those graduating near the usual age (over 16½) he found that 16 per cent more of the younger group graduated from college, and 19 per cent more took one or more years of graduate work. The young group married over a year younger, and had fewer divorces. And twice as many of the younger group were highly successful vocationally. Results to date of the Fund for the Advancement of Education, and of the Ohio State University investigations, are similar; these last studies show both those entering young and those taking a four year program in three years doing better in college, *and* having more successful careers after, than matched cases of the same ability but entering at the usual time or taking the usual four years for a degree (1, 4). And in most of the investigations to date the accelerates were not carefully selected as capable of rapid progress, or given guidance in acceleration: also, they moved forward mostly by these least satisfactory methods—grade-skipping or lengthened school year. There is every reason to suppose that better selection, guidance, and methods would bring yet better outcomes. For instance, 25 per cent more of a group of bright freshmen selected as capable of acceleration and given guidance in so doing finally obtained a degree than a controlled group not accelerating. A more effective education in *less* time— how can this be explained? Presumably because more rapid progress is normal for the gifted, and the beginning of adult career (and marriage and responsible citizenship) without long delays is biologically sound. There are of course certain obvious advantages, as that saved time and funds leave more of both for advanced training. There are also motivational gains of possible pervasive importance. It is in the American tradition, and stimulating to the bright and ambitious youngster, that there be opportunity to get ahead. The lockstep negates all that. You may have heard the jibe that a certain state penitentiary had a major advantage over the neighboring university: you could get out of the pen sooner if you did well. *Wise means for "acceleration" are legitimate opportunities for the able to forge ahead, which encourage a general climate of enterprise and lively effort.*

In Résumé and Final Application

Numerous studies of human development thus show that able youngsters should progress in school faster than the lockstep rate of a grade a year, not only because they develop faster but to prevent too long drawnout education from delaying productive careers. Wise methods of acceleration expedite progress without hampering social adjustment. With acceleration, more able students complete advanced training; they get into productive careers earlier. And these careers tend to be more fruitful. In addition, congested schools are relieved to some degree. It seems a not unreasonable estimate that each year there remain in the secondary schools perhaps 300,000 bright youngsters who ought well to have been graduated. *More trained men, sooner, at less cost,* to counter the Russian technological threat! Clearly such a program calls for frequent appraisals from the primary years to graduate school, continuing guidance, and informed educational statesmanship.

REFERENCES

1. *Bridging the gap between school and college.* New York: The Fund for the Advancement of Education, 1953.
2. Lehman, H. C. *Age and achievement.* Princeton, N.J.: Princeton Univer. Press, 1953.
3. Meyerhoff, H. A. United States shortage: scientists. *U. S. News and World Report,* 1954, 36, 46–49.
4. Pressey, S. L. *Educational acceleration: appraisals and basic problems.* Columbus, Ohio: Ohio State Univer., 1949.
5. Terman, L. M. The discovery and encouragement of exceptional talent. *American Psychologist,* 1954, 9, 221–230.
6. Terman, L. M. (Ed.) *Genetic studies of genius.* Vol. 4. Terman, L. M., & Oden, Melita H. *The gifted child grows up.* Stanford, Calif.: Stanford Univer. Press, 1947.

Measuring the Quality of a College or University[1]

DEWEY B. STUIT

1961

The problems encountered in measuring the attributes or qualities of an educational institution do not differ basically from those encountered in the measurement of the attributes or behavior of the individual. Members of the group here assembled have spent a great deal of time and effort in the development of instruments designed to measure behavior and in the interpretation of the results obtained by use of these instruments. In assessing the quality of a college or university, as in measuring the behavior of an individual, one must first decide upon the dimensions to be measured, then the necessary instruments must be developed and, finally, appropriate reference points or bench marks must be established for the interpretation of results. In a very real sense, of course, the behavior of an institution is ultimately determined by the behavior of the individuals associated with that institution. For these several reasons, therefore, the measurement of the quality of an educational institution does not confront one with tasks which are totally new and different, and much of what we have learned about measurement in recent decades has direct application to the assessment of the quality of our colleges and universities.

A major thesis of this paper is that the quality of an institution should be determined by measuring its products—what the institution does by way of developing the talents and attributes of its students and what it does to encourage productivity in its faculty. The primary business of colleges is the education of students; in the case of universities, equal emphasis is usually placed upon scholarly productivity and perhaps to a somewhat lesser degree, special services rendered to the state and nation. Whatever the prod-

[1] The writer wishes to acknowledge his indebtedness to Norman Frederiksen and Gerald C. Helmstadter who collaborated with him in the writing of the report, *Survey of College Evaluation Methods and Needs*, submitted to the Carnegie Foundation for the Advancement of Teaching. The present paper is based in considerable part on that report.

ucts of an institution may be, their quality (and sometimes quantity) should be measured to determine the institution's adequacy or excellence. It isn't the beauty of the ivy on the walls, the splendor of the buildings, or even the size of the budget that counts; rather, it's what happens to students, and in the case of universities, what they produce by way of research and the extra services they render to society.

The next question is: how does one measure these products? The answer to the latter question is far from simple. First, one must know the objectives of the institution. What changes in student behavior does the college or university aim to produce? What level of competence are the students expected to reach? What emphasis does the institution place upon scholarly productivity? What services does it aim to provide for the community— city, state, region, or nation?

Second, one must reach a decision about the measuring instruments to be employed. Will the chief reliance be placed on tests which purport to measure changes in student behavior—in knowledge, critical thinking, attitudes, and appreciations? Will the "success" of students following college graduation be used as a measure of quality? Will research productivity be measured by the number and quality of books and articles written by the faculty? Will service be measured by the number of speeches given, conferences attended, or letters written? Or, instead of using these more or less objective indices, will outcomes be measured or assessed exclusively by the intuitive judgments of those deemed to be competent judges?

Third, one must allow for the quality of student input. A college or university with a highly selective admissions policy will show up with better results in achievement tests and will graduate more illustrious alumni, not necessarily because of the high quality of education at that institution but at least in part because of the high level of talent enrolled. Very successful coaches of intercollegiate athletics not infrequently admit that the "secret" of their success is recruiting. Likewise, one of the major reasons explaining the success of a college's alumni is careful selection of the freshman class. This problem, namely, the differences in quality of input, can, of course, be dealt with statistically; nevertheless it is a factor which must be recognized in institutional evaluation and has been seriously neglected in some earlier studies.

One could proceed indefinitely to recite the many problems involved in trying to measure objectively the products of institutions. These problems are formidable, and one could rather easily convince oneself that the difficulties inherent in this approach are insurmountable. Many of our institutions of higher education, for example, are liberal arts colleges, hence one ought to have available some means of measuring the major outcomes of a liberal education. Likewise, there is need for suitable instruments to measure instructional outcomes in each of the many professional programs found on the campuses of our colleges and universities. Admittedly, these measurement problems are difficult and complex, but perhaps no more complex than the problems which exist in other fields. Placing a satellite in orbit would probably have been looked upon as a well-nigh impossible task twenty-five years ago. Now we take it as a matter of course. In my judgment, there is no overriding reason to believe that the measurement problems involved in the evaluation of colleges and universities are so difficult that they cannot be solved in due time.

While I would hope that our long-range goal would be that of developing the necessary instruments and techniques for assessing the quality of an institution by measuring directly the quality of its products, at the moment we do not have the necessary instruments and techniques which would permit us to use this approach exclusively. I believe that at the moment we could use that method in part, but we must also use other approaches.

If one cannot do an acceptable job of assessing the quality of an institution by measuring the quality of its products directly, the next best thing is to measure the factors or dimensions which appear to correlate significantly with the quality of the product and which are educationally meaningful. Common sense, plus suppporting evidence from such studies as reported in *The Evaluation of Higher Institutions* (2), suggests first that certain factors or dimensions appear to be rather closely associated with institutional quality and are educationally meaningful. Among these factors are: 1) the objectives, 2) curriculum, 3) experience and training of the faculty, 4) quality of teaching, 5) aptitude and achievement of students, 6) number and quality of personnel services, and 7) adequacy of the library. There is also some evidence that amount and quality of institutional research (reference is not being made here to research in subject-matter fields) and institutional tone or atmosphere are related to academic quality. In addition, such factors as financial circumstances, physical plant, administrative organization, and athletic policy have been studied as dimensions of institutional quality, particularly by accrediting agencies.

If one were interested in the maximum economy of effort in evaluating an institution, it would seem best to concentrate on measuring the quality of the faculty and the changes which occur in students. However, since the nature of what one seeks to measure in the faculty and students is conditioned by the institution's objectives, one can hardly omit the statement of objectives from the evaluation process. Because of their positive relationship to the quality of an institution, it seems appropriate to spend a few moments discussing the three dimensions mentioned, plus one other—intellectual atmosphere.

Objectives: The curriculum, the student personnel services, library resources, laboratory equipment, and extracurricular activities—in short, the entire educational program of a college or university, should be an outgrowth of its educational objectives. Although nearly every college catalogue contains some statement of objectives, it is not always clear that the curricular offerings and related educational activities are planned to implement these stated objectives.

It would seem, therefore, that one of the first steps in any program of institutional evaluation, whether conducted by the institution itself or some outside agency, should be that of assessing the quality of its stated objectives. Among the critical questions which should be asked are the following: 1) Are the institution's objectives appropriate for the student body and community which it seeks to serve? 2) Are its objectives stated with sufficient precision so one can determine what student behaviors the institution is seeking to develop? 3) Were sound procedures used in arriving at its objectives? 4) Are the institution's objectives expressed clearly enough so they can be translated into curricular offerings and other types of learning experiences? 5) To what extent is the institution, particularly its faculty, concerned about its objectives?

Any institution of quality should have a statement of objectives which can be examined or inspected for adequacy—but this is not enough for purposes of evaluation. What institution "A" needs to know is how appropriate its objectives appear to be when compared with those of institution "B"; this holds true for each of the other dimensions by which its objectives can be measured. Although it is sometimes said that each institution should be evaluated with respect to its own objectives, no institution is in a class completely by itself. It can always be compared with one or more quite similar institutions. Colleges and universities should be evaluated in terms of the objectives which they are seeking to achieve, but this evaluation should be accomplished by grouping institutions with similar programs and purposes and then making comparisons within these homogeneous groups. In my judgment it is incorrect to say that an institution is so nearly unique that it cannot be compared with any other institution.

Faculty: If the most distinguishing characteristic of an institution is its curriculum, it could be said, perhaps, that its greatest claim to fame is the quality of its faculty.

The chief questions which should be asked in evaluating a particular institution are the following: 1) How do the training and experience of its faculty compare with those of sister institutions? 2) How do its faculty members compare in scholarly productivity with those in similar institutions? 3) How do the attitudes of its faculty members toward scholarship, teaching, and students compare with those of other faculties? 4) How is the morale of its faculty? 5) How do the community, professional, and other service activities of its faculty compare with faculty members elsewhere?

The individual administrator or faculty committee wrestling with the problem of faculty evaluation works under a considerable handicap. The experienced administrator is able to draw upon his own observations of colleges, but in most cases, such observations are limited to a small and possibly unrepresentative list of institutions. For this reason, normative data collected from sister institutions can be very helpful in making a self-study of the faculty and also in the appointment and promotion process.

A praiseworthy beginning was made by the North Central Association in the 1930's in providing data of this sort, particularly with reference to such factors as number of Ph.D.'s on the faculty, years of teaching experience, and number of scholarly papers and books published. More recently, completed tabulations have appeared from time to time in the *North Central Association Quarterly*. While simple, tabular data regarding academic degrees, years of experience, and number of scholarly publications produced by the faculty may be subject to misuse, the availability of such statistics would be generally helpful. At the present time, an individual institution can make such comparisons only by examining college catalogues or by writing letters to many individual institutions. If these statistical data could be supplemented with some attitude and morale factors regarding faculty members, a genuinely helpful set of data would be provided for purposes of evaluating colleges and universities.

There seems little doubt, however, that we need better methods of evaluating faculty and administrative personnel than are generally available at the present time. The work of Clark in identifying the members of the American Psychological Association who were judged to have made the greatest contribution to their profession would seem to offer considerable promise. This type of study ought to be carried out in a number of other areas. The results of a comprehensive study of several professional fields would be very helpful in assessing the quality of faculties, especially at our universities.

Students: It is a well known fact that the quality of students as measured by scholastic aptitude tests varies considerably from college to college. Although most colleges and universities would prefer to enroll students of high scholastic aptitude, it is generally agreed that higher education should not be limited exclusively to the intellectually elite. One of the chief characteristics of American higher education is its diversity—in purposes, curriculum offerings, physical facilities, and also in types of students enrolled —but this does create problems in evaluating institutions.

Some of the questions which may well be asked of an institution regarding its students follow: 1) Considering its location, facilities, and purposes, is it drawing the size of student body which would be expected for an institution of its type? 2) How do its students compare in academic aptitude with the students enrolled in institutions in its classification? 3) Assuming that its courses and teaching procedures are the equivalent of those in sister institutions, how do the achievements of its students compare with those in other schools—test scores, honors won, number going on to graduate and professional schools, etc.? 4) How is the morale of the students in comparison with that of students on other campuses? 5) How do the educational, social, and cultural backgrounds of the students compare with those in sister institutions?

In the early years of the use of the American Council on Education Psychological Examination, reports of the average scores at different institutions were published in the *Educational Record*. After a few years, this practice was discontinued, and at the present time, the general policy is not to publish the average scores of students at specific institutions. In some state and national testing programs it is, of course, quite easy for the individual college or university to determine how it compares with other institutions of its type, but this information is not usually available to the general public. Granted that it might not be advisable to publish, by name, the average scores in aptitude and achievement tests for students at different institutions, it would be extremely helpful to have such information available in a handbook on an anonymous basis—grouped by types of institutions. The same would be true regarding drop-out rates, honors won by students, success of graduates, etc. The availability of such data would be very helpful in institutional evaluation.

Intellectual Atmosphere: Over and above the quality of the faculty, the richness of the curriculum, the adequacy of the physical facilities, and possibly even the effectiveness of teaching in the classroom is a factor or dimension which one may call the intellectual climate prevailing on a particular campus. Although this dimension may be somewhat vague or nebulous, experienced educators would probably agree that there are noticeable differences in the intellectual tone of our campuses. The recent work of Pace and Stern (7) and Thistlethwaite (8), among others, lends support to the view that the climate which prevails on the campus is related to the quality of the institution's work, at least as measured by such a criterion as Ph.D. productivity.

Illustrative of the sorts of questions which pertain to the intellectual climate of a campus are the following: 1) Do students, faculty, and administration appear to place intellectual attainment at the top of their scale of values? 2) Are extracurricular and service activities given priority over academic attainments? 3) Do students and faculty feel that they have freedom to express themselves without fear of censorship? 4) Is the unorthodox point of view welcomed on the campus or is it only tolerated or even discouraged? 5) Is there much campus debate or discussion about serious intellectual matters or fundamental issues facing our society?

Up to the present time, no association of colleges or universities or any accrediting agency has made a serious attempt to assess this nebulous quality of a total institution. It is, of course, the sort of dimension which no one institution can very well study by itself. Any single college or university making a serious self-study may gain some insight into the intellectual tone of the campus, but it would be very easy to miss or overlook this quality unless one compared the situation prevailing on the local campus with that existing elsewhere.

Since it is generally recognized that the intellectual atmosphere varies from campus to campus and that this factor may be important in its effects upon the work of the institution, it would seem that more systematic efforts should be made to collect information about it and to publish it in such a way that each college or university could tell about where it stood with respect to this dimension. Samplings of faculty and student opinions obtained by some of the instruments recently developed, reports on the sorts of administrative controls which are exercised, statements of factors considered in the appointment and promotion of faculty members, and similar types of data could be collected and evaluated so as to place a particular institution on a scale of "goodness" or "badness" of the intellectual climate prevailing on the campus.

In recent years, colleges and universities have been questioned about the degree to which they have encouraged serious intellectual work. We ought to have data which provide answers to such questions. Fortunately, some excellent research on this subject has been completed during the past five or six years and is going forward at the present time.

The principal techniques which have been employed to date in institutional evaluation are the personal interview and the questionnaire. Accrediting agencies, for example, have required institutions to supply an extensive body of information by answering questions put to them either in oral or written form. Judgments concerning the quality of institutions have then been reached in large part on the basis of the information collected through personal visits and the use of questionnaires.

Despite the fact that aptitude tests, achievement tests, attitude scales, and similar types of measuring instruments have been widely used in higher education, the results obtained by means of these instruments have not been used systematically in institutional evaluation. There is considerable evidence in the literature of personnel work which casts doubt on the adequacy of the interview and related observational procedures as data-gathering devices—and yet, these methods more than any others have been and are being used in institutional evaluation, particularly in accrediting. Inevitably, some use of interviews and observational procedures, and extensive use of questionnaires, will always be required. In addition, if colleges and universities are to be given assistance in self-evaluation, they should have available the results obtained from large-scale testing programs so the individual institution can see how it compares with sister institutions. The individual or collective judgments of one or more interviewers are simply not adequate for this purpose.

In recent years, a number of follow-up studies have been made which would seem to have a considerable application in institutional evaluation. Particularly to be noted are the studies by Knapp and Greenbaum (6), Knapp and Goodrich (5), and Havemann and West (3). Holland (4) and Thistlethwaite (8) have made some significant studies which take into consideration the role of student aptitude in the evaluation of institutions.

Many individual colleges and universities have made significant follow-up studies of their own graduates. Very frequently, however, these studies have been incomplete and have failed to serve their purpose because of lack of normative data. If, for example, a particular liberal arts college discovers that 30 per cent of its freshmen do not return for the sophomore year, that 15 per cent of its graduates go on for graduate work, that 25 per cent of its applicants for medicine are accepted for admission, and that 10 per cent of its graduates go into teaching, what do these statistics mean? The answer is that they are not very meaningful until compared with the performance of students at similar institutions. When studied in the light of "norms of performance," they become meaningful and useful not only to the institution itself, but also to prospective students.

Obviously, there are many problems involved in making over-all evaluations of institutions. One of the problems has been referred to earlier, namely, the different levels of student scholastic aptitude in different institutions. This problem can be dealt with statistically as shown by Holland (4) and Thistlethwaite (8). Another problem is that of differences in institutional objectives. Again, this can be dealt with by a very careful homogeneous grouping of institutions having similar purposes and programs. Still another is the lapse of time factor. However, if it is agreed that institutions should be evaluated on the basis of their products, that is, the extent to which the "aimed for" changes in student behavior are achieved, then it would seem that evaluations of the follow-up type should play an important role in measuring the quality of colleges and universities.

The four dimensions of institutional quality that have been briefly discussed in this paper do not exhaust the list of factors that are positively correlated with the quality of the institution's products. Adequate evidence concerning these four factors, particularly the quality of the faculty and the performance of students, would go far toward making possible valid and reliable evaluations of colleges and universities. The major problems are those of devising adequate measuring instruments and of assembling the necessary normative data.

As stated earlier in this paper, the interview and the questionnaire have received the most extensive use in institutional evaluation, and these techniques will continue to be used in the future. A great deal of research has already been done on interviewing, but not in relation to institutional evaluation. Questionnaires have also been studied extensively, particularly with reference to the wording of questions and the recording of data. No doubt a good deal could be done to improve the questionnaires used in evaluation studies, checking the validity of items, weeding out the nonessential, and facilitating the recording of data.

In the North Central study of the 1930's, *The Evaluation of Higher Institutions* (2), a good deal of use was made of ratings. There would seem to be a continuing place for ratings, particularly when evaluating the institution's objectives, curriculum, and personnel services. The type of rating device to be used, the instructions prepared for evaluators, and the conversion of ratings to some scale score such as percentiles are all problems which are deserving of study. Since rating scales call for human beings to serve as measuring instruments, it is important that more research be done on ways and means of preparing the raters to perform their particular rating tasks.

In addition to improved methods of observational assessment there is an urgent need for instruments that will measure the changes in behavior that occur in students as a result of their educational experiences. Some tests of this nature are already available, but much could be done to improve them for use in institutional studies. In the case of liberal arts colleges, for example, it would be highly desirable to have available a test battery measuring the major outcomes of a liberal education. Intensive work ought to be started on such a test battery; similar instruments are needed in many professional training programs.

Development and experimentation should not be limited to tests that measure intellectual outcomes alone, although these tests should receive the primary emphasis. There should also be better instruments to measure changes in attitudes and appreciations occurring during college years, for these are the outcomes frequently stressed in liberal education. These types of instruments may not yet be ready for wide-scale use, but intensive research on them should be encouraged.

Finally, there is a great need for normative or comparative data. Some of these data consist of nothing more than enumerations or listings of various items—withdrawal rates of students, degrees held by faculty members, number of students going on to graduate school. Test scores constitute another form of normative data. The important point is that the collection of these data, arranging them in appropriate form, and then distributing them to the members of homogeneous groups of institutions, would serve a very useful purpose. Quite apart from possible uses in institutional evaluation, such as accrediting, the availability of such normative data would be extremely helpful to institutions in making self-studies.

I now return to the note on which I started, namely, that the measurement problems involved in the assessment of individuals and of institutions are not basically different. In both instances we need definitions or working hypotheses about what we are seeking to measure, we need effective measuring instruments, we need normative data, and we need interpretative skill in arriving at a meaningful interpretation of the results. Why, then, may we ask, despite the excellent research completed in recent years, haven't we made more progress in institutional evaluation? Perhaps the answer lies in certain peculiarities which distinguish institutional from individual evaluation.

First, within our own circle, perhaps it should be admitted that we in higher education have evidenced a certain unwillingness to face facts as objectively as we should. Most of us like to feel that we are doing a good job and, at times, conveniently overlook the defects which exist in our own institutions. If we were to gather the sorts of data suggested in this paper, we might disclose some facts which would not be welcomed by many American colleges and universities.

Second, I think we have a fear, partly legitimate, that data of the sort described in this paper would be subject to misuse. A failure to interpret the data properly, or a twist of emphasis here or there, intentional or unintentional, might result in harm to a particular institution. Actually, I believe that this danger should be accepted as a challenge on our part to do a better job of explaining higher education to the public.

Third, there is the problem of our measuring instruments. Our present procedures for the assessment of institutional quality are lacking in precision. A good deal of research should be done on them. Nevertheless, one should not wait for the development of perfect instruments. If this were done, we would never make progress in institutional evaluation.

Finally, there is a reluctance on the part of institutions, including some very good ones, to devote time and effort to collect the sorts of data needed in a thorough evaluation. Even though it might take some class time and some extra consultation and deliberation, I believe that time spent in careful evaluation would be well spent.

The problem before us is a challenging one. We in America have some of the best colleges and universities in the world. We also have our share of poor ones. Our country has great need for quality in higher education. I believe that institutional evaluation such as proposed in this paper would help to raise the level of our colleges and universities and enable them to contribute more significantly to our strength as a nation and to our way of life.

REFERENCES

1. Clark, K. E. *America's psychologists: a survey of a growing profession.* Washington, D.C.: American Psychological Association, 1957.
2. *The evaluation of higher institutions.* Vols. 1, 2, 3, 4, 5. Chicago: Univer. of Chicago Press, 1937.
3. Havemann, E., & West, Patricia S. *They went to college.* New York: Harcourt, Brace & World, 1952.
4. Holland, J. L. Undergraduate origins of American scientists. *Science,* 1957, 126, 433–437.
5. Knapp, R. H., & Goodrich, H. B. *Origins of American scientists.* Chicago: Univer. of Chicago Press, 1952.
6. Knapp, R. H., & Greenbaum, J. J. *The younger American scholar: his collegiate origins.* Chicago: Univer. of Chicago Press, 1953.
7. Pace, C. R., & Stern, G. G. An approach to the measurement of psychological characteristics of college environments. *Journal of Educational Psychology,* 1958, 49, 269–277.
8. Thistlethwaite, D. L. College environments and the development of talent. *Science,* 1959, 130, 71–76.

4 · IMPROVING CONSTRUCTION AND USE OF EDUCATIONAL TESTS

FOLLOWING THE DISCUSSION of broad educational issues in Chapter 3, we may now turn to papers dealing more directly with the development and use of tests in educational settings. In the opening paper, Ebel describes a University Examination Service designed to help college faculties to improve their examining procedures. He wisely includes a discussion of "procedural strategy" for avoiding resistance and gaining acceptance of the service by faculty members, as well as an analysis of obstacles to the improvement of course examinations. Test-analysis techniques suitable for use in this situation are described and illustrated.

The next three papers were presented at a panel entitled "Improving Measurement through Better Exercise Writing." All three analyze and illustrate techniques of effective item writing in the preparation of achievement tests. Diederich discusses item writing in the humanities, Nedelsky in the natural sciences, and Engelhart in the social sciences.

A common criticism of the ubiquitous multiple-choice item is that this item type is likely to emphasize memory for isolated factual details, superficial familiarity with technical terminology, and other relatively trivial instructional objectives. It is certainly true that multiple-choice items dealing with this type of knowledge are relatively easy to construct and are likely to predominate in objective achievement tests produced by unskilled item writers. One way to guard against this pitfall is to prepare a two-way table, listing topics to be covered along one axis and type of learning to be tested along the other. Besides memory for factual details, other learning objectives can thus be specified, such as the application of knowledge to new problems, critical evaluation of conclusions, understanding of experimental design, artistic and literary appreciation, and the like. By recording in advance the number of items wanted in each cell of this table, as determined by the relative importance of topics and learning objectives in the area under examination, the test constructor can counteract the tendency to let ease of item writing determine coverage.

That multiple-choice items *can* be written so as to test many complex and subtle types of learning is clearly exemplified in the stimulating set of papers presented at this panel. A by-product of these discussions, particularly evident in Diederich's paper, is their demonstration of the basic similarity between testing techniques and teaching techniques. The very name, "exercise writing," suggests this dual function to which the resulting items can be put.

Lennon's paper is concerned with the improvement of test manuals, particularly those designed for use by school teachers who administer group tests of intelligence, aptitude, or achievement. Focusing on the understanding of test results, Lennon points to the widening gap between technical developments in test construction and the interpretation of scores by the test user. Voiced in 1953, this observation is strongly reminiscent of one of the major points in the 1936 *Memorandum,* prepared at the first Conference of State Testing Leaders (Ch. 1). Lennon cites similar conclusions reached in two surveys of educational testing, both published in 1953. Apparently this particular difficulty had not lessened over the intervening years—nor did it do so during the subsequent decade. In the hope that clarifying test manuals might help the situation, Lennon considers the content that should be included in a test manual and reports data on readability and comprehensibility of typical manuals.

How an Examination Service Helps College Teachers to Give Better Tests

ROBERT L. EBEL

1953

I. DESCRIPTIVE BACKGROUND

May I begin by giving a brief description of the Examinations Service of the State University of Iowa. It was established in April 1943 under the leadership of Professor E. F. Lindquist. The first director of the service, Professor Paul Blommers, was largely responsible for organizing and equipping it, and for setting up its procedures.

Currently, the Examinations Service occupies several small rooms in the principal office building of the university. The staff consists of seven clerical employees, a graduate assistant, and the director. Multilith duplicators, IBM scoring machines and typewriters, Monroe calculators, and the usual desks, filing cabinets, and storage cupboards constitute the principal items of equipment. The service operates on an annual budget for salaries and supplies of approximately $30,000.

One of the principal functions of the Examinations Service is to relieve university instructors of the mechanical and clerical burdens involved in duplicating, scoring, and analyzing course examinations. Each year, a few examinations are constructed as special projects, but this is not one of the main functions of the service. Its principal responsibility is to provide, upon request, assistance and advice on technical problems involved in the construction, administration, and interpretation of examinations of all types. Another area of responsibility is the administration of special testing programs, such as entrance examinations and various achievement testing programs. Special individual testing for the purposes of guidance and counseling is the function of a separate office.

115

II. Procedural Strategy

The long-range goal of the Examinations Service is to contribute to the effectiveness of the university's educational programs by improving the quality of the testing done. The strategy for achieving this objective involves three main considerations. The first is to make it as convenient as possible for college instructors to give good tests. No charge is made for any of the services offered. The offices are centrally located on campus. Service is rendered as promptly as possible, and pains are taken to prevent errors.

The second consideration is to avoid any suggestion of interference with the instructor's independence with respect to his own examination procedures. The service is operated on a voluntary, permissive basis. If an instructor chooses to give a speed test when a power test seems more appropriate, or to call for raw scores reported as 100 less the number of errors, rather than as the number of correct answers, or to weight each multiple-choice item four times as much as each true-false item in his test, we may inquire the reason for his procedure, but it is his preference, not ours, which determines how the job will be done.

It may seem somewhat inconsistent that a service established to improve examination practices should cooperate in carrying out unimproved practices. Yet it appears that helpful service offers the best opportunity for gradual improvement. College professors are human and cherish their feelings of adequacy and independence. However much their methods need mending, they do not like to be told so directly. Further, they feel some distrust for those they call "educationists." Many of us who work in the field of educational measurement have backgrounds of public school teaching or hold degrees from colleges of education. We could not succeed, even if we tried, in *imposing* upon faculty members our ideas of what is right and proper in educational measurement.

The third consideration is to maintain free and friendly communication with staff members. They receive notices regarding the extent and availability of the service. They are sent bulletins dealing with such matters as item writing, test administration, and the interpretation of item-analysis data. Opportunities to consider examination problems with departmental faculties and with individual staff members are welcomed.

III. Basic Problems

Having given this brief description of our organization and service, may I turn next to consideration of some of the basic problems we have encountered in our efforts to help college teachers give better tests. It is emphatically asserted by wounded students and harassed professors and generally agreed by impartial observers, that college testing practices need improvement. In a recent survey of student opinions of teaching in our College of Liberal Arts, the item on which instructors were ranked lowest was "Quality of Examinations." This low rating may be explained in part as defensive rationalization by students who received lower grades than they expected or desired. But, I am convinced, it also indicates that there is very great room for improvement in many of our classroom tests. What has stood in the way of more rapid improvement? It seems to me that certain common attitudes and misconceptions on the part of college teachers constitute the chief barriers.

To begin with, there are some professors who do not take the responsibility of evaluating student achievement seriously. They regard testing and grading as nonessential administrative red tape, largely divorced from the essential process of education. Since, in their view, the whole process is unimportant, it is unnecessary for them to expend much time or effort to achieve high validity or precision in the process. Such professors often solve the problem of grading according to the principle of least annoyance. "Give few low grades and you will have few complaints from the students, and hence there will be few occasions for outsiders to question your grading procedure."

It is interesting to note that the same professors who shun the onerous tasks of accurately evaluating student achievement in their own classes are likely, quite inconsistently, to object very strenuously to the consequences of similar behavior by other teachers. "My students can't read or write," they cry in anguish. "How did they ever pass freshman English?" Sometimes a professor finds himself in this unhappy predicament. He is serving on the doctoral examination committee of a very weak candidate. Ready to object strenuously, and possibly to cast a negative vote, he suddenly discovers that, in the recent past, he has himself rewarded the student's mediocre talents with a grade of A.

The second obstacle to the improvement of college tests is the refusal of many professors to acknowledge the importance of objectivity in the evaluation of achievement. Note that we *did not say,* "the importance of objective tests." Such tests are valuable, but they do not provide the only pathway to objective measurement. Evaluation is objective to the degree that equally competent observers can agree in their evaluation of a particular achievement. Our thesis here is that no measurement or evaluation, however obtained, is worth anything if it is not objective in some degree. To put it another way, only that component of a measurement or evaluation which can be verified by independent observation can serve any useful purpose.

Strange as it may seem, there exists a considerable group among college professors who reject the idea that objectivity is an essential ingredient in good evaluation. Two subspecies of this group may be recognized. The first is composed of those who worship the mystical goddess of intangibility. The second consists of those who are certain that any judgment which differs from their own must be wrong.

Here is a professor who bases his evaluation on a student's extended discussion of a rather vague topic. He prefers this procedure because, as he says, it yields occasional flashes of insight into how the student's mind is working. If these flashes please him, he is likely to give the student an A. It bothers him not at all that an equally competent professor, failing to receive these same flashes, or valuing them less, might give the same paper a C. The first professor may know that his grade of A will be placed on record together with the A's assigned by a great many other instructors, and that when such grades are combined to give an over-all indication of achievement, each A is assumed to have essentially the same meaning as any other A. But the obvious inference from these facts that some sort of common standards (objectivity) in grading are required seems to have escaped him. Our Examinations Service does very little in the way of analysis of essay tests, not because such analyses would be impossible to perform, but rather because many users of essay tests are subjectivists who fail to see any significance in such analyses.

A third major obstacle to the improvement of college tests lies in the emphasis upon testing for recall of course content and the neglect of testing the attainment of course objectives. Some of the poorest examinations we handle come from the older academic fields where students are simply asked to recall this fact or that statement which was presented during the course. Some of the best tests come from professors of medicine and law. Concrete case situations are described and the examinee is required to make decisions concerning treatment or procedures.

We hold it to be a fundamental principle of good educational achievement testing that a test should measure as directly as possible as many as possible of the ultimate objectives of instruction in the course. We have little patience with those who assert that many of the important outcomes of instruction are intangible. Does this mean that no one can observe them? If so, they cannot possibly be of any importance, except in the internal life of the particular individual. And none of us can possibly be concerned about the internal life of another individual except when it manifests itself in overt behavior. I strongly suspect that many of those who insist upon the importance of intangible outcomes of education are simply using it as a shield for their reluctance, or inability, to describe specifically what a given course of instruction ought to accomplish.

Many college instructors have seriously limited and distorted notions concerning what can be measured in well constructed tests of educational achievement. Having had limited experience with objective-type questions, they assume that only the recall of factual details, or, worse still, the recognition of names and verbal symbols, can be tested with such a device. You frequently hear it asserted that "we do not yet know how to measure certain important outcomes of education." This may be true, but I am convinced that most of the difficulty is due to inability to define precisely what is to be measured. I learned recently of a college instructor who was seeking help in measuring leadership potential. He felt the measurement specialists were being evasive and uncooperative when they persisted in asking him precisely what he meant by "leadership potential."

A fourth obstacle to the improvement of college tests arises from the reluctance of many professors to recognize the inherently relative character of most measurements of educational achievement. Many of them feel quite strongly that the standards they should employ are set by the subject matter itself, and are best interpreted and applied by one who possesses expert knowledge of that subject matter. They would deny that the best basis for judging whether a given student's achievement is superior or inferior is a comparison of his achievement with that of other students in the same class, course, or grade group. The latter type of relative evaluation they refer to, somewhat disdainfully, as "grading on the curve."

This preference for presumably absolute external standards seems to be based on several misconceptions. One is that standards of achievement are inherent in the subject matter. If they are, they are extremely elusive. Repeated attempts to set minimum standards of achievement in various subject matter areas seem to have demonstrated quite convincingly that such standards are arbitrary, depending largely on the preferences and judgments of the individuals concerned with establishing them.

A second misconception is that standards set by an expert instructor are likely to represent more stable standards than those based on group performance. Again, experience has demonstrated quite clearly that equally competent instructors in the same subject matter have quite different standards, both qualitative and quantitative. Further, any given instructor's standards are likely to shift markedly as time passes.

It is easy for an instructor to delude himself about the absoluteness of his standards when he relies on subjective processes of evaluation. So long as essay tests prevailed, an instructor could claim absoluteness and still see to it that not too many students failed. His standard of 70 per cent correctness for a passing grade *seems* to be independent of group performance, but actually may not be. If too many students seem to be getting scores below 70, the instructor can quietly shift his basis for calculation without letting any one else know about it.

With objective tests, however, such a readjustment is much more obvious. The decline of percentage grading (and the 70 per cent pass mark) following the growth of objective testing was no accident. It came about, in part at least, because of the great difficulty of building an objective test which a consistent and reasonably large number of students could pass when the minimum was set at 70 per cent correctness.

Another misconception is that relative standards based on student performance tend to be too low. The use of relative standards does not, however, imply fixed percentages of A's, or F's, or any other grade. These proportions can be set independently of the group performance. The point is that consideration should be given to that performance so the standard will not be too high or too low. Others have feared that relative grading will encourage academic "slow-downs." Students might say to one another, "If none of us performs at capacity, it will be easier for all of us to pass." So far as I know, there is no empirical evidence to support this argument, and even the logic of it appears shaky when one considers the strength and prevalence of individual aspirations toward academic achievement.

Four obstacles to more rapid improvement of classroom tests at the college level have been mentioned. These are 1) failure to recognize the importance of measurement, 2) failure to see the need for objectivity, 3) emphasis on content details, and 4) preference for allegedly "absolute" standards of achievement. These are essentially problems of attitude and orientation. But there is another serious obstacle or problem of a different type. It is lack of knowledge of appropriate techniques of measurement and lack of skill in their application. May we consider briefly what an examinations service can do to help solve this problem.

IV. Test Analysis

Detailed test analysis has proved to be one of the most useful avenues for progressive improvement of the tests constructed by classroom instructors. Its possesses the two very important characteristics of objectivity and impersonality. Following test analysis, it is not necessary for the test specialist to make critical comments concerning the test. Such criticisms are obvious and implicit in the data presented. Instead of placing the test specialist in the role of judge and critic, the use of test analysis places him in the role of consultant and adviser working with the instructor to solve a common problem.

You have been issued sample copies of some of the materials we use in the test analysis [reproduced on pp. 124–127.—Ed.]. May I direct your attention first to the test analysis report form [p. 124]. You will note that two major test characteristics, relevance and discrimination, are the subject of analysis. These are the most important qualities that an educational achievement test can possess. Most of the suggestions for improved test construction relate to these two basic qualities, either directly or indirectly. In order to improve the relevance of their tests, instructors are urged to write items based on course objectives rather than on content details, to emphasize useful and important information rather than trivial or esoteric details, and to test the student's understanding and ability to apply rather than his recognition or recall of details. When item writers are urged to choose questions of moderate difficulty, to express them clearly, to make sure that there is one best response, but that each of the alternative answers has some basis for plausibility, the purpose is to improve the discriminating power of the individual items and hence, the test as a whole.

Evaluation of the relevance of a test is a difficult matter which is largely a responsibility of the subject matter specialist rather than of the test specialist. However, it is possible to roughly classify the items with respect to the type of achievement they call for, on the basis of very little subject matter competence. This is what we attempt to do in our analysis of relevance. Six categories of relevance are recognized: content details, vocabulary, facts, generalizations, understanding, and applications. These constitute an ascending scale of values. That is, we regard items dealing with the understanding and application as being much more valuable than those dealing in general with content details or vocabulary. While it is often difficult to be sure where a particular item ought to be classified, the usual effect of the classification process is to show quite clearly where the emphasis of the test as a whole lies. One of the main purposes of this analysis for relevance is to make each instructor directly aware of the desirability of writing more items which deal with generalizations, understanding, and applications.

The so-called ideals listed in the second column of the test analysis report are practical ideals rather than "ideal" ideals. Their purpose is to indicate the desired emphasis without giving any instructor the impression that his test is hopelessly inadequate. The second sheet in the appended material [p. 125] is a relevance worksheet filled in with data from a specific test. A copy of this classification of items is returned to the instructor along with the test-analysis report giving the over-all distribution of emphasis.

The lower half of the test analysis report sheet is concerned with the discrimination of individual items and of the test scores as a whole. The index of item discrimination used in this report is the U-L index suggested by Johnson (2). It is based upon the number of correct responses to an item in upper and lower 27 criterion groups, and is defined as the difference between the number of successful responses in upper and lower groups divided by the maximum possible difference. It is an index which favors items of near 50 per cent difficulty, but for most tests of educational achievement this is an advantage rather than a handicap. Separate indices of item difficulty are reported to the instructor, to aid him in analyzing the causes of low discriminating power among certain items, but they are not used as a basis for selecting the best items or of indicating the over-all quality of the items. This is done on the basis of the U-L index alone. One should remember that the frame of reference for this analysis is classroom testing. In wide-scale achievement testing programs, where tests are designed to cover a range of grades, more attention would certainly need to be given to the distribution of item-difficulty values.

If all of the items in the test possess high relevance to the objectives of instruction, then the only other necessary quality for the test scores as a whole is reliability. It is well known that the standard deviation (or variance) of test scores is an important factor in the reliability of those scores, and that the general level of scores, as indicated by the mean, has some bearing on the variance obtainable. Data on all of these matters are reported to the instructor. A copy of the score analysis worksheet is included in the appended material [p. 127]. The reliability coefficient it calculates is based on Angoff's simplification of Kuder-Richardson formula 8 (1, p. 10). At least one competent statistician has questioned the superiority of this formula over the more familiar Kuder-Richardson formula 20. On the other hand, this formula gives results identical to those obtained from K-R 20 when all items are equally difficult. When the items differ in difficulty, this formula has the advantage of an upper limit of 1.00, while that of K-R 20 is less than 1.00. At the moment, I am prepared to argue that Angoff's formula provides the best reasonably convenient estimate of test-score reliability that can be derived from a single test administration. The issue between the two may be of considerable theoretical importance. Practically, the coefficients yielded are not widely different.

We have developed a table [p. 128] to simplify the computation of item variances and the so-called "true item variances" which are needed in this reliability formula. The table is entered with response counts obtained in the usual upper-lower 27 per cent item-analysis procedure. You will note that a blank row was left at the top of this table and at the left of it. This permits a clerk to enter directly the *number* of correct responses corresponding to a *percentage* of correct responses for any given size of upper and lower criterion groups. When this has been done, it is possible to obtain the values of total item variance and "true" item variance working directly from the response counts which the scoring machines produce. Since we would be performing an item analysis in any case, we have found this approach to calculation of test reliability much simpler and more convenient than the split-halves technique.

The probable error of measurement of each test is calculated primarily to call the instructor's attention to the magnitude of such errors, even with well-constructed tests. Instructors are cautioned, however, against regarding this probable error as a direct index of the quality of the test. Some highly unreliable test scores, which also show low variability, turn up with very low probable errors of measurement.

V. CONCLUSION

It has been our purpose, in this brief presentation, to describe some of the facilities available in the Examinations Service at the University of Iowa, to outline some of the procedures used in improving examinations, to discuss some of the obstacles to more rapid improvement, and to describe specifically our test analysis procedures. In these efforts to help college teachers give better tests, we have gained a little ground, but there is ample room for earnest and imaginative efforts on our campus, and on others as well, for many years to come.

REFERENCES

1. Angoff, W. H. Test reliability and effective test length. *Psychometrika,* 1953, 18, 1–14.
2. Johnson, A. P. Notes on a suggested index of item validity: the U-L index. *Journal of Educational Psychology,* 1951, 42, 499–504.

University Examinations Service   State University of Iowa

TEST ANALYSIS REPORT

Test Title _Security Transactions)_ k = _100_ Job Number _6314_

Group Tested _Class students)_ N = _57_ Date of Test _2-2-53_

Time Limit _2 hr._ Calculator _Dorothy_ Checker _Ruth_

Characteristic	Ideals	Observed	Rating
I. Relevance			
A. Content details	0%	2%	OK
B. Vocabulary	less than 20%	6%	good
C. Facts	less than 20%	16%	OK
D. Generalizations	more than 10%	11%	OK
E. Understanding	more than 10%	5%	Low
F. Applications	more than 10%	60%	good
II. Discrimination			
A. Item			
1. High (.41 and up)	more than 25%	22%	OK
2. Moderate (.21 to .40)	more than 25%	41%	good
3. Low (.01 to .20)	less than 15%	30%	High
4. Zero or Negative	less than 5%	7%	OK
B. Score			
1. Mean	(a) 62.5	64.60	good
2. Standard Deviation	(b) 12.5	9.05	Low
3. Reliability	more than .70	.80	good
4. Probable Error		2.71	
III. Speededness			
A. Percent of Complete Papers	more than 90%	100%	good

(a) Midpoint of range between highest possible and expected chance score.
(b) One-sixth of range between highest possible and expected chance score.

University Examinations Service   State University of Iowa

RELEVANCE WORKSHEET

Test Title _Security Transactions_ k= _100_ Job Number _6314_

Group Tested _Class students_ N= _51_ Date of Test _2-2-53_

Time Limit _2 hrs._ Classifier _Ebel_ Checker _____

A. Content Details _52, 99_
    k = _2_
    % = _2_

B. Vocabulary _1, 2, 5, 23, 70, 81_
    k = _6_
    % = _6_

C. Facts _3, 9, 16, 27, 28, 46, 47, 48, 49, 50, 51, 64, 73, 74, 78, 100_
    k = _16_
    % = _16_

D. Generalizations _6, 10, 19, 34, 44, 45, 54, 56, 82, 91, 92_
    k = _11_
    % = _11_

E. Understanding _15, 17, 32, 53, 79,_
    k = _5_
    % = _5_

F. Applications _4, 7, 8, 11, 12, 13, 14, 18, 20, 21, 22, 24, 25, 26, 29, 30, 31, 33, 35, 36, 37, 38,_
    k = _60_   _39, 40, 41, 42, 43, 55, 57, 58, 59, 60, 61, 62, 63, 65, 66, 67, 68, 69, 71,_
    % = _60_   _72, 75, 76, 77, 80, 83, 84, 85, 86, 87, 88, 89, 90, 93, 94, 95, 96, 97, 98_

125

DISCRIMINATION WORKSHEET

Test Title _Security Transactions_ k= _100_ Job Number _6314_

Group Tested _Class students_ N= _57_ Date of Test _2-2-53_

Time Limit _2 hr._ Calculator _Dorothy_ Checker _Ruth_

Highly Discriminating Items Number _22_ Percent _22_

.85_____	.90_____	.95_____
.70_____	.75_____	.80_____
.55_____	.60 _100,_	.65 _10, 57_
.46 _7,13,14, 16,21,36, 62, 65,85_ .48_____		.50 _88, 95,_
.40 _3 11, 27 35, 63 66, 77, 90_ .42_____		.44_____

Moderately Discriminating Items Number _41_ Percent _41_

.34_____	.36_____	.38 _56, 72, 73, 75, 94, 97_
.29_____	.30 _93,_	.32 _17, 22, 23, 32, 39, 47, 50,53_
.26_____	.27 _1,5,6, 9, 20, 40, 43, 51, 59, 78_ .28_____	
.23 _67, 69, 70, 77, 80, 83, 91, 92,_	.24_____	.25_____
.20 _19, 25, 26, 41, 45, 64, 58, 61,_	.21_____	.22_____

Poorly Discriminating Items Number _30_ Percent _30_

.17_____ _87, 89, 96, 99,_	.18_____	.19_____
.13 _4, 15, 18, 38, 42, 55, 60, 64, 82,_ .15_____		.16_____
.07 _29 30, 48, 52, 74, 81, 86,_	.09_____	.11_____
.01_____	.03_____	.05_____
.00 _2, 12, 31, 37, 44, 49, 71, 76, 84,_	.00 _98,_	.00_____

Negatively Discriminating Items Number _7_ Percent _7_

-.01_____	-.03_____	-.05_____
-.07 _24,_	-.09_____	-.11 _8, 28, 33, 34, 68,_
-.15_____	-.20_____	-.25_____
-.30_____	-.35_____	-.40 _46,_
-.50_____	-.60_____	-.80_____

SCORE ANALYSIS WORKSHEET

Test Title _Security Transactions_ k: _100_ Job Number _6314_

Group Tested _Class students)_ N: _57_ Date of Test _2-2-53_

Time Limit _2 hr._ Calculator _Dorothy_ Checker _Ruth_

I. Basic Data

N	ΣX	ΣX^2		k	Σpq	$\Sigma r_{it}^2 pq$
20	1103	61239		15	2.92	.49
20	1314	86237	-	20	3.78	.47
17	1265	94538		20	3.35	.38
				20	3.84	.60
				25	4.31	.68
57	3682	242512		100	18.20	2.62

II. Statistics

Mean (M) $= \dfrac{\Sigma X}{N}$ $= \dfrac{3682}{57}$ $= 64.5965$

Variance (σ_t^2) $= \dfrac{\Sigma X^2}{N} - M^2$ $= \dfrac{242512}{57} - (64.5965)^2$ $= 81.8886$

Standard Deviation (σ_t) $= \sqrt{81.8886}$ $= 9.0492$

Reliability (r_{tt}) $= \dfrac{\sigma_t^2 - \Sigma pq}{\sigma_t^2 - \Sigma r_{it}^2 pq}$ $= \dfrac{81.89 - 18.20}{81.89 - 2.62}$ $= .8035$

Probable Error $(P.E._{meas})$ $= .6745 \; \sigma_t \sqrt{1 - r_{tt}} = .6745 \times 9.0492 \times .4433$ $= 2.7057$

127

TABLE OF TOTAL ITEM VARIANCE (pq) AND "TRUE" VARIANCE ($r^2_{tt}pq$)

Prepared by Robert L. Ebel, University Examinations Service, State University of Iowa

Example: If an item is answered correctly on 75% of the upper group papers and on 30% of the lower group papers, its total variance is .25 and its "true" variance is .05. These values, summed over all k items in the test, may be used with the variance of the test scores σ^2_t to find the reliability coefficient, α_1, or α_2, of the scores.

$$\alpha_1 = \frac{\sigma^2_t - \Sigma pq}{\sigma^2_t - \Sigma r^2_{tt}pq}$$

$$\alpha_2 = \frac{k}{k-1} \cdot \frac{\sigma^2_t - \Sigma pq}{\sigma^2_t}$$

Each cell gives total item variance / "true" variance ($\times 100$).

Upper P (columns) versus **Lower P** (rows)

Lower P \ Upper P	00	03	06	09	12	15	18	21	24	27	30	33	36	39	42	45	48	51	54	57	60	63	66	69	72	75	78	81	84	87	90	93	96	99
00	00/00	01/00	03/00	04/00	06/00	07/00	08/00	09/00	11/01	12/01	13/01	14/02	15/02	16/02	17/03	17/04	18/04	19/05	20/06	20/07	21/08	22/09	22/10	23/11	23/12	23/13	24/14	24/16	24/17	25/19	25/20	25/22	25/23	25/25
03	01/00	03/00	04/00	06/00	07/00	08/00	09/00	11/00	12/01	13/01	14/01	15/01	16/02	17/02	17/03	18/03	19/04	20/05	20/05	21/06	22/07	22/08	23/09	23/10	23/11	24/12	24/14	24/15	25/16	25/17	25/19	25/20	25/22	25/23
06	03/00	04/00	06/00	07/00	08/00	09/00	11/00	12/00	13/00	14/01	15/01	16/01	17/01	17/02	18/02	19/03	20/03	20/04	21/05	22/06	22/06	23/07	23/08	23/09	24/10	24/11	24/13	25/14	25/15	25/16	25/18	25/19	25/20	25/22
09	04/00	06/00	07/00	08/00	09/00	11/00	12/00	13/00	14/00	15/00	16/01	17/01	17/01	18/02	19/02	20/03	20/03	21/04	22/04	22/05	23/06	23/07	23/08	24/09	24/10	24/11	25/12	25/13	25/14	25/15	25/16	25/18	25/19	25/20
12	06/00	07/00	08/00	09/00	11/00	12/00	13/00	14/00	15/00	16/00	17/01	17/01	18/01	19/01	20/02	20/02	21/03	22/03	22/04	23/05	23/05	23/06	24/07	24/08	24/09	25/10	25/11	25/12	25/13	25/14	25/15	25/16	25/18	25/19
15	07/00	08/00	09/00	11/00	12/00	13/00	14/00	15/00	16/00	17/00	17/00	18/01	19/01	20/01	20/01	21/02	22/02	22/03	23/03	23/04	23/05	24/05	24/06	24/07	25/08	25/09	25/10	25/11	25/12	25/13	25/14	25/15	25/16	25/17
18	08/00	09/00	11/00	12/00	13/00	14/00	15/00	16/00	17/00	17/00	18/00	19/00	20/01	20/01	21/01	22/02	22/02	23/02	23/03	23/04	24/04	24/05	24/06	25/06	25/07	25/08	25/09	25/10	25/11	25/12	25/13	25/14	25/15	24/16
21	09/00	11/00	12/00	13/00	14/00	15/00	16/00	17/00	17/00	18/00	19/00	20/00	20/00	21/01	22/01	22/01	23/02	23/02	23/03	24/03	24/04	24/04	25/05	25/06	25/06	25/07	25/08	25/09	25/10	25/11	25/12	25/13	24/14	24/15
24	11/01	12/01	13/00	14/00	15/00	16/00	17/00	17/00	18/00	19/00	20/00	20/00	21/00	22/00	22/01	23/01	23/01	23/02	24/02	24/03	24/03	25/04	25/04	25/05	25/06	25/07	25/07	25/08	25/09	25/10	25/11	24/12	24/12	24/13
27	12/01	13/01	14/01	15/00	16/00	17/00	17/00	18/00	19/00	20/00	20/00	21/00	22/00	22/00	23/01	23/01	23/01	24/01	24/02	24/02	25/03	25/03	25/04	25/04	25/05	25/06	25/06	25/07	25/08	25/09	24/10	24/10	24/11	23/12
30	13/01	14/01	15/01	16/01	17/01	17/00	18/00	19/00	20/00	20/00	21/00	22/00	22/00	23/00	23/00	23/01	24/01	24/01	24/01	25/02	25/02	25/03	25/03	25/04	25/04	25/05	25/06	25/06	25/07	24/08	24/09	24/09	23/10	23/11
33	14/02	15/01	16/01	17/01	17/01	18/01	19/00	20/00	20/00	21/00	22/00	22/00	23/00	23/00	23/00	24/00	24/01	24/01	25/01	25/01	25/02	25/02	25/03	25/03	25/04	25/04	25/05	25/06	24/06	24/07	24/08	23/08	23/09	22/10
36	15/02	16/02	17/01	17/01	18/01	19/01	20/01	20/00	21/00	22/00	22/00	23/00	23/00	23/00	24/00	24/00	24/00	25/01	25/01	25/01	25/01	25/02	25/02	25/03	25/03	25/04	25/04	24/05	24/06	24/06	23/07	23/07	22/08	22/09
39	16/02	17/02	17/02	18/02	19/01	20/01	20/01	21/01	22/00	22/00	23/00	23/00	23/00	24/00	24/00	24/00	25/00	25/00	25/01	25/01	25/01	25/01	25/02	25/02	25/03	25/03	24/04	24/04	24/05	23/05	23/06	22/07	22/07	21/08

Statistical table (paired confidence-limit values; each cell shows two stacked numbers). Row labels 42–99 at left; 20 data columns.

n																				
42	17/10	17/09	16/09	15/08	15/07	14/07	13/06	12/05	11/05	10/05	10/04	09/03	08/02	08/02	07/02	07/02	06/01	05/01	04/01	02/00
45	20/08	19/08	20/07	18/07	18/06	17/06	16/05	15/04	15/04	14/03	13/03	12/02	11/02	11/02	09/01	08/01	07/00	07/00	05/00	02/00
48	21/07	20/07	20/06	19/05	18/05	18/04	17/04	16/03	15/03	15/03	13/02	13/02	12/01	11/01	10/01	09/00	07/00	07/00	05/00	04/00
51	22/06	21/05	21/05	20/04	19/04	19/03	18/03	17/02	17/02	16/02	15/01	14/01	13/01	12/01	11/01	10/00	09/00	07/00	06/01	04/00
54	22/05	22/05	21/04	21/04	20/03	20/03	19/02	18/02	18/01	17/01	16/01	15/01	14/00	13/00	12/00	11/00	10/00	09/00	07/00	06/01
57	23/05	23/05	23/04	22/04	21/03	21/03	21/02	20/02	19/01	19/01	18/01	17/00	16/00	15/00	14/00	13/00	12/00	11/00	08/01	07/02
60	24/04	23/04	23/04	23/03	22/02	22/02	21/01	21/01	20/00	20/00	19/00	18/00	17/00	16/00	15/00	14/00	13/00	11/01	09/01	07/02
63	24/03	24/03	23/02	23/02	23/02	22/01	22/01	21/01	21/01	20/00	19/00	19/00	18/00	18/00	16/00	15/00	14/00	13/01	11/02	08/02
66	24/03	24/02	24/02	23/02	23/01	22/01	22/01	21/00	21/00	20/00	19/00	19/00	18/00	17/00	16/00	15/00	14/00	13/01	11/02	09/03
69	25/02	24/02	24/02	24/01	23/01	23/01	22/00	22/00	21/00	21/00	20/00	19/00	19/00	18/00	17/00	16/01	15/01	13/02	12/02	10/04
72	25/02	25/02	24/01	24/01	24/01	23/00	23/00	22/00	22/00	21/00	21/00	20/00	19/00	19/01	18/01	17/02	16/02	15/03	13/03	11/05
75	25/02	25/01	25/01	24/01	24/00	24/00	23/00	23/00	22/00	22/00	21/00	21/00	20/00	19/01	18/01	17/02	16/03	15/03	14/03	11/05
78	25/01	25/01	25/01	25/00	24/00	24/00	24/00	23/00	23/00	22/00	22/00	21/00	21/01	20/01	19/01	18/02	17/02	16/03	15/03	12/05
81	25/01	25/01	25/00	25/00	25/00	24/00	24/00	24/00	23/00	23/00	22/00	22/01	21/01	21/01	20/02	19/02	18/03	17/04	15/04	13/06
84	25/00	25/00	25/00	25/00	25/00	24/00	24/00	24/00	23/01	23/01	22/01	22/02	21/02	21/02	20/03	19/03	18/04	16/05	14/07	
87	25/00	25/00	25/00	25/00	25/00	25/00	24/01	24/01	23/01	23/02	22/02	22/03	21/03	20/04	19/05	18/06	17/06	15/07		
90	25/00	25/00	25/00	25/00	25/00	25/00	25/01	24/02	24/02	23/03	23/03	22/04	21/05	20/06	18/07	17/09	15/08			
93	24/00	25/00	25/00	25/00	25/00	25/01	25/02	25/02	24/03	24/04	23/04	23/05	22/06	21/07	20/07	19/08	16/09			
96	24/00	24/00	25/00	25/00	25/01	25/02	25/03	25/03	25/04	24/05	24/06	23/07	22/08	21/10	19/11	17/09				
99	14/13	15/14	16/15	16/15	17/16	18/17	19/18	20/19	21/20	21/20	22/21	23/23	24/23	24/24	25/21	24/19				

ITEMS ILLUSTRATING CATEGORIES OF RELEVANCE

A. CONTENT DETAIL

". . . 'title' is a formal word for a purely conceptual notion; I do not know what it means and I question whether anybody does, except perhaps legal historians." Statement of

(1) Charles Clark
(2) Felix Frankfurter
(3) Harry Chase
*(4) Learned Hand

B. VOCABULARY

A security interest in a chattel, created by a bailment for the purpose of securing the payment of a debt, is properly called

(1) equitable chattel mortgage
(2) deposit of title bonds
*(3) pledge
(4) equitable conditional sale
(5) conditional sale

C. FACT

The title of the mortgaged personal property is held in Iowa by

*(1) the mortgagor
(2) the mortgagee

D. GENERALIZATION

Probably the outstanding recent development in the area of the conditional sales contract is

*(1) its gradual coalescence with the mortgage security devise
(2) the development of the right to bar the equity of redemption

(3) the inequitable treatment meted out to it by the courts of equity
(4) its total replacement of the chattel mortgage

E. UNDERSTANDING

If a creditor ever got your advice on loan arrangements, you might recommend the taking of a deed absolute in form rather than a mortgage as security for a loan because (most persuasive reason)

*(1) the debtor will have certain procedural hurdles to overcome if he comes in seeking to get the deed declared a mortgage
(2) the creditor can move on the property on default
(3) the creditor can sell, after default, to a third party free and clear and get the market value
(4) by taking a deed absolute in form, the creditor can obviate the necessity of foreclosure and thus eliminate the equity of redemption

F. APPLICATION

A married to B. A alone mortgaged certain property. On A's death, B asserted her right to her statutory share in the property. She claimed a one third interest in the realty. She can redeem by

*(1) paying off the entire mortgage
(2) paying off her pro rata share
(3) having the court divide the property

130

Exercise Writing in the Field of the Humanities

PAUL B. DIEDERICH

1957

I am indebted to the next speaker, Leo Nedelsky, a former colleague in the Office of the University Examiner at the University of Chicago, for an illustration of a classic type of test-exercise in the humanities. When he graduated from high school in China as a refugee from Russia, the final examination was quite an occasion. Candidates had to appear in a public place several hours a day for a whole week and answer any questions that the townspeople wanted to ask. Leo was almost caught by the Archbishop of the Orthodox Church, a kindly old man then in his ninety-third year. After the examination had proceeded for some time, the Archbishop indicated that he would like to ask the young man a question. "Young man," he said, "when the soldiers opened Christ's side with the lance, why did both water and blood come forth?" Leo was stuck; he was not prepared for this question. But as he put his head down and appeared to be thinking furiously, it occurred to him that the old man was really in his dotage, and if he could only postpone his reply for about a minute, the Archbishop might forget what he had asked. He therefore continued thinking, and after a suitable pause, raised his head as though inspiration had struck and replied, "Your Reverence, when the soldiers opened Christ's side with the lance, *both* water and blood came forth!" "That's right," said the Archbishop benignly. "A prize pupil!" Leo said that, as he glanced around the table, he saw a black-bearded Jesuit gazing intently at him as though to say, "We need that boy in our Order!" It is something to be said for this form of examination, that, although Leo might have had theological objections, that Jesuit was undoubtedly right.

For all its merits, this form of test-exercise has all but disappeared except in the archaic ceremonial of the oral examination for the Ph.D. Coming down closer to our own time, the sort of test-exercise that is still most commonly used in the humanities is well illustrated by a story that my old professor of the Bible at Harvard, Kirsopp Lake, told in one of his last lectures. It was the day before our final examination, and I think he tried to ease the tension by saying, "Gentlemen, I had a remarkable dream last night. I dreamed that I was sitting on a cloud at Judgment Day, watching all the tribes of earth assemble. They all came together into a great plain and sat down. Then, out of the circumambient mist, a great hand arose and began writing on a celestial blackboard in letters large enough for all the world to read. It wrote out the Ten Commandments, and then—in typical examination fashion—it added: 'Students choose six.' "

These two types of questions pretty well cover the history of examining techniques in the humanities down to our own time. To carry on the story from that point, I obviously have an enormous field to cover in a very brief time. It usually takes me a semester. With your permission, therefore, I shall pass over the fields of art and music with only a brief comment on each, chiefly because they require so much testing time per item before I could make them come alive for you. I should have to have at least tape recordings and slides, and I prefer a live pianist and original works of art loaned from some museum. If I had the pianist, it would not be difficult, but it would take a good deal of time for her to play snatches of 20 very familiar melodies, like "My country, 'tis of thee" and "Old Black Joe." In about half of these excerpts, I should coach her to insert one definite, but not too obvious, error. You would mark each excerpt "C" if it was correct, and "E" if it contained an error. If I wanted to increase the difficulty, I might ask you to indicate what was wrong with each excerpt that you marked "E": to mark it "1" if the error was in the melody, "2" if it was in the harmony, "3" if it was in the rhythm, and "4" if it was in the expression or emphasis—that is, in the relative loudness or softness of the notes.

If you were too sophisticated for this simple exercise, I might ask her to play the little tune from Haydn on which both Handel and Brahms wrote variations. I should then ask her to play the basic variation by each composer, tell you who wrote it, and ask you to tell me the chief difference between the two styles out of four or five suggested differences. Then I would have her play perhaps ten or twelve variations in a random order: some by Handel, some by Brahms, some by neither, and some on the wrong tune. You can see how this sort of thing can get quite complex. If I started you analyzing fugues and telling me what the different voices were doing, I should soon have you hanging on the ropes.

If there is time, as there is in a course, although not in an examination, I like to make a point about any great work in sonata form by playing a complete sonata, quartet, or symphony and substituting one movement that does not belong: that comes out of a similar work by the same composer, written at about the same period of his development. One might think that when a composer writes a work in four movements, he writes one tune for the first movement, another for the second, another for the third, and another for the fourth, and then puts the four tunes together, with perhaps some relationship in key or mood. I am convinced that nothing like this happens; he writes basically the same tune in four different ways—although sometimes, I admit, it takes a good deal of subtlety to recognize it as the same tune. What any sensitive musician can do at once, however, is to recognize it if you put in the wrong minuet, the wrong slow movement, or the wrong finale—and not because he has any previous acquaintance with the work, but simply because they don't belong; they won't fit. I have found this sort of exercise very good for demonstrating the underlying unity of a classic composition in four movements.

For the visual arts, one of the simplest techniques is to use four projectors that can throw four slides at once on a large screen, and ask a series of questions about them that can be answered with the number of the correct slide, or with "None of them." For example, at the humblest level: which one was a watercolor? Which was an oil? Which was a fresco? Which was a wash drawing? If they represent well-marked historical styles, which was Italian of the High Renaissance? Which was Dutch? Which was eighteenth-century French? Which was eighteenth-century English? All such works, of course, must be previously unknown to the students. At a slightly deeper level, one might show three works by one painter and one by a contemporary in a different style, such as three by Cezanne and one by an Impressionist. The painting that does not belong with the others will stick out like a sore thumb to a sensitive student, but others will see no difference. One can ask all sorts of questions about techniques and about the composition: for example, in which is the basic form of the composition a rectangle? a pyramid? a diagonal? an S-curve? Which makes the most obvious use of contrasting textures? Which one is basically two-dimensional? Which is organized in a series of planes? There is hardly any limit to the number of questions one can ask in the form, "Which painting does A?" "Which painting does B?" If the paintings have clear-cut differences, and if the questions are perceptive, the answers will reveal a good deal of sensitivity to what is going on in a work of art.

I should next like to turn to the field of history as it relates to the humanities, hoping to leave a clear field for Max Engelhart to deal with history as it relates to the social sciences. You will see the difference, I hope, in the kind of illustration I shall use. The sort of outcome I have in mind has no large social significance; it is not a necessary ingredient of good citizenship; it has, rather, a personal significance, and is an ingredient in one's philosophy. Less pompously, it is a part of that general stock of ideas that a man carries around in his head that determine what objects and events in everyday life will strike him as significant, or interesting, or puzzling, or dangerous, or good. Among these ideas, I would place a high value on a sense of the past and of its continuing influence on the present.

For example, I once read in a book of popular scientific essays the statement that the average person must take the existence of a man like Julius Caesar on faith, or on authority. To a man educated in the humanities, that statement is preposterous. I am sure that at least two-thirds of you have in your pocket or in your purse some tangible evidence that Julius Caesar existed and left us something that we use every day. It is something that you can take out and hold in your hand. It even has the name, Julius, printed on it, although in an English form that you may not at first recognize. The place in which his name is printed is peculiarly appropriate in view of his life history. What is it?

I could nudge you closer to the answer by writing the names of our last four months on a blackboard: September, October, November, December. Then I would erase the "ber," on the ground that it is nothing but a shiver, and would have left four good Latin words: *septem, octo, novem,* and *decem.* We have other forms of these same words in *septet, octet, novena,* and *decimal.* What do they mean? Obviously, seven, eight, nine, ten. But why do we call our ninth month the seventh, our tenth month the eighth, and so on? Did somebody lose count? That is hardly likely. We can get a clue as to what probably happened by writing out the Latin names of the months immediately preceding these four: *Julius* and *Augustus mensis,* our July and August. Do the names *Julius* and *Augustus* ring a bell? Certainly: Julius and Augustus *Caesar.* But how did their names happen to get into our calendar and displace all the following months by two months? At this point I allow a little time for research. Someone usually looks up the encyclopedia article on "Calendar" and discovers that, when Julius Caesar was campaigning in Egypt in 48 and 47 B.C., he was not too preoccupied with the charms of Cleopatra to notice that the Egyptians had a much better calendar than the Romans. Consequently, when he returned to Rome in 46, he brought along not only Cleopatra but an Egyptian astronomer named Sesogines, and with his help worked out essentially the calendar we use today. His successor, Augustus, secured its adoption throughout the Roman Empire, and either he or his followers apparently saw to it that the names Julius and Augustus were forever enshrined in it, disregarding the protests of the mathematicians that the names of the last four months would all be two numbers off from their proper numbers. Augustus may have explained that it had to be that way because Julius was born during the month we now call

July in his honor—and by a surgical procedure that we still call a "Caesarean section."

If I wanted to make this exercise just a bit more complicated, I might ask you why we called this calendar the "Julian Calendar" down to about the time of George Washington in English-speaking countries, and still later in countries dominated by the Greek Orthodox Church, but then shifted over to a slightly modified calendar that we call the "Gregorian Calendar." One of the chief differences between them is that our present dates are 11 days off the corresponding Julian dates. If you look in old history books, you will see that George Washington was born on February 11 (Old Style) or on February 22 (New Style), obviously the Julian and Gregorian dates. One of the best exercises in semantics I know is to have a class argue about the date on which he was "really" born. If we accepted the Julian date, it would make quite a difference in the time of the annual meeting of the American Association of School Administrators. Why did we change? What was done to prevent losing 11 days again? Did it work?

A still more complicated problem is that all our names for the months are Roman, while all our names for the days are Anglo-Saxon, yet each of our days corresponds planet for planet with the Roman names. *Solis dies* and *lunae dies,* day of the sun and day of the moon, Sunday and Monday, are obvious examples. Wednesday, which is Woden's day, is less obvious, but his planet was Mercury, as you can see in the Latin *Mercuri dies* or the French *mercredi.* Thursday is obviously Thor's day; he was "the thunderer," as you can see in the German name for this day, *Donnerstag.* But so was Jupiter the thunderer; hence this day was *Jovis dies,* the day of Jove, in Latin, or *jeudi* in French. All the other day names are Anglo-Saxon equivalents of the gods or planets for whom the Romans named their days. When do you think the Anglo-Saxons had a chance to pick up the Roman names for the days and then translate them into their own language? They did not invade England until the Roman Occupation had ended, and they had little if any contact with the Romans on the continent. And why didn't they translate the months?

If you are wondering how I would put problems like these into multiple-choice form, the truth is that I wouldn't bother. I'd give my classes some linguistic data, some historical data, a little time for research, ask them a series of questions, and let them answer in essay form, perhaps after some preliminary discussion. You may be disappointed because you know that the grading of a single essay is unreliable as a test or examination. But I am not talking about a test; I am talking about exercises for a course; and after I get sixteen to twenty such exercises over a period of a year, and grade them the way I grade them, the reliability of the cumulative total score can easily exceed .9. Please note that the program does not require me to talk exclusively about multiple-choice tests: the topic is "Exercise Writing."

I might carry this same line of thinking into a somewhat different outcome of the humanities that I call a sense of the interconnection of ideas, especially across languages and cultures. For example, when I learned that the new tranquilizing drugs had been given the ugly name, *ataraxics,* I greeted it as an old friend. It was the ringing battle-cry of my fighting days in college, the watchword of the Epicureans, *Ataraxía,* which may be translated, "Do not be disturbed!" Why it had such an appeal for young men I have never figured out. But I found the same idea expressed in Horace's motto: "Nil admirari," which may be translated, "Don't be swept off your feet!" There is even a hint of it in the Biblical, "Take no thought for the morrow," but that is really a different idea: it means trusting in God, not in your own inner resources. But later on the same idea is picked up in Castiglione's ideal for a courtier, which he called *Sprezzatura,* and in the seventeenth-century French ideal of the *honnête homme.* Coming down to our own time, I think we have the same idea on a somewhat different plane in Oxford reserve and Harvard indifference. It may be something basic in the code of the gentleman that has perennial appeal for youth. Our young men in one of their moods seem to be groping for "the still point of the turning world."

Here, again, I would not attempt to put such an exercise into objective form unless I had some compelling reason, such as having to give a test to 50,000 candidates. For a class it would be better just to give a list of these slogans, perhaps with translations, and ask what they had in common, why they have such an appeal for youth, and which one is farthest out of line with the others, as I believe the Biblical passage to be.

But I had better give some attention to objective exercises, and for that purpose I shall choose a poem, because nowhere else can I find so much meaning in such compact form. This one is called *Spring and Fall,* and was written by Gerard Manley Hopkins. It appears to be addressed by a mature man to a young girl, and hence, the title might be taken to refer to youth and age. I hope to convince you before we are through that this is definitely an error. *Spring* may well refer to youth, but *fall* in this title has a much more sinister meaning than "age." It is a moot point whether one can ask objective questions about a poem without lacerating it. I believe that one can elicit a very sensitive reading of a poem by objective questions. In fact, when anyone asks me whether I really understand a very difficult poem, like one of Eliot's *Four Quartets,* I have to answer, "I don't know. I haven't yet got around to making up a test on it."

It might be better to begin by reading the poem straight through, but it is rather puzzling and would not "get across" at first reading. Hence, we shall take it by pairs of lines and ask somewhat abbreviated objective questions about them.

> "Margaret, are you grieving
> Over Goldengrove unleaving?"

Here are two puzzles. What is "unleaving"? Staying? Failing to produce leaves? Unfolding leaves from buds? Or shedding leaves? The only one of these that might cause a young child to grieve is shedding leaves—in autumn. Hence Goldengrove can hardly be a particular flower or shrub, but just a patch of woods in autumn, with its characteristic golden color.

> "Leaves, like the things of man, you
> With your fresh thoughts care for, can you?"

Here the syntax is a bit tangled for the sake of the rhyme, but it obviously means, "Can you, with your fresh thoughts, care for leaves, like the things of man?" We should get at the ability to unravel the syntax by a grammatical question. What would be the *opposite* of "the things of man"? The things of woman? The things of children? Abstract ideas? Probably it is "the things of nature," because what she is caring for at this time is the falling leaves, and the poet expresses some surprise that she can care for these things, which are certainly things of nature, just as she cares for the things of man.

> "Ah, as the heart grows older
> It will come to such sights colder
> By and by, nor spare a sigh
> Though worlds of wanwood leafmeal lie."

The puzzle here is the interesting formation, "leafmeal," which I have never seen anywhere else. We have to figure it out by analogy. Is it like oatmeal, cornmeal, last meal, or piecemeal? The first three would be ridiculous, but the last suggests a clue. "Piecemeal" means "piece by piece." Can "leafmeal" then mean "leaf by leaf?" It certainly makes sense, for that is the way the leaves would be lying. The word "wanwood" is not in any dictionary, British or American, which is small enough to lie on my desk, and it is hardly worth tracking down in anything larger or more specialized since it obviously has to be some kind of dead foliage which is lying in great quantities, leaf by leaf, upon the ground. As Margaret grows older, she will not spare a sigh at such a sight.

> "And yet you *will* weep *and* know why."

As the poem is usually printed, the poet has indicated a strong stress on *will* and on *and* by accent marks. This is a first-rate puzzle, since the poet has just said that she will come to such sights colder and will not spare them so much as a sigh. If she then breaks down and weeps, with no reason given for the change in mood, there is a flat contradiction.

The only way out of it that I can see is that she is weeping now, over the falling of leaves; the poet has tried to comfort her by telling her that by and by she won't care; but she refuses to be comforted: she goes right on weeping and wants to know why she is weeping. This is the *volitional* use of *will,* as in "He *will* do it no matter what you say." It might be translated, "In spite of what I have been saying, you insist on weeping and on knowing why." I can't see any way in which it could be weeping in the future, for he has just said that in the future she not only won't weep; she won't even sigh. Now he begins to tell her why.

> "Now no matter, child, the name:
> Sorrow's springs are the same."

He doesn't want to tell her just the *name* of what she is weeping for, since now it would probably mean nothing to her; and anyway, the ultimate source of all sorrow is the same ("sorrow's springs").

> "Nor mouth had, no, nor mind, expressed
> What heart heard of, ghost guessed:"

We have to do a bit of translating here. "Your heart heard of, and your spirit guessed, what had not been stated in words or even formulated as an idea." I should simply ask, "Which of the following is the best reading of lines 12–13?"

> "It is the blight man was born for,
> It is Margaret you mourn for."

Here is the ultimate answer to the question of why the young girl is weeping. In the falling of the leaves she has unconsciously glimpsed a symbol of her own death, far off in the future: "the blight man was born for." It is really not the falling leaves she mourns for, but for herself, even though it is only what her heart told her, and her spirit guessed; it had never been explained to her in words, nor even entered her mind as an idea. That is why sorrow's springs are the same, for the ultimate source of all sorrow is death. It is also why the name is no matter, now, for it would mean nothing to her, but in her heart she has already guessed it.

If anyone now wants to interpret the title, "Spring and Fall," as "Youth and Age," he must have a sentimental aversion to the obvious interpretation, once we have puzzled it out, which is "Youth and Death"—the latter symbolized by the falling leaves. There are very few interpretations of a cryptic poem that one can absolutely rule out as untenable, but I believe "age" in the title of this poem is one of them. There is no clear reference to old age anywhere in the poem. True, as her heart grows older, she will no longer weep at the falling of leaves, but that could well occur by the age of twelve. The poet is represented as somewhat older than the girl, but there is no reason to suppose that he is very old: he might be a man of thirty. The girl is certainly not weeping about *his* age: "It is the blight man was born for,/It is Margaret you mourn for." That seems to me an unmistakable reference to death.

I have now used up my allotted time and have discussed only five topics: a few techniques for getting at sensitivity to what is going on in a musical composition or a work of art; a few informal ways of revealing understandings that are peculiarly characteristic of the humanities: namely, a sense of the past, and a sense of the interconnection of ideas; and, finally, some objective means of eliciting a sensitive response to a philosophical poem. Since I should use the same types of items to reveal more than a superficial grasp of any prose passage, literary, philosophical, or historical, I hope that in some way or other I have touched upon the chief fields usually associated with the humanities. To attempt a comprehensive coverage of such a vast domain, so differently conceived and differently taught in different institutions, would obviously be absurd in a brief talk. I can only hope that I have left you with a few testing ideas that are fairly representative of the spirit of this great domain.

Exercise Writing in the Natural Sciences

Leo Nedelsky

1957

This paper is concerned with general principles to be used in writing test exercises, especially objective test exercises, in natural sciences. Most examples will be drawn from physics, the field in which the author feels most at home; the generalizations which these examples are to illustrate, however, should be applicable to any of the natural sciences.

Exercise Variety

In these relatively enlightened times it may be safe to assume that the test writer has before him a list of clearly stated objectives, i.e., a description of the kinds of knowledge and abilities the test is to measure. It is well, however, to look into the origin of the list. The most important function of a science test, perhaps its only defensible function, is to predict the student's behavior when faced with a situation in which an understanding of science is useful and important. Such a situation, which we shall call a criterion situation, may occur in the student's academic career, his life as a citizen, or his work as a scientist.

One way to test the student's criterion competence, i.e., competence to deal with a criterion situation, is to present the student with realistic problems, i.e., with situations that closely resemble those he is likely to face in the future. A test of this "synthetic" sort is quite valid but also almost prohibitively cumbersome and expensive, for genuine problems facing a scientist or a citizen are usually very complex and not of the paper-and-pencil type. Further disadvantages of such a test lie in the difficulty of assembling an adequate sample of problems and of communicating about the precise nature of the test and students' "scores."

Another way is first to analyze the complex competence to solve genuine problems into its constituents, and then to test for the more important but

140

still tractable of these. Such an "analytic" test has all the usual shortcomings of an analytic representation of complex and incompletely understood phenomena: neither are all the constituents known nor would they add up to the whole. In addition, some of the more important constituents, such as habits of thought and attitudes, cannot be conveniently or accurately measured. Those shortcomings of an analytic test which result from the unavailability of a complete analysis of a complex competence are probably best alleviated by including in the test exercises that, in the aggregate, evoke in the student a great variety of mental processes in varied patterns.

We are here concerned with the analytic type of test. The list of objectives is the list of presumed constituents of the criterion competence. As has been suggested in the last paragraph, the test writer can in some respects transcend statements of objectives and come closer to the criterion competence by varying test exercises as widely as the limits of the formally stated objective permit. Thus, for example, in testing for the ability to interpret physics data the following variations are possible: the data may be graphical, numerical, or verbal in form; the content may be, for instance, mechanics or heat; the student may be asked to draw possible conclusions, to assess the accuracy or consistency of the data within themselves or with other data, or to estimate the cogency of the data as evidence for a generalization. The form of the test may also vary: it may be essay or objective.

EXERCISE WRITER'S PREPARATION

If the variety of exercises described in the preceding paragraph is not to be merely haphazard, the exercise writer should not only know the subject matter tested but also have some understanding of what is involved in solving a genuine scientific problem at a level of sophistication higher than that of the students. As will be shown below, he must also know the extent and the range of the students' knowledge, abilities, and general intelligence. He must even know their method of preparation, enough at least to be able to judge the degree of novelty a particular test exercise will have for them. Finally, the exercise writer must have some notion of the more common methods used by the students in solving various exercises.

OBJECTIVE AS FUNCTION OF THE EXERCISE AND OF THE STUDENTS

Having described the prerequisites for writing an exercise, we shall skip the actual technique of producing its first version and deal instead with the general methods of criticizing an already written exercise. The key question is, of course, what a particular exercise measures. This question we shall assume to be equivalent to the following one: If the exercise is successfully performed by a group of students and unsuccessfully by another group, what is the main difference in the abilities of the two groups? It seems clear at the outset that the answer depends on the choice of the whole group. We shall nevertheless labor the point at some length because of the prevalent misconception that the ability measured by a test is a function of the test alone. Some test makers seem to think, for example, that a test designed to pick out promising college material from among the students of an eastern preparatory school can do the same job effectively when given to the students of a rural school in the South. We shall illustrate our point by an example.

A group of students is presented with the following exercise:

It is possible to hear the sound of a fountain behind a brick garden wall although the fountain cannot be seen. This phenomenon

A—can

B—cannot

be explained on the basis that long waves are diffracted more than short waves.

The group will be divided into two subgroups: those who pass by choosing the right response, A, and those who fail. In what respect do these subgroups differ? That is, what relative ability or knowledge does the exercise test for?

If the group consists of graduate students of physics of a Spanish university, it seems clear that the two subgroups will differ in their ability to read English, for it may be safely assumed that all members of this group possess the requisite mastery of physics but that only some know English. Next, let us suppose that the group consists of students thoroughly trained in the theory of wave motion but accustomed to using the terms bending and spreading in place of the term diffraction. The two subgroups are most likely to differ in their knowledge of terminology. Let our next group consist of students who have had a year of physics, a good discussion of diffraction of both light and sound, but no treatment of the relevant similarities between them. Let us assume that most of these students know that sound waves are longer than those of light. The two subgroups are most likely to differ in their ability to surmise that the principles of diffraction are applicable to the situation described in the exercise, an ability which may be considered a part of the more general ability to relate generalizations to specific situations. Let our last group consist of students to whom the particular test situation—sound of a fountain behind a wall—was explained in class or textbook. The ability to recall the situation may be influenced by a variety of factors, especially if the explanation was not emphasized. The main difference between the two subgroups is hard to determine and may not depend on anything educationally significant. An exercise writer who uses situations very similar to those in the textbook even in a test of pure information is on slippery ground.

It is sometimes argued that every pair of subgroups discussed in the preceding paragraphs exhibits the same important difference—the passing group knows the answer to the question while the failing group does not—and that, in measuring the general mastery of physics, it is a matter of secondary importance *how* the various students arrive at the correct answer. It seems that this argument is based on at least two questionable assumptions. One of these is the assumption that it is important to know the answer to the question of the exercise. Surely, unless the student is going to be a landscape gardener or fountain builder, we are interested in his ability to answer not this particular question but this *kind* or class of question, the basis of the classification being the objective to be measured. Let us assume, however, that it *is* important for the student to know the answer to some particular question, for of course there are such questions in science. Granted this, the second false assumption in the argument which we are criticizing is that it is important that the student know the answer on the date of the examination. For if we are interested in the retention of knowledge, in the student's ability to answer the question some months after the examination date, such ability will depend crucially on how the student was able to arrive at the correct answer in the first place.

We freely admit that to make our point clear we have chosen groups that are extreme in their differences. It is nevertheless quite generally true that a given test will measure different abilities if used with different groups. It is the examiner's responsibility reliably to determine what the differences are and consequently what conclusions from test results are justified. The specifications given to the exercise writer must include a description of the group or groups that will take the test.

NECESSARY AND SUFFICIENT ABILITIES

We have argued above that, in general, the relative scores of the members of a group will depend only on the factors with respect to which the group is heterogeneous. For example, our group number one was homogeneous at the requisite level of mastery of physics, but presumably heterogeneous with respect to the ability to read English. If it is desired to know the relative standing of the members of a group with respect to an ability, the principal ability of the exercise, this ability should clearly be a necessary one for doing the exercise, and the group should be fairly homogeneous with respect to all other auxiliary necessary abilities. The homogeneity of the group, relative to auxiliary abilities that an exercise requires, is best attained by writing the exercise in such a way that the level of the required auxiliary abilities is quite low, i.e., below that of the great majority of the group. If a single grade is to be assigned on an achievement test, it may be sufficient to keep the required auxiliary abilities below the barely passing level. In all cases, however, it is not enough to assert that the students ought to possess the auxiliary abilities; it is necessary to ascertain that the great majority of them in fact do.

In the exercise under consideration the necessary abilities are English, terminology, certain knowledge of sound and light and diffraction, and, finally, the ability to relate this knowledge to a particular situation. Let us now assume that the latter is the ability we want to measure, and that we have a realistic group consisting of students who have had one year of college physics, including the study of diffraction, but who are not likely to have discussed the particular test situation in class. If it seems likely that a sizable fraction of the group, say one-fourth, does not know what diffraction means, the term may be explained or omitted from the exercise. Either of these emendations will make the group properly homogeneous relative to the auxiliary ability of the knowledge of terminology but will make the exercise either longer or less clear to those who do know the term. For such a group it may be better to write an altogether different exercise. The most effective compromise between a reliable measure of an ability and a test of a practical length is determined by the group for which the test is designed.

Besides being necessary, the principal ability of the exercise also ought to be *sufficient* for dealing with the exercise. The following simple example will clarify the meaning of necessity and sufficiency. The student is asked: "What is the product of 3 and 7?" The ability to multiply is not here necessary because the problem can be solved by addition. Nor is it sufficient, for the term "product" must be understood. It should be clear that it is to make the principal ability sufficient or effectively sufficient that the auxiliary abilities must be kept at a low level. If the principal ability is necessary but not sufficient, those who can do the exercise have the ability and those who can't may or may not have it. If the ability is sufficient but not necessary, those who can't do the exercise don't possess the ability and those who can may or may not have it. In achievement testing, both the necessity and sufficiency conditions must be strived for, but often one has to be satisfied with a more modest claim that the ability tested for is likely to be very helpful in dealing with the exercise.

STUDENTS' MENTAL PROCESSES AND VALIDITY

There are statistical methods that help us find out just what ability an exercise measures. They all involve correlations between the exercise and a test whose validity is known to be high. Such tests are not usually available, however, for the more complex educational objectives, and the exercise writer must still mainly depend on his surmise of the students' mental activities while working on the exercise. One of the guides toward identifying the measured ability is a formal analysis of the test exercise. If, for example, in an objective item, the term "data" seems to be applicable to the information given the student, and if the responses among which he is to choose can be legitimately characterized as "interpretations" of the data, it is usually assumed that the exercise measures the ability to interpret data. Studies at Chicago (1) indicate, however, that students vary a great deal in the method of arriving at the right response. Some of them read the stem— in our case, the data and the question—arrive at some interpretation, and look among the prepared responses for a similar one. Others test each response in turn against the data and reject the inconsistent ones. If the inconsistencies can be established by inspecting parts of data only, the right response can be chosen without understanding even the general trend of the data. Not only in this example but generally, the abilities required in going from the question to the responses and vice-versa are quite different. It is in general impossible, for example, to use objective exercises for a reliable and consistent differentiation between the old standbys, "Ability to interpret data" and "Ability to apply principles." It is therefore better to use a classification of objectives that depends on the nature of the situation as defined by both the question and the responses and to use "interpretation of data" and "application of principles" exercises only to insure variety (5, Chs. 2 and 3).

HOMOGENEITY OF RESPONSES

Although there are many ways in which students attack objective exercises, in almost all of them the rejection of wrong responses seems to play an important role. If, therefore, the exercise is to measure a specific ability, this ability must be the key one not only in recognizing the right response but also in rejecting the wrong ones. This requires a certain *homogeneity* among the responses. Thus, e.g., if the exercise is to measure the ability to estimate the cogency of facts as evidence for a theory, the responses should all be correctly stated facts and differ among themselves only in their value as evidence. If, on the contrary, the wrong responses contain data that are factually false but that, if true, would have been good evidence, the exercise may or may not measure straight knowledge, but its reliability of measuring the principal ability is reduced.

The "ability-homogeneity" of responses has other values that may transcend that of insuring the purity of the ability measured. We believe that the main advantage of objective test exercises is their ability to define the problem for the student with a precision that is entirely out of reach of essay exercises. The definition must start with the stem, i.e., the part that precedes the responses. The stem must be so suggestive or directive that it guides the student's thinking into proper channels and even enables him to anticipate the general form of the responses. Stems like "Which of the following is true?" may produce tension and start some speculations in the student's mind—perhaps in connection with the preceding item—that are merely distracting. The very first response must further define the problem or, in many cases, even complete its definition. After reading it, the better students should be able to formulate a response that resembles closely in form and substance the right response—it may of course be the first one. And when the student who has the relevant ability comes upon the right response, he should recognize it as such and give only casual attention to the following responses. To this end in particular and to increase the general directiveness of the stem, the stem may well include hints as to the nature of the responses. For example, "All of the following responses are factually correct. Choose the one that contains the most convincing (or best established, or most precise) evidence for the theory." Or, "None of the responses below is strictly correct. Choose the one that deviates from the correct response through being too general (or too specific, or quantitatively inaccurate)." The problem of communication is a thorny one; every part of the exercise must contribute to the student's understanding of what the problem is and what kind of answer, as to form, content, precision, etc. is expected of him. The argument in this paragraph should make it clear why we have avoided using the term "distracter," a term that applies with such damning accuracy to many wrong responses in the existing tests.

Homogeneity of responses also contributes to economy of effort and time. Time allowance for objective items is usually indecently short. Yet it is patently impossible to test the student's thinking ability without allowing him to think. If the student's problem is to evaluate the cogency of evidence, he should be allowed to concentrate on that problem without being sidetracked into estimating the reliability of data or other matters. Nor should he be on the lookout for verbal traps. The "onlys," "nevers," and other words so frequently used to differentiate between the right and wrong responses should be prominently displayed. If underlining such words ruins the exercise, chances are it was not very good to begin with.

Homogeneity of responses relative to the ability measured helps define the problem, concentrates the student's attention on it, and reduces his tension. A similarity in the *form* of the right and the wrong responses, i.e., in their length, presence of qualifying words and phrases, the degree of technicality, and in other essentially superficial respects, should help prevent successful guessing based on the auxiliary ability of test-sophistication. Ideally, responses should differ in nothing but a single quality; in the above example this quality is their cogency as evidence for the theory.

THE BEST AND THE CORRECT RESPONSE

In natural science, as in other disciplines, it is nearly impossible to give a strictly correct answer to any but the most trivial question in less than a page. In order to decide how correct the best response should be we must again recall that the main function of an exercise is to divide the students into two groups that differ in a particular ability. The response marked right should then have appeal to those who have this ability. It is therefore at best useless to increase the accuracy of the best response by adding qualifications whose absence would not be noticed by the great majority of the students, say by B+ students and those below. For an obvious example, the relativistic and quantum mechanical corrections or qualifications are out of place in a test over a one-year physics course. It is of course true that the absence of certain qualifications may disturb an exceptionally well-informed student. This is to be preferred, however, to changing the exercise so as to lower its discriminating power for the rest of the class. For, as qualifying phrases are added to make the best response more nearly correct, two difficulties arise. First, a large number of students become puzzled by the presence of the over-refined qualifications, and second, making the formal attractiveness of wrong responses approximately equal that of the best response becomes more difficult. The optimum correctness of the best response must therefore vary with the caliber of the students. We are thus reminded once more that the really effective test is tailor-made to fit a particular population.

In some exercises it is preferable not to have the best response correct even in the modest sense of the preceding paragraph. It is then of course usually desirable to warn the students of this fact. By using as the right response one that is not correct but is merely the best of those available, it may be possible to force the student to do more profound thinking. For example, the best response in the following exercise is A:

Exercise: Which of the following is the best definition of *Potential Energy?* (None of the definitions is strictly correct)
A—The energy which a body possesses because of its position.
B—The energy which a body at rest possesses because of its position.
C—The maximum energy which a body can acquire.
D—The energy which a body possesses before it starts doing work.
E—The energy which enables a body to do work.

If the right response were made more correct by including elastic potential energy, its form might easily become so like that in textbooks, that the exercise could be worked by rote memory. As it stands, the exercise is likely to discriminate between those who understand the term, potential energy, and those who don't. It may be remarked in passing that the responses of this exercise lack in formal homogeneity because two of them, A and B, are "paired," i.e., have a close similarity, while the rest of the responses are not. Students soon learn that paired responses are more likely to contain the right one.

Teachers are almost invariably unhappy about incorrect answers even if they are shown good statistical evidence that the exercise correlates highly with the teachers' own choice of good students. Their arguments against incorrect best responses vary from good to bad, the bad ones being more frequent. An example of a good argument is that since we have no accurate knowledge of the mental processes involved in the criterion situation, i.e., in resolving a genuine scientific problem, or those used in the test situation, we should hold firmly to the few similarities between the two situations that are under our control. Thus in a criterion situation of almost any sort it is a statement of the correct definition or law that is useful; therefore similarly correct statements should be used in test situations. There is a good deal of truth in this analysis, although it should be noted that the choice of the best approximation concerns the scientist and the citizen more often than the choice between the correct and the wrong. A less good argument, based on the uncontestable truth that tests are valuable tools of instruction, claims that therefore they should contain nothing but the truth. What the student is likely to learn from a test, however, is not an isolated fact or generalization, for the test is encompassed in a few pages and a few hours as compared to the hundreds of pages of the text studied over a period of months. The most effective role of the test as a teaching instrument is rather to let the student know in an emphatic manner what the objectives of the course are. Another questionable argument runs as follows: "I told

my students that 'the energy which a body possess because of its position' is
not a correct definition of potential energy. It is not fair to ask them to accept it." Our reply to this teacher would be that the only physics test that is
fair to the students is the one that reliably identifies those of them who understand physics. The question is rather whether the exercise in question is
fair or kind to the teacher. On this point we would say first, that fallibility
of teachers and texts is not a bad thing for students to learn, and second,
that the teacher should have given his class a deeper criticism of the quoted
definition than merely calling it wrong. Whatever the worth of the arguments against exercises with incorrect best responses, it should be clear that
writing such exercises does require a steady hand.

THE WRONG RESPONSES

The prevalent criterion for a wrong response seems to be that it should
be wrong and yet plausible. As we have indicated before, this requirement,
although necessary, is not enough. If the student is asked to choose among
conclusions from some data, the wrong responses should be wrong only in
their relation to the data. Of course even if the wrong responses are homogeneous in this respect, there are still degrees and kinds of wrongness that
are possible. The degree of wrongness determines the difficulty of the item
and sets the main discrimination line, e.g., between A and B or between D
and F students. The *kind* of wrongness determines the auxiliary abilities
that are helpful in finding the right response. Thus, for example, if the
wrongness in the preceding example is that of going beyond data, students
who have such a weakness will be more attracted to the wrong responses
than, say, students who have the weakness of being over-cautious. Besides
these two, there are many other weaknesses that make wrong responses,
and sometimes the right response, unequally attractive to students who possess the principal ability in an equal degree. Two common ones are distrust
of theory and over-reliance on quantitative data. A play on various students' weaknesses to make wrong responses attractive to them is often
justified and, in fact, can seldom be avoided. It is necessary, however, that
the prevalent weaknesses be sampled fairly. Such sampling is controlled
primarily by the nature of the wrong responses and, to a smaller degree, of
the right response if it deviates, as it usually must, from the strictly correct
one.

Although it is difficult, and unnecessary, to have a single exercise discriminate at several levels of ability, it is quite easy and useful to make it
discriminate at two levels by making one or two of the wrong responses so
wrong that only failing students should be attracted by it. Let us call such a

response an F-response, and the right response, R-response. Let the number of F-responses a student chooses be called his F-score, and similarly for R. It will amost always be found that the R-minus-F scores are more reliable than the R-scores; F-scores may discriminate more reliably between F-students and the rest than any other scores. It should be noted that for students who make a try at every exercise, the reliability of the usual right-minus-wrong scores is identical with that of the R-scores. F-scores are also useful for establishing absolute standards for passing performance (3, 4).

SPONTANEITY

If the strongest argument for objective tests is that they make it possible to make clear to the student what is expected of him, the strongest argument for the essay test—we are not here considering the ability to express oneself—is that it calls for a spontaneously produced answer. Since all criterion situations call for greater spontaneity than is required in the usual objective test, the latter, if not supplemented by an essay test, must be modified to decrease such discrepancy in some of the exercises. An objective exercise that comes closest to this requirement is one in which the student reads the statement of the problem, decides on the right answer, and then searches for it among the prepared responses. Such a procedure can never be enforced but it can be made more profitable than any other. To this end, the stem must be very directive and the responses nondirective or even nonevocative, i.e., nonsuggestive.

The following exercise has nonevocative responses. The student is asked to solve two simultaneous equations: $3x + 2y = 17$ and $x - y = 9$. If the responses were pairs of values of x and y, some students would find it easier not to solve the equations but rather to substitute the pairs of values into the equations. If, on the other hand, the correct response is given as $x + y = 5$, and the wrong ones similarly, a solution of two simultaneous equations is the only way to the right answer, and solving the given two is by far the quickest way.

Numerical science problems lend themselves well to the technique of nonevocative responses. For example, each response may list just the second digit of a numerical answer. Or, the student may be asked to compute two quantities, or two formulas, and asked to choose among responses that are ratios of the two. In qualitative exercises, a similar result may be achieved by making the analysis of each response, without first solving the problem of the exercise, as much of a chore as solving the problem. The following exercise, in which, to save space, we show only two responses, may serve as an illustration:

Exercise: This exercise involves two steps. First, decide what law of nature is most directly useful in explaining the following fact: A brick can be pulled along a fairly smooth surface by means of a string; the string would break, however, if jerked sharply. Second, choose that one of the following phenomena for which this law of nature provides an explanation.

A—A glass tube dropped from a height of 10 feet breaks if it falls on a concrete sidewalk but will not break if it falls on a soft ground.

B—It is impossible to lift oneself by pulling up on one's own hair.

Most students will find that the most efficient way to deal with the above exercise is to follow the directions which suggest giving a spontaneous answer to the first question. Directions to the students must of course always be scrupulously honest in the sense of indicating the easiest path to the right response. We note that the second part of the stem in the above exercise is not at all directive. This is the usual price we must pay for introducing spontaneity into objective exercises. A more elaborate but also easier method to combine the more advantageous aspects of the essay and objective exercises is described in another article (2).

SUMMARY

An effective test must be tailor-made for a particular population. The degree and range of the students' abilities determine: the optimum correctness of the best response; the degree and kind of wrongness of the wrong responses; the level of the auxiliary abilities necessary for working the exercise. This level should be below that of the great majority of the students.

The definition of the ability measured by an exercise should hold true for all the prevalent methods of solution used by students; e.g., the method of eliminating wrong responses.

The principal ability of the exercise should be both necessary and sufficient for working the exercise.

Test exercises measuring a particular ability should exhibit as great variety as is consonant with the definition of the ability. They can vary in content, form, type of analysis required, difficulty, and auxiliary abilities.

The situation on which an exercise is based should not be similar to the textbook ones.

Abilities auxiliary to a group of items should be sampled fairly by these.

The stem of an exercise should contain a clear statement of the problem and even suggest the desired kind of solution.

Responses should be homogeneous relative to the principal ability and in their form.

The technique of using incorrect best responses is useful but difficult.

It is easy and desirable to include among wrong responses some that are attractive to failing students only.

It is possible to make an objective exercise evoke in the students nearly spontaneous answers by making this process the most economical one for dealing with the exercise.

REFERENCES

1. Bloom, B. S., & Broder, Lois J. *Problem-solving processes of college students: an exploratory investigation.* Chicago: Univer. of Chicago Press, 1950.
2. Nedelsky, L. Evaluation of essays by objective tests. *Journal of General Education,* 1953, 7, 209–220.
3. Nedelsky, L. Absolute grading standards for objective tests. *Educational and Psychological Measurement,* 1954, 14, 3–19.
4. Nedelsky, L. Ability to avoid gross error as a measure of achievement. *Educational and Psychological Measurement,* 1954, 14, 459–472.
5. Nedelsky, L. *Science teaching and testing.* New York: Harcourt, Brace & World, 1965.

Exercise Writing in the
Social Sciences

Max D. Engelhart

1957

In discussing the art of exercise writing in the social sciences, it seems wise to limit the discussion to exercises useful in evaluating certain important objectives of a college level general course in social science. Many of the suggestions made also have application to more specialized courses in the social science field on both the high school and college levels. Before considering the writing of exercises, it is desirable to characterize briefly what constitute, in my judgment, desirable instructional objectives, methods of instruction, and subject-matter content of a social science general course.

Instructional Objectives in Social Science

As in other subjects, the instructional objectives of such a course may be classified under the headings of 1) knowledge, 2) intellectual skills, and 3) ideals, attitudes, interests, and appreciations. Under the first heading can be listed knowledge or understanding of specific facts, terminology, and principles. We may also include knowledge of the methods of inquiry in social science and how social science can contribute to the making of choices between values, without determining, as science, which values to choose.

Under intellectual skills, we may include the skills required in making discriminations and comparisons and in organizing knowledge in ways which contribute to understanding of relationships. We may include the skills required in reading discussions of social problems or issues with comprehension and with sensitivity to the logic, or lack of logic, of what is read, presuming that these discussions are of varying points of view, or are based on evidence of varying relevance and dependability. Under intellectual skills we may include the ability to analyze a social problem, to recognize assumptions and to propose hypotheses, to obtain relevant data from appropriate sources, and to arrive at warranted conclusions. Especially important is the acquisition of the ability to predict and to compare the consequences of different courses of action. This objective is fundamental to the critical evaluation of social policies essential to effective citizenship.

There are, of course, no sharp boundaries between the levels of objectives just mentioned. This is also true of the classification of objectives in the *Taxonomy of Educational Objectives* by Bloom and others (2). Furthermore, an exercise may evaluate the attainment of different specific objectives, given different learning experiences.

We shall not here be concerned with the formulating of essay questions nor with the evaluation of ideals, attitudes, interests, and appreciations. In the bibliography of this paper the speaker has listed the provocative article of V. M. Sims entitled "The Essay Question is a Projective Technique" (9) and John Stalnaker's scholarly chapter on essay examinations in Lindquist *et al., Educational Measurement* (10). A comprehensive program of measurement in a social science general course should include some amount of essay testing, the writing of papers on social problems, and the evaluation of change in social attitudes and beliefs. Levi's *General Education in the Social Studies* (8) is one source of information with respect to such evaluation.

The Content and Methods of Social Science Instruction

Where teaching is restricted to the imparting of the content of a text, in fairness to the students, evaluation should be restricted to measurement of the information they have thus obtained. On the other hand, instruction which justifies the use of exercises measuring intellectual skills should provide for the development of such skills. In addition to the explicit recognition of these skills as objectives, instruction should give students numerous opportunities to acquire and practice them. In class discussion and in written assignments, thought-provoking problems should frequently be presented. The instructor should be constructively critical of the thinking done by students whether in recitation or in written work. While much time must be devoted to the imparting of knowledge by an instructor and to its acquisition by students, instruction can include development of understanding of the nature of assumptions and hypotheses, and of the elements of logical reasoning. Students should be expected to use terms with precision and to support their answers with evidence. Problems and issues should be analyzed in class so that students may be trained in identifying problems or issues, in recognizing assumptions, in determining what kinds of data are needed to support or disprove hypotheses, and what methods are useful in collecting and in interpreting the data. From time to time instruction should include the comparing and contrasting of facts, ideas, principles, and generalizations earlier learned with those being learned so that the student is able to organize his knowledge in ways which will prove helpful in solving new problems.

While there are numerous sources of information concerning the methodology of social science instruction, reference will be made only to two recent and challenging books—*Theory and Practice of the Social Studies* by Earl Johnson (6) and *Teaching High School Social Studies* by Maurice Hunt and Lawrence Metcalf (5). The latter should be of equal interest to teachers of the social studies on the college level. It is unique in its applications of field psychology to learning in social science. It strongly advocates the use of content relevant to areas of conflict and of contradictory beliefs both within persons and between persons, such as: social class; race and minority group relations; sex, courtship, and marriage; and religion and morality. Whether or not these particular areas are included, the content of the social science general course should include areas in which there are important controversial problems and issues. *Contemporary Social Issues* by Lee, Burkhart, and Shaw, (7) and *Basic Issues of American Democracy* by Bishop and Hendel (1) are examples of sources in which students may read selections presenting opposing points of view on numerous problems and issues. *Society and Man* by Weinberg and Shabat (11) is unique in that its authors have shortened and rewritten, in language understandable to students but acceptable to the original authors, research studies and basic writings of noted authorities in the social science field.

Unless the students have had previous instruction relevant to fundamental concepts and principles of sociology, economics, and government, it is possibly unwise to base a general course on such a "problems" text alone. There may be, however, concurrent use of a systematic text and a problems text. While instruction and class discussion should be concerned with problems and issues, it is more effective to deal intensively with a relatively few problems or issues in relation to more systematic content and in relation to social science methods of inquiry, than to deal with numerous problems or issues superficially. With all of the preceding as introduction, let us turn to the art of exercise writing in the social sciences.

THE ROLE OF THE TEACHER IN EXERCISE WRITING

While it would seem logical to insist that exercise writing begin with a carefully formulated and detailed list of specific objectives and a detailed analysis of the subject matter content to be covered, it is my experience that such a formal approach is seldom effective with a group of teachers. It should be emphasized, however, that a less formal approach with the underlying goal of gradual development toward adequate definition of objectives and representative sampling of content can lead, after a number of semesters, to the production of exercises compatible with a wide range of objectives. There will be an increasing emphasis on intellectual skills or critical thinking in the social science field both in instruction and in evaluation of the goals of instruction.

After numerous exercises have been written by the various teachers of a group, its members should critically evaluate each other's work. When different instructors key exercises independently, discussion of disagreements with respect to correct answers can stimulate improvement of the content and phraseology of the exercises. Group evaluation of exercises may result in the elimination of exercises relevant to trivial content or to content uniquely taught by one of the teachers. Group evaluation may also result in the organization of an examination representative of the content of the course and of the objectives it is desired to evaluate. After the examination has been given and subjected to item analysis, the item difficulties, expressed as percentages of correct response, make it possible for each teacher to evaluate achievement in terms of specific objectives. The item difficulties and the item-test correlations are also of great help to teachers in revising series of exercises for future use. It is especially true of social science exercises that knowledge of the percentage who choose each answer, both correct and incorrect, contributes significantly to the improvement of faulty exercises.

THE WRITING OF MULTIPLE-CHOICE EXERCISES

As in other fields, the writer of multiple-choice exercises in social science should observe a number of precautions. The introductory part of each exercise—the "item stem"—should present the problem of the exercise. This promotes both clearer understanding of the problem of the exercise and the use of briefer answers, which often may be no more than single words or phrases. Such exercises are more economical of testing time, and since more exercises can be used, the total test may be more valid and reliable. Unless the exercise begins with a question, each answer should complete the item stem grammatically. One of the answers should be definitely correct and the other answers should be plausible although incorrect. (In exercises of the best-answer type one of the answers should definitely be the best.) Frequently, incorrect answers, or "distracters" can be true in themselves, but not relevant to the problem set by the item stem. Often an exercise writer can produce good distracters by anticipating the kinds of answers students are likely to select when applying the wrong information or the wrong kind of thinking to the problem. Precision in the use of English and the ability to express complex ideas in brief and simple phraseology are desirable attributes of an exercise writer. Some of the suggestions just made may be illustrated by quoting two multiple-choice exercises.

1. Authorities on marriage deplore the American "idealistic belief in romantic love." A young couple characterized by this belief will be more likely to have a successful and happy marriage if also characterized by
   A. a belief in the double standard of morality.
   B. a willingness to take risks.
   C. emotional maturity and adaptability.
   D. a belief in the contractual concept of marriage.
   E. physical attractiveness.

2. A large increase in total spending by consumers, business, industry, and government will probably not cause inflation if
   A. government bonds are sold only to individuals.
   B. interest rates on loans are reduced.
   C. production of goods increases in proportion to spending.
   D. less money is saved by individuals.
   E. money is placed in circulation as needed for spending.

CLASSIFICATION OR KEY-LIST EXERCISES

While many and sometimes all of the exercises in a social science examination may be of the multiple-choice type and "self-contained" in the sense that a given exercise is not a member of a series of related exercises, it is frequently effective to use series of items of the classification or key-list types. In my judgment, items of these types can be useful in evaluating understanding of relationships and ability to make comparisons and discriminations. The expectation of such series of items, ranging more widely over content than self-contained multiple-choice exercises, can motivate students to organize their knowledge, an advantage sometimes claimed for essay testing by persons critical of objective tests.

Suppose, for example, that in a social science course, instruction has been concerned with the characteristics of liberal democracy, communism, and fascism, and that the instruction has included some discussion involving the contrasting and comparing of these ideologies. Then a series of exercises such as the following is appropriate:

After each item number on the answer sheet, blacken *one* lettered space to designate that the item is characteristic of the theory of

A   liberal democracy.
B   communism.
C   facism.
D   both communism and fascism.
E   both liberal democracy and communism.

1. There should be respect for individual personality in both the ends and means of government.
2. Freedom and equality are meaningful only in a classless society.
3. A temporary dictatorship may precede the establishment of a "stateless" society.
4. The ultimate goal is freedom and equality for all in a democratic society.

Recall of the comparisons made during instruction may enable many students to classify such items correctly. Something more than mere recall is needed, however, if the items are not in the same words used by the instructor and if the student has to select the ideas that are relevant from a wide range of information. In writing such exercises a number of precautions should be observed. The categories should be related, but mutually exclusive. If, for example, the categories pertaining to liberal democracy, communism, and fascism had included socialism it would be difficult to classify such an item as "Advocates collective ownership of the means of production." Careful wording of the categories is extremely important. The word "theory" was included in the directions since it was evident to the writer of this series that the students could become confused if they thought of practices rather than theories. The items should not include long, involved, and qualified complex sentences.

In thinking critically about some controversial problem or issue in the social field, students need to become alert to arguments that a protagonist for one side of the issue will use to support his side and the arguments he will advance against the other side. Consider in this connection the following key-list categories and a few of the items to be classified in accordance with them:

Imagine two persons debating the relative merits and limitations of presidential and parliamentary governments. After each item number on the answer sheet, blacken *one* lettered space to designate that the item is an argument advanced

    A in support of presidential government.
    B in opposition to presidential government.
    C in support of parliamentary government.
    D in opposition to parliamentary government.

1. Such a government is especially designed to prevent a dangerous concentration of power.
2. Such a government should respond more quickly to the expressed will of the people.
3. Experience shows that a government which permits the executive and the legislative to become rivals for power retards governmental action.
4. Such a government is especially ineffective where there are several political parties.

EXERCISES RELEVANT TO QUOTED MATERIAL

In evaluating intellectual skills, it is effective to use series of multiple-choice exercises or key-list items relevant to brief selections quoted within the examination itself or assigned to students for critical reading prior to the examination. Selections presenting different points of view or advocating different courses of action are particularly useful. On occasion, exercises following a brief selection may call for student analysis of its content in relation to that of one or more other selections earlier assigned. In a recent examination, a paragraph from *American Community Behavior* by Jessie Bernard attributes minority group conflict to competition for jobs and scarce consumer goods including housing. Three of the multiple-choice exercises following this paragraph expect the student to compare its thesis with the points of view on minority group relations expressed by Robert Redfield, T. V. Smith, and Gunnar Myrdal in selections earlier studied. One of the exercises follows:

1. In his *American Dilemma,* Myrdal disagrees with the above writer in that Myrdal
    A. opposes racial discrimination.
    B. explains discrimination in terms of inconsistent social values.
    C. ignores the role of economic factors in causing racial prejudice.
    D. favors a certain degree of inequality as being socially healthy.

Each answer in the following exercise is quoted from a paragraph from Jefferson's first inaugural address presented above the exercises:

1. In view of Hamilton's beliefs with respect to our government, it is likely that he would consider least desirable
   A. "Equal and exact justice to all men."
   B. "The support of the state governments in all their rights."
   C. "The supremacy of the civil over the military authority."
   D. "The honest payment of our debts."

When two or three brief selections advocating contrasting points of view or differing courses of action are quoted within an examination, they may be followed by multiple-choice exercises or by key-list items. For example, one selection may be a quotation from Edmund Burke's "Address to the Electors of Bristol," while the other may be a paragraph by Speaker Rayburn on the importance to a legislator of respecting the wishes of his constituents. A series of items may follow such directions as:

For each of the following items, blacken *one* lettered space if the item is one with which
   A   Burke would agree.
   B   Rayburn would agree.
   C   both would agree.
   D   neither would agree.

Certain things need to be considered in selecting material for quotation within a social science examination. In addition to relevance to instruction and elements of novelty, the quoted material should not be of unreasonable length. It should say much in little space. In some cases it is necessary to adapt rather than to quote literally. Often it is desirable to substitute words or phrases more readily understood by students. On one occasion, "the architectural drawing of a benevolent welfare state" was changed to "the idea of a welfare state." Frequently, modification of the quotation may be guided by the exercises written. Sentences which do not contribute to the solution of any exercises may be omitted if the omission does not impair the major thought of the selection. Sometimes an exercise can be keyed more readily if a word or phrase is modified. When a quotation has been changed as described above, the citation of its source should begin "Adapted from. . . ."

Some of the exercises pertaining to quoted selections may evaluate "background" knowledge of facts, terminology, principles, or conditions relevant to the quoted material, but not defined or explained therein. While certain of the exercises may be written to evaluate knowledge, other exercises may be written to evaluate the acquisition of the intellectual skills characteristic of critical thinking. For example, an exercise may call for the identification of a central issue or problem:

1. The basic problem of all government involved in the situation described above is
   A. free enterprise vs. socialism.
   B. democracy vs. dictatorship.
   C. individual freedom vs. the welfare of society.
   D. government by an elite vs. government by the masses.

Another exercise may have to do with the identification of an assumption or a hypothesis. For example:

1. The above paragraph describes how interviewers collect data to be used in predicting which party will win an election. The *basic* assumption made is that
   A. the persons interviewed have sound reasons for voting as they plan to do.
   B. the persons interviewed are well informed with respect to the merits of the candidates.
   C. all age groups in the population are represented.
   D. the persons interviewed are representative of all the voters on election day.

Examples are given below of exercises calling for the identification in a quoted selection of bias, prejudice, and propaganda devices; of inconsistencies in an argument; and of limitations in the data presented, or in the techniques used in collecting them.

1. In describing Mr. Brown's argument, one can justifiably say that
   A. he was consistently factual.
   B. he was logical and precise.
   C. he used propaganda devices.
   D. he discussed both sides of the issue.

2. Although Mr. Brown is for "free enterprise," he is inconsistent in asking for
   A. an elimination of the excess profits tax.
   B. reduction of government expenditures.
   C. elimination of subsidies for farmers.
   D. government insurance of home loans made by private agencies.

3. The data reported in the table show that a greater proportion of children from broken homes become delinquent than other children.

The importance of this factor could be better evaluated if we knew
A. the comparative intelligence of delinquent and nondelinquent children.
B. the economic status of the homes of both types of children.
C. the educational opportunities of both types of children.
D. all of the above.

4. The author of the experiment summarized above concludes that children learn more efficiently when motivated by praise rather than reproof. We would be more confident of the results of this experiment had the experimenter
A. had the pupils alternately praised and reproved during instruction.
B. used a control group of pupils of equivalent initial ability subjected to reproof.
C. used an equivalent control group neither praised nor reproved.
D. tested a different hypothesis.

Certain exercises may require discrimination between expressions of fact, opinion, or value judgments:

1. Instead of stating a fact, the sentence in the paragraph which expresses a belief or opinion begins
A. The price of agricultural products . . .
B. The government should . . .
C. The surplus of wheat . . .
D. Last year, exports of wheat . . .

Other exercises may call for identification of inferences supported or contradicted by data in a table, a graph, or summarized in a paragraph:

1. The data given in the graph could be used to argue that
A. industrial profits are too high.
B. price controls should have been retained longer after the close of World War II.
C. the supply of consumer goods has decreased in recent years; hence, prices are high.
D. a depression is inevitable.

2. Judging from the figures reported in the article, it is correct to conclude that
A. consumers are buying more goods, but at lower prices.
B. consumers are buying less goods.
C. manufacturers intend to increase their sales efforts.

D. one-fourth of the manufacturers are decreasing output although customers are plentiful.

An exercise may evaluate the ability to recognize the need for additional evidence or of the effect of new evidence in accepting or rejecting some conclusion stated in the quotation:

1. We could more justifiably accept the conclusion that slum children are less intelligent than children from more privileged environments if we knew that the investigator had
   A. tested larger samples of both types of children.
   B. used a test that is fair for both types of children.
   C. done both of the above.
   D. done neither of the above.

2. We could most justifiably accept the author's conclusion that the Taft-Hartley Act has served to "enslave" workers if we knew that
   A. labor leaders in general oppose this Act.
   B. opinions of plant managers were obtained.
   C. the status of workers had actually declined since its adoption.
   D. a survey was made of the opinions of a representative sample of workers.

Frequently, an exercise should call for the identification of the consequences or effects of given courses of action. For example:

1. If the sales tax advocated by the author of the above quotation were to be adopted, which of the following would be likely to happen?
   A. Less money would be collected by means of the income tax.
   B. People with large incomes would suffer more than people with small incomes.
   C. People with small incomes would suffer more than people with large incomes.
   D. The burden of the tax would be proportionate to income.

CONCLUSION

A variety of types of objective exercises have been discussed and illustrated and numerous suggestions have been made concerning the art of writing them. An effort also has been made to emphasize relationships between social science instruction and evaluation. The question may be raised as to how we know that such exercises measure more than factual recall. It is evident from study of the exercises that knowledge is an important factor in their solution. It seems to me that it is also legitmate to infer that many of the intellectual skills functioning in critical thinking are also evaluated, assuming that social science instruction has been of the character described.

REFERENCES

1. Bishop, H. M., & Hendel, S. *Basic issues of American democracy.* New York: Appleton-Century-Crofts, 1956.
2. Bloom, B. S., *et al. Taxonomy of educational objectives: the classification of educational goals; handbook 1, cognitive domain.* New York: David McKay, 1954.
3. Chausow, H. The organization of learning experiences to achieve more effectively the objective of critical thinking in the general social science course at the junior college level. Unpublished doctoral dissertation, Univer. of Chicago, 1955.
4. Dressel, P. L., & Mayhew, L. B. *General education: explorations in evaluation.* Washington, D.C.: American Council on Education, 1954.
5. Hunt, M. P., & Metcalf, L. E. *Teaching high school social studies.* New York: Harper & Row, 1955.
6. Johnson, E. S. *Theory and practice of the social studies.* New York: Macmillan, 1956.
7. Lee, R. L., Burkhart, J. A., & Shaw, V. *Contemporary social issues.* New York: Crowell, 1955.
8. Levi, A. W. *General education in the social studies.* Washington, D.C.: American Council on Education, 1948.
9. Sims, V. M. The essay examination is a projective technique. *Educational and Psychological Measurement,* 1948, 8, 15–31.
10. Stalnaker, J. M. The essay type of examination. In E. F. Lindquist (Ed.), *Educational measurement.* Washington, D.C.: American Council on Education, 1951. Pp. 495–530.
11. Weinberg, M., & Shabat, O. E. *Society and man.* Englewood Cliffs, N.J.: Prentice-Hall, 1956.

The Test Manual as a Medium of Communication

ROGER T. LENNON

1953

The fact that this discussion of the test manual as a medium of communication is part of a program devoted to the general topic "Making Test Results Meaningful" dictates that we concern ourselves with problems of transmittal, via test manuals, of those knowledges and skills that will enable test users to comprehend, evaluate, and make more effective use of test results. The inclusion of the topic "Making Test Results Meaningful" in this conference betrays our awareness that test results in many instances are less meaningful to users than they might be, and our hope that at least some increase in understanding can be effected through improved test manuals. Few will question the need for better understanding of test results by the user. Durost, in summarizing trends in testing a year ago, noted that "Technical developments in test construction have outrun practice and there is a widening gulf between the test maker and the test user" (2). Traxler, reporting on a recent survey of testing practices in large cities, states that the major problem in testing is now that of communication, including the communication of the test maker's knowledge about the uses and misuses of appraisal instruments to the actual users of tests (3). How soundly based is the hope that we shall be able to improve this situation appreciably by improving test manuals is another matter, and the one with which this paper will be largely concerned.

In the remarks that follow, I have in mind particularly manuals for achievement, intelligence, and aptitude tests; and when I speak of the "test user," I am thinking generally of the classroom teacher, the guidance counselor, and the supervisor, rather than of the psychologist, the director of research, or the test specialist.

The problem of the test manual as a medium of communication has two aspects: what is to be communicated, and how it may best be communicated. Let us consider each of these in turn.

165

Content of the manual. What *must* a test manual include? What information is necessary in order that test results be meaningful? There is substantial agreement at least as to the topics that ought to be covered, if not as to the detail with which each should be treated. This agreement has been fairly well summarized in the American Psychological Association's set of technical recommendations for test manuals (1). As a minimum, a manual should include specific directions for giving and scoring a test, and information on how to interpret results, on validity and reliability, and on the purpose and construction of the test.

Few will deny that all these kinds of information have a contribution to make toward a better understanding of test results and toward enhanced meaningfulness of the results. We may well wonder, however, whether the information usually included under these headings is what the ordinary teacher or counselor needs to make the test results meaningful for him. For test results to be meaningful to a test user, it is necessary that he be able to see connections between the test results and problems which are real and urgent for him—to perceive how the test results are related to the goals for which he is striving. In my judgment, information about item validities, errors of measurement, selection of norm groups, and the like, does not help the user to see these connections—in fact, may set up a barrier to such understanding by focusing undue attention on the technicalities.

When we ask what information is necessary in order that test results be meaningful, we must also ask: meaningful for whom? For the teacher? For the director of research? For the counselor? For the administrator? Each is seeking something different in the results, each has his own purposes in mind. Information that will add to the meaningfulness of the results for one may not for another. The effort to meet the needs of these various audiences, differing as they do in training, understanding, and test sophistication, greatly complicates the task of preparing a satisfactory manual, both from the standpoint of providing sufficiently for all their needs, and with respect to the level of presentation.

If it be true, as some feel, that manuals do not provide as much technical information as the specialist needs for adequate evaluation of a test, it is far more certain that they do not provide enough assistance to the teacher or counselor in the proper use of the tests. How much help can a teacher derive from the average achievement test manual with respect to using results in such matters as marking and grading, improvement of instruction, motivation of pupils, diagnosis, and remediation? The teacher needs more specific recommendations, more concrete illustrative material than is ordinarily provided on these applications of test data.

Lest you misinterpret what I am saying as a recommendation to reduce the amount of technical information in favor of the how-to-do-it type of content, let me hasten to say that the solution certainly does not lie in the direction of providing less technical information, even though we may suspect that such information goes unread or uncomprehended by the majority of test users, but rather in the provision of more of the kind of information that relates the test results to the user's own needs and problems.

The attempt to provide all the kinds of assistance that all types of users need has one inevitable consequence—the unending expansion of test manuals. This poses a most difficult problem, the possible solutions to which we cannot even begin to consider here. Whatever the proposed solution—whether it be reorganization of material within the manual, relegating technical data to an appendix, publication of extensive manuals not included in test packages, or publication of several items to take the place of the traditional manual, all of which have been resorted to—it leaves something to be desired for adequacy of communication. Until it is safe to assume considerably more training in measurement than the typical teacher or counselor possesses at the present time, the need for more extensive accessory material for tests than can conveniently be provided will persist.

Let us now turn from consideration of *what* the manual should communicate, to the *how* of its communication. Can the ordinary user read, comprehend, and apply information as typically set forth in a test manual? How may manuals be improved in this respect?

Readability of test manuals. We have explored the matter of readability of manuals by computing Dale-Chall readability indices for the manuals for a group of achievement, intelligence, and aptitude tests. The tests involved—all widely used—are those of five different publishers, and I may say that there was remarkably little variation among them in the matter of readability. I believe these manuals to be reasonably representative. The average manual was found to be, on the whole, of about eleventh- or twelfth-grade reading difficulty, which would hardly appear to be beyond the level of the ordinary teacher. Within any manual, readability of content varies appreciably from one part to another. Those sections that consist of the specific directions for administering and scoring tend to be the easiest; those sections that have to do with technical aspects of a test—standardization data, reliability, item and test validity, etc.—are, as we would expect, more difficult. In this sample of manuals the more difficult sections were of college graduate level of reading difficulty, according to the Dale-Chall values. We may safely assume that material of this level of difficulty will be skipped or inadequately comprehended by substantial proportions of typical test users.

Can test manuals be written more simply, so that they will communicate more effectively to users of relatively limited measurement background? I have no doubt that they can—within limits. The fact that the various manuals which we studied were so similar in readability causes me to suppose that the level of readability is pretty much inherent in the nature of the material, rather than a reflection of the literary talent of the author. Technical concepts, usually of a quasi-mathematical character, and specialized vocabulary, cannot and should not be avoided entirely in any adequate treatment of the development of a test and interpretation of results. We must be willing either to presuppose enough training in measurement to equip the user with adequate background for understanding this technical information, or to acknowledge that this information in manuals will not contribute greatly to the meaningfulness of results.

Comprehensibility. The fact that material is readable, of course, does not guarantee that it will in fact be read and comprehended. In an effort to obtain some insight into how well typical users actually understand the content of a test manual, we have recently conducted a study of the extent to which teachers could read, comprehend, and apply information presented in the manual for the new edition of *Stanford Achievement Test.* We prepared a 68-item test covering information specifically set forth in this manual and administered it to two groups of teachers taking summer-session courses in tests and measurements. Prior to taking the test, the examinees had been directed to read the manual carefully, as if they were going to give the tests, and were further told that they would be tested on their knowledge of the content of the manual. In reading the manual they would, therefore, probably have been at least as highly motivated as the ordinary teacher preparing to give and score the test. They took the test on the manual first as a closed-book examination without access to the manual and later with the benefit of the manual at hand.

The results under either condition evinced a disappointing level of mastery of the content of the manual. The average percentage correct on the items of the test under the open-book condition was a little over 60. Only one item was answered correctly by all examinees, despite the fact that the answer to actually every item was readily obtainable in the manual.

We have studied the results of this test item by item in order to get some clues as to the sources of difficulty and nature of misunderstandings. I must confess that I have been unable to arrive at any generalizations in which I would repose much confidence—in fact, some of the results I find inexplicable. But I venture at least these few observations:

1) Items requiring some operation—e.g., conversion of scores to grade equivalents or percentile ranks, calculation of months above or below

norm—were harder than items requiring merely location of information. This finding we interpret as evidence of the limitations of the printed word as a medium for developing skills. Verbal directions for carrying out operations that are essentially quite simple frequently may create an impression that these operations are complicated and, by an odd paradox, the more complete and careful the directions, the greater the likelihood that they will seem hard. An operation which can be demonstrated very easily may in verbal presentation appear disturbingly complex. This fact highlights the importance of workshops, teachers' meetings, and in-service training programs, in which the operations of administering, scoring, and interpreting test results can be demonstrated, and in which teachers who are to be using tests may have an opportunity to perform the necessary operations under supervision. It further suggests the desirability of additional visualization in manuals themselves.

2) Items requiring the reading of tables proved difficult. For example, an item reading, "The most reliable of the nine subtests in the Intermediate Battery is ?", to be answered by reference to a simple table of reliability coefficients, was answered correctly by fewer than half the examinees; and other table-reading items were similarly hard. This indicates the necessity of textual description of tabular data, and of provision of examples of how tables are to be used. Again, *show-how* and supervised practice seem called for.

3) Some items answered almost verbatim in the text of the manual were missed by surprisingly large percentages of the subjects. To illustrate, consider the item:

"An examiner should never cut short the time specified for a test even though all pupils have finished." T or F

which was answered correctly by only 60 per cent of the examinees. The pertinent statement in the manual reads, "If all pupils or all but two or three in a class finish before the stipulated time has elapsed, time may be called."

It is impossible to suppose that the problem here is one of readability or comprehensibility of the material as presented. One must seek the explanation in the attitude, or set, or motivation, which the user, or in this case the examinee, brings to the task of reading the manual. It is hard to believe that the average teacher, if sufficiently interested, could not locate in a test manual information of the kind called for in the question just cited. Perhaps our real problem is that of discovering why they are not interested and how this interest can be stimulated—which brings us back to the principle earlier stated, that testing and test results take on meaning when the user sees them in relation to his own needs and problems.

Information of the kind revealed in this study is disconcerting, if not entirely unexpected; but it is necessary for any realistic appraisal of what test manuals can reasonably be expected to do, and as a basis for their improvement. I am glad to note, in this connection, that Roger Allison of Educational Testing Service has been making a somewhat similar study of the usefulness of the manual for the ACE Psychological Examination. He has prepared two forms of a test intended to reveal the extent to which teachers or counselors can make effective use of ACE results on the basis of information presented in its manual. He has, moreover, solicited their opinion about the adequacy of various sections of the manual, further information they would like to have included, etc. His findings, as far as I know, have not yet been made public.

To summarize: we have considered the test manual as a means of transmitting to the user the information and skills he needs if the results are to be meaningful and useful to him. The following points have been advanced:

1) There is unquestionably an urgent need for better communication from test maker to test user, if test results are to be made more meaningful to the average user.

2) The test manual can be made a more effective communication medium, and can contribute more to better understanding of test results.

3) The meaningfulness of test results to the average user will be enhanced if the manual concerns itself to a greater extent with relating test results to the user's problems and needs, and demonstrates specifically and concretely the kinds of actions indicated by the results.

4) The readability of test manuals, and presumably their comprehensibility, can be improved; but it is neither possible nor desirable to avoid technical material.

5) Dependence on the test manual alone for proper understanding and use of test results is inadequate. Not only must more formal training in measurement be encouraged as vital for proper use of test results, but such formal work should be supplemented by workshops and other in-service training, if teachers, counselors, and supervisors are to derive maximum benefit from tests.

REFERENCES

1. American Psychological Association Committee on Test Standards. Technical recommendations for psychological tests and diagnostic techniques: preliminary proposal. *American Psychologist,* 1952, 7, 461–475. [Final version published by American Psychological Association in 1954 and revised edition published in 1966—Ed.]
2. Durost, W. N. Modern trends in testing and guidance. In A. E. Traxler (Ed.), *Modern educational problems.* Washington, D.C.: American Council on Education, 1953. Pp. 111–120.
3. Traxler, A. E. The status of measurement and appraisal programs in large city school systems—a questionnaire survey. *Educational Records Bulletin,* 1953, No. 61, 75–84.

5 · TESTING IN THE PROFESSIONS

THE PAPERS presented in this chapter may be regarded from two levels. First, they illustrate the development and use of tests for the selection and evaluation of personnel in several professional fields. Second, each paper makes a methodological or theoretical contribution to broader testing problems, independently of the specific contexts in which the tests were developed.

The application of testing techniques to various professions has been discussed repeatedly at Invitational Conferences, beginning in 1946 with a report of tests designed for accountants at different training levels, and a description of tests for engineering school applicants developed by the Graduate Record Office. The 1950 conference included a session on the construction and validation of tests for admission to schools of law, dentistry, and medicine, as well as a later report on the accounting test project. The papers reproduced in the present chapter, given between 1958 and 1963, include Kelly's paper on medical school students, Hubbard's on National Board certification for the practice of medicine, Frederiksen's on elementary school principals, and Ryans' on elementary and high school teachers.

With regard to broader implications, Kelly's study highlights the need for criterion analysis. Drawing upon the intercorrelations he obtained among 54 criterion variables and 100 predictors, Kelly provides a convincing demonstration of the multidimensionality of criteria and the uniqueness of criterion measures. Criterion analysis should precede the development of any prediction battery for at least two reasons. First, most practical criteria, such as success in a professional school or in the subsequent practice of the profession, are multifaceted; and different facets are likely to require a different set of predictors. Second, criterion analysis often reveals the unreliability of certain criterion measures or their irrelevance to stated professional objectives. Under these circumstances, the criterion needs to be improved in its own right, as well as to provide a better measure against which to validate potential predictors. An interesting by-product of Kelly's research is the finding that sociometric peer ratings provide more satisfactory criterion measures than supervisory ratings for the same traits. This result corroborates what has been found with peer ratings in several other contexts.

Hubbard describes an objective technique for measuring a set of skills as complex and elusive as "clinical competence" in the practice of medicine. Adapting some of the procedures of programmed teaching, this technique automatically informs the examinee about the consequences of his decisions and enables him to use this information in making each subsequent decision in a step-by-step progression. While assessing diagnostic and treatment skills in realistic situations, the ingenious testing procedure described is highly controlled and suitable for mass testing programs.

The in-basket test discussed by Frederiksen represents another attempt to assess complex and relatively intangible skills—in this case, administrative performance. Simulating the familiar "in-basket" found on the administrator's desk, this technique provides a set of incoming letters, memoranda, reports, and similar items. After preliminary orientation regarding the simulated job context, the examinee is to handle all the matters in his in-basket as he would in real life, except that all his actions must be recorded in writing. Besides describing the testing technique, Frederiksen reports a factor analysis of the resulting scores designed to identify major dimensions of administrative behavior in this context, as well as some of the variables associated with it. It should be added that the in-basket technique has also been adapted for testing administrators in other settings, such as business executives and Air Force officers in administrative positions.

Ryans' paper provides a brief summary of the monumental "Teacher Characteristics Study" conducted under the auspices of the American Council on Education. After describing the data-gathering procedures, Ryans reports factorial analyses identifying the dimensions along which teacher behavior can be classified, as well as results on some correlated personal characteristics. Like Kelly, he gives considerable attention to the criterion problem. Not only does he, too, find criterion multidimensionality and technical difficulties in the way of obtaining satisfactory criterion measures, but he also discusses other, special problems in the assessment of effective teaching. Pre-eminent among these problems is the interaction between teacher characteristics and other types of variables, including pupil characteristics, grade level, subject taught, and cultural milieu. Such interaction simply means that the teacher characteristics associated with the most effective teaching will vary with the intellectual and emotional characteristics of pupils, as well as with other contextual variables. The same teacher may be highly effective in one context and quite ineffective in another. Such interaction is similar to that encountered in other distinctly interpersonal occupations, as illustrated by research on the effectiveness of therapists in clinical psychology and of first-line supervisors in industry.

Alternate Criteria in Medical Education and Their Correlates

E. LOWELL KELLY

1963

INTRODUCTION

The concern of the medical profession with testing and with the more general problem of assessment is threefold:

1) in the evaluation of applicants seeking a license to practice medicine in a state;
2) in the evaluation of applicants to medical schools;
3) in the evaluation of the outcomes of medical education.

The right to practice medicine is a privilege controlled by licensure in each of the states and territories. Although requirements vary widely from state to state, practically all require the completion of a specified program of medical education leading to some type of doctoral degree (in most cases the M.D.) *and* satisfactory performance on an examination designed to evaluate medical knowledge and competence. Such examinations ordinarily consist of a number of parts and are collectively called "State Boards." Since these examinations are typically constructed and graded locally, it is not surprising that their nature varies widely from state to state. Furthermore, because of the jealousy of the states in guarding the right to grant licenses to practice in each state, any physician moving from one state to another, or one who wishes to practice in two adjacent states simultaneously, finds it necessary to submit to two or more unique sets of examinations. While a few states have entered into reciprocal agreements (i.e., agreed to recognize the validity of the other's licensing examination), such reciprocation is sufficiently rare as to have led to the development of the program of National Board examinations.

The need for, and use of, tests in the evaluation of applicants to medical schools is of more recent origin. Those of you who are familiar with the history of the medical profession will remember that, until relatively re-

176

cently, medicine, like law, was an art acquired by apprenticing oneself to an older and more experienced member of the profession, reading a few books, and passing the state licensing examination. There were a few medical schools associated with certain of our older universities, but only a relatively small proportion of the practicing physicians of the day ever attended them. During the nineteenth century there was a very rapid growth in the number of colleges and schools offering professional training in medicine, but a large proportion of them were proprietary, with the result that their owners were more interested in attracting students for the tuition which they would bring with them than for their aptitude for the study of medicine. This state of affairs is reflected by the fact that in 1904 there were twice as many medical schools in the United States as there are in 1964! As a result of the survey of medical education sponsored by the Carnegie Foundation, which culminated in the famous Flexner report (2), two very significant changes occurred in professional training for medicine: (*a*) the standards of medical education were markedly increased; and (*b*) the medical schools began more and more to seek an affiliation with a university. Today there are only a few nonaffiliated schools remaining.

Although medical practitioners had always been accorded a fairly high status in their communities, these developments served to enhance further the prestige associated with medicine as a profession. As a result, membership in the profession became the aspiration of many more young people than could be accommodated in recognized medical schools. Thus, the faculties of these institutions found themselves confronted with the necessity of selecting the most promising applicants for the study of medicine. It is not surprising, therefore, that medical schools were among the first to utilize a professional aptitude test. The present Medical College Admission Test (MCAT), which was developed in 1927, was an outgrowth of the Moss Medical Aptitude Test and the Professional Aptitude Test (9). Since 1935 it has been given every year in several hundred premedical schools to at least 90 per cent of all applicants for admission to medical schools throughout the United States.

The affiliation of medical schools with universities and, even more important, the introduction of extensive components of basic science teaching in the medical curriculum led to an increasing concern on the part of medical school faculties with the evaluation of student achievement and assigning grades. There is fully as much disagreement among medical school professors as among teachers everywhere about the best methods of evaluating students and assigning grades. In fact, it was inevitable in these professional schools, where grades are so important in determining not only survival but assignment to internships and other professional opportunities, that there would be much ferment and discussion regarding the comparative values of oral versus written tests, of objective versus essay tests, of tests emphasizing short-term versus long-term learning, of whether grades should represent progress made as a result of taking a course or the absolute level of accomplishment upon course completion, of whether grades should be given primarily for factual learning or for the demonstration of professional skills, and so on.

While the ratio of the number of applicants to the number of available places in the admission class has declined over the last few years, medical schools are generally more concerned with the selection of their students than are universities and colleges or even other professional schools. This is true for two very good reasons. First, the high cost of constructing, equipping, and staffing medical schools results in a very high per-student societal investment as compared with other types of educational institutions. Second, because of the integral nature of the curriculum in medicine, it is generally not feasible for medical schools to admit students in the second, third, and fourth years. Thus, any beginning student who does not succeed in the program leaves a gaping and costly hole in an establishment geared for a certain number of students. This, in turn, subjects the institution to public criticism for not turning out as many doctors as it was tooled up to do. The typical college or university may regret the loss of an entering freshman but it can always fill its upper classes with transfer students and thus utilize to the fullest the educational resources of the institution. The result is that neither the institution nor society is so painfully aware of the importance of good selection of beginning students as are medical schools.

Still another unique situation has contributed to the extensive concern of medical schools with testing. To a degree that is not true of any other category of professional education, the Association of American Medical Colleges monitors and coordinates the typical multiple applications of medical school candidates and provides feedback concerning the quality of students entering each medical school. This has served to sensitize the admissions committees of medical schools to very wide differences in both the quantity and quality of applicants to different schools. The result is that medical schools in general probably invest more time and money in the evaluation of applicants than any other educational institution. For example, most medical schools have fairly large admissions committees whose members are responsible for interviewing all applicants to the school (4, 5) and make an eventual decision to admit or not admit an applicant only after an extended staff conference regarding each applicant.

These, then, are the factors that have combined to develop an increasing concern on the part of the medical profession with the problems of testing.

My personal involvement in the problem of selecting medical students began about a dozen years ago, just about the time that Fiske and I completed our project on the selection of graduate students in clinical psychology (7). I was approached by the late Wayne Whittaker, assistant dean of the University of Michigan Medical School and Chairman of the Admissions Committee, who asked me to work with him to improve the selection of students for our medical school. Because I found that he and his committee were deeply concerned with selecting not only students who would succeed academically, but also those who would become good physicians willing to accept social responsibilities commensurate with society's investment in them, I was delighted to accept his invitation to participate in a collaborative study.[1] With a small research grant we carried out a preliminary study of the senior class of 1952 and planned a more intensive study of students entering in the fall of 1952—the class that graduated in 1956. The findings, which I am reporting here, are based, for the most part, on 112 of the 181 members of the class of 1956. The fact that this group does not represent the entire class was primarily a function of class schedules rather than any biased selection of the sample.

Our broad objective was simply to try to improve the over-all quality of the students selected to receive medical training. In the hope of identifying variables that should be considered at the time of the selection decision, we made an intensive study of the "mistakes" of the admissions committee, i.e., those students who had been admitted but failed in the course of their training. We eventually accumulated data regarding 100 potential predictor variables.

For our criteria, we began, of course, with the most convenient and frequently used index of academic performance, the grade point average (GPA). Medical educators, like others, are free to admit that academic grades are not the only, and perhaps not the most important, criterion of success in medical education. Nevertheless, grades are regarded as important by both students and staff, and successful academic performance, especially in the first two years (preclinical), is a *sine qua non* for developing one's clinical skills in the later years of medical training. Therefore, as soon as the first-year grade point average had become available for the class, correlational analyses were begun.[2]

Twenty-three of the 100 predictor variables were found to be significantly correlated ($P < .05$) with the first-year GPA. Two variables, All

[1] I have purposely postponed publication of certain of the findings until changes in staff, curriculum, and grading practices will make it impossible to point an accusing finger at any specific department or faculty member!

[2] The writer gratefully acknowledges the assistance of Gordon Bechtel, Lillian Kelly, and Leonard Uhr who served as research assistants at various stages of the study.

Pre-med. Grades and Pre-med. Science Grades, tied for first place as the best predictor of this criterion, both yielding an r of $+.61$. This variable was also significantly predicted by the four subscores of the MCAT with coefficients ranging from .25 to .30. Offhand, this would seem to reflect a relatively satisfactory state of affairs. However, members of the admissions committee were not satisfied. Even with validity coefficients of this magnitude, considerable error of prediction remains, and, as noted above, the desire not to lose already admitted students is very strong. Of greater concern to members of the admissions committee, however, was the finding that their individual ratings of the applicants yielded validity coefficients lower than that provided by a simple average of all premedical grades. The actual coefficients of five members ranged from $+.27$ to $+.59$ in spite of the fact that the ratings were made by persons who had had an opportunity to study the entire premedical transcript, review the profile of MCAT scores, read the letter of recommendation, and discuss each case at a staff conference at which the interview impressions of at least one of the committee members were reported.

Quite obviously, something was wrong. There were two possibilities: (a) members of the admissions committee were not identifying and/or properly weighting relevant items from the large mass of information available to them; or (b) the criterion of first-year grades was not the appropriate one against which to check the validity of their individual judgments. I am sure that you can guess which of these alternatives was chosen by members of the admissions committee. While they were, of course, concerned with evaluating the aptitude of the student to successfully complete the prescribed course work of the medical curriculum (i.e., earn satisfactory grades), they were much more concerned, they insisted, with selecting those applicants who also had the other characteristics essential to becoming a good physician. It would, therefore, be necessary to secure additional and very different criterion measures of success in medicine before the unique validities of the ratings derived from this elaborate admissions procedure could be properly evaluated.

During the next three years much time and effort were devoted to the development and acquisition of alternative measures of achievement and performance in medicine. Eventually data became available for 54 criteria.

With 100 predictor variables and 54 criterion variables, several alternate modes of analyses suggested themselves and, thanks to the availability of the high speed computer, several of them were carried out. In this paper we shall be primarily concerned with an analysis of the resulting 5,400 correlations between the 100 predictors and the 54 criteria. More specifically, we shall concern ourselves with the relative utility of the predictors, i.e., the number of alternate criteria which they predict, and with the significant correlates of each of the 54 criteria. I have intentionally selected the term *correlates* of the criteria rather than *predictors* because of the obvious limitations of the present study with respect to generalizability. With such a large number of variables and an N of only 112, it would have been possible to have computed spuriously high multiple correlations to predict many of the criteria, correlations that would certainly have shrunk markedly if the resulting regression equations had been applied to another class. Furthermore, it must be remembered that I am reporting data not only for a single class but also for but one medical school. In view of the known differences not only in the quantity and quality of applicants but in selection procedures used by different schools, any attempt to make generalizations regarding predictive value of specific variables for other institutions would be extremely hazardous. In spite of these limitations, I believe that our findings are worthy of serious attention, not because of their immediate applicability to the problem of selection, but rather because of their implications for the problems of testing and measurement in all educational institutions, of which the medical school is but one example.

POTENTIAL PREDICTOR VARIABLES

Table 1 lists the 100 potential predictor variables selected for analysis; also shown is the number of the 54 criteria with which each variable showed a correlation of at least .20, i.e., a value yielding a *P* of < .05. Since there were 54 possible significant correlations for each predictor variable, chance alone would yield an expectancy of two to three such correlations for each predictor.

Part A of Table 1 lists 12 predictor variables which have been labeled Intellectual and Cognitive. This category includes premedical grades, MCAT scores, and ratings by the five individual members of the admissions committee, since these ratings appear to be primarily determined by the premedical academic record. Similarly, the month of acceptance is included in this category of variables because of the practice of according early admission to the applicants rated most favorably by the admissions committee. In general, it will be noted that these intellectual and cognitive variables yield significant correlations with a fairly large proportion of the 54 criterion variables.

Part B of Table 1 lists the 88 noncognitive predictor variables used. The first subgroup of these includes 19 background variables derived from analysis of the application blank or the transcript of premedical college training. As will be noted, most of this group of variables predict more

Table 1

100 Potential Predictor Variables of Performance in Medicine and the Number of 54 Alternative Criteria with which Each was Significantly Correlated

A. Intellectual and Cognitive Variables

	No. of Criteria		Strong VIB Variables	No. of Criteria
1. All Pre-Med. Grades	28	1.	Artist	7
2. Pre-Med. Science Grades	27	2.	Psychologist	9
3. Rating: Adm. Comm. Member No. 1	26	3.	Architect	8
4. Rating: Adm. Comm. Member No. 2	30	4.	Physician	2
5. Rating: Adm. Comm. Member No. 3	23	5.	Osteopath	5
6. Rating: Adm. Comm. Member No. 4	20	6.	Dentist	4
7. Rating: Adm. Comm. Member No. 5	9	7.	Veterinarian	10
8. Month Accepted	17	8.	Mathematician	7
9. MCAT: Verbal	17	9.	Physicist	7
10. MCAT: Quantitative	9	10.	Engineer	5
11. MCAT: Modern Society	15	11.	Chemist	10
12. MCAT: Science	14	12.	Production Manager	2
		13.	Farmer	7
B. Noncognitive Variables		14.	Aviator	6
		15.	Carpenter	6
Background Variables		16.	Printer	12
		17.	Math-Physical Science Teacher	11
1. Year of Birth	8	18.	Industrial Arts Teacher	8
2. Own a Car	4	19.	Vocational Agriculture Teacher	7
3. Father's Occupation	8	20.	Policeman	10
4. Father's Education	8	21.	Forest Service Man	4
5. Mother's Education	4	22.	YMCA Physical Director	4
6. Per Cent Self-supporting	5	23.	Personnel Director	0
7. Reported Estimate of Summer Earnings	8	24.	Public Administrator	2
		25.	YMCA Secretary	1
8. Reported Estimate of Religious Activity	3	26.	High School Social Science Teacher	6
9. Amount of Pre-Med. (3 or 4 yrs.)	5	27.	City School Superintendent	1
10. Marital Status	2	28.	Minister	4
11. Month Application Submitted	4	29.	Musician	2
12. Height	3	30.	CPA	10
13. Weight	3	31.	Senior CPA	4
14. No. of Credit Hrs. English	3	32.	Accountant	1
15. No. of Credit Hrs. Foreign Language	2	33.	Office Manager	2
16. No. of Credit Hrs. Inorganic Chemistry	8	34.	Purchasing Agent	2
		35.	Banker	8
17. No. of Credit Hrs. Organic Chemistry	4	36.	Mortician	10
18. No. of Credit Hrs. Physics	3	37.	Pharmacist	6
19. No. of Credit Hrs. Biology	12	38.	Sales Manager	9
		39.	Real Estate Salesman	7
Cattell 16 Personality Factor Questionnaire Variables		40.	Life Insurance Salesman	6
		41.	Advertising Man	7
		42.	Lawyer	5
1. Cyclothymia	8	43.	Author-Journalist	4
2. General Intelligence	4	44.	President, Manufacturing Concern	6
3. Ego Strength	4	45.	Interest Maturity	3
4. Dominance	17	46.	Occupational Level	2
5. Surgency	5	47.	Masculinity-Femininity	1
6. Super-Ego	1	48.	"Anxiety"	9
7. Adventurous Cyclothymia	12	49.	"Theoretical Values"	8
8. Emotional Sensitivity	5	50.	"Economic Values"	4
9. Paranoid	8	51.	"Self-Confidence"	2
10. Hysterical Unconcern	1	52.	"Sociability"	5
11. Sophistication	11			
12. Anxious Insecurity	4		*McQuitty Health Index*	7
13. Radicalism	10			
14. Independent Self-Sufficiency	12			
15. Will Control & Stability	1			
16. Nervous Tension	10			

than a chance number of the 54 criteria. Note that the number of credit hours in biology appears to be the best of these predictors, yielding significant correlations with 12 of the 54 criteria. There follows an extensive list of measures of personality characteristics and interests. The first block includes the 16 scores derived from the Cattell 16 Personality Factor Questionnaire (1). The labels given these factors correspond to the positive or high scoring end of each scale. Incidentally, these Cattell scores were based on an administration of the test to the class as seniors, whereas the 52 scores derived from the Strong Vocational Interest Blank (10) and all other variables of Table 1 were based on instruments administered before admission to medical school, i.e., under conditions which led applicants to perceive them as a part of the total process of admissions.

The first 47 variables derived from the Strong VIB are the familiar vocational interest scores which were coded on the basis of numerical scores rather than letter grades. In general, high scores reflect a pattern of interests highly congruent with those of persons successfully engaged in each profession or occupation. Variables 48 to 52 were also derived from responses to the Strong VIB, using empirically derived scoring keys to assess personality variables alternatively measured by the Taylor Manifest Anxiety Scale (11), the Allport-Vernon-Lindzey Study of Values (3), and the Bernreuter Personality Inventory (12). Finally, the McQuitty Health Index (8) was based on responses to a self-report form developed to assess personality integration.

Although none of these noncognitive variables correlated significantly with a very large number of the 54 criteria, it will be noted that most of them yield more than a chance number of significant correlations. Thus, 9 or more of the 54 criteria were found to be significantly correlated with the Cattell factors of Dominance, Adventurous Cyclothymia, Sophistication, Radicalism, Independent Self-Sufficiency, and Nervous Tension. A fairly impressive number of significant correlations also appeared for the interest patterns of Psychologist, Veterinarian, Chemist, Printer, Math-Physical Science Teacher, Policeman, CPA, Mortician, and Sales Manager. Finally, the "Anxiety" score derived from the Strong yielded nine significant correlations with criterion measures.

THE CRITERIA AND THEIR CORRELATES

Table 2 summarizes the 54 criteria used in this study. Shown also for each criterion is the number of the potential cognitive and noncognitive predictor variables with which it was significantly correlated. Column 3 in-

TABLE 2

The Correlates of 54 Alternative Criteria of Performance in Medicine

Criteria	No. of Significant r's with: 12 Cognitive Variables	88 Noncognitive Variables	Highest Correlated Variables[a] Cognitive		Noncognitive	
A. Grades						
1. 1st-yr. GPA	12	11	Pre-Med. Grades	.61	Veterinarian	.24
2. 2nd-yr. GPA	12	8	Pre-Med. Grades	.56	"Anxiety" (VIB)	.30
3. 3rd-yr. GPA	11	4	Pre-Med. Grades	.47	"Anxiety" (VIB)	.31
4. 4th-yr. GPA	6	5	Pre-Med. Grades	.31	Hrs. Biology	−.22
					Dominance	−.22
5. Over-all GPA	12	8	Pre-Med. Grades	.57	"Anxiety" (VIB)	.28
6. Public Health (2nd yr.)	5	7	Pre-Med. Grades	.45	Pharmacist	.26
7. Medicine (4th yr.)	5	1	Month Accepted	−.33	Hrs. Foreign Language	.22
8. Surgery (4th yr.)	5	2	MCAT: Quantitative	−.20	Dominance	−.36
9. Obstetrics & Gynecology (4th yr.)	0	4	Cattell General Intelligence[b]	.13	"Theoretical Values" (VIB)	−.25
					Self-Sufficiency	−.25
10. Pediatrics (4th yr.)	7	6	Pre-Med. Grades	.38	Hrs. Biology	−.31
11. Psychiatry (4th yr.)	0	12	MCAT: Verbal	.14	Mother's Education	.28
B. Nationally Administered Tests						
1. Cancer Examination	11	18	MCAT: Modern Society	.45	"Anxiety" (VIB)	.44
National Boards						
2. Medicine	7	12	MCAT: Science	.37	Insecurity	.24
3. Surgery	12	29	MCAT: Science	.40	Adventurous Cyclothymia	−.38
			Pre-Med. Grades	.40		
4. Obstetrics & Gynecology	10	6	Pre-Med. Grades	.39	Public Administrator	.28
5. Public Health	10	5	MCAT: Science	.42	Farmer	.22
6. Pediatrics	10	10	MCAT: Science	.40	Banker	−.27
7. Nat'l Boards: Total	10	25	MCAT: Science	.48	Printer	.32
C. State Boards						
1. Anatomy	8	4	Month Accepted	−.38	Adventurous Cyclothymia	−.24
2. Histology & Embryology	6	8	Rating: Adm. Comm. Member No. 4	.30	Lawyer	.28
3. Physiology	0	8	MCAT: Verbal	.14	Own a Car	−.25
4. Chemistry & Toxicology	4	7	MCAT: Verbal	−.21	Physician	−.31
5. Bacteriology	2	30	Rating: Adm. Comm. Member No. 5	.29	Sales Manager	−.38
6. Pathology	0	8	Cattell General Intelligence[b]	−.30	Dominance	−.32
7. Hygiene	7	5	Rating: Adm. Comm. Member No. 5	.34	Hrs. Organic Chemistry	−.27
8. Practice	0	8	MCAT: Modern Society	.17	"Theoretical Values" (VIB)	−.24
9. Medical Jurisprudence	0	12	Cattell General Intelligence[b]	−.26	Father's Occupation	.30

[a] An r of .20 is significant at the .05 level.
[b] Cattell's General Intelligence is, strictly speaking, a noncognitive variable derived from questionnaire responses.

TABLE 2 (Continued)

Criteria	No. of Significant r's with: 12 Cognitive Variables	88 Noncognitive Variables	Highest Correlated Variables[a] Cognitive		Noncognitive	
C. State Boards (Continued)						
10. Eye, Ear, Nose, & Throat	0	0	MCAT: Science	.13	Occupational Level	.19
11. Obstetrics	1	1	MCAT: Verbal	−.21	Weight	−.21
12. Surgery	8	3	Pre-Med. Science Grades	.24	Surgency	−.31
13. Gynecology	0	5	MCAT: Verbal	−.14	Hrs. Physics	.27
14. Materia Medica	0	1	MCAT: Modern Society	.19	Further Education	.20
D. Sociometric Choices as Seniors						
1. Camping Companion	1	6	MCAT: Science	−.23	Self-Sufficiency	−.33
2. Office Partner	3	17	Pre-Med. Grades	.28	Chemist	−.29
3. Research Promise	8	10	Pre-Med. Grades	.41	Dominance	−.27
4. Intimate Friend	0	10	MCAT: Verbal	−.12	Mortician	.31
5. Physician to Own Family	6	9	Pre-Med. Science Grades	.39	Dominance	−.31
6. Colleague Hosp. Staff	4	8	Pre-Med. Grades	.30	Dominance	−.26
7. Hospital Teaching Staff	7	4	Pre-Med. Science Grades	−.40	Self-Sufficiency	−.23
8. Highest Income	1	21	MCAT: Quantitative	−.21	Sales Manager	.37
9. Personal Satisfaction as G.P.	2	20	MCAT: Verbal	−.29	Father's Education	−.47
10. Med. Sch. Teacher	7	1	Pre-Med. Grades	.35	Nervous Tension	.23
11. Interest in Public Health	4	15	Pre-Med. Grades	.32	Dominance	−.32
12. Willing to Accept Salaried Position	0	16	MCAT: Quantitative	.14	Height	−.31
13. Disease (i.e., Specialty) Orientation	3	13	Rating: Adm. Comm. Member No. 2	.31	Father's Education	.47
14. Hospital Administrator	4	7	Pre-Med. Grades	.32	Radicalism	−.23
E. Internship Ratings						
1. Personal Appearance	1	1	MCAT: Modern Society	−.22	Amount of Religious Activity	.23
2. Desire to Learn	5	17	Pre-Med. Science Grades	.32	Math-Physical Science Teacher	.36
3. Over-all Medical Knowledge	4	7	Pre-Med. Grades	.23	Dominance	−.32
4. Diagnostic Competence	0	12	Pre-Med. Grades	.19	Math-Physical Science Teacher	.32
5. Integrity	1	11	MCAT: Quantitative	−.20	Math-Physical Science Teacher	.25
6. Sensitivity to Patients' Needs	0	10	MCAT: Modern Society	−.18	Dominance	−.30
7. Ability to Inspire Confidence	0	2	Pre-Med. Grades	.11	Dominance	−.26
8. Over-all Promise	0	0	Pre-Med. Grades	.11	Sales Manager	.17

[a] An r of .20 is significant at the .05 level.

dicates the cognitive variable, and column 4 the noncognitive variable, yielding the highest correlation with each of the criteria.

These 54 criteria have been grouped into five categories, A through E. Those in A require little further description than is provided by their names. The grade in the second-year course in Public Health was selected as a criterion because this course at the time was generally regarded by the students as both difficult and not very relevant to their training. The several fourth-year course grades presumably reflect the faculty's best evaluation of the performance of the medical student in the clinical, as contrasted with the preclinical, years of medicine. As far as could be determined, these grades were based not so much on tests as on the impressions made by the student as a participant in ward rounds, conferences, and seminars.

As will be noted, the best predictor of medical school grades throughout the four years is the Pre-med. Grades (Average). Of the noncognitive correlates, the "Anxiety" score derived from the Strong VIB appears most frequently. Whereas there is a relatively high intercorrelation (about .80) between the grade point averages for the first three years of medical school, the situation for the fourth-year course grades is quite different. First-year and fourth-year grades correlate only .53 and the median intercorrelation among the six fourth-year grades is only .22. It is therefore not surprising that a very different pattern of correlates emerges for these fourth-year course grade criteria. As will be noted in several instances, a noncognitive variable is more closely associated with grades in these courses than a cognitive variable, suggesting the degree to which these grades are assigned on the basis of impressions made by the students while on a particular service and thus are more a function of the student's personality characteristics than of his intellectual performance.

Category B of the criteria includes scores made by the students on nationally administered objective tests. In general it will be noted that performance on these objective tests at the end of medical training is predicted by most of the cognitive predictor variables, best by the MCAT Science score and Pre-med. Grades. It is of considerable interest, however, that grades on these objective tests are also significantly correlated with several noncognitive predictor variables. For example, 29 of the 88 noncognitive variables are significantly associated with National Board scores in Surgery, the correlation with one of them being almost as high as that of any cognitive variable.

We now turn to a consideration of the criteria listed in Part C of Table 2, marks on the State Board examination (State Boards), required for licensure in Michigan. As contrasted with the National Boards, which are objective examinations, these are typically essay examinations prepared by experienced and often older physicians who volunteer to prepare and grade examinations in each of the 14 subject matter areas. Whereas the median intercorrelation among the scores on the National Boards is +.51, the modal intercorrelation among the scores on the 14 parts of the State Board examination is zero; the median is only .10; and 16 of the intercorrelations are negative! This being the case, it is not surprising to find markedly different patterns of correlates of the grades on the various subparts of the State Boards. For 7 of the 14, we note no significantly correlated cognitive predictor variable. And in general for each a noncognitive variable correlates about as highly as a cognitive variable, suggesting that even though these are written examinations, marks are determined in part by the student's personality characteristics: interest, values, and background variables.

Part D of Table 2 lists 14 variables derived from Sociometric Choices made by members of the class of 1956 near the completion of their medical training. In our search for more relevant criteria (and for criteria more predictable from the ratings of the medical admissions committee!) we decided to capitalize on the rather extensive opportunities which medical students have to become acquainted with each other's strengths, weaknesses, and special competences. In brief, these sociometric ratings were collected as follows: all members of the senior class were assembled in one room, provided with a list of all members of their class, and before they knew what was to follow, they were asked to star the names of the 40 fellow class members whom they felt they knew best. They were next asked to select the three most desirable (or most likely) and the three least desirable (or least likely) persons out of this group of 40 fitting each of the categories indicated by the labels associated with these 14 criteria (Cf. Table 2, Part D). The score for each student on each criterion was simply the algebraic sum of the number of positive and negative choices on each item.

It is of interest to note that practically all of these sociometric criteria are significantly associated with far more than a chance number of the potential predictor variables. In fact, most of them can be predicted about as well as any of the categories of criteria. Furthermore, the pattern of the significant correlates seems to make sense in that those sociometric criteria most obviously associated with intellectual performance are most likely to be correlated with cognitive variables, whereas those primarily related to social acceptability are more often correlated with noncognitive variables. Finally, the pattern of the correlates makes sufficiently good sense to suggest that these sociometrically derived criteria may have considerable validity for real-life performance.

Our final effort to secure additional and still more relevant criteria of performance as a physician is reflected in the Internship Ratings listed in

Part E of Table 2. With the assistance of a number of members of the medical school staff, these eight variables were selected as those believed to be most relevant and the most ratable by the supervisors of medical school graduates during their year of internship. We note immediately that these criterion measures tend to be less often significantly correlated with the predictor variables than was the case for sociometric criteria. Only two of them, rated "Desire to Learn" and "Over-all Medical Knowledge," have more than a chance number of correlates among the cognitive predictors. Although each of them tends to be more closely associated with some non-cognitive predictor than with a cognitive one, the general magnitude of the correlations tends to be low. Finally, we note that for the most global of these ratings, "Over-all Promise," there are no significant correlates whatsoever. Apparently this rating, made by many different supervisors in different internship settings, reflects such a composite of unsystematically weighted values as to result in it not being significantly related to any of the 100 predictor variables.

In summary, most of the criteria were found to have a number of correlates among predictor variables available before admission to medical school. In fact, most of the criteria could be resonably well predicted by the weighted combination of some subset of predictor variables. Unfortunately, however, because of the relatively low intercorrelations among the alternative criteria, a different set of predictor variables would be needed to select applicants likely to rank high on alternate criteria. We have already noted the extremely low intercorrelations among parts of the State Board examination. The problem of the validity of alternate criteria is even more dramatically demonstrated by examination of the intercorrelations of presumably alternative criteria of the same type of accomplishment. For example, the fourth-year course grade correlations with National Board scores are as follows: Pediatrics .37, Medicine .33, Surgery .19, Obstetrics and Gynecology .12. And, as might be expected, neither of these criterion measures correlates significantly with State Board examinations bearing the same label! Under the circumstances, it is somewhat surprising that most of these criteria are at all predictable from data obtained before admission to medical school.

THE CRITERION CORRELATES OF THE MOST PROMISING PREDICTOR VARIABLES

From Table 1, we noted that those variables listed in category A, Intellectual and Cognitive, are generally the most promising predictors of a large number of criterion variables. In fact, all 12 of them yield significant correlations with 9 or more of the 54 criterion variables, most typically appearing as the best predictor of the more intellectually loaded criterion measures. The most promising intellectual predictor for this particular group of students was the average of all premedical grades, rather than the average of the premedical science grades only, as members of the admissions committee had anticipated. In general, the ratings of the members of the admissions committee, here categorized as intellectual or cognitive variables, showed significant correlations with a fairly large number of criterion variables but most typically with those which might be categorized as reflecting intellectual or academic accomplishment rather than those reflecting performance as a physician. Only rarely did these ratings of individual committee members turn out to be as predictive of any criterion as one or more of the pieces of information available to the person making the rating!

The most likely explanation of this attenuated potential validity of clinical judgments of academic performance appears to be a function of the background variable B 19 of Table 1. The number of credit hours in biology is the only one of these background variables associated with as many as nine criterion variables. Since the medical school at that time required all applicants to present 12 credits of biology, this variable represented the extent to which applicants presented credit hours in biology in excess of this minimal requirement. Many premedical students, especially if their over-all academic record is not good, are encouraged to take additional credits in biology as an indication of their strong interest in medicine and because of the prevalent opinion that members of the admissions committee would be favorably impressed with a transcript reflecting elected courses in biology. This turns out to have been the case. In general, the ratings of the members of the admissions committee tend to be positively correlated with the number of hours of biology. However, this same variable, number of hours in biology, yielded a significantly negative correlation with 12 of the 54 criteria! These correlations were as follows: State Boards Hygiene $-.22$; 2nd-yr. GPA $-.27$; 3rd-yr. GPA $-.24$; 4th-yr. GPA $-.22$; Over-all GPA $-.23$; 2nd-yr. grade in Public Health $-.20$; 4th-yr. grade in Pediatrics $-.31$; National Cancer Exam. $-.23$; National Boards of Medicine $-.23$; National Boards Public Health $-.20$; National Boards Pediatrics $-.22$; National Boards Over-all $-.21$. In a word, the potential validity of the clinical prediction of academic success was seriously attenuated by the fact that the members of the admissions committee were noting the number of hours of biology as a relevant predictor but weighting it positively rather than negatively!

Of the noncognitive variables, the one yielding the largest number of significant correlations with the criteria used was Cattell's factor labeled Dominance-Ascendance versus Submissiveness. These correlations were as follows: State Boards Physiology −.23; State Boards Pathology −.32; Office Partner −.24; Worthy Recipient of Research Grant −.27; Intimate Friend −.21; Physician to Own Family −.31; Colleague-Hospital Staff −.26; Hospital Teaching Staff −.20; Personal Satisfaction as General Practitioner −.37; Interest in Public Health −.32; Hospital Administrator −.23; 4th-yr. GPA −.22; 4th-yr. grade in Surgery −.36; Desire to Learn −.27; Over-all Medical Knowledge −.32; Sensitivity to Patients' Needs −.30; Ability to Inspire Confidence −.26. Since a high score on this variable reflects a tendency to be self-assertive, boastful, conceited, aggressive, and pugnacious, it appears that those students characterized by submissiveness, modesty, and complacency are more likely to be positively evaluated on these generally noncognitive criterion variables. Another personality variable measured by the Cattell 16 PF shows a similar pattern of negative correlations with 12 of the criterion measures. It is Adventurous Cyclothymia, representing a continuum characterized by adventurous versus shy, timid; gregarious versus aloof; and frank versus secretive. In general, withdrawn cyclothymia seems to be more highly prized in this particular subculture, the only significant positive correlation being .29 with the sociometric choice, Likely to Make the Highest Income.

Four additional scores from the 16 PF yielded significant correlations with 10 or more of the criterion variables. These were: Sophistication (all positive correlations except with State Boards Gynecology); Radicalism (generally negative correlations except with National Boards Over-all); Independent-Self-Sufficiency (generally positive correlations with intellectually loaded criteria and negative ones with sociometric choices involving interpersonal relations); and Nervous Tension (generally positive correlations with intellectually loaded criteria).

Of the 52 variables derived from the Strong VIB, 7 were found to be significantly correlated with 9 or more of the criteria. Psychologist scores are typically negatively correlated with sociometric choices; Veterinarian scores are positively correlated with 10 criteria, including Physician to Own Family; Chemist scores are negatively correlated with several sociometric choices but positively with Disease or Specialty Orientation, Willingness to Accept Salaried Job, and National Boards scores; Policeman scores are positively correlated with 10 criteria, mostly sociometric choices and intern ratings. CPA scores typically yield negative correlations with criteria. Sales Manager scores are negatively correlated with State Boards in Bacteriology, Interest in Public Health, Willingness to Accept a Salaried Job, National Boards in Surgery, and National Boards Over-all; Sales

Manager scores are positively associated with State Boards in Practice, Likely to Make Highest Income, 4th-yr. grade in Psychiatry, and Sensitivity to Patient Needs as rated by the Intern Supervisor.

Another Strong VIB score, Printer, proved to be a relatively good predictor of several different criteria, with correlations as follows:

State Boards Bacteriology	.31
Sociometric Research Promise	.21
Interest in Public Health	.20
Six National Boards Scores	.25 to .32
Intern, Over-all Medical Knowledge	.29
Intern, Diagnostic Competence	.31

By contrast, Strong VIB scores for Physician yielded but two significant correlations: −.31 with State Boards in Chemistry and Toxicology and −.21 with sociometric choice as Office Partner. The most likely explanation of the lack of validity of this score is that this group of subjects, both as the result of self-selection and the selective process of admission, was so homogeneous with respect to the interest pattern measured by the Physician key that there was little opportunity for covariance to occur.

Finally, the Anxiety score derived by scoring the Strong VIB responses with a specially developed key yielded a consistent array of positive correlations with nine criterion variables all heavily loaded with intellectual and academic accomplishment. Interestingly enough, this variable seems to be tapping something different than the Nervous Tension factor of Cattell 16 PF, which was more likely to be positively correlated with sociometric choices.

DISCUSSION

In view of the known uniqueness of many of the criterion measure employed, it is encouraging to discover that so many of the predictor variables showed significant and often meaningful correlations with so many criteria. Obviously, however, any practical program of student selection would require some consensus on the part of a faculty regarding the relative importance and hence the manner of weighting alternative criterion measures before making a decision regarding predictor variables. Fortunately, factor analyses of our criterion variables indicate that there are probably not more than five or six really meaningful dimensions involved. *If* satisfactory measures of this limited set of criteria could be developed, it is highly probable that even better predictive devices could be developed than the ones used in this study, e.g., premedical grades might well be weighted by the median

Scholastic Aptitude Test (SAT) score of freshmen admitted to each premedical college; the parts of the MCAT could be designed to predict more specific criteria; empirically derived keys for the Strong VIB might well provide more useful scores than the occupational keys now available, etc.

Obviously, however, no test or test battery and no statistical technique can answer the fundamental question of what kind of a physician the faculty of a given medical school wishes to produce. Given a multidimensional criterion, which appears to be the case, and relatively nonoverlapping sets of predictor variables for each, the "yes-no" decision required in student selection must in the long run depend on the hierarchical ranking and weighting of the criterion dimensions by the faculty concerned.

The findings of the study here reported strongly suggest that wise decisions regarding the product desired cannot be arrived at by any amount of staff discussion of the problem in the abstract. Only with the aid of an ongoing program which monitors the characteristics of applicants selected and rejected and of the criteria used to assess success in both the school and in practice, and which feeds back the interrelationships among these variables, will a staff be in the position of knowing to what degree its stated objectives are being attained. Fortunately, with the ready availability of modern computers, such an ongoing program of "quality control" is now entirely feasible for any medical school. Obviously, at least one appropriately trained professional person is needed to identify the essential variables, to collect and analyze the data in a systematic fashion, and to interpret the results back to the faculty members concerned (6).

While the findings of this study of a single class in one medical school do not justify any recommendations regarding specific procedures to be used in the selection of medical students, they do point to a number of more general conclusions, each with implication for measurement in all institutions involved in professional training:

1) The criterion problem is both important and complex. Instead of a neat unidimensional criterion, it appears likely that there are several relatively unrelated criterion dimensions of success in professional education and practice. Since each of these dimensions is likely to be regarded as important by subgroups of the faculty and by segments of the society which the profession serves, it is essential that improved measures of these criterion dimensions be developed.

2) It appears likely that reasonably valid predictions of alternate criteria of professional performance can be made on the basis of data obtainable before admission to the professional school, but a different subset

of predictor variables will obviously be required to predict uncorrelated criteria.

3) In view of the limited number of applicants for professional education (an applicant to medical school currently has better than one chance in two of being accepted by *some* medical school within a couple of years) and by virtue of the differential pattern of predictor variables correlated with alternate criteria of performance, it is simply not feasible for any school to attempt to select applicants who will rank high on all criterion dimensions. This suggests the possible desirability of an explicit decision on the part of the staff of each professional school with respect to the particular dimension(s) of professional performance which that school wishes to maximize both in its program of student selection and its program of instruction. Alternatively, larger professional schools may wish to consider the establishment of clearly differentiated programs of professional training with the consequent implications for using different variables in student selection and expecting very different kinds of professional performance in the graduates of the alternative programs of education.

REFERENCES

1. Cattell, R. B. *The Sixteen Personality Factor Questionnaire.* Champaign, Ill.: Institute for Personality and Ability Testing, 1957.
2. Flexner, A. *Medical education in the United States and Canada.* New York: Carnegie Foundation for the Advancement of Teaching, 1910, Bulletin No. 4.
3. Garman, G. D., & Uhr, L. An anxiety scale for the Strong Vocational Interest Inventory: development, cross-validation, and subsequent tests of validity. *Journal of Applied Psychology,* 1958, 42, 241–246.
4. Kelly, E. L. An evaluation of the interview as a selective technique. *Proceedings of the 1953 Invitational Conference on Testing Problems.* Princeton, N.J.: Educational Testing Service, 1953. Pp. 116–123.
5. Kelly, E. L. A critique of the interview. *Journal of Medical Education,* 1957, 32, No. 10, Part 2, 78–84.
6. Kelly, E. L. Multiple criteria of medical education and their implications for selection. *Journal of Medical Education,* 1957, 32, No. 10, Part 2, 185–196.
7. Kelly, E. L., & Fiske, D. W. *The prediction of performance in clinical psychology.* Ann Arbor, Mich.: Univer. of Michigan Press, 1951.

8. McQuitty, L. L. Health Index 46 and 47. Unpublished manuscript. East Lansing, Mich.: Michigan State Univer., ND.

9. Moss, F. A. Aptitude tests in selecting medical students. *Personnel Journal,* 1931, 10, 79–94.

10. Strong, E. K., Jr. *The Vocational Interest Blank.* Palo Alto, Calif.: Consulting Psychologists Press, 1959.

11. Taylor, Janet A. A personality scale of manifest anxiety. *Journal of Abnormal and Social Psychology,* 1953, 48, 285–290.

12. Tussing, L. An investigation of the possibilities of measuring personality traits with the Strong Vocational Interest Blank. *Educational and Psychological Measurement,* 1942, 2, 59–74.

Programmed Testing in the Examinations of the National Board of Medical Examiners

JOHN P. HUBBARD

1963

Ten years have now passed since the National Board of Medical Examiners came to Educational Testing Service for advice and help in converting our time-honored essay tests to the more modern techniques of multiple-choice testing. The change was accompanied by the cries of those who chose not to understand multiple-choice testing and the criticism of those who, understanding the tests, still did not like them. Nevertheless, with the assistance of those such as John Cowles, then a member of ETS, convincing evidence soon accumulated to demonstrate the gains that had been achieved in the reliability and validity of our written examinations (1, 2). The new examinations prospered, and after relying heavily upon the experience, the facilities, and the excellence of ETS for a period of five years, we were bold enough to strike out on our own. We added to our staff highly qualified individuals from the field of psychometrics, and now, after another five years, we have welcomed this opportunity to return to ETS at this Conference to describe and—not without some trepidation—to ask for your critical comments about a testing method developed by the National Board.

I have chosen for the title of this presentation, "Programmed Testing." Let me make it clear, however, that I do not wish to become involved in prevalent debates over programmed teaching. Rather, this title is intended to suggest that this new testing method has certain features that are similar to those of programmed teaching. Whether one follows Skinner down the linear path, or prefers the branching program method of Crowder, the essential characteristic of programmed teaching, with or without machines, appears to be a step-by-step progression toward carefully constructed goals. Each step calls for specific knowledge. The student must already have the knowledge or he must master it before he may progress to the next step.

Similarly, in the testing method that I wish to describe to you, the examinee proceeds in a step-by-step fashion through a sequential unfolding of a series of problems. It is this feature that has, we believe, justified the terminology of our title "Programmed Testing."

Since any test must be viewed in the light of the purpose for which it is designed, let me summarize briefly the objectives of National Board examinations. Our primary objective is to determine the qualification of individual physicians for the practice of medicine. A physician, having successfully completed the extensive series of National Board examinations, may present his certificate to the licensing authority of the state in which he wishes to practice and obtain his license without further examination. If the physician has not elected to take National Board examinations, he must go before the state medical examining board, and if, later in his medical career, he should move to another state, he may be required to repeat this performance perhaps years after he had thought to leave qualifying examinations far behind him. National Board certification is a permanent record and, with few exceptions, permits physicians to move from one state to another without repeated examinations.

This was the initial purpose of the National Board, but it is not its only function. Following the change to multiple-choice testing, and as the reliability, validity, and impartiality of these examinations gained recognition, medical school faculties began to see in these examinations a means of measuring their students class by class and subject by subject, and comparing the performance of their students in considerable detail with the performance of other medical school classes across the country. Thus, these examinations have come to be used widely as extramural evaluations of medical education throughout the United States.

Our examinations are set up in three parts. Part I is a comprehensive two-day examination in the basic sciences usually taken at the time that a medical student is completing his second year of medical school. Part II is a two-day examination in the clinical sciences, designed for the student at the end of the fourth and final year of the medical school curriculum. The third and final part—our Part III—is designed for those who have passed Parts I and II, who have finished their formal medical school courses, have acquired the M.D. degree, and have had some intern experience. It is this Part III examination that is the subject of this presentation today.

Whereas Parts I and II are looked upon as searching tests of knowledge and the candidate's ability to apply his knowledge to the problem in hand, the Part III examination is designed to measure those attributes of the well-trained physician that, rather glibly, we call "clinical competence." It has been the long-standing conviction of the National Board that, before we certify an individual to a state licensing board as qualified for the practice of medicine, we should—if we can—test his ability as a responsible physician. Can he obtain pertinent information from a patient? Can he detect and properly interpret abnormal signs and symptoms? Is he then able to arrive at a reasonable diagnosis? Does he show good judgment in the management of patients?

Historically, the National Board sought to answer these questions by means of a practical bedside type of oral examination based upon the candidates' examination of carefully selected patients. In earlier days with few candidates and few examiners, this procedure was effective. More recently, with thousands of candidates, thousands of patients, and thousands of examiners, we found ourselves running into a difficulty that you will be quick to recognize. We were dealing with three variables: the examinee, the patient, and the examiner. Here we had two variables, the patient and the examiner, that we were unable to control at the bedside in order to obtain a reliable measurement of the examinee.

Approximately four years ago, we felt compelled to face up to the necessity of developing a better test of clinical competence or admitting defeat and abandoning the effort. Therefore, we undertook a two-year project with the support of a research grant from the Rockefeller Foundation and the cooperative help of the American Institute of Research. The first step in this project was to obtain a realistic definition of the skills that are involved in clinical competence at the intern level, since it is this level of competence that our Part III examination is intended to measure. The method used for this definition was the critical incident technique under the direct guidance of John C. Flanagan. By interviews and by mail questionnaires, senior physicians, junior physicians, and hospital residents throughout the country were asked to record clinical situations in which they had personally observed interns doing something that impressed them, on the one hand, as an example of good clinical practice and, on the other hand, an example of conspicuously poor clinical practice. A total of 3,300 such incidents were collected from approximately 600 physicians. This large body of data provided a rich collection of factual information that constituted a profile of the actual experience of interns. We had arrived at a well documented answer to the question of *what to test*. The next step—and a formidable one—was to determine *how to test* the designated skills and behaviors of interns.

Many methods were explored. Motion pictures of carefully selected patients were introduced to eliminate the two variables that had vexed us in the traditional bedside performance. The patient, projected on the screen, became constant, and the examiner appeared in the form of pretested, multiple-choice questions about the patient. This method has stood up well under the test of usage and continues as a part of the total examination.

A second method—that which we have called "Programmed Testing"—was evolved to test the intern in a realistic clinical situation where he is called upon to face the unpredictable, dynamic challenge of the sick patient. In real life, the intern may be called to see a patient who, let us say, has just been admitted to the medical ward of the hospital. The intern sees the patient and studies the problem; he obtains information from the patient; he performs a physical examination; and he must then decide upon a course of action. He orders certain laboratory studies, and the results of these studies may then lead him to definitive treatment. The patient's condition may improve, or perhaps worsen, or be unaffected by the treatment. The situation has changed; a new problem evolves; and again decisions and actions are called for in the light of new information and altered circumstances.

In the testing method, as we have developed it, a set of some four to six problems related to a given patient simulates this real-life situation in a sequential, programmed pattern. The problems are based upon actual medical records, and may follow the patient's progress for a period of several days, several weeks, or even months until eventually, as in real life, the patient improves and is discharged from the hospital, or possibly has died and ends up on the autopsy table. At each step of the way, the examinee is required to make decisions; he immediately learns the results of his decisions, and with additional information at hand, proceeds to the next problem.

I believe at this point you are detecting certain similarities between the design of this test and the methods of programmed teaching—a step-by-step progression to the goal, each step accompanied by an increment of information upon which the next step depends.

Essential to the methodology of this form of testing, as in the case of programmed teaching, is the concealing of additional information until the examinee has made his decision and has earned the right to have the additional information. We, therefore, first turned to the tab test method. But the tab test, with the tearing off of bits of paper to reveal the underlying information, seemed to us difficult to produce for mass testing and awkward for the examinee.

We also gave serious consideration to the technique for the testing of diagnostic skills described by Rimoldi in a series of papers (4). Again, a clinical situation is presented and the candidate is offered a number of steps that might be taken to arrive at the correct diagnosis. Each choice appears on a separate card on the back of which is information pertinent to the selected choice. In Rimoldi's hands, the scoring of this test depends not only upon the nature of the choices selected but also the order in which the choices are made. This test, although it has many interesting features, also appeared difficult to handle for mass testing and furthermore does not altogether meet our objectives for a thorough evaluation of diagnostic acumen and judgment in the management of patients.

We then devised the present method, the idea for which has recognizable origins in the tab test and the Rimoldi test but uses a different technique. Instead of tearing off bits of paper or flipping over cards to find the appropriate information, we have concealed the information under an erasable ink overlay. The examinee first studies the problem and a carefully prepared list of possible courses of action. He then makes his decisions and turns to a separate answer booklet where he finds a series of inked blocks each numbered to correspond to the given choices. He removes the ink for selected choices with an ordinary pencil eraser, and the results of his decisions are revealed.

At first we had considerable difficulty in finding a printing technique that would permit erasure of the overlying ink block without, at the same time, erasing the underlying information. With the help of an interested specialty printer, a method was developed that has the genius of simplicity. The answers—the results of decisions—are printed and numbered serially in an answer book. A thin acetate layer is laminated on the pages of the answer book, and on top of the cellophane layer, blocks of ink are applied to cover the underlying printing. The ink is of a special formula so that when dry, it can be removed easily by an eraser or scraper. The acetate interphase layer protects the underlying printing.

The method is readily adaptable to mass testing and also has the advantage of being foolproof for scoring purposes. The examinee has no way of putting ink back over an answer. If, when he sees the results of his decision, he finds that he has made a wrong choice or if mistaken choices become apparent as the solution to the problem unfolds, he is stuck with the choices he has made. He cannot change his answers and he cannot cheat by peeking ahead under tabs or on the back of cards. His responses, whether right or wrong, are clearly apparent for the scorer to count.

I shall have more to say about scoring, but first a word about content. The complexities of the clinical situations contained in these tests are such as to make them very difficult to describe—especially, I might add, for a nonmedical audience. If, however, I may take a leaf from ETS tests, an oversimplified example may be helpful. I have frequently seen on ETS tests an oversimplified example of a multiple-choice item: Chicago is (A) a state, (B) a city, (C) a country, (D) a continent, (E) a village. Just as ETS would, I am sure, resent any implication that this gives a fair impression of the potential of multiple-choice testing, so too the oversimplified example we use for purposes of instruction to the examinee is not to be looked upon as any indication of the difficulty and complexity of the problems in the actual test.

Figure 1, the front cover of one of these tests, is shown to indicate that carefully worded instructions are read aloud by the proctor at the beginning of the test. The candidate is told that the test is based upon his judgment in the management of patients. He is told that initial information is given for each patient and that following the initial information a numbered list of possible courses of action constitutes the first problem for this patient. He is not told how many courses of action are considered correct; his task is to select those courses of action that he judges to be important for the proper management of this patient at this point in time. After he has arrived at a decision on a course of action, he must turn to the separate answer booklet and erase the ink rectangle numbered to correspond to his choice, and the result of his action will appear under the erasure. He is told that information will appear under the erasure for incorrect as well as correct choices. If, for example, he has ordered a diagnostic test, the result of the test will appear under his erasure whether or not the selected test should have been ordered. After having completed the first problem for the first patient, he then goes on to the second problem for the same patient and so on throughout the test.

Figure 2 shows the back page of the test booklet. Before breaking the seal of the booklet, the candidate is given a chance to familiarize himself with the method and to practice on two simplified problems related to one patient. At the top of the page is a brief description of a patient who is brought to the emergency room of the hospital in a comatose condition. From the information given, any medical student would recognize the coma as due to diabetes (just as any ETS examinee would recognize that Chicago is a city). The first problem for this patient then offers nine courses of action that call for immediate decision. Three of these nine choices constitute proper management at this point: selection of these three and only these three choices leads to a perfect score for this problem; and, for this sample problem, the key to the perfect score is included on the page in order to give the candidate some feeling of confidence in his understanding of the method.

NATIONAL BOARD OF MEDICAL EXAMINERS

PART III — SECTION C

GENERAL INSTRUCTIONS

This test is based upon the management of a number of patients. You are given the opportunity to order diagnostic studies and procedures, to prescribe therapy, and to make decisions regarding each patient. The patients are identified as Patient A, Patient B, Patient C, etc.

A series of problems is associated with each patient. For example, the problems concerning Patient A are identified as Problem A-1, Problem A-2, Problem A-3, etc. The problems for each patient must be undertaken in the order in which they are presented.

Initial information is given for each patient in the printed test booklet. Following the initial information, the first of a series of problems (Problem A-1) for that patient (Patient A) is presented. This problem consists of a numbered list of possible courses of action arranged in random order. You are not told how many courses of action are considered correct; for each problem, your task is to select all of those courses of action that you judge to be indicated for this patient at this point in time.

First, read all of the courses of action listed in the problem. Then select a study or procedure that you judge to be indicated, turn to the separate answer booklet, erase the blue rectangle numbered to correspond with this choice, and the result of this action will appear under the erasure. The information you receive may lead you to select other courses of action within the same problem, or you may decide to select other courses of action quite independent of results already obtained.

Information may appear under your erasure for incorrect as well as correct choices. If, for example, you have ordered a chemical test, the chemical value may appear, or if you have ordered a procedure, the results may be given. For some incorrect choices, the words "not indicated" or "order cancelled" will appear under the erasure.

Your score on a given problem will depend upon your judgment in the selection of indicated courses of action. You will be penalized for errors of commission (selection of actions that are not indicated) and for errors of omission (failure to select indicated actions). In scoring, any erasure in a rectangle, no matter how slight, will be treated as a total erasure.

After you have completed Problem A-1, and bearing in mind the additional information resulting from your decisions, proceed in similar manner with Problem A-2, etc.

For the purpose of illustration and practice, there are two simplified problems on the back cover of this booklet. Erase opposite your selected choices for these sample problems and the results of your decisions will appear. You may then erase all the rectangles for these sample problems in order to see the results of other choices. In this illustration only, the correct answers are made available at the conclusion of each problem.

Do not break seal until you are told to do so.

FIG. 1. *Front cover of test booklet with detailed instructions for the candidate.*

SAMPLE PATIENT

You are called to the emergency room of the hospital to see a comatose patient. You find a man about 40 years old, unaccompanied by family or friends. There is no obvious evidence of trauma. There is Kussmaul breathing and the breath has an acetone odor. The skin is dry. The eyeballs are soft to palpation. Examination of the heart and lungs shows nothing abnormal except for labored respiration and a rapid, regular heart rate of 120 per minute. The abdomen is soft. There is no evidence of enlarged liver or spleen or abnormal masses. Deep tendon reflexes are somewhat hypoactive bilaterally. The rectal temperature is 98.0°F (36.7°C). Blood pressure is 100/70 mm Hg.

You would immediately

SAMPLE PROBLEM S-1

1. Order serum calcium determination

2. Order carbon dioxide content determination

3. Measure venous pressure

4. Catheterize

5. Perform lumbar puncture

6. Order blood sugar determination

7. Order electroencephalogram

8. Order electrocardiogram

9. Request neurological consultation

For Problem S-1 the correct answers are:

SAMPLE PROBLEM S-2

You would now

10. Order digitalis

11. Order morphine sulfate

12. Order insulin

13. Order coramine

14. Start intravenous infusion with normal saline

15. Withdraw 500 ml of blood by phlebotomy

16. Admit patient immediately to cardiac ward

17. Admit patient immediately to neurosurgical service

18. Admit patient immediately to medical service

19. Keep patient in emergency room for further observation

For Problem S-2 the correct answers are:

FIG. 2. *Back cover of test booklet with sample problems.*

3. Measure venous pressure

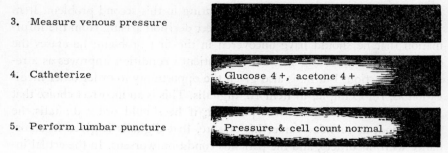

4. Catheterize   Glucose 4 +, acetone 4 +

5. Perform lumbar puncture   Pressure & cell count normal

FIG. 3. *Enlargement of items 3, 4, 5 of sample problem
showing erasures for items 4 and 5.*

Figure 3 is an enlargement of choices 3, 4, and 5 in this list. Choice No. 4 is one of the essential procedures. It is shown here with the erasure having been made and the answer revealed. The examinee has decided to catheterize the patient to test the urine, and the urine is found to contain large amounts of glucose and acetone, characteristic of the condition with which he is dealing. Let us now assume that he did not recognize diabetes as the cause of the patient's coma and he decided to select choice No. 5 and to perform a lumbar puncture. His erasure for this choice would reveal the words "pressure and cell count normal." Thus, in very realistic fashion, we are simulating a situation with which an intern might be confronted in the middle of the night when the decisions are entirely his own with no senior physician looking over his shoulder and saying, "No, do not do a lumbar puncture." He makes his decision, he performs the action, and obtains the results. He may or may not realize as the problem unfolds that the procedure was unnecessary or ill-advised.

Having made his decisions for the immediate steps to be undertaken for this patient, he then proceeds to the second problem. Figure 4 shows an en-

10. Order digitalis   Condition worse

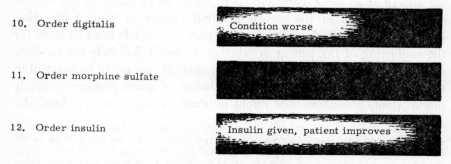

11. Order morphine sulfate

12. Order insulin   Insulin given, patient improves

FIG. 4. *Enlargement of items 10, 11, 12 of sample problem
showing erasures for items 10 and 12.*

largement of Items 10, 11, and 12 appearing in this second problem. Item 12 reads "Order insulin." This is a correct decision arising from the information that he should have uncovered in the first problem; he erases the corresponding block and sees that the patient's condition improves as a result of his action. But he is also given the opportunity to order other medication as, for example, in Item 10, digitalis. This is an incorrect choice that would reflect error in the first problem; if he should order digitalis, he would find, as revealed under his erasure, that digitalis is given in accordance with his orders, and the patient's condition worsens. In the actual internship situation, it might not be until the following morning, when the patient is seen by the Chief of Service, that the intern learns of his error in ordering digitalis. The members of our Test Committee, who are physicians prominent in their respective fields and with considerable experience in this manner of testing, sometimes become rather fanciful in the wording of the results of the examinee's actions, particularly with regard to incorrect decisions. One examiner suggested that if the examinee selected a choice that would be considered a fatal error, he should find under the erasure "You have just killed your patient; go on to the next patient."[1]

Now, to turn to the scoring of this test. Let me remind you, as stated earlier, that the basic function of National Board examinations is to serve as a qualification for the general practice of medicine. After having passed the final test of clinical competence in Part III, the candidate is certified and we say in effect: We have examined this individual as carefully as we know how and we consider him qualified to assume responsibility for the medical care of patients. Therefore, although we are interested in excellence, we are mainly concerned with the identification of those few who cannot be considered safe to practice on their own. The focus of this examination is, therefore, on the lower end of the distribution curve.

After having carefully studied several different formulas for the scoring, we arrived at an error scoring to count both sins of omission and sins of commission. Each of the several hundred choices of courses of action offered in the test is classified as to whether it definitely must be done for the well-being of the patient or whether it should definitely not be done and if done would be a serious error in judgment that might be harmful to the patient. A third category includes choices of action that are relatively unimportant, procedures that might be done or might not be done, de-

---

[1] The example of the patient with diabetic coma, oversimplified for purposes of demonstrating the test technique, gives no adequate representation of the test content in the actual examination. Examples of more complicated problems, taken from National Board examinations, will be provided upon request to the author (133 South 36th Street, Philadelphia, Pa.).

pending upon local conditions and customs. A candidate who fails to select a choice considered mandatory or who selects a choice considered harmful receives an error score. The choices in the equivocal middle ground receive no score.

Thus, we are dealing with a test and a scoring procedure that are quite different from the usual multiple-choice method in which the examinee is offered a number of choices and directed to select the one best response. Here we offer him a number of choices and require him to use his best judgment in selecting those that he considers important for the management of the patient. Usually, as in a practical situation on the medical ward, he recognizes a number of actions that should definitely be done and other actions that should definitely not be done. His responses are, therefore, interrelated. If he is on the right track, he makes a number of correct decisions among the available choices; then, by his erasures, he gains the information necessary for the proper management of the patient in the next problem and the next set of choices. If he starts off on the wrong track in this programmed test, he may compound his mistakes as he proceeds and he may become increasingly dismayed as he learns from his erasures the error of his ways. But, if he discovers that he is on the wrong track, he has a chance to change his course, although he cannot undo the mistakes he has already made, again a situation rather true to life.

Finally, a brief summary of the statistical analysis of this testing procedure. As you have probably already noted, both the structure of the test and the manner in which we are now scoring it are such as to affect the reliability adversely. In our desire to simulate real-life situations, we have included within each problem a varying number of interrelated responses. Furthermore, there is interdependency between one problem and the next. To return to the two sample problems, anyone who knows anything about diabetic coma would decide to do the three procedures coded as correct for the first problem and he would avoid other procedures coded as incorrect. Then, having confirmed the diagnosis in the first problem, he would have no doubt about the further management of the patient in the second problem. The interdependency of responses within each problem and from one problem to the next has the effect of decreasing the number of points upon which the test score is built and, consequently, decreasing the reliability of the test.

We have studied at some length the balance between the objective to simulate real-life situations in this sequential manner of testing and the objective to obtain high or reasonably high reliability. While the reliability of our tests of Part I and Part II is quite consistently between .80 and .90, the internal consistency measure of reliability for this portion of Part III for the first few administrations has been in the range of .40 to .70 with a mean of .53. We are now taking several steps that may be expected to increase the reliability. The test has been lengthened; the number of items for the next administration in January 1964 has been increased from approximately 200 to approximately 400. The examiners, the experts who construct the tests, are learning from the item analyses the need for more discriminating judgment in categorizing each choice as right, wrong, or equivocal. The task is quite different and considerably more arduous than the more familiar task of deciding on the one best among five choices. On the other hand, the examiners find themselves on somewhat more familiar ground and feel that they are dealing with practical situations in a more realistic manner than when they are faced with the necessity of a single best choice.

We have also looked closely at the correlation between this programmed test of clinical competence in Part III (taken after 6 to 12 months of internship) and the multiple-choice tests of knowledge of clinical medicine in our Part II (taken before internship). The correlation between this portion of Part III and the total Part II was .42 and 1962 and .35 in 1963. Corrected for attenuation, the correlation between these two tests in 1963 would have been .53. These correlations, positive and yet moderate, reflect about the degree of relationship we would expect between medical knowledge and additional elements of clinical competence that are inevitably based upon medical knowledge.

In conclusion, let me summarize by saying that we have developed a testing method that promises to open up new dimensions in evaluating professional competence. We have described this technique as "Programmed Testing" because of features that are similar in principle to "Programmed Teaching," that is to say, a step-by-step progression to carefully designed objectives, each step accompanied by an increment of information essential to the sequential unfolding of the problems. The method is far from perfect and needs continuing refinement. It has, however, yielded results that give us reason for increasing confidence in our ability to evaluate effectively certain skills and qualities of professional competence, skills and qualities that we consider essential for certification of a physician's readiness to assume independent responsibility for the practice of medicine.

ADDENDUM. A more recent paper (3) describes the total test of clinical competence of which the "Programmed Test" is one portion. During 1965 the total test (Part III of the National Board examinations) achieved a reliability of .87 and the "Programmed Test" portion had a reliability of .82.

REFERENCES

1. Cowles, J. T., & Hubbard, J. P. Validity and reliability of the new objective tests: a report from the National Board of Medical Examiners. *Journal of Medical Education,* 1954, 29 (6), 30–34.
2. Hubbard, J. P., & Cowles, J. T. A comparative study of student performance in medical schools using National Board examinations. *Journal of Medical Education,* 1954, 29 (7, Part 1), 27–37.
3. Hubbard, J. P., Levit, Edithe J., Schumacher, C. F., & Schnabel, T. G., Jr. An objective evaluation of clinical competence—new technics used by the National Board of Medical Examiners. *The New England Journal of Medicine,* 1965, 272, 1321–1328.
4. Rimoldi, H. J. A. Rationale and applications of the test of diagnostic skills. *Journal of Medical Education,* 1963, 38, 364–368.

In-Basket Tests and Factors in Administrative Performance

NORMAN FREDERIKSEN

1960

The purpose of the study which I will describe was to learn more about performance in educational administration. There is a tendency, in evaluating administrators, to think in terms of one over-all dimension of goodness or badness. We felt that formulating the evaluation problem in terms of one variable was too simple. One of our purposes was to try to identify some major dimensions of administrative behavior; another was to discover how such dimensions might be related to a variety of other measurable characteristics of people.

The study was a cooperative one, done by staff members of Teachers College, Columbia University, and Educational Testing Service. When I say *we,* I am referring to Daniel Griffiths of Teachers College, Director of the Project; John K. Hemphill of ETS, Associate Director; Glen Stice, Research Associate at ETS, and myself. The study was supported by a grant to Teachers College from the Cooperative Research Program of the U.S. Office of Education.

One difficulty encountered when one tries to study behavior on the job is that it is impossible to tell whether variation in performance should be attributed to differences among the subjects or to differences among the jobs. In this study, we eliminated the job as a source of variation by simulating a school and community and giving each one of the 232 subjects the job of being principal of the same simulated school. Enough information about this school and community was provided that subjects could reasonably be expected to take action on the administrative problems presented to them.

The subjects of the investigation were 232 elementary school principals. They came from school districts all over the United States, and they constituted quite a varied group in terms of age, experience, and ability.

The test is a fairly elaborate one, requiring five days to administer. About twenty people were tested at one time. The test began on Monday morning, when the examinees were introduced to the school of which each was to be the new principal. The simulated school is Whitman School, located in Jefferson in the hypothetical state of Lafayette. Each subject was temporarily given a new name, Marion Smith. The subjects were instructed that they were not to play a role, that each was to bring to the new job his own background of experience, his own knowledge and personality. During the test, he was to perform the duties of the new principal of Whitman School.

The participants spent the first day and a half in learning about Whitman School and its community. First, a film strip was presented which gave the participants an over-all view of Jefferson. Then the principals were given an opportunity to study the Jefferson School-Community Survey which had recently been completed by the School of Education at Lafayette State. Next, the group viewed a sound color film which took the subjects inside Whitman, where they saw the faculty and children at work. The subjects were given personnel folders for the teachers and staff, a floor plan of the school, and a staff roster. Study guides were provided to direct the subjects' study of the materials.

On Tuesday morning, the indoctrination was continued with additional material for study, including a Staff Handbook, the School Board Handbook, excerpts from the Lafayette school law, copies of the most recent school census, a class size list, the school calendar, and a report of achievement test scores. All this printed material became the principals' files throughout the week. The examinees also listened to tape recordings of school board meetings and conversations involving teachers and parents.

At the end of the day and a half of orientation, the subjects had as much information as would be expected of a new principal in an actual situation. It was now reasonable to expect the subjects to take action on problems arising in the administration of the school.

The balance of the week was devoted to work sessions in which each Marion Smith performed the duties of the principal of Whitman School. All the participants were presented with the same set of administrative problems under the same conditions. Each new principal was given memo pads, letterheads, paper, pencils, and paper clips. He was instructed merely to be the principal. He was not to say what he *would* do—he was to *do* it. He actually wrote memos, called meetings, prepared agendas, made notes in preparation for interviews, and the like.

The primary method of presenting problems in our study was the in-basket test. Such a test consists of facsimiles of the letters, memoranda, and other contents of the in-basket such as is found on every administrator's desk. Figures 1, 2, and 3 show some in-basket items and the responses to them made by one of our subjects. Four in-basket tests were presented, each requiring a half-day session. About thirty-two problems were included in each in-basket; they were chosen in the light of a theoretical formulation of the job of an elementary school principal.

In addition to the desk work involved in the four in-baskets, the subjects were required to participate in committee work, observe the work of teachers shown in kinescopes, and react to conference situations presented by means of tape recordings.

This is a very brief description of a rather elaborate situational test. The

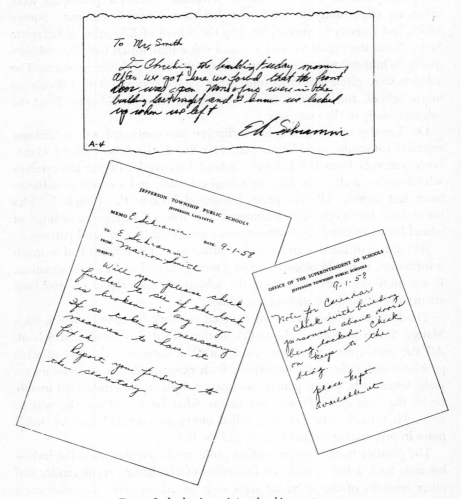

FIG. 1. *In-basket item A-4 and subject responses.*

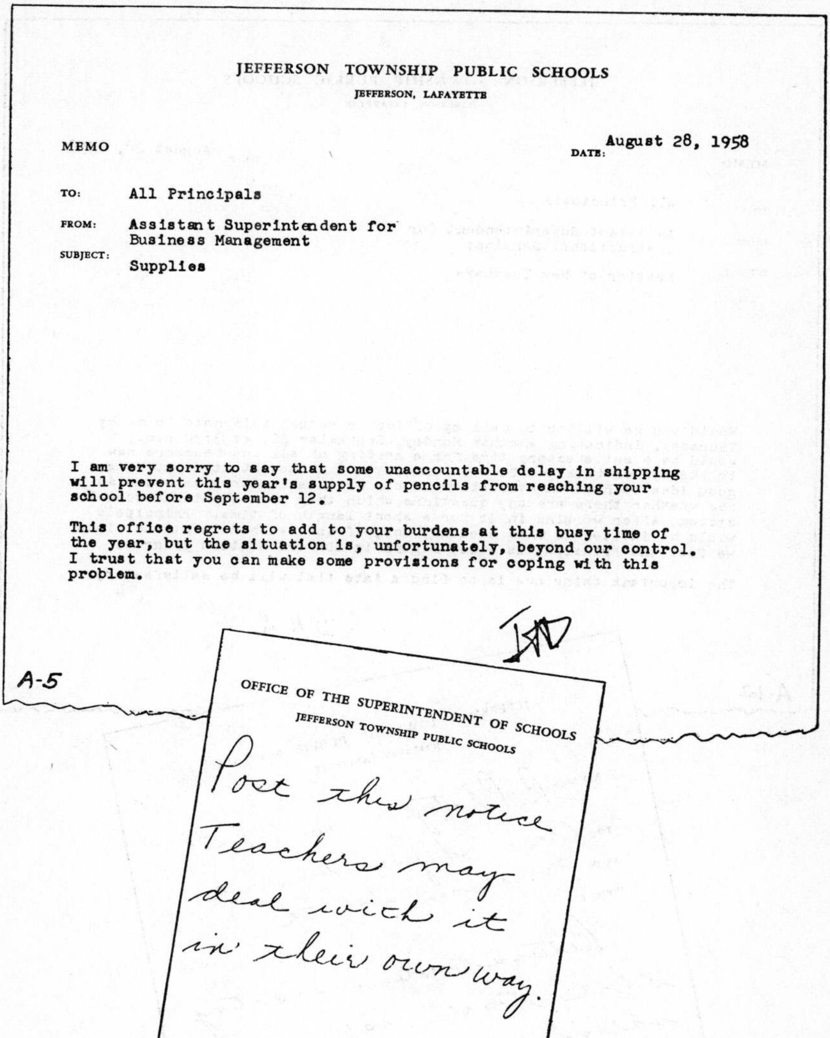

JEFFERSON TOWNSHIP PUBLIC SCHOOLS
JEFFERSON, LAFAYETTE

MEMO

DATE: **August 28, 1958**

TO: All Principals

FROM: Assistant Superintendent for
Business Management

SUBJECT: Supplies

I am very sorry to say that some unaccountable delay in shipping
will prevent this year's supply of pencils from reaching your
school before September 12.

This office regrets to add to your burdens at this busy time of
the year, but the situation is, unfortunately, beyond our control.
I trust that you can make some provisions for coping with this
problem.

A-5

OFFICE OF THE SUPERINTENDENT OF SCHOOLS
JEFFERSON TOWNSHIP PUBLIC SCHOOLS

*Post this notice
Teachers may
deal with it
in their own way.*

FIG. 2. *In-basket item A-5 and subject response.*

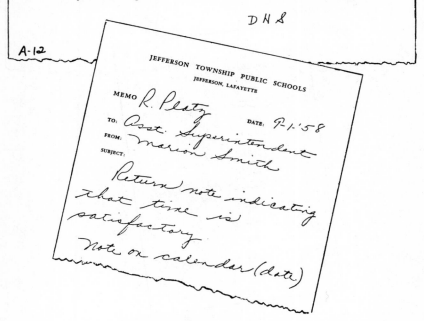

JEFFERSON TOWNSHIP PUBLIC SCHOOLS
JEFFERSON, LAFAYETTE

MEMO   DATE: August 28, 1958

TO: All Principals

FROM: Assistant Superintendent for
        Instructional Services

SUBJECT: Meeting of New Teachers

Would you be willing to call my office or return this note to me by
Thursday, indicating whether Monday, September 22, at 3:30 p.m.,
would be a satisfactory time for a meeting of all the teachers new
to the system this year? Dr. Donnelly and I thought it might be a
good idea to have an evaluation of our orientation program and also
see whether there are any questions which they have about the school
system, after working in it for a short length of time. Principals
would be invited to this meeting, too, if they wished to attend since
we feel the Principal is a key figure in the orientation program.

The important thing now is to find a date that will be satisfactory.

                              D N S

A-12

JEFFERSON TOWNSHIP PUBLIC SCHOOLS
JEFFERSON, LAFAYETTE

MEMO R. Platz

TO: Asst. Superintendent   DATE: 9-1-'58

FROM: Marion Smith

SUBJECT:

Return note indicating
that time is
satisfactory

Note on calendar (date)

FIG. 3. *In-basket item A-12 and subject response.*

participants tell us that the situation was realistic and that they built up vivid images of the people involved. Each participant received the same opportunities to learn the background, and each was presented with the same problems under identical conditions. Therefore, we can attribute differences in behavior to the participants rather than to variations among jobs.

Each principal left an envelope full of memos, letters, reminders, instructions to his secretary, appointment calendars, and the like. How can this material be scored?

The first step towards developing a scoring procedure was to examine in-basket responses to see how respondents differ. As a result of such examination by a number of observers, a large pack of cards was collected, each card containing a statement of some kind of difference observed in the way the principals behaved. The cards contained phrases like "compulsive," "postpones decisions," and "makes unwarranted assumptions." A second source of ideas for scoring categories came from theories of administration and leadership, especially the theories of the Director and Associate Director of the project.

Eventually, all these modes of behavior were collapsed to make the 68 scoring categories shown in Table 1. A scoring manual was written, providing appropriate definitions and rules for scoring. Each in-basket problem can be thought of as an opportunity to display the behavior described by the category. On the score sheet a *one* or a *zero* was recorded under each category heading, for each problem, to indicate whether or not the behavior did occur. A total of 132 problems was scored for each of the 68 categories.

The in-baskets were scored by eight scorers, each scoring a different half-in-basket. Reliability was determined by correlating the scores obtained from the odd-item scorers with the scores for the even-item scorers, and correcting for length. Thus, the reliabilities reflect both scoring accuracy and amount of consistency in the principals' behavior. The reliabilities which resulted varied from zero to .97, as shown in Table 1.

The 40 categories which are double-starred in Table 1 were chosen for use in the next phase of the analysis. These categories had reliabilities of .52 or higher and a median reliability of .78. The intercorrelations of these 40 scores were computed, and the matrix of intercorrelations was factored. Eight factors were retained; they account for almost all of the common variance among the scores. Rotations were made graphically to produce an oblique factor matrix with simple structure. Table 2 presents the category scores having loadings of .25 or more on each of the factors.

Factor A is called *Exchanging Information*. This interpretation seems quite clear on the basis of the four scores with the highest loadings.

TABLE 1
Reliability of In-Basket Category Scores

Category	Relia-bility	Category	Relia-bility
**Estimated number of words written	.94	**Work scheduled for same or next week	.83
**Number of items not attempted	.97	**Work scheduled—no time specified	.83
**Number of courses of action (usual)	.92	**Leading action	.90
Rejection of test conditions	.59	**Terminal action	.86
**Number of subordinates involved as individuals	.84	**Follows lead by subordinates	.77
**Number of subordinate groups involved	.69	**Follows lead by superiors	.71
**Number of superiors involved	.60	**Follows lead by outsiders	.61
**Number of outsiders involved as individuals	.73	**Follows pre-established structure	.67
Number of outside groups involved	.44	Coordination	.41
**Unusual action	.52	**Initiates a new structure	.78
Recognizes good work	.71	Delegates completely	.31
**Aware of poor work	.65	Delegates partially with control	.24
**Carelessness or minor error	.69	Delegates partially without control	.59
Socially insensitive	.38	**Gives directions or suggestions	.83
**Relates to background material or other items	.75	Refers to superiors	.17
**Conceptual analysis	.70	**Communicates face-to-face	.86
Prejudges, unwarranted assumptions, inappropriate	.35	**Communicates by telephone	.74
Uses human values	.43	**Communicates by writing	.90
Uses physical values	*	**Gives information to subordinates	.66
**Uses program values	.65	Gives information to superiors	.24
**Discusses with subordinates	.84	**Gives information to outsiders	.58
Discusses with other principals	.39	Explains actions to subordinates	.53
Discusses with superiors or outsiders	.58	Explains actions to superiors	.19
**Asks subordinates for information or opinion	.81	Explains actions to outsiders	.18
Asks superiors for information or opinion	.41	**Courtesy to subordinates	.91
Asks outsiders for information or opinion	.46	Courtesy to superiors	.53
**Requires further information for deciding	.68	**Courtesy to outsiders	.55
**Delays, postpones, or temporizes	.81	**Informality to subordinates	.92
**Arrives at a procedure for deciding	.80	Informality to superiors	.64
Contingent decision	.38	Informality to outsiders	.00
**Concluding decision	.78	Backs up staff	.06
**Tentative or definite plans only	.92	Improves staff	*
**Work scheduled for same or next day	.77	Improves working conditions	*
		Sets a deadline	.36
		Follow-up or feedback planned	.01

* Reliability estimates were not computed because of the extremely low frequency of these scores.
** These items were used in the first factor analysis.

TABLE 2
Factor Loadings of In-Basket Category Scores

Factor A: Exchanging Information

Asks subordinates for information, opinion, or advice	.50
Gives information to subordinates	.45
Requires further information for deciding	.34
Gives information to outsiders	.31
Number of subordinate groups involved	.29
Number of usual courses of action	.25

Factor B: Discussing Before Acting

Work scheduled—time unspecified	.63
Discusses with subordinates	.62
Communicates face-to-face	.60
Initiates a new structure	.48
Arrives at a procedure for deciding	.46
Tentative or definite plans only	.40
Number of items attempted	.40
Discusses with superiors or outsiders	.39
Number of usual courses of action	.36
Requires further information for deciding	.31
Number of subordinate groups involved	.29
Follows lead by subordinates	.29
Follows lead by superiors	.29
Terminal action	−.25

Factor C: Complying with Suggestions Made by Others

Concluding decision	.73
Number of items attempted	.68
Follows lead by subordinates	.65
Terminal action	.59
Follows lead by superiors	.50
Follows pre-established procedure	.48
Communicates by writing	.45
Number of words written	.33
Number of subordinates involved	.31
Gives directions or suggestions	.31
Gives information to subordinates	.28
Number of usual courses of action	.27
Informality to subordinates	.27
Number of subordinate groups involved	.26

Factor D: Analyzing the Situation

Uses program values	.82
Conceptual analysis	.75
Aware of poor work	.28

Factor E: Maintaining Organizational Relationships

Number of superiors involved	.54
Discusses with superiors or outsiders	.42
Number of outsiders involved	.41
Relates to background materials or other items	.37
Follows lead by outsiders	.26
Communicates by telephone	.26
Delays, postpones	−.38

Factor F: Organizing Work

Work scheduled for same or next week	.51
Work scheduled for same or next day	.50
Follows pre-established procedure	.30
Relates to background information or other items	.25
Work scheduled—time unspecified	−.48

Factor G: Responding to Outsiders

Gives information to outsiders	.44
Courtesy to outsiders	.44
Follows lead by outsiders	.41
Number of outsiders involved	.31
Carelessness or minor error	.30
Awareness of poor work	−.31

Factor H: Directing the Work of Others

Leading action	.64
Communicates by writing	.59
Courtesy to subordinates	.57
Gives directions or suggestions	.47
Courtesy to outsiders	.40
Carelessness or minor error	.31
Number of subordinates involved	.28
Communicates by telephone	−.30
Tentative or definite plans only	−.67

Factor B we call *Discussing Before Acting*. Again the interpretation is clear from the scores with the highest loadings. The "new structure" in *Initiates a new structure* is likely to be a committee or other discussion group; the "procedure" in *Arrives at a procedure for deciding* is likely to be a discussion.

Factor C might appear to involve precipitate and aggressive action from the categories *Concluding decision* and *Terminal action*. But the two categories, *Follows lead by subordinates* and *Follows lead by superiors,* also have high loadings. The actions and decisions are thus likely to be made in compliance with suggestions; hence the name *Complying with Suggestions Made by Others*.

Factor D has very high loadings on two categories. The factor is called *Analyzing the Situation* because it appears to involve broad situational analysis of in-basket problems.

Factor E has loadings on categories which imply concern about superiors and outsiders, and the negative loading on *Delays or postpones* implies prompt action. We call this factor *Maintaining Organizational Relationships*.

Factor F is *Organizing Work,* and it is characterized particularly by care in specifying in advance quite exactly when one's work is to be done.

Factor G is called *Responding to Outsiders* because the four categories with the highest loadings all have to do with people outside the organization. We might think of this factor as reflecting concern about community relations.

Factor H is interpreted as *Directing the Work of Others*. Giving directions to subordinates is likely to be done in writing rather than orally, and courtesy is often used, apparently to soften the blow.

A second-order factor analysis revealed two factors which we call X and Y. The saturations of the individual scoring categories were determined, and those saturations of category scores which are .50 or higher are shown in Table 3.

Factor X has high saturations on a number of scores having to do with productivity—number of words written, number of courses of action taken, number of people involved, and so on. There are negative loadings on such categories as *Delays or postpones* and *Plans only*. We call this second-order factor *Amount of Work Done in Handling Items*.

Factor Y is a bipolar factor with negative loadings on *Concluding decisions* and *Terminal action* and positive loadings on a variety of scores having to do with deciding how to proceed, getting informed, and having discussions; hence the name *Preparation for Decision vs. Taking Final Action*.

The Factor Y loadings shown in Table 3 represent the extremes of a

TABLE 3

Second-Order Factor Loadings of In-Basket Category Scores

Factor X: Amount of Work Done in Handling Items	
Number of words written	.67
Number of usual courses of action	.65
Number of outsiders involved	.60
Gives directions or suggestions	.57
Number of subordinates involved	.57
Communicates by writing	.56
Leading action	.53
Gives information to subordinates	.52
Follows lead by superiors	.51
Factor Y: Preparation for Decision vs. Taking Final Action	
Arrives at a procedure for deciding	.69
Requires further information for deciding	.64
Work scheduled for same or next day	.61
Discusses with subordinates	.60
Asks subordinates for information or advice	.56
Communicates face-to-face	.55
Initiates a new structure	.54
Work scheduled for same or next week	.54
Concluding decisions	−.52
Terminal action	−.62

continuum which has a rather marked similarity to certain theories of decision-making. Table 4 identifies six theoretical stages in the process of decision-making. In the parallel columns are shown some selected category scores and their loadings on Factor Y. The agreement between the theoretical formulation and the empirical findings is rather striking. This is, of course, no verification of the theory that one goes through these stages in reaching a decision. There is clear indication, however, that a principal's characteristic behavior in response to a standard set of administrative problems can be described in terms of his position on the continuum of decision development.

A large number of other variables—ratings, inventory scores, ability measures, and so on—was also available. The relation of the factor scores to these other variables is a matter of considerable interest. Therefore, the intercorrelations of 120 variables were computed. The variables included in-basket category scores, ability measures, personality inventory scores, ratings, interest measures, tests of professional knowledge, and biographical items.

It is, of course, possible merely to compute the correlations between factor scores and other variables; but such an approach is possibly misleading because the factors are substantially correlated and hence contain variance

TABLE 4

Stages in Decision-Making

Stage in Decision-Making	In-Basket Score	Loading on Factor Y
1. Recognizes a problem		
2. Prepares to clarify the problem	Arrives at a procedure for deciding	.69
	Requires further information for deciding	.63
3. Initiates work on the problem	Work scheduled for same or next day	.61
	Discusses with subordinates	.60
	Asks subordinates for information	.56
	Leading action	.41
4. Organizes and judges facts and opinions	Conceptual analysis	.24
	Tentative or definite plans only	.16
	Delays, postpones	.15
5. Selects alternative solutions	Follows lead by superiors	.09
	Follows lead by subordinates	−.10
6. Decides and acts	Concluding decision	−.51
	Terminal action	−.62

which is shared by other factors. A factor-analytic approach to the problem was adopted, at the suggestion of Ledyard R Tucker, which makes it possible, in effect, to determine the relationship of each variable to the part of each factor not shared by other factors. For example, *Amount of Work* influences in varying degrees the scores on all the eight factors; it would be desirable to learn the relationship between variables and factors with the effect of *Amount of Work* ruled out. The method employed resulted in the computation of coefficients which are proportional to the correlations with the unique part of each of the eight factors.

The procedure is as follows: the 120×120 matrix was factored. An orthogonal factor matrix composed of the first ten factors was rotated to form an oblique matrix having a factor structure as nearly as possible like that found for the original in-basket factor analysis. Coefficients were computed which reflect the relative relationship of each of the 120 variables to each of eight oblique reference vectors, each vector corresponding to one of the eight in-basket factors. These coefficients are proportional to the correlations with the unique portion of the corresponding factor. Similar estimates of correlations with second-order factors were computed. We will merely indicate briefly a few salient findings.

Table 5 shows the relationships of several cognitive measures with in-basket factors. We see that both of the second-order factors (Columns 9 and 10) have fairly high relationships with the tests. *Amount of Work* is related to a variety of cognitive abilities, while *Preparation for Decision* relates especially to the School Administration test. The signs of the correlations in Column 10 show that high-ability people tend to prepare for decision rather than to take action.

TABLE 5

Relationships of Cognitive Ability Tests to In-Basket Test Factors

	In-Basket Test Factors									
	1	2	3	4	5	6	7	8	9	10
Cognitive Ability Tests	Exchanging Information	Discussing	Complying with Suggestions	Analyzing Situation	Maintaining Relationships	Organizing Work	Responding to Outsiders	Directing Work of Others	Amount of Work	Preparation for Decision
Reasoning	.02	.03	.48	.34	−.15	.07	−.31	−.22	.28	.13
Subtraction and Multiplication	.43	−.14	.00	−.25	.14	.09	.12	−.26	.38	.21
Vocabulary	.39	−.14	.06	.15	.03	−.06	−.12	−.31	.33	.24
Concealed Figures	.04	.16	.47	.22	−.22	.11	−.13	−.24	.30	.24
Mathematics Aptitude	.06	.04	.49	.24	−.13	.18	−.17	−.30	.34	.16
School Administration and Supervision	.36	−.09	.15	.18	.01	.04	−.23	−.28	.41	.45
NTE Science and Mathematics	.07	.09	.48	.33	−.21	.02	−.27	−.27	.28	.19

The other columns show relationships with the unique parts of the eight in-basket factors—the part remaining after the variance due to second-order factors is removed. The coefficients in the first eight columns, therefore, cannot be attributed to *Amount of Work* or to *Preparation for Decision*.

There are a number of high positive coefficients, particularly in Columns 1 and 3. People who characteristically exchange information (Column 1) are high on Verbal and Number factors and on the test of school administration. The relationships with *Complying with Suggestions* (Column 3) involve a completely different set of tests, particularly tests of reasoning. Perhaps the compliance factor is not weak submission, but involves logical evaluation of suggestions.

Coefficients in Columns 7 and 8 are mostly negative. Those principals who were responsive to outside pressures and who were characterized by actively directing the work of their subordinates tended to be the less able principals.

Table 6 gives relationships between in-basket factors and some selected scores from Cattell's 16 Personality Factor Questionnaire. The personality scores do not predict the second-order factors; but there are a number of high relationships with the unique parts of the primary factors. Look at Column 5, for example. Principals who typically try to maintain good organizational relationships tend to be friendly, adventurous rather than shy,

TABLE 6

Relationships of Personality Measures to In-Basket Test Factors

	In-Basket Test Factors									
	1	2	3	4	5	6	7	8	9	10
Personality Measures	Exchanging Information	Discussing	Complying with Suggestions	Analyzing Situation	Maintaining Relationships	Organizing Work	Responding to Outsiders	Directing Work of Others	Amount of Work	Preparation for Decision
Friendly vs. Aloof	.21	−.09	−.29	−.28	.51	−.14	−.15	−.18	−.01	.01
Emotional Maturity vs. Lack of Frustration Tolerance	.15	.28	−.09	−.10	.12	−.36	.08	−.03	.12	.07
Dominance vs. Submission	−.14	.03	.12	.30	.14	.03	−.37	−.12	−.03	.09
Adventurous vs. Shy	.03	.19	−.26	.01	.50	−.33	−.23	−.07	−.02	.08
Emotional Sensitivity vs. Tough, Practical	.34	−.07	−.21	−.28	.22	−.11	.12	−.19	.10	.05
Suspicious vs. Trusting	−.30	−.16	.36	.18	.14	.45	−.13	.00	−.02	−.13
Sophistication vs. Rough Simplicity	−.12	−.10	.09	.30	.02	−.02	−.35	.01	−.08	−.03
Anxious Insecurity vs. Placid Self-Confidence	−.21	−.28	.25	.14	−.35	.55	−.01	.03	−.11	.00
Nervous Tension	−.21	−.30	.39	.22	−.30	.60	−.22	−.14	−.10	.04

TABLE 7

Relationships of Biographical Information to In-Basket Test Factors

	In-Basket Test Factors									
	1	2	3	4	5	6	7	8	9	10
Biographical Information	Exchanging Information	Discussing	Complying with Suggestions	Analyzing Situation	Maintaining Relationships	Organizing Work	Responding to Outsiders	Directing Work of Others	Amount of Work	Preparation for Decision
Experience in Education	.09	−.18	−.49	.01	.08	.04	.44	.28	.04	.01
Years of Academic Preparation	−.01	.02	.08	.08	−.08	−.01	−.15	.04	.03	.14
Age	.02	−.15	−.43	.05	.06	.02	.40	.28	.00	−.05
Sex[a]	.45	.17	−.60	−.42	.22	−.07	.50	−.03	.08	.13

[a] Positive correlation indicates greater frequency among females.

and free from anxiety and nervous tension. Look at Column 6. Principals who typically plan their work for specific days and hours tend to lack frustration tolerance and to be shy, suspicious, anxious, and nervous. Anxious people appear to exhibit a compulsive pattern of behavior in handling in-basket problems.

Table 7 shows relationships of in-basket factors with some biographical information items. Again the second-order factors are unrelated to the predictors, but the unique parts of the primary factors have high relationships with certain of the items. Years of college training have nothing to do with any of the factors; but age, experience, and sex do. *Complying with Suggestions* (Column 3) is typical of inexperienced young men. *Responding to Outsiders* (Column 7) is characteristic of older women with prior job experience in education.

The simulation of a standard job in educational administration through the use of in-baskets has proved to be successful as a method of collecting records of administrative performance that can be scored reliably; and it yields scores useful in providing a better understanding of some of the dimensions of performance in such a situation. The method of factoring that was employed appears to be a powerful technique for isolating important aspects of behavior and examining their relationships with other measures.

Measurement and Prediction of Teacher Effectiveness[1]

Davⁱᴅ G. Ryans

1958

Proper consideration of even some of the more obvious problems associated with the definition, measurement, and prediction of teacher effectiveness would be an exhausting undertaking. What I shall attempt is to review sketchily a few of the complexities facing researchers who try to study teaching competency; then briefly to summarize some high spots in research conducted by the Teacher Characteristics Study; and finally, to suggest some tentative conclusions about identifiable conditions and characteristics that may be associated with teacher effectiveness.

SOME BASIC ISSUES

The basic concern of research on teacher effectiveness is, of course, prediction. We seek to determine how and to what extent various data descriptive of teachers (e.g., verbal responses, overt acts, biographical information, etc., all of which may be subsumed under *teacher characteristics*) are either 1) antecedents or 2) concomitants of some behavior agreed to be a component of some criterion of teaching competence.

The extent to which such relationships can be uncovered depends, of course, not only on the real, or latent, relationships which may obtain, but also on: 1) how unambiguously and operationally the *agreed-upon* criterion can be defined, and how validly and reliably estimates of the criterion can be obtained; 2) how unambiguously the teacher characteristic under study can be identified and how validly and reliably it can be measured; and 3) what the purposes and hypotheses of the research are and how adequately it has been designed, taking into account sampling,

[1] A fuller report of the research summarized in this paper was subsequently published in Ryans, D. G. *Characteristics of teachers: their description, comparison, and appraisal.* Washington, D.C.: American Council on Education, 1960—Ed.

control, and replication. I should like to deal briefly with these three areas of problems.

Criterion Measurement

Recently I attempted to outline different methods of obtaining criterion data relative to teacher effectiveness. The major categories included: *a*) direct measurement of *ongoing* teacher behavior (e.g., time sampling involving replicated systematic observation); *b*) indirect measurement based on preserved records of ongoing teacher behavior (e.g., tape recordings); *c*) indirect measurement by nontrained observers, based on recall of teacher behavior and assessment thereof (e.g., ratings by students, administrators, peers, etc.); *d*) measurement of a product (student behavior) of teacher behavior; and *e*) measurement of concomitants (secondary criterion data) of the criterion of teacher effectiveness.

These different approaches to measurement vary in nature of rationale employed to support them, in reliability of the criterion data produced, and in the order of obtained relationships between criterion estimates and specified predictors—this last observation, of course, merely bearing testimony to the fact that most criteria are very complex and any one set of estimates is likely to be very incomplete with respect to the over-all criterion.

Approaches to the measurement of a criterion of teacher effectiveness thus involve the evaluation of 1) teacher behavior *in process,* 2) a *product* of teacher behavior, or 3) *concomitants* of teacher behavior. Measurement of ongoing behavior of the teacher is the most direct approach; measurement of products and of concomitants is less direct and more subject to the effects of confounding conditions.

Concomitants (which, in a sense, may be thought of as secondary criterion data) usually are not acceptable for criterion measurement when direct measurement of behavior in process or the measurement of isolable products of teacher behavior can conveniently be used. However, in investigations involving extensive sampling and where other measurement approaches are impractical, the use of known correlates as substitutes for process or product data frequently is defensible.

Of the measurement approaches employing observation and assessment only *time sampling involving replicated systematic observation by trained observers* produces sufficiently reliable data to recommend its use in fundamental research, although less well-controlled variations (e.g., ratings by students) may be employed when only coarse discrimination (e.g., "best" and "poorest" teachers with respect to some criterion component) is required, and when the larger expected error is recognized and accepted. Various assessment techniques have been developed, among which the more reliable and promising appear to be 1) graphic scales with operationally, or behaviorally, defined poles and/or units; 2) observation check lists; and 3) forced-choice scales. The chief shortcoming of observation and assessment techniques has been lack of reliability, a shortcoming that research has indicated can fairly readily be overcome with care to definition and to scale development, and with adequate training of the observers or judges.

Product measurements (estimates of the behavior or achievement of the pupils of teachers) have been widely acclaimed as desirable criterion data, but have been infrequently used in the study of teacher effectiveness. Actually, the seeming relevance and appropriateness of the measurement of pupil behaviors and their products as indicators of teacher performance may be more apparent than real, for the producers of (or contributers to) pupil behavior, or pupil achievement, are numerous, and it is most difficult to designate and parcel out the contribution to a particular "product" made by a specified aspect of the producing situation, such as the teacher. We also must note that the facets of the product criterion (various understandings, skills, and attitudes, etc. in various content fields and areas of personal behavior) are similarly numerous, and each must be capable of valid measurement and of at least partial isolation for study. The comparability of estimates of various components or aspects of a product (pupil achievement, for example) also becomes a special problem when student behavior or achievement is employed as a criterion of teacher effectiveness. And when measurement of the product is accomplished by obtaining estimates of student change (i.e., pretest-posttest data) the problem of variable potential gain (students who score high on the initial measurement being closer to their "ceilings" than students who originally score low are to theirs) is particularly plaguing to the researcher. However, if the rationale of the product (student performance) criterion is accepted, and if the complex control problem presented by a multiplicity of producers and the multidimensionality of the criterion can be satisfactorily coped with, student change becomes an intriguing approach to the measurement of teacher effectiveness.

In dealing with any of the several approaches to measuring the criterion, the researcher must be thoroughly familiar with, and guard against, the various sources of criterion measurement bias, particularly those which have to do with incompleteness and contamination of the obtained data.

Predictor Measurement

I shall pass very quickly over the problem of obtaining estimates of the predictors. The chief technical problems faced here are those familiar to educational research and measurement workers, namely validity and reliability. The prediction of a criterion may be very seriously limited by the reliability of estimates of the predictor employed in a study. And, unless the researcher has a pretty clear idea of the meaning of his predictor estimates and the conditions or traits they actually represent, interpretation of predictor-criterion relationships may be pretty risky.

It is important to note that similarly *named* predictor measures (e.g., estimates of teacher empathy, or leadership, or understanding of children) used in different investigations do not necessarily refer to the same underlying characteristic of the teacher. Quite apart from sampling errors, they do not necessarily yield similar relationships with estimates of a specified criterion dimension. Discrepancies in findings reported in the literature sometimes may be traced to this lack of agreement in operational definition of the predictor, in addition to criterion inadequacies and lack of control of relevant variables.

Research Objectives and Design

Still another set of conditions that contribute to variability in the nature and degree of association which may be obtained between hypothesized predictor measures and measures of a criterion of teacher effectiveness has to do with research objectives and the approach to the predictor-criterion relationship incorporated in the research design. Such questions as the following should be (but frequently are not) considered by the researcher:

1) Does the investigation purpose to determine *a*) concomitant or *b*) antecedent-consequent relationships?

2) Is prediction of the criterion of teacher effectiveness attempted from single bits of information (e.g., answers to a single questionnaire, test, or inventory item) or from scores based on combinations of such bits of information forming sets of homogeneous items, or scales? (And, if the latter, does the combination of bits involve equal or differential weighting?) An extension of this question involves the question of whether prediction of the criterion is determined from a single predictor alone or from a combination of predictor scores, weighted perhaps in light of multiple regression weights.

3) Is the derivation of predictors (original selection of items, or combinations of items, as predictors of the criterion) based upon experience with a single sample, or has replication been employed involving multiple samples of teachers?

4) Is prediction directed at a) additional random samples of the same population as the samples employed in deriving the predictors (e.g., cross validation) or b) samples of populations other than that from which the predictors were derived, employing either a) the same criterion measure (validity generalization) or b) a different criterion measure (validity extension)?

5) Is prediction attempted for predictor data and criterion data which have been collected at approximately the same time, or when the obtaining of criterion data has been delayed and carried out with a considerable time interval separating the collection of the two sets of estimates?

6) Is prediction attempted when the predictor data are obtained under "incentive" conditions (e.g., in connection with selection for employment) or under "nonincentive" conditions (e.g., as in basic research)?

7) Is prediction attempted for selected criterion dimensions singly (e.g., effective classroom discipline) or for a composite criterion made up of a number of heterogeneous components or dimensions (e.g., over-all teaching effectiveness)?

8) Is prediction of teacher effectiveness attempted on an actuarial or group basis, or is the concern prediction for particular (individual) teachers?

Still other aspects of the prediction problem might be noted, but these are representative of some of the major considerations involved in the over-all design of studies of the predictor-criterion relationship.

TEACHER EFFECTIVENESS AND THE TEACHER CHARACTERISTICS STUDY

When, near the beginning of this discussion, I referred to methods of obtaining criterion data relative to teacher effectiveness, I avoided definition of the term "teacher effectiveness." If I were pressed, I might say that I believe teaching is effective to the extent that the teacher acts in ways that are favorable to the development of basic skills, understandings, work habits, desirable attitudes, value judgments, and adequate personal adjustment of the pupil. But even such an operational-appearing definition is really very general and abstract and is not easily translatable into terms relating to specific teacher behaviors. Embarrassing as it may be for professional educators to recognize, relatively little progress has been made in rounding out this definition with the details that are necessary for describing competent teaching or the characteristics of effective teachers for a specific educational situation or cultural setting. Granted, most educators and most parents do have some idea of what constitutes effective teaching. These conceptualizations, however, usually are very vague and far removed from specific observable behaviors of teachers. Frequently even such hazy ideas are highly individualized, with very little agreement existing among different persons. One is reminded of the old, familiar fable of the blind men who perceived an elephant in widely varying manners depending on the part of the elephant's body that each one touched.

Relativity of Teacher Effectiveness

Disagreement and ambiguity with respect to the description of teacher effectiveness are to be expected and cannot be entirely avoided because competent teaching undoubtedly is a relative matter. A person's concept of a "good" teacher depends, *first,* on that person's acculturation, his past experience, and the value attitudes he has come to accept, and, *second,* on the aspects of teaching that may be foremost in his consideration at a given time. Pupil F, therefore, may differ widely from pupil G in his concept of the essential attributes of an effective teacher. If pupil F is bright, academically minded, well adjusted, and independent, he may value most the teacher who is serious, rigorously academic, and perhaps relatively impersonal. If pupil G, on the other hand, is more sensitive and requires considerable succorance, he may find the teacher just described not at all to his liking and indeed literally "impossible." In the mind of pupil G, the better teacher may very well be one who is somewhat less exacting from an academic standpoint, but who is characteristically sympathetic, understanding, and the like.

Answers to the question, "What is an effective teacher like?" also may vary to a degree with the particular kind of teacher one chooses to consider. It does not seem unreasonable to hypothesize that, even if it were possible to agree upon a generalized definition of effective teaching which would be acceptable to a number of different cultures, and if our thinking might be objectified to the point where effective teaching could be described on a factual basis, "good" teachers of different grades or different subject matters still might vary considerably in personal and social characteristics and in various domains of classroom behavior.

The concept of competent teaching must, therefore, be considered to be relative to at least two major sets of conditions: 1) the social or cultural group in which the teacher operates, involving social values which frequently differ from person to person, community to community, culture to culture, and time to time; and 2) the grade level and subject matter taught. It is not surprising, then, to note the difficulties that have confronted those seeking to establish criteria of teacher effectiveness, the dearth of testable hypotheses produced in such research as has been undertaken, and a general lack of understanding of the problem of the characteristics of effective teachers. One very important reason why effective or ineffective teachers cannot be described with any assurance is the wide variation in tasks performed by the teachers and in value concepts of what constitutes desirable teaching objectives.

But in addition to these considerations, and important in its own right as a deterrent to the study of teacher effectiveness, is the fact that there is a lack of any clear knowledge of the *patterns of behaviors* that typify individuals who are employed as teachers. It seems probable that, without losing sight of the importance of developing means for recognizing "good" teachers, attention of the researcher might first more properly and profitably be directed at the identification and estimation of some of the major patterns of personal and social characteristics of teachers. This represents the point of departure for research conducted by the Teacher Characteristics Study.

In the Teacher Characteristics Study, considerations of the effectiveness, or value, of particular teacher behaviors were to a large extent disregarded. Instead, attention was focused on the study of possible teacher-behavior dimensions, such dimensions being hypothesized to represent generalized trait continua. From this point of view, teacher-behavior variables are assumed to consist of clusters of relatively homogeneous (positively intercorrelated) behaviors, such component behaviors being of the nature of *simple predicates,* capable of operational definition.

Implied in this approach is the assumption that a teacher may be described in terms of a position on a particular behavior dimension, such description being essentially factual and relating to observable manifestations of overt behavior or else to responses known to be correlated with some behavior pattern to a degree that may permit indirect estimation of the behavior.

The Teacher Characteristics Study

The Teacher Characteristics Study was sponsored by the American Council on Education and generously supported by The Grant Foundation. During the six years of the Study, approximately 100 separate research projects were carried out and over 6,000 teachers in 1,700 schools and about 450 school systems participated in various phases of the research. Some of the basic studies involved extensive classroom observation (by trained observers) of teachers, with the purpose of discovering significant patterns of teacher behavior. Other activities of the project had to do with the development of instruments (paper and pencil tests and inventories) for the identification of individuals characterized by different levels of specified patterns of *a*) classroom behavior, *b*) attitudes and educational viewpoints, *c*) verbal intelligence, and *d*) emotional stability. Still other investigations were concerned with the comparison of defined groups of teachers (e.g., elementary teachers and secondary teachers, married and unmarried teachers, etc.), from the standpoint of their observable characteristics.

Basically, the Teacher Characteristics Study had three major purposes: 1) to analyze and describe patterns of teacher classroom behavior and the manifestations of certain value systems and cognitive and emotional traits of teachers; 2) to isolate and combine into scales significant correlates (provided by responses to self-report inventories concerned with the teacher's preferences, experiences, self-appraisals, judgment, and the like) of some major dimensions of teacher behavior; and 3) to compare American teachers (in terms of the teacher characteristics described by the Study) when they had been classified according to a number of conditions.

Pursuance of these objectives involved development of techniques for the reliable assessment of classroom behavior, determination (largely through factor analysis) of some major patterns of teacher behavior, development of instruments made up of materials hypothetically related to teacher classroom behavior dimensions and other personal and social characteristics of teachers, the empirical derivation of scoring keys for such instruments in light of response-criterion correlations, and finally, comparison of defined groups of teachers.

Patterns of Classroom Behavior

As a result of the direct observation and assessment of teacher classroom behavior and subsequent statistical analyses of the measurement data, several interdependent patterns of teacher behavior were suggested. Three in particular appeared to stand out in separate factor analyses of elementary and secondary teachers:

T.C.S. Pattern X_o—understanding, friendly *vs.* aloof, egocentric, restricted teacher behavior

T.C.S. Pattern Y_o—responsible, businesslike, systematic *vs.* evading, unplanned, slipshod teacher behavior

T.C.S. Pattern Z_o—stimulating, imaginative, surgent *vs.* dull, routine teacher behavior

Pattern scores X_o, Y_o, and Z_o, derived from observers' estimates of teacher behaviors in the classroom, appeared to possess sufficient reliability to permit comparisons of teacher groups with respect to these patterns and, also, to justify their use for criterion purposes in attempting to identify inventory responses that might be used to predict teacher classroom behavior.

Among elementary school teachers, patterns X_o, Y_o, and Z_o were highly intercorrelated and each also seemed to be highly correlated with pupil behavior in the teachers' classes. Among secondary school teachers, the intercorrelations of the three patterns were lower, that between patterns X_o (friendly) and Y_o (organized) being of a very low order. The teacher classroom-behavior patterns and pupil behavior were much less highly correlated among secondary teachers as compared with elementary teachers.

Elementary and secondary teachers, as major groups, differed hardly at all with respect to mean assessments on patterns X_o, Y_o, and Z_o. However, Grade 5–6 women teachers, represented by a relatively small sample, were assessed somewhat higher on the several classroom behavior patterns (particularly on Y_o) than teachers of other elementary grades. Among secondary school groups, social studies teachers received the highest mean assessment on pattern X_o (friendly behavior) and women mathematics teachers (with women social studies teachers not far behind) on pattern Y_o (businesslike behavior). Teachers over 55 years of age received distinctly lower mean assessments on pattern X_o (friendly), and also slightly lower with regard to pattern Z_o (stimulating), than younger teacher groups. Among elementary teachers, the mean assessments on the classroom behavior patterns X_o, Y_o, and Z_o were slightly but insignificantly higher for married, as compared with single, teachers. Among secondary mathematics-science teachers, single teachers received higher mean assessments than did those who were married. With respect to English-social studies teachers, single teachers were assessed higher than married teachers on pattern Y_o, but slightly lower on patterns X_o and Z_o. In general, differences between teacher groups compared on the observed classroom behavior patterns X_o, Y_o, and Z_o were not pronounced. However, it is of interest to note that scores on the Teacher Characteristics Schedule (to be described shortly), based on keys (X_{co}, Y_{co}, and Z_{co}) derived to predict these classroom behavior patterns, frequently distinguished different teacher groups more sharply and with greater assurance than did the X_o, Y_o, and Z_o observation data.

Patterns of Values, Verbal Ability, and Emotional Stability

Inevitably, the Teacher Characteristics Study sought other evidences of teacher behavior in addition to those provided by assessments of overt classroom behavior. To extend the understanding of conative and cognitive aspects of teacher behavior, and to permit the more complete investigation of relationships between teacher characteristics and specified conditions of teaching, the study undertook a number of researches directed at analyses of teachers' attitudes, their educational viewpoints, their verbal intelligence, and their emotional adjustment, and attempted to develop direct-inquiry instruments for estimating from a teacher's responses his status relative to such behavior domains.

In one set of studies, a number of opinionnaires relating to teachers' attitudes toward groups of persons encountered in the school were developed, and the organization of teacher attitudes was studied through factor analysis. In keeping with the results of the factor analyses, the study centered its attention chiefly on the attitudes of teachers toward pupils, their attitudes toward administrators, and their attitudes toward fellow teachers and nonadministrative personnel.

The educational viewpoints of teachers with respect to curricular organization and scope, pupil participation and class planning, academic achievement standards, etc. also were investigated (separately for elementary and secondary teachers) through the employment of direct-inquiry type of items and factor analysis of the intercorrelations among responses. The patterns of viewpoints which emerged were not clear-cut, and there seemed to be some justification for considering teachers' educational beliefs from the standpoint of a single continuum, oversimplified perhaps by its designation as a "traditional-permissive" dimension.

To obtain estimates of the verbal understanding of teachers, vocabulary and verbal analogy items were constructed, experimentally administered, and the responses analyzed, the procedure culminating in the selection of a small number of highly discriminating items comprising a "verbal ability" scale. In a similar way, materials were prepared and analyzed to obtain items for providing estimates of the emotional stability of teachers. And, to aid in the detection of "tendency to make a good impression" when dealing with responses to direct-question type of materials, a set of items intended to measure probable validity-of-response of teachers also was assembled.

Various studies and comparisons of the attitudes, educational viewpoints, verbal understanding, and emotional adjustment of teachers were undertaken in the course of the development of such measuring devices as those noted above. Some of these results were extremely interesting, but I shall not attempt to go into them here. I shall move on to a description of our efforts to obtain indirect estimates of teacher classroom behaviors and other characteristics from correlated inventory responses.

An Inventory for Indirect Estimation

In the interest of providing more readily obtainable estimates of teacher classroom behaviors, and also estimates of teacher attitudes, viewpoints, verbal ability, and emotional stability which might be less susceptible to the response set of giving socially acceptable responses, efforts of the Teacher Characteristics Study were directed at the derivation of correlates scoring keys applicable to the items of the Teacher Characteristics Schedule. The Teacher Characteristics Schedule was an omnibus self-report inventory based upon some 25 originally separate instruments. In its final form, it consisted of 300 multiple-choice and check-list items relating to personal preferences, self-judgments, frequently engaged-in activities, biographical data, and the like.

Employing as criteria a) observers' assessments of teacher classroom behaviors X_o, Y_o, and Z_o, and b) scores on the direct response scales relative to teacher attitudes, viewpoints, verbal intelligence, and emotional stability, hundreds of response analyses were carried out (thanks to SWAC, our first high speed computer at UCLA). Response-criterion correlations were obtained for each response to each item of the Teacher Characteristics Schedule under a variety of conditions. Correlates scoring keys, employing responses associated with the criterion behaviors as signs or symptoms of behavior, thus were derived for a large number of teacher groups. The most generally applicable sets of scoring keys (and those most frequently used in other phases of the Study's research) were the all-elementary teacher keys, the all-secondary teacher keys, and the combined elementary-secondary teacher keys.

Reliability data for the correlates scoring keys and various kinds of validity data, relating particularly to the friendly (X_{co}), businesslike (Y_{co}), and stimulating (Z_{co}) keys, were obtained. Generally speaking, the reliability coefficients fell between .7 and .8, and the validity coefficients were of varying magnitude depending upon the kind of validity investigated, the particular behavior estimated, and the teacher group from which the key was derived and to which it might reasonably be applied. Concurrent validity coefficients for correlates scores on classroom behavior patterns X_o, Y_o, and Z_o typically were between .2 and .4; predictive validity coefficients were positive, but generally low, seldom exceeding .2. Intercorrelations among scores resulting from application of the several correlates scoring keys estimating classroom behaviors, attitudes, educational viewpoints, verbal intelligence, and emotional stability, and correlations between Schedule scores and observers' assessments indicated 1) substantial relationships among the correlates data, and 2) prediction of observed classroom behaviors principally by the scales specifically developed for that purpose (X_{co}, Y_{co}, and Z_{co}).

"High" and "Low" Teachers Compared

I shall not deal here with the numerous comparisons of teachers which were made in light of the Teacher Characteristics Schedule data collected. But I do want to mention a study we conducted which was concerned with identifying teachers who fell into one of three groups: one group comprised of teachers each of whom had received observer assessments one standard deviation or more above the mean on each of the three classroom behavior patterns X_o, Y_o, and Z_o; another made up of teachers who were all within two-tenths of a standard deviation on either side of the mean on the three different classroom behavior patterns; and a third group made up of teachers all of whom received observers' assessments one standard deviation or more below the mean on each of the three classroom behavior patterns. After having identified these teachers, we attempted to determine some of the distinguishing characteristics, in terms of Teacher Characteristics Schedule responses, of the different groups. Here, I suppose, we were approaching the problem of over-all teacher effectiveness. We were attempting to discover responses of generally high-assessed teachers which distinguished them from generally low-assessed teachers. I shall summarize some of the more notable characteristics for combined elementary and secondary teachers which distinguished the high group from the low and the low group from the high. There was a general tendency for "high" teachers to: be extremely generous in appraisals of the behavior and motives of other persons; possess strong interest in reading and literary affairs; be interested in music, painting, and the arts in general; participate in social groups; enjoy pupil relationships; prefer nondirective classroom procedures; manifest superior verbal intelligence; and be above average in emotional adjustment. Turning to the other side of the coin, "low" teachers tended generally to: be restrictive and critical in their appraisals of other persons; prefer activities which did not involve close personal contacts; express less favorable opinions of pupils; manifest less high verbal intelligence; show less satisfactory emotional adjustment; and represent older age groups.

Obviously, the description I have been able to give of the Teacher Characteristics Study is very sketchy. I have not been able to get down to some of the really interesting findings such as those related to comparisons of teacher groups and interrelationships among teacher behaviors. I will, however, be able to incorporate some of our findings in the concluding section which follows.

Some Probable Correlates of Teacher Effectiveness

It is indeed presumptuous and dangerous to speak out boldly about conditions and teacher characteristics associated with teacher effectiveness. However, based upon the findings of various researches conducted by the Teacher Characteristics Study and an accumulation of investigations which have appeared in the literature over a period of years, certain threads of fact do seem discernible. But the conclusions and inferences are still, at best, tentative—they are more in the nature of hypotheses for which some support has been found in our American midtwentieth-century culture. We also must recognize that changing educational values in the future reasonably may lead to changes in the patterning of teacher behaviors and to further revision of our understanding of predictors of teacher effectiveness.

The following generalizations regarding the relationship between teacher characteristics, as predictors, and teacher effectiveness, as a criterion abstracted from various criterion measures reported in the literature, appear to be in order.

1) Characteristics and conditions of the teacher which are likely to be *positively correlated* or associated with teacher effectiveness in the abstract include: measured intellectual abilities, particularly verbal intelligence; achievement in college courses; general cultural and specific subject-matter knowledge; professional information (knowledge of education and teaching); practice teaching marks; emotional adjustment; attitudes favorable to students or pupils; generosity in appraisals of the behaviors and motives of

other persons; interest in reading and literary matters; interest in music and painting; participation in social and community affairs; early experiences in caring for children and in teaching (e.g., reading to children, taking class for teacher); history of teaching in family; size of school and size of community in which presently teaching; and cultural level of community in which teaching. 2) Extensiveness of general and/or professional education, enrollment in particular professional courses, and personal appearance appear to bear very little relation to the abstracted criterion of general teacher effectiveness. 3) Elementary teachers and secondary teachers, as groups, do not seem to differ greatly when an over-all view of teacher effectiveness is taken. However, elementary teachers do seem to show superiority when selected aspects of criterion behavior having to do with warmth, permissiveness, and favorable attitudes toward children are considered. Secondary teachers are superior from the standpoint of verbal understanding. Within the elementary school, Grade 5–6 teachers tend toward superiority on several criterion dimensions; within the secondary school, English and social studies teachers show a similar tendency. 4) Age of the teacher and amount of teaching experience seem to manifest an over-all negative relationship with teaching effectiveness, although there is evidence of curvilinearity, increase in effectiveness appearing to be positively correlated with age and experience during early years of teaching careers. 5) Sex differences in over-all teacher effectiveness do not appear to be pronounced, but the classroom performance of women teachers seems to be more organized and businesslike than that of men, and men teachers seem to be very distinctly more emotionally stable. 6) For teachers of all grades and subjects considered together, differences in effectiveness between single and married teachers are small. However, within the elementary school, the evidence appears to favor married teachers. At the secondary level results are somewhat mixed, with unmarried teachers as a group apppearing to be superior with respect to such criteria as businesslike classroom behavior, permissive viewpoints, and verbal understanding, but with married teachers showing superior emotional adjustment.

Certain characteristics, then, do seem to be associated with certain dimensions of teacher behavior and teacher effectiveness, although the extent of obtained relationships frequently has not been high. It is important here to recall that 1) relationships and differences which have been noted are in terms of averages for groups of teachers; and 2) any obtained relationship is limited by, and may be expected to vary with, conditions such as those noted earlier. The usefulness of research findings pertaining to the prediction of teacher effectiveness will be greatest when the results are considered in an actuarial context, rather than in attempting highly accurate prediction for given individuals, and when variations in relationship found among different classifications of teachers, and with use of different approaches to the predictor-criterion relationship, are taken into account.

APPENDIX: PREDICTABILITY OF TEACHER EFFECTIVENESS

The notes which follow have to do with general considerations relating to conditions which probably should be taken into account both in the design and the interpretation of research on teacher effectiveness. Some of these are derived from rational analysis of the problems involved, but many also have substantial support from empirical data.

1) The predictability of teacher effectiveness undoubtedly is affected by the *multidimensionality of the criterion*. There is accumulating evidence that prediction can be accomplished with better-than-chance results for specified dimensions or components of the criterion. On the other hand, the prediction of over-all teacher effectiveness is possible only to the extent that some general agreement can be reached regarding the dimensions comprising "over-all effectiveness" (involving, of course, acceptance of a common set of educational values) and how they should be combined to form a composite. Teachers effective with regard to one aspect of the criterion may not be effective when judged by other criterion dimensions.

2) The predictability of teacher effectiveness varies depending on the *degree of control* it is possible to exert in dealing with the multiplicity of predictors and the multidimensionality of the criterion.

3) The predictability of the criterion varies with the *kind of measure* employed in obtaining the criterion data.

4) The predictability of the criterion varies with the *adequacy* (reliability and validity) *of measures* of a) the criterion and b) the predictor variables.

5) The predictability of the criterion is so limited by conditions associated with measurement of the criterion, measurement of predictors, and practical conditions, that relationships representing common variance of perhaps one-fifth or one-fourth of the total variance probably approach the maximum to be expected except in chance instances.

6) The predictability of a dimension of the criterion of teacher effectiveness from a specified predictor probably varies depending upon the

cultural milieu which provides the setting for an investigation, particularly the values and objectives prominent in the teacher training curriculum at the time the teachers studied were in college.

7) Predictability of the criterion varies directly with the degree of similarity between the sample with respect to which predictors are derived, and the sample to which the predictors are applied in attempting to determine predictor-criterion relationships.

8) Predictability of a criterion dimension varies with the *particular teacher population* (e.g., Grade 1–2 women teachers, men science teachers, etc.), or student population, studied. Effective teaching methods may differ from one grade level to another and from course to course.

9) Predictability of the criterion varies inversely with the *time interval* separating the obtaining of predictor measurements and criterion measurements.

10) Predictability of the criterion probably varies depending upon the association of *incentive or nonincentive conditions* with the obtaining of predictor data.

11) The regression of predictor measurements on criterion measurements frequently is *curvilinear* (e.g., positive correlation between amount of teaching experience and certain criterion measures of effectiveness of secondary school teachers during first five years or so, followed by leveling off and decline in criterion estimates with extensive experience).

12) Prediction of teacher effectiveness must be considered largely in the *actuarial* sense; individual prediction, as generally is the case in attempting to predict human behavior, is much more limited and is accomplished with a lesser degree of confidence.

PART II

PSYCHOMETRIC THEORY
AND METHOD

Psychometric Theory and Method

6 · NORMS, UNITS, AND SCALES

A TOPIC OF CONTINUING INTEREST at the Invitational Conferences concerns the improvement of norms and the development of suitable units and scaling procedures for reporting test scores. In Chapter 1, several papers on this topic were cited from the 1938, 1939, and 1940 conferences. In his 1963 paper, Lennon again calls attention to some of the problems discussed at these early conferences, for which an adequate solution has not yet been found. He begins by showing that considerable progress *has* been made in norming technology, particularly as it relates to the selection of large, representative norming samples and to the identification of relevant subject characteristics. Nevertheless, an examination of the norming procedures followed in the standardization of six widely used intelligence and achievement test batteries reveals that the normative samples used in different tests still vary in important respects. As a means of achieving better comparability among scores obtained with different tests, Lennon reiterates the appeal for an anchor test voiced by Cureton at the 1940 conference.

Angoff addresses himself to the broader problem of score comparability, inquiring into the possible development of equivalency tables for converting scores from different tests. While Lennon is concerned chiefly with what can be done in advance to make test norms comparable, Angoff considers principally what can be done to render scores comparable after test standardization. He differentiates between the relatively simple problem of transforming a system of units, as in conversion among parallel forms of the same test, and the more vexing problem of converting scores across tests of different functions. The latter is more characteristic of the conversion of scores on tests designed for the same purpose by different publishers. Such conversion among nonparallel tests presents a number of methodological problems, which Angoff analyzes with thoroughness and clarity.

The next two papers, by Cronbach and Lindquist, are concerned with the use of norms for two specific purposes for which educational achievement tests are commonly employed. Cronbach considers the evaluation of the

241

achievement test score of an individual pupil with reference to the score expected from his initial status, prior to receiving relevant instruction. This problem is related both to the measurement of change and to the establishment of differentiated subgroup norms. Lindquist, on the other hand, raises a question regarding the applicability of the usual individual norms to the evaluation of schools. For this purpose, he calls for distributions of school averages in each achievement test. Without this information, administrators are likely to reach misleading conclusions about the relative performance of their schools, since the variability of school averages is less than the variability of the individual scores in terms of which published norms are customarily reported.

Gardner discusses the scaling of test scores, with special emphasis on the role of the reference population in this process. After briefly surveying different types of scaled scores, he describes his own K scores, which are based on the assumption that overlapping grade distributions can be more accurately represented by Pearson Type III curves than by a normal curve. Gardner reports data from the standardization of the Stanford Achievement Test supporting the hypothesis that grade distributions are in fact skewed. He also uses the data from two editions of this test, standardized 12 years apart, to illustrate the stability of the K scores obtained with different but comparable reference populations.

Norms: 1963

ROGER T. LENNON

1963

I have found it convenient to organize my remarks under two topics, which I shall refer to as norming theory, on the one hand, and norming technology, on the other.

As to norming theory, I shall have relatively little to say—and this for the best of reasons, namely, that the past decade has seen little development in this area. Where the literature abounds with theoretical treatment of validity and reliability, it is almost devoid of systematic treatment of norming; the words "norms" and "norming," for example, have not even appeared in the index of the *Annual Review of Psychology* for the past three years.

Indeed, some of you may even wonder what I have in mind when I speak of "norming theory." Surely, you will say, everyone knows what norms are and why we need them; what more is there to it than that? Perhaps I can make my meaning clear by recalling that the administration of a test to an individual or a group can, in most instances, be thought of as akin to the conduct of a scientific experiment. Performance on a test, when interpreted according to suitable norms, serves as evidence supportive or not supportive of a hypothesis: this pupil has or has not made progress in reading during the past school year; the group using this textbook has made significantly greater progress than comparable students spending the same amount of time on this subject; etc. Now the inferences or conclusions that are drawn from this experiment-like testing are obviously conditioned by attributes of the norming group; but we have little in the way of a body of general principles relating test interpretation to norm group characteristics, little spelling out of the relations between norms, let us say, and test validity, little *theory,* in a word, of norming. I shall go no further in developing this concept; for purposes of this paper, suffice it to report, as I did a moment ago, that the past decade has been productive of very little advance in this area.

243

But if it appears that the past decade has been disappointing with respect to advances in norming theory, the picture with respect to norming technology and current practice is a more encouraging one. I discern at least four lines of development:

1) Applications of sampling theory to test standardization, particularly as reflected in the work of Frederic M. Lord, have pointed the way to more efficient data-gathering designs.

2) We have added substantially to our knowledge about community and school system variables related to performance on achievement and general mental ability tests. Jack C. Merwin (3), some three years ago, reviewing the literature on community and school characteristics related to test performance, found some eighty-odd relevant studies; a decade ago, there was scarcely a score. The work of John C. Flanagan and his associates in Project Talent (2) has already eventuated in a wealth of information about characteristics related to performance on various types of tests at the secondary school level, some corroborative of earlier findings, and some raising questions about certain assumptions hitherto widely acted upon in definition of norming populations.

3) There is a general willingness on the part of the major test-making agencies to commit the resources required for adequate test standardization, at least with respect to their most important test series.

4) The major test publishers, several years ago, began to give serious consideration to the use of a common anchor test in norming their respective tests, as a device for heightening comparability among the norms. This enterprise has moved forward less rapidly than it should have, a state of affairs for which, I regret to say, I am as much responsible as any one individual.

By way of documenting these points, and as introduction to additional points that I shall make, I ask you to bear with me while I read to you excerpts from the descriptions of the standardization programs for six of the most widely used batteries of tests.

TEST A

The basic procedure for ruling out bias . . . was to select a stratified sample of communities on which to base the norms. Communities were stratified on a composite of factors which have been found to be related to the measured intelligence of children in the community. Each community which volunteered to serve in the normative testing was evaluated with respect to the factors of: 1) per cent of adult illiteracy; 2) number of professional workers per thousand . . .; 3) per cent of home ownerships; and 4) median home rental value. On the basis of a composite of these factors each community was classed as: Very High, High, Average, Low, or Very Low. All the pupils present in each grade in the community were to be tested. . . .

TEST B

. . . schools in the norm sample were so chosen that the representation from each of nine regions is similar to the proportions in the United States. . . . At the inception of the standardization program . . . a random sample of all school superintendents in the country was chosen; the superintendents were asked if they were willing to participate in some phase of a long-range standardization program. . . . The selection of schools was random from all available schools in the region.

TEST C

More important than the sheer number of students tested, however, is the degree to which they adequately represent the total national public school population at those grades. U. S. school enrollment data were obtained showing distributions of students by geographic region. Apportionment according to community size within each geographic region was based on 1960 census figures for the distribution of population among communities of various sizes. Invitations to participate in the standardization program were then extended to appropriate school systems, so selected that the group as a whole would typify the national population. . . . Eighty-five school systems in thirty-seven states participated in the . . . standardization program. . . . All cooperating school systems were asked to test complete classroom groups from one or more schools so chosen as to be representative of the community.

TEST D

The total pupil enrollment in public elementary . . . and secondary . . . schools in the United States is the reference population on which the norms . . . are based. . . . Data in the Biennial Survey of Education 1952–54, and general educational, social, cultural and economic conditions were considered in grouping states with similar characteristics into geographical regions. Specific characteristics considered were: average expenditures per pupil for instructional purposes, length of school term, and type of school organization. . . . Community size was the second factor used for stratification control. . . . The norming samples for all grades within a given level

. . . were independent. Thus, any single school contributed to only one grade for any single level of the test. No one school, however, was permitted to contribute to samples for two successive grades, even though they were for different levels of the test. . . . A total of 672 school systems were contacted. A total of 69,354 pupils from 341 school systems in 48 states were included in the norming sample.

TEST E

[The] . . . norms purport to describe the achievement of pupils "representative" of the nation's public school population. . . . Authors and publisher sought to obtain a norm group that would match the national school population with respect to certain characteristics known or assumed to be related to achievement. . . . These characteristics include size of school system, geographical location, type of community, . . . intelligence level of pupils, and type of system (segregated or non-segregated). . . . Each field representative . . . was asked to designate . . . twenty school systems meeting specifications that would yield a properly representative total norm group. . . . A total of 225 systems accepted the invitation and carried through all the necessary phases of the program. . . . Included in this group are public school systems from 49 states; the number of pupils tested in the standardization program was over 500,000.

One additional control, relating to age, was exercised in the selection of the final norm group. . . . Pupils falling outside this range [18-month modal or typical for each grade] were excluded from the norm group. . . . The final age-controlled sample included between 91% . . . and 81% . . . of the total grade group. Each participating system was required to test its entire enrollment in regular classes in at least three consecutive grades. . . .

TEST F

The population to which the norms apply includes all students in grades nine through twelve in regular daily attendance at public high schools throughout the United States. . . . The sample on which the norms are based was drawn . . . so as to reflect the regional distribution and the community-size distributions. A preliminary sample of school systems was chosen strictly at random from each of the 36 strata. The number of systems chosen from each stratum was based on the average high school enrollment per grade within that stratum. This preliminary sample of 714 systems included approximately three times as many students as were demanded by the sample specifications. The head administrative official in each of these 714 school systems was sent a registered letter in which the details of the standardization program were outlined and his cooperation solicited. Over two hundred school systems responded affirmatively. . . . In multiple-building systems either *all* buildings or *randomly selected* buildings were included in the sample. . . . All pupils in all grades in the cooperating schools were tested. . . . A total of 366 schools in 254 school systems participated in the standardization project.

I do not cite these particular standardization projects as examples of either good or bad practice in norming tests; much less do I propose to criticize any features of any one of these programs. I adduce them rather as representative of current practice on the part of major test publishers with respect to standardization of their more important test offerings. The six excerpts are, by intent, chosen from publications of the six major test publishers; the excerpts are mostly verbatim, but not complete; three are for achievement batteries, three for general ability tests.

It seems to me quite clear from the descriptions that the norming in each of the instances cited must be judged to be a planful, earnest, and informed attempt on the part of the respective authors and publishers to develop appropriate norms, an effort implying in every instance substantial commitment of time and resources. I may observe in passing that the author-publisher expenditure is likely to be in excess of forty or fifty cents for each case tested in the standardization of a group test (and very much higher in the case of an individual test), and you can readily appreciate the size of the commitment in these norming programs, involving as they did tens or even hundreds of thousands of pupils. It is no longer possible to say, as it might have been twenty years ago, that the norms represent adventitious collections of available test scores bearing only accidental relationship to an accurate description of the test performance of definable groups of pupils. At least with respect to the tests involved here—and they would collectively represent a large fraction of the testing done in elementary and secondary schools—such shortcomings as the norms may possess, either viewed individually or in relation to one another, do not stem from carelessness, lack of sophistication, or unwillingness to devote the resources needed to do respectable norming.

But shortcomings are in evidence; the norms do leave much to be desired, at least when viewed across tests. There are discernible marked differences with respect to the population whose achievement or ability the norms purport to describe. These differences arise from: the variables considered important as stratifying variables; sampling procedures; the proportions of voluntary cooperation forthcoming; the degree of control over administration and scoring; and other critical characteristics. It is impossible to state on a priori grounds the effect that such differences may have in introducing systematic variations among the several sets of norms, but there are good reasons for supposing that the differences in norms ascribable simply to these variations in norming procedures are not negligible. When we consider that to such differences from test to test there must be added differences associated with varying content, and with the time at which standardization programs are conducted (including the time of the school year), the issue of comparability, or lack of it, among the results of the various tests may begin to be seen in proper perspective. Empirical data reveal that there may be variations of as much as a year and a half in grade equivalent among the results yielded by various achievement tests; variations of as much as 8 or 10 points of IQ among various intelligence tests are, of course, by no means uncommon.

Some of you may feel that this lack of comparability among results of various tests is not really a matter of great concern—that as long as a school or school system consistently uses a given test or test series, it need not be too distressed that some other test or series would yield somewhat different results. If there be any such among you, may I cite for you a situation presently prevailing in the state of California, to the distress of both California educators and the test publishers. The California legislature, in response to public clamor over the quality of education in that state, enacted legislation prescribing the administration of ability and achievement tests in grades five, eight, and eleven, on an annual basis, to all public school pupils in the state. The state education department issued implementing regulations, which, in a wholly laudable attempt to provide for a measure of local autonomy in the selection of evaluation instruments, established an approved list of about half a dozen ability tests and an equal number of achievement tests from which local school districts might choose the instruments to be used. School districts are required to submit results to the state education department, which, in turn, is charged with the responsibility of preparing a summary of pupil achievement for the state for submission to the state board of education and presumably to the legislature and public. Now imagine the task that confronts the state education department in attempting to combine into a single summary the results, noncomparable as they are known to be, from a variety of tests. How can this agency discharge this responsibility and give to the legislature and the public a clear picture of pupil attainments? Must it undertake its own study of equivalence among the half dozen-or-so measures? This is an expensive and complicated undertaking, the results of which would in any case be subject to serious limitations. Must it resort to the alternative of requiring use of the same instrument by all school districts? I for one could consider this to be undesirable on various educational grounds.

Is this a state of affairs that we in testing should be willing to accept with complacency? I do not believe we should; I do not believe we have to. To do so, in my opinion, is to court growing lay and professional disbelief that measurement can provide worthwhile answers to important educational questions. Neither do I think, as do some within and without the testing field, that these vexing problems of norming should prompt us to repudiate the notion of national norms as an unattainable, unrealistic, and meaningless goal. For both general mental ability or scholastic aptitude measures and for achievement tests, there is surely a place and a need for a single, comprehensively based, broadly descriptive set of norms, whatever additional needs may also exist for data descriptive of particular samples of the general population. Rather, the proper direction for us now to take would seem to me to be along the path of a collaborative attack on the norming problem by the major test-producing agencies. I think each of us publishers should be willing to sacrifice whatever competitive advantage one or another of us may have felt he enjoyed by virtue of the superior norming of his tests, for the sake of the great gains in test interpretation that would flow from adoption of common definitions of norms populations and norming methods. We might even succeed in having schools give pre-eminence in selecting tests to considerations of content, validity, and reliability.

Exactly 23 years ago this very day, speaking in this very forum, Edward E. Cureton[1] read a paper on norms that has not, in my opinion, been surpassed by any subsequent paper on this issue. Cureton called for a general adoption by test-making agencies of a system of anchoring their respective tests to a common scale. He urged the development of a basic anchor test, its standardization on a genuinely representative sample of the general population, and the equating of intelligence tests and achievement tests of all publishers to this common scale. The attainment of this state of affairs would mark, in Cureton's words, "the date of maturity of educational and mental measurements as a science, and of educational guidance and counseling as a profession" (1, p. 300). We are, alas, not yet at this level of maturity, by Cureton's definition.

While I have no reason to suppose that any appeal that I might make along these lines will be more potent than Cureton's (save only that the need for some such development is now far more evident than it was in 1940), I would like to close my remarks with a similar call to concerted action now by the major test-making agencies. Surely we now know enough about the characteristics of communities and school systems related to performance on achievement and mental ability measures, and are sufficiently

[1] Cited in Chapter 1. A revised version of this paper has been published (1)—Ed.

close to common understanding of the proper general population on which to develop norms, to enable us to agree on a generally acceptable definition of the population whose test performance we seek to describe; to specify the distribution of this population on measures of economic status, cultural status, educational effort, and caliber of pupil population, plus other demographic features to which norming samples will be made to conform; to push ahead with the creation of an anchor instrument that will serve as a defining variable for all standardization groups at least for tests in the general cognitive domain, and thus to bring our collective efforts to that level of maturity for which Cureton pleaded. As we value the concept of a science of measurement of human abilities, let us take at least these steps to make our efforts more deserving of the label "scientific."

REFERENCES

1. Cureton, E. E. Minimum requirements in establishing and reporting norms on educational tests. *Harvard Educational Review*, 1941, 11, 287–300. (Revision of paper read at Conference of State Testing Leaders, New York, November, 1940.)
2. Flanagan, J. C., Davis, F. B., Dailey, J. T., Shaycroft, Marian F., Orr, D. B., Goldberg, I., & Neyman, C. A., Jr. *The American high school student*. Final report for Cooperative Research Project No. 635, U.S. Office of Education, Department of Health, Education, and Welfare. Pittsburgh, Pa.: Project Talent Office, Univer. of Pittsburgh, 1964.
3. Merwin, J. A review of literature on community and school system characteristics related to achievement. Unpublished study, Univer. of Minnesota, 1962.

Can Useful General-Purpose Equivalency Tables Be Prepared for Different College Admissions Tests?

WILLIAM H. ANGOFF

1962

In recent months complaints have been heard from various sources that the amount of testing that is going on these days is excessive and burdensome to the schools. These complaints are primarily directed at the kind of testing that has been called "external," by which is meant the testing that is demanded of students and schools by agencies external to the schools—e.g., colleges requiring standardized information regarding the abilities of students who are applying either for college entrance or for college scholarships. One solution that has been offered for this excessive testing calls for the computation of equivalency tables which would allow the conversion of scores obtained on the test of one publisher to the score scale of another publisher. A grander solution that has been suggested is to convert the scores on tests produced by all publishers to a single, common score scale. These conversions would presumably make it possible for a school to administer to its students only one test and then to submit to each college admissions officer or scholarship agency a converted score reported in terms of the score scale that is considered acceptable by that agency. In this way, it is claimed, the student would be spared the repeated testing that is now ordinarily required of him.

The validity of the claim that external testing today is excessive has been examined thoroughly, I am sure, and I doubt that I could add anything significant here to that discussion. However, you may be interested to know, if you do not already know, of an excellent article written by Frank B. Womer (5) of the University of Michigan for the Fall 1961 issue of the *North Central Association Quarterly,* in which he discusses the "Pros and Cons of External Testing" thoroughly and quite objectively, I believe. You may also know of a study conducted by the College Entrance Examination Board in 1960 in which the use of tests in the eleventh and twelfth

251

grades was surveyed (1). However, aside from the question that external testing is excessive, what I would like to consider here is the adequacy of the proposed solution—of equivalency tables that would relate the tests of all publishers.

This solution has some obvious attractions. It also has some objectionable features which may be summarized by saying that such tests will not necessarily be parallel forms—that is, they will not necessarily be measuring precisely the same function—and that in such instances it is not possible to provide a unique conversion that will be appropriate for all groups who are likely to take the tests or for all purposes for which the tests are likely to be given. It is of course reasonable to equate the tests of different publishers when these tests are known to be parallel. And quite possibly some *are*. On the other hand, it is more than likely that in the majority of instances they are not, since they were not constructed with that intention in the first place.

Before going on to consider the problems of equating tests of different function, it may be helpful to say what we mean when we talk about the equating of scores on tests of the *same* function. In this case, in the conversion of scores from one form to a parallel form of a test, say from one form of the American Council on Education (ACE) Psychological Examination to another, or from one form of the College Board Scholastic Aptitude Test (SAT) to another, we have simply the problem of transforming the system of units. We ordinarily consider this problem as one that is directly analogous to the problem of conversion from centimeters to inches, from centigrade to Fahrenheit, from pounds to grams, and so on. On the other hand, the question of converting scores across tests of *different* function is another matter. Here we are concerned with the problems of conversion from one kind of dimension to something quite different—from the scale of inches to the scale of pounds, for example. This is not necessarily an extreme or unreasonable example. For instance, the correlation between height and weight for adults of the same age is in the region of the low .50's. The correlation between observed scores on two tests of mathematical ability—SAT-Mathematical and ACE-Quantitative, for example—both of which, it should be pointed out, were designed to be predictive of scholastic success in the quantitative areas, is in the low .60's. The true-score correlation between these tests is not much higher—around .70. On the face of it, it seems unreasonable to ask for a conversion from inches to pounds. Why then, is it not similarly unreasonable (or at least *almost* as unreasonable) to ask for a conversion from SAT-M to ACE-Q? Yet requests for this conversion are not at all unusual.

Even in the conversion of scores across tests of the *same* function we can enumerate at least four sources of error. One source of error lies in the unreliability of the measuring instruments themselves, and affects the stability of statistics obtained in the collection of data. A second source of error lies in the design of the equating experiment and the method of treating the data: the various methods of equating are not equally reliable. A third source of error lies in the choice of samples used to establish the conversion line. Different samples will yield lines that differ randomly from one another. Finally, there is a source of error that is characteristic of any statistical enterprise—the error associated with the size of the study sample. Obviously, larger samples will yield more reliable data.

Nevertheless, in spite of all these kinds of error, it is reasonable, in the equating of parallel forms of a test, to postulate a unique "true" line and to consider that errors resulting from the unreliability of tests, from design and method, and from the sampling of people only cause random departures from this true line. On the other hand, the problem of "comparable" scores, that is, the conversion of scores of *different* function, has additional complexities. Here, as in the physical analogy in which we convert height to weight, the request for equivalent scores rests on an inappropriate premise—that there is *a single* conversion system—a unique system that exists and needs only to be estimated with the use of appropriate data. While it is certainly true that one can estimate or predict by means of a regression equation the most likely weight of an individual of a given height, or predict scores on the SAT from knowledge of scores on the ACE, in neither case can the prediction be considered simply a transformation of unit systems. Furthermore, just as regression systems will differ, depending on various considerations like the conditions of measurement and the characteristics of the group measured, so will conversion lines which purport to translate scores across tests of different function differ—and they will differ systematically, that is, in a predictable fashion, depending on certain known considerations.

For one thing, different conversion lines will result, depending on the particular definition of comparability employed. For example, one might ask what the most likely score on one test would be, given a particular score on the other. This would be one definition. Or one might equate standard-score deviates on the two tests. Or one might equate equivalent percentiles. These would be other definitions. Or one might, for example, equate scores that yielded equal predicted scores on one criterion or another. Here the use of different prediction criteria might yield different conversions. There is probably an unlimited number of definitions, each one conceivably yielding a different conversion. In contrast to this multiplicity of conversions for nonparallel tests, all methods or definitions of equivalent scores for *parallel* tests should lead to the same conversion equation—that is, except for random error of the kind described before.

Second, different lines will result when different populations are used to form the basis for deriving the tables of comparable scores. For example, there will be one conversion line between Verbal and Mathematical test scores at the college entrance level for boys and quite another for girls. This fact is immediately apparent if one examines the mean scores of boys and girls on the Verbal and Mathematical sections of the SAT. Girls characteristically score slightly higher than boys on Verbal but considerably lower than boys on Mathematical. The conversion line between Verbal and Mathematical scores when derived from the data for boys would be much different from the conversion line derived from the data for girls. As another illustration of the same general point we might consider some data collected by Majorie Olsen (4) in a study in which an attempt was made to predict Graduate Record Examinations (GRE) Aptitude Test scores from College Board SAT scores earned three and four years earlier. In this study it was found that students who later majored in liberal arts scored 40 points higher on SAT-Verbal than students who later majored in engineering. On SAT-Mathematical, however, the picture was considerably different. Here, the students who later majored in liberal arts scored 45 points lower than students who later majored in engineering. The data available on the GRE Aptitude Test four years later showed the same picture, even more pronounced. Here, the students who had majored in liberal arts scored 56 points higher than the engineers on GRE-Verbal. On GRE-Quantitative, however, the engineers scored 76 points higher than the liberal arts students. While these results may not be too surprising, they do point up the fact that any so-called equating between tests of different function, say between SAT-Verbal and SAT-Mathematical or between GRE-Verbal and GRE-Quantitative, would not necessarily yield the same results for different kinds of groups. When we consider the problem from a slightly different point of view, we recognize that conversion lines for tests of different function *must* be different for different groups if the groups show different profiles on the two tests. One might even say that because they reveal group characteristics and are not independent of the groups on which they are based, these kinds of conversions are themselves another way of representing group profiles.

A third reason for the nonuniqueness of comparable scores is the fact that differential selection will have a pronounced and predictable effect on the conversions. Let us suppose, for example, that we collect data on the SAT and the ACE for a group of individuals in order to construct a conversion table from scores on one of these tests to scores on the other, and let us suppose also that these individuals have been explicitly selected on the SAT. The distribution of resulting SAT scores will, of course, be sharply curtailed. The distribution of ACE scores, on the other hand, will be only moderately curtailed. A conversion line derived from these data could be far different from a line derived from a group of unselected students, or from a group of students who were selected on ACE. Even if the students have not been selected on one of the two tests, but on some third variable, say high school grades, their resulting distributions on the two tests and consequently the conversion of scores on the two tests could be considerably altered. This is so because the two score distributions will be unequally curtailed in rough proportion to the correlation of the two tests with the selection variable. The test that correlates more highly with the selection variable is the test on which the distribution of scores will be more drastically affected by the selection. The unequal effect of this selection is what causes the conversion for the selected group to be different from the conversion for the original unselected group. In contrast, scores taken from parallel tests of equal length will be equally affected by selection on a third variable, since they would correlate equally with that variable. The result is that there would be no predictable effect on the conversion equation.

I should emphasize that these problems are inherent in the derivation of a system of comparable scores, that is to say, in the conversion of scores on nonparallel tests, and that they do not replace or preclude the kinds of sources of error that were mentioned before in connection with equivalent scores that are taken from parallel forms. The problems of comparable scores exist *in addition to* the problems of equivalent scores.

By referring to appropriate data, it can be demonstrated quite readily that conversions for nonparallel tests are not unique, but depend in each case on the nature of the group used to establish the conversion. Table 1 shows two sets of conversions between ACE-Quantitative and SAT-Mathematical, one based on a group of 333 male students, the other based on a group of 582 women, both enrolled in the liberal arts curriculum at a large western state university. Clearly, each of the ACE-Q scores listed in the column at the left yields two converted scores that differ from each other appreciably. If it were necessary to convert these two tests to a single "common currency," so to speak, to be used for students of both sexes, there would be considerable doubt as to which one of these two conversions would be the proper one to use. In contrast, Table 2 also shows two sets of

TABLE 1

Conversions from ACE-Quantitative
to SAT-Mathematical

ACE-Q Scores[a]	SAT-M Scores		
	Men Liberal Arts	Women Liberal Arts	Difference
6	250	226	24
9	333	299	34
12	416	373	43
15	499	446	53
18	582	519	63
21	665	592	73
24	748	665	83

[a] Special scale for ACE; Mean = 13, Standard Deviation = 4.

conversions for the same two groups of students, this time for tests that correlate more highly, ACE-Linguistic and SAT-Verbal. The results in Table 2 are entirely different from those in Table 1. Here, because the tests are more similar, in terms of what they measure, than are ACE-Quantitative and SAT-Mathematical, the conversions are in much greater agreement.

It may give concrete value to the points that have been made here if we constructed a special set of illustrative data. Let us say that we have two college admissions tests (X and Y) and that we construct a table for converting scores from the scale of one test to the scale of the other. For the sake of the illustration, let us say that the table was constructed on the basis of data that yielded a mean of 50 and standard deviation of 10 on one test (Test X) and a mean of 500 and standard deviation of 100 on the other

TABLE 2

Conversions from ACE-Linguistic to SAT-Verbal

ACE-L Scores[a]	SAT-V Scores		
	Men Liberal Arts	Women Liberal Arts	Difference
6	322	316	6
9	393	383	10
12	464	450	14
15	535	518	17
18	605	585	20
21	676	652	24
24	747	719	28

[a] Special scale for ACE; Mean = 13, Standard Deviation = 4.

TABLE 3

Conversions for Imperfectly Correlated Test Scores,
Before and After Incidental Selection

X Scores	Corresponding Y Scores		
	Before Selection	After Selection	Difference
20	200	298	98
30	300	376	76
40	400	453	53
50	500	531	31
60	600	609	9
70	700	687	13
80	800	764	36

test (Test Y). The conversion based on these data would comprise the figures in the second column of Table 3. Now let us curtail the lower 40 per cent of the distribution of these students on a third test (Test Z)—let us say that these 40 per cent were rejected for admission at a college—and let us develop a conversion for Tests X and Y on the basis of the selected students. Let us say, finally, that Tests Z and X correlate .60, and that Tests Z and Y correlate .95. We can estimate that the 60 per cent of the group who were selected for admission will have a mean of 53.9 and a standard deviation of 8.9 on Test X and a mean of 561 and a standard deviation of 69 on Test Y. The conversion based on these data appears in the third column of Table 3. The differences between the two conversions appear in the fourth column. Obviously, these differences are not inconsiderable. Which of these two, then, is the appropriate conversion, and is it appropriate under all circumstances? Clearly, neither one is appropriate under all circumstances for the reason that the tests are not parallel forms.

Added to the systematic effects on comparable score conversions that were discussed earlier—namely, the definition of the kind of comparability in question; the choice and size of the group which would be used to establish the conversion; and finally, the related effects of selection—there are still other problems to face when we consider the equating of nonparallel tests. Particularly important are the problems of interpretation. For example, there is the danger that converted scores will be assumed to possess the reliability and validity of the scale of scores to which they are converted. While it should go without saying that scores on one test, however well they may be converted to another scale, retain all the basic characteristics of the original test, many test users will assume that, once converted, they should behave in all respects like the test whose scale they have adopted.

Obviously, this assumption is unjustified. It becomes evident that this is not an insignificant concern when we reflect that this kind of misinterpretation favors the publisher of the poorer, less reliable test. And it is probably safe to say that scores on the less reliable test would more often be converted to the scale of the more reliable test than vice versa.

Related to this is the very real worry that the existence of tables of comparable scores will favor the test that is readily available for purchase and is sanctioned by the publisher for administration under less secure and less carefully controlled conditions. Here, too, it is more likely that this test would be the one that is converted to the scale of the test in which only the highest standards of control are permitted in and out of the testing room than vice versa. Since it is also reasonable to assume that the test that is administered under less stringent conditions is the one that is likely to yield the higher score, it is easy to see that the candidate, say, for college admission, who is given the test under these conditions is the one who stands to gain in comparison with a competing candidate who is required to take the more secure test.

Another kind of error occurs in the interpretation of converted scores when regression methods are used for establishing the conversion line between two tests. Predicted scores are regressed, that is, they have a reduced standard deviation; original scores are unregressed. The pooling of these two kinds of data, one taken from actual obtained scores and the other taken from regressed scores, would be improper. Yet it is for the very purpose of pooling such data, or at least, considering them in conjunction, that conversion tables are ordinarily called for. Let us say, for example, that we have a conversion of this sort from ACE to SAT. It is interesting to note here that, to adopt the winning strategy, good students would be well advised to take the test that does not undergo this type of conversion—the SAT, that is—since, by doing so they will avoid the unfavorable effects of regression, in which scores at the upper end of the scale are characteristically depressed. *Their* scores will depend only on their own high level of performance. Poor students, on the other hand, would be well advised to take the ACE, because in the conversion to the SAT their scores would naturally be regressed upward toward the mean. Thus, by following this advice and taking advantage of statistical laws, they manage to achieve a higher score than they deserve—that is, a higher score than would be earned by students of the same ability who are not given this advice. It is important also to note that the lower the correlation between these tests the greater the extent of the regression and the greater the effect of the strategy. The other side of this coin is also worth noting: The good student would be ill advised to take the ACE because his score would also regress in the conversion process, but downward toward the mean.

There are other situations as well where it would be to a student's advantage to take into consideration the effects of regression. Suppose, for example, a table of comparable scores were developed for two tests of dissimilar validity by defining as equivalent those scores that yielded equal predicted scores on some single criterion, say college grades. Since scores on both tests would inevitably regress toward the mean and since the regression would be more pronounced for the less valid test, it is clear that the winning strategy for the poor student would be to take the less valid test, because it is on this test that his scores would undergo the greater upward regression. The opposite strategy would be appropriate for the good student. His scores would necessarily regress downward in the conversion process, but if he were circumspect and took the more valid test he would insure himself against substantial loss due to the effects of regression.

In spite of all that has been said so far, there are times, nevertheless, when it is reasonable and appropriate to derive tables of comparable scores for tests of different function. The methods of deriving these tables are much like, and in most instances identical to, the methods of equating scores on parallel tests. The ideal plan for equating would be one in which we would select a sample of individuals to whom we would administer both Forms X and Y and see to it that practice on the first form administered did not affect performance on the second form. However, since the ways of doing this are not immediately apparent, we find it more convenient to divide the group into random halves and give Form X to one half of the group and Form Y to the other half of the group. Then, making the assumption that there are no systematic differences between the groups, we equate the means and standard deviations on the two tests to produce a linear equation relating the two sets of scores. This procedure in effect says that we consider equivalent (or, in the present discussion, comparable) those scores that correspond to equal standard-score deviates. Or, if we wish, we can say that we consider comparable those scores that correspond to equal percentiles. Now, if the distributions on Form X and on Form Y have the same shape, then this latter procedure will result in a straight-line conversion quite similar to the one first described, which assumes that differences in shape are of no consequence. On the other hand, if the distributions are different, then this latter conversion will be curvilinear. Still another method is one in which half the group takes Form X followed by Form Y, the other half taking Y followed by X. Here the assumption is made that the effect of practice is constant and unrelated to score level, and also that the effect on Form Y performance (in terms of standard scores) is the same as the effect on Form X performance. Finally, the conversion between X and Y is achieved by averaging the means and variances on Form X and also on Form Y and setting them equal. Incidentally, the problem of practice effect is a troublesome one in the case of parallel tests. It is particularly troublesome in the case of nonparallel tests for the reason that, just as it is logically awkward to compare *performance* on tests that are not designed to measure the same thing, similarly it is logically awkward to compare *changes* on tests that are not designed to measure the same thing.

All other methods of equating that are known to be in frequent use involve the use of anchor tests in one way or another and are variations of a basic method developed by Ledyard R Tucker[1] and also by Frederic M. Lord (3)—but with different sets of assumptions. In all of these methods the tests X and Y are given to different groups; the function of the anchor test, which is given to both groups, is to adjust for any differences that may be observed in them. Most of these methods may also be used for deriving comparable scores between tests of different function. More recently—within the last two or three years—a method has been suggested by Lord[2] for making use of anchor tests in estimating frequency distributions for groups on tests that were not actually taken by those groups. This method has been adopted for use with the equipercentile method of equating tests, a method which heretofore was possible only in those situations where the tests could be administered to random groups. I should also add that anchor test scores may be used in a method of equipercentile equating that has been suggested by E. F. Lindquist.[3] In this method, scores on two tests are taken to be equivalent if they are found to be equivalent to the same score on an anchor test.

If we attempt to adapt these methods of equating to the problem of nonparallel tests and consider the restriction that was discussed before, that such a conversion is applicable only to the specific conditions under which it was derived, we find that the following questions are pertinent: 1) How similar are the tests for which comparable scores are to be developed? 2) How appropriate is the group on whom the table of comparable scores is based when one considers the person or the group for whom the table is to be used? And, 3) how much error can we safely tolerate in the particular use we have in mind? These questions are intentionally phrased in terms of degree, because this issue, like so many others, depends on the considera-

---

[1] The derivations for Tucker's equations can be found in Gulliksen (2, pp. 299–304).
[2] Personal communication.
[3] Personal communication.

tions of degree. Categorical answers are inappropriate. Thus, in considering the first of these three questions, if the tests are extremely different—if, say, one is a test of quantitative skills and the other is a measure of interest in sports—then, clearly, it would be absurd to contemplate a conversion that would make any sense at all. On the other hand, if one is a verbal test heavily loaded with items of the definition type, while the other is a test of reading comprehension, then it is certainly reasonable to consider a table of comparable scores for these two tests.

With regard to the second question, if the group on whom the table is based consists of seniors majoring in literature, and the group for whom we wish to use the conversion consists of high school sophomores enrolled in a manual training course, then obviously the use is inappropriate. On the other hand, if the groups are both freshmen in liberal arts in colleges that are similarly selective, then the use is probably appropriate.

The third question, which calls for a commitment to a maximum tolerable error, is fundamental to the entire issue. Commitments regarding the amount of difference between the tests that may be allowed and commitments regarding the difference that may be allowed between the groups under consideration depend ultimately on the demands for precision that are implied by the purpose of the conversion table.

Ordinarily we are confronted with the situation where the tests and the use for which a table of comparable scores is required may not be questioned or altered. In such instances we are free to choose the kind of group we wish to use in forming a conversion table, in order to achieve a degree of error that we say we are willing to tolerate. Three such groups are: 1) the national norms group; 2) a set of differentiated norms groups; and 3) the local norms group. A fourth method—of basing a table of comparable scores on a group of people for whom data happen to be convenient and available—is simply to go through the motions of deriving a table of comparable scores without considering its meaning. The usefulness of such a table—if there is any—is extremely restricted.

Of the various kinds of comparable scores, the one based on differentiated norms groups is probably the most defensible. This procedure would yield a number of conversion tables, each based on, and appropriate for, a different norms group. If the tests are measures of the same psychological function, then the various conversion tables will, for all practical purposes, be the same. However, if the tests are measuring different functions, then there will be as many conversions as there are distinguishable and different norms groups. Each conversion, like a profile, will be descriptive of the group on which it is based and applicable only to that group. The user will be forced to choose the appropriate table with care, keeping in mind the group for which he intends to use it and the purpose for which it is to be applied.

The local norms approach to comparable scores is similar to the one involving differentiated norms, and is in general as highly recommended for the purpose of comparable scores as are local norms distributions themselves for the purpose of evaluating relative status. Here the cautions that need to be exercised are: 1) that the group has not been directly selected on either of the scores involved in the conversion; 2) that there are sufficient cases to yield reliable conversions; and 3) that they be applied only in the school where they were developed or in schools known to be similar to it.

The national norms approach is probably the least satisfactory of all, for the reason that it is not likely to be highly appropriate except when the tests in question are quite similar in function. Its primary advantage, however, is that it is the most readily applied method of obtaining rough conversion tables, if for no other reason than the fact that national norms for tests are generally readily available. The significant concern here is that none of the students on whom the comparable scores are based took both the tests in question, and that the norms groups for the different tests may not have been selected in the same fashion in order to satisfy even approximately the requirement of randomly equivalent groups that is ordinarily imposed in parallel-forms equating. And even if they were so selected, there is enough unreliability in norms samples to introduce serious errors in the tables of comparable scores. There are situations in which errors of given magnitude are tolerable in norms, but not at all tolerable in tables of comparable scores—again, of course, depending on the intended use of the tables.

I would like also to mention a method that is appropriate for developing comparable scores for situations in which candidates are permitted to take the particular test that is most appropriate to their own curricular background or interests. As applied to the achievement tests in the College Board program, the procedure is to correlate the SAT-Verbal and Mathematical scores with each achievement test, and use them in combination as a composite control or anchor test in estimating the achievement test performance of a group with certain defined characteristics, as measured by the SAT. The purpose of all this statistical work is to relate the scores on the various achievement tests to one another and to the SAT-Verbal and Mathematical scale, and to enable us to say, for example, that a 600 score on the French test is comparable, in the sense defined by the statistical method, to a 600 score on the physics test. Obviously, there are logical difficulties in expressing this comparability, as there would be with any comparability, and perhaps more than there would be with most. However, because of the way in which the achievement test scores are used, and have to be used, by the admissions officers, some kind of comparable scores must be prepared. And of the various kinds that are available, this one, which balances out the effects of differential selection for each of the groups that take the various achievement tests, has obvious advantages.

Another approach to the question of comparable scores involves the use of the ordinary correlation and prediction model. This method has at times been suggested for use with tests at the same grade level in order to provide interchangeable scores on different tests. However, as described earlier, it is clearly inappropriate here because it fails in its very purpose. One of the scores is actual and the other is regressed; they cannot be interchanged. On the other hand, when the tests are designed for different grade levels, then the method does have merit. For example, an attempt has been made to use the regression model for relating scores on the Cooperative School and College Ability Test taken in the early years of secondary school to scores earned on the SAT in the twelfth grade. Since these results will be used solely as predictions—to enable students to get a preliminary idea of how well they may expect to do on a test used to select college freshmen—and not to merge or compare them with actual scores, the dangers that were described as inherent in regressed scores are not present here. Furthermore, since the presentation lays great stress on the presence of errors of estimate, it is felt that misinterpretations will be kept to a minimum.

In general, the different uses of comparable scores require different levels of precision. Where, for example, the need for comparable scores arises from a desire to use scores on different tests interchangeably for admissions purposes, the highest degree of precision is required for comparability. Otherwise, a college which gives serious consideration to test scores in admissions decisions might find itself admitting too large a proportion of applicants from one group or another because of the use of an inappropriate conversion table. On the other hand, when scores on different tests are used interchangeably for placement purposes, the demand for precision is less serious, since erroneous placements can be corrected early in the course. Also, the use of conversion tables for estimating the comparative abilities of *groups* of individuals is one that does not ordinarily require a high degree of precision. For one thing, in such comparisons the careers of individuals are seldom at stake (as would be true in admissions decisions). For another, it is a characteristic of conversions that there is relatively little error at the mean. In contrast to this, conversions of scores for individuals of high or low ability are much more likely to be in error.

It probably bears repetition that the problem of comparable scores is simply another one of many other problems about which it is impossible to make categorical evaluations that hold fast in all situations. If the decisions that are made on the basis of a table of comparable scores are made in the central region of the distribution, if the tests are relatively similar in function, if they have approximately equal reliabilities and validities, and finally, if generalizations are restricted to the kind of group that formed the basis of the conversion in the first place, these are the conditions that allow the free use of comparable scores. To demand that all these conditions hold is undoubtedly unrealistic and unnecessarily restrictive as well. At the same time, if, in any instance, too few of these conditions are operative, then testing organizations would probably do well to heed the advice that they like to give their test users, and proceed with caution.

REFERENCES

1. Campbell, H. W., Gibel, Inge B., & Pearson, R. *A survey of the use of test in the 11th and 12th grades.* New York: College Entrance Examination Board, 1960.
2. Gulliksen, H. *Theory of mental tests.* New York: Wiley, 1950.
3. Lord, F. M. Equating test scores—a maximum likelihood solution. *Psychometrika,* 1955, 20, 193–200.
4. Olsen, Marjorie. Relationship between Graduate Record Examinations Aptitude Test and Scholastic Aptitude Test. Unpublished manuscript, Educational Testing Service, Princeton, N.J., 1961.
5. Womer, F. B. Pros and cons of external testing programs. *North Central Association Quarterly,* 1961, 36, 201–210.

Norms and the Individual Pupil

LEE J. CRONBACH

1948

Achievement tests are most often used to evaluate the educational development of a pupil. The teacher or counselor who refers to a norm table receives insufficient help, because the table does not give an adequate answer to the question, "Is this pupil doing as well as we should expect of him?" Often, the teacher must stop with the judgment that John is doing superior work, and that, since John is a superior student, everything must be in order. But John might be much less above average than his ability permits. And Sam, who is a below average student, may be dismissed without further thought, whereas a careful study of the evidence might show that he was really performing "over his head," or falling below reasonable expectation for such a subaverage student.

I would propose that we consider practical methods of providing achievement norms for different types of students. For some purposes, we need merely to compare the pupil with a large and representative group of the same age or grade who have had comparable experience. But usually we wish to decide if he is doing as well as others *like himself*. The teacher has been able, in the past, to look at the results for his class and, if they fell below the tabled norms, to stop with the easy evaluation that his group was weak to start with. If he had measures showing just how weak his pupils were initially, and we could supply evidence of how such weak pupils have performed in the standardizing groups, we would help him and impel him to think far more rigorously about the adequacy of the educational program he is operating.

This suggestion boils down to the following procedures. One or more reference tests would be given. As reference we might use a measure of mental age, of general educational development in the field, or a pretest of the sort we are norming. Then the evaluating test would be given. We would prepare a scatter diagram relating the evaluating test, on the Y-axis, to the reference test, on the X-axis. By plotting best-fit lines through the median of each vertical array, through the ninetieth percentile of each array, and so on, we would be able to provide a simple chart of norms. The teacher would interpret the performance of a pupil by entering the chart with his X-score and reading his standing on the achievement test in comparison to others equal to him on the reference test.

This is not especially complicated for the teacher. Trimble and I (3) worked on methods of this sort with pretest-posttest data for certain Progressive Education Association tests and found that such graphic norms are readily interpreted. The proposal does involve additional work for the test standardizer, but in many cases the essential data are available in his files and the analysis can be done with little cost.

The first question we need to consider is: What shall we use as a reference test? The general answer would be: any variable likely to be correlated with performance. We already apply the principle of differentiated norms when we prepare separate norms for sex, age, or grade groups. Ordinarily, the most helpful reference test would be a measure of mental age (not IQ) or a pretest of the behavior being evaluated. When several tests are given simultaneously, as in a fall testing program, performance in each ability measured might well be referred against "general mental ability" or "verbal ability" as a reference. The producers of the Differential Aptitude Tests, for example, have normed all their tests on the same sample and could easily produce charts of differentiated norms. I would suggest a broad search for helpful reference variables. Allison Davis'[1] studies suggest strongly that separate norms for pupils of various social-class levels would stimulate teachers to do better teaching. If a pupil, although not outstanding according to general norms, is found to be quite superior considering his impoverished social background, a teacher is far more likely to put her heart into stimulating him. Other variables may prove equally significant for reference purposes.

This proposal does not conflict with the very desirable current trend toward providing separate norms for various types of schools or various curricula. But there are some interesting studies of how various types of pupils profit from different modes of instruction. They show that a particular change of method may lower the learning expectancy of one pupil while raising that of another. So there is a strong argument for norms by types of pupils within norms differentiated by curricula.

For what tests should we differentiate norms? In general, whenever there is a significant correlation between an achievement test and a sensible refer-

[1] See Eells, Davis, *et al.* (1)—Ed.

ence variable. In fact, I would go further and provide differentiated norms for all guidance tests. One interprets mechanical aptitudes, for example, in relation to general academic ability, when making recommendations to a boy. Differentiated norms would reduce the subjectivity of such pattern interpretation.

Let us consider the relation of this proposal to the popular profile method. Profiles are becoming more useful as we get more sets of tests with norms based on comparable groups. But profiles are easily misinterpreted because of the regression fallacy. The differentiated norm chart automatically takes care of the factor of regression, and in that way is able to avoid the pitfalls of the achievement quotient.[2] And by emphasizing differential interpretation, I hope it would make test designers more conscious of the need for high reliability. The interpretation of profiles is severely complicated when the tests in the profile are unequally reliable, because the profile of true scores differs from that of the raw scores. Finally, I may refer to our common experience that a test profile changes markedly when a different norm group is used. It appears sound to contend that the most meaningful profile is that derived by comparing the pupil with others like himself.

I recognize that I am passing over endless technical complications involved in this proposal. Some of these are: How can you standardize when every publisher will use a different test as a reference variable? How do you make a sensible reference variable out of such a complex mixture as general mental ability? How can you keep the system within bounds, when there are several possible reference variables for a given achievement test? How can you use growth norms, when the time interval between tests varies from school to school? And so on. But the main point is that we are giving test users only a portion of the information that would be valuable to them, and that we could give them a lot more if we tried, with little extra cost. I wouldn't worry too much if our next type of norms is still only approximately utopian.

My concern about differential norms has been enhanced through recent experience with the Rorschach test. That, of course, is a test where norms are in an exceedingly primitive stage. I have been using the test with superior adolescents and adults: people with IQ's in the range of 120 to 160. When I try to make sense of a given score, all that is available to me is

---

[2] Since the original publication of this paper, various sorts of expectancy tables and differentiated norms have appeared in test manuals; a particularly good example is found in the manual for the California Achievement Tests. It should be noted that scores expressed as deviations from a regression line do not necessarily correspond closely to the deviation scores that would be obtained if true scores on the measures were available (2); but this appears not to be a problem when deviations are converted to percentiles within an array.

some investigator's finding that the normal person of a given age gives, say, 35 to 50 per cent F responses. Now I find my cases giving 60 to 80 per cent F responses. What do I conclude? Only that they are different from the norm group. But I knew that to start with. The question I need to answer is whether my subjects differ, in the emotional characteristics the Rorschach allegedly reveals, from other people of the same high intellectual ability. There is no solution save to go out and prepare separate norms for a representative sample of highly superior individuals. While the Rorschach is certainly off our beaten track, I suspect that the same problem, in less striking form, is handicapping interpretation of much more prosaic tests of mathematics, interpretation of literature, and social attitudes.

REFERENCES

1. Eells, K., Davis, A., *et al. Intelligence and cultural differences.* Chicago: Univer. of Chicago Press, 1951.
2. Harris, C. W. (Ed.) *Problems in measuring change.* Madison, Wisc.: Univer. of Wisconsin Press, 1963.
3. Trimble, H. C., & Cronbach, L. J. A practical procedure for the rigorous interpretation of test-retest scores in terms of pupil growth. *Journal of Educational Research,* 1943, 36, 481–488.

Norms of Achievement
By Schools

E. F. Lindquist
1948

What I have to say is not at all profound, and I should be able to say it in just two or three minutes. As elementary as is the observation I have to make, however, judging from current test standardization practices and from the literature on testing, it is one that is sorely in need of stressing even in as sophisticated a group as this one.

What I wish to do is to put in a plug for a special type of norm for educational achievement tests. It is a type of norm which, in consideration of the major uses generally made of achievement tests, should always be provided with tests of that character, but one which in actuality is very rarely provided.

Let me remind you first of two major uses which we generally claim for educational achievement tests. First, we claim that these tests will provide the teacher and counselor with a more adequate and dependable basis for the educational guidance of the individual pupil and for the individualization of instruction. Second, we claim that these tests will be useful to the school administrator as a partial basis for evaluating the content and methods of instruction, or in curriculum evaluation in general.

Now with reference to the first of these purposes, quite obviously we need norms that are descriptive of the distributions of measures of achievement of pupils. We interpret a pupil's score by comparing it with the scores of other pupils in the relatively homogeneous population to which he belongs. The second purpose, however, is the evaluation of *group*, not of individual, achievement. What the principal wants to know is, "How are we doing as a school?" or "How does this grade group compare in *average* achievement in relation to other similar grade groups?" Quite obviously, what is needed here is a type of norm that is descriptive of distributions of measures of group achievement, i.e., of distributions of school averages, not of distributions of individual pupil scores.

Since such norms are rarely provided, what the school principal does is to attempt to interpret his grade averages or grade medians in terms of the norms that *are* provided—norms descriptive only of distributions of pupil scores. What he really does, without often knowing that he is doing so, is to assume that the school averages are distributed just as are individual pupil scores. School averages, of course, are much less variable than pupil scores (although not as much less as many may assume), and he immediately makes wrong interpretations of his results on that account. A school average that coincides with the 75th percentile in the pupil score distribution, for example, might be a remarkably high average, but since it is "at the 75th percentile," it might not be regarded as high by the principal. What he does would not be so serious, however, if there were a constant relationship between the variability of school averages and the variability of pupil scores. In that case he could at least tell on what tests his school did well in relation to other schools, and could rank the tests in order of the relative performance of his school, even though he would be misled as to the true relative performance on any one test. Actually, however, the relationship is not constant, but varies widely from subject to subject and from one grade level to another.

I have with me here some data concerning the relative variability of individual pupil scores and of school means for 34 widely used achievement tests. I am not going to read all of these data to you but will just give you a sample of them. They are all based on large numbers of cases—in no instance upon less than 193 schools, in some cases as many as 400, and in no case less than 6,000 pupils—so the results are quite stable so far as sampling errors are concerned.

The tests include tests of elementary school achievement, such as the Iowa Tests of Basic Skills, and tests of high school achievement, such as the Cooperative subject achievement tests.

In the first place, let me say that, in every case, the variability of school means is far larger than would be the variability of means of random samples of the same size drawn from the same total population. If, in any case, one were to make a simple analysis of the total variance into "between schools" and "within schools" components, one would find that the "between schools" variance is from two to ten times as large as that which could be accounted for by random sampling alone. The ratio would vary greatly, however, from test to test.

In third-grade arithmetic (Iowa Tests of Basic Skills) the ratio of the 10th to the 90th percentile range for school averages and for pupil scores is exactly .5. For sixth-grade arithmetic it jumps to .55, but for third-grade language it is .36. For a high school physics test the ratio is .61, while for a United States history test at the same grade level it is .37. In general, the ratio seems to be largest where the opportunity to learn what is tested is relatively restricted to the classroom and to the formal school curriculum, and to be least where the achievement measured might more often result from out-of-school experiences and informal learning.

Well, I think I have said enough to make my point. School averages are less variable than pupil scores, but much more variable than the means of random samples. More important, the relative variability of school averages differs markedly from test to test and grade to grade. If school administrators, then, are to interpret properly measures of *school* achievement for purposes of curriculum evaluation or for the evaluation of group achievement in general, they must be supplied with norms specifically adapted to that purpose—i.e., they must have norms descriptive of distributions of school *averages* for defined populations of schools, just as for the interpretation of individual achievement they now have norms descriptive of distributions of pupil scores for defined populations of pupils.

The Importance of Reference Groups in Scaling Procedure

ERIC F. GARDNER

1952

It is commonly accepted that a single, isolated test score is of little or no value. For a score to have meaning and be of social or scientific utility, some sort of frame of reference is needed. A number of different frames of reference have been proposed and been found to have value. In view of the fact that this session is devoted to a consideration of the scaling of tests *with* and *without* emphasis on a reference population, it is the purpose of this paper to present some of the more common scaling methods, and to comment on the role played by the underlying population.

ROLE OF POPULATION IN SCALING TEST SCORES

A familiar frame of reference is provided by the performance of individuals in a single well-defined group on a particular test at a particular time. Two commonly used types of scales have been derived within such a frame of reference. The simplest are ordinal scales, such as percentile scores, in which the scale number describes relative position in a group. The simplicity of percentile scores is also their limitation: they do not have algebraic utility. The second type are interval scales where an effort has been made to obtain algebraic utility by definition. The T scores of McCall represent an interval scale where equal units have been defined as equal distances along the abscissa of a postulated normal population frequency distribution.

A second type of frame of reference is provided by the test performance of individuals belonging to well-defined subgroups where the subgroups have a specific relationship to each other within the composite group. Within this frame of reference, both ordinal and interval scales have been derived. Initially, the basic problem is to obtain ordinally related subgroups, such as grades one to nine or age groups from a specified population for the scaling operation. Age scores and grade scores provide ordinal scales that have had wide utility in the elementary grades. Attempts have been made to obtain the merits of an algebraically manipulatable scale by utilizing ordinal relationship of subgroups but introducing restrictions in terms of the shape of the frequency distributions. Efforts to obtain interval scales within such frames of reference have been made by Flanagan (1) in the development of the Scaled Scores of the Cooperative tests, and by the speaker in the development of K scores (3). Cooperative Scaled Scores are based on the assumption of overlapping normal distribution of ability groups, and K scores on the assumption that overlapping grade distributions can be represented by Pearson Type III curves.

The importance of the particular reference population which is used to determine any such scales cannot be overemphasized. A person scoring at the 84th percentile or obtaining a T score of 60 in an arithmetic test where the score is calculated for a typical seventh grade is obviously not performing equally to one whose standing at the 84th percentile on the same test is calculated for a below-average seventh grade. Likewise, a pupil with a vocabulary grade score of 5.2 obtained from a representative sample of fifth graders in, say, Mississippi, is certainly not comparable to a pupil making a score of 5.2 based on a national, representative sample. The importance of the particular population in determining the fundamental reference point and size of unit is stressed by the originators of both Cooperative Scaled Scores and K scores. The ratio between the variabilities of overlapping groups in both Scaled Scores and K scores is a function of the areas cut off in samples of the overlapping groups by the same points in each of the overlapping distributions. Hence, this important characteristic of the basic units in each type of scale depends upon the particular sample selected since it is highly probable that overlapping distributions selected from different populations will have different amounts of overlap at points along the scale.

Psychophysical scaling procedures are also sometimes applied to achievement testing. It is to be noted that resulting scales such as sensed difference units which are based on just-noticeable-differences or equally-often-noted-differences are a function not only of the pupils tested, but also of the sample of persons making the required judgments.

PROPERTIES OF SCALE DEPENDENT UPON PURPOSE AND DERIVATION

Tests scores are used by administrators, teachers, and research workers to make comparisons in terms of rank, level of development, growth, and trait differences among both individuals and groups. Hence many types of scales have been developed depending upon the intended use. Each is consistent within itself, but the properties of the scales are not completely consistent from one type of scale to another. For example, a grade scale is not appropriate for measuring growth in a function, unless one is willing to accept the assumption that growth is linearly related to grade. K scores, which were designed to provide an interval scale for measuring growth during the elementary school within a particular school subject, are not comparable from one school subject to another, unless one is willing to assume a common growth for all the subjects being compared. Furthermore, the adoption of a uniform standard deviation of seven K units for fifth-grade distributions defines as equal the variability of fifth-grade performance in all functions. The scaling of the Binet items involves the assumption of a linear relationship between Mental Age and Chronological Age. As valuable and useful as the Binet scale has been for the purpose for which it was designed, it has obvious limitations when we try to infer the "true" nature of intellectual growth.

SCALING STABILITY IN LARGE REPRESENTATIVE POPULATIONS

Scales derive their properties in two ways—by definition and experimental verification. Using K scores as an example, let us consider two desirable properties of a scale: 1) that it shall be invariant with respect to the sample of items used, and 2) that it be invariant with respect to the population used in its derivation. The first property is inherent in the definition of K scores and in the specific definitions of other scores, such as Cooperative Scaled Scores. That is, since K scores are defined by the amount of overlap between adjacent grade distributions, any test of a function that will reliably rank the scaling sample in the same way will give rise to exactly the same set of K scores.

For example, the K scores obtained from Stanford Achievement Word Meaning test data would be identical to the K scores obtained from the Metropolitan Vocabulary test data, provided all children in the grade range scaled were ranked in the same order by both tests.

The second property mentioned is not necessarily inherent in K scores in terms of their derivation. With suitable attention to sampling problems, it is reasonable to expect to obtain scales with reproducible properties from one sample to another. In contrast, such reproducibility is not expected from population to population. There are, however, practical situations in which it would be useful to have a scale invariant with respect to more than

TABLE 1

K Score Means, Standard Deviations, and Skewnesses for Each Grade at End of School Year on Stanford Achievement Test Form D, Arithmetic Reasoning, Given in 1940, and Form J, Given in 1952

Grade	Mean K Score		Difference between grade means		Standard Deviation		Skewness	
	Form D (1940)	Form J (1952)	Form D (1940)	Form J (1952)	Form D (1940)	Form J (1952)	Form D (1940)	Form J (1952)
9	100.0	100.0			11.5	18.1	.73	.86
			2.2	5.3				
8	97.8	94.7			11.2	16.3	.86	.85
			6.5	8.4				
7	91.3	86.3			8.8	11.7	.85	.68
			5.0	7.6				
6	86.3	78.7			8.8	8.8	.38	.45
			5.8	5.2				
5	80.5	73.5			7.0	7.0	.53	.32
			5.2	5.6				
4	75.3	67.9			4.9	6.0	.34	.23
			4.9	5.6				
3	70.4	62.3			4.1	4.2	−.06	−.34
			4.4	4.8				
2	66.0	57.5			3.2	3.3	.16	−.01

a single population. For example, since achievement tests are used for measuring growth and comparing the performance of groups over a long period of time (8 to 10 years), it would be desirable to have a scale that would be invariant with respect to national samples taken annually. Any such property of K scores or any other scale must be established on an empirical or experimental basis. Such stability from one population to another is evidenced in recent efforts to apply K-score scaling to the 1952 edition of the Stanford Achievement Test.

Grade means, differences in grade means, grade standard deviations, and grade skewnesses expressed in K units determined from the performance of the national normative sample obtained in 1952 on Form J of the 1952 revision of the Stanford Achievement Test are compared in Table 1 with the corresponding statistics expressed in K units determined from the 1940 national normative sample on Form D of the Stanford Achievement Test.

A K unit is defined as one-seventh the standard deviation of the national grade five frequency distribution in any trait where Pearson Type III curves have been fitted to it and to the adjacent grades in such a way that the proportion of cases in each grade exceeding each raw score is the same as that found in the original data. The mean performance of children in the

United States after completing the ninth grade was selected as the reference point, and assigned a K score of 100.

The 1940 sample in terms of which the 1948 K units were defined consisted of approximately 50,000 cases, and was itself a 20 per cent random sample selected from about 300,000 pupils to whom the Stanford Achievement Test (Form D) was administered at the end of the school year in 1940. The sample appeared representative of the national elementary school population with respect to sex, IQ, age, and geographical location.

The sample in terms of which the 1952 K units for arithmetic reasoning were defined consists of approximately 94,000 cases, and was selected from a sample of about 460,000 pupils to whom the 1952 Stanford Achievement Test (Form J) was administered in April and May 1952. Communities were selected to give a representative national sample in terms of size and geographical location according to the United States census. All pupils in at least three consecutive grades in those communities were tested, and a 20 per cent sample of these examinees was taken at random from each class tested within those communities.

In order to compare the results obtained when K units in arithmetic reasoning were derived independently from each population, let us now examine: 1) the average growth in arithmetic reasoning from grade to grade; 2) the extent to which the variability in arithmetic reasoning changes as children progress through the grades; 3) the effect of progress on the skewness of the grade distributions; and 4) whether the fitted curves approximate normal curves.

Although it is commonly believed that growth in specific subjects in the elementary and junior high schools is not constant from grade to grade, the objective verification of this belief has been difficult due to lack of an interval scale extending over the range of grades. The differences in mean achievement (in terms of K scores) of successive grades of the 1940 sample and the 1952 sample in arithmetic reasoning are given respectively in the fourth and fifth columns of Table 1. These differences are indicative approximately of the amount of growth in the trait measured in the particular grade listed.[1]

The relative change in variability of the performance of children in successive grades has also been difficult to determine, due to the lack of an in-

---

[1] However, since the pupils in each grade were different from those in other grades, these differences in grade means may be considered as growth only to the extent that we are willing to consider, for example, the present third graders as comparable to what the second graders will become a year hence. True growth could be determined by measuring the same children with comparable instruments in terms of K units at different grade levels as they progress through school.

terval scale extending over the range of grades. The standard deviation in terms of K units of each grade in arithmetic reasoning for the 1940 sample and the 1952 sample are given in columns six and seven of Table 1.

One of the major findings presented in a paper given at the 1948 Invitational Conference on Testing Problems (2) was the *consistent increase* in variability in two arithmetic traits from the second grade to the ninth in contrast with two verbal traits in which the standard deviations were *nearly constant*. The present study supports the previous finding concerning increased variability from grade to grade in arithmetic reasoning. The standard deviation in grade two is 3.3 K units, while in grade nine it has increased to 18.1 K units. Thus one of the several implications one can draw is that as children progress through the grades, the problems of the arithmetic teacher increase in that the groups become more heterogeneous.

The skewness of each grade for each sample is given by columns eight and nine. In the 1948 paper, no consistent skewness trends comparable to those observed for grade standard deviations were evidenced. In the present situation, there does appear to be an increase in skewness from grade to grade, with a single reversal between grades two and three. These data coupled with the previously reported data (2) would lead one to believe that the assumption of normality for every grade distribution is not as tenable a hypothesis as the assumption that the grade distributions are skewed.

The data in Table 2, which were published in the *Proceedings of the 1948*

TABLE 2

K Score Means, Standard Deviations, and Skewnesses for Each Grade at End of School Year on Stanford Achievement Test, Form D, Paragraph Meaning, Given in 1940

Grade	Mean K Score	Difference between grade means	Standard Deviation	Skewness
9	100.0		8.0	.29
		3.7		
8	96.3		7.5	.44
		3.4		
7	92.9		7.0	.50
		3.7		
6	89.2		7.2	−.39
		4.1		
5	85.1		7.0	−.10
		4.8		
4	80.3		6.7	.18
		6.5		
3	73.8		7.1	−.40
		6.6		
2	67.2		6.4	.31

Invitational Conference on Testing Problems (2, p. 74), have been included to show the contrasting results obtained between arithmetic functions (arithmetic reasoning) and a second function (paragraph meaning) when measurements are made in terms of K scores.

Considering the facts that different tests were used, and also samples from different populations reflecting the lapse of a 12-year period which included World War II with resulting dislocations of pupils and teachers and many curriculum changes, it seems to the author that discrepancies in the *pattern of differences* in grade means and grade variabilities in the two sets of arithmetic reasoning data are minor compared with the general pattern of agreement.

ROLE OF POPULATION IN SCALING INDIVIDUAL ITEMS

The problems involved in the scaling of individual test items are similar to those of scaling test scores in that an item may be considered as a test that represents a smaller sample of behavior than the total test score. One of the most widely used scales in which individual items were scaled is the Terman-Merrill scale for the Stanford Binet (5). Items were located on this scale as a result of the performance of well-selected age groups. In his recently developed latent structure analysis, Lazarsfeld (4) has presented scaling methods that involve the assumption of a polynomial trace line for each item. The responses of the sample of people to the item are used to determine the parameters necessary to define the scale. In all cases, the empirical data that define the scale are dependent upon the reference population used.

In some instances, scaling based on total test score is preceded by a scaling or partial scaling of items. In the Stanford Achievement Test, difficulty indices for each item were computed for well-defined and well-described grade groups. A test composed of these items was then administered to a national sample of each grade group, and various types of scales based upon the total score were obtained.

GENERAL CONSIDERATIONS

In conclusion, this paper has attempted to achieve two objectives: 1) to review some of the more common scaling techniques and emphasize the importance of the role of the reference population; and 2) to illustrate that stable results can be obtained with different large reference populations, as shown by an empirical study on the comparability of arithmetic reasoning

K scales based on two national samples of elementary school children taken 12 years apart and obtained from two distinct, though similar, instruments.

It is to be noted that not only in the argument of this paper but in the development of *K* scores (our major illustration), the reference populations have assumed major and fundamental importance. The acceptance of comparable scales utilizing different methods, different populations, or both is dependent upon empirical verification.

Situations where there is internal consistency within a number of frames of reference, but inconsistency of properties from one frame of reference to another, are not unique to scaling. There are excellent analogies in the field of geometry. The geometries of Euclid, Riemann, and Lobachevsky, each of which is based on a different postulate about parallel lines, are consistent internally, but have certain properties that are inconsistent from one geometry to another. Each of these geometries has its own value and utility as a logical model. The utility of any particular one is determined by the appropriateness or adequacy of the basic postulates to the problem at hand.

One of the objectives of the scientist is to bring together, reconcile, and synthesize as many theories and concepts as possible. In the testing field, we follow the usual pattern of establishing scales to fit a particular need, and then attempt to synthesize the properties of the various scales designed for different purposes. On occasion, we find that for complete synthesis we either have to abandon a desirable property or utilize an unacceptable relationship.

Although we continually strive for a single scale with the maximum of desirable properties, it would seem inadvisable to abandon useful scales designed for a specific purpose merely because they are not adequate for additional purposes for which they were not designed.

It should be emphasized that the adoption by a test user of any one of the scales available does not exclude the use of any of the others. In fact, the use of more than one type of scale leads to more adequate interpretation of results in most situations.

REFERENCES

1. Flanagan, J. C. *The Cooperative achievement tests: a bulletin reporting the basic principles and procedures used in the development of their system of scaled scores.* New York: Cooperative Test Service, American Council on Education, 1939.

2. Gardner, E. F. Value of norms based on a new type of scale unit. *Proceedings of the 1948 Invitational Conference on Testing Problems.* Princeton, N.J.: Educational Testing Service, 1949. Pp. 67–74.

3. Gardner, E. F. Comments on selected scaling techniques with a description of a new type of scale. *Journal of Clinical Psychology,* 1950, 6, 38–43.

4. Lazarsfeld, P. F. The logical and mathematical foundation of latent structure analysis; the interpretation and computation of some latent structures. In S. A. Stouffer (Ed.), *Studies in social psychology in World War II.* Vol. 4. *Measurement and prediction.* Princeton, N.J.: Princeton Univer. Press, 1950. Pp. 362–472.

5. McNemar, Q. *The revision of the Stanford-Binet scale: an analysis of the standardization data.* Boston: Houghton Mifflin, 1942.

7 · RELIABILITY, VALIDITY, AND HOMOGENEITY

FROM THE OUTSET, test reliability has been a topic of concern at the Invitational Conferences. The papers by Richardson in 1940 and Horst in 1941 were cited in Chapter 1. At the 1946 conference, Thorndike surveyed methodological problems in the measurement of reliability, with special reference to the experimental procedures followed in gathering the raw data with which reliability coefficients are computed. Among the questions considered were: whether to sample time, situations, or other parameters; whether to measure reliability separately in subgroups at different ability levels; and whether to report the absolute consistency of an individual's score or the consistency of his relative position in a group. Special problems encountered in measuring the reliability of speed tests and of tests significantly affected by learning or by insight were also examined.

In 1963, Thorndike was again invited to discuss test reliability. In the opening paper of this chapter, he reports on developments during the seventeen-year interval. Finding no significant innovations in data-gathering procedures, Thorndike concentrates on changes in conceptual formulation and in corresponding mathematical models. He contrasts the classical concept of reliability in terms of "true score" and "error of measurement" with the newer concept based on the sampling of a universe of possible scores, and he discusses the difficulties met in defining this universe. He also notes that the application of the sampling concept leads ultimately to the merging of reliability and validity into a single concept of generalizability. With regard to mathematical models, he points out that the change to a sampling concept has been paralleled by a shift to analysis of variance and intraclass correlation.

As noted in Chapter 1, validity has received somewhat less attention than reliability at the Invitational Conferences. Particularly in the early years, the predominant interest at the conferences was in achievement tests, where questions of validity are relatively minor and present rather atypical problems. The first scheduled paper on validity was that given by Rulon at the 1946 conference. In it, Rulon discussed several aspects of content validity, although he did not employ this term. It was not until the publication of the *Technical Recommendations* in 1954 that these procedures were formally designated as content validation.

Gulliksen's 1950 paper, reproduced in this chapter, again concentrates on the validation of achievement tests. His discussion, however, has broader implications for criterion analysis as a whole, since the procedures he proposes for evaluating achievement tests are applicable to the evaluation of any criterion measure, such as school grades or supervisory ratings. In this paper, Gulliksen introduces his concept of "intrinsic validity of a criterion." Reversing the usual direction of validation, he shows how achievement tests (or other criterion measures) can be evaluated in terms of their relationships to aptitude or predictor tests. Other procedures he recommends include an analysis of the effects of training or experience upon criterion measures and an examination of the relation between immediate criterion measures and the individual's subsequent performance in related tasks.

Carroll's paper, given at the same 1950 symposium on procedures for the evaluation of achievement tests, is concerned with the general problem of test homogeneity. This is a concept that is often confused with either reliability or validity. It should actually be defined and measured in its own right, as an important test characteristic that influences the meaning of test scores. When items are highly heterogeneous, the same total score may represent a very different performance pattern on the part of different individuals. Carroll shows the difficulties encountered with certain previously proposed indices of homogeneity, and goes on to develop a more generally applicable technique.

In the next paper, Saunders describes the utilization of moderator variables to improve the predictive validity of tests. Essentially, a moderator variable may be regarded as any population characteristic (such as age, sex, socioeconomic level, or scores on other tests) that in turn affects the validity of a given test. Thus if the population is divided into subgroups in terms of such a variable, the validity of the same test may differ widely from one subgroup to another. Today, moderator variables are of particular interest because of the widespread concern regarding the use of tests with various subgroups of the general population, especially culturally disadvantaged subgroups. The empirical investigation of moderator variables in the interpretation of test scores is a more constructive approach than the evasive procedures of so-called culture-free tests. Saunders' illustrations are taken from personality variables; but his techniques could be used equally well with demographic and background variables.

In the last paper of the chapter, Anastasi gives a rapid overview of developments in the measurement and interpretation of validity since the publication of the first edition of the *Technical Recommendations* in 1954. In contrast to discussions of validity at early Invitational Conferences, this paper concentrates on the validation of aptitude and personality tests rather than achievement tests. Five topics pertaining to test validity are singled out for special consideration: construct validation, decision theory, moderator variables, synthetic validity, and response styles.

Reliability

ROBERT L. THORNDIKE

1963

The issues of test reliability may be approached, it has seemed to me, at three levels. The first of these is the verbal level of formulation and definition of the concept. A second level is that of mathematical model-building, leading to specification of a set of formulas and computational procedures by which the parameters specified in the model are to be estimated. A third level is that of experimental data-gathering procedures, under which certain tests are given to certain subjects at certain times and treated in certain ways to yield scores that are the raw materials to which we apply our formulas and computational procedures.

Developments in the past seventeen years appear to have been primarily at the first two of these levels. In fact, Oscar Buros, addressing the American Educational Research Association last year, expressed the view that the last thirty-five years have been retrogressive, so far as our empirical procedures for appraising reliability are concerned. He exhorted us to return to the virtuous ways of our forefathers and stick to the operation of testing the individual with two or more experimentally independent tests, in order to get the data which permit generalizations about precision of measurement over occasions as well as over test items, and to this I can only say "Amen." He urged us not to backslide from the high standards of precision that Truman Kelley laid down for us in 1927, and to this I would comment, "It all depends." But my point is that I am not aware of any distinctive proposals for new patterns of data-gathering that call for our special attention today, though it is always well that we be aware of the limitations of the methods we are using.

Turning now to verbal formulation, perhaps the major trend has been toward increasingly explicit formulation of the concept that performance on a test should be thought of as a sample from a defined universe of events, and that reliability is concerned with the precision with which the test score, that is, the sample, represents the universe. I shall not try to be a historian, but will merely note that this idea has been made fairly explicit by Buros, by Cronbach, by Tryon, and probably by others.

What we may call the "classical" approach to reliability tended to be conceptualized in terms of some unobservable underlying "true score" distorted in a given measurement by an equally unobservable "error of measurement." The corresponding mathematical models and computational routines were procedures for estimating the magnitude, absolute or relative, of this measurement error. The formulation in terms of sampling does away in one lightning stoke with the mystical "true score," somehow enshrined far above the mundane world of scores and data, and replaces it with the less austere "expected value" of the score in the population of values from which the sample score was drawn.

Now what are the implications, the advantages, and possibly the limitations of this "sampling" conception over the classic "true score and error" conception?

For myself, I cannot say that the advantage lies in simplification and clarification. This notion of a "universe of possible scores" is in many ways a puzzling and somewhat confusing one. Of what is this universe composed? Suppose we have given Form A of the XYZ Reading Test to the fifth graders in our school and gotten a score for each pupil. Of what universe of scores are these scores a sample—of all possible scores that we might have gotten by giving Form A on that day? Of all possible scores that we might have gotten by giving Form A sometime that month? Of all possible scores that might have been gotten by giving Forms A or B or C or other forms up to a still-unwritten Form K on that day? Of scores on these same numerous and presumably "parallel" forms—and we shall have to ask what "parallel" means under a sampling conception of reliability—at some unspecified date within the month? Of scores on the whole array of different reading tests produced by different authors over the past twenty-five years? Of scores on tests of some aspect of educational achievement not further specified?

As soon as we try to conceptualize a test score as a sample from some universe, we are brought face to face with the very knotty problem of defining the universe from which we are sampling. But I suppose this very difficulty may be in one sense a blessing. The experimental data-gathering phase of estimating reliability has *always* implied a universe to which those data corresponded. Split-half procedures refer only to a universe of behaviors produced at one single point in time, retest procedures to a universe of responses to a specific set of items, and so forth. Perhaps one of the advantages of the sampling formulation is that it makes us more explicitly aware of the need to define the universe in which we are interested, or to acknowledge the universe to which our data apply. Certainly, over the past thirty years, all of us who have written for students and for the test-using public have insistently harped upon the nonequivalence of different operations for estimating reliability, and emphasized the different universes to which different procedures referred.

The notion of a random sample from a universe of responses seems most satisfying and clear-cut when we are dealing with some unitary act of behavior, which we score in some way. Examples would be distance jumped in a broad jump, time to run 100 yards, speed of response on a trial with a reaction time device, or number of trials to learn a series of nonsense syllables to a specified level of mastery. In these cases, the experimental specification of the task is fairly complete. Thus, for the 100-yard run, we specify a smooth, straight, well-packed cinder track, a certain type of starting blocks, certain limitations on the shoes to be worn, a certain pattern of preparatory and starting signals, and a certain procedure for recording time. A universe could then be the universe of times for a given runner, over a certain span of days, weeks, or months of his running career. Data from two or more trials under these conditions would give us some basis for generalizing about the consistency of this behavior for this defined universe. We could also extend the universe if we wished—to include wooden indoor tracks for example, or to include running on grass, or running in sneakers instead of track shoes—and sample randomly from this more varied universe. As conditions were varied, we might expect typical performance to vary more widely and precision to be decreased.

We are usually interested in estimating precision for each of a population of persons, rather than just for some one specific person, and so we are likely to have a sampling from some population of persons. The nature of that population will also influence estimates of precision, and so it will be important that the population be specified as well as the conditions. Precision of estimating time to run 100 yards is probably much greater for college track stars than for middle-aged professors—for whom one might occasionally get scores approaching infinity. But it would be possible to specify the population of individuals fairly satisfactorily, as well as the population of behaviors for a given person. Within this at least two-dimensional universe, we could sample in a presumably random fashion, and we could then analyze our sample of observations to yield estimates of the relative precision with which a person could be located within the group or the absolute precision with which his time could be estimated in seconds.

When we are dealing with the typical aptitude or achievement test, however, in which the score is some type of summation of scores upon single items, the conception of the universe from which we have drawn a sample becomes a little more fuzzy. Here, fairly clearly, we are concerned with a sampling not only of responses to a given situation but also of situations to be responded to. How shall we define that universe? The classical approach to reliability tended to deal with this issue by postulating a universe of equivalent or parallel tests and by limiting the universe from which our sample is drawn to this universe of parallel tests. Parallel tests may be defined statistically as those having equal means, standard deviations, and correlations with each other and with other variables. But they may also be defined in terms of the operations of construction, as tests built by the same procedures to the same specifications. If we adopt the second definition, statistical characteristics will not be identical, but the tests will vary in their statistical attributes to the extent that different samples of items all chosen to conform to a uniform blueprint or test plan will produce tests with somewhat differing statistical values.

But some of the recent discussions seem to imply a random sampling of tests from some rather loosely and broadly defined domain—the domain of scholastic aptitude tests, or the domain of reading comprehension tests, or the domain of personal adjustment inventories. Clearly, these are very vague and ill-defined domains. A sampling expert would be hard put to delimit the universe or to propose any meaningful set of operations for sampling from it. And in the realm of practical politics, I question whether anyone has ever seriously undertaken to carry out such a sampling operation. One might argue that the data appearing in the manual of the XYZ Reading Test, showing its correlations with other published reading tests, are an approximation of such a domain sampling. But how truly does the set of tests, taken collectively, represent a random sampling from the whole domain of reading tests? One suspects that the tests selected for correlating were chosen by the author or publisher on some systematic and nonrandom basis—because they were widely used tests, because data with respect to them were readily available, or for some other nonrandom reason.

We note, further, that as we broaden our conception of the universe being sampled from that of all tests made to a certain uniform set of specifications to all tests of a certain ability or personality domain, we begin to face the issue of whether we are still getting evidence on reliability or whether we are now getting evidence on some aspect of construct validity. But, once again, perhaps we should consider it a contribution of the sampling approach that it makes explicit to us and heightens our awareness of the continuity from reliability to validity. Cronbach offers the single term "generalizability" to cover the whole gamut of relationships from those within the most restricted universe of near-exact replications to those extending over the most general and broadly defined domain, and develops a common statistical framework which he applies to the whole gamut. Recognition that the same pattern of statistical analysis can be used whether one is dealing with the little central core, or with all the layers of the whole onion, may be useful. On the other hand, we may perhaps question whether this approach helps to clarify our meaning of "reliability" as a distinctive concept.

A third context in which the random sampling notion has been applied to the conceptualization of reliability has been the context of the single test item. That is, one can conceive of a certain universe of test items—let us say the universe of vocabulary items, for example. A given test may be considered to represent a random sampling drawn from this item universe. This conception provides the foundation for the estimation of test reliability from the interrelations of the items of the sample, and thus to a somewhat more generalized and less restrictive form of the Kuder-Richardson reliability estimates.

But here, again, we encounter certain difficulties. These center on the one hand upon the definition of the universe and on the other upon the notion of randomness in sampling. In the first place, there are very definite constraints upon the items which make up our operational, as opposed to a purely hypothetical, universe. If we take the domain of vocabulary items as our example, we can specify what some of these constraints might be in an actual case. First, there is typically a constraint upon the format of the item —most often to a five-choice multiple-choice form. Second, there are constraints imposed by editorial policy—exemplified by the decision to exclude proper names or specialized technical terms, or by a requirement that the options call for gross rather than fine discriminations of shade of meaning. Third, there are the constraints that arise out of the particular idiosyncrasies of the item writers: their tendency to favor particular types of words, or particular tricks of distracter construction. Finally, there are the constraints imposed by the item selection procedures—selection to provide a predetermined spread of item difficulties and to eliminate items failing to discriminate at a designated level. Thus, the universe is considerably restricted, is hard to define, and the sampling from it is hardly to be considered random.

Presumably we could elaborate and delimit more fully the definition of the universe of items. Certainly, we could replace the concept of random sampling with one of stratified sampling, and indeed Cronbach has proposed that the sampling concept be extended to one of stratified sampling. But we may find that a really adequate definition of the universe from which we have sampled will become so involved as to be meaningless. We will almost certainly find that in proportion as we provide detailed specifications for stratification of our universe of items, and carry out our sampling within such strata, we are once again getting very close to a bill of particulars for equivalent tests. Just as random sampling is less efficient than stratified sampling in opinion surveys or demographic studies when stratification is upon relevant variables, so also random sampling of test items is less efficient than stratified sampling in making equivalent tests. Analytical techniques developed on the basis of random sampling assumptions will make a test appear less precise than it is as a representation of a population of tests which sample in a uniform way from different strata of the universe of items. It is partly in this sense that the Kuder-Richardson Formula 20 and the other formulas that try to estimate test reliability from item data, or from such test statistics as means and variances (which grow out of item data), are lower-bound estimates of reliability. They treat the sampling of items as random rather than stratified. They assume that differences in the factor composition of items either do not exist, or are only such as arise by chance.

Sometimes the facts suggest that this may be approximately the case. Thus, Cronbach (2) compared the values that he obtained for tests divided into random halves and those divided into judgmentally equivalent halves for a mechanical reasoning test, and found an average value of .810 for random splits and .820 for parallel splits. For a short morale scale the corresponding values were .715 and .737. But frequently a test is fairly sharply stratified—by difficulty level, by area of content, by intellectual process. When this is true, correlation estimates based on random sampling concepts may seriously underestimate those that would be obtained between two parallel forms of the test, and consequently the precision with which a given test represents the stratified universe.

These reactions to random sampling as applied to tests and test items were stimulated in part by Jane Loevinger's presidential address to Division 5 at the recent American Psychological Association meetings (6), and I gladly acknowledge the indebtedness, without holding her responsible for anything silly that I have said.

The shift in verbal formulation to a sampling formulation is compatible with a shift in mathematical models of reliability to analysis of variance and intraclass correlation models. These models have, of course, been proposed for more than twenty years, but they have been more systematically and completely expressed in the past decade.

The most comprehensive and systematic elaboration of this formulation of which I am aware is the one distributed in hectographed form by Oscar Buros (1), and available for $1.00 from the Gryphon Press. I confess my own limitation when I say that I find this presentation pretty hard to follow. I hope that others of you will be either more familiar with or more facile at picking up the notation that Buros has used, and will be able to pick from the host of formulas that are offered the one that is appropriate to the specific data with which you are faced.

One great virtue of analysis of variance models is their built-in versatility. They can handle item responses that are scored 0 or 1, trial scores that yield scores with some type of continuous distribution, or, where more than one test has been given to each individual, scores for total tests. They can deal with the situation in which the data for each individual are generated by the same test or the same rater, and also the situation in which test or rater vary from person to person. This latter situation is one of very real importance in many practical circumstances. How shall we judge the precision of a reported IQ when we do not know which of two or more forms of a test was given? How shall we appraise the repeatability of a course grade when the grade may be given by any one of the several different instructors who handle a course? If we have more than a single score for each individual, even though the scores are based on different tests or raters for each individual, we can get an estimate of within-persons variation. And whenever we have an estimate of within-persons variation we have a basis for judging the precision of a score or rating as describing a person. Clearly, with only two or three or four scores per person, the estimate of within-persons variance is very crude for a single individual. We must be willing to assume that the within-persons variance is sufficiently uniform from person to person for a pooling of data over persons to give us a usable common estimate of variance from test to test for each single individual. Having such an estimate, we can express reliability either as the precision of a score for an individual stated in absolute terms or as the precision of placement of an individual relative to his fellows.

As various writers have shown, the conventional Kuder-Richardson formulas emerge as special cases of the more general variance analysis approach. Likewise, the adjustment of correlational measures of reliability for test length are derivable from general variance analysis formulas.

I shall not try to recite to you a set of formulas today, because this would serve no good purpose. Rather, let me direct you to Tryon's 1957 article in the *Psychological Bulletin* (7), Buros' available if unpublished material (1), and Cronbach's article in the *British Journal of Statistical Psychology* (3). These, plus Horst's (5) and Ebel's (4) articles in *Psychometrika* should give you all the formulas you can use.

In closing, let me raise with you the question of how much you are willing to pay for precision in a given measurement. The cost is partly one of time and expense. But, given some fixed limit on time and expense, the cost can then be a cost in scope and comprehensiveness. We can usually make gains in precision by increasing the redundance and repetitiveness of successive observations. The more narrowly a universe is defined, the more adequately a given length of test sample can represent it. With all due respect to the error of measurement, we must recognize that it is often the error of estimate that we are really interested in. To maximize prediction of socially useful events, it may be advantageous to sacrifice a little precision in order to gain a greater amount of scope. Precision and high reliability are, after all, a means rather than an end.

REFERENCES

1. Buros, O. K. Summary of definitions, basic concepts, and formulas in the schematization of test reliability. Highland Park, N.J.: The Gryphon Press, 1963. (Hectographed)
2. Cronbach, L. J. Coefficient alpha and the internal structure of tests. *Psychometrika*, 1951, 16, 297–334.
3. Cronbach, L. J., Rajaratnam, N., & Gleser, Goldine C. Theory of generalizability: a liberalization of reliability theory. *British Journal of Statistical Psychology*, 1963, 16, 137–163.
4. Ebel, R. L. Estimation of the reliability of ratings. *Psychometrika*, 1951, 16, 407–424.
5. Horst, P. A generalized expression for the reliability of measures. *Psychometrika*, 1949, 14, 21–31.
6. Loevinger, Jane. Person and population as psychometric concepts. Presidential address to Division 5, American Psychological Association, September, 1963.
7. Tryon, R. C. Reliability and behavior domain validity: reformulation and historical critique. *Psychological Bulletin*, 1957, 54, 229–249.

Evaluation of Achievement Tests in Terms of External Statistical Relationships

HAROLD GULLIKSEN

1950

Let us consider the relationship of an achievement test to various possible types of external criteria. It seems to me that an achievement test may be evaluated first in terms of its relationship to a total battery of aptitude tests. Second, it may be evaluated in terms of its relationship to training, practice, experience, or drill in the subject concerned. And third, it may be evaluated in relationship to future performance of the individual in various related tasks.

With respect to the first method of evaluating the relationship of the achievement test to a battery of aptitude tests, we may point to several concrete illustrations of this type of study. We usually think of the aptitude test standing or falling in terms of its relation to a criterion. I propose here that the criterion should stand or fall in terms of its relation to aptitude tests. For example, in studying the relationship of the Basic Navy Battery to grades in service schools it was found that the U. S. Navy Reading Test correlated well with grades in Gunner's Mates Schools. Steps were taken to introduce more practical work on assembling and disassembling the guns and to place less emphasis on a study of manuals in the training and testing of gunner's mates (4, 5). Such a change in the criterion resulted in a decreased validity for the Reading Test and an increased validity for some of the mechanical-type tests. Grades in Torpedoman School correlated high with Reading and the General Classification Test, and low with mechanical knowledge—an inappropriate pattern for Torpedoman grades. An increase in the validity of the Mechanical Knowledge Test and a drop in the validity of the Reading and General Classification Tests followed the introduction of achievement tests in the Torpedoman School (8, p. 308).

Another concrete illustration of the use of a set of validity coefficients for making an initial appraisal of a criterion is furnished by the Navy Basic Engineering School (8, pp. 305–309). The first eye-opener to an unsatisfactory situation was the fact that an arithmetical reasoning test gave the highest correlation with final grades in the Basic Engineering School. Mechanical knowledge and mechanical comprehension tests gave the lowest correlation with these final grades. This state of affairs was extremely peculiar in view of the fact that arithmetic constituted *one*-seventh, and shop work *four*-sevenths of the curriculum. Investigation of grades showed that the standard deviation of the grades covering the one week of arithmetic was about 8.0; the standard deviation of grades for approximately four weeks devoted to shop work was about 2.5. Averaging one-seventh arithmetic (standard deviation 8.0) with four times as much shop work (standard deviation 2.5) gave a final grade which correlated in the high .80's with arithmetic and in the .50's with shop work. It would, of course, have been possible to suggest that grades in shop work be multiplied by a factor of 100 or so to increase their weight. However, a study among different instructors showed that the ratings of shop work intercorrelated from −.11 to .55. Clearly the problem was to develop more precise ratings before allowing them to determine the major portion of the grade. This was done in terms of better rating scales and various gauges and calipers to measure accurately the precision of the product.[1] The result was a highly reliable set of ratings of shop performance which were judged by the chiefs to be ratings of important characteristics. A recheck on the correlation of various aptitude tests with grades after institution of this program showed that the mechanical knowledge tests had the highest correlations and the arithmetical reasoning tests the lowest correlations with final grades (8, p. 307). Here we have a case where the interrelationships among part scores, the inspection of the curriculum, the judgment of the instructors, and the pattern of validity coefficients from selection tests all gave a consistent picture. The initial picture was strongly indicative of a *low intrinsic validity* of basic engineering grades. In the final picture all the evidence pointed toward a *higher intrinsic content validity* of basic engineering grades.

Comprehensive Factor Study of Criterion and Predictor Variables

Extending the idea of the previous section we see that the most information about the criterion would be afforded if a comprehensive matrix of intercorrelations including both criterion and predictor variables were available. A representative set of predictor variables should be included so that

---

[1] The major part of this work was done by Nicholas A. Fattu on NDRC Project N-106 of the Applied Psychology Panel. This Project was conducted by the College Entrance Examination Board at the request of the Bureau of Naval Personnel.

the investigator will be able to inspect both the high *and low* validity coefficients to be certain that this pattern is reasonable. Also a variety of modes for assessing different aspects of the criterion must be used in order to determine the dimensionality of the criterion variables and the extent to which the various expert judgments agree and disagree.

As yet there are very few factor studies which include an attempt both to analyze and represent various *aspects* of the criterion and to include a representative list of a variety of predictor variables (2, 3, 6, 7).

It seems to me that such studies are the major means now at the psychologist's disposal for evaluating what may be called the intrinsic validity of a criterion. They would enable us to see the extent to which ideas regarding the nature of the criterion and the nature of the predictors were correct. For example, a differential validity study has found that the best predictor of grades in Latin is a clerical aptitude test (1, p. E-14). This fact might be considered relevant to the view that Latin constitutes a valuable mental discipline in clear thinking.

Let us now consider possibilities of evaluating achievement tests in terms of their relationship to some type of training or practice in the material. Here we would need to utilize parallel achievement tests, one given before and one after the training or practice. Clearly the experts' judgment regarding the content of these tests is corroborated if the students *do not* know the material before training and *do* know it afterwards. However, if the material is known before training or is not known after training the expert judgment would bear reconsideration. I do not have any rules to suggest concerning the amount of improvement that should be expected as a result of training—whether good students should improve to the same extent or a greater or lesser extent than poor students. However, the behavior of the material with reference to instruction or practice seems to me to be a matter that must be investigated carefully in the case of every achievement test.

The third type of evaluation suggested is in terms of future performance on related tasks. Here again we must depend primarily on the judgments of experts in the field concerning the expected relationship between the test and subsequent performances. For example, if instruction in high school English is supposed to improve a person's ability to write personal letters or to do adequate work in English in college, then the relationship between various achievement tests in English and agreed-upon desirable future outcomes could be studied. The studies in each case would depend, it seems to me, primarily on the type of claims that were made for the achievement test in question. For example, if Latin teachers seriously maintain that one studies Latin because he thereby becomes better in English, it is relevant to study the relationship between future performance in English for students who have had and who have not had Latin, and for those who have done well in Latin and poorly. If the English teacher does not make this claim, and if no one else makes it, then such a study is not relevant for evaluation of achievement tests in Latin.

Concluding, then, I would feel that considerably more attention should be paid to some of the external relationships of achievement tests; their relationships to subsequent relevant achievement; their relationship to training, practice, or drill in the field; and the fact that achievement tests may be evaluated in terms of their relationship to batteries of aptitude tests.

REFERENCES

1. Bennett, G. K., Seashore, H. G., & Wesman, A. G. *Differential Aptitude Tests Manual.* (1948 ed.) New York: The Psychological Corporation, 1948.
2. Carroll, J. B. The factorial representation of mental ability and academic achievement. *Educational and Psychological Measurement,* 1943, 3, 307–332.
3. Comrey, A. L. A factorial study of achievement in West Point courses. *Educational and Psychological Measurement,* 1949, 9, 193–209.
4. Frederiksen, N. Statistical study of the achievement testing program in gunner's mates schools. Navpers 18079, 1948.
5. Frederiksen, N., & Monroe, A. E. The development of achievement tests for gunner's mates schools. OSRD Report No. 5259, Project N–106, Report No. 17, 1945.
6. French, J. W. The description of aptitude and achievement tests in terms of rotated factors. *Psychometric Monograph No. 5.* Chicago: Univer. of Chicago Press, 1951.
7. Sisk, H. L. A multiple factor analysis of mental abilities in the freshman engineering curriculum. *Journal of Psychology,* 1939, 9, 165–177.
8. Stuit, D. B. (Ed.) *Personnel research and test development in the Bureau of Naval Personnel.* Princeton, N.J.: Princeton Univer. Press, 1947.

Evaluation of Achievement Tests in Terms of Internal Statistics

JOHN B. CARROLL

1950

One of the most interesting questions to ask about an achievement test is the question of its *homogeneity*. When we ask this question, we may be concerned with whether all the items of the test measure the same ability, *or* we may be concerned with whether a test has sampled the information contained in a homogeneous field. For example, we may be asked whether an American history test contains a representative sample of the body of facts contained in a given syllabus of a course in American history, and whether the items uniformly measure achievement in learning this particular syllabus.

Unfortunately, most discussions of test homogeneity thus far have dealt with ability tests; that is, with tests intended to measure the level of difficulty that can be mastered by the examinee. Now, some achievement tests are intended to place the examinee on a continuum of task difficulty—e.g., a vocabulary test—but a large number of achievement tests are *not* so intended. Rather, they are designed to measure the examinee's total knowledge of an area. The score is merely an expression of the probability that the subject can pass any item—we don't necessarily care which items he passes. A valid measure can be obtained even if the items do not vary in difficulty (item difficulty being measured by the proportion passing each item). How can we measure the homogeneity of such an achievement test?

I shall return to this question later, but let us review some proposals which have been made regarding the homogeneity of ability tests. We see at once that there are several different ideas of what is meant by homogeneity. One technique of determining homogeneity is the factor analysis of the items of a test. From the standpoint of factor analysis, if the common factor variance of the items is traceable to only one factor, the test would be said to be homogeneous. Notice this, however: unreliability of the items would not affect one's conclusion regarding the homogeneity of the test, so long as the item intercorrelations constituted a matrix of rank one. If the matrix were of higher rank, the technique would presumably enable one to sort out the items into two or more homogeneous sets, if the data so permitted. Nevertheless, the study of the homogeneity of test items by factor analysis meets several obstacles. Aside from the rather exhaustive labor required, there is the question of what kinds of correlation coefficients should be factored. On this question, I have advocated the use of tetrachoric correlation coefficients, corrected, if necessary, for the effect of chance success. In a paper (1) read at the last American Psychological Association meeting, I attempted to demonstrate techniques for determining the factorial purity of an ability test. The Seashore pitch discrimination test was my example; it was found to be about as factorially pure as one might desire. The items acted homogeneously in placing the examinee on a single difficulty continuum. Nevertheless, my techniques are complicated, and require a number of assumptions.

A somewhat different approach is adopted by Jane Loevinger in her monograph, "A Systematic Approach to the Construction and Evaluation of Tests of Ability" (2). First, she is careful to point out that she restricts her discussion to "a specific class of tests: power tests of ability." She defines a perfectly homogeneous test of an ability as one "such that, if A's score is greater than B's score, then A has more of some ability than B, and it is the same ability for all individuals A and B who may be selected." From this she deduces that when the items of a homogeneous test "are arranged in order of increasing difficulty, every individual will pass all items up to a certain point and fail all subsequent items." She proposes an index of homogeneity based on the variance of scores relative to the variances of perfectly homogeneous and heterogeneous tests. Now, Loevinger's concept of a homogeneous test implies that the test measures a *difficulty continuum*. It is analogous to Guttman's idea of a perfectly reproducible scale. It must be pointed out that unreliability of items from any cause will depress Loevinger's index. For example, the index cannot have a value of unity unless all items are perfectly discriminating. Consequently, it is likely to be misleading. I applied Loevinger's index to my data on the Seashore pitch discrimination test, and found a value of only .08. Loevinger's index can be corrected for some sources of unreliability. For the Seashore test data, an estimate of the homogeneity corrected for the effect of chance success is .42, and this still does not correct for the effect of an imperfect operating characteristic. (I must omit discussion of the correction techniques, because that is not my present concern.) The point still remains that Loevinger's homogeneity is the homogeneity of a difficulty continuum, and it is depressed by unreliability due to any source.

We do not yet have available a simple and effective index of the homogeneity of an ability test. Nevertheless, let us now turn to the problem of measuring the homogeneity of achievement tests. It is obvious that either the factor analysis approach or Loevinger's approach will yield a decision of test heterogeneity when applied to many types of achievement tests, particularly those whose items do not vary greatly in difficulty. It must be that a different kind of homogeneity is implied here.

I would like you to imagine a hypothetical model of a test that might be regarded as a homogeneous achievement test. Suppose we have a number of individuals who have been given an opportunity to learn a number of facts. At the time of testing for knowledge of these facts, each individual is conceived to have a true score represented by the probability, p_i, that he will pass any item. The value of p_i varies from individual to individual, but whatever its value, it applies uniformly to all items. In the sense that the probabilities are uniform over the items, the test is said to be homogeneous. Starting from any series of true individual p_i values, it is possible to work out the expected variance of observed individual scores and the variance of item difficulties. I developed a hypothetical series of data for this case, using random numbers to decide whether my hypothetical individuals passed the items. Now, I would call this test perfectly homogeneous, but Loevinger's index of homogeneity was only .32. Even this figure is spurious, because the items vary in difficulty only by chance; Loevinger's index tends to be biased positively because of chance variations in item difficulties.

We can also think of the case where for any individual the probabilities of passing the items vary in a systematic manner. For example, the probability of passing any one item might be always proportional, or otherwise functionally related, to the probability of passing any other item. We can still call the test homogeneous because of the systematic variation of the individual-item probabilities. This type of model takes care of the homogeneous achievement test whose items vary in difficulty.

I have some data on a test that seems to exemplify this model. The test is Thurstone's Word-Number Memory test, and while it would ordinarily be regarded as an ability test (of the memory factor) it is, as it were, an achievement test in a nutshell, because it tests the subject's knowledge of 20 word-number associations to which he has just been exposed in a learning period. The total score is the number of items recalled, and from the many factorial studies of memory tests, this score measures the rote learning factor in a highly valid manner. In order to see whether the items of the test are functioning homogeneously in the production of the total score, I wanted to find whether the p_{ij}'s were systematically related. By p_{ij} I mean the proportion of persons at the ith ability level passing item j (whose difficulty, p_j, is measured as the proportion of the total group passing the item). To get reasonably accurate measures of p_{ij}, we often have to combine individuals in a sufficient range of ability to build up the number of cases. I tabulated the p_{ij}'s for the 20 items at 6 ability levels, and thus obtained a 6 x 20 matrix. Arranging the rows and columns in order of the marginal proportions, it was evident that some law governed the entries. In fact, it turned out that when the logarithms of the p_{ij}'s were taken, the resulting matrix had a rank very nearly equal to 1. The rows and columns, in other words, were proportional. Furthermore, it seemed that the following equation was satisfied, at least within small errors:

$$\log p_{ij} = W \log p_i \, U \log p_j,$$

where W and U are proportionality constants, and p_i and p_j are the marginal proportions. (I don't know whether this equation can be rationalized; at the moment, it is purely empirical.) Thus, knowing an individual's ability level and the "difficulty" of the item for the whole group, it was possible to estimate quite accurately the probability that an individual of that ability level would pass the item. The prediction was so close that the correlation between the predicted and obtained p_{ij}'s was .95. Even this correlation is not so high as it might be because of the sampling error that we would expect for the obtained proportions. In any case, I propose to say that this result indicates that the items of the test are homogeneous.

Thus, whenever we can predict, to a high degree of accuracy, the probability that an individual of ability level i will pass an item of difficulty level j, the test will be called homogeneous. A possible measure of homogeneity is the correlation between the obtained p_{ij}'s and the predicted p_{ij}'s, adjusted for the expected sampling variance of the obtained p_{ij}'s.

Now, the interesting thing is that this formulation can be extended to ability tests measuring a difficulty continuum. Take any test, whether you think it's an ability test or an achievement test, and make a three dimensional plot, using these variables as coordinates:

- *a*) the ability level of the individual, based on total test score;
- *b*) the over-all difficulty of each item; and
- *c*) the proportion of individuals at a given ability level passing an item of given difficulty.

If the resulting swarm of points is systematic—e.g., following a slanted plane, or a curved surface—and if the variation of the points from the fitted surface is not beyond what one might expect by chance variation, the items of the test will be said to be homogeneous. Furthermore, items that show significant deviations of their p_{ij}'s from the fitted surface will be indicated as nonhomogeneous with the generality of the items.

There remains the problem of the fitting of surfaces to the three-dimensional swarm of points. I have not had enough experience with this method to give you any discussion of this beyond two statements: a function of the form

$$\log p_{ij} = W \log p_i \, U \log p_j$$

is likely to be satisfactory and convenient for achievement tests. For an ability test, the normal ogive will perhaps generate the best fitting surface.

To sum up, I am proposing that homogeneity be defined as a property of a test such that the probability that an individual of a given ability level will pass an item of a given difficulty level is uniformly predictable within expected sampling errors for all items and all ability levels. In this sense, homogeneity is *not* the same as the property that concerns the function of a test in placing individuals along a difficulty continuum. A perfect measure of a difficulty continuum is necessarily homogeneous by the foregoing definition. But an achievement test whose items do not vary in difficulty could also be perfectly homogeneous by this definition.

REFERENCES

1. Carroll, J. B. Problems in the factor analysis of tests of varying difficulty. *American Psychologist,* 1950, 5, 369. (Abstract)
2. Loevinger, Jane. A systematic approach to the construction and evaluation of tests of ability. *Psychological Monographs,* 1947, 61, No. 4 (Whole No. 285).

The "Moderator Variable" as a Useful Tool in Prediction

DAVID R. SAUNDERS

1954

This paper is intended to be partly informative and partly persuasive. From the information standpoint, I hope to supply you with answers to three main questions: What is a moderator variable? How do you use a moderator variable? Why should you, anyway? The persuasive aspect of the paper is obvious in the third question, just as in the title. It is an important aspect, because much of the information I can give you is neither very new nor very complicated.

Moderator variables have been used for many years by our friends in economics and agriculture to help in fitting regression surfaces to their data. In these applications, the moderator effect is typically just one of many that are possible with a multivariate, curvilinear regression based on a polynomial expansion. Our economic and agricultural friends don't need, and don't seem to have, any special name for it. Our biological friends might be tempted to suggest the name "synergistic variable," but this is a term that already has a lot of additional scientific connotations that we want to remain neutral on.

So far as I know, Gaylord and Carroll (3) were the first to use a moderator variable in psychology. They called it a "population control variable," and presented a paper on it during the 1948 American Psychological Association meetings. The term "population control variable" is a good one, because it suggests a very important application. But it is a bad term to the extent that it tends to blind us to a number of other equally important applications, which I will touch on. The term "moderator variable" seems to be general enough in its meaning, and still not to be loaded with too many undesirable connotations.

Well—we have just christened this thing, but have only hinted at what it is. Let's look at some examples. By now, I've managed to think of dozens of attractive hypothetical examples, but I'll spare you these, and emphasize two examples that have been fully worked out and cross-validated.

The first example is the one that originally led me to think a moderator variable might be an important concept. Frederiksen and Melville (2), at Educational Testing Service had just shown that interests were less predictive of academic success for "compulsive" people than for "noncompulsive" people. For this discussion, we can ignore the measures that were used to define interests, success, and compulsiveness, except to note that they *all* were regarded as continuous variables. Frederiksen and Melville's experimental design, nevertheless, had to be the analysis of covariance; the total experimental sample was arbitrarily divided near the median compulsiveness score to produce two groups—called "compulsives" and "noncompulsives." The relations between interests and success were compared for these groups, and were found to differ significantly in the slopes of the regression lines. This was done separately for ten different interests as predictors.

This example is typical of many situations in which the use of a moderator variable should be considered. In this particular kind of situation, the term "population control variable" would also be apt. Clearly, what we are after is a means of treating compulsiveness as the continuous variable that it is—a means of avoiding the arbitrariness of dichotomizing or otherwise dividing the population into *smaller* pieces—a means of maintaining the integrity of the total population, while still maintaining a statistical control on each individual's membership in one of a continuous, infinite series of subpopulations defined by his compulsiveness score. In short, we will allow the meaning of his interest score to be "moderated" by his compulsiveness score.

Mathematically, this turns out to be extremely simple to do. Suppose we start with an ordinary, linear regression using several variables. Keeping everything in standard scores, we would write the equation:

$$y = \sum_{i=1}^{k} \beta_i x_i,$$

where y is our criterion, and β_i is the beta-weight for predictor x_i. Now, suppose that β_i, instead of being a constant, is itself a linear function of a series of moderator variables, z_j's. If we plug this into our equation, and do a little rearranging, we immediately find that we can write:

$$y = \sum_{i=1}^{k} a_i x_i + \sum_{j=1}^{l} b_j z_j + \sum_{ij} c_{ij} x_i z_j.$$

This would be just another linear regression if it were not for the last term, involving the products of the x's and the z's. If we want to, we can always choose origins of measurement for the x's and z's that will make everything drop out of this equation *except* the products and a constant term.

It is evidently these product terms that are inextricably tied up with the use of a moderator variable. And that is all that has happened. So long as there is a clear separation of the x's and z's, we cannot have any use for squared variables, let alone terms of higher power. All we have to do to fit the model to data is to find the appropriate xz product (or products) for each subject, and treat it (or them) as new independent predictors in any standard multiple correlation technique. Of course, we cannot introduce a product variable into a battery unless both of its factors are already there.

There are many interesting mathematical sidelights to this thing, but if I want to persuade you that moderator variables are useful and practical, we'd better go back to our examples.

We took the data that Frederiksen and Melville (2) had collected, and computed the products of the interest predictors with compulsiveness for each individual subject. Then we ran multiple correlations, first adding compulsiveness to the interest predictor, and then adding their product to the battery (3).

For three of the ten interest predictors studied, the simple addition of compulsiveness to the battery gave a significant increase to the multiple R. In these three cases, the compulsiveness score happened to act as a suppressor variable. A moderator variable is different from a suppressor variable, though they both typically have zero zero-order relation to the criterion; a moderator variable does not have to have zero-order correlations with even the predictor.

Back to the example. In five of the remaining seven instances, addition of the appropriate product score to each battery of two measures resulted in a further significant increase in the multiple R. The sign of the beta weight for the third term was correctly predicted from the hypothesis in all ten of the ten instances. You will recall that the hypothesis told us at which end of the compulsiveness scale to look for good predictions.

These results looked promising. So we moved the scene of operations from Princeton to Rochester; from a group of self-referred counselees to a larger group tested routinely during Freshman Week; from Strong Vocational Interest Blanks scored with weighted responses to scoring with unit weights. The criterion was still freshman grade average for engineering majors, and the moderator was still the Accountant Interest score of the

Strong, as a measure of compulsiveness. Insofar as the same or similar interest scores were available to try as predictors, we were able to cross-validate all but one of the statistically significant findings from Princeton.

In this example we have observed that in the more significant instances, the predictive contribution of the moderator effect is just as great as the initial contribution of the interest variable predictor. This may not seem like saying much, but note that Frederiksen and Melville (2) reported correlations ranging from zero to over .50 for subgroups of the same population that were formed by using a pair of compulsiveness measures. Even when a moderated regression model does not lead to much increase in the multiple R, it does lead to quite different predictions for some individuals, and should be used if its effect is even statistically significant. These predictions may differ in standard error, as well as in the expected value itself.

In the second main example that I want to discuss here, *neither* the moderator *nor* the predictor has been shown to have a significant zero-order correlation with the criterion! In this situation, the predictor and moderator lose their separate identity, and a name like "population control variable" becomes more awkward to use. In this example, there is no significant multiple R until the product term is introduced; then it jumps to values like .45. This example is based on some of Fiedler's recently reported work on the influence of leader-keyman relations on small group effectiveness. Many of you may have seen this written up in *Time* magazine recently, even if you missed Fiedler's APA presentation, and haven't yet seen his report to the Office of Naval Research (1).

The gist of it is this. Suppose you are the formally designated leader of a small group or team. There is probably someone in the group who is your right-hand man—your principal subordinate or keyman. If you are the kind of person who generally has warm feelings for most people, for whom similarities among other people are more important than differences, it will pay you and your group for you to maintain a relative aloofness from your group, and especially from your keyman. On the other hand, if you tend to think of others you like as being different from those you dislike, it will pay to do the opposite: namely, for you to cultivate strong sociometric ties with your group, and especially with your keyman.

Here, then, are two variables you need to measure to predict a particular leader's effectiveness in a particular group. While neither variable is related to the criterion, their product has a substantial negative correlation with it. The results happen to be psychologically very sensible, and they can probably be used to counsel leaders towards a more effective style of leadership, and to predict what groups will respond best to given styles of leadership.

These two examples have been very different in many respects, but they do have two things in common in addition to their featuring of important moderator effects. For one thing, they both feature noncognitive variables as predictors—and as moderators, if you still care which is which. It seems to me that we can expect to find examples of this kind relatively more easily, but cognitive examples are still a real possibility. For instance, if we could obtain a meaningful coefficient of reliability for an individual's test score independently of the group within which he happened to be tested, it would probably moderate any predictions made from the test score itself.

In the second place, both these examples were initially studied by breaking a total sample up into subgroups. There are many studies that have been carried this far, and then reported in tedious detail for lack of an organizing concept, such as the moderator variable provides. For the past three years, I have made it a point at the APA meetings to seek out studies of this kind; I have always found my fill without going very far afield. For some reason, studies involving the "authoritarian personality syndrome" seem to be in particular need of something like a moderator variable. But no more so, I would say, than people who do configural scoring or make clinical judgments on the basis of personality tests.

There is one last topic on my agenda. Assuming you have decided to look for moderator effects, what is the best way to go about it? There are at least four methods to consider. 1) You can start with a good hypothesis. This is always a good idea. 2) If you don't have one handy, you can look for one by studying a few cases intensively, and seeking out variables whose interpretation seems to depend on other variables. 3) You can do the same thing with larger groups of cases by looking for sets of subgroups within which correlations are significantly different. 4) You can do the same thing with items instead of variables, by testing the interaction variance of a pair of items against a criterion. This fourth approach is a whole technique in itself, and I wish there were time to tell you about it. It capitalizes on the electronic computers; it can be generalized beyond pairs of items; and it brings the old idea of keying patterns of response to several items into a new perspective.

REFERENCES

1. Fiedler, F. E. The influence of leader-keyman relations on combat crew effectiveness. Urbana, Ill.: Group Effectiveness Research Laboratory, Univer. of Illinois, 1954. (Technical Report No. 9, Contract No. N6–ori–07135.)

2. Frederiksen, N., & Melville, S. D. Differential predictability in the use of test scores. *Educational and Psychological Measurement,* 1954, 14, 647–656.

3. Gaylord, R. H., & Carroll, J. B. A general approach to the problem of the population control variable. *American Psychologist,* 1948, 3, 310. (Abstract)

4. Saunders, D. R. Moderator variables in prediction. *Educational and Psychological Measurement,* 1956, 16, 209–222.

Some Current Developments in the Measurement and Interpretation of Test Validity

ANNE ANASTASI

1963

Within the past decade, psychologists have been especially active in devising novel and imaginative approaches to test validity. In the time allotted, I can do no more than whet your appetite for these exciting developments and hope that you will be stimulated to examine the sources cited for an adequate exposition of each topic. I have selected five developments to bring to your attention. Ranging in scope from broad frameworks to specific techniques and from highly theoretical to immediately practical, these topics pertain to: construct validation, decision theory, moderator variables, synthetic validity, and response styles.

CONSTRUCT VALIDATION

It is nearly ten years since the American Psychological Association published its *Technical Recommendations* (1) outlining four types of validity: content, predictive, concurrent, and construct. As the most complex, inclusive, and controversial of the four, construct validity has received the greatest attention during the subsequent decade. When first proposed in the *Technical Recommendations,* construct validation was characterized as a validation of the theory underlying a test. On the basis of such a theory, specific hypotheses are formulated regarding the expected variations in test scores among individuals or among conditions, and data are then gathered to test these hypotheses. The constructs in construct validity refer to postulated attributes or traits that are presumably reflected in test performance. Concerned with a more comprehensive and more abstract kind of behavioral description than those provided by other types of validation, construct validation calls for a continuing accumulation of information from a variety of sources. Any data throwing light on the nature of the trait under

307

consideration and the conditions affecting its development and manifestations contribute to the process of construct validation. Examples of relevant procedures include checking an intelligence test for the anticipated increase in score with age during childhood, investigating the effects of experimental variables such as stress upon test scores, and factor analyzing the test along with other variables.

Subsequently the concept of construct validity has been attacked, clarified, elaborated, and illustrated in a number of thoughtful and provocative articles by Cronbach and Meehl (14), Loevinger (30), Bechtoldt (6), Jessor and Hammond (28), Campbell and Fiske (11), and Campbell (10). In the most recent of these papers, Campbell (10) integrates much that had previously been written about construct validity and gives a well-balanced presentation of its contributions, hazards, and common misunderstandings. Referring to the earlier paper prepared jointly with Fiske (11), Campbell again points out that in order to demonstrate construct validity we need to show not only that a test correlates highly with other variables with which it should correlate, but also that it does not correlate with variables from which it should differ. The former is described as convergent validation, the latter as discriminant validation.

In their multitrait-multimethod matrix, Campbell and Fiske (11) proposed a systematic experimental design for this twin approach to validation. Essentially what is required is the assessment of two or more traits by two or more methods. Under these conditions, the correlations of the same trait assessed by different methods represent a measure of convergent validity (these correlations should be high). The correlations of different traits assessed by the same or similar methods provide a measure of discriminant validity (these correlations should be low or negligible). In addition, the correlations of the same trait independently assessed by the same method give an index of reliability.

Without attempting an evaluation of construct validity, for which I would urge you to consult the sources cited, I should nevertheless like to make a few comments about it. First, the basic idea of construct validity is not new. Some of the earliest tests were designed to measure such theoretical constructs as attention and memory, not to mention that most notorious of constructs, "intelligence." On the other hand, construct validity has served to focus attention on the desirability of basing test construction on an explicitly recognized theoretical foundation. Both in devising a new test and in setting up procedures for its validation, the investigator is urged to formulate psychological hypotheses. The proponents of construct validity have thus tried to integrate psychological testing more closely with psychological theory and experimental methods.

With regard to specific validation procedures, construct validation also utilizes much that is not new. Age differentiation, factorial validity, and the effect of such experimental variables as practice on test scores have been reported in test manuals long before construct validity was given a name in the *Technical Recommendations*. As a matter of fact, the methodology of construct validity is so comprehensive as to encompass even the procedures characteristically associated with other types of validity (see 2, Ch. 6). Thus the correlation of a mechanical aptitude test with subsequent performance on engineering jobs would contribute to our understanding of the construct measured by this test. Similarly, comparing the performance of neurotics and normals is one way of checking the construct validity of a test designed to measure anxiety. Nevertheless, construct validation has stimulated the search for novel ways of gathering validation data. Although the principal techniques currently employed to investigate construct validity have long been familiar, the field of operation has been expanded to admit a wider variety of procedures.

The very multiplicity of data-gathering techniques recognized by construct validity presents certain hazards. As Campbell puts it, the wide diversity of acceptable validational evidence "makes possible a highly opportunistic selection of evidence and the editorial device of failing to mention validity probes that were not confirmatory" (10, p. 551). Another hazard stems from misunderstandings of such a broad and loosely defined concept as construct validity. Some test constructors apparently interpret construct validation to mean content validity expressed in terms of psychological trait names. Hence they present as construct validity purely subjective accounts of what they believe (or hope) their test measures.

It is also unfortunate that the chief exponents of construct validity stated in one of their articles that this type of validation "is involved whenever a test is to be interpreted as a measure of some attribute or quality which is not 'operationally defined'" (14, p. 282). Such an assertion opens the door wider for subjective claims and fuzzy thinking about test scores and the traits they measure. Actually the theoretical construct or trait assessed by any test can be defined in terms of the operations performed in establishing the validity of the test. Such a definition should take into account the various external criteria with which the test correlated significantly, as well as the conditions that affect its scores. These procedures are entirely in accord with the positive contributions of construct validity. It would also seem desirable to retain the concept of criterion in construct validation, not as a specific practical achievement to be predicted, but as a general name for independently gathered external data. The need to base all validation on data rather than on armchair speculation would thus be re-emphasized, as would the need for data external to the test scores themselves.

Decision Theory

Even broader than construct validity in its scope and implications is the application of decision theory to test construction and evaluation (see 2, Ch. 7; 13; 25). Because of many technical complexities, however, the current impact of decision theory on test development and use is limited and progress has been slow.

Statistical decision theory was developed by Wald (37) with special reference to the decisions required in the inspection and quality control of industrial products. Many of its possible implications for psychological testing have been systematically worked out by Cronbach and Gleser in their 1957 book, *Psychological Tests and Personnel Decisions* (13). Essentially, decision theory is an attempt to put the decision-making process into mathematical form, so that available information may be used to reach the most effective decisions under specified circumstances. The mathematical procedures required by decision theory are often quite complex, and few are in a form permitting their immediate application to practical testing problems. Some of the basic concepts of decision theory, however, can help in the reformulation and clarification of certain questions about tests.

A few of these concepts were introduced in psychological testing before the formal development of statistical decision theory and were later recognized as fitting into that framework. One example is provided by the well-known Taylor-Russell Tables (36), which permit an estimate of the net gain in selection accuracy attributable to the use of a test. The information required for this purpose includes the validity coefficient of the test, the selection ratio, and the proportion of successful applicants selected without the use of the test. The rise in proportion of successful applicants to be expected from the introduction of the test is taken as an index of the test's effectiveness.

In many situations, what is wanted is an estimate of the effect of the test, not on proportion of persons who exceed the minimum performance, but on the over-all output of the selected group. How does the level of criterion achievement of the persons selected on the basis of the test compare with that of the total applicant sample that would have been selected without the test? Following the work of Taylor and Russell, several investigators addressed themselves to this question. It was Brogden (8) who first demonstrated that the expected increase in output or achievement is directly proportional to the validity of the test. Doubling the validity of the test will double the improvement in output expected from its use. Following a similar approach (see 27), Brown and Ghiselli (9) prepared a table whereby mean standard criterion score of the selected group can be estimated from a knowledge of test validity and selection ratio.

Decision theory incorporates a number of parameters not traditionally considered in evaluating the predictive effectiveness of tests. The previously mentioned selection ratio is one such parameter. Another is the cost of administering the testing program. Thus a test of low validity would be more likely to be retained if it were short, inexpensive, adapted for group administration, and easy to give. An individual test requiring a trained examiner and expensive equipment would need a higher validity to justify its retention. A further consideration is whether the test measures an area of criterion-relevant behavior not covered by other available techniques.

Another major aspect of decision theory pertains to the evaluation of outcomes. The absence of adequate systems for assigning values to outcomes is one of the principal obstacles in the way of applying decision theory. It should be noted, however, that decision theory did not introduce the problem of values into the decision process, but merely made it explicit. Value systems have always entered into decisions, but they were not heretofore clearly recognized or systematically handled.

Still another feature of decision theory is that it permits a consideration of the interaction of different variables. An example would be the interaction of applicant aptitudes with alternative treatments, such as types of training programs to which individuals could be assigned. Such differential treatment would further improve the outcome of decisions based on test scores. Decision theory also focuses attention on the important fact that the effectiveness of a test for selection, placement, classification, or any other purpose must be compared not with chance or with perfect prediction, but with the effectiveness of other available predictors. The question of the base rate is also relevant here (33). The examples cited provide a few glimpses into ways in which the application of decision theory may eventually affect the interpretation of test validity.

MODERATOR VARIABLES

A promising recent development in the interpretation of test validity centers on the use of moderator variables (7, 19, 21, 22, 23, 24, 35). The validity of a given test may vary among subgroups or individuals within a population. Essentially the problem of moderator variables is that of predicting these differences in predictability. In any bivariate distribution, some individuals fall close to the regression line; others miss it by appreciable distances. We may then ask whether there is any characteristic in which those falling farther from the regression line, for whom prediction errors are large, differ systematically and consistently from those falling close to it. Thus a test might be a better predictor of criterion performance for men than for women, or for applicants from a lower than for applicants from a higher socioeconomic level. In such examples, sex and socioeconomic level are the moderator variables since they modify the predictive validity of the test.

Even when a test is equally valid for all subgroups, the same score may have a different predictive meaning when obtained by members of different subgroups. For example, if two students with different educational background obtain the same score on the Scholastic Aptitude Test, will they do equally well in college? Or will the one with the poorer or the one with the better background excel? Moderator variables may thus influence cutoff scores, regression equation weights, or validity coefficients of the same test for different subgroups of a population.

Interests and motivation often function as moderator variables in individual cases. If an applicant has little interest in a job, he will probably do poorly regardless of his scores on relevant aptitude tests. Among such persons, the correlation between aptitude test scores and job performance would be low. For individuals who are interested and highly motivated, on the other hand, the correlation between aptitude test score and job success may be quite high. From another angle, personality inventories like the Minnesota Multiphasic Personality Inventory (MMPI) may have higher validity for some types of neurotics than for others (19). The characteristic behavior of the two types may make one more careful and accurate in reporting symptoms, the other careless or evasive.

A moderator variable may itself be a test score, in terms of which individuals may be sorted into subgroups. There have been some promising attempts to identify such moderator variables in test scores (7, 19, 21, 24). In a study of taxi drivers conducted by Ghiselli (21), the correlation between an aptitude test and a criterion of job performance was only .22. The group was then sorted into thirds on the basis of scores on an occupational interest inventory. When the validity of the aptitude test was recomputed within the third whose occupational interest level was most appropriate for the job, it rose to .66. Such findings suggest that one test might first be used to screen out individuals for whom the second test is likely to have low validity; then from among the remaining cases, those scoring high on the second test are selected.

Even within a single test, such as a personality inventory, it may prove possible to develop a moderator key in terms of which the validity of the rest of the test for each individual can be assessed (24). There is also evidence suggesting that intra-individual variability from one part of the test to another affects the predictive validity of a test for individuals (7). Those individuals for whom the test is more reliable (as indicated by low intra-individual variability) are also the individuals for whom it is more valid, as might be anticipated.

SYNTHETIC VALIDITY

A technique devised to meet a specific practical need is synthetic validity (4, 29, 34). It is well known that the same test may have high validity for predicting the performance of office clerks or machinists in one company and low or negligible validity for jobs bearing the same title in another company. Similar variation has been found in the correlations of tests with achievement in courses of the same name given in different colleges. The familiar criterion of "college success" is a notorious example of both complexity and heterogeneity. Although traditionally identified with grade point average, college success can actually mean many different things, from being elected president of the student council or captain of the football team to receiving Phi Beta Kappa in one's junior year. Individual colleges vary in the relative weights they give to these different criteria of success.

It is abundantly clear that: 1) educational and vocational criteria are complex; 2) the various criterion elements, or subcriteria, for any given job, educational institution, course, etc. may have little relation to each other; and 3) different criterion situations bearing the same name often represent a different combination of subcriteria. It is largely for these reasons that test users are generally urged to conduct their own local validation studies. In many situations, however, this practice may not be feasible for lack of time, facilities, or adequate samples. Under these circumstances, synthetic validity may provide a satisfactory approximation of test validity against a particular criterion. First proposed by Lawshe (29) for use in industry, synthetic validity has been employed chiefly with job criteria, but it is equally applicable to educational criteria.

In synthetic validity, each predictor is validated, not against a composite criterion, but against job elements identified through job analysis. The validity of any test for a given job is then computed synthetically from the weights of these elements in the job and in the test. Thus if a test has high validity in predicting performance in delicate manipulative tasks, and if such tasks loom large in a particular job, then the test will have high synthetic validity for that job. A statistical technique known as the J-coefficient (for Job-coefficient) has been developed by Primoff (34) for estimating the synthetic validity of a test. This technique offers a possible tool for generalizing validity data from one job or other criterion situation to another without actually conducting a separate validation study in each situation. The J-coefficient may also prove useful in ordinary battery construction as an intervening step between the job analysis and the assembling of a trial battery of tests. The preliminary selection of appropriate tests is now done largely on a subjective and unsystematic basis and might be improved through the utilization of such a technique as the J-coefficient.

Response Styles

The fifth and last development I should like to bring to your attention pertains to response styles. Although research on response styles has centered chiefly on personality inventories, the concept can be applied to any type of test. Interest in response styles was first stimulated by the identification of certain test-taking attitudes which might obscure or distort the traits that the test was designed to measure. Among the best known is the social desirability variable, extensively investigated by Edwards (15, 16, 17, 18). This is simply the tendency to choose socially desirable responses on personality inventories. To what extent this variable should also reflect the tendency to choose common responses is a matter on which different investigators disagree. Other examples of response styles include acquiescence, or the tendency to answer "yes" rather than "no" regardless of item content (3, 5, 12, 20); evasiveness, or the tendency to choose question marks or other indifferent responses; and the tendency to utilize extreme response categories, such as "agree strongly" and "disagree strongly."

We can recognize two stages in research on response styles. First there was the recognition that stylistic components of item form exert a significant influence upon test responses. In fact, a growing accumulation of evidence indicated that the principal factors measured by many self-report inventories were stylistic rather than content factors. At this stage, such stylistic variance was regarded as error variance, which would reduce test validity. Efforts were therefore made to rule out these stylistic factors through the reformulation of items, the development of special keys, or the application of correction formulas.

More recently there has been an increasing realization that response styles may be worth measuring in their own right. This point of view is clearly reflected in the reviews by Jackson and Messick (26) and by Wiggins (38), published within the past five years. Rather than being regarded as measurement errors to be eliminated, response styles are now being investigated as diagnostic indices of broad personality traits. The response style that an individual exhibits in taking a test may be associated with characteristic behavior he displays in other, nontest situations. Thus the tendency to mark socially desirable answers may be related to conformity and stereotyped conventionality. It has also been proposed that a moderate degree of this variable is associated with a mature, individualized self concept, while higher degrees are associated with intellectual and social immaturity (31, 32). With reference to acquiescence, there is some suggestive evidence that the predominant "yeasayers" tend to have weak ego controls and to accept impulses without reservation, while the predominant "naysayers" tend to inhibit and suppress impulses and to reject emotional stimuli (12).

The measurement of response styles may provide a means of capitalizing on what initially appeared to be the chief weaknesses of self-report inventories. Several puzzling and disappointing results obtained with personality inventories seem to make sense when re-examined in the light of recent research with response styles. Much more research is needed, however, before the measurement of response styles can be put to practical use. We need more information on the relationships among different response styles, such as social desirability and acquiescence, which are often confounded in existing scales. We also need to know more about the interrelationships among different scales designed to measure the same response style. And above all, we need to know how these stylistic scales are related to external criterion data.

The five developments cited in this paper represent ongoing activities. It is premature to evaluate the contribution any of them will ultimately make to the measurement or interpretation of test validity. At this stage, they all bear watching and they warrant further exploration.

REFERENCES

1. American Psychological Association. *Technical recommendations for psychological tests and diagnostic techniques.* Washington, D.C.: American Psychological Association, 1954. (Revised edition published in 1966.)

2. Anastasi, Anne. *Psychological testing.* (2nd ed.) New York: Macmillan, 1961.
3. Asch, M. J. Negative response bias and personality adjustment. *Journal of Counseling Psychology,* 1958, 5, 206–210.
4. Balma, M. J., Ghiselli, E. E., McCormick, E. J., Primoff, E. S., & Griffin, C. H. The development of processes for indirect or synthetic validity—a symposium. *Personnel Psychology,* 1959, 12, 395–420.
5. Bass, B. M. Authoritarianism or acquiescence? *Journal of Abnormal and Social Psychology,* 1955, 51, 616–623.
6. Bechtoldt, H. P. Construct validity: a critique. *American Psychologist,* 1959, 14, 619–629.
7. Berdie, R. F. Intra-individual variability and predictability. *Educational and Psychological Measurement,* 1961, 21, 663–676.
8. Brogden, H. E. On the interpretation of the correlation coefficient as a measure of predictive efficiency. *Journal of Educational Psychology,* 1946, 37, 65–76.
9. Brown, C. W., & Ghiselli, E. E. Per cent increase in proficiency resulting from use of selective devices. *Journal of Applied Psychology,* 1953, 37, 341–344.
10. Campbell, D. T. Recommendations for APA test standards regarding construct, trait, or discriminant validity. *American Psychologist,* 1960, 15, 546–553.
11. Campbell, D. T., & Fiske, D. W. Convergent and discriminant validation by the multitrait-multimethod matrix. *Psychological Bulletin,* 1959, 56, 81–105.
12. Couch, A., & Keniston, K. Yeasayers and naysayers: agreeing response set as a personality variable. *Journal of Abnormal and Social Psychology,* 1960, 60, 151–174.
13. Cronbach, L. J., & Gleser, Goldine C. *Psychological tests and personnel decisions.* Urbana, Ill.: Univer. of Illinois Press, 1957. (Revised edition published in 1965.)
14. Cronbach, L. J., & Meehl, P. E. Construct validity in psychological tests. *Psychological Bulletin,* 1955, 52, 281–302.
15. Edwards, A. L. *The social desirability variable in personality assessment and research.* New York: Dryden, 1957.
16. Edwards, A. L., & Diers, Carol J. Social desirability and the factorial interpretation of the MMPI. *Educational and Psychological Measurement,* 1962, 22, 501–509.
17. Edwards, A. L., Diers, Carol J., & Walker, J. N. Response sets and factor loadings on sixty-one personality scales. *Journal of Applied Psychology,* 1962, 46, 220–225.
18. Edwards, A. L., & Heathers, Louise B. The first factor of the MMPI: social desirability or ego strength? *Journal of Consulting Psychology,* 1962, 26, 99–100.
19. Fulkerson, S. C. Individual differences in response validity. *Journal of Clinical Psychology,* 1959, 15, 169–173.

20. Gage, N. L., Leavitt, G. S., & Stone, G. C. The psychological meaning of acquiesence set for authoritarianism. *Journal of Abnormal and Social Psychology,* 1957, 55, 98–103.

21. Ghiselli, E. E. Differentiation of individuals in terms of their predictability. *Journal of Applied Psychology,* 1956, 40, 374–377.

22. Ghiselli, E. E. The prediction of predictability. *Educational and Psychological Measurement,* 1960, 20, 3–8.

23. Ghiselli, E. E. Differentiation of tests in terms of the accuracy with which they predict for a given individual. *Educational and Psychological Measurement,* 1960, 20, 675–684.

24. Ghiselli, E. E. Moderating effects and differential reliability and validity. *Journal of Applied Psychology,* 1963, 47, 81–86.

25. Girshick, M. A. An elementary survey of statistical decision theory. *Review of Educational Research,* 1954, 24, 448–466.

26. Jackson, D. N., & Messick, S. Content and style in personality assessment. *Psychological Bulletin,* 1958, 55, 243–252.

27. Jarett, R. F. Per cent increase in output of selected personnel as an index of test efficiency. *Journal of Applied Psychology,* 1948, 32, 135–145.

28. Jessor, R., & Hammond, K. R. Construct validity and the Taylor anxiety scale. *Psychological Bulletin,* 1957, 54, 161–170.

29. Lawshe, C. H., & Steinberg, M. D. Studies in synthetic validity. 1. An exploratory investigation of clerical jobs. *Personnel Psychology,* 1955, 8, 291–301.

30. Loevinger, Jane. Objective tests as instruments of psychological theory. *Psychological Reports,* 1957, 3, 635–694.

31. Loevinger, Jane. A theory of test response. *Proceedings of the 1958 Invitational Conference on Testing Problems.* Princeton, N.J.: Educational Testing Service, 1959. Pp. 36–47.

32. Loevinger, Jane, & Ossorio, A. G. Evaluation of therapy by self-report: a paradox. *Journal of Abnormal and Social Psychology,* 1959, 58, 392–394.

33. Meehl, P. E., & Rosen, A. Antecedent probability and the efficiency of psychometric signs, patterns, or cutting scores. *Psychological Bulletin,* 1955, 52, 194–216.

34. Primoff, E. S. The J-coefficient approach to jobs and tests. *Personnel Administration,* 1957, 20, 34–40.

35. Saunders, D. R. Moderator variables in prediction. *Educational and Psychological Measurement,* 1956, 16, 209–222.

36. Taylor, H. C., & Russell, J. T. The relationship of validity coefficients to the practical effectiveness of tests in selection: discussion and tables. *Journal of Applied Psychology,* 1939, 23, 565–578.

37. Wald, A. *Statistical decision functions.* New York: Wiley, 1950.

38. Wiggins, J. S. Strategic, method, and stylistic variance in the MMPI. *Psychological Bulletin,* 1962, 59, 224–242.

8 · MULTIVARIATE PROCEDURES IN TEST CONSTRUCTION

THE PAPERS in this chapter are among the most technical in the book. They provide a sample of the type of problems encountered by the research psychometrician when dealing with a multiplicity of variables. In the first paper, French examines the rationale of differential testing, i.e., testing for purposes of classification rather than selection. It is this type of testing that underlies decisions as to which of several occupations or academic courses an individual can most profitably pursue. French compares multiple discriminant analysis with the multiple regression method, discusses the validation of tests for differential prediction, and considers the problem of restriction of range in essential variables within natural criterion groups.

Approaching differential prediction from another angle, Tiedeman uses the rationale of the multiple discriminant function in developing a model for profile analysis. In both aptitude and personality testing, psychometricians have turned more and more to profile scoring, which preserves the pattern of an individual's subtest scores rather than combining them into a single, global score. Tiedeman tackles the problem of measuring the degree of similarity between an individual's profile and the modal profiles of any number of criterion groups.

The last three papers, spanning an interval of fifteen years, deal with factor analysis. Eysenck provides a picture of the state of the art as it looked in 1949, before high-speed computers had had a significant impact upon factor-analytic techniques. After describing three examples of the application of factor analysis to psychometric problems, Eysenck discusses limitations and misuses of the method. Some of the limitations cited are rapidly being overcome today through the utilization of refined techniques made possible by high-speed computers.

In a paper bubbling with enthusiasm, Kaiser introduces the reader to some of the major break-throughs in factor-analytic technique that have occurred since 1960 and for which he and his associates have been largely responsible. These include scale-free procedures of factor analysis—some of which also provide a unique solution for factor scores—and an ingenious solution for the oblique rotation problem.

Another significant innovation is discussed by Tucker in his paper on multimode factor analysis. For some time, psychometricians have been familiar with certain variants of traditional factor-analytic techniques, which utilize the correlations among persons or among occasions, rather than the correlations among tests. With Tucker's multimode factor analysis, data such as these—classified in three or more independent ways—can be subjected to a single composite factor analysis. This procedure thus permits the discovery of interactions among the different sets of factors identified through the separate classifications. Such interactions are illustrated in the "core box" given in each of the examples reported by Tucker.

The Logic of and Assumptions Underlying Differential Testing

JOHN W. FRENCH

1955

Let us start my discussion of differential testing by taking a typical practical problem in which differential testing applies. Suppose a student has the choice of entering fields A, B, or C, where A, B, and C are either academic courses or occupations. Let us assume that we have given suitable batteries of tests to previous groups of students, and have followed up those students to obtain a quantitative measure of how successful or how happy the students became in pursuing A, B, and C. For this criterion measure of success or satisfaction, even a dichotomy would be satisfactory.

Now, we are asked by the student which field we would recommend for him: A, B, or C. Our choice of the statistical techniques to apply should depend on what the student wants to know. He probably doesn't know exactly what he wants to know. However, I think we can assume that he would like to enter the field in which he would be most happy, most successful, or both. This means he needs information such as: 1) his chance of obtaining a certain level of success or satisfaction in each field, and 2) his chance of obtaining greater success or satisfaction in one field as compared to that in any other field.

Let me compare two statistical techniques that are recommended for developing test batteries useful in guidance work: multiple discriminant analysis and multiple regression.

Those who recommend multiple discriminant analysis in this kind of guidance work attempt to answer the student's problem by showing him how much resemblance there is between his own test scores and the average test scores for people in fields A, B, or C. It is suggested to the student that he enter the field in which his colleagues would have test scores most closely resembling his own. If the criterion groups for fields A, B, and C were chosen from among successful people in their respective fields, it is expected that the student will also be successful when associated with the group that he most closely resembles. How successful? What chance does he have of not being successful? Is he likely to be more successful in one field than in another? Multiple discriminant analysis doesn't answer these questions. It is an excellent technique for detecting membership in a group, for handling the very elusive problems of classification based on qualitative differences. But it does not answer the question: "How well will I do if I take a job as a dog catcher?" Although discriminant analysis cannot answer this kind of question, it does have a place in guidance work. It is probably the best available method in cases where criterion scores are unavailable or so restricted in range that multiple regression would give only a distorted picture. I shall discuss this limitation of multiple regression later.

Validity coefficients rather than score patterns are the stock-in-trade for those who have satisfactory criterion scores available to them and who want to give what seems to me to be the direct answer to the student's problem. This is the multiple regression method. It provides predictions that indicate to the student his chances for attaining a given amount of success in A, B, and C, and differential predictions that indicate his chances for being more successful in one field than in another.

Let us look at the data in an actual case so that we can compare a counselor's advice based on multiple discriminant analysis with a counselor's advice based on multiple regression. Tables 1 and 2 present small portions from each of two larger tables. The rows in the two tables represent four aptitude scores: Perceptual Speed (this is mainly speed in finding given symbols in a mass of distracting material), Mechanical Knowledge (this is a knowledge of mechanical techniques and equipment), Carelessness (this is the numbers of errors made on speeded tests; a high score indicates many careless errors), and Speed of Judgment (this is the number of simple choices made within a short time limit; no attention is paid to the correctness of the subject's judgments or to the nature of his preferences). The columns in the tables represent groups of vocational high school students who later became, respectively, office workers, beauty operators, carpenters,

TABLE 1

Validity of Factor Scores for Job Training Criteria

Factor	Office Workers	Beauticians	Carpenters	Mechanics
Perceptual Speed	.46	—	—	—
Mechanical Knowledge	—	—	.39	.36
Carelessness	—	.33	—	− .27
Speed of Judgment	.31	.37	—	− .23

TABLE 2

Mean Factor Scores for Students Who Entered the Four Jobs

Factor	Office Workers	Beauticians	Carpenters	Mechanics
Perceptual Speed	58	52	47	47
Mechanical Knowledge	39	39	55	58
Carelessness	48	50	48	51
Speed of Judgment	53	51	48	49

and mechanics. The first two groups are girls, the second two are boys. Table 1 gives the validity coefficients for vocational shop course grades. Blanks occur in the table where the coefficients were nonsignificant. Table 2 gives the mean test scores for the four groups of students. For convenience of interpretation, the means have been converted so that 50 is the general mean of all groups and 10 is the standard deviation.

For the office worker group, Perceptual Speed and Speed of Judgment look good from the standpoint of the validity coefficients. Therefore, multiple regression would choose office workers who had high scores on these two aptitudes. Future office workers also have the highest mean scores on these two factors. Therefore, multiple discriminant analysis would guide into office jobs girls who had high scores on Perceptual Speed and Speed of Judgment. Thus, here is a case where both multiple regression and multiple discriminant analysis would select the same people for the job.

For mechanics, the validity coefficients recommend high Mechanical Knowledge, Carefulness (that is, there is a negative validity for number of careless errors), and Slowness of Judgment (there is a negative validity for number of choices made). The means, on the other hand, show that the criterion group of mechanics had high mechanical knowledge, but they were the most careless of the four groups and were speedier of judgment than the carpenters. This is a situation where multiple regression would guide different boys into mechanics than would multiple discriminant analysis.

For beauticians and carpenters, the two methods would also select somewhat different kinds of people.

Which method is the more suitable? Let me reply by asking a leading question. Do we want to encourage speedy, careless boys to go into mechanics just because mechanics are speedy and careless now, even though speed and carelessness correlate negatively with performance ratings?

I have tried to point out how two theoretical models for differential testing are related to the practical problem of counseling. The multiple regression techniques, when made possible by the nature of the data, seem to be more suitable, at least in view of the kind of discussion I have been advancing. Let me now turn to a discussion of some of the theory bearing upon the accuracy and the limitations of predicting amount of success by the multiple regression techniques.

There are two ways for measuring the effectiveness of differential testing that make pretty good sense to me. By inspecting the equations involved, it is possible to understand what things need to be maximized or minimized to attain the most accurate discriminations.

Paul Horst has developed a number of general formulas in this area. William Mollenkopf (3) has worked out a formula for the validity of a battery in predicting a difference between two criteria, a and b. This formula is Formula 1 given below. R_{d*d} is the validity of the differential prediction; that is, the correlation between d^* (the predicted difference) and d (the observed difference). Stars in this notation mean "predicted." R_{a*a} is the validity of the battery for criterion a, and R_{b*b} is the validity for criterion b; r_{a*b*} is the correlation between the predicted criterion scores, and r_{ab} is the correlation between the observed criterion measures.

Formula 1. Mollenkopf's formula for the validity of the prediction of a difference.

$$R_{d*d} = \frac{\sqrt{R^2_{a*a} + R^2_{b*b} - 2R_{a*a}R_{b*b}r_{a*b*}}}{\sqrt{2(1 - r_{ab})}}$$

It is clear from the equation that the validities for the two criteria should be high. The correlation between actual criteria, r_{ab}, depends upon what particular criteria are involved, and so is not in the experimenter's control. The critical point for Mollenkopf's equation is that the correlation between predictions should be as low as possible. Let me translate this demand of the equation into terms of direct interest to the constructer of the test battery. Let us suppose that each test in the battery had the same validity for criterion a as it had for criterion b. For example, suppose we are trying to discriminate between plumbing and carpentry. Perhaps a mechanical test has a high validity for both. Let's say a verbal test has a low validity for both. Then the same tests and same weights would be used to predict success in both plumbing and carpentry. The predictions for any one person would be exactly the same. r_{a*b*} would be 1.00, and, according to Formula 1, the validity of differential prediction would be zero. On the other hand, if each test has a very different validity for plumbing from what it has for carpentry, the predictions for the two criteria will be made on the basis of different tests or very differently weighted tests. The correlations between predictions, r_{a*b*}, will be a minimum. That is, it is a critical requirement for each test to have different validities for the different criteria. This differential validity is more likely to occur if the tests in the battery are highly independent one from another. Use of pure-factor tests or factor scores is one way to heighten chances of reaching this goal. The validity coefficients in Table 1 indicate that here is an instance where some success was attained in finding for each test widely different validities for the different criteria.

It is perhaps wise to remind ourselves here not to lose sight of the fact that good general prediction is also useful in counseling. That is, the student not only wants to know in which job he will do best, but he also wants to know how well he is likely to do. One should, therefore, consider the inclusion of some highly valid tests of mixed factorial content. There is a real danger of losing high general prediction when one is trying too hard to get good differential prediction.

Another way of judging the effectiveness of differential prediction that makes good sense to me was first described by T. L. Kelley (2) and later developed by Segel (4) and by Bennett and Doppelt (1). Suppose two persons stand at exactly the same level on some aptitude. When these two people are tested for this aptitude by fallible tests, there will be a difference between the scores they receive. If the testing is done repeatedly, a distribution of differences will evolve. This distribution of differences may be said to be entirely attributable to chance, since there is actually no difference between the aptitude levels of the two people. In the case where a real difference in aptitude level does exist, the observed differences in scores will be greater; they will be partly attributable to chance, and partly a reflection of the real difference in aptitude level. The effectiveness of differential testing can be stated in terms of the proportion of observed differences that are not attributable to chance. If the two variables in question are highly related, the real differences will be small. Therefore, the proportion that is *not* accounted for by chance will be low. If the two variables are relatively independent, the real differences will be large. If the tests are highly reliable, the chance differences will be small, and the proportion *not* accounted for by chance will be high.

For computing the proportion *not* accounted for by chance, Bennett and Doppelt (1) presented an easy-to-use nomograph. Kelley (2) presented a table yielding the desired proportion when entered by Formula 2 given below. In this value, the numerator gives the standard error of differences caused by the unreliability of the tests, and the denominator gives the over-all standard error of differences found between test scores. In the equation,

r_{1I} and r_{2II} are the reliabilities of the tests, and r_{12} is the correlation between the test scores.

Formula 2. Kelley's formula for a value used in obtaining the proportion of differences not accounted for by chance.

$$\frac{\sigma_{d.\infty\omega}}{\sigma_d} = \frac{\sqrt{2 - r_{1I} - r_{2II}}}{\sqrt{2 - 2r_{12}}}$$

While this formula was worked out for pairs of individual tests, there is no reason why it cannot be applied to pairs of test batteries. When we are interested in prediction, the batteries used for two criteria will usually overlap, because one or more of the tests are likely to be valid for both criteria. The correlations between the predictions for the two criteria are likely, therefore, to be high. The correlation between predictions is analogous to the r_{12} in the formula. The formula shows that it is critical to keep this correlation down. This can only be done by having relatively independent tests weighted as differently as possible in the prediction equations. This means that here again each test must have widely different validities for different criteria.

There is one very disturbing matter that seems fitting to discuss in connection with the foregoing remarks about highly differential validities, and about the choice between multiple regression and multiple discriminant analysis. It is something that tends to befuddle the multiple regression approach to differential prediction.

Let's say we are trying to predict success as a mechanic. In view of the correlations appearing in Table 1, the regression equation for this prediction will include a considerable weighting of Mechanical Knowledge and a smaller negative weighting of Carelessness and Speed of Judgment (or positive weighting of Carefulness and Slowness of Judgment). Now let's suppose that a hypothetical factor X was also, for some obvious psychological reason, absolutely essential for mechanics, so essential that all mechanics need it in a high degree. This factor X might be some such thing as a willingness to get all messed up with dirty grease. The range of scores on factor X would be at a high level, and very restricted in extent. This would make the observed validity coefficient for factor X low, perhaps so low that factor X would not enter into the prediction equation for mechanics at all. Suppose we used only the factors with high validities to make our predictions. Then we might predict that a certain student would do well as a mechanic, because he is high on Mechanical Knowledge and low on Carelessness and Speed of Judgment. Nevertheless, he might fail completely, because he lacked factor X.

This kind of error can be avoided in either of two ways. One way would be to apply a special cutting score in cases of variables like factor X. For example, a student would be given no prediction for success as a mechanic unless his factor X score fell within the range of the criterion group of mechanics for factor X. That is, unless the student is willing to get messed up with dirty grease, you don't predict his success as a mechanic at all. If his factor X score was in the proper range, his success in mechanics would then be properly predicted by the regression equation computed from uncorrected validity coefficients. For such individuals, whose factor X scores were already known to be within this high range, the amount of factor X possessed by them might be sufficient for success as a mechanic, and therefore not important in predicting amount of success. That is why the low validity coefficient of factor X would be appropriate, provided factor X was used separately to eliminate those whose scores on it are low.

The General Aptitude Test Battery (GATB) takes this matter into account through the rules it uses for selecting the "key aptitudes" upon which the qualification of individuals for jobs is based. Among these rules are the provisions that aptitudes should be considered as "key aptitudes" for a particular job if the mean score for people in that job is high relative to the mean score of the general population, and if the standard deviation of the scores for people in that job is low relative to that for the general population. By selecting "key aptitudes" in this way, GATB is giving extra weight to the aptitudes that are thought to be so important to a job that their range of scores for people on the job is high and restricted. The added weight given to such aptitudes will quite properly tend to offset the lowering of the observed validity coefficient due to restriction of range.

Now, let's examine again what we are really doing when we use a variable for guidance just because its mean is high for a particular criterion. Let's also examine what we are really doing when we correct for restriction of range. In the example I mentioned, it turned out that mechanics have a high mean in carelessness, even though the criterion values correlate negatively with carelessness. If we guide students into mechanics just because they resemble our criterion group of mechanics, we are assuming erroneously that it is good for mechanics to be careless. Let's say we have found that some people who tried to be mechanics but could not make the grade were low on factor X. This would show factor X to have positive validity, even though validity coefficients may not have revealed it. Or perhaps there is some psychological or practical reason that makes it logically apparent that mechanics should be high on factor X. If either of these things is so, it would be reasonable to guide into the mechanical trades only those students who were high on factor X.

Now, take the case where we do *not* have an independent study showing the validity of any aptitude with restricted range, and do *not* have any particular psychological reason for being sure that high scores on any aptitude are necessary for mechanics. If restriction of range on any one aptitude is extreme, we must, as I mentioned before, limit our predictions based on that aptitude to persons whose scores fall within the restricted range. If, on the other hand, restriction of range is, say, no greater than 50 per cent, it is possible to use the known range for mechanics and the known range for the total population to correct the obtained validity for restriction of range. When the corrected validity coefficient is used, the aptitude with a restricted range of scores should take its proper weighting in the regression equation, and any student, whether within the restricted range or not, can be given a prediction as to the amount of success he could expect if he entered mechanics.

This is all very satisfactory if the regression is linear. However, if there are no mechanics with low scores on factor X, we will not be able to tell whether it is linear. The lower part of the scatter plot of factor X scores versus mechanics criterion values does not exist. Linearity in this lower part of the scatter plot cannot be proved, but must be assumed in order to extrapolate the regression line to accommodate students with low values of factor X. If restriction is not more than 50 per cent, the assumption is probably not more dangerous than many of the assumptions we have to make in the field of testing. However, some accuracy of prediction is lost by having to extend the regression line out beyond the range that served to locate it experimentally. Not only do such predictions of scores suffer from the usual error variance of the distribution of actual scores above and below the regression line, but there is also error variance resulting from errors in the determination of the slope of the regression line. Such errors become increasingly serious as the predictor score recedes from the mean of the criterion group. Snedecor (5, p. 120) gives the formula for this variance. This is Formula 3 given below. The separate error variances are additive. The "*1*" in the parentheses is the usual error variance around the regression line.

Formula 3. Snedecor's formula for the standard error of a prediction for predictor scores not close to the mean of the criterion group.

$$S\overline{Y} = \sigma^2{}_{y.x}(1 + 1/N + X^2/\Sigma X^2)$$

"$1/N$" represents the error in locating the mean through which the regression line must pass, and "$X^2/\Sigma X^2$" represents the error variance caused by errors in the slope of the regression line.

How serious a reduction in the accuracy of prediction is this? If, for example, the range of a predictor is restricted 50 per cent because the criterion group consists of very high-scoring people on the predictor, a few students asking for guidance could be as far as eight standard deviations from the mean of the criterion group. Although this would be extreme, let's find out what the accuracy of prediction would be. With 100 cases, $X^2/\Sigma X^2$ would equal .64, $1/N$ would be .01. The error variance, then, would be 65 per cent higher than the error variance for cases near the mean. The standard error of the predictions would be 29 per cent higher. This is enough to be considered, but is not very serious, even for extreme cases, as long as restriction of range is not over 50 per cent, and as long as there are a reasonable number of cases in the experiment.

Again and again, it seems that there is not one best method for doing something. The method depends upon the practical purpose. If a student wants to know how well he will succeed if he goes into mechanics, you should tell him how much he resembles the typical mechanic only if that is all you are able to tell him. Otherwise tell him what he wants to know. Estimate his likelihood of attaining a given amount of success. If a predictor has a restricted range for some criterion, *don't* correct for restriction of range if you consider people outside the range to be unqualified anyway, but *do* correct for restriction of range if you want to get the best prediction for people outside the range. The statisticians and psychometricians offer us an impressive inventory of formulas from which to choose. However, this does not always make the choosing easy. For me, I think it's like being a little boy facing the horrendous problem of choosing exactly the right piece of candy from a great big box.

REFERENCES

1. Bennett, G. K., & Doppelt, J. E. The evaluation of pairs of tests for guidance use. *Educational and Psychological Measurement,* 1948, 8, 319–325.
2. Kelley, T. L. A new method for determining the significance of differences in intelligence and achievement scores. *Journal of Educational Psychology,* 1923, 14, 321–333.

3. Mollenkopf, W. G. Predicted differences and differences between predictions. *Psychometrika,* 1950, 15, 409–417.

4. Segel, D. *Differential diagnosis of ability in school children.* Baltimore: Warwick & York, 1934.

5. Snedecor, G. W. *Statistical methods applied to experiments in agriculture and biology.* (4th ed.) Ames, Iowa: Collegiate Press, 1946.

A Geometric Model for the Profile Problem[1]

DAVID V. TIEDEMAN

1953

Not less than five papers (1, 5, 8, 10, 12) published during the past five years are introduced by a statement that psychologists are increasingly becoming interested in the problem of studying the similarity of the psychological profile of an individual to some reference profile. This independent collaboration of interest in the problem is reassuring to a person like myself who has been working on this problem for the past year. This work is being conducted by the Educational Research Corporation under a contract between the Corporation and the United States Government, represented by Lloyd G. Humphreys,[2] Director of Research, Personnel Research Laboratory, Human Resources Research Center, Lackland Air Force Base. Phillip J. Rulon of Harvard University is the principal investigator for this project. I am indebted to Professor Rulon for many of the ideas discussed in this paper. However, responsibility for these remarks is completely mine.

Cronbach and Gleser (5), and Kogan (10) indicate that psychological profiles are studied for several reasons. However, the lists in both of these papers have the comparison of an individual with a group as a common purpose. In the short time available, I shall deal with just this problem. I do this not only because a model for a set of observations on individuals grouped together by some common *known* characteristic or characteristics is useful for vocational guidance, psychological diagnosis and prognosis, and anthropology, but also because any treatment of data designed to isolate types when the classification is *unknown* should be consistent with the model appropriate when the classification is *known*.

In order to reason from a concrete example, let us presume that the Air Force has administered experimentally an Activity Preference Inventory to

[1] This research was supported in whole or in part by the United States Air Force under Contract No. AF 18(600)-361 monitored by Director of Research, Personnel Research Laboratory, Lackland Air Force Base, San Antonio, Texas. Permission is granted for reproduction, translation, publication, use, and disposal in whole or in part by or for the United States Government.

[2] Now at University of Illinois, Urbana, Ill.—Ed.

all airmen inducted during a given month. The Activity Preference Inventory has a scale consisting of 30 pairs of activities, one member of the pair being an indoor activity, and the other member of the pair being an outdoor activity. Each airman must indicate preference for one activity of each pair. The score is a number of preferences for outdoor activities. The Inventory also has a second set of 35 pairs of activities, one member of the pair being a solitary activity, and the other member of the pair being a convivial activity. Airmen must indicate preference for one or the other activity in each pair, and the score is the number of preferences for convivial activities. Thus, each airman has two scores, X_1 and X_2.

The scores on the Activity Preference Inventory are not made available to career counselors during the career counseling of the airmen. Each airman is counseled and assigned to an Air Force specialty in the ordinary manner. After a time sufficient for airmen to assume duties of their specialties and for the Air Force to judge its satisfaction with the performance of the airmen in their specialties, airmen who were satisfied with, and were performing satisfactorily in, a specialty were classified according to that specialty. G groups or specialties resulted from this classification. Provided the bivariate distributions for each specialty are not all coincidental, the Air Force now has data for inferring the regions of an outdoor and convivial activity preference reference plane from which later satisfactory and satisfied airmen in each of these G specialties arise. From information such as this, we wish to determine the similarity of the outdoor and convivial activity preferences of a new airman to the outdoor and convivial activity preferences of airmen later satisfied with, and satisfactorily performing in, *each* of the G specialties.

Now consider the case of Tom Basic, who, when tested at induction, indicated preference for 18 outdoor and 19 convivial activities. If we define a test plane by constructing Cartesian reference axes such as those in Figure 1,[3] we may indicate all the information concerning the outdoor and convivial activity preferences of Tom Basic by placing a point in the test plane at the intersection of a line parallel to the convivial axis through the point representing 18 outdoor activity preferences, and a line parallel to the outdoor axis through the point representing 19 convivial activity preferences. The information that Tom Basic prefers 18 outdoor and 19 convivial activities is then called the *coordinates* of the point for Tom Basic. Thus, the scores X_i, where i takes the values 1 and 2, define a point in the test plane. Cronbach has referred to this model in at least three of his papers

[3] Figures, Tables, and Equations are in the Appendix at the end of the article on pp. 343–354.

(3, 4, 5). Cattell (2) refers to the model in his book on personality; Osgood and Suci (12) found the model useful in resolving some of the problems concerned in the analysis of semantic data; and Gaier and Lee (8) mention the model in a recent review. This form of representation of the set of scores is familiar to psychologists, since they have been making scatter diagrams for some time. However, it seems to be only recently that consistent attention has been given to this conceptualization of the profile of an airman.

We may, of course, indicate the two coordinates for Tom Basic on parallel reference axes, as in Figure 2. If we do this, we have a *profile*.

Let us suppose that, among the airmen to whom the Air Force administered the Activity Preference Inventory experimentally, 85 of them later became satisfactory and satisfied Clerk-Typists. The records of outdoor and convivial activity preferences of these 85 airmen are sorted from the records for all the airmen tested in the experiment, and recorded in a roster such as that of Table 1. If the outdoor and convivial activity preferences of these later satisfactory and satisfied Clerk-Typists are taken from Table 1 and enclosed in two sets of parallel lines as they are in Figure 3, and if the labels for rows and columns are deleted, the result is called a *matrix*. The score matrix, which has been designated X_1 in Figure 3, conveys exactly the same information as the roster for Clerk-Typists reported in Table 1. The matrix, however, has an advantage over the roster in Table 1; it immediately implies that the pairs of numbers like [10, 22], [14, 17], and so on, are coordinates of 85 points in the test plane. Cartesian representation of the matrix is given in Figure 4.

Figure 4 represents all information available to the Air Force concerning the meaning of expression of preference for outdoor and convivial activity for later presence in, satisfaction with, and satisfactory performance in, the Clerk-Typist specialty. The figure suggests: 1) that later satisfactory and satisfied Clerk-Typists tend to be found in the upper left portion of the test plane; 2) that the joint preferences for outdoor and convivial activities of later satisfactory and satisfied Clerk-Typists are more dense in the region of the test plane near the *centroid* of the Clerk-Typist group; 3) that the density of outdoor and convivial activity preferences of Clerk-Typists becomes less as one moves in all directions from the centroid; and 4) that dispersion along the new reference axis labeled x_{112} is more widespread than dispersion along the new reference axis x_{122}.

We noted earlier that a profile resulted from representation of the coordinates of the outdoor and convivial activity preferences of Tom Basic on parallel reference axes. In a similar way, we may form the profiles of outdoor and convivial activity preferences for each of the 85 Clerk-Typists, as in Figure 5. However, in Figure 5 we have not connected the outdoor activity coordinate of each airman with his convivial activity coordinate. Therefore, it is impossible to tell in Figure 5 which outdoor activity preferences are associated with which convivial activity preferences. Hence, we have *Profile Problem 1*: How may the joint preferences of each airman be represented? To represent the joint preference of each airman on a profile results in such a mess between the two profile stalks that the profile for Tom Basic, when plotted with respect to the profiles for Clerk-Typists, becomes obscure.

Because of this fact, we frequently indicate only two profiles when we wish to compare the profile for Tom Basic with those for Clerk-Typists. The two profiles are the profile for Tom Basic and the profile for the centroid of the Clerk-Typist group, as indicated in Figure 6. Figure 6 suggests immediately *Profile Problem 2*: How may the similarity of an airman to airmen in a particular specialty be expressed? In order to answer this question, let us note first that all of the 85 airmen whose outdoor and convivial activity preferences are represented in the test plane in Figure 4 and on profile axes in Figure 5 have the *same* label. Each one of these 85 airmen is a later satisfactory and satisfied Clerk-Typist. And yet, Figures 4 and 5 indicate that these 85 airmen expressed outdoor and convivial activity preferences at the time of induction that were neither coincidental nor collinear. This condition has occurred so frequently in my experience, and I am sure in yours as well, that I suggest we accept it, summarize it, and even give it the formal name, "axiom." Let's have the axiom read as follows:

Axiom 1. Points representing pairs of psychological observations on airmen grouped according to a common designation will ordinarily be dispersed about the centroid in a space of dimensionality two.

This axiom does no more than formalize for bivariate data the principles of individual differences and reliability that most of us accept.

Application of this axiom to the example under discussion results in a feeling of relaxation concerning the bivariate dispersion of outdoor and convivial activity preferences of the 85 airmen later classified as satisfactory and satisfied Clerk-Typists, as represented in Figure 4. All of these airmen *are* of the same kind. However, the outdoor and convivial activity preferences of all of these airmen are *not* of the same kind. Our task may then be stated this way: How likely is it that a random point (X_1, X_2), whose coordinates are the two test scores, will have a Clerk-Typist label associated with it?

An answer to this question necessitates a definition of similarity. Obviously, our definition of similarity cannot be so rigorous that points must be coincidental. If such a definition of similarity were employed it would result in missing almost all of the later satisfactory and satisfied Clerk-Typists. Cronbach and Gleser's index of eccentricity (5, p. 5) and Cattell's coefficient of pattern similarity (1) treat as similar all points lying on a circle centered at the centroid of the group. I have already indicated that wider dispersion along the x_{112} axis in Figure 4 than along the x_{122} axis is to be expected in the outdoor and convivial activity preferences of later satisfactory and satisfied Clerk-Typists. Consequently, if I were to define as similar points lying on a circle centered at the centroid of the Clerk-Typist specialty, I would be treating as similar points that occur with different relative frequences in the profiles for later satisfactory and satisfied Clerk-Typists. In order to overcome this difficulty, I define similarity in terms of equal probability of occurrence of a point within a specialty. This definition is a second fundamental tenet of my remarks and consequently I also state it as an axiom.

Axiom 2. Similar profiles within a specialty are those that occur with the same probability.

In order to apply this axiom to a comparison of the outdoor and convivial activity preferences of Tom Basic with those of later satisfactory and satisfied Clerk-Typists, it is necessary to specify the regions of equal probability in the test plane of Figure 4. Obviously, it is impossible to do this from the empirical data of Figure 4 itself, since there is no consistent location of points that occur with a frequency of 3, a frequency of 2, or a frequency of 1. Therefore, we turn to a theoretical distribution.

Figure 5 indicates that it is reasonable to assume that both the outdoor and convivial activity preferences of a large sample of later satisfactory and satisfied Clerk-Typists are distributed normally. Figure 4 indicates that the regression is approximately linear. When both conditions pertain, the bivariate distribution is distributed in a bivariate normal manner. Consequently, *we will assume that outdoor and convivial activity preferences of a large number of later satisfactory and satisfied Clerk-Typists will be distributed normally with means similar to that of this sample and with dispersion matrix similar to that of this sample.*

The dispersion matrix may be computed directly from the raw score matrix X_1 given as Figure 3 by defining both a matrix of means, as illustrated in Equation 1, and a matrix of number of cases, as illustrated in Equation 4, and performing the matrix operations indicated by Equations 2, 3, and 5.

For the Clerk-Typist data, the operations result in the dispersion matrix given as Equation 6. The matrix indicates that dispersion along the outdoor activity preference reference axis is somewhat greater than dispersion along the convivial activity preference reference axis, and that outdoor and convivial activity preferences are related positively to a small degree. Consequently, variation along the reference axis x_{112} in Figure 4 is greater than variation along the reference axis x_{122} in that figure. The dispersion matrix is, of course, a direct function of the raw score matrix, since it was computed from Equation 7, the expanded way of writing Equation 5. Thus, when treated in the right way, the score matrix X_1 reports all the information concerning outdoor and convivial preferences that is of psychological significance for inferring later duty as a Clerk-Typist. I say this with complete confidence because the indoor-outdoor and solitary-convivial scales of the Activity Preference Inventory are a figment of Professor Rulon's imagination as influenced by Professor Kelley's work on activity preferences, and data for Clerk-Typists were obtained by throwing dice to approximate specification of the matrix of means and the dispersion matrix.

In a bivariate normal distribution, the probability, $P(X_1, X_2)$, that a point, (X_1, X_2), drawn at random from the bivariate distribution will be from a small area surrounding the point is given by Equation 8, where the symbols μ, σ, and ρ have their usual meaning of population mean, standard deviation, and correlation respectively. For fixed values of these parameters, the probability depends only upon the quantity in the braces of Equation 8. This quantity is copied in Equation 9, and is called χ^2, following Pearson (13).

Since we do not know the values of the parameters in Equation 9, we choose their maximum likelihood estimates, sample means, standard deviations, and correlation. Computation of the correlation coefficient itself is not necessary, because if the matrix variable x_1 is defined as it is in Equation 10, χ^2 may be computed directly from Equation 11. I have written the subscript "1" after χ^2 in Equation 11 because this is the χ^2 for the deviation scores with respect to the means of the Clerk-Typist, or first, specialty. Equation 11 indicates that there are a number of values of the matrix variable x_1 that yield the same value of χ^2. The locus of points with equal values of χ^2 is that of an ellipse with center at the centroid of the Clerk-Typist group. The ellipse is symmetric about the Kelley (9) principal components of the Clerk-Typist data. Two of the set of iso-frequency ellipses are shown in Figure 7.

I have used the symbol χ^2 to denote the value obtained from the triple matrix product in Equation 11 because the distribution of this χ^2 is the same as the distribution of χ^2 used ordinarily in tests of independence or in tests of goodness of fit. The number of degrees of freedom associated with this χ^2 is the number of variates, in our illustration, two. Consequently, a value of χ^2 computed from Equation 11 may be evaluated in terms of probability from any of the tables of χ^2 commonly available. If greater accuracy for the relative frequency of the χ^2's which exceed a given χ^2 is desired, use Table IX of Pearson's *Tables for Statisticians and Biometricians, Part I* (13, pp. 22–23).

Thus, $\sqrt{\chi^2}$ is the distance in the Mahalanobis (11) sense of a point from the centroid for a specialty which is consistent with Axioms 1 and 2, and contains all of the psychological meaning for later presence in, satisfaction with, and satisfactory performance in, the Clerk-Typist specialty inherent in the matrix $\mathbf{X}_1$. If χ^2 is computed for every point in the bivariate Gaussian distribution, and if a frequency distribution of these χ^2's is determined, it is possible to compute the percentile rank of each χ^2 value. If computation is done such that a χ^2 of zero corresponds to the percentile rank 100, the percentile rank will indicate the per *cent* of points in the bivariate distribution beyond the cont*our* ellipse upon which a point with a given χ^2 value falls. For this reason, Rulon, Bryan, and I (15) have called this percentile rank a "centour" score. The centour score is not only a percentile index of distance, but also an estimate of the relative frequency with which the outdoor and convivial activity preferences of Clerk-Typists will exceed the χ^2 of the point representing the outdoor and convivial activity preferences of a given airman, provided outdoor and convivial activity preferences of Clerk-Typists reasonably approximate a bivariate Gaussian distribution. Thus, the centour score indicates the per cent of actual Clerk-Typists that will be assigned to some specialty other than the Clerk-Typist specialty if assignment to other specialties is made for values of the Clerk-Typist χ^2 equal to or greater than the value associated with a given point.

If we now evaluate Equation 11 for the 18 outdoor and 19 convivial activity preferences of Tom Basic, we get 3.8423 as the value of χ^2 for the comparison of the profile for Tom Basic with those for later satisfactory and satisfied Clerk-Typists. The χ^2's for approximately 15 per cent of the later satisfactory and satisfied Clerk-Typists exceed this value of χ^2. Thus, Tom Basic expressed preference for outdoor and convivial activities of a type whose discrepancy from the centroid of the Clerk-Typist specialty was exceeded by the discrepancies of 15 per cent of the later satisfactory and satisfied Clerk-Typists. If all airmen with a discrepancy this large or larger were excluded from the Clerk-Typist specialty, approximately 15 per cent of those who would normally become satisfactory and satisfied Clerk-Typists later would be excluded from that specialty.

The centour score permits interpretations of this nature for all points in the test plane. Centour scores may be summarized in a table such as Table 2. Table 2 contains the percentile equivalents of the distances of a sample of points in the test plane from the centroid for the Clerk-Typist specialty. Such information is quite useful in the career counseling of airmen.

This model is developed in terms of a single specialty. When the outdoor and convivial activity preferences of airmen who later became satisfactory and satisfied Aircraft & Engine Mechanics are assembled, they may be written as a new matrix of scores, as in Figure 8. The matrix X_2 is written without influence on the matrix X_1. The scores indicated in the rows of the matrix in Figure 8 represent the coordinates of a point in a test plane such as Figure 9 for each of the later satisfactory and satisfied A&E Mechanics. Figure 9 is constructed by adding a new set of points to the previous Figure 4. Figure 9 indicates that the location of the point representing the outdoor and convivial activity preferences of an airman in the test plane is related to later identification as a Clerk-Typist or an A&E Mechanic. Figure 9 indicates also that the meaning of outdoor and convivial activity preferences is different psychologically among later satisfactory and satisfied A&E Mechanics than it was among later satisfactory and satisfied Clerk-Typists. Among later satisfied and satisfactory A&E Mechanics, dispersion of outdoor and convivial activity preferences is greater along the axis x_{212} than it is along the axis x_{222}. This information is implied in the matrix X_2, but is not explicit.

In order to make the information of matrix X_2 explicit, it is necessary to form both a matrix of means and a matrix of number of A&E Mechanics, as has been done in Equations 12 and 14, respectively. The dispersion matrix for the A&E Mechanic group may then be computed from Equations 13 and 15. If the matrix variable x_2 is formed for every pair of scores X_1 and X_2 according to Equation 16, equal frequency points in the test space for the A&E Mechanic specialty lie on one of the set of homothetic ellipses given by Equation 17, provided the bivariate distribution of outdoor and convivial activity preferences of A&E Mechanics is reasonably normal. Addition of two of this new set of homothetic ellipses to Figure 7 results in Figure 10.

For Tom Basic, evaluation of Equation 17 gives 0.2629 as the value of χ^2 for the comparison of his point with those for A&E Mechanics. This χ^2 is exceeded by the χ^2's of approximately 88 per cent of the A&E Mechanics. Hence the centour score for Tom Basic's point compared with the A&E Mechanic distribution is 88. It indicates that the χ^2 of Tom Basic's point is exceeded quite frequently by the χ^2's of the points of later satisfactory and satisfied A&E Mechanics.

We now know that the centour score of the point for Tom Basic is 15, when compared to the later satisfactory and satisfied Clerk-Typists, and 88, when compared with the later satisfactory and satisfied A&E Mechanics. Tom's preferences for outdoor and convivial activities are more typical of those of later satisfactory and satisfied A&E Mechanics than they are of later satisfactory and satisfied Clerk-Typists.

Centour scores for comparison with A&E Mechanics may be added to Table 2, as they have been in Table 3. Table 3 contains all information from the outdoor and convivial activity preferences expressed by an airman at induction for inferring later presence in *either* the Clerk-Typist or the A&E Mechanic specialty.

In this brief consideration of a second specialty, I have indicated sufficient steps for extension of the logic to a third, fourth, and so on to the last or G group by means of induction. Computations specified by Equations 12–17 are simply repeated for each new group added. Table 3 may be augmented by a new row in each of the row blocks associated with a particular convivial activity preference score for each group.

The centour score model for inferring group membership provides implicit answers for Profile Problems 3 and 4. *Profile Problem 3* is: On what type of scales should profiles be represented? Centour scores are based upon the assumption that the bivariate distribution of each group is normal. Thus, the scale on which profiles are represented and the scale on which Cartesian representation of profile information is plotted should be such that an approximate bivariate normal distribution results in *each* group. When the distribution of each variate is normal in the group, and when regression is linear in the group, a bivariate normal distribution results for the group. Therefore, the basic requirements for the scale on which each variate is represented are that it produce an approximately normal distribution in *each* of the groups with which the profile for an airman is to be compared, and that it be related linearly to other variates in *each* group. Raw scores themselves may fulfill these properties. However, if the raw scores do not fulfill these properties, some transformation similar to the transformation used by Flanagan (7) in the construction of his Scaled Scores for the Cooperative tests may provide the desired conditions. The transformation is necessary for only those variates that do not fulfill both conditions in *each* group.

Profile Problem 4 is: On which group should profiles be standardized? In the comparison of a point with specialty 1, the comparison should be in terms of scores standardized on specialty 1. In comparison of a point with scores for specialty 2, the standardization should be in terms of scores for specialty 2, and so on, to the last, or G[th], specialty.

The centour score model has a further advantage of considerable importance. Equation 17 does not depend on the number of variates on which each individual is observed. Equations 12–16 need only be augmented appropriately for every variate added. Pearson (13, p. xxiv) has indicated that all points on the ellipsoid defined by the generalized form of Equation 17 are equally probable in a multivariate normal distribution. The value of the centour score can then be determined from a table of χ^2 with degrees of freedom equal to the number of variates or from Pearson's tables (13).

The volumes necessary to bind the tables of centour scores that would result from even as few as four or five variates and three or four groups will undoubtedly lead to immediate efforts to reduce the number of variates. In my opinion, these efforts will be most fruitful if they start from this model and evaluate the efficiency of the reduced number of variates with this model as the standard of efficiency. The Rao-Tukey-Bryan multiple discriminant function should not be overlooked in efforts at reduction.

The centour score conversion of χ^2 is, I believe, the index most useful in guidance work, especially of a vocational guidance nature. In work of this kind, I believe that the counselor should be aware of the realities of the ratios of individuals in various jobs, and that these realities should influence the interpretation of centour scores. However, I do not believe that the ratios given by numbers currently in jobs should have the influence on the interpretation of centour scores that they would have if the ratios were to be incorporated in this model, and if they were to affect classification regions in a test space such as that depicted in Figure 10. The introduction of these ratios into the interpretation of centour scores is, of course, necessary for the classification or assignment of men instead of their guidance. The introduction of these ratios will increase the efficiency of classification of men. However, boundaries of these classification regions are still functions of Equation 17. Therefore, this equation is one that must be determined whether the data are to be used for guidance purposes or for classification purposes. If the data are to be used for classification purposes, the centour scores need to be modified by the proportion of men in the specialty before classification is done. If the centour scores are to be used for guidance purposes, it is my feeling that each counselor should exercise his own judgment in dealing with the question of the ratio of men in each specialty.

In the development of the model, I have stated two axioms. One axiom expressed the faith that the observations of individuals sharing a common classification will contain multivariate dispersion of the observations about the centroid. The second axiom defined as similar those points within the common classification that occur with the same probability. With these two tenets in mind, I suggest that you trace the locus of points in a test plane resulting from efforts to describe psychological types by person-to-person comparison, mean scatter, vocabulary scatter, the selection of similar profiles, Cronbach and Gleser's index of distance (5), Cattell's coefficient of pattern similarity (1), and duMas' coefficient of profile similarity (6). If you do this, you will find the loci of points inconsistent with either or both of the axioms I have stated. In this situation, you are forced to abandon either the techniques as a means of isolating types or the axioms as a description of what you would expect the bivariate distributions for a type to be. Personally, I have questioned the techniques.

I indicated earlier that I considered it desirable to have an adequate model for inferring a known classification from a knowledge of psychological characteristics because I felt that efforts to develop an unknown classification system on the basis of multivariate observations should be consistent with the model appropriate to the known classification.

I wish that I could offer a solution to the problem of resolving a multivariate set of N points into the multivariate distributions of G types which is consistent with my two axioms. Someday I hope that someone will. If anyone is interested in thinking about this problem, I can at least share a lead with him. On pages 300–306 of Rao's recent book (14) you will find that Rao treats the problem of resolving a mixed series into two Gaussian components. Rao indicates that a solution of this problem for the case of a single variate and two groups in terms of the method of moments was discussed by Karl Pearson as early as 1894. The solution of this problem requires estimation of the two means, the two standard deviations, and the proportion of mixture from the data on the single variate of the mixed series. Rao gives an adaptation of Pearson's method. Rao further discusses the problems of sexing osteometric material on the basis of multiple measurements. These solutions should, I think, receive the attention of more psychologists.

REFERENCES

1. Cattell, R. B., r_p and other coefficients of pattern similarity. *Psychometrika*, 1949, 14, 279–298.
2. Cattell, R. B. *Personality: a systematic theoretical and factual study.* New York: McGraw-Hill, 1950.
3. Cronbach, L. J. "Pattern tabulation": a statistical method for analysis of limited patterns of scores, with particular reference to the Rorschach test. *Educational and Psychological Measurement,* 1949, 9, 149–171.

4. Cronbach, L. J. Statistical methods for multi-score tests. *Journal of Clinical Psychology,* 1950, 6, 21–26.
5. Cronbach, L. J., & Gleser, Goldine C. *Similarity between persons and related problems of profile analysis.* Urbana, Ill.: Bureau of Research and Service, College of Education, Univer. of Illinois, Technical Report No. 2, April 1952.
6. duMas, F. M. The coefficient of profile similarity. *Journal of Clinical Psychology,* 1949, 5, 123–131.
7. Flanagan, J. C. *The Cooperative achievement tests: a bulletin reporting the basic principles and procedures used in the development of their system of scaled scores.* New York: Cooperative Test Service, American Council on Education, 1939.
8. Gaier, E. L., & Lee, Marilyn C. Pattern analysis: the configural approach to predictive measurement. *Psychological Bulletin,* 1953, 50, 140–148.
9. Kelley, T. L. *Essential traits of mental life.* Cambridge, Mass.: Harvard Univer. Press, 1935.
10. Kogan, L. S. Statistical methods. In D. Brower & L. E. Abt (Eds.), *Progress in clinical psychology.* Vol. 1, (Sect.2). New York: Grune & Stratton, 1952. Pp. 519–535.
11. Mahalanobis, P. C. On the generalized distance in statistics. *Proceedings of The National Institute of Science, India,* 1936, 12, 49–55.
12. Osgood, C. E., & Suci, G. J. A measure of relation determined by both mean difference and profile information. *Psychological Bulletin,* 1952, 49, 251–262.
13. Pearson, K. (Ed.) *Tables for statisticians and biometricians, Part I.* (2nd ed.) London: Biometric Laboratory, University College, 1924.
14. Rao, C. R. *Advanced statistical methods in biometric research.* New York: Wiley, 1952.
15. Tiedeman, D. V., Bryan, J. G., & Rulon, P. J. *The utility of the airman classification battery for assignment of airmen to eight Air Force specialties.* Cambridge, Mass.: Educational Research Corporation, 1951. (Reprinted by Educational Research Corporation, March 1953.)

APPENDIX

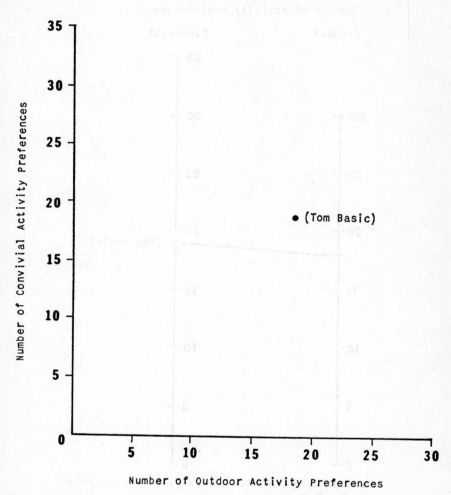

FIG. 1. *Cartesian representation: outdoor and convivial activity preferences*—Tom Basic.

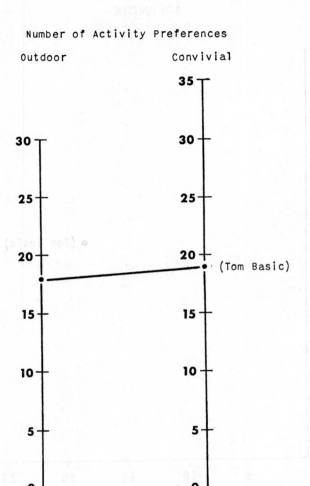

FIG. 2. *Profile representation: outdoor and convival activity prefer-*
ences—Tom Basic.

TABLE 1

Outdoor and Convivial Activity Preferences of Later
Satisfactory and Satisfied Clerk-Typists

Airman No.	Number of Activity Preferences	
	Outdoor	Convivial
1	10	22
2	14	17
3	19	33
.	.	.
.	.	.
.	.	.
85	16	24

$$\mathbf{X_1} = \begin{Vmatrix} 10 & 22 \\ 14 & 17 \\ 19 & 33 \\ \cdot & \cdot \\ \cdot & \cdot \\ \cdot & \cdot \\ 16 & 24 \end{Vmatrix} \quad \text{(85 rows)}$$

FIG. 3. *Matrix representation: outdoor and
convivial activity preferences*—Clerk-Typists.

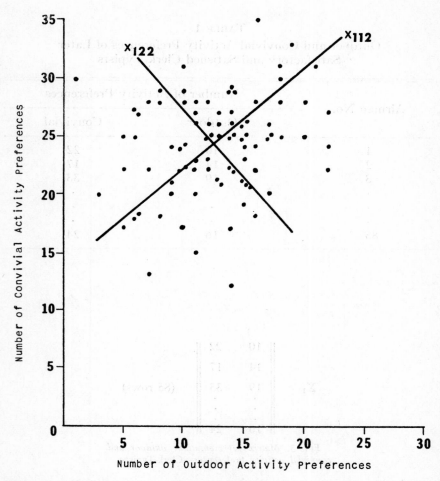

FIG. 4. *Cartesian representation: outdoor and convivial activity preferences*—Clerk-Typists.

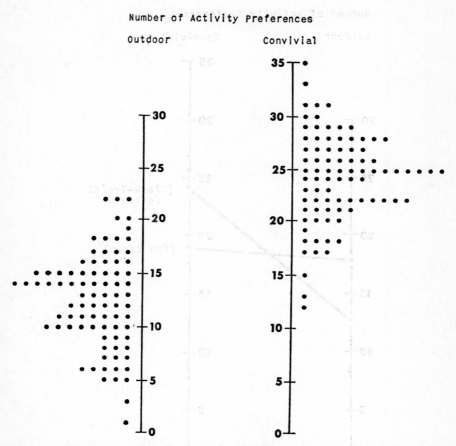

Number of Activity Preferences

Outdoor   Convivial

FIG. 5. *Profile representation: outdoor and convivial activity preferences*—Clerk-Typists.

347

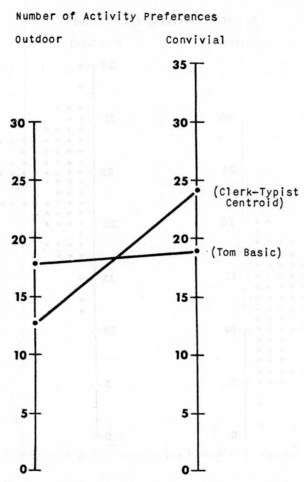

FIG. 6. *Profile representation: outdoor and convivial activity preferences*—Tom Basic and Clerk-Typist Centroid.

$$\bar{\mathbf{X}}_1 = \begin{Vmatrix} 12.5882 & 24.2235 \\ 12.5882 & 24.2235 \\ 12.5882 & 24.2235 \\ \cdot & \cdot \\ \cdot & \cdot \\ 12.5882 & 24.2235 \end{Vmatrix} \quad \text{(85 rows)} \qquad [\text{Eq. 1}]$$

$$\mathbf{x'}_1\mathbf{x}_1 = \mathbf{X'}_1\mathbf{X}_1 - \bar{\mathbf{X}}'_1\bar{\mathbf{X}}_1 = \Sigma_1 \qquad [\text{Eq. 2}]$$

$$\Sigma_1 = \begin{Vmatrix} \sum_{p=1}^{n_1} x^2_{p_1} & \sum_{p=1}^{n_1} x_{p_1}x_{p_2} \\ \\ \sum_{p=1}^{n_1} x_{p_2}x_{p_1} & \sum_{p=1}^{n_1} x^2_{p_2} \end{Vmatrix} \qquad [\text{Eq. 3}]$$

$$N_1 = \begin{Vmatrix} \sqrt{85} & 0 \\ 0 & \sqrt{85} \end{Vmatrix} \qquad [\text{Eq. 4}]$$

$$D_1 = N_1^{-1}\Sigma_1 N_1^{-1} \qquad [\text{Eq. 5}]$$

$$D_1 = \begin{Vmatrix} 20.006920 & 4.562629 \\ 4.562629 & 18.573564 \end{Vmatrix} \qquad [\text{Eq. 6}]$$

$$D_1 = N_1^{-1}(\mathbf{X'}_1\mathbf{X}_1 - \bar{\mathbf{X}}'_1\bar{\mathbf{X}}_1)N_1^{-1} \qquad [\text{Eq. 7}]$$

$$P(X_1, X_2) = \frac{1}{2\pi\sigma_1\sigma_2(1-\rho^2)^{1/2}} e - 1/2\left\{\frac{1}{1-\rho^2}\left[\left(\frac{X_1-\mu_1}{\sigma_1}\right)^2 - \right.\right.$$
$$\left.\left. 2\rho\left(\frac{X_1-\mu_1}{\sigma_1}\right)\left(\frac{X_2-\mu_2}{\sigma_2}\right) + \left(\frac{X_2-\mu_2}{\sigma_2}\right)^2\right]\right\} dX_1 dX_2 \quad [\text{Eq. 8}]$$

$$\frac{1}{1-\rho^2}\left[\left(\frac{X_1-\mu_1}{\sigma_1}\right)^2 - 2\rho\left(\frac{X_1-\mu_1}{\sigma_1}\right)\left(\frac{X_2-\mu_2}{\sigma_2}\right) + \left(\frac{X_2-\mu_2}{\sigma_2}\right)^2\right] = \chi^2 [\text{Eq. 9}]$$

$$\mathbf{x}_1 = \|(X_1 - \bar{\mathbf{X}}_1) \quad (X_2 - \bar{\mathbf{X}}_2)\| \qquad [\text{Eq. 10}]$$

$$\mathbf{x}_1 D_1^{-1}\mathbf{x'}_1 = \chi^2_1 \qquad [\text{Eq. 11}]$$

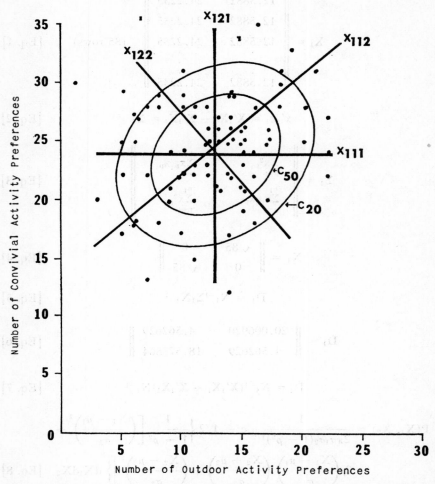

Fig. 7. *Cartesian representation: outdoor and convivial activity preferences*—Clerk-Typist Centour Specialty Psychographs.

350

TABLE 2
Centour Scores: Outdoor and Convivial Activity Preferences
(*Clerk-Typists*)

	Number of Activity Preferences						
	Outdoor						
Convivial	0	5	10	15	20	25	30
35	*	*	02	04	02	*	*
30	*	05	27	40	16	02	*
25	01	20	80	86	25	02	*
20	02	20	58	45	09	01	*
15	01	05	10	06	01	*	*
10	*	*	*	*	*	*	*
5	*	*	*	*	*	*	*
0	*	*	*	*	*	*	*

* Centour ≤ 0.5

$$\mathbf{X}_2 = \begin{Vmatrix} 20 & 27 \\ 21 & 15 \\ 15 & 27 \\ \cdot & \cdot \\ \cdot & \cdot \\ 19 & 16 \end{Vmatrix} \quad \text{(93 rows)}$$

Fig. 8. *Matrix representation: outdoor and convivial activities preferences*—A&E Mechanics.

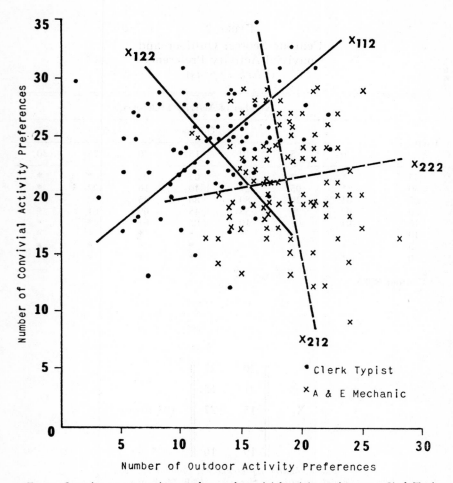

FIG. 9. *Cartesian representation: outdoor and convivial activity preferences*—Clerk-Typists and A&E Mechanics.

$$\bar{\mathbf{X}}_2 = \begin{Vmatrix} 18.5376 & 21.1398 \\ 18.5376 & 21.1398 \\ 18.5376 & 21.1398 \\ \cdot & \cdot \\ \cdot & \cdot \\ 18.5376 & 21.1398 \end{Vmatrix} \quad \text{(93 rows)} \qquad [\text{Eq. 12}]$$

$$\mathbf{X'}_2\mathbf{X}_2 - \bar{\mathbf{X}}'_2\bar{\mathbf{X}}_2 = \Sigma_2 \qquad [\text{Eq. 13}]$$

$$N_2 = \begin{Vmatrix} \sqrt{93} & 0 \\ 0 & \sqrt{93} \end{Vmatrix} \qquad [\text{Eq. 14}]$$

$$D_2 = N_2{}^{-1}\Sigma_2 N_2{}^{-1} \qquad [\text{Eq. 15}]$$

$$\mathbf{x}_2 = \big\| (\mathbf{X}_1 - \bar{\mathbf{X}}_1) \quad (\mathbf{X}_2 - \bar{\mathbf{X}}_2) \big\| \qquad [\text{Eq. 16}]$$

$$\mathbf{x}_2 D_2{}^{-1}\mathbf{x'}_2 = \chi_2{}^2 \qquad [\text{Eq. 17}]$$

TABLE 3

Centour Scores: Outdoor and
Convivial Activity Preferences
(*Clerk-Typists and A&E Mechanics*)

Specialty	Convivial	\multicolumn{7}{c}{Number of Activity Preferences / Outdoor}
		0	5	10	15	20	25	30
C-T	35	*	*	02	04	02	*	*
A & E		*	*	*	01	01	*	*
C-T	30	*	05	27	40	16	02	*
A & E		*	*	01	11	12	02	*
C-T	25	01	20	80	86	25	02	*
A & E		*	*	05	46	61	11	*
C-T	20	02	20	58	45	09	01	*
A & E		*	*	05	57	90	19	01
C-T	15	01	05	10	06	01	*	*
A & E		*	*	02	21	38	09	*
C-T	10	*	*	*	*	*	*	*
A & E		*	*	*	02	05	01	*
C-T	5	*	*	*	*	*	*	*
A & E		*	*	*	*	*	*	*
C-T	0	*	*	*	*	*	*	*
A & E		*	*	*	*	*	*	*

* Centour ≤0.5

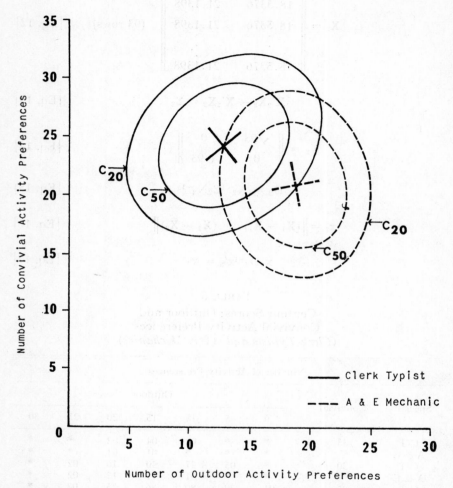

FIG. 10. *Cartesian representation: centour specialty psychographs*—Clerk-Typist and A&E Mechanic.

Uses and Limitations of Factor Analysis in Psychological Research

H. J. EYSENCK

1949

Factor analysis has been much criticized by orthodox statisticians as well as by idiopathically-minded psychologists, although for different and frequently opposite reasons. These criticisms often stem from inadequate understanding—inadequate understanding of the assumptions involved and the statistical methods used on the part of the "idiopaths," and inadequate understanding of the purposes underlying its use on the part of the statisticians. As always, the uses and limitations of a mathematical method of analysis depend on the purposes it is designed to serve. In the case of factor analysis, there appear to be two main purposes: 1) to discover taxonomic principles in a field in which so little is known that no reasonable hypotheses can be set up and tested, and 2) to test deductions made from taxonomic hypotheses in a field studied sufficiently to allow the setting up of promising theories. In both cases, it will be seen, the problem is one of taxonomy or classification; factors are conceived as principles of classification that allow us to order our field of study in a way determined by the properties of the material with which we are dealing, rather than in terms of subjective preference, intuition, or on the basis of common sense.

It will be clear that factor analysis is differentiated from all the orthodox procedures of statistics—determination of significance of differences, analysis of variance and covariance, discriminant function analysis, sequential analysis, and so forth—by the fact that where all the orthodox procedures test the null hypothesis as regards differences between certain groups which are known a priori, or in terms of previous experimental investigation, factor analysis attempts to answer the much more fundamental question: "What are the principles of classification which obtain in this particular field, and according to which experimental groups ought to be selected for the determination of significant differences?"

This differentiation links up with the fundamental problem in mental testing, namely, that of validity. We must distinguish very clearly between two types of validity, which we may tentatively call lower-order validity and higher-order validity. The usual textbook definition of validity as "agreement with a criterion" refers to lower-order validity, and is essentially an engineering concept. If we select a simple criterion, such as number of bolts soldered per hour, or number of accidents per month, we can easily determine the "validity" of a given test by correlating it with the criterion. But while such a determination may have a certain amount of practical usefulness in human engineering, its scientific value is almost precisely nil.

The difficulty of this conception of "validity" is brought out clearly when we apply it to truly psychological concepts such as "intelligence," or "extraversion," or "suggestibility." Here we have either no criterion at all, or a multiplicity of criteria which do not correlate very highly with each other. We must, therefore, look for a criterion to decide which of the many criteria to use, a procedure that gives rise to an infinite regress of looking for criteria to decide which of several criteria to use in deciding which is the correct criterion, and so forth.

Once this situation arises in which no clear-cut external criterion is available—and this is the case in connection with every genuinely psychological concept I know of—we must have recourse to some form of higher-order concept of validity. Such a concept can only derive from the adoption of the internal-consistency approach; in other words, as in every other science, the isolated fact acquires meaning only in relation to other facts; and interpretation, measurement, and conceptualization become possible by coordinating the isolated facts in a system capable of functional development through the use of the hypothetico-deductive method (4). It is not claimed that factor analysis is the only possible variant of this internal-consistency approach; it is merely claimed that at the present stage of development of mental testing procedures, no other method is available that will answer the taxonomic, classificatory questions that arise. Nor is it claimed that factor analysis is perfect in its present form; all of us who have used it on any large scale will agree that there are many aspects of it that require improvement or even drastic overhauling. But for the type of problem I have outlined, there simply does not appear to be an alternative, although that does not mean that we should not go on looking for one that is free of the admitted difficulties attending the factorial approach.

Two brief examples will illustrate the use of factorial methods in relation to the two main purposes I mentioned at the beginning. The first purpose related to the discovery of taxonomic principles in a field in which so little is known that no reasonable hypothesis can be set up and tested. In our early work on factors determining aesthetic preferences, we made an attempt to discover the reasons underlying preferences for different types of poetry (1). The literature threw no light on this problem, and consequently a factor-analytic design was set up. Some thirty poems, each relatively short, were ranked in order of preference by our subjects; these rankings were correlated and factor analyzed. Two factors emerged, without rotation, which could be interpreted very clearly on the basis of the poems most liked and most disliked by the subjects having high positive or negative saturations respectively on these factors. The first factor divided those who like a simple rhyming scheme (a-b, a-b), a regular, evenly accentuated rhythm, and a clearly defined ending to each line from those who like complex rhyming schemes, irregular, uneven rhythms, and lines that continue from one to the other without clear breaks. I do not want to waste time by discussing the second factor also; one factor will illustrate my point sufficiently. Starting from a position in which we have no guiding principles as to how we should classify our material, we emerge with a clear-cut hypothesis determined essentially by the internal organization of the preference judgments. This hypothesis allows of disproof and of functional development; we have tested it by predicting preference for poems not contained in our original sample, and we have developed it functionally by showing that similar principles of organization obtain in preferences for pictures, jokes, statues, and other aesthetic objects, and by showing that this simplicity-complexity factor is correlated with temperament (2). Many other examples could be given, but I think this one is sufficient to illustrate our point that factor analysis may give rise to classificatory hypotheses.

As an example to illustrate our second claim, namely, that factor analysis can be used to test a classificatory hypothesis, I may perhaps quote our studies in suggestibility (3). The hypothesis was set up that eight well-known tests of suggestibility measured one and the same underlying variable, which might be identified with this concept of suggestibility. Intercorrelations were run among the eight tests, and a factor analysis performed. The analysis showed that two factors were needed to account for the observed correlations within the limits of the sampling error, and that the tests were grouped in the two-dimensional space of this two-factor pattern in such a way that four tests—the body-sway test originated by Hull, the Chevreul Pendulum test, and two arm-levitation tests—constituted one group, while tests of the Binet type—progressive lines, progressive weights, etc.—constituted the other group. These two groups were entirely uncorrelated, the angle of separation between the centroids passing through them being almost exactly 90°. The original hypothesis is conclusively disproved, and the hypothesis suggested that we are dealing with two separate types of suggestibility which we called "primary" and "secondary," or "ideomotor" and "sensory" suggestibility. When this new hypothesis was tested by using different populations and additional tests (such as a measure for hypnotizability and a variety of tests of the sensory kind), the deductions made were confirmed in each instance (5). Here, then, we have an example of how factor analysis can be used to disprove a hypothesis, namely, that of a general factor of suggestibility; how it can suggest instead another hypothesis; and how it can be used to test this new hypothesis.

A third possible use of factor analysis may lie in a field in which it has not hitherto been used to any significant extent, namely, that of the description of social groups. It is customary to describe individuals and groups in terms of scores on psychometric tests; thus, a group of Democrats may be more "radical" than a group of Republicans in terms of some measure of radicalism-conservatism. However, it is possible that differences between groups may be apparent more in the organization of component attitudes than in over-all scores. Two groups may not differ with respect to "radicalism" as measured, but they may show differences with regard to the pattern of intercorrelations between the component attitudes. Factor analysis appears to be the preferred method for disclosing and quantifying such differences in organization, and it has been used in this way in our studies into the organization of social attitudes as determined by political party, age, sex, education, and nationality.

If these are the uses of factor analysis, what are its limitations? One serious limitation lies in the lack of statistical criteria of significance for factor loadings, for variances, and for residuals. While we have approximations, and at least one method (namely, that of Lawley) which permits of the application of such criteria, nevertheless the absence of practicable and accurate methods for estimating significance is a serious business. Another limitation is implied in the outline of the use of factor analysis given above —the evidence given by factorial methods is often suggestive rather than definitive, permissive rather than conclusive. However, factor analysis shares this limitation with almost all other scientific research methods.

While these limitations are admitted, others, also often suggested by critics, are not. The fact that factor analysts do not always agree, for instance, is no more a criticism of factor analysis, and does not set up any more necessary limitations than does the fact that the respective schools started by Weierstrass and Kronecker in mathematics hold diametrically opposed views on the nature of such a fundamental concept as numbers limit the usefulness of mathematics. The fact that factor analysis makes certain assumptions regarding linearity and the additive nature of its variables does not constitute a necessary limitation, as these assumptions can be tested, and as methods of factor analysis not dependent on them can be envisaged. The fact that factorial analyses often give results that are plainly absurd constitutes a limitation of factorial analysis only in the sense that this statistical method does not guarantee success, when inappropriately used and inexpertly handled, any more than does calculus or any other mathematical technique. Factor analysis requires just as insightful statement of the problem, just as careful design of the experiment, and just as skillful interpretation psychologically of the results as does any other technique; if used in any other way, it will prove misleading and unhelpful. Its limitations, insofar as they are not merely of a temporary technical nature, are defined by its purposes—while useful and indeed essential for certain purposes, it throws no light on other types of problems, and does not attempt to displace other methods more adequate for their solution. In other words, like all scientific methods, its usefulness is not universal, but circumscribed, and only the mature judgment of the expert can decide whether in a given situation it is likely to give him the answer he wants.

REFERENCES

1. Eysenck, H. J. Some factors in the appreciation of poetry, and their relation to temperamental qualities. *Character and Personality,* 1940, 9, 160–167.
2. Eysenck, H. J. The experimental study of the "good Gestalt"—a new approach. *Psychological Review,* 1942, 49, 344–364.
3. Eysenck, H. J. Suggestibility and hysteria. *Journal of Neurology, Neurosurgery and Psychiatry,* 1943, 6, 22–31.
4. Eysenck, H. J. *Dimensions of personality.* New York: Macmillan, 1949.
5. Eysenck, H. J., & Furneaux, W. D. Primary and secondary suggestibility: an experimental and statistical study. *Journal of Experimental Psychology,* 1945, 35, 485–503.

Psychometric Approaches to
Factor Analysis[1]

HENRY F. KAISER

1964

The title of this paper is seemingly delimiting: apparently I am only to talk about the "psychometric" side of factor analysis. This restriction gives substantial pause for thought, for what indeed does "psychometric" mean? Is it unduly restrictive?

First, the term can be used in a negative sense, so that I am not to be concerned with recent developments on the statistical (inferential) side of factor analysis; consequently, I shall not talk about sampling distributions, tests of significance, and all the rest of the jargon associated with the problem of making probabalistic inferences from samples of individuals to populations of individuals; we shall consider that populations of individuals are available or, more realistically, that our sample-population inferences are nonprobabilistic. Therefore, let us first consider the psychometric side of factor analysis as a concern for what indeed *is* the mathematical model of factor analysis, and how, algebraically, one thinks about it. Louis Guttman once said informally, "We have to clean up the algebra of factor analysis before we can, appropriately, hand it over to the statisticians." My successor on this program, Ledyard Tucker, has many times said essentially the same thing. Since these two gentlemen are undoubtedly the two heaviest of the heavyweights in the theory of factor analysis, restricting consideration to the nonstatistical side is, in all likelihood, not entirely a sterile enterprise.

The term "psychometric," though, has an important, and somewhat more pretentious, meaning—with connotations that are distinctly of a scientific, inferential nature. Often hidden in the maze of algebra and computations of factor analysis is the fact that these procedures are ultimately rather explicitly concerned with inferences about domains of scientific con-

---

[1] This paper was prepared while the author was the L. L. Thurstone Distinguished Fellow, Psychometric Laboratory, University of North Carolina.

tent, i.e., that we are faced with the important problem, beyond merely statistical description, of attempting to infer the nature of the structure of a large—usually arbitrarily large—battery or universe or domain of variables or tests on the basis of a limited sample (*selection* might be a better word) of variables. In this sense, factor analysis might be called "psychometric inferential," and an explicit concern for this kind of scientific inference is indeed the first problem of factor analysis.

Before I get down to brass tacks, allow me to delimit myself in a way not suggested by my title. I shall restrict myself to considerations of what might be called traditional—or exploratory—factor analysis. I can illustrate this by giving two extreme kinds of situations in which factor analysis is applied. Often, a consultant is confronted with a seemingly sincere "investigator" who presents a large table of numbers and wants to "do" a factor analysis, and for which the apparent principal justification for proposing to do this deed is that the large table just referred to is neatly written out. At the other extreme is the proposed factor-analytic investigation for which every variable to be included has been subjected to the most searching rationalization and, with this case, the hope is that very specific hypotheses can be adjudicated definitively. The former extreme is, of course, to be eschewed, while for the latter, there are perhaps more powerful techniques available (some of which are factor analytic in nature, thanks to Tucker and Guttman). Thus, I would like to put in a plug for steering a middle course, and suggest that factor analysis as it is usually known enjoys its greatest justification as an exploratory technique, by which the variables under consideration all enjoy a reasonably well-rationalized, but not necessarily certain, probability of belonging to the scientific domain of interest, and the structure of which is essentially unknown.

From this viewpoint, factor analysis is an unpretentious "bringer of preliminary order out of well-perceived chaos," a technique capable of generating ideas rather than providing final answers. Thus, be reasonably—not compulsively—careful in planning a factor-analytic investigation. But don't take your results with such seriousness as to preclude further—probably more penetrating—analysis.

It is convenient to divide the theoretical problems of factor analysis into two groups: 1) those concerned with finding an interesting factor space, the so-called communality problem, and 2) those concerned with finding an interesting basis (coordinate system) for the interesting factor space, the so-called rotation problem. It is almost accurate to say that these two problems, conceptually, are independent of one another. First, then, the communality problem.

D. N. Lawley (12) in 1940 gave what we now recognize as one definitive solution to the problem of factoring. This is his famous maximum likelihood solution. Subsequently, much work has been done with his procedures, particularly by Lawley himself, and by Rao (14) who, in clarifying and specializing the method, renamed it "canonical factor analysis." It is perhaps best described in Rao's terms as the solution of a certain problem in canonical correlation, and operationally as a principal-axes solution of a *rescaled,* reduced correlation matrix. That is, the correlation matrix, with communalities in the diagonal, then has the variances of the variables changed in a way to solve a problem in canonical correlation. The result of this rescaling, or change of metric, has the most important property of leading to solutions that are invariant under *any* rescaling: the solution is scale-free, different from many traditional factoring methods (e.g., that anachronism, the centroid method).

Now, the Lawley-Rao method, in particular, rescales in the metric of the unique parts of the observable variables, but to obtain this profoundly important property of securing scale-free solutions, it is sufficient (but not necessary) to rescale in the metric of the unique parts; one can go to the other extreme and rescale in the metric of the common, or communality, parts of the observable variables. John Caffrey and I noticed this a couple of years ago; more accurately, we noticed nothing more than that one could write down an eigenequation paralleling Rao's—and wondered if it meant anything. Apparently it does, for in groping for a rationalization for our writing Rao with backwards rescaling, we found that we were, in solving this affair, determining common factors that successively have maximum reliability in the generalized Kuder-Richardson sense: i.e., factors with maximum "alpha," to use Cronbach's term.

For those of you who are interested in more detail in these two scale-free procedures for finding arbitrary factors, let me refer you to our paper, "Alpha Factor Analysis" (10). I like to think that this paper is quite readable; I would be the first to admit that our very psychometrically oriented procedure undoubtedly enjoys its principal justification today because it was provoked by attempting to imitate the work of Lawley and Rao. I would hope that those who read our paper will be able to provide Caffrey and me with more incisive understanding of what is going on.

Both attacks described above for the communality problem were developed most fundamentally under what might be called the "pure" factor-analytic model of L. L. Thurstone. As many are aware, there are other models, factor analytic in flavor, giving factor-analytic results in practice, but which are not strictly factor analysis. I refer here to the monumental work of Hotelling (6) in his component analysis, and to the monumental work of Guttman (2) in his image analysis. My reference above to the problem of finding an "interesting factor space" rather than a "common factor space" was deliberate: I most certainly do want to talk about both component analysis and image analysis, because practically these methods will yield results that differ only minutely from those obtained under the pure factor-analytic model, while they enjoy many elegant technical simplifications, and in practice have the tremendous advantage of being capable simply of solving the factor-score problem. In "pure" factor analysis the factor-score problem is insoluble (more accurately, a unique solution does not exist).

I do not have the time to describe Guttman's image analysis; I will only assert—and refuse to stand for any arguments—that his basic 1953 *Psychometrika* paper (2) is required reading for the serious student, for all who aspire to be lifted out of the primordial mire which preceded it. Now, Guttman did not explicitly develop his ideas with direct reference to work-a-day factor analysis; this link was provided by Harris (4) in the most important paper to appear in the last ten years on the communality problem. It is also required reading.

What Harris accomplished was to bring together many of the provocative psychometric properties of image analysis, and show their intimate relationship to Rao's version of maximum likelihood factor analysis—again probably better termed "canonical factor analysis." The crucial insight here was brought about again by rescaling: in order to obtain a scale-free solution, Harris rescaled in the metric of the anti-images (the analog of unique parts in factor analysis), and provided us, right down the line, with the image-analytic version of canonical factor analysis. Most important practically, in this context, Harris solved the "number of factors" question, but I shall defer talking about this until I summarize the communality problem below.

The three solutions described above, 1) Rao-Lawley canonical factor analysis, 2) Kaiser-Caffrey alpha factor analysis, and 3) Guttman-Harris image analysis, let me reiterate, all have the elegant property of yielding factors invariant under changes of scale—one no longer need be concerned about units of measurement, as the same results are obtained regardless. Initial factoring procedures that do not have this property deserve only one treatment: the ash can. What, then, about the popular use of Hotelling's principal component analysis, which does *not* have this property? The rule of thumb of taking only such components of the *correlation* matrix with latent roots or eigenvalues greater than one—proposed years ago by me

(7) originally for no really good theoretical reason—has disdainfully been referred to as "Little Jiffy" by some of my thoughtful colleagues. It turns out, though, in a component-analysis setting (no unique factors postulated), that if we maximize Cronbach's coefficient alpha rather than Hotelling's variance-accounted-for, Little Jiffy can be rescued from the ash can of non-scale-free solutions; more exactly, if we maximize alpha, we automatically rescale into the correlation matrix associated with any covariance matrix and, thus, are able to determine scale-free components. So, more or less after the fact, we can add a fourth scale-free procedure—the popular Little Jiffy—for determining an interesting factor space.

These four methods can be summarized in the following two-by-two table:

Canonical Factor Analysis	Image Analysis (à la Harris)
Alpha Factor Analysis	Principal Components (Little Jiffy)

All four procedures involve principal-axes solutions, with rescaling; all four are scale free. The two on the left are "pure" factor analysis, and may be obtained operationally by iterating on the solution immediately to the right. The two on the right in this sense are first approximations to those on the left, and while they are not factor analysis in the strict sense, they do yield very similar results to their counterparts. They have the substantial advantage of giving factors that are linear combinations of the observable variables and, thus, of yielding scores on the derived variables or "factors" with no fuss—in stark contrast to the absence of a unique solution for factor scores in the purely factor-analytic solutions.

Probably the most important side of the communality problem in practice is the hoary old question of the "number of factors." In the foregoing two-by-two table, the number of factors that come out "naturally" in the first row, for canonical factor analysis and for image analysis à la Harris, is Guttman's (3) classic strongest-lower-bound, empirically "too many"—about half the number of variables observed. For the second row—alpha factor analysis and principal component analysis of the correlation matrix (Little Jiffy)—the number of factors that come out "naturally" is Guttman's (3) classic weaker-lower-bound, the number of eigenvalues greater than one of the correlation matrix, usually about the "right" number.

I might say that Guttman's weaker-lower-bound, in giving *about* the "right" number, can sometimes give too few, and underfactoring is a catastrophe. His stronger-lower-bound, which invariably gives too many, can never lead to this disaster of underfactoring; overfactoring is usually only a mild irritant, which may be cured by careful thought. I wish that I were able more successfully to promote this idea, but generally practitioners want exactly the "right" answer for the number of factors to be given without careful thought, and that, gentle readers, is as unattainable as Eldorado.

I'm not going to reveal which of the four solutions discussed above is the right one; the question really is without meaning. I *will* say that four is a somewhat smaller number than the myriad of techniques one is confused by in the earlier literature.

The result is an interesting factor space, preferably found by one of the four methods just reviewed. Its basis, however, is not interesting—being some variety of (rescaled) principal axes—so this original basis should be changed by a linear transformation, i.e., it should be "rotated." What is the current state of this general problem? For objectivity's sake, I shall restrict myself to analytic methods; consistent with considering factor analysis in its traditional, exploratory vein, I shall also consider that I am going in "blind," searching for a structure, rather than testing for the existence of a postulated structure.

In this venture, I first distinguish the so-called "orthogonal" from the so-called "oblique" case, according to the kind of restrictions I place on the transformation matrix. This distinction usually—but not always—bears a one-to-one relation to whether I restrict the transformed factors to being uncorrelated or not.

In the orthogonal case, present criteria are almost invariably of the form:

$$Q - wK = \text{maximum}$$

where Q is the quartimax function (13), and K is the function which, in conjunction with a weight w of one, turns the criterion into varimax. More generally, this weight w controls the variability in the variance contributions (column sums of squares) of the factors; at one extreme, for $w = -\infty$, we have principal factors; for $w = 0$, quartimax; for $w = 1$, varimax; for $w =$ one-half the number of factors, Saunders' (15, 17) "equamax;" and for $w = \infty$, all factors have exactly equal column sums of squares. Recently, I have looked at this class of criteria with some care, particularly at values of w greater than one, in the hope of obtaining orthogonally rotated factors with more nearly equal variance contributions—a hope generated by the concern of some investigators who have expressed little doubts here and there as to the ubiquity of varimax. Unfortunately, I have been able to prove that it is always possible, for any trans-varimax solution where w is chosen greater than one, even by a smidgen, to produce examples in which utter catastrophe occurs, and two pure, independent, uncorrelated clusters will be subjected to a 45° rotation. I have also looked at criteria in this class where w is generated by the data; here I have been able to prove that the factorial invariance (in simple cases) that obtains for varimax cannot, in general, occur. I must conclude that within this class of solutions, varimax best does the deed. But here "best" has mostly a negative connotation: the old reliable work-horse varimax will never result in catastrophe, while other criteria in this class, perhaps better in specific problems, can be disastrous in others.

It appears, then, that further progress in the orthogonal case must come from an entirely fresh start. The most promising development that I know of occurs tangentially in Peter Schönemann's (18) recent doctoral dissertation at the University of Illinois. He may have something very good for us in the near future.

Analytically, in the "pure" sense of writing down some to-be-optimized function of the loadings to be obtained via a nonorthogonal transformation, the oblique case has been quiet for about five years. The last serious effort in this line of thought, initiated by John Carroll (1) and followed up by David Saunders (16), Kern Dickman, and me (11), was something dubbed "binormamin" by Dickman, and presented by the two of us at the 1959 American Psychological Association meetings. We discarded it, more or less, because of the simply awful computational problems involved, and because of its apparent sensitivity to the number of factors retained (it would seem to collapse the factor space if you gave it a dirty look). There has been a minor revival of interest now that we have the super-speedy computers to do the job (9); it appears that some of our initial concern was overly pessimistic. The one positive statement I can make about it is that when it works, it works fine—better, say, than the earlier oblimax and oblimin criteria. In general, though, *any* analytic, oblique criterion is not to be trusted routinely to give adequate results because of the apparent lack of our ability to apply the constraint of nonsingularity on the transformation matrix in the traditional approach to oblique "rotation."

The terrible terror of singular transformations in the oblique case was resolved in the summer of 1963 when Harris suggested to me that we apply orthogonal transformations to deliberately rescaled and then "mis-scaled" principal-axes solutions. Patting him gently on the head, I pointed out that this was of course illegal. Smiling serenely, he decimated my conservatism by pointing out that after such transformations, all the preliminary scaling can be taken out very easily with nonsingular diagonal matrices. The result? All possible transformations, and thus all possible factor-analytic solutions—involving uncorrelated or correlated factors—for a given factor space can be obtained with orthogonal transformations. This is a Big Break-through, for being able to reduce the entire rotation problem simply to one of applying orthogonal transformations makes the problem really tractable for the first time. Already Harris has brought this entirely new framework to bear in solving definitively the problem of cluster analysis. Further applications will undoubtedly be forthcoming soon. Be prepared: read "Oblique Factor Analytic Solutions by Orthogonal Transformations" (5).

I shall stop now. Let me close on an optimistic note. I don't think I'm becoming senile when I say that, psychometrically, the period of the algebraic explication of traditional, exploratory factor analysis is drawing to a close. We are near to having things well enough in hand to give the model to the statisticians. Perhaps pretentiously, I think I can say that we psychometricians are like Galton, who, when having the correlation coefficient sufficiently under control conceptually, turned the thing over to Karl Pearson.

REFERENCES

1. Carroll, J. B. An analytical solution for approximating simple structure in factor analysis. *Psychometrika*, 1953, 18, 23–38.
2. Guttman, L. Image theory for structure of quantitative variates. *Psychometrika*, 1953, 18, 277–296.
3. Guttman, L. Some necessary conditions for common-factor analysis. *Psychometrika*, 1954, 19, 149–162.
4. Harris, C. W. Some Rao-Guttman relationships. *Psychometrika*, 1962, 27, 247–263.
5. Harris, C. W., & Kaiser, H. F. Oblique factor analytic solutions by orthogonal transformations. *Psychometrika*, 1964, 29, 347–362.
6. Hotelling, H. Analysis of a complex of statistical variables into principal components. *Journal of Educational Psychology*, 1933, 24, 417–441; 498–520.
7. Kaiser, H. F. The varimax method of factor analysis. Unpublished doctoral dissertation, Univer. of California, 1956.
8. Kaiser, H. F. The varimax criterion for analytic rotation in factor analysis *Psychometrika*, 1958, 23, 187–200.
9. Kaiser, H. F. The application of electronic computers to factor analysis. *Educational and Psychological Measurement*, 1960, 20, 141–151.
10. Kaiser, H. F., & Caffrey, J. Alpha factor analysis. *Psychometrika*, 1965, 30, 1–14.

11. Kaiser, H. F., & Dickman, K. Analytic determination of common factors. *American Psychologist,* 1959, 14, 425. (Abstract)
12. Lawley, D. N. The estimation of factor loadings by the method of maximum likelihood. *Proceedings of the Royal Society of Edinburgh,* 1940, 60, 64–82.
13. Neuhaus, J. O., & Wrigley, C. The quartimax method: an analytical approach to orthogonal simple structure. *British Journal of Statistical Psychology,* 1954, 7, 81–91.
14. Rao, C. R. Estimation and tests of significance in factor analysis. *Psychometrika,* 1955, 20, 93–111.
15. Saunders, D. R. An analytic method for rotation to orthogonal simple structure. Princeton, N.J.: Educational Testing Service, Research Bulletin 53–10, 1953.
16. Saunders, D. R. The rationale for an "oblimax" method of transformation in factor analysis. *Psychometrika,* 1961, 26, 317–324.
17. Saunders, D. R. Trans-varimax: some properties of the ratiomax and equamax criteria for blind orthogonal rotation. *American Psychologist,* 1962, 17, 395. (Abstract)
18. Schönemann, P. H. A solution of the orthogonal Procrustes problem with applications to orthogonal and oblique rotation. Unpublished doctoral dissertation, Univer. of Illinois, 1964.

Experiments in Multimode
Factor Analysis[1]

LEDYARD R TUCKER

1964

Multimode factor analysis is being developed to help meet the needs for a procedure to search for, and to represent, relations existing in data from observations that may be classified according to several identifying attributes. Initial discussions of this development appear in the monographs *Problems in Measuring Change,* edited by Chester Harris (8); and *Contributions to Mathematical Psychology,* edited by Norman Frederiksen and Harold Gulliksen (9).

An example of the simplest case for an identifying attribute of observations would be when a single test is administered to a group of individuals. The scores on this test constitute our observations, and each observation is identifiable by the individual. Thus, the individuals constitute an identifying classification of these observations, or a mode of identifying classification. An alternative example is when a single individual is given a large number of tests. Then each score can be identified by the test. The group of tests now constitutes a mode of identifying classification. A step up in complexity of classification occurs when, say, a group of people is given a group of tests. Now each score is identified by the person and by the test, thus involving two modes of identifying classification. These data may be recorded in a table with a row for each individual and a column for each test. Each score is recorded in one cell of such a table. Traditional factor analysis was developed to systematize and represent relations in such data.

A next step upward in complexity occurs when, for example, a group of individuals is given a battery of tests on a number of different occasions. This means that each score must be identified by the individual, the test, and the occasion, thus constituting three modes of identifying classification.

[1] The research reported in this paper was jointly supported by the University of Illinois and the Office of Naval Research under contract Nonr 1834 (39).

These data may be thought of as being recorded in a three-dimensional table, such as the data box illustrated in Figure 1, where there is a row in mode 1 for each occasion, a column in mode 2 for each test, and a layer in mode 3 for each individual. Each cubicle of this box contains one test score. Multimode factor analysis is being devised to treat data such as those in this data box.

An extensive variety of situations can be conceived that involve three or more modes of identifying classification. First is the example just discussed. A second example occurs when a number of individuals are rated on a number of traits by a number of other individuals; an analysis of such data will be presented. An alternative to the preceding example is when each of a number of individuals is rated on a number of personality traits in different kinds of situations. An extended example would involve four modes: persons, traits, occasions, and situations. In this example, occasions might be interpreted as particular periods of life, such as entering first grade, in the middle of first grade, and toward the end of first grade. The situations might be: in the classroom, on the play yard, at home, etc. Such a study might have extended relevance to developmental psychology. A third example could be when individuals are learning a complex task on which a number of different scores can be taken on a number of trials. Such data constitute our second example to be presented. The third example of analysis to be presented involves individuals imagining that they are in a number of different situations, and indicating the extent of response for different modes of responding while in these situations.

Figure 2 presents a schematic representation of the three-mode factor model. There is a factor matrix for each mode of identifying classification, mode 1 on the left, mode 2 at the right, and mode 3 as if in depth. Each of these factor matrices relates the observed variables of the mode of identifying classification or factor variables for the mode. Thus, if method of rat-

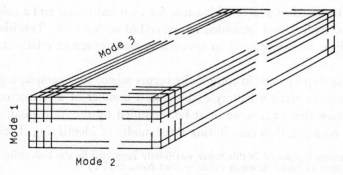

FIG. 1. *The data box.*

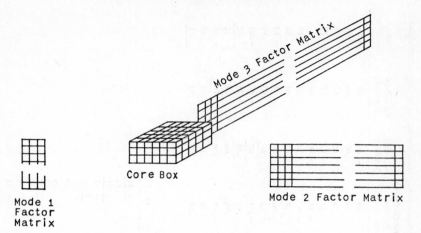

FIG. 2. *Schematic representation of the three-mode factor model.*

ing constitutes mode 1, the rows of the mode 1 factor matrix would be the various methods of rating, and the columns would be conceptual methods of rating. The observed methods would be described in terms of their relation to these conceptual methods of rating. For the three examples to be described, mode 3 will be considered to be the individuals on whom the observations were made, so that columns of the mode 3 factor matrix in Figure 2 represent the actual individuals. The rows of this matrix represent conceptualized or idealized individuals.

One of the developments beyond the procedures described in the monograph *Contributions to Mathematical Psychology* (9) is a procedure by which allowance can be made for errors of measurement and other influences that affect the measures for each particular combination of variables in mode 1 and mode 2. This raises a problem analogous to the communality problem in traditional factor analysis, and results in an indeterminacy of the entries in the mode 3 factor matrix. This is analogous to the factor score problem. The three factor matrices are tied together by a small core box which gives the relations among the three types of idealized entities. A point of interest is that the new procedure utilizes a matrix of mean cross products between variables analogous to the Campbell and Fiske multitrait-multimethod matrix (1). The examples will present the mode 1 and mode 2 factor matrices and the core box for each case.

Consider Table 1. This presents the results of an analysis of multitrait-multimethod data. These data were collected by E. Lowell Kelly and Donald Fiske (5) as part of a research project on the selection of clinical psychologists conducted at the University of Michigan. Data were supplied by Donald Fiske. The analysis was conducted by Edward Hoffman (4) while

TABLE 1
Analysis of Multitrait-Multimethod Data

Mode 1: Methods Factor Matrix

Rating Method	General	Self
Staff	.76	-.18
Teammate	.65	-.13
Self	.46	.48

Mode 2: Trait Factor Matrix (Rotated)

Variable	Social Adaptable	Serious Conscientious	Inquiring Intellect	Emotional Control	Self-Assertive
4 Cheerful—Depressed	.75	-.10	-.06	.34	-.07
6 Attentive to people—Cool, aloof	.68	.15	.00	.09	-.08
20 Frank, expressive—Secretive, reserved	.61	.10	.02	.07	.05
10 Good natured, easy going—Self-centered, selfish	.55	.24	-.03	.19	-.38
11 Talkative—Silent, introspective	.50	-.13	-.06	.05	.32
12 Adventurous—Cautious	.41	-.07	.10	.24	.13
5 Serious—Frivolous	-.17	.68	.01	.03	.10
17 Conscientious—Not conscientious	.14	.60	.00	.01	-.10
8 Broad interests—Narrow interests	.02	.13	.64	.05	-.10
18 Imaginative—Unimaginative	.24	-.04	.60	-.07	-.03
21 Independent minded—Dependent minded	-.14	.22	.38	.25	.32
7 Unshakable poise—Easily upset	.05	.08	.06	.75	.11
16 Placid—Worrying, anxious	.29	-.09	.00	.70	-.16
15 Self-sufficient—Dependent	-.08	.26	.16	.53	.18
3 Assertive—Submissive	.00	.04	.04	.04	.61

Core Box

Person Factor	Social Adaptable	Serious Conscientious	Inquiring Intellect	Emotional Control	Self-Assertive
1 General	1.56	-.34	.25	-.11	1.31
Self	.01	.06	-.03	-.14	.12
2 General	.12	1.25	-.05	-.05	-1.01
Self	-.09	-.26	-.30	.05	-.07
3 General	.21	.17	1.45	.05	1.01
Self	-.10	-.11	-.12	-.19	-.20
4 General	.16	.18	.16	.50	.30
Self	.33	.37	.48	.60	.29
5 General	-.05	.41	.27	.75	-.43
Self	-.10	.04	-.12	-.26	.29
6 General	.17	-.48	-.04	.91	.04
Self	-.20	-.37	-.10	.05	-.17

he was a graduate student at the University of Illinois. The methods of rating constitute mode 1; these methods are ratings by the staff, by the teammates, and by the trainee himself. The mode 1 factor matrix is given at the upper left. Two factors were extracted, a general factor and a factor related to the self-ratings. These factors are unrotated, principal axes. Note that the staff- and teammate-observed methods of rating are very similar whereas the self-rating depends in part on the general and in part on the specific idealized rating method for the self.

Five factors were found for mode 2 having to do with the different traits that were rated. From the 22 traits that actually were rated, 15 were selected. These 15 traits were to represent the 5 recurring factors identified by Fiske (3). The first factor strongly apparent was the social adaptability factor, the second was the factor of seriousness or conscientiousness, the third trait factor was an inquiring intellect, whereas the fourth appeared to be emotional control. The fifth factor was less well defined, but appears to be related to self-assertiveness.

Entries for the core box are given in the lower middle section of the table. The first person factor is characterized by high values for social adaptability and self-assertiveness as rated on the general rating method factor. A person who was describable as high on the first person factor and near average on the remaining person factors would be rated highly social-adaptable and highly self-assertive. All other ratings would be near average. Another person characterized by a low value in the first person factor would tend to be low in social adaptability and low in self-assertiveness when rated by the general rating factor. All self-ratings would be near average. The second person factor is characterized by a high positive loading on seriousness and conscientiousness, and a high negative loading on self-assertiveness when rated by the general rating factor. The third person factor also involves the general rating factor, and positive values for an inquiring intellect and self-assertiveness. The fourth person factor brings in the self-rating method factor to a greater extent where the individuals high on this factor rated themselves high on inquiring intellect and emotional control. The fifth and sixth person factors involve the emotional control as rated on the general rating factor with different combinations of seriousness-conscientiousness and self-assertiveness. It is of considerable interest that the self-rating factor is involved to a marked extent only in one of the person factors, factor four. This person factor may represent the difference between the way a person views himself and the way others view him. We may summarize the results, then, as indicating a fairly strong communality of ratings by the different rating methods in the general factor, with the self-ratings diverging in part only toward the self-rating factor. The trait factors are relatively clear and identifiable. The person factors indicate an area within which the self-ratings diverge from the ratings by the staff and teammates.

Results for our second example are given in Table 2. The data for this analysis were taken from the *Psychological Monograph* by James Parker and Edwin Fleishman on "Ability Factors and Component Performance Measures as Predictors of Complex Tracking Behavior" (7). The tracking device employed was constructed so as to simulate roughly the display characteristics and control requirements of an airborne radar intercept mission. Time of the tracking performance of each subject was divided into a number of trials. On each trial four measures were taken: a measure of horizontal error, a measure of vertical error, a sideslip error, and a time-on-target measure. Data for ten of the trials were presented in the form of correlations in a matrix analogous to the Campbell and Fiske multitrait-multimethod correlation matrix. A consequence of using correlations in this situa-

TABLE 2

Analysis of Complex Tracking Task Measures

Mode 1: Scoring Measures Factor Matrix			Mode 2: Trials Factor Matrix				
Measure	Direction Errors	Sideslip Control	Trial	Very Early	Middle Early	Middle Late	Very Late
Horizontal error	2.51	−.10	1	1.09	−.03	−.01	−.02
Vertical error	2.50	.01	2	1.39	.02	.01	.00
Sideslip error	−.13	2.39	3	.30	1.16	.00	.07
Time-on-target	2.58	1.08	4	−.03	1.26	.51	−.05
			5	.06	.83	.85	−.06
			6	−.02	.39	1.13	.06
			7	.00	−.02	.83	.65
			8	−.03	.04	.36	1.10
			9	−.03	.01	.03	1.49
			10	.06	−.03	−.03	1.38

		Core Box			
Person Factors	Measure Factors	Very Early	Middle Early	Middle Late	Very Late
1	Direction	.154	−.002	.001	.003
	Sideslip	.017	.008	.008	−.012
2	Direction	−.009	.182	−.028	.002
	Sideslip	.021	−.052	.050	−.004
3	Direction	.001	.001	.201	.003
	Sideslip	.001	.015	−.003	.006
4	Direction	.000	−.014	.028	.147
	Sideslip	.007	−.002	−.002	−.014
5	Direction	−.005	−.009	.008	.000
	Sideslip	.210	.044	−.031	.002
6	Direction	.004	−.012	.014	−.001
	Sideslip	.000	.083	.186	.033
7	Direction	−.011	.013	−.015	.015
	Sideslip	.001	−.028	.056	.192

tion is that the analysis involves consistencies in deviations from the mean learning curve for each measure.

Mode 1 was concerned with the scoring measures. Again, there were two factors. This time, one of the factors was related to direction errors involving the horizontal errors, the vertical errors, and the time-on-target. The second measure factor was related to sideslip control involving the sideslip error and time-on-target. These two factors indicate a marked distinction between the two aspects of control in this tracking test.

The mode 2 factor matrix is for trials, and appears at the upper right of Table 2. Four factors were apparent, one for very early learning, a second for middle early, a third for middle late, and a fourth for very late trials. These trial factors constitute standard patterns for discrepancies from the mean learning curves.

The core box is in the bottom portion of the table. There are seven person factors, representing seven dimensions of individual differences in performance on this complex tracking task. The first four person factors involve the direction error factor. The first person factor is for very early performance on direction errors; the second is for middle early performance on direction errors; the third emphasizes the middle late direction errors; and the fourth factor tends to emphasize the very late direction errors factor. The fifth, sixth, and seventh factors are concerned mainly with the sideslip control: the fifth factor involving very early performance on sideslip control; the sixth factor being related mostly to middle early and middle late performance on sideslip control; and the seventh factor being related to the very late performance on sideslip control.

A major point of interest is the almost complete disassociation in the person factors of effects of the direction errors factor and the sideslip control factors. Only during the middle late trials factor does there seem to be an interaction between the direction errors and the sideslip in discrepancies from the mean learning curves for the measures. This independence should be important to our theoretical considerations of such learning tasks, and to our attempts to measure performance on them. If similar independence of measure factors were observed for other learning tasks, serious doubt would exist as to the equivalence of a number of learning experiments when different measures of performance were employed in these experiments.

The results in Table 3 are taken from an analysis by Joseph Levin (6) of situation versus mode-of-response rating data collected by Norman Endler, J. McV. Hunt, and A. J. Rosenstein (2). Mode 1 involves the mode of response. There are 14 different listed modes of response given in the upper

TABLE 3
Analysis of Situation-Mode of Response Rating Data

Mode 1: Mode of Response Factor Matrix

Mode of Response	Distress	Exhilaration	Autonomic
2 Get "uneasy feeling"	.68	−.02	−.05
1 Heart beats faster	.63	.10	−.04
3 Emotions disrupt actions	.46	−.04	.10
6 Perspire	.34	−.03	.18
8 Enjoy the challenge	−.04	.77	.00
12 Seek experiences like this	−.05	.73	.05
4 Feel exhilarated and thrilled	.11	.60	−.02
5 Want to avoid situation	.34	−.38	.03
13 Have loose bowels	−.15	.01	.55
7 Need to urinate frequently	.07	.09	.49
11 Get full feeling in stomach	.05	.05	.42
14 Experience nausea	.02	−.09	.41
9 Mouth gets dry	.21	−.03	.31
10 Become immobilized	.23	−.05	.25

Mode 2: Situations Factor Matrix

Situation	Interpersonal	Inanimate	Unknown to Subject
5 Speech before large group	.55	−.10	.03
10 Interview for important job	.52	−.03	.04
8 Competitive contest	.46	.09	−.14
11 Final exam in important course	.33	.09	.05
2 New date	.31	−.12	.30
4 Ledge high on mountain side	−.06	.56	.01
9 Alone in woods at night	.07	.47	−.06
7 Sailboat on rough sea	−.01	.42	.08
3 Psychological experiment	.00	.03	.54
1 Auto trip	.01	.04	.38
6 Counseling Bureau for personal problems	.20	.04	.36

Core Box

Person Factors	Response Factors	Situation Factors		
		Interpersonal	Inanimate	Unknown to Subject
1	Distress	.40	.39	.22
	Exhilaration	−.05	−.11	.03
	Autonomic	.41	.37	.23
2	Distress	−.07	−.29	.20
	Exhilaration	.29	.44	.32
	Autonomic	.19	.05	.33
3	Distress	−.22	.30	−.16
	Exhilaration	.37	−.19	.19
	Autonomic	−.01	.37	−.15

portion of the table. Eleven situations are shown in the middle section of the table. The task of each subject was to imagine that he was in each of these listed situations and to rate the extent that he would respond for each of the modes of response. The rating scales were from 1 to 7. The ratings were standardized over individuals for each mode of response within each situation.

The mode of response factor matrix for mode 1 is given in the upper portion of the table. The four modes of response listed first have high loadings on a factor called Distress or General Distress. The next four modes of response have high loadings on a factor that could be called Exhilaration. And the last six modes of response are grouped under a factor that might be called Autonomic responses.

The factor matrix for situation is given for mode 2 in the center of the table. Five of the situations tend to group under a factor that could be called Interpersonal situations. Three more of the situations have high loadings on the second situation factor, which might be called Inanimate situations. The last three situations load highly on the third factor, which puzzled us for some time, but seemed to have a common characteristic in that the subject is, as it were, going into a situation whose exact nature is unknown to him.

The results in the core box at the bottom of the table are especially interesting. There appear to be three person factors, which could be characterized as idealized persons. The first person seems to react with both General Distress and Autonomic reactions to all three types of idealized situations. A negative person in this person factor would not be distressed nor have Autonomic reactions to these idealized situation factors. Persons characterized by either high positive loadings on the first person factor or high negative loadings on this first person factor would be about average as to Exhilaration responses to the conceptual situation factors. The second idealized person would be characterized by Exhilaration to all three types of situations, especially the Inanimate, and a negative amount of Distress to this Inanimate situation, while he would show Distress and Autonomic reaction to the Unknown to Subject factor. The person with a high negative loading on the second person factor would have the reverse effects. For the third person factor, there is an interesting differentiation drawn between the Interpersonal and the Inanimate situation factors. A person high on this third person factor would be exhilarated by the Interpersonal and have a negative Exhilaration for the Inanimate. This person would have negative distress for the Interpersonal situations and about average Autonomic reaction. In contrast, for the Inanimate situations, he would be positively distressed and have positive Autonomic reactions. The Unknown to Subject situations are more like the Interpersonal situations to this individual, but the reactions are not quite so extreme.

These results appear to me to reflect rather commonplace observations as to different types of people: one, a very shy person; two, a person who is generally exhilarated; and three, a kind of person who gives contrasting Exhilaration responses to Interpersonal and Inanimate types of situations. I submit that the existence of these types of people raises real problems in the development of psychological theory as related to the situation and the responses of individuals to these situations. The psychological theory must be sufficiently complex to take into account the various kinds of individuals involved. It does not appear that a simplified general theory will be adequate. A postscript that must be made for this study is that the data are the ratings by the subjects when they *imagine* themselves in the particular situations. A much more extensive study in which the individuals were actually placed in these situations and measures of their responses made would be desirable.

In the three studies reported, the factor matrices for modes 1 and 2 tend to confirm previous results and observations. The values in the core box, however, tend to bring out newer statements of relation. One might take the view that the mode 1 and 2 factor matrices are dealing with relations of a more surface type, and that the core box is dealing with deeper and more subtle relations. These relations in the core box should have more general effects on the phenomena being observed. One might argue, then, that the relations indicated in the core boxes should be of greater general interest in understanding the phenomena. It is my belief that the core boxes for the three analyses presented do indicate general effects of considerable interest in the content area of the observations made.

REFERENCES

1. Campbell, D. T., & Fiske, D. W. Convergent and discriminant validation by the multitrait-multimethod matrix. *Psychological Bulletin,* 1959, 56, 81–105.
2. Endler, N. S., Hunt, J. McV., & Rosenstein, A. J. An S-R inventory of anxiousness. *Psychological Monographs,* 1962, 76, No. 17 (Whole No. 536).
3. Fiske, D. W. Consistency of the factorial structures of personality ratings from different sources. *Journal of Abnormal and Social Psychology,* 1949, 44, 329–344.

4. Hoffman, E. L., & Tucker, L. R. *Three-way factor analysis of a multitrait-multimethod matrix.* Technical Report, Department of Psychology, Univer. of Illinois, 1964. (Mimeographed)
5. Kelly, E. L., & Fiske, D. W. *The prediction of performance in clinical psychology.* Ann Arbor, Mich.: Univer. of Michigan Press, 1951.
6. Levin, J. *Three-mode factor analysis.* Technical Report, Department of Psychology, Univer. of Illinois, 1963. (Mimeographed)
7. Parker, J. F., Jr., & Fleishman, E. A. Ability factors and component performance measures as predictors of complex tracking behavior. *Psychological Monographs,* 1960, 74, No. 16 (Whole No. 503).
8. Tucker, L. R. Implications of factor analysis of three-way matrices for measurement of change. In C. W. Harris (Ed.), *Problems in measuring change.* Madison, Wis.: Univer. of Wisconsin Press, 1963. Pp. 122–137.
9. Tucker, L. R. The extension of factor analysis to three-dimensional matrices. In N. Frederiksen and H. Gulliksen (Eds.), *Contributions to mathematical psychology.* New York: Holt, Rinehart & Winston, 1964. Pp. 109–127.

9 · NATURE AND DEVELOPMENT OF INTELLECTUAL TRAITS

THE PAPERS in this chapter throw light from several angles on the nature and development of intellectual traits. In a 1956 paper entitled "A New Look at the Curve of Intelligence," Bayley questions several traditional beliefs about both "intelligence" and "growth curves." Citing data from her own longitudinal studies as well as from research by other investigators, she shows that the composition of intelligence (as measured by intelligence tests) changes with age, and that the component abilities develop at different rates. She also cites the results of longitudinal studies on adults, in which test performance continued to improve well into the fifties, although the extent of improvement varied from one function to another. Bayley concludes with a discussion of environmental conditions affecting intellectual development, with special reference to parental attitudes and child-rearing practices.

The next two papers are taken from a panel on the nature of the verbal factor as used in aptitude-test batteries, presented at the 1948 Invitational Conference. Reflecting the rising influence of factor analysis and the increasing tendency to measure separate intellective factors, this panel concentrated on the verbal factor because of its predominant role in both intelligence-test performance and educational achievement. It should be noted, however, that in the late 1940's the proliferation of factors through factorial analyses of narrower and narrower domains was in full swing. Accordingly, the remarks of all the panelists clearly indicated their awareness that they were dealing with a group of verbal factors rather than a single factor.

Davis considers briefly three ways in which the verbal factor could be defined for educational testing purposes, and illustrates each with an appropriate multiple-choice item. While cautioning against the use of esoteric words to increase item difficulty, he favors limiting the verbal factor to the range and precision of word meanings that the individual can differentiate.

Examining the verbal factor from a different point of view, Turnbull recommends four approaches designed to increase our understanding of this ability: extension of research to include spoken as well as written communication; developmental study of age changes in verbal factors; comparison of verbal factors in different cultural groups; and exploration of relationships between verbal factors and personality characteristics.

The next paper, by Carroll, is much broader in its orientation. While again drawing upon the verbal domain for illustrations, Carroll provides an excellent discussion of the nature and origin of intellective factors in general. Given in 1961, this paper reflects the growing sophistication of psychologists in the interpretation of factors. Especially noteworthy is Carroll's discussion of the possible role of differential learning experiences in the development of factors.

The last three papers in the chapter are concerned with creativity—a type of behavior traditionally identified with high intelligence but rarely incorporated in standard intelligence tests. Each paper approaches the topic from a distinctly different angle. This diversity is especially noteworthy in view of the similarity of professional background of the three speakers—all are psychometricians closely identified with the application of statistical techniques to psychological research and test development.

Thurstone's paper was a special invited address given in 1950, prior to the widespread surge of creativity studies. In it, Thurstone describes the state of psychological knowledge about creativity at that time—which was virtually nonexistent—and presents a number of stimulating hypotheses about creative behavior. He emphasizes the distinction between creative talent and "intelligence" as identified through available intelligence tests and school achievement. This distinction points up a semantic difficulty destined to bedevil creativity research for some years to come. It represents one more demonstration that the term "intelligence" has acquired so many meanings as to be of little use for communication purposes. Terminology aside, Thurstone's paper offers provocative insights into creative behavior, which have provided many hypotheses for subsequent investigators in this elusive area.

The papers by Guilford and Thorndike were given in 1962 at a session on creativity. During the twelve-year interval separating these papers from Thurstone's, creativity research had flourished in many centers. Its methodology ranged from intensive clinical studies of highly creative individuals to factorial analyses of large test batteries designed to measure the many facets of creative behavior. The subjects investigated covered nearly the whole life span, from preschool children to mature leaders in various fields. Guilford's paper provides an overview of the most relevant factors identified in his long-term Aptitudes Project at the University of Southern California. Guilford notes that the divergent-production factors, which predominate in creative behavior, are largely absent from traditional intelligence or academic aptitude tests. In his own comprehensive model of the "structure of intellect," however, he includes divergent-production abilities together with other abilities commonly classified under "intelligence." One of the chief outcomes of the Aptitudes Project has thus been a redefinition of intelligence to include creative abilities.

Thorndike opens his paper with a systematic examination of the concept of creativity and of the difficulties in the way of defining creativity so that it is amenable to research. He then reports his own re-analyses of published data from creativity studies, which indicate more extensive overlap between "creativity" tests and traditional "intelligence" tests than had generally been recognized. Thus it appears that the reaction against identifying creativity with "high IQ" and academic achievement may have gone too far. Although some investigators have given the impression that the two domains are uncorrelated or even negatively correlated, test correlations across these domains prove to be almost as high as those within the creativity domain.

A New Look at the Curve
of Intelligence

NANCY BAYLEY

1956

In the past thirty years, the accepted form of the age curve of intelligence has become pretty well stabilized, as the result of a number of studies in which many people of different ages were tested. Miles (25) set the pattern, which follows the course of increasing scores to the early twenties, followed by a consistent but slower decline throughout the adult years. Subsequent studies have followed this pattern with minor variations. Notable among them are the studies of Jones and Conrad (19), Wechsler (40), and Foulds and Raven (11).

In recent years, repeated tests on the same persons as they grow older have yielded scores that do not follow this pattern, but indicate that at least some intellectual abilities may continue to increase slowly to 50 years of age or older. These, among other findings on early development, such as the instability of infant scores, are forcing us to reconsider the whole subject of age changes in intellectual abilities. As a part of this reconsideration, we need to review the methods by which intelligence can best be tested and evaluated at different ages and levels of complexity. We must investigate the limitations of current tests and develop more adequate and discriminating ones.

THE COMPLEX NATURE OF INTELLECTUAL ABILITIES

It is, of course, understood that the "curve of intelligence" is derived from performances on tests that measure samples of the whole range and variety of mental abilities. This means that all of the following discussion presupposes that the tests must be validated and revalidated, as occasion requires and permits, against useful outside criteria of intelligent behavior. That is, if we wish to know the nature of intellectual change over time, we must insure that we are using a valid measure of intelligence. It may be necessary, also, for us to re-evaluate our criteria of intelligence.

In formulating any adequate theory of the nature of intelligence, it seems to me necessary to take into consideration the fact that the human organism, in all of its aspects, undergoes continual processes of change throughout its life span. These changes are more rapid at some periods of life than at others, and in some processes than in others. They involve increments and decrements in size and waxing and waning of functions. They also involve developmental increases in complexity, and processes of maturation of both structure and function, followed eventually by retrogressions, declines, and other manifestations of senescence.

In the field of intelligence, these processes are complex and difficult to work with, and hence have been only partially mapped out. For one thing, the concept of intelligence is very general, and covers a variety of intellectual functionings. It is necessary, then, for an adequate appraisal of the course of intelligence from birth to old age, that we consider not only the course of general intelligence, but also age changes in mental organization, and that we try to identify and independently to measure the various intellectual functions. When this has been done, it will become possible to trace the developmental changes in each function or factor, and to see how each fits in to any general, over-all curve.

Of course, many investigators have been working on the problem of analyzing intelligence into its component parts. Early in the history of intelligence testing, efforts were made both to define intelligence and to construct tests that would sample and score separately its different aspects. At first the various intellectual faculties to be tested were selected on an a priori basis. But with experience, and the help of statistics, we have found ways of isolating and measuring relatively discrete intellectual functions.

Considerable work has been done on what seems to me the logical approach to building new test batteries, i.e., through the use of such methods as factor analysis, cluster analysis, or analysis of variance. But very few investigators have actually applied the results of such analyses to construct factorially independent scales. A notable exception, of course, is the series of Thurstone tests of Primary Mental Abilities (39). Following from such a start as this, by successive constructions, analyses, and additions of test items and test areas, we can hope to tease apart and thus to identify, measure, and label the different components of intelligence. Something very like this process has been reported recently by Guilford (14) who presents an elaborate scheme for what he calls "the structure of intellect." He reports systematic attempts to detect and to organize into a conceptual frame the various factors of intellect. With this schema as a basis, new types of function are hypothesized or identified, and appropriate tests are devised to measure them. It seems to me that Guilford reports the kind of research we badly need if we are to differentiate and understand the various intellectual processes that make up "intelligence." But in his elaborate analysis, he does not take into consideration the further complications of age and maturational differences.

However, a number of investigators are interested in this developmental aspect of intelligence, and with the instruments available several studies have been made on age changes in intellectual ability and in mental organization (13). Much of this work has been done on tests of cross-sectional samples: that is, on tests administered once to persons of different ages. But there are very pertinent data now available from a number of longitudinal studies in which the same persons have been tested repeatedly as they grew older. None of these longitudinal studies covers the entire age span, but some start as early as one month of age and others continue through 50 years and even later. By splicing together some of these data, it should be possible to construct longitudinal age curves of several different intellectual factors.

A Suggested Age Curve of Intelligence

Any curve of intelligence will be dependent upon the behavioral components included in the test scores on which it is constructed. The general curve that I presented in 1955 in an article, "On the Growth of Intelligence" (4), is based on total scores of fairly comprehensive tests. To the extent that these tests are broadly inclusive and representative of "general intelligence," this curve might be thought of as representing the usual course of age changes in general intellectual capacity.

Everyone agrees that intelligence grows throughout infancy and childhood, though with the accumulation of records we have had to move along (from a start at 13 years) the age at which growth was assumed to stop. As for the *form* of the childhood curve, minor differences from one investigator to another are probably related to differences in tests and sampling, but there is the further problem of constructing comparable units of growth. In the tentative curve I constructed, for the period one month to 25 years, I used the test scores of the Berkeley Growth Study. It was necessary to splice together the scores from a number of different tests by converting the scores into standard deviation units based on the mean and SD of the 16-year scale scores on the Wechsler-Bellevue test.

This part of the curve shows rapid acceleration in the first year, and again a moderate acceleration between 8 and 10 years. After about 10 years the rate slows down so that by 25 the increment is very gradual. Freeman and Flory's (12) curve, although based on units derived in a different way, is similar to the Berkeley Growth Study curve for the ages it covers, 8 to 17 years. According to the VACO[1] curve, there is accelerated growth between about 10 and 12 years. This is later than the Berkeley Growth Study period of rapid growth. However, different tests were used, and when the subtests of the VACO are considered, each has a different course of growth with different ages of greatest increment.[2]

By fitting on to the Berkeley Growth Study curve the curves of either Owens' Iowa data or of the scores made on the Concept Mastery Test by the spouses of Terman's Gifted Study subjects, it was possible to construct a 50-year curve from just two longitudinal samples. Rather than choose between them, I put both adult studies onto the curve. Each one contributes something that the other lacks. The Alpha test probably samples a wider variety of abilities, but the Concept Mastery Test offers more possibility of expansion into higher scores. Also, the Terman study subjects covered a sufficiently wide range of ages tested so that it was possible to plot approximate scores by age at five-year intervals from 20 to 50 years. Thus, from the Terman material it appears that a relatively greater proportion of this adult growth occurs between 20 and 25 years, with the subsequent increments relatively smaller, and constant.

Of course, this curve can be viewed only as a tentative one based on limited tests and limited samples. In constructing more adequate curves, we need to take into account many things. For example, different mental functions appear to have different rates of growth with different ages at maximal contribution to the total. In order to spell this out, we need to have both more clearly defined and more adequately measured subtests or "factors."

CHANGING COMPONENTS OF THE CURVE

It seems to me probable that in the early part of the curve the independent factors tend to occur successively with simultaneously developing and operating factors appearing only after some complexity of intellectual functioning has been achieved. For example, in the Berkeley Growth Study, both the early age trends in standard deviations and the patterns of correlations for consistency of scores indicate age changes in the nature of abilities. These changes are also shown by Hofstaetter's (15) factor analysis of my table of correlations for consistency of scores from birth through

---

[1] The battery employed by Freeman and Flory, consisting of vocabulary, analogies, completion, and opposites tests—Ed.

[2] It is interesting to note that the childhood period of acceleration in both of these studies comes *before* the adolescent spurt of physical growth in boys. For the Berkeley study, it occurs in both sexes at the same age and is over before physical acceleration starts.

18 years (2). He obtained three distinct factors that operate successively. The first, which he named "Sensory-Motor Alertness," is predominant for the first two years, with a very high loading at months 7 through 12. The second factor, "Persistence," is high from 2 to 4 years, while the third, "Manipulating Symbols," accounts for most of the variance after 4 years. The three factors are about equal in weight at two years.

This use of the total scores gives evidence for some age-specific factors and even indicates the beginnings of concurrent factors that operate over longer segments of growth. The total scores are made up from a variety of behaviors which could represent several different factors. Support for only general factors in infancy is lent by the study of Richards and Nelson (31) who factored the Gesell Scale scores for 80 infants at 6, 12, and 18 months. In this scale, they included gross motor coordinations that are left out of the California First-year Mental Scale. The fact that they obtained just two factors, "Alertness" and "Motor Ability," would make it appear that I had already separated the factorially independent functions in the first year by putting the gross motor coordinations into a Scale of Motor Ability. Therefore, the "Sensory-Motor Alertness" factor of Hofstaetter and the "Alertness" factor of Richards and Nelson appear to be practically identical. This factor may very well represent the lion's share of "intelligence" for the first 9 months. After this, Hofstaetter's factors II and III appear to be operating concurrently for a while.

I shall not attempt to cover the work on factor analysis of intelligence tests. There are others here far more able to do this. But it may be of interest to consider a few isolated bits from longitudinal studies that it seems to me contribute to our understanding of this general problem.

Freeman and Flory's (12) longitudinal data show different slopes of increment for their four subtests and evidence for different ages at highest ability. Relative to the means and SD's of the 17-year scores, the Analogies score has shown most change during the nine-year interval, 8 to 17 years, with Opposites scores gaining second. The slopes of these curves indicate that they have approached close to their mature status. The slower-gaining Vocabulary and Completion tests appear to be still gaining at 17 years (3).

Some data based on retest scores on the Wechsler-Bellevue for my small Berkeley Growth Study sample may be relevant in this same connection. This test was given at four ages (16, 18, 21, and 25 years), the number for the first three testings ranging from 35 to 45. So far, 24 have been given the test at 25 years. For the Full Scale and for the Verbal and Performance halves, there is no indication that these young adults have reached their intellectual ceiling. But for this group, the subtests of the Wechsler-Bellevue are unequal both in difficulty and in the slopes of their age curves (6). Each appears to be following a different course of change with age. These differences show up most clearly when constant subsamples are selected, so that the same cases are included at all ages used in the growth curves.

Other subsamples, selected to be homogeneous in certain respects, show interesting differences in scores and growth rates. For example, in a division by sexes, boys and girls do about equally well on the Full Scale, but the boys are better on the Verbal, and the girls on the Performance Scale.

The group was divided into higher and lower intelligence halves on the basis of their average scores at 16, 17, and 18 years. The highly intelligent group was found to do equally well on the Verbal and Performance parts of the test. The lower-scoring less "intelligent" half, however, does much less well on the Verbal than on the Performance Scale. Both highs and lows exhibit increasing scores, but with some indication that the high group is approaching a ceiling. This ceiling is at least in part due to a lack of top in the Wechsler-Bellevue scale.

If we consider the 11 subtests separately, for constant subsamples, the greater differences between the higher and the lower intelligence groups occur in the six Verbal tests. Among the five Performance tests, the two groups differ most in Picture Arrangement and Block Design (tests that require organization of spatial relations) and least in Picture Completion and Digit Symbol substitution (tests that require recognition of patterns). Those subtests in which the highs do not show continued increase in scores are tests in which they have already reached the upper limits of the scale. The lows show continued growth in most subtests, but appear to have reached their top capacities in the Vocabulary and Block Design subtests, and possibly Picture Arrangement. We may have here some indications of differential growth according to level of ability.

These comparisons are on a very small sample, and on a test that is not completely adequate for such purposes. The data therefore are only suggestive, but they do seem to indicate some probable differences in ability-tied growth rates for different intellectual functions. However, credence may be lent to these differences by the fact that they are in general congruent with those found by H. E. Jones (18) for the Adolescent Growth Study for a similar age range on the subtests of the Terman Group Test of Mental Ability.

To carry the picture beyond 25 years we may turn to the consideration of age changes in both cross-sectional and longitudinal studies.

The cross-sectional studies tend to agree in the finding that some abilities, such as information and word knowledge, are maintained with little or no loss to an advanced age, while other abilities such as arithmetic, analogies, and organization of spatial relations decline with age (after 20 or 30) at varying rates (17). Those functions that drop off most rapidly in the older subjects appear to differ with the tests used, and to some extent with the populations studied. The more recent the studies and the more complete the population sample included, the less do scores drop with advancing age. Other differences in age trends are often found to be related to the general intellectual level of the subjects and to the amount of their education.

In the longitudinal studies, however, there is an invariable finding that the scores in at least some subtests are higher on the second testing. The earlier of these reports, such as the studies of Freeman and Flory (12) and R. L. Thorndike (38), were usually on tests of young adults, mostly college students in their late teens and early twenties. But more recently, repeat test scores have been secured on adults at later ages. These also show increased scores earned at the later testing after the subjects have grown older, with intervals of 12 to 30 years between tests. I should like here to summarize some of these studies.

Owens (27) repeated the Army Alpha test on 50-year-old men who had taken this same test 31 years before as college freshmen, and found an increase in tested ability at the later age, with greatest increase in the Information test, and least in Arithmetic. Bayley and Oden (7) found increases on repeat tests after a 12-year interval for gifted adults on Terman's difficult Concept Mastery Test (35). When these scores were expressed in standard deviation units for each subtest at its initial administration, there was twice as much increase in the Synonym-Antonym (or word-knowledge) half as in the Analogies (or abstract relationships) half of the test. The increases occur in all age groups tested (20 to 50 years), though they are least in the Analogies test for the older ages. Nisbet (26) reports repeat tests, after a lapse of about 23 years, on 141 teachers in Aberdeen, Scotland, who were first tested as postgraduate students when about 22 years old. On a timed verbal group test (Simplex Group Intelligence Scale), improvement occurred on all 14 subtests; the increase was significant in all but one. Greatest increases, expressed in SD of the first testing, were in Substitution, .71 σ; Vocabulary, .67 σ; and Number Series, .65 σ; they were least in Digit Memory, .16 σ; Verbal Rearrangement, .21 σ; and Analogies, .26 σ. H. E. Jones (18) has reported increased scores on the Terman Group Test of Mental Ability between the 16½-year tests and retests at 33 years for 83 cases of the Berkeley Adolescent Growth Study. He found smaller gains in the lowest-scoring quartile of his population and in those subtests involving problem solving. The greatest gains were in Vocabulary.

Thus, the studies cited, both the cross-sectional and the longitudinal, show similar age trends in changing organization. At the older ages, the subjects do relatively better in tests of information and word knowledge and less well in tests of reasoning and seeing relationships.

EVALUATING INTELLECTUAL CHANGES IN ADULTS

The difference between the two methods of study is found in comparisons of the actual scores. In the longitudinal studies the subjects nearly always do better at the later testing, when they are older, on most of the subtests, as well as on total scores. Although the longitudinal studies were made on different populations and used different tests, they agree in finding that different intellectual functions show varying amounts of increase, ranging from no change to as much as a standard deviation between test and retest. In no instance do these studies show the precipitous decline in scores after ages 25 to 30 that occurs in most cross-sectional studies of age differences.

Let us consider some of the things that could account for this difference.

1) When subjects of different ages are tested at one time, there is the problem of selecting comparable samples. Apparent changes in relative scores could be artifacts of differential sample selection for subjects of different ages. In the older age groups, there may be selective elimination of certain segments of the population through deaths or through lack of cooperation. It is true that when a complete population is tested, e.g., a whole Vermont community (19) or an entire prison population (9), the curve of intelligence scores shows less decline with age. We might conclude that when willingness to be tested is a selective factor, the brighter older persons are less cooperative about taking tests, or else more adept at finding excuses. In any event, when the same persons are retested at successive ages, whatever the selective factors in sampling, we do have a constant sample.

2) But with a constant sample there is the ever-present problem in psychological testing: the inescapable fact that a test is never the same for a person the second time he takes it. When comparing retests, it is necessary to take into account possible practice effects and generally increased familiarity with the testing procedures. However, in many studies practice effects are of little import. When the elapsed time between tests has been as much as 12 to 30 years (as in the Owens, the Nisbet, and the Bayley and Oden studies), it seems obvious that there can be very little, if any, direct memory of problems and their solutions from the first to the second test. Also, when alternate test forms are used, there may be very little increase after

short intervals. I have, for example, some data on practice effects of the Concept Mastery Test. There was practically no carry-over from one form to the other after an interval of only one or two weeks for the sample of 148 on which the two forms of the scale were equated. The difference was less than two points, or about 1/15 of the SD of scores.

3) Another important difference between the longitudinal and cross-sectional data is the *temporal* one. Perhaps this has not been given enough weight. In cross-sectional studies, all tests are given at the same time, while in longitudinal studies not only do the same subjects grow older before their retests, but with the lapse of time they have all experienced the same general changes in the environment, and have been responding to similar changes in such things as world events and means of communication.

It is relevant here to point out that the scores earned on the Concept Mastery Test by Terman's Gifted Study subjects who were tested only once increased just as much in the 12-year interval, 1939–40 to 1950–52, as did the scores of the twice-tested subjects. Of the men who missed the first administration of the test but took it in 1950–52, 129 earned scores averaging half an SD above the mean for the men tested in 1939. A similar increase over the 1939 means was found for 98 Gifted Study women who were first tested in 1950–52. For each testing date, the means of the once-tested and twice-tested groups are very similar. Thus, there appears to have been no selective factor differentiating the groups: whether or not a subject was tested in 1939, in 1951, or in both years was pretty much a matter of his geographical availability. Furthermore, for these bright people, the average scores earned at the later date and older age were evidently not dependent on the experience of having taken the Concept Mastery Test at the earlier date. In general, then, it seems to me that we should consider very seriously the possibility that at least some kinds of intelligence may very well continue to improve slowly from 20 to 50 years or later.

ENVIRONMENTAL DETERMINERS IN INTELLECTUAL GROWTH

So far, I have touched only briefly on the whole array of potential influences on intellectual growth that we may classify as environmental. This is a very general term, including both emotional climate and opportunities for intellectual stimulation, and for practice in intellectual activities such as reasoning and problem solving. No organism develops in complete absence of stimulation, and up to a certain stage in infancy, the minimal requirements for life furnish adequate stimuli to afford normal development. Ordinarily, the human infant's environment is much richer than these minimal conditions. The infant responds to those parts of his environment that are relevant for his degree of maturity (neural, sensory-motor, perceptual, and organizational). Also, as he grows, the actively healthy child will interact with his surroundings, seeking stimulation to the extent of his capacities to utilize and cope with it. Those who are inherently gifted may well be the ones who continue to seek out and to find challenging intellectual problems and experiences in any normal life situation. However, there are probably here also inherent individual differences in this kind of active intellectual curiosity. Granting this, we may further explore the possibility that extreme environmental deprivation or depressing emotional climate could restrict the growth of even the most intellectually alert, while optimal intellectual stimulation and emotional climate could enhance the development even of those with little inherent drive or capacity.

If we assume the relevance of these variables to the growth of intelligence, then we need to study the conditions of their effects on the course of mental development. We should inquire what kinds of emotional climate are optimal at what ages, what effects the attitudes of responsible adults such as parents and teachers have on intelligence, and whether certain attitudes are more important at some ages than at others. We should inquire further: What kinds of intellectual stimulation, or "environmental enrichment" are optimal for infants, preschoolers, children, adults? Is deprivation at certain stages crucial in determining whether development will be normal? That is, are there environmental "critical stages" for mental growth analogous to those embryological stages at which trauma can result in such deformities as cleft palate, ovarian agenesis, or possibly Mongolism and other conditions associated with feeblemindedness?

We have now some relevant information offering tentative answers to some of these questions, but so far most of the information is based on casual observations or on studies that have not been sufficiently well designed and controlled to give us definitive answers.

A number of reports (8, 34) suggest the retarding effect on infants of life in institutions that offer little in either normal parental care or mental stimulation. But we do not yet know either the amount or generality of this effect, or on the other hand, what are the crucial aspects in regard to type of care, the nature of deprivation, or the ages at which the child experiences them. The fact that institutions do not invariably depress intelligence is brought out by Rheingold (29) who studied the effects of a significant care-taking mother-figure on 6-month-old institutional babies. The six babies she cared for 40 hours a week for eight weeks, compared with six control babies, showed no significant differences in IQ at the end of care.

There are studies that show significantly low IQ's for children in backward rural communities (33, 42). The studies of racial differences in intelligence are plagued with the problems of environmental impoverishment in certain racial groups.

The many comparisons that show a correlation between socioeconomic factors and IQ have made clear the fact of the relationship, but give little information about the specific ways in which such factors might affect mental growth.

Studies of the relation between intelligence scores and such personality factors as emotional tone, effort, and persistence usually show a moderate positive correlation in young children. But so far we have little information on the effect of long-term emotional influences on the growth curve of intelligence. However, we do have reports of the differential effects of praise and blame on learning, and the depressive effect of anxiety on achievement in school (28). Ability to learn is often classed as one form of intelligence.

In the Berkeley Growth Study (1), as well as in other studies, such things as the children's emotional tone and generally optimal conditions for testing yield r's with IQ that are in the neighborhood of about .30 (24, 16, 43). However, when we considered individual children, and for each child correlated his "Optimal" and "Attitude" scores with his intelligence ratings for series of 10 to 15 ages, we found a wide spread of r's from +.77 to −.46, with a mean of +.20. Evidently the children differed in the effect of current emotional state on performance, and for some children other factors (presumably maturational and hereditary) were of predominant importance for mental growth (1).

As for the long-term effects of emotional climate, Schaefer, Bell, and I are now in the process of getting some tentative information from the Berkeley Growth Study (32). Personality characteristics of the mothers, relevant to their behavior toward these children, have been rated. The ratings were made on a scale designed for use with descriptive protocols of the mothers, made at the times they came with their children for the tests when the children were between one month and 3 years of age. Some of these behavior traits were found to be relatively stable over a 10-year period that could be compared. The most stable of the maternal traits are: cooperativeness; use of fear to control the child; irritability; and tendencies to ignore the child, to reject the homemaking role, to evaluate the child positively, to express affection toward the child, to treat him as an equal, and to be strict with him. The 32 traits could be clustered into two main variables, which we have labeled by the "good" end of the scale, (*a*) Positive Attitudes, and (*b*) Autonomy of the Child. The few correlations we have computed with intelligence indicate that there are relations with these maternal variables, but that the nature of the relationship changes with the age of the child. If these preliminary findings should hold up, it would appear that during the first year of life, higher scores tend to be earned by babies whose mothers are intrusive, dominating, and punitive, while by the time they reach school age the reverse is true and the high-scorers' mothers are characterized as cooperative, evaluating their children positively, expressing affection toward them, and allowing them autonomy as individuals.

This analysis is still so incomplete that I hesitate to mention it. But there are other studies that corroborate it in a general way, though they are not directly comparable in methods or in the variables used. For example, Macfarlane, Allen, and Honzik (24) report correlations between children's mental test scores and the number of their problems (as reported by the mothers). At 21 months and at 3 years the r's with IQ tend to be positive, but from 4 through 14, the r's are negative (around $-$ .30), indicating a tendency after 3 years for high IQ to go with fewer problems. There are no direct correlations reported here between the IQ's and parental attitudes. However, in another paper (16) the same authors report individual cases whose IQ's appear to be related to parental behaviors. Wittenborn (43), working on data from the Yale Clinic of Child Development, reports some r's between 5-year Binet IQ and certain characteristics of adoptive parents. These r's also vary around .30 with the adoptive parents' Ambition, Education-Occupation, and Age-Duration of Marriage. These variables probably reflect some enduring attitudes and expectations of the parents.

If we were to develop an environmental criterion of conditions fostering high intelligence, it might be composed of scores on some of the following variables: 1) Characteristics of the parents (or responsible adults) in respect to: (*a*) understanding of the child's capacities and readiness for tasks of given difficulties, (*b*) willingness to grant the child autonomy relative to his capacities, (*c*) ability to offer stimulating experiences without overly strong pressures to high achievement, and (*d*) warm affectionate acceptance of child as an individual in his own right. 2) Environmental opportunities geared to the child's stage of development. These last will include good teaching and varieties of experience, perhaps through such media as radio and television, as well as through travel and discussions of ideas.

Wechsler (41) has discussed the possible causes of the differences between the 1939 and 1955 age curves of intelligence as measured by the two forms of his scale. The 1955 curve is at most ages higher than the earlier one, and scores do not start to drop until after 30 years. In addition to the usual reasons (sampling, educational level, and test-wiseness) for this generally increased performance, he offers a fourth of a very different kind. To quote from his abstract:

Finally, one may posit that the improved performance of the American adult on tests of intelligence could be due in part to the improving general health and virility of the population during the last two decades. Advances in medical and social hygiene have seemingly not only served to increase life expectancy but extended the period of intellectual as well as physical vigor into later maturity.

We find some support for this suggestion of Wechsler's from studies of children's nutritional status. Many studies report low positive r's with IQ of such variables as size, health, and physical maturity (10, 20, 36). It is, therefore, quite possible that generally improved health and living conditions in recent years are reflected not only in generally greater physical size, but also in greater and more prolonged mental vigor.

I should like to suggest to Wechsler that he go a step further, and if his hypothesis is true, then possibly his curve falls off after 30 because, in his cross-section sample, his older subjects have not had the advantage of growing up in this generally more healthful world.

Another step beyond this is to suggest that not only is the physical environment improved in the last two decades, but also the psychological environment. Perhaps in addition to more years of schooling for more people we have actually progressed in our educational effectiveness, grade for grade. Also, it seems rather obvious that the general environment in which children are now growing up is richer: there is more knowledge available and better communication of it; travel is easier; and more children can, with less trouble, have varied experiences. Possibly also our knowledge of child training and mental hygiene is influencing parental practices in a healthful way.

If these things are true in any significant degree, and if progress in mental and physical health continues, it may become necessary repeatedly to construct new norms for intelligence every decade or so. Furthermore, in considering age changes in older people, we may need to evaluate their scores according to norms standardized at appropriate calendar years, rather than for age only.

REFERENCES

1. Bayley, Nancy. Factors influencing the growth of intelligence in young children. *Yearbook of the National Society for the Study of Education,* 1940, 39, Part II, 49–79.
2. Bayley, Nancy. Consistency and variability in the growth of intelligence from birth to eighteen years. *Journal of Genetic Psychology,* 1949, 75, 165–196.
3. Bayley, Nancy. Development and maturation. In H. Helson, in association with S. H. Bartley, *et al., Theoretical foundations of psychology.* New York: Van Nostrand, 1951. Pp. 145–199.
4. Bayley, Nancy. On the growth of intelligence. *American Psychologist,* 1955, 10, 805–818.
5. Bayley, Nancy. A consideration of age changes in mental organization. *Primer Congreso Panamericano de Gerontologia* (Book of Abstracts). Ciudad Universitaria, Mexico. 1956, 31.
6. Bayley, Nancy. Data on the growth of intelligence between 16 and 21 years as measured by the Wechsler-Bellevue Scale. *Journal of Genetic Psychology,* 1957, 90, 3–15.
7. Bayley, Nancy, & Oden, Melita H. The maintenance of intellectual ability in gifted adults. *Journal of Gerontology,* 1955, 10, 91–107.
8. Bowlby, J. Maternal care and mental health. *World Health Organization Monograph Series,* 1951, No. 2.
9. Corsini, R. J., & Fassett, Katherine K. Intelligence and aging. *Journal of Genetic Psychology,* 1953, 83, 249–264.
10. Ebert, E., & Simmons, K. The Brush Foundation study of child growth and development. I. Psychometric tests. *Monographs of the Society for Research in Child Development,* 1943, 8, (No. 2).
11. Foulds, G. A., & Raven, C. J. Normal changes in the mental abilities of adults as age advances. *Journal of Mental Science,* 1948, 94, 133–142.
12. Freeman, F. N., & Flory, C. D. Growth in intellectual ability as measured by repeated tests. *Monographs of the Society for Research in Child Development,* 1937, 2, (No. 2).
13. Garrett, H. E. A developmental theory of intelligence. *American Psychologist,* 1946, 1, 372–378.
14. Guilford, J. P. The structure of intellect. *Psychological Bulletin,* 1956, 53, 267–293.
15. Hofstaetter, P. R. The changing composition of "intelligence": a study of *t*-technique. *Journal of Genetic Psychology,* 1954, 85, 159–164.
16. Honzik, Marjorie P., Macfarlane, Jean W., & Allen, Lucile. The stability of mental test performance between two and eighteen years. *Journal of Experimental Education,* 1948, 17, 309–324.
17. Jones, H. E. Age changes in adult mental abilities. *Old age in the modern world.* London: E. & S. Livingstone, Ltd., 1955. Pp. 267–274.

18. Jones, H. E. Trends in mental abilities. (Paper read in a symposium at the 1955 meeting of the American Psychological Association) *American Psychologist,* 1955, 10, 405.

19. Jones, H. E., & Conrad, H. S. The growth and decline of intelligence: a study of a homogenous group between the ages of ten and sixty. *Genetic Psychology Monographs,* 1933, 13, 223–294.

20. Knobloch, Hilda, & Pasamanick, B. Further observations on the behavioral development of Negro children. *Journal of Genetic Psychology,* 1953, 83, 137–157.

21. Lorge, I. The influence of the test upon the nature of mental decline as a function of age. *Journal of Educational Psychology,* 1936, 27, 100–110.

22. Lorge, I. Schooling makes a difference. *Teachers College Record,* 1945, 46, 483–492.

23. Lorge, I. Aging and intelligence. *Journal of Chronic Diseases,* 1956, 4, 131–139.

24. Macfarlane, Jean W., Allen, Lucile, & Honzik, Marjorie P. *A developmental study of the behavior problems of normal children between twenty-one months and fourteen years.* Vol. 2. Berkeley, Calif.: Univer. of California Press, 1954.

25. Miles, W. R. Psychological aspects of ageing. In E. V. Cowdry (Ed.), *Problems of aging: biological and medical aspects.* (2nd ed.) Baltimore: Williams & Wilkins, 1942, Pp. 756–784.

26. Nisbet, J. Family environment and intelligence. *Eugenics Review,* 1953, 45, 31–40.

27. Owens, W. A. Age and mental abilities: a longitudinal study. *Genetic Psychology Monographs,* 1953, 48, 3–54.

28. Palermo, D. S., Castenada, A., & McCandless, B. R. The relationship of anxiety in children to performance in a complex learning task. *Child Development,* 1956, 27, 333–337.

29. Rheingold, Harriet L. The modification of social responsiveness in institutional babies. *Monographs of the Society for Research in Child Development,* 1956, 21, (No. 63).

30. Ribble, Margaret A. Infantile experience in relation to personality development. In J. McV. Hunt (Ed.), *Personality and the behavior disorders.* Vol. II. New York: Ronald Press, 1944. Pp. 621–651.

31. Richards, T. W., & Nelson, V. L. Abilities of infants during the first eighteen months. *Journal of Genetic Psychology,* 1939, 55, 299–318.

32. Schaefer, E. S., Bell, R. Q., & Bayley, Nancy. Quantification of maternal behavior and consistency of mother-child interaction. *American Psychologist,* 1956, 11, 404. (Abstract)

33. Sherman, M., & Henry, T. R. *Hollow folk.* New York: Crowell, 1933

34. Spitz, R. A. An inquiry into the genesis of psychiatric conditions in early childhood. I. Hospitalism. *Psychoanalytic Study of the Child,* 1945, 1, 53–74.

35. Terman, L. M. *Concept Mastery Test (Manual).* New York: The Psychological Corporation, 1956.

36. Terman, L. M., & Oden, Melita H. *The gifted child grows up.* Stanford, Calif.: Stanford Univer. Press, 1947.

37. Thorndike, E. L. *The measurement of intelligence.* New York: Bureau of Publications, Teachers College, 1927.

38. Thorndike, R. L. Growth of intelligence during adolescence. *Journal of Genetic Psychology,* 1948, 72, 11–15.

39. Thurstone, L. L. Primary mental abilities. *Psychometric Monographs,* 1938, No. 1.

40. Wechsler, D. *The measurement of adult intelligence.* (3rd ed.) Baltimore: Williams & Wilkins, 1944.

41. Wechsler, D. Recent changes in rate of decline of intelligence test scores of the American adult. *Primer Congreso Panamericano Gerontologia* (Book of Abstracts). Ciudad Universitaria, Mexico. 1956, 267–268.

42. Wheeler, L. R. A comparative study of the intelligence of East Tennessee mountain children. *Journal of Educational Psychology,* 1942, 33, 321–334.

43. Wittenborn, J. R., *et al.* A study of adoptive children: III. Relationships between some aspects of development and some aspects of environment for adoptive children. *Psychological Monographs,* 1956, 70, No. 3 (Whole No. 410).

Delimiting the Verbal Factor

Frederick B. Davis
1948

Everyone recognizes that high ability in the verbal factor denotes facility with words, and that low ability in this factor denotes the reverse, but not everyone has precisely the same conception of what facility with words means. To some, it connotes ability to remember word meanings and to make increasingly fine distinctions among them. In her diary, Dorothy Wordsworth has recounted an amusing conversation between Samuel Coleridge and her brother regarding the best adjective to use for describing a waterfall called the Linn. Coleridge hesitated among *sublime, majestic,* and *grand.* He was making fine distinctions among the precise connotations of those three adjectives, any one of which might well have completely satisfied a less sophisticated literary craftsman, or, to put it in the terminology of measurement which we are using this morning, men with lower scores in the verbal factor.

A measurement of memory for word meanings may be accomplished by means of test items like the following:

inviolable:
(A) unapproachable
(B) undefiled
(C) virtuous
(D) not violent
(E) sacred

The degree of precision with which the ability to make distinctions among words is measured can be increased simply by incorporating decoys in the items that are closer and closer to the exact meaning of the correct answer. Unfortunately, many tests of this kind have obtained greater and greater difficulty in their component items by employing esoteric words with decoys of little plausibility rather than by employing useful words with ingenious and attractive decoys. Examples of esoteric words that have been used are *syzygy* (which is the last word in the vocabulary test of the

California Test of Mental Maturity), and *umbel*. These are typical of the highly specialized words that have sometimes been included in general vocabularly tests used to measure the verbal factor.

Some people have thought of the verbal factor as ability to determine the precise meaning of a word from its context. This has led them to avoid verbal items of the kind cited above, and to test the meanings of words as they appear in sentences or even in paragraphs or stories. Ordinarily, the context provided by short phrases or sentences is mere window dressing that serves no useful purpose, but I have presented evidence that a mental skill independent of memory for word meanings does indeed seem to exist when genuine dependence on context is actually required for obtaining the meaning of an unknown word, or for obtaining the meaning of a word like *lead*, which may be pronounced "lĕd" or "lēd," depending on the meaning indicated by the context.

A third group of people has conceived of the verbal factor chiefly as the ability to manipulate words in combination and to reason with them. Measurement of this ability has often been accomplished by means of items like the following:

Who is to *when* as *Mary* is to

(A) time
(B) Jane
(C) 8 p.m.
(D) person
(E) girl

Needless to say, there are other concepts of the verbal factor. Thurstone, for example, has noted the existence of a verbal factor that he has described as word fluency.

I would like to see the verbal factor defined rather narrowly as an index of both range and precision of word meanings, and to suggest that it be measured by means of cleverly contrived multiple-choice items in the format of the first item quoted above. The verbal factor would then be divorced in large measure from the reasoning abilities involved in items of the word-analogy type or of the opposites type. These reasoning abilities are probably important enough to warrant assigning separate names to them. They may be so nearly identical with the reasoning-in-reading factor identified in two separate batteries of reading tests that they can be conveniently included in that factor's variance.

It is likely that measures of both the verbal factor and of the reasoning-in-reading elements, as I have defined them, will prove to have substantial social utility. The contextual-meaning skill may also prove to be worthy of separate measurement. The extent to which these separate measures correlate to markedly different degrees with various criteria of real consequence will, however, determine whether they are worthy of separate measurement.

The Relationship Between Verbal Factor Scores and Other Variables

WILLIAM W. TURNBULL

1948

Preceding speakers have pointed out that studies of "the verbal factor" have shown it to be much more complex than had been supposed originally, with an undetermined number of factors (at least four or five) appearing where only one was originally known.

The immediate problem for attack is, presumably, the surer identification of these factors involved in the use of words. Work of this kind will provide an important part of the answer to the problem implied by the title of this discussion: "Defining the nature of the verbal factor. . . ."

It will be my purpose to present briefly four approaches other than the refinement of the factors that can be isolated through studies of the intercorrelation of written verbal tests—four approaches that I believe will be required in reaching a more complete definition of the nature of the "verbal factor" or, should we rather say, the "word factors." These approaches will constitute attempts to describe the word factors in relation to external variables as well as in relation to each other.

The first approach is the extension of studies to include media of communication other than writing. Passing mention of this need has been made by Taylor (3) in the discussion of his study, and some work has been done by British investigators in tracing fluency through speech as well as in written work. Studies are needed to determine whether or not the factors found in speaking and in the comprehension of speech are similar to, or the same as, those found for tests based on reading and writing.

A second approach is the study of the genetic development of the word factors. Studies relating age and the organization of mental abilities have, of course, been made by Thurstone and by others. As new abilities or characteristics are brought to light, however, there is a need for repetition of such studies; and we now require investigations of the word factors as they

403

are exhibited by very young children. At what age can we differentiate these factors, and how do their interrelationships change with age?

A third approach is the study of the relation between cultural influences and the development of the word factors. We should discover whether or not the same factors are found in different cultures or subcultures. Does Factor *W* operate in verbal tests prepared in Oriental languages? (*W*, you will recall, involves the ability to produce words that have some formal characteristic in common, such as the same first letter. Is there an analogous ability in languages based on independent, pictorial units rather than on an alphabet?) Then, within a society in which a given set of word factors has been identified, we need to know whether or not some subcultures are more propitious than others for the growth of word abilities, in general and differentially. It is fairly well conceded that there is a large, general effect of experiential background on word skills. Is this effect more pronounced for some word abilities than for others? Are some environments favorable to the development of one of the word abilities and unfavorable to the development of others? A study of systematic variation between word abilities in relation to experiential background would provide an effective supplement to the evidence gained from factor analysis as to the independence of the word factors.

A fourth type of investigation will be that in which an attempt is made to relate word factors to personal characteristics other than mental abilities as usually conceived. Here the work of Stephenson should be mentioned. In an article published some fifteen years ago, Stephenson (2) indicated positive results in an attempt to relate fluency scores and types of mental disturbance. The manic phase of manic-depressive psychosis had particularly strong relations with fluency, as might be hypothesized. Cattell (1) felt even earlier that written fluency tests were strongly related to a characteristic that he named "surgency"—a temperament trait in terms of which, of course, normal as well as disturbed subjects can be described. In the light of our growing knowledge of the dimensions of the word-factor field, and the refinements in testing instruments made possible by the recent factor studies, this earlier work should perhaps be redone in an effort to relate temperament traits to the more specifically delineated word factors.

When these approaches to the definition of the verbal factor (or word factors) have been taken, we shall, I believe, have a good picture of its dimensions and of its place in the psychological economy.

REFERENCES

1. Cattell, R. B. Temperament tests. II. Tests. *British Journal of Psychology,* 1933, 24, 20–49.
2. Stephenson, W. Spearman factors and psychiatry—introductory. *British Journal of Medical Psychology,* 1934, 14, 101–105.
3. Taylor, C. W. A factorial study of fluency in writing. *Psychometrika,* 1947, 12, 239–262.

Factors of Verbal Achievement

JOHN B. CARROLL

1961

Factor analysis is indeed a perennial favorite as a subject for discussion at these conferences. I was asked to consider the implications of factor analysis for achievement testing, with special reference to skills and knowledges in the verbal domain. My title, "Factors of Verbal Achievement," may sound as if I am going to rattle off a catalogue of such factors. This is not what I intend to do. Instead, I want to consider some general questions about the role of factor analysis in studying and measuring achievement. I shall illustrate my points in connection with the verbal domain, but they are equally applicable in other domains. I shall, of course, restrict my attention to factor-analytic work conducted by *R*-technique as applied to our relations of test variables over persons.

What does factor analysis really do? The pat answer is that it isolates a series of underlying "dimensions" of individual differences, and makes it possible to describe a large set of test scores in terms of a relatively small number of such dimensions. Given a set of tests, the use of factor analysis helps one understand what kinds of things are being measured, and provides an account of the "structure" of the domain under study. An attempt is made to "interpret" the separate factors or dimensions, and some of the more venturesome of the factor-analytic guild have even attempted to draw inferences from factor-analytic results about the structure of the intellect itself.

I must say that I have been steadily losing sympathy for such a way of thinking about factor-analytic results. The notion of "dimensions" may be a convenient one when we are trying to understand the geometric representation of the factor-analytic model, but it makes less and less sense as a faithful way of describing behavior. It deflects attention from a better and more realistic description, a description, by the way, that may help in the resolution of certain mathematical aspects of factor analysis.[1]

[1] For example, the description urged in this paper would tend to minimize the importance of attempting to find any definite minimum rank for a matrix of correlations; rather, the

406

Essentially, any factor-analytic study has to do with a series of behaviors or responses as embodied in a set of tests or other measuring instruments or procedures. The factor-analytic procedure examines, as it were, all the possible pairs of these behaviors, and identifies clusters of responses whose frequencies of joint occurrence in a given sample of individuals are greater than the frequencies of joint occurrence for other pairs of responses. The important datum is the frequency of joint occurrence of responses. The factor analysis might find, for example, that correct responses to two mathematics test items are more likely to co-occur than the responses to two items, one of which concerns mathematics and one of which concerns history.

There are a number of technical difficulties which I will pass over as not really relevant to my argument. It must be pointed out, for example, that most factor-analytical studies do not study single responses but, rather, groups of responses embodied in tests. The net effect of this is artificially to construct metrics relating to the co-occurrence of certain sets of responses, the only justification being a certain significant degree of internal consistency among the responses in a set, as established by item-analysis techniques.

Factor analysis would be of more generalized import if it restricted itself to studies of sets of items considered singly, but this has usually been regarded as impractical because of the large numbers of items one would have to consider, and for other reasons. Another technical problem concerns the statistical treatment of joint occurrence data. One does not ordinarily enter joint occurrence data into a factor analysis, but instead uses some statistical measure of "relationship"; I have considered this problem in my recent presidential address to the Psychometric Society (3).

I believe these technical problems, in any case, can be resolved in a way that will embrace the present analysis, in which I wish to emphasize that the essential data of factor analysis are the joint frequencies of pairs of behaviors, or classes of behavior, in a specified sample of individuals, and that the "factors" of factor analysis really correspond to sets of responses whose joint occurrences are conspicuous in comparison to those of other possible sets of responses. The "factor loadings" of a test variable on a factor may be regarded as being functions of the magnitudes of its joint frequencies of occurrence with other variables in the set.

When we try to "interpret" a factor, therefore, we should attempt to consider the source of the frequencies of co-occurrence. That is, why do the responses clustering in a factor appear together?

---

question is one of ascertaining how many of the *n* dimensions into which a matrix can be factored are significantly associated with identifiable sources of variance. This description also supports the notion of correlated, nonorthogonal, primary factors corresponding to correlated sources of variance which give rise to clustering within sets of responses.

There are many possibilities. Among these are: 1) the learning or the performance of one response is prerequisite to, or implied in, the performance of another (this is most frequently the case where it is found that the items can be scaled in the Guttman sense); 2) the learned behavior represented in one response has transferred to the other response; and 3) because of the accidents of personal history or because of the common experience of certain numbers of the group of persons, there was a higher probability that both of any pair of responses were learned together than that either would have been learned alone.

Note, now, that this last possibility makes no appeal to any psychological considerations about the two responses; it merely refers to the actuarial fact of their co-occurrence, beyond chance, in the particular sample under study. I suspect that this account will often apply to the sets of responses included in many so-called "achievement" tests. And if it is correct, a demonstration of it could be brought about on an experimental basis. Indeed, given a series of behaviors, one could arrange a training situation so as to obtain any particular factor structure that one might desire. For example, suppose I have 50 randomly assorted nonsense syllables, and suppose that I wish to establish a training program so that there will be five factors of achievement, each represented by a specified set of 10 nonsense syllables. All I have to do is to arrange my 50 syllables into the five lists of 10 nonsense syllables apiece, and then proceed to give the subjects in my experimental group different amounts of training on the five lists. For example, random halves of the group would get either much or little training on the first list, different random halves would get much or little training on the second list, etc. This would be an easy experiment to do; it might truly be worth doing if it would enlighten anybody (7).

The model developed here is similar, I think, to any situation in which one analyzes a series of achievement tests. An appropriately designed factor-analysis study in a high school could yield an English factor, a Social Studies factor, a Physics factor, a Chemistry factor, and perhaps even a Driver Education factor, among others. These factors could exist solely by virtue of the fact that these courses of study consist of a series of responses that are learned together (or not learned together, in the case of the failing students).

Actually, there are few factorial studies that have been restricted to "achievement tests" covering distinct courses or syllabi and, therefore, it is difficult to cite cases illustrating the design described here. No matter—the same type of interpretation in terms of joint learning of responses can be applied to factorial studies of aptitude tests, intelligence tests, and the like, for all of these can be regarded as achievement tests of a special kind. It must be remembered that the distinction between achievement tests and other types of tests is largely one of purpose, intended use, and scope of content, rather than any qualitative difference in type of content. If, therefore, I now turn my attention to a scrutiny of some of the better established "factors" of intelligence and aptitude tests in the verbal domain, it will now be understood that my title, "Factors of Verbal Achievement," is not inapplicable. Some of the mystique which has surrounded factor-analytic results needs to be torn away. "Factors" as entities have been over-hypostatized. They cannot and must not be regarded as putative "things," which somehow exist in whatever bodily structures may be responsible for behavior.

Take, for example, the question which has sometimes been formulated as that of whether abilities tend increasingly to specialize with age. Some evidence has been interpreted as showing that they do. If so, is it not better to consider this result a manifestation of the fact that in our culture the learning experiences of individuals tend to become gradually more and more heterogeneous?

Another example is afforded by the apparent contrast between British and American results in the study of intelligence tests. If British results have found a larger place for a general intelligence factor g than American results, could this not be a reflection of a greater uniformity of learning experiences in British grammar schools—uniformity, that is, in content, if not also in teaching method or quality of learning?

I offer these only as speculations; there exists no clear-cut evidence for either of them.

Let us turn our attention, then, to some of the factors of verbal achievement. The basic hypothesis we shall be examining is that whenever we identify a "factor" through factor-analytic procedures, the source of this variance is to be found in differential learning experiences. Actually, in this brief talk I can do little more than to suggest how this hypothesis could be investigated.

Take first the well-known V factor, the "verbal knowledge" factor. A variety of tests—all essentially "achievement tests"—seek to determine whether various verbal responses have been previously learned. I have in mind vocabulary tests, verbal comprehension tests, grammatical usage tests, and the like; morphological, syntactical, and lexical aspects of language are all involved, as well as certain kinds of language habits, which are better studied in terms of conditional probabilities than in terms of linguistic analysis.

There are many obvious reasons for the joint learning or nonlearning of the responses involved in these tests. One stems from the fact that the members of the English-speaking community are exposed to widely varying amounts and qualities of English. Among the influences that determine the amount and quality of English to which a child or adolescent will be exposed are the following: socioeconomic class, language ability, and occupational status of parents; rank among siblings; sex; and type of child rearing. In addition, there are the person's (learner's) interests and temperament which engender more or less exposure to, and handling of, verbal materials.

In any case, the very structure of language insures a clustering of the responses in a factorial sense. In a representative group, the joint frequency with which any two verbal responses will be present will be greater than the joint frequency of any one verbal response and any nonverbal response (for example, a mathematical or a spatial response).

It is strange, but true, that even now we can cite no thorough-going, all-inclusive, factor-analytic study of all the ordinary English language skills; therefore, we have had to piece together our knowledge from a variety of studies. It is now pretty certain, however, that there are separate "factors" for the traditional language modes, that is, reading, writing, speaking, and listening.

Reading, whether measured in terms of speed or of comprehension, is probably closest to the traditional V factor; that is, it is highly correlated with the V factor, and in many studies indistinguishable because of lack of clear study design. It is reasonable for reading ability to be factorially similar to verbal knowledge because verbal knowledge tests tap the kinds of responses that are more likely to be learned through reading than through listening. Furthermore, most verbal knowledge tests are printed tests that require reading.

Listening ability, studied extensively in a recent thesis at Harvard by Spearritt (8), seems to be fairly well distinct from verbal knowledge and reading ability, even though correlated. Apparently the learning experiences that make one able to listen to auditorily presented verbal material are sufficiently specific as not to correlate highly with reading comprehension. It is quite plausible that individuals have different degrees of experience in listening to and understanding material presented in oral form.

Recent studies at Harvard (6) have also shown that there are several factors in the domain of speaking ability, keyed to the various types of situation in which speaking is required—ranging from private conversation and interviews to public speaking occasions. Learning experiences in these several situations vary, it would seem, giving rise to distinct factors.

Much the same sort of situation may exist in the field of writing ability, which has perennially been regarded as one of the most elusive things to measure. That is, writing ability may be a matter of situational control, with achievement varying according to the kind of task that is set.

Insofar as good writing depends upon knowledge of language responses —morphological, syntactical, and lexical—it will be found related to the verbal knowledge factor V; indeed, in some studies of the College Entrance Examination Board, it appears that verbal knowledge tests are more satisfactory measures of writing ability than writing tasks themselves. We have not yet been able to measure the reasoning and organizational aspects of good expository and creative writing independently of writing itself, perhaps because the two are inextricably bound together. The many studies showing that the teaching of formal grammar is practically irrelevant to writing ability suggest that formal grammar knowledge constitutes a set of achievements attained quite apart from experience in writing (9). Strangely enough, I do not know of any factorial studies which have concerned themselves with formal grammar, as distinct from the usual type of grammatical usage test. There is much investigation yet to be done in the realm of grammar and its relevance to English composition, the learning of foreign language, etc. I would suggest further experimentation with the kind of "grammatical sensitivity" test to be found in my Modern Language Aptitude Test (4), because it seems to me that this test, which measures ability to identify grammatical functions and patterns (without any knowledge of formal grammar or terminology), may be of greater relevance to the kinds of responses called for in English composition.

The so-called Word Fluency Factor W is an interesting example of a factor which has been masquerading as some sort of special ability but which, I believe, can in large part be interpreted as the result of certain kinds of learning experience. Tests of the W factor, you will recall, are the ones that require the subject to rearrange letters in anagrams tests, to think of words beginning and ending with certain combinations of letters, and the like. Is it not possible that an individual's experiences with the phonetic correspondences of letters and letter combinations—that is, with "phonics" —may have much to do with his ability to perform the kinds of tricks demanded on tests of the W factor? There exist tests of "phonic skill" which, one may hypothesize, would show a substantial correlation with tests of the W factor (1). The problem is to identify the sources of the learning experiences that are responsible for performance on these tests; perhaps they could be identified only by finding out how the individual learned to read. Was he taught phonic skills, or was he allowed to learn to read primarily by whole-word recognition techniques?

In some fields of verbal achievement, it would appear that learning experiences are rather highly specific to certain kinds of situations. Take, for example, the "Naming" factor which has been identified by me and several investigators (2). It appears whenever the subject is required to give names to a series of stimuli. Can it be that such an ability—the ability to do this rapidly, that is—is acquired as the result of specific practice, perhaps in early childhood? It would take rather an elaborate longitudinal study to find out, I am afraid. Similar remarks could probably be made for a number of other factors of verbal ability—for example, Expressional Fluency, Associational Fluency, and Ideational Fluency as described, for example, by John French (5) in his kit of reference tests for factor studies.

Of course, even after we have accounted for as much of the variance in all these factors of verbal achievement as possible on the basis of differential learning experiences, there might be some residue traceable to genetic or constitutional factors. It would be satisfying, however, to get these factors solidly tied in with the processes of learning. Even more satisfying would be to find out to what extent these factors are subject to training: that is, to posttest learning experiences. This is an exciting prospect for future experimental work. At the moment, one cannot find much evidence of activity in this area. It is perhaps regrettable that we are all just too busy making and analyzing tests to leave time for that.

REFERENCES

1. Brown, Grace M., & Cottrell, Alice B. *Stanford Diagnostic Phonics Survey (research edition)*. Palo Alto, Calif.: Consulting Psychologists Press, 1958.
2. Carroll, J. B. A factor analysis of verbal abilities. *Psychometrika*, 1941, 6, 279–308.
3. Carroll, J. B. The nature of the data, or how to choose a correlation coefficient. *Psychometrika*, 1961, 26, 347–372.
4. Carroll, J. B., & Sapon, S. M. *Modern Language Aptitude Test*. New York: The Psychological Corporation, 1959.
5. French, J. W. (Ed.) *Kit of selected tests for reference aptitude and achievement factors*. Princeton, N.J.: Educational Testing Service, 1954. [Rev. ed.: French, J. W., Ekstrom, Ruth B., & Price, L. A. (Eds.) *Kit of refer-*

ence tests for cognitive factors. Princeton, N.J.: Educational Testing Service, 1963—Ed.]

6. Marge, M. Home background influences on the development of oral communication skills in children. Unpublished doctoral dissertation, Harvard Univer., 1959.

7. Skager, R. W. The effects of two training procedures on the differentiation of numerical ability. Unpublished doctoral dissertation, Univer. of California, Los Angeles, 1961.

8. Spearritt, D. A. A factorial analysis of listening comprehension. Unpublished doctoral dissertation, Harvard Univer., 1961.

9. Strom, Ingrid M. Research in grammar and usage and its implications for teaching writing. *Bulletin of the School of Education, Indiana University,* Vol. 36, No. 5, September 1960.

Creative Talent

L. L. THURSTONE
1950

One of the most important educational problems is to encourage creative talent, to learn how to find it, and how to train it. We need creative talent in all fields of life. Creative talent is in demand in science, the fine arts, industry, and in the professions. In comparison with the social importance of this kind of talent, we have not done much to learn about it.

At the very beginning of this paper, we must admit that little is known about creative talent. We have in mind here the intellectual and temperamental traits that characterize people who are able to formulate problems and to find original solutions. Because of the importance of creative talent, it seems worthwhile to study it experimentally. We shall consider a number of hypotheses about the conceivable nature of creative talent and the types of observation and experiment by which it might be investigated.

Let us first try to delimit the problem as far as we can in the present state of knowledge. Perhaps the first thought that comes to mind is to investigate anecdotal material concerning the work of geniuses. If we should focus attention on such studies, we should also select some living geniuses and study them at work. To limit investigation to the study of geniuses is probably not a profitable way to proceed.

Let us begin with the working hypothesis that creative talent is qualitatively the same at all levels: in the trades and in the professions, as well as in the rare and extreme forms that we call genius. Most men in the professions and in business do creative thinking. Of course, some do more than others. We assume that the thinking that leads to the solution of problems at the professional level is qualitatively the same as that which characterizes the work of geniuses. The difference may be one of power. If this working hypothesis is sound, then we can learn much about creative thinking by studying the working habits of professional men and the conditions that seem to favor the successful solution of problems. Such study might be cooperative. We might study our work habits in relation to successful problem solving. A few hypotheses will be mentioned that we might keep in mind in watching ourselves at work. Such inquiries can lead to clues that may eventually be useful for understanding creative work, whatever its nature may turn out to be.

Before eliminating the upper extreme of genius from our inquiry, let us correct a common misunderstanding about creative talent. It is rather common in the field of mental measurement to discuss the distribution of intelligence in terms of a normal curve. At one end of this curve, we indicate the low intelligence of those unfortunates who do not have enough mental endowment to get along in competitive society. They are the idiots and the imbeciles. Then, at the upper end of the distribution, it is rather common to indicate the range of genius. This is a serious error. If genius represents extremely high gifts for creative thinking, then it is not synonymous with intelligence. To be extremely intelligent is not the same as to be gifted in creative work. This may be taken as a hypothesis.

It is a common observation in the universities that those students who have high intelligence, judged by available criteria, are not necessarily the ones who produce the most original ideas. All of us probably know a few men who are both creative and highly intelligent, but this combination is not the rule. One does not expect to find creative talent in a stupid person, but there may even be some doubt about this statement because creative talent in one field can be associated with general mental endowment that is mediocre. There is undoubtedly a positive correlation between creative talent and intelligence, so that geniuses are usually in the upper half of the general intelligence distribution.

The confusion between intelligence and creative talent is common. For example, Quiz Kids are often referred to as geniuses. They would undoubtedly score high in memory functions, including incidental memory and rote memory. But it is doubtful whether they are also fluent in producing original ideas. If they were, then the problem of selecting creative talent would be simple. Other examples are the students who complete their college degrees at an early age. Experience does not indicate that they later produce the ideas that advance our civilization. On the other hand, we should expect to find an occasional genius among them.

Those who supervise doctor's and master's dissertations in the universities often have occasion to speculate about this problem. A doctor's dissertation is, by definition, "a contribution to knowledge." As instructors, we work hard to make an occasional contribution to knowledge, but it is difficult to insist that the inexperienced student do likewise. There is good reason why dissertations are often referred to as "pieces" of research—often trivial pieces. Although a tremendous volume of dissertation research is being poured out from the universities every year, it does not offer any solution to the problem of defining creative talent.

It will probably be agreed among experienced teachers that it is not the student with the highest scholarship who produces the most interesting and original ideas in the laboratory. Students who have creative ideas are sometimes erratic and undependable. They might argue that scholarship represents a certain degree of intellectual docility. Although there seems to be some conflict between scholarship and creative talent, they are probably positively correlated. Several primary factors of memory have been indicated in factorial studies. Incidental memory seems to be independent of the ability to memorize paired associates, and these seem to be different from visual memory as primary factors. Men who excel in producing original ideas should be studied as to the several memory factors.

It might seem plausible to formulate the hypothesis that people who are creative tend to be generous towards ideas. Perhaps they should be characterized as openminded. Although this hypothesis has some face validity, it will probably be found that creative people do not excel in openmindedness.

By way of further delimiting the problem, we might consider the hypothesis that scientific talent and creative talent are not the same. It seems possible for a man to have good scientific talent without being creative. By scientific talent we mean here the ability to handle competently the concepts and methods of a science or profession without the ability to produce new ideas that are commensurate with mastery of subject matter.

Let us turn next to a tentative formulation of differentiating criteria for the creative act. The solution to a problem is usually characterized by a moment of insight in which the significant question is asked and perhaps solved in the same moment. The moment of insight is the critical moment. The thinking that precedes the moment of insight is different from the thinking that follows that moment. We might define the moment of insight as the main characteristic of work that is called creative. It does not necessarily follow that a problem which is so solved is important. A problem that is solved by the creative act of one man may be solved quite casually and routinely by another man with different experience and training. It is the nature of the psychological processes that should determine whether we call the act creative. A creative act may be dead wrong. That is not known until the new idea has been tested.

It is in the nature of creative work that it has some novelty or invention. Whether society considers the idea to be novel has nothing to do with the case. The act is creative if the thinker reaches the solution in a sudden closure which necessarily implies some novelty for him. Problem solving in a moment of insight may involve almost any kind of content. The idea may be artistic, mechanical, or theoretical. The creative idea may be administrative if it solves an organizational problem. It may be a new football play or a clever chess move or a new slogan.

If the creative act is identified by a sudden closure of insight, it is of psychological interest to consider the nature of the thinking that precedes the closure and the thinking that follows it. The thinking that precedes the closure is in the nature of worrying about the problem. In that stage, the thinker may have some feeling for the nature of the solution, which is not yet verbalized. He may be able to say that a solution should look like this, but not like that. He may be able to say that such and such things are associated with the solution, which is still unknown, and that certain other things seem to him to be irrelevant. The thinker may be haunted by the problem so that he deserves no credit for working at it. Because the solution has not been verbalized, it is difficult for him to discuss it, even though he may have some feeling for the nature of the solution which is to be found. It is as if the partial solution were essentially affective in nature. The solution to a problem is often so embarrassingly simple that it can be explained in a few minutes of a lecture. Instead of pride in the new idea, there might even be some hesitation in admitting the very considerable cost in time and effort. The work that follows the moment of insight may require months or years of drudgery and hard work in testing and developing the new idea.

After an idea has been found relating to the solution of a problem, it can usually be verbalized. At this stage, we can begin to apply the various tools that we have been taught: the scientific methods, experimental designs, and deductive logic. The object is then to test the idea with all the rigorous procedures at our disposal. The method of attack is then quite explicit. Sometimes the solution of a problem consists of a succession of inventions, and it happens not infrequently that the principal contribution in problem solving is in the design of the experimental equipment itself. Our principal concern is not with the later deductive stages in the solution of each problem. We are interested here primarily in the psychological processes that precede each of the sudden closures at which the significant ideas appear. Most of the instruction in scientific methods is concerned with the testing of an idea, but this instruction has very little to offer in teaching students how to produce ideas. It is this prefocal stage of the process of problem solving that specially needs investigation.

Although we seem to be unable to teach ourselves and our students how to produce ideas in problem solving, it may be worthwhile to consider some of the attitudes that favor the production of ideas. In teaching graduate students, many of us have had occasion to observe them as well as ourselves in the work of problem solving. We shall consider a few hypotheses concerning the attitudes that seem to favor the production of fruitful ideas and other attitudes that seem to stifle them. Some students have the characteristic that when a strange problem or idea is presented, their first reaction is negative. Some very bright students seem to be able to show immediately by clear logical reasoning that the proposed idea is wrong. Sometimes the proof is so convincing that one is tempted to discard further thought about the new proposal. Even when this negative attitude is associated with high intelligence, the result is not likely to be creative. The more promising candidate is one who examines the new and queer proposal. He toys with it and speculates what the implications might be, if it could be demonstrated. Because of the very novelty of the proposal, his impulse is to wish that it could be shown to be true. He asks, in effect, how the world would be different if the proposal could be sustained. This observation leads one to wonder whether those who are inventive and creative should preferably have a certain amount of gullibility.

Some years ago, Walter Dill Scott, when he was at Carnegie Institute of Technology, had a test in which he asked the candidate to write some of the implications of a number of strange hypotheses. What would be the practical consequences if we had eyes both in the front and the back of our heads? He might ask the candidate to enumerate some practical consequences if we could swim more easily than we could walk. Scott's purpose was to determine the candidate's fluency of ideas. Some such procedures might be tried in relation to the present problem, but we would probably find that mere fluency of ideas does not adequately represent creative talent. Fluency in seeing implications may be an important characteristic of creative ability. Some forms of fluency may signify intelligence without implying creative talent.

Even if we cannot teach students how to produce ideas, as we can teach them how to test ideas, we might be able to accomplish something by encouraging them, as well as ourselves, to adopt attitudes that favor the production of ideas. Students often have difficulty in selecting dissertation problems. When a student asks us to suggest a dissertation problem, we might encourage him to ask a lot of questions about the field of his scientific interest. I sometimes suggest that he take as an exercise the writing of twenty dissertation proposals in the course of the following week. Sometimes the student is startled by this assignment because he has the attitude that any single idea would be welcome. Our ways of teaching are partly responsible for this type of difficulty.

It seems proper to encourage students to be critical in reading the literature, but the cultivation of such an attitude has disadvantages. When students review a paper or a monograph, they often assume that their task is to tear the paper to pieces and to make the author look foolish, if it is possible to do so. Often their appraisal of a paper stops there. If a student reviews the literature with the attitude of tearing it to shreds, the resulting attitude is not wholesome for his own work. It might be better to ask him to review some papers or monographs that he is enthusiastic about. In presenting a monograph, he would then pay attention to what the author was really trying to do, what he actually did, and how far he succeeded. In criticizing a paper either because of the formulation of the problem or because of experimental and analytical errors, the student could be encouraged to suggest what he would have done with the same problem. In this way, the student's work on the literature would be more constructive than if we merely remain satisfied because he has a critical attitude in reading. If courses were always concerned with ideas and what to do with them, with occasional support from the literature, the student would have less difficulty in selecting one of these ideas for his own dissertation.

One of the attitudes that seems to favor the resolution of a problem can be called the method of solving a problem by denying it. One can ask whether the formulated problem, or the half-way solution that may be available, contains some hidden premise that is implied and taken for granted, but which is unnecessary for the real goal. One can try to state explicitly everything that has been assumed and which has not previously been made explicit. If any restrictive assumption or premise can be found that we are taking for granted without saying so, and if that premise or restrictive condition can be thrown out, then the solution sometimes appears. For this reason, it may be a good policy not to put anything in writing, not even diagrams on scratch paper, until the central problem seems to be solved. The casual sketch may inadvertently commit further thinking to some restrictive error. I asked Professor Barnard in our mathematics department about a problem. He told me that he would think about it. A few days later, he came to me with a solution, but he told me that it was trivial, and that very likely I had some assumptions that were irrelevant, or else I had not told him about some restrictive conditions that I had taken for granted. The solution that he proposed satisfied the question that I had asked. He was right in his inference that I had not really stated my problem completely.

A hypothesis that should be considered in the experimental study of problem solving is that the moment of insight is often, perhaps always, in relaxed and dispersed attention. Sometimes sudden closure appears after leaving a problem in disgust, or the closure will suddenly intrude when attention is distracted.

In recent years, Mrs. Thurstone and I have been working on various scoring problems. The use of tests is markedly affected by the considerable labor of scoring, especially with hand scoring. It is a practical problem to reduce the labor of hand scoring to a minimum. The use of a separate stencil for every page of every test is a complication that should be eliminated, if possible. A simple solution appeared as a sudden closure in a familiar but apparently irrelevant percept. In this percept, a picket fence across the street was seen through a window screen at our house. There was an optical interference effect somewhat analogous to beating in sound. In this effect, the window screen was seen as a universal scoring screen and the picket fence represented a printed half-tone surface. Here the percept was affected by the problem, even though the problem was not focal in consciousness at the moment of closure. Attention was dispersed and relaxed. The universal stencil does not need to be fitted to any exact location on the test paper, and the same stencil can be used for all kinds of tests. The answer spaces can be arranged in any desired patterns with the same stencil. The first thought after this closure was naturally that one should have thought of something so simple a long time ago.

I have tried one type of experiment several times with complete failure. On several occasions, I have left my work on a problem to walk around the block and to give attention to other things in the hope of inducing a solution by voluntarily dispersed attention. I learned that dispersed attention in problem solving cannot be faked.

Experimental studies should be made to ascertain what kinds of mental work are done best under conditions of muscular tension with concentrated attention, and what kinds of mental work can be done best with dispersed and relaxed attention. Such studies may bear on problem solving. A related and important educational problem is to determine whether the most productive results are obtained by a driving course of instruction where all the student's time is devoted to lesson learning. Another method would be to alternate periods of intense lesson learning with periods in which the student is asked to do problem solving with the same material at a leisurely tempo and without any pressure of speed. Ordinary scholarship examinations would appraise the lesson learning, but not the gains in productive abilities with the newly learned material.

We don't ordinarily hear about how professional men get their useful ideas, but there is much anecdotal material on how discoveries have been made. Such stories often sound as if discoveries were quite accidental. It is more likely that the investigators had previously identified themselves with a problem in terms of which they interpreted some accidental effect. Scientific discoveries at all levels are probably not so accidental as they look to the casual observer.

When creative work is studied experimentally, serious attention should be given to the inductive factor. This is one of the most interesting of the primary factors that have been identified so far because it has been shown to transcend the nature of the content, including verbal, numerical, and spatial material. One hypothesis that should be considered is that ability in the primary factor for induction may be closely related with problem-solving ability. All of the tests that have been designed for the primary factor of induction require the subject to discover the rule or principle in the material that he is working with. It does seem that this ability should be close to, if it is not identical with, the ability for creative work. Although the inductive factor is an important component in intelligence with high saturation in the second-order general factor in intelligence, it probably does not alone represent creative talent. If the inductive factor which is heavily saturated in intelligence were the same as creative ability, then there should be a higher correlation between intelligence and creative talent than has actually been found. Problem solving probably represents more than induction. Frequently it consists in reformulating the problem itself and then solving the new problem.

The scientific study of creative work will probably encounter a set of questions more or less analogous to those that marked the scientific study of intelligence. First comes to mind the question whether creative talent is some general factor, which can operate in many different media, or whether there are different factors of creative intelligence in the different fields. In exploratory studies of creative work, it might be well to start with the working hypothesis that creative talent is a general factor, or that it can be treated as such in first approximation. This corresponds more or less to the way in which Spearman started his analytical work on intelligence. We shall then postulate a general factor for creative work, or perhaps a group of factors which express themselves in different media. Whether a creative person becomes a poet or machine designer or composer or physicist would then depend on the various primary abilities of his intelligence.

We should consider the hypothesis that this talent is not confined entirely to the cognitive or intellective domain. It might very well happen that creative work is characterized mainly by the combination of intellective functions with certain temperamental characteristics. If this should be the case, then we should fail if we confine our efforts entirely to cognitive and intellective functions. The distinction between cognitive and temperamental traits is not so clear as used to be believed. They overlap quite definitely. An example is the first closure factor, which is well indicated by Gestalt-completion tests and by mutilated-words tests. The informal observation has been made that those who are especially fluent in the first closure factor are temperamentally more alert, quick, and active, and more quickly responsive than those who rate lower in the first closure factor. We cannot make this judgment about the second closure factor, which has other temperamental associates. Those who excel in the second closure factor seem to be more frequently deliberate in manner. However, these are only rough observations which have not yet been checked against actual performances.

In studying normal functions, it is sometimes useful to turn to the extremes of pathology. In factorial studies of the primary mental abilities, we have found it useful to include in the experimental groups the most extreme differences in the abilities to be analyzed. Applying the same principle here, we should profit by gaining information about the work of geniuses. We should not confine ourselves to them because they might be very individualistic subjects that would be hard to manage. By analogy, one might expect to find that ordinary people who have creative talent in some line would tend to be somewhat individualistic, and this probably agrees with general observation. It may also be found that creative people are on the whole less outgoing and sociable than the average, but one can think of exceptions to such a hypothesis.

Many years ago, I had the privilege of working rather closely with a man who is certainly known to be a genius, and I am trying to recall in the present context some of his intellectual and personality characteristics. Immediately after receiving an engineering degree at Cornell, I went to work with Thomas Edison as one of his laboratory assistants. I talked with him daily and had good opportunity to observe his work habits. He was a man of many strong convictions, and he did not seem to have much admiration for university education. It seemed to me that one of his most outstanding characteristics was a tremendous fluency of ideas. For every experimental failure he seemed to produce three more experiments to try. In this sense, he seemed to be tireless. The cot in his office was probably used for lying down to think about his problems as often as it was used for sleep. Thomas Edison seemed to have a startling fluency of ideas often spread far from the immediate problem. He seemed to have an absolutely endless array of stories. Few of them were fit for publication. Especially relevant to our present problem is the great fluency in proposing alternative solutions to a problem. This fluency of ideas should certainly be investigated in this context, but I suspect that there may be different kinds of fluency and that all of them may not be equally relevant to creative work. Another characteristic of Edison's was the casual way in which he treated experimental failures. These seemed to be merely part of the day's work and the signal for starting another experiment.

In setting up experimental studies of creative work, it would seem best to arrange for two groups: an experimental group of men who have demonstrated creative talent to a marked degree; and a control group at the same intellectual level but with less productive or inventive talent. In order to make sure that inventive talent is really distinguished from other intellectual traits, the control group should consist of men who have high scholarship and intelligence, and who are capable of profound critical appraisal in the same field as the more productive group. Both groups should be comparable in professional prestige.

One naturally considers the availability of graduate students in the universities for studies of creative talent and originality. There are serious limitations to such a proposal. In studying individual differences among graduate students in their ability to produce ideas, we must necessarily depend on the judgments of their teachers. To make judgments about students as to their originality is so different from the customary academic judgments about scholarship that there is some question whether we can trust available judgments for this kind of study. We can be sure at the outset that scholarship grades will have only imperfect positive correlation with the desired ratings for originality. It should be a major part of a research program to obtain rather extensive and systematic judgments of the originality of men in various fields, and to make close comparisons with the judgments of these men when they were students some years ago. Some illuminating results might be obtained from such a study, which could be a part of a major research program.

One study might be made with students in musical conservatories where they could be rated on originality and promise in musical composition. Similar studies might be set up in art schools and in schools of architecture. The college curricula in engineering and in medicine are so crowded that there may not be adequate opportunity to judge the originality of students. It would be especially promising to have studies of originality in organizations such as the Bell Telephone laboratories or the Westinghouse and General Electric laboratories. In such organizations, there should be good opportunity to differentiate between the originators and the men whose intellects turn more readily to critical and evaluative tasks and administrative duties. Such organizations could not survive and produce if they consisted only of innovators.

In judging men as to originality, we must deal with the inevitable conflict between the standards of our day and those of the next generation. In the musical conservatories and in the art schools, there might be some erratic young artists of doubtful status at the present time who will be the leaders twenty years from now. We shall certainly make errors in rating young talent. Every field of endeavor has such errors, but they are probably more common in some fields than in others. Work in the physical and biological sciences can be checked more promptly as to its potentialities than original work in the fine arts. Although every field is subject to errors of this kind, they are probably less frequent in the natural sciences than in the fine arts.

It should not be necessary to wait for the results of scientific studies on creative talent before taking some action about this problem. Considerable improvement can probably be made in the selection and training of university students by giving serious consideration to creative talent. For a number of years, I was chief examiner at the University of Chicago when the undergraduate college was reorganized. Scholarships were awarded annually on the basis of competitive examinations. At one time, there was discussion about how the examination should be appraised for the scholarship awards. The simplest procedure was merely to add up the total number of points that the student had earned with equal weighting for the four divisions: namely, the physical sciences, the biological sciences, the humanities, and the social sciences. This naturally gave the advantage to those students who were good lesson learners over a wide range of content. It seemed more plausible that we would select a larger number of future leaders in the various fields by following a different procedure. According to this proposal, we should require only a minimum of attainment in the four fields in order to assure communication with the student at the college level. This should be the minimum requirement for eligibility. The applicant should be expected to show marked attainment in some one field. The third requirement should be some evidence that the applicant has produced something new on his own initiative. This might be some production in musical composition or in poetry or in the design and construction of scientific apparatus, some useful invention, an article or publication on some general social issue. It might even be some clever business enterprise that showed initiative and originality. The appraisal of the applicants would, of course, require the pooled efforts of university faculty groups in their respective fields. One of the objections was that these appraisals could not be reduced to machine scoring. The more serious objection was based on educational policy, namely, that we should bet on the student who could demonstrate good scholastic performance over the whole range of the college curriculum. We would probably be selecting a larger proportion of future leaders in the various fields by the policy that emphasizes independent creative effort, even though it would require more faculty participation.

There have been various proposals for the selection of university students by centrally controlled examination methods. It would probably be an error to adopt any wholesale method of awarding university scholarships by means of uniform national examinations. It would be better to allow every community to select its quota of scholarship awards by various methods of selection, subject to minimum admission standards that would be set by each college. The standards would vary with the communities and with the colleges.

In setting up experimental studies in this field, we should certainly include objective tests of temperamental characteristics, as well as tests of the primary factors that seem to be important. These should include the two closure factors, the several space factors, the inductive factor, and several memory factors. Some of the perceptual functions may be differentiating for creative talent. Some characteristics of perseveration may be diagnostic.

One more hypothesis concerning the possible nature of creative talent and a proposed type of experimental study of it will be considered. According to one theory of intelligence (3), the psychological act originates in the essentially affective and nonverbalized, nonfocal motivations and needs of the individual. The development of the psychological act towards final overt expression consists in successive particularizations. Each of these successive steps can be regarded as a choice point or bifurcation. If the choice point is in focal consciousness, then the decision is subject to rational control and it is fully conscious. If the choice-point decision is made unconsciously in the particularization of the act, then the choice is determined instinctively or by intuition, habit, or chance. According to such a theory, a high intelligence is indicated by a choice point that becomes focal in consciousness at an early stage of the act so that a wide range of possible overt expressions is under conscious control. If the act develops under great pressure of motivation or emergency, then it will develop to nearly overt definition before it becomes focal in consciousness, and the act is then likely to be impulsive and relatively less intelligent. We might now make an additional interpretation for this theory of intelligence. It seems plausible that there should be individual differences in the ability to be in some kind of rapport with the unconscious stages of the act, even before it becomes focal in consciousness. Imaginative people might have some kind of rapport with their own unconscious thinking before it becomes focally conscious. It might be possible for a person to have the ability for a high degree of abstraction, in that his acts are subject to conscious deliberation at their early stages, and still not be in rapport with his own unconscious thinking. Such a person would be intelligent and even profound, but possibly not creative.

This hypothesis could be experimentally investigated. In one type of experiment, we might start with a set of several hundred cards with a word on each card. There might be a code of several rules by which a number or a letter is associated with each word. Consider a case where only four digits are used, namely, 1, 2, 3, and 4. Man-made objects might have the even digits 2 or 4. Large objects might have the digits 1 and 2. Whatever the code is, it should refer to the meanings of the words. The subject might be asked to guess a number for each presented word. The first ten or fifteen cards would be presented with their correct digits. The next ten or fifteen cards would be presented without any digit, and the subject would be asked to guess for each card. The next set of cards would have the digits given. In this way, alternate sets would have the response given for each word, and alternate sets would require the subject to guess. No word should ever be repeated unless it is done intentionally to give the subject the impression that he is doing a memory test. It is easy to determine for each experimental setup the probability of a correct guess. After a while, the subject might say that the word *elephant* should perhaps have the number 1, that he does not really know why, and that he is merely guessing. One might tabulate the proportion of correct guesses for the successive groups of cards. When the subject sees the principle, he will have all the responses correct, and the experiment is then of no further interest. Our interest would be in the proportion of correct guesses before the moment of insight. This type of study was done as a doctor's dissertation by one of my students (1). Marked individual differences were found. Some subjects continued at the probability level until suddenly the insight appeared, after which the performance was, of course, perfect. Other subjects showed a marked gain in the number of guesses up to 65 per cent correct before the moment of insight appeared. One hypothesis would be that those who show this gain in the guessing of right answers before insight have more imagination than those who do not show such a gain. It will be recognized that this experiment is similar to current experiments on concept formation. Instead of dealing with a general process of concept formation, we would be interested in individual differences in learning before insight. Experimental work of this sort should be leisurely with ample response time for each guess. The subject's ability to guess right more often than wrong, even when he feels that he is guessing, is the characteristic of special interest in this problem.

If a research program on problem solving is undertaken by the College Entrance Examination Board, I fear that a reorientation will be necessary as regards the criterion. The conventional criterion of college scholarship would not be adequate. Furthermore, in the exploratory studies which would be necessary to solve this problem, it is almost certain that the ordinary objective scoring methods will have to be relaxed. It is almost certain that machine scoring must be ruled out. It may eventually be possible to conduct a test for originality and creative talent with tests that can be machine scored, but it would be a serious error to impose any such restriction on research.

The recent presidential address on creative talent by Guilford (2) at the American Psychological Association is a very well-considered discussion of the problem. Some of his major considerations are the same as those we have discussed here. Guilford has proposed a rather complete factorial analysis of a large number of tests that represent various hypotheses concerning creative talent. The present paper has attempted only to outline some exploratory studies that might be concurrent with Guilford's more complete and formal program.

In this paper we have considered some working hypotheses that might be helpful in initiating the scientific study of creative talent. First, we may start with the tentative assumption that creative talent is qualitatively the same at all levels of problem solving. The creative act may be characterized by the moment of insight that is often preceded by nonverbalized, prefocal thinking. The moment of insight is normally followed by explicit and deductive thinking in testing the new idea. The prefocal thinking before insight should be studied in order to gain understanding about problem solving as a form of thinking. A hypothesis has been considered that the moment of insight can be expected in dispersed attention more often than in concentrated attention. A research program on creative talent should put the main emphasis on what happens before insight. It is not enough merely to describe the curiosities of creative product.

We might consider creative talent as determined, in a descriptive way, by the rapport that the actor has with his own preconscious thinking. This hypothesis can be considered as an extension of an earlier theory of intelligence according to which intelligence is defined by the degree of incompleteness of the act at which it can become focal in consciousness. This rapport can be studied experimentally.

The hypothesis should be considered that creative talent is in large part determined by the temperamental characteristics that are associated with intellect. It would probably be an error to look for creative talent exclusively in the cognitive or intellective domain. Even though we know little about creative thinking, we can encourage students as well as ourselves to cultivate those attitudes that favor problem solving, including tolerance for that which is novel. Experimental studies should be on two major problems, namely, to inquire about the nature of the thinking that leads to a moment of insight, and to investigate empirically how to differentiate creative talent by objective and experimental procedures. It is conceivable that we may discover how to select people with creative talent before we learn much about the nature of that kind of talent. Serious consideration might be given to a plan of teaching that alternates between intensive lesson learning and the leisurely application of the new material to original problems. Finally, let me urge a realization of the importance of this problem, because the creative talent in our population is our greatest national asset.

REFERENCES

1. Bouthilet, Lorraine. The measurement of intuitive thinking. Unpublished doctoral dissertation, Univer. of Chicago, 1948.
2. Guilford, J. P. Creativity. *American Psychologist,* 1950, 5, 444–454.
3. Thurstone, L. L. *The nature of intelligence: a biological interpretation of mind.* New York: Harcourt, Brace & World, Inc., 1924.

Potentiality for Creativity
and Its Measurement

J. P. GUILFORD

1962

"Creativity," like "love," is a many-splendored thing. Small wonder that few have ventured to define it. At a conference on creativity a few months ago, each of the thirty-odd members was asked to write a list of his free associations to the word *creativity*. The results were almost as varied as the personalities of those present.

We gain a little bit if we take a first step toward discrimination, namely, the distinction between creative potential and creative production. Creative production, in the popular sense, is the aspect that catches general public fancy because the creative person's output is so frequently in the form of tangible products, such as a poem, a novel, a musical composition, an invention, a painting, a scientific theory, or a philosophical system.

To a psychologist who is interested in the mental operations that lead up to the emergence of the creator's product, the criteria of creative production must be of a different kind. There is agreement that the tangible product must have some novel aspects. The thinking that leads to that product also has novel aspects. In either case, it is these novel aspects that justify the label "creative." We are not concerned here with the operational criteria by which novelty can be gauged. What I wish to point out is that on the way to his final, *public* product, the creative thinker arrives at numerous *psychological* products. In focusing attention on the public product, we overlook the numerous ideas that the inventor had and discarded. From the psychological point of view, those generated ideas also have many chances of being novel.

In simplest terms, an individual's potential for being creative is his readiness to produce novel ideas or psychological products. In this we should include the production of old ideas in new connections. His readiness depends upon many things. An essential part of his preparation is in the form of specific items of information that are available to him from his memory storage. But, as we know, having the information is not sufficient. It is what the person does with the information that is important. When we speak of creative potential, we usually have in mind the dispositions that enable a person to use his information in new ways. Some of these dispositions are abilities or aptitudes, while others are traits of interest, needs, attitudes, and temperament. The emphasis upon aptitudes in this paper should not be interpreted to mean that these other kinds of traits are thought to be of negligible consequence.

Our investigations of creative potential at the University of Southern California have been directed mainly at the aptitude aspects, in part because they have been conducted in an Aptitudes Project, and in part because of the belief that an understanding of the aptitudes will also give us much information regarding the nature of creative thinking itself. From the standpoint of aptitudes alone, creative potential has proven to be considerably more complex than was expected. We did not expect to find a single, universal key to successful creative thinking, but we were not prepared to find so many facets to the subject.

Considering first the interpreted psychological factors found in the analysis of tests with meaningful, verbal content, the basic traits most clearly related logically to creative thinking include three fluency factors, two flexibility factors, and an elaboration factor. All of these factors are recognized as falling in the same psychological category of divergent-production abilities. They have in common the fact that in measurement of these abilities, the tests present the examinee with a certain item, or items, of information, and he is to generate from the given information some other items of information. In every case, multiple responses are called for, all different. In many cases, the produced items were probably never previously learned in association with the given information, for example, in a test calling for the activity of forming titles to apply to a given story plot. Information thus comes from memory storage, but out of its stored contexts; in other words, by way of transfer. I have elsewhere elaborated on a transfer theory of creative thinking (2).

The fluency factors pertain to *efficiency* of recall under these general circumstances. They differ from one another in terms of the kind of psychological product involved. Ideational fluency pertains to the rapid generation of units of verbal or semantic information—single ideas or units of thought, such as words to fit a described class of meanings. Associational fluency pertains to the rapid generation of semantic units to fulfill a relationship, having given a specified relation (e.g., a relation of similarity, opposition, part-whole, etc.) and a given unit. Expressional fluency pertains to the production of connected discourse, in the form of phrases and sentences. The psychological product involved is recognized as a semantic system.

Flexibility factors have to do with the *lability* or *fluidity* of stored information. The factor first recognized as spontaneous flexibility is now thought to be a matter of flexibility with regard to classes of information. In tests of this kind of flexibility, the examinee must shift his responses readily from one class to another. It has been said that some uncreative people are suffering from a disease known as hardening of the categories. Such a malady may be a matter of low degree of spontaneous flexibility.

The factor first called "originality" was later recognized as a kind of flexibility, described as *adaptive* flexibility. In one test, the examinee who suggests a relatively large number of clever plot titles earns a high score for this factor. To the fable of the fox and the grapes, for example, if he gives the titles "The fox griped about grapes," or "The sweet grapes turned sour," his titles are regarded as clever because he has produced what we call transformations. A transformation is a change or alteration in meaning or interpretation, a redefinition of some kind. Turning old interpretations of information into new ones makes possible new and different uses of what one knows.

Elaboration means building upon given information to round out a structure, to make it more detailed, or to extrapolate in new directions. Proceeding naturally from what is already given is a matter of producing implications. The given information suggests the first step to be taken, and each completed step helps to determine the following ones. The ability to produce a variety of implications is also in the category of divergent production.

We have just seen that the six divergent-production abilities dealing with meaningful, verbal information differ only in the kinds of products of information involved—units, classes, relations, systems, transformations, and implications. These are the kinds of psychological products mentioned early in this paper. They are not restricted to divergent production, but have very general application to intellectual abilities in all other operation categories—cognition, memory, convergent production, and evaluation. It is the relative variety and novelty of the products found in divergent production that link this category of abilities logically with creativity. When we have learned how new products come into existence, how familiar products become transformed, and how known products enter into new connections, we shall know a great deal about creative thinking.

I have mentioned only six divergent-production factors, all pertaining to verbal information. Most likely there are other sets of six, nonverbal, divergent-production abilities parallel to them. One set pertains to (visual) figural information, of which five have been demonstrated. A second set pertains to symbolic information, of which five have also been demonstrated. Thus, we have the important general inference that successful creative performance, to the extent that it depends upon aptitudes, is not equally promising in all fields of information. Potential for creative production in the arts is not the same thing as that in mathematics or that in writing, to say nothing of potential for creative handling of problems involving human relations.

It would be incorrect to say that only the divergent-production abilities contribute to success in creative performances. It appears that in the other four operation categories in the structure of intellect (3), we shall find sets of abilities parallel to those in the operation category of divergent production. Thus, in each operation area there is a set of transformation abilities which may contribute to creative potential, particularly in the areas of cognition and convergent production. Convergent production is a matter of generating a single right answer to given information, but it is sometimes necessary to do some searching around or to achieve a transformation in order to arrive at that answer.

In our initial study of creative abilities, we hypothesized and we found a factor interpreted as sensitivity to problems, a factor that has been repeatedly verified. In terms of placement in the structure of intellect, this factor has been recognized as an ability to evaluate implications; for example, seeing the faults in the working of a common appliance or of a social institution. The discovery of a category of evaluative abilities has opened many new possibilities of thinking about thinking. It should have been obvious before that we evaluate just about everything we perceive, or know, or do. Observers of the creative thinking of experts commonly report a terminal period of verification, which, in part, means evaluation. Actually, evaluative operations may occur, and probably do, at any step of the way in thinking, wherever we can gain any feedback information.

Reflection upon the total event of a creative production of some degree of complexity shows how similar that total process is to the commonly held picture of complex problem solving. The category of problem solving even applies to the production of objects of art, for the psychoanalysts tell us that in working toward his product, the artist is attempting to solve a personal problem by externalizing a phantasy. The amount of creativity involved in solving any kind of problem is proportional to the amount of novel production the problem solver shows, or to the degree of novelty in his solution.

Creative problem solving involves considerable trial-and-error behavior.

Except for instances in which the given information in the problem is sufficient to lead directly to one right answer, every trial is an act of divergent production, and the seeing of an error is an act of evaluation. Thus, trial-and-error behavior is an interplay of divergent production and evaluation, ending when some product is evaluated as acceptable. The thinker who can vary his potential solutions easily and extensively has an advantage in getting around to suitable solutions. In everyday life, most problems have no one right answer; there are many answers, a number of which are more or less suitable.

The more able the individual, the more he can produce trial information of high quality, with a higher probability of success. His over-all indulgence in trial-and-error thinking is, therefore, relatively less. But in view of the necessity for at least some trial and error, and the amount of divergent production that this requires, we should give much more attention to facility in this kind of mental activity and its assessment. Certainly, the person who can think of only one possible answer to a problem is much less likely to solve it than the person who can think of several. A number of investigators have found that tests of divergent production account for many cases of so-called overachieving, when achievement is assessed in terms of standard achievement tests. The same kind of tests may also be found to account for many cases of underachievement.

Standard tests and scales of intelligence have practically nothing to contribute to assessment of divergent-production abilities. For example, factor analyses of the Wechsler scales have thus far failed to show any such relationships. Recently I indulged in some armchair analysis of the 140 tests in the 1960 Stanford revision of the Binet scale, from which comes the impression that, in spite of the great surface variety of the tests, there is an overwhelming weighting with tests of cognitive abilities, with some attention to a few of the factors of memory, convergent production, and evaluation. Only 5 of the 140 tests appear to offer any appreciable divergent-production variance.

Current, standard, academic aptitude tests have been constituted along the lines of intelligence scales. They therefore emphasize much the same factors, and neglect the great majority of the intellectual abilities. It cannot very well be claimed that the neglected abilities are of little importance, for there has been little investigation of the relation of most of those abilities to performance in or out of educational institutions. Many of the neglected abilities should be potentially important in connection with various academic subjects and various occupational activities. For example, some recent data that I have seen show that scores from a few divergent-production tests are correlated with criteria of creative performance of public relations personnel and of advertising copy writers (1), with coefficients as high as .60. The criteria of creativity were essentially rankings of personnel by their superiors.

What is the implication of all this for assessment of academic aptitude? Not being so close to this problem as many of you are, I am not so well prepared to draw up an extensive list of implications. I will mention two or three things that I think should be done.

Believing in proceeding on a foundation of research findings, I would urge that extensive efforts be made to discover the phases of academic learning to which each of the basic intellectual aptitudes is relevant, and which of the aptitudes are important to development in each academic subject. At the University of Southern California, we are engaged in a two-year investigation of potentially relevant factors for learning ninth-grade algebra. We are planning to follow this with similar studies of other school subjects.

Although some of the neglected intellectual abilities are quite possibly touched upon in current achievement tests, this is on an incidental basis. As rapidly as research findings become available on the relevance of new aptitude factors, there should be appropriate revisions of academic aptitude batteries. Present batteries should be examined for redundancies, of which I am sure there are a number, replacing parts with measures of new relevant factors. It is well known that current batteries are by no means equally predictive of achievement in all curricula and in all courses of study. Achievement tests may touch upon many of the deficiencies of aptitude batteries, but they cannot do justice to them.

In introducing tests of divergent-production abilities, some technical difficulties will be encountered. Thus far, we have failed to find machine-scorable aptitude tests of these abilities. It is doubtful that any such tests exist, but with application of ingenuity, something may be done about it. Outside the divergent-production area, we have employed a few completion tests also, but it is probable that they can be replaced with machine-scorable tests.

Some of you may be alarmed at the possible large number of intellectual factors that may need to be given attention in the assessment of academic aptitude. I suggest that we save such misgivings until we know how many factors are relevant and how much weight needs to be given to them.

Until such time as measures of creative aspects of aptitude can be included in aptitude batteries, something can be done in the way of gathering information regarding creative promise and in the way of predicting creative production of students. Such information could be used less formally than aptitude scores are used and includes certain biographical signs of creative promise, such as self-initiated or spontaneous extracurricular activities in the form of scientific investigation, writing, or composing. The use of nonaptitude measures is another possibility. MacKinnon and his group at the University of California have shown that the most creative architects and scientists are distinguished by means of interest and temperament inventories (4). The information they have concerns concurrent validity; presumably predictive validity is also promising.

Thus, although immediate prospects of selecting and placing students with superior creative potential are not certain, future prospects, with the possibilities of using various kinds of information, including aptitude measures, appear to be reasonably bright. The least that we should aim to do is to determine what oversights exist in present aptitude batteries.

REFERENCES

1. Elliott, J. M. Advancing our methods for measuring creative abilities. *Information Service for A.N.A. Members.* New York: Association of National Advertisers, May 1962.
2. Guilford, J. P. Some theoretical views of creativity. In H. Helson & W. Bevan (Eds.), *Theories and data in psychology.* Princeton, N.J.: Van Nostrand. (In press)
3. Guilford, J. P., & Merrifield, P. R. The structure of intellect model: its uses and implications. *Reports from the Psychological Laboratory,* No. 24. Los Angeles: Univer. of Southern California, April 1960.
4. MacKinnon, D. W. Fostering creativity in students of engineering. *Journal of Engineering Education,* 1961, 52, 129–142.

Some Methodological Issues in the Study of Creativity

ROBERT L. THORNDIKE

1962

One feels put in a somewhat uncomfortable, perhaps even untenable position when called upon to look critically at the research on creativity. As one reads the reports in this field one encounters frequent references to the importance for creativity of a complete openness to any idea, and of the lethal impact upon the creative act of an evaluative and critical approach to life. So, from this point of view, the critic is condemned before he starts to being at best noncreative and at worst anticreative—in the physicist's sense of antimatter—that is, to being a force that destroys creativity. But if this be true, I must just make the best of it, and trust that this will be a creative critique, so that it won't destroy creativity, but only call attention to some possible directions for creativity research.

For the moment, let us forgo any formal definition of creativity. We may need to back into the issue of definition as we proceed further with the problem of evaluation.

As a point of departure, let us raise the question of whether research should focus on the creative act or the creative individual. From some points of view, the specific act or unitary sequence of acts is the attractive unit of study. Thus, we might get protocols from the poet as he writes a poem, or from the engineer as he plans a device permanently to eliminate leaky faucets. We might examine the paintings produced by a class of first-graders, or the compositions written by high school seniors. But how are we to determine when a creative act has taken place? Is creativity a matter of kind or degree? Do we identify creativity through the process or the product?

The product is, of course, much more convenient to study. It is there and can be examined at leisure. We can replicate judgments so as to get the needed degree of reliability—though the replication may not do much to improve the validity of the resulting judgments. We can divorce our evalua-

436

tion of the product from possibly irrelevant attributes of the producer, such as his or her personal charm, his or her group membership.

But can we judge creativity from a product? We may be able to appraise excellence in a product by some implicit or explicit criteria of excellence. We can almost certainly appraise unusualness of a product, if that appeals to us as an indicator of creativity. And we can certainly very readily appraise sheer voluminousness of production, which sometimes seems to be offered in lieu of excellence. However, the production of even a good product need not constitute a highly creative act for the individual. What proportion of the stories of even the most gifted raconteur are new creations as he tells them, or are even of his own original devising? In every field, the skilled and well-trained workman may turn out products that are technically excellent, but that involve little of what we would consider to be creativity in the producing.

And even the statistically rare need not be creative as far as the specific individual is concerned. Unless we know his individual history, we cannot be sure but that he is feeding back to us rather mechanically something he saw or heard only a day or two before. Before we can make any sure appraisal of the creativity of a production by an individual, we need to know intimately the microstructure of past experience of that individual so that we may evaluate the product against the background of that past experience. Whether an act is creative, in the sense of representing a novel synthesis *for that individual*, depends not only upon the product produced, but also on the past history of the producer. This holds true equally of all tasks that aspire to appraise "thinking" or "problem solving" on the part of an individual. One man's problem solution is another man's habituated response.

It would seem, then, that we can appraise the unusualness of a product, or the excellence of the product, in terms of certain criteria; but it is questionable whether we can appraise the creativity of a specific product. Creativity lies in the relationship beteen the product and the producer. To study creativity in an act, it seems that we must return to the process and study that process.

There have been a number of attempts to study the creative process over the years. Some have been based on retrospective reports by particularly successful creators or problem solvers, some upon concurrent observation of somewhat lesser souls. These have brought out a number of recurrent features in creation and problem solution—the need for intense immersion in a problem, the role of preconscious activity during a period of withdrawal from the task, the frequently sudden redirection and restructuring of perceptions, and the like. Do the features frequently described in the creative process give us a basis for categorizing acts as creative or noncreative, or for scaling them with respect to degree of creativity?

If we were to combine features of observable behavior with concurrent verbalization of his mental content by the subject, and add to this a retrospective self-analysis by the subject, we could probably separate those acts that called for only a routine application of available knowledge or skill from those that called forth a genuinely new synthesis of experience. But we could not do this perfectly nor completely. It might even be possible to achieve some consistency in sorting acts into several categories of an ordered series with respect to a dimension of automatic and routine vs. productive and novel. For the person who is interested in studying the situational factors influencing creativity or the effect of different kinds of experiences or training upon the creativity of behavior, such a crude scaling might have value. Thus, it might be possible to distinguish those effects of experience that lead to effective routinizing of certain skills, such as applying the congruency theorems of geometry or using Roget's *Thesaurus* in writing limericks, from those that lead to a freer and more spontaneous attack upon novel problems. It might be possible to judge whether the character of the individual's mental processes changed as a result of the training, or whether the training merely provided a larger foundational background of knowledge or skill to which essentially the same processes were applied. It might at least make it possible to weed out from among the products of an individual—which we might then want to evaluate for their excellence—those that were routine reproductions of habituated responses. However, an enterprise of this sort would be extraordinarily laborious. Whether the yield would justify the labor may well be questioned.

Let us turn our attention now from the act to the person. The question now centers on whether it is meaningful to attempt to identify individual differences in creativity among persons, and whether "creative," used as a rather global term to characterize a person, has meaning.

Once again, it would be possible, in theory at least, to describe differences between persons either in terms of process or of product. Is the creative person to be identified as the person who frequently engages in creative acts—acts in which he restructures and recombines the components of his experience, producing syntheses that are novel to him and compatible with the demands of the situation? Or is the creative person to be identified as the individual who frequently produces good products—good art, science, or social invention—"good" in the sense of being approved or valued by society?

In the case of the person, I suspect that we shall rarely find it feasible to evaluate creativity in terms of process. It hardly seems practical to get the type of evidence about individuals that would give us an adequate basis for judging individual differences in frequency or quality of creative acts. Our appraisal is almost certain to fall back in large part on the products the individual has produced, and be a judgment of some quality in these products. The products could, of course, be those produced within a circumscribed time and set of circumstances—that is, under essentially test conditions, as when an essay is written on an examination, or a defined test of "fluency" or "originality" is administered. But here, as elsewhere, we tend to think of tests as predictors of, rather than criteria of, life performance. What investigators have often relied upon is some type of global evaluation of real-life productions. Persons knowledgeable in the field, be it one of the arts, one of the sciences, or one of the professions that are neither art nor science, are asked to nominate or rate colleagues with respect to their contribution to the field.

There is no question that with some degree of agreement specialists can appraise individuals in their own field with respect to some composite of excellence. Individuals differ in the reputation that they have with their colleagues. Some are more favorably perceived than others. Certainly, if psychologists, or any other group, were asked to rate one another on creativity, there would be some nucleus of agreement. The stickier question is whether colleagues could discriminate "creativity" from "productivity," "visibility," or "general reputation." Do ratings and nominations for "creativity" only have a certain amount of general validity as indicators of professional reputation, or do they have *specific, differential* validity in picking out those who are creative from among all those who are professionally successful and visible? What would be the correlation, corrected for rater unreliability, between ratings for creativity and ratings for some other indicator of general reputation? Our general experience of the halo in ratings does not make us too optimistic about the prospects for a valid differential rating.

When we use any term to designate an attribute of an individual, be it abstract intelligence, sociability, or creativity, the distinct label implies that there exists a set of behaviors of the individual that can be grouped together because they exhibit a common quality. Furthermore, if the label is a useful one, the set of behaviors that it designates can be differentiated from the sets designated by other labels. Thus, we expect the sociable person to choose to be with other people, and to express pleasure in being with them. We distinguish this set of behaviors from the set to which we apply the term "ascendant," because the sociable person will in many cases show no tendency to take a leadership role, but will be content with merely being in and a member of a group.

We may appropriately ask how well the attribute "creativity" meets these joint criteria of designating a reasonably extensive set of behaviors that 1) have some degree of coherence, and 2) can be distinguished from other sets of behaviors.

The question may be asked in relation to the activities of life. The question will then be phrased: Does the person who behaves creatively in one type of life situation tend also to show creative behavior in others? To what extent is the inventive scientist also a creative amateur in music, art, or writing? To what extent does the original architect also exhibit ingenuity and improvisation in interpersonal relations?

To obtain dependable evidence on such life performances would certainly be extraordinarily difficult. As a matter of fact, in many fields, it is certainly difficult to make a diagnostic judgments that discriminate between a *creative* performance and a *competent* one. And it is perhaps unreasonable to expect comparable performance in different fields. It could be argued with some plausibility that a person who finds an outlet for his creativity in one direction may have no need to show creativity in others. If this be so, then either we must apply some modifier to the label "creative"—i.e., creative in art, creative in physical science, creative in corporate finance, creative in home decorating—thus specifying more limited subsets, or we must unite these subsets on the basis of the correlates of their creative behavior.

A good deal of the research on individuals identified by some type of nominating procedure as being creative has focused upon the characteristics of these creative individuals or, in other words, upon the correlates of creativity. Thus, this has been one main focus of effort for MacKinnon and his associates (5) at the California Institute of Personality Assessment and Research. They report, for example, that on the Barron-Welsh Art Scale not only outstanding architects but also outstanding writers, scientists, and mathematicians tend to choose complex, asymmetrical, and "messy" line drawings in preference to simple, symmetrical, and (judging from the illustrative examples) "sterile" ones. A number of other uniformities are reported for groups selected as leaders in different fields, and become the basis for affirming a degree of generality to creativity. These uniformities arise from the assessment approach that is espoused by the California group. The comprehensive assessment is clearly fruitful in suggesting hypotheses as to correlates of creativity, but here perhaps as dramatically as anywhere the limitations of the assessment approach as a design for *testing* hypotheses become apparent. As Gough (2) pointed out, in developing some multiple correlations in the high .90's with rating criteria on a group of engineers, with over 100 items of data for a sample of 45 cases, some mighty dramatic relationships can be generated. The critical issue is whether the relationships will be maintained in a new sample of cases. And an adequate stock of new cross-validation cases is difficult to come by when the persons are such rare birds as some of the California groups of highly evaluated architects, writers, and mathematicians. We face something of a dilemma. We are loath to accept lesser degrees of talent in order to get numerically convincing samples, and yet we feel the pressure for verification of reported findings. The value conflict between the hypothesis generator and the hypothesis tester is in some ways parallel to the discrepancy between the perceptual and judgmental modes alleged to characterize the more and the less creative. Hypothesis testing certainly has less of a flavor of creativity, but still has an essential role in the fabric of science.

In the test domain, as distinct from the life-activities domain, the question as to the meaningfulness of a general rubric of "creativity" can be raised somewhat more incisively. We may ask whether there is a variety of different test behaviors that 1) seem reasonably to pertain to the concept of "creativity," 2) are associated so that a person who tends to exhibit one also tends to exhibit the other, and 3) are distinct from other sets of test behaviors, such as the set to which we have applied the term "abstract intelligence."

The issue we raise is closely analogous to the issue that has been raised with respect to the concept of intelligence, around which so much research and controversy have centered. Though ways of interpreting the facts in the domain of intelligence have differed, there would be general agreement as to the basic facts, I believe. The essential points are that although there is a degree of specialization of intellectual functioning, so that tests within a specific region of content or process correlate more highly than those from different regions, still the correlations across regions are appreciably positive. It is these uniformly positive correlations, whether conceptualized as g, or a second-order factor among the primary factors, or as an overlapping of group factors, that give some substance to the general concept of abstract intelligence and some reasonableness to pooling a set of subtests into a common score.

We may appropriately ask whether there is another broad second-order factor in the test domain, distinct from the traditional g, to which the term "creativity" can appropriately be applied. The existence of such a distinct factor is strongly implied in the publications by Getzels and Jackson (1), and by Torrance (7), among others; and Guilford and his associates (3) have fairly sharply differentiated between tests of convergent and divergent thinking. How well does this differentiation of two broad cognitive domains hold up in practice?

I have re-analyzed some of the published data to try to get a partial answer to these questions. The first set of data I examined were the correlations reported in Table 1 of Getzels and Jackson's recent book *Creativity and Intelligence* (1). Getzels and Jackson emphasize the lack of correlation between the traditional intelligence test and the measures that they used to appraise creativity. However, the intercorrelations of the five "creativity" tests were themselves not very high. It is of some interest to extract a first factor from this table of correlations, and compare the factor loadings of the several tests. The results are shown in Table 1. Thus, we see that on the

TABLE 1

First Factor Loadings of Getzels and Jackson's
"Creativity" Tests and IQ

Test	Boys	Girls
Word Association	.69	.70
Uses	.47	.48
Hidden Shapes	.58	.60
Fables	.41	.42
Make-up Problems	.58	.72
IQ	.52	.50
Average	.54	.57

first factor common to these six measures, the factor loadings are all fairly modest, and the loading for the conventional intelligence test falls about midway among the "creativity" tests.

However, these data are less than ideal for answering the question of the factor structure of the intelligence and creativity domains because they include only one undifferentiated measure of intelligence. More comprehensive sets of data are provided in some of the studies by Guilford and his associates (4, 8). I have re-analyzed certain of these by somewhat primitive methods to explore the point at issue. In general, what I have done is to take the two tests with highest factor loadings on a given factor to represent that factor. Partly on personal judgment, and partly from the discussion provided by the authors, I have classified the factors as old-line or convergent-thinking factors or as new-type, divergent-thinking (i.e., "creativity") factors. I have prepared a miniature correlation table, made up of just these pairs of tests, for each factor, rearranged so as to appear in the two designated broad clusters. Then I have found the average correlation for each test, first with the tests of other factors within its own domain, and then with all the tests in the other domain. The first correlation provides an indication of the extent to which a test "hangs together" with its own domain, and the second, an indication of the extent to which it overlaps the other domain, or the extent to which the domains themselves are indistinguishable.

In Table 2, you see the results for this analysis applied to a factor analysis of the domain of verbal fluency carried out by Guilford and Christensen (4). This study appeared to yield three factors that would be considered old-line, convergent factors—to wit, Verbal Comprehension, General Reasoning, and Eduction of Conceptual Correlates. Five new-style, divergent factors appeared to emerge, labeled Originality, Expressional Fluency, Ideational Fluency, Word Fluency, and Associational Fluency. The average correlations are shown in the body of the table. Thus, the across-factors correlation for the old-line tests was .435, while for the new-type tests, it was .267. The average across-domains correlation was .238. The Word Fluency and Associational Fluency tests correlated slightly higher with the convergent than with the rest of the divergent tests.

If we conceptualize these findings in terms of an orthogonal two-factor structure, assuming that what is common to the old-line tests is some sort of a g factor (here pretty heavily saturated with a verbal component), that what is common to the old-line and new-style tests is entirely this same g, and that whatever more there is tying together the new-style tests is our D-C (divergent or creativity) factor, we get the factor structure shown at the bottom of Table 2 as representing the average test in each of the two clusters. That is, the average old-line test has a loading of .66 on g, which accounts for $43\frac{1}{2}$ per cent of the test variance. The average new-style test has loadings of .36 on g and .37 on D-C, accounting for roughly 13 and 14 per cents of variance, respectively. Our second broad factor has reality, but the tests in its domain are only about one-third as saturated with it as the old-line tests are saturated with g.

A second analysis was made based on the factor analysis of creative-thinking abilities by Wilson, Guilford, and others (8). This was a rather more extensive battery, providing six presumably old-line and eight new-style factors. The results of the initial analysis are shown in Table 3. Both broad factors appeared more weakly in this set of data, perhaps because the content of the test materials ranged more widely. However, the old-line cluster shows an average across-factors correlation of .23, and the new-

TABLE 2

Average Correlation Across Factors: Verbal Fluency Study
(Guilford and Christensen, 4)

Divergent Factors

Factor	Test No.	Average Correlation	
		Divergent	Convergent
Originality	35 36	.155 } .255 .355	.196 } .245 .294
Expressional Fluency	24 28	.303 } .270 .238	.174 } .198 .221
Ideational Fluency	17 19	.340 } .265 .190	.260 } .158 .057
Word Fluency	2 5	.228 } .250 .271	.260 } .290 .320
Associational Fluency	7 22	.239 } .294 .350	.286 } .300 .314
Average		.267	.238

Convergent Factors

Factor	Test No.	Average Correlation	
		Divergent	Convergent
Verbal Comprehension	15 38	.263 } .236 .209	.520 } .478 .436
General Reasoning	34 40	.274 } .202 .129	.510 } .398 .286
Eduction of Conceptual Correlates	11 12	.289 } .276 .263	.466 } .439 .412
Average		.238	.435

	Convergent Tests	Divergent Tests
Factor g	.66	.36
Factor D-C	—	.37

TABLE 3
Average Correlation Across Factors: Creative-Thinking Study
(Wilson et al., 8)

Divergent Factors

Factor	Test No.	Average Correlation	
		Divergent	Convergent
Word Fluency	53	.135 ⎫ .126	.268 ⎫ .250
	28	.118 ⎭	.232 ⎭
Associational Fluency	39	.204 ⎫ .190	.125 ⎫ .158
	11	.175 ⎭	.190 ⎭
Ideational Fluency	6	.098 ⎫ .143	−.025 ⎫ .003
	8	.188 ⎭	.031 ⎭
Originality	7	.159 ⎫ .103	.059 ⎫ .006
	19	.047 ⎭	−.046 ⎭
Adaptive Flexibility	16	.042 ⎫ .070	.250 ⎫ .234
	17	.097 ⎭	.218 ⎭
Spontaneous Flexibility	10	.155 ⎫ .188	.089 ⎫ .086
	22	.220 ⎭	.083 ⎭
Redefinition	29	.062 ⎫ .102	.184 ⎫ .139
	31	.141 ⎭	.094 ⎭
Sensitivity to Problems	24	.173 ⎫ .154	.075 ⎫ .052
	25	.134 ⎭	.030 ⎭
Average		.14	.12

Convergent Factors

Factor	Test No.	Average Correlation	
		Divergent	Convergent
Verbal	33	.154 ⎫ .128	.274 ⎫ .231
	43	.102 ⎭	.188 ⎭
Numerical	50	.136 ⎫ .135	.242 ⎫ .269
	52	.134 ⎭	.296 ⎭
Perceptual	38	.102 ⎫ .109	.188 ⎫ .223
	47	.116 ⎭	.258 ⎭
Visualizing	35	.101 ⎫ .076	.268 ⎫ .229
	51	.052 ⎭	.190 ⎭
Reasoning	34	.146 ⎫ .136	.284 ⎫ .260
	44	.125 ⎭	.236 ⎭
Closure	37	.067	.140
Average		.12	.23

	Convergent Tests	Divergent Tests
Factor g	.48	.25
Factor D-C	—	.28

style cluster an average of .14. The average across-domains correlation was .12. Again, conceptualizing this in a two-factor structure, we find a g factor of .48 for the old-line tests, while the new-style tests have average loading of .25 on g, and .28 on D-C. Though all loadings are reduced, the relative values are quite comparable to those for the other study. What is common among the divergent-thinking or creativity tests can be divided about equally between the conventional cognitive factor and some other factor that does not appear in the old-line tests. This new factor accounts for about a third as much of the common variance of these tests as the g factor does for the conventional tests.

A further examination of Table 3 suggested that certain of the factors might be misplaced. The Word Fluency and Adaptive Flexibility tests showed markedly stronger affiliations with the old-line than with the new-style tests. Perhaps the limits of the clusters should be redefined. This has been done in Table 4 by shifting the Word Fluency and Adaptive Flexibility tests to the old-line convergent cluster. The effect has been to increase appreciably both the homogeneity and independence of the remaining cluster. The average within-cluster correlation rises to .185, while the between-clusters correlation drops to .077. The factor loadings for these redefined clusters are shown at the bottom of the table. The reduction in the g loading and increase in the D-C loading for the smaller group of new-style tests can be noted. The g factor now accounts for only a little over 2 per cent of the variance, while the D-C factor accounts for 16 per cent—about two-thirds as much variance as the g factor accounts for in the old-line tests.

I would very much like to apply this same type of critical (if not creative) analysis to the tests that Torrance (6) has been developing at Minnesota. So far, I have not encountered a set of data that lent themselves to this approach. Though Torrance has expressed commendable concern about rater reliability in appraising the protocols from his tests, I have not encountered the same type of concern about trait reliability; that is, the consistency with which his tests measure some common attribute to which a common designation may legitimately be applied. Though Torrance specifically disavows intending to produce a test to produce a "Creativity Quotient" that would constitute a characterization of an individual, he often uses a team of his tests as if they did produce one, or at least as if they had enough in common to justify pooling them into a single composite score. I would suggest that a good deal of further study of the behavior domain is needed before this is done.

The analyses that I have reported to you here suggest that there is some reality to a broad domain, distinct from the domain of the conventional in-

TABLE 4

Modified Average Correlation Across Factors: Creative-Thinking Study
(Wilson et al., 8)

Divergent Factors

Factor	Test No.	Average Correlation — Divergent	Average Correlation — Convergent
Associational Fluency	11	.163 } .180	.194 } .172
	39	.198	.151
Ideational Fluency	6	.136 } .188	−.020 } .007
	8	.241	.034
Originality	7	.178 } .123	.071 } .017
	19	.068	−.037
Spontaneous Flexibility	10	.177 } .230	.090 } .082
	22	.282	.074
Redefinition	29	.030 } .107	.175 } .125
	31	.184	.075
Sensitivity to Problems	24	.202 } .182	.080 } .059
	25	.161	.038
Average		.185	.077

Convergent Factors

Factor	Test No.	Average Correlation — Divergent	Average Correlation — Convergent
Verbal	33	.087 } .099	.299 } .242
	43	.111	.186
Numerical	50	.082 } .076	.260 } .283
	52	.070	.306
Perceptual	38	.067 } .074	.194 } .220
	47	.081	.246
Visualizing	35	.054 } .036	.260 } .219
	51	.019	.178
Reasoning	34	.105 } .102	.280 } .252
	44	.100	.225
Closure	37	.044	.149
Word Fluency	28	.108 } .121	.232 } .246
	53	.134	.259
Adaptive Flexibility	16	.020 } .049	.240 } .232
	17	.078	.224
Average		.077	.235

	Convergent Tests	Divergent Tests
Factor g	.485	.156
Factor D-C	—	.401

telligence test, to which the designation "divergent thinking" or "creative thinking" might legitimately be applied. However, they suggest that this is a rather more nebulous and loosely formed domain than that of conventional intellect. If this be true, an adequate domain measure, which clearly brings out this general characteristic relatively unencumbered by variance due to error or to specific factors, will be hard to come by. Different creativity measures will be less equivalent and interchangeable than different intelligence measures. We will be well advised to use the term "test of creativity" with even more circumspection than we are learning to use in speaking of "test of intelligence." But at the same time that we urge a considerable degree of caution, we can all applaud the attempts to develop a new and potentially fruitful field of appraisal.

REFERENCES

1. Getzels, J. W., & Jackson, P. W. *Creativity and intelligence.* New York: Wiley, 1962.
2. Gough, H. G. Techniques for identifying the creative research scientist. In D. W. MacKinnon *et al., Proceedings of Conference on "The Creative Person,"* Oct. 13–17, 1961. Berkeley, Calif.: Institute of Personality Assessment and Research, Univer. of California.
3. Guilford, J. P. A revised structure of intellect. *Reports from the Psychological Laboratory,* No. 19. Los Angeles: Univer. of Southern California, April 1957.
4. Guilford, J. P., & Christensen, P. R. A factor-analytic study of verbal fluency. *Reports from the Psychological Laboratory,* No. 17. Los Angeles: Univer. of Southern California, September 1956.
5. MacKinnon, D. W., *et al. Proceedings of Conference on "The Creative Person,"* Oct. 13–17, 1961. Berkeley, Calif.: Institute of Personality Assessment and Research, Univer. of California.
6. Torrance, E. P. Current research on the nature of creative talent. *Journal of Counseling Psychology,* 1959, 6, 309–316.
7. Torrance, E. P. *Educational achievement of the highly intelligent and the highly creative: eight partial replications of the Getzels-Jackson study.* Research Memorandum BER–60–18, Bureau of Educational Research, Univer. of Minnesota, September 1960.
8. Wilson, R. C., *et al.* A factor-analytic study of creative-thinking abilities. *Psychometrika,* 1954, 19, 297–311.

PART III

SPECIAL PROBLEMS IN THE ASSESSMENT OF INDIVIDUAL DIFFERENCES

10 · CULTURAL DIFFERENTIALS IN TEST PERFORMANCE

IN THE OPENING PAPER of this chapter, given at a 1949 panel on the influence of cultural background on test performance, Anastasi examines some implications of cultural differences for test construction. She observes that the decision to retain or eliminate cultural differentials from test scores depends upon the purpose for which the test was designed. Examples are cited to illustrate opposite item-selection procedures followed with regard to sex and socioeconomic differences in the development of both aptitude and personality tests. Some tests have been designed so as to magnify group differences, others to minimize them. When the criterion behavior that tests are designed to predict is itself culturally loaded, eliminating culturally loaded content from a test may serve only to reduce its validity.

In another paper from the same panel, Turnbull reports data showing the specificity of urban-rural differences in test performance. The group differences found in mean scores varied in amount and even in direction from one type of test content to another. Moreover, item analyses showed that these group differences in performance differed significantly among individual items of each type. These results, obtained with young men applying for a college-level training program, corroborate earlier findings with school children from urban and rural areas. Turnbull also cites evidence to show that the predictive validity of tests need not be affected by differences in performance level among cultural groups.

Cultural influences were again discussed at the 1952 Invitational Conference, in a panel dealing with "Techniques for the Development of Unbiased Tests." The next two papers were presented at this panel. In a critique of the approach followed by Eells, Davis, Havighurst, and their associates at the University of Chicago, Lorge argues that to eliminate group differences from test scores is not the way to reduce bias among test users. When test items are selected only because they fail to differentiate between specified groups, the resulting test may prove not to be a valid measure of any useful function. Lorge also notes that the use of tests that fail to reveal existing group differences is not likely to produce improvement in the cultural conditions that caused the differences. Amid the confusion and tumult currently associated with the testing of culturally disadvantaged persons, the points made by Lorge in this paper appear even more cogent than they did in 1952.

Rulon addresses himself more specifically to problems encountered in the construction of tests for cross-cultural use. He points out that most non-verbal tests employed for cross-cultural testing measure different functions from those measured by verbal tests or required in academic and other intellectual pursuits. After summarizing the major defects of previously developed cross-cultural tests, Rulon describes the Semantic Test of Intelligence (STI) constructed by him and his co-workers at the Harvard School of Education. While utilizing simple and widely familiar pictorial content, this test is designed to measure the learning of semantic symbols and syntactical relations.

By 1964, general concern with the problems of cultural deprivation had risen sharply. At that year's Invitational Conference, the entire afternoon session was devoted to papers on testing and research with culturally dissimilar populations. The last two papers in this chapter, by Fifer and by Wolf, were selected from this session. Fifer reports an investigation of first-grade public school children in New York City, classified into four ethnic groups (Chinese, Jewish, Negro, Puerto Rican) and two socioeconomic levels (Middle and Lower). Specially developed nonreading tests of verbal, reasoning, numerical, and spatial abilities were administered individually to all subjects. Results are analyzed so as to reveal group differences in both level and pattern of abilities, as well as interactions between the two independent variables investigated, viz., ethnic background and social class.

Wolf's paper explores a relatively neglected approach to the understanding of cultural influences. In view of the growing recognition of the effect of environmental conditions upon behavioral differences, Wolf emphasizes the need for instruments to measure environments. After noting the scarcity and inadequacy of available instruments in this field, he describes the development of new measures designed to assess specific aspects of a child's home environment that are likely to influence his general intelligence and academic achievement. From a technical standpoint, this paper provides an excellent model for the construction of other environmental scales, concerned with the development of other abilities or personality traits. From another angle, the empirical findings of such a study have important implications for the planning of compensatory educational programs for culturally disadvantaged children.

Some Implications of Cultural
Factors for Test Construction

ANNE ANASTASI

1949

Any discussion of the influence of cultural background on test performance involves at least two distinct questions. First, to what extent is test performance determined by cultural factors? Second, what shall we do about it?

In considering the first question, it is important to remember at the outset that culture is not synonymous with environment. Although this distinction should be obvious, some writers apparently forget it when drawing conclusions about heredity and environment. For example, environmental factors may produce structural deficiencies that in turn lead to certain types of feeblemindedness. Research on microcephaly, hydrocephaly, and several other varieties of mental deficiency associated with brain damage has yielded a growing body of evidence for the role of prenatal environmental factors in the development of these conditions. Yet these types of mental deficiency would certainly not be classified as cultural in their etiology. Nor are they remediable in the individual case by education or by the manipulation of other cultural factors. Of course, the environmental factors leading to the development of these structural deficiencies may themselves be culturally influenced in the long run. Some day, we may know enough about them to control them through maternal nutrition, prenatal medical care, and the like. But such factors would represent an *indirect* cultural influence on behavior, mediated by organic deficiencies. Moreover, any such improvement in cultural conditions could have only a long-range effect, and would not help the individual in whom the organic deficiency is already present.

Cultural factors do, however, affect the individual's behavior in many direct ways. Psychologists are coming more and more to recognize that the individual's attitudes, emotional responses, interests, and goals—as well as what he is able to accomplish in practically any area—cannot be discussed independently of his cultural frame of reference. Nor are such cultural influences limited to the more complex forms of behavior. There is a mass of evidence, both in the field observations of anthropologists and in the more controlled studies of psychologists, to indicate that "cultural differentials" are also present in motor and in discriminative or perceptual responses.

Now, every psychological test is a sample of behavior. As such, psychological tests will—and should—reflect any factors that influence behavior. It is obvious that every psychological test is constructed within a specific cultural framework. Most tests are validated against practical criteria dictated by the particular culture. School achievement and vocational success are two familiar examples of such criteria. A few tests designed to serve a wider variety of purposes and possibly to be used in basic research are, in effect, validated against other tests. Thus when we report that a given test correlates highly with the number factor, we are actually saying that the test is a valid predictor of the behavior common to a group of tests. If we had no number tests in the battery, we could not have found a number factor. The type of tests included in such a battery—however comprehensive the battery may be—reflects in part the cultural framework in which the experimenter was reared. It is obvious that no battery samples *all* possible varieties of behavior; and as long as a selection has occurred, cultural factors are admitted into the picture.

In the construction of certain tests, special consideration has been given to cultural group differences in the selection of test items. The practices followed with regard to items showing significant group differences may be illustrated, first, with reference to *sex differences*. Insofar as the two sexes represent subcultures with distinct mores in our society, sex differences in item performance may be regarded as cultural differentials. The Stanford-Binet (8, cf. Ch. V) is probably one of the clearest examples of a test in which sex differences were deliberately eliminated from total scores. This was accomplished in part by dropping items that yielded a significant sex difference in per cent passing. It is interesting to note, however, that it did not prove feasible to discard all such items, but that a number of remaining items that significantly favored one sex were balanced by items favoring the other sex. The opposite procedure was followed in the construction of the Terman-Miles Interest-Attitude Analysis (9), as well as in other similar personality tests designed to yield an M-F Index. In these cases, it was just those items with large and significant sex differences in frequency of response that were retained.

Another type of group difference that has been considered in the selection of test items is illustrated by the so-called *culture-free tests,* such as the International Group Mental Test (4), the Leiter International Performance Scale (7), and R. B. Cattell's Culture-Free Intelligence Test (1, 2). In these tests, a systematic attempt is made to include only content universally familiar in all cultures. In actual practice, of course, such tests fall considerably short of this goal. Moreover, the term "culture-common" would probably be more accurate than "culture-free," since at best, performance on such items is free from cultural *differences,* but not from cultural *influences.*

As a last example, let us consider *socioeconomic level* as a basis for the evaluation of test items. One of the objectives of the extensive research project conducted by Haggard, Davis, and Havighurst (3, 6) is to eliminate from intelligence tests those items that differentiate significantly between children of high and low socioeconomic status. On the other side of the picture, we find the work of Harrison Gough (5) in the construction of the Social Status Scale of the Minnesota Multiphasic Personality Inventory. In this scale, only those items were retained that showed significant differences in frequency of response between two contrasted social groups.

It is apparent that different investigators have treated the problem of cultural differences in test scores in opposite ways. An obvious answer is that the procedure depends upon the purpose of the test. But such an answer may evade the real issue. Perhaps it is the purpose of the test that should be more carefully examined. There seems to be some practical justification for constructing a test out of items that show the maximum group differentiation. With such a test, we can determine more clearly the degree to which an individual is behaviorally identified with a particular group. It is difficult to see, however, under what conditions we should want to study individual differences in just those items in which socioeconomic or other cultural group differences are lacking. What will the resulting test be a measure of? Criteria are themselves correlated with socioeconomic and other cultural conditions. The validity of a test for such criteria would probably be lowered by eliminating the "cultural differentials." If cultural factors are important determiners of behavior, why eliminate their influence from tests designed to sample and predict such behavior?

To be sure, a test *may* be invalidated by the presence of uncontrolled cultural factors. But this would occur only when the given cultural factor affects the test without affecting the criterion. It is a question of the *breadth* of the influence affecting the test score. For example, the inclusion of questions dealing with a fairy tale familiar to children in one cultural group and not in another would probably lower the validity of the test for most criteria. On the other hand, if one social group does more poorly on certain items because of poor facility in the use of English, the inclusion of these items would probably *not* reduce the validity of the test. In this case, the same factor that lowered the test score would also handicap the individual in his educational and vocational progress, as well as in many other aspects of daily living. In like manner, slow work habits, emotional instability, poor motivation, lack of interest in abstract matters, and many other conditions that may affect test scores are also likely to influence a relatively broad area of criterion behavior.

Whether or not an item is retained in a test should depend ultimately upon its correlation with a *criterion*. Tests cannot be constructed in a vacuum. They must be designed to meet specific needs. These needs should be defined in advance, and should determine the choice of criterion. This would seem to be self-evident, but it is sometimes forgotten in the course of discussions about tests. Some statements made regarding tests imply a belief that tests are designed to measure a spooky, mysterious "thing" which resides in the individual and which has been designated by such terms as "Intelligence," "Ability Level," or "Innate Potentiality." The assumption seems to be that such "intelligence" has been merely overlaid with a concealing cloak of culture. All we would thus need to do would be to strip off the cloak and the person's "true" ability would stand revealed. My only reaction to such a viewpoint is to say that, if we are going to function within the domain of science, we must have operational definitions of tests. The only way I know of obtaining such operational definitions is in terms of the criteria against which the test was validated. This is true whether a so-called practical criterion is employed or whether the criterion itself is defined in terms of other tests, as in factorial validity. Any procedure, such as the discarding of certain items, that raises the correlation of the test with the criterion, enables us to give a more precise operational definition of the test. But we cannot discard items merely on the basis of some principle that has been laid down a priori, such as the rule that items showing significant group differences must be eliminated. If this procedure should lower the validity coefficient of the test, it could have neither practical nor theoretical justification.

It is also pertinent to inquire what would happen if we were to carry such a procedure to its logical conclusion. If we start eliminating items that differentiate subgroups of the population, where shall we stop? We could with equal justification proceed to rule out items showing socioeconomic differences, sex differences, differences among ethnic minority groups, and educational differences. Any items in which college graduates excel elementary school graduates could, for example, be discarded on this basis. Nor should we retain items that differentiate among broader groups, such as national cultures, or between preliterate and more advanced cultures. If we do all this, I should like to ask only two questions in conclusion. First, what will be left? Second, in terms of any criterion we may wish to predict, what will be the validity of this minute residue?

REFERENCES

1. Cattell, R. B. A culture-free intelligence test: I. *Journal of Educational Psychology,* 1940, 31, 161–179.
2. Cattell, R. B., Feingold, S. N., & Sarason, S. B. A culture-free intelligence test: II. Evaluation of cultural influence on test performance. *Journal of Educational Psychology,* 1941, 32, 81–100.
3. Davis, A., & Havighurst, R. J. The measurement of mental systems (Can intelligence be measured?). *Scientific Monthly,* 1948, 66, 301–316.
4. Dodd, S. C. International Group Mental Tests. Unpublished doctoral dissertation, Princeton Univer., 1926.
5. Gough, H. G. A new dimension of status: I. Development of a personality scale. *American Sociological Review,* 1948, 13, 401–409.
6. Haggard, E. A., Davis, A., & Havighurst, R. J. Some factors which influence performance of children on intelligence tests. *American Psychologist,* 1948, 3, 265–266. (Abstract)
7. Leiter, R. G. *The Leiter International Performance Scale, Vol. 1.* Santa Barbara, Calif.: Santa Barbara State College Press, 1940.
8. McNemar, Q. *The revision of the Stanford-Binet scale: an analysis of the standardization data.* Boston: Houghton Mifflin, 1942.
9. Terman, L. M., & Miles, Catharine C. *Sex and personality: studies in masculinity and femininity.* New York: McGraw-Hill, 1936.

Influence of Cultural Background on Predictive Test Scores

WILLIAM W. TURNBULL

1949

For convenience in attacking the broad question before this panel, I should like to limit my discussion to tests used for the purpose of prediction. In imposing this limitation, however, I feel that I am not greatly restricting the field of inquiry, since in the final analysis most test scores derive their utility from their predictive significance.

If we consider tests whose use is frankly predictive, two questions of interest are: first, when people of different cultural backgrounds take the same test, how do their scores compare? And second, are differences in level of test performance of different cultural groups associated with similar differences in the subsequent behavior those scores were supposed to predict?

In an approach to the first of these questions, I should like to report on an unpublished study that Henry Chauncey and I carried out some years ago. The purpose of this study was to discover the manner in which students from different geographical areas and different sizes of communities differed in their performance on types of questions commonly used in tests of scholastic aptitude.

The test used was the first Army-Navy College Qualifying Test. This examination included four sections, consisting of verbal, scientific, reading, and mathematical material, respectively. The verbal section included questions relating to word meaning, word usage, and the like in the form of opposites, analogies, and definitions in completion form. The second, or "scientific" section, was composed of questions of the so-called commonsense science type. The technical information needed to answer them was not great, and for the most part intelligent scientific interest and alert observation would prove as valuable as scientific training. The third section of the test consisted of paragraphs of rather general nature, each followed by questions on its content, while the mathematical section (the last section of

458

the test) was designed to test numerical reasoning, presupposing a background of arithmetic, elementary algebra, and rudimentary geometry.

The test was given in 1943 to over 300,000 students all over the country as a screening device for the college training programs of the Army and Navy. All of the persons tested were male, were 17–21 years of age, and had reached or passed the senior year of secondary school.

From the mass of answer sheets, eight subgroups were segregated, first by taking all answer sheets from the four regions of New York State, Alabama and Georgia combined, Iowa and Nebraska combined, and California; and then by separating within each region the answer sheets of students in large and in small communities. A large community was defined as one with a population of 150,000 or more and a small community as a nonsuburban community below 5,000 in population. For convenience, these groups were called urban and rural respectively. (I will readily agree that these terms are not rigorous, since not all students attending school in a community of fewer than 5,000 souls come from farm homes, although a substantial proportion of them do.) Finally, from each of the eight groups (two sizes of community within four geographical areas), a random sample of 500 answer sheets was drawn.

Please note particularly that the samples were far from random or representative samples of the total student population of the age range 17–21 in the four regions. They represent merely the extremes on a scale of population size, within groups that had voluntarily taken the qualifying tests; and there is no basis for ascribing representativeness to the samples.

The main results of this study have been put in graphic form in Figures 1 and 2. Looking at Figure 1, we see first the very conspicuous depression of all values for Alabama-Georgia, particularly in the rural areas (represented by the dotted line). Since the scale here is expressed in tenths of a standard deviation for the total group, it is evident that the rural Alabama-Georgia candidates scored about three-fourths of a sigma below their rural New York cousins. For the urban groups, the regional differences are less striking, but are still present. Next, notice that the solid lines tend to slope *downward* to the right, while the dotted lines tend to slope *upward* to the right. This is seen clearly from the chart where the composite rural-urban comparison is made (see Fig. 2), with all four regions averaged together. Evidently, the students from large communities were much more facile verbally than those from small communities, whereas in mathematical ability their superiority was slight, and in terms of ability to answer common-sense science questions, the two groups were equal.

An analysis of variance showed that the differences in total test perfor-

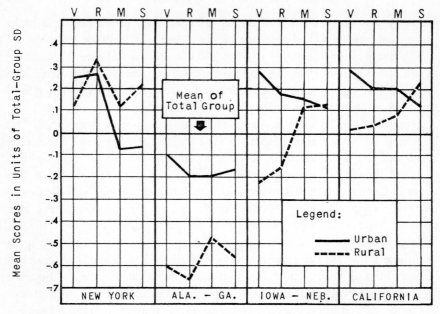

FIG. 1. *Army-Navy College Qualifying Test: rural-urban differences by regions.*

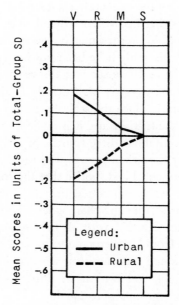

FIG. 2. *Army-Navy College Qualifying Test: rural-urban differences.*

mance according to geographical region were statistically significant, as were the differences in performance according to size of community. There were significant differences between states in the relationship of the ability of persons from large communities to that of persons from small communities. And finally, rural-urban differences varied significantly according to the kind of test material used, as illustrated in the second graph.

As a further step in this investigation, separate item analyses were completed for the eight subgroups on ten items from each test section, in an attempt to discover whether the lower scores of the rural group resulted from generally poorer performance on the items within a given test section or from failure on particular items. I shall not take time to report in detail on our findings, but an analysis of variance showed that the item-difficulty differences between the groups varied significantly from one item to another. That is, the order of item difficulty was not the same for boys from small communities as for boys from large cities. In the case of the verbal section of the test, the variance of item difficulties by community sizes was considerably larger than would have been required for significance at the 1 per cent level, and for the other three sections was significant at better than the 5 per cent level. Similarly, the differences in performance of geographically distinct groups varied significantly from item to item.

The fact that the differences between groups depend on the individual test questions considered, rather than merely on the type of test material, is of crucial importance for the argument as to the cause of the differences. For if the differences were common to all items of one type or one factor, we might argue that the different groups had inherited different patterns of abilities and that these patterns reflected themselves directly in the test section scores. But one would scarcely argue for differential inheritance of ability to solve individual questions within such a homogeneous factor as verbal, where the dependence of rural-urban differences on the particular test question asked was most clearly indicated. The conclusion must be that whether or not there were inherited mental differences between our groups from large and small communities, and from state to state, environmental differences must have caused certain of the differences in test performance: specifically, the intergroup differences in order of item difficulty within a single test section.

If one grants that some test questions are relatively harder than others for persons in a specified cultural group, the next question is: what shall we do about it? Should we build tests that minimize the intercultural difference in scores, or that maximize that difference, or shall we trust to chance to bring us out somewhere in the middle?

It is my contention that on a predictive test any score difference between groups whose backgrounds differ should be judged not good or bad, not right or wrong, but useful or not useful, valid or invalid for the prediction of future behavior. We must specify the criterion we wish to predict, and then justify intergroup equality or inequality of test scores on the basis of its effect on prediction.

Relatively little attention has been given to the question of the effect on prediction of score differences between cultural groups. The results of a few investigations (3, 4) are available, and they show in general that the rather haphazard mixing of items favorable to various subcultures has so far resulted in tests that differentiate usefully among cultural groups, if one's purpose is to predict the criteria used in these studies.

In a study of data reported in Frederiksen and Schrader (2), a comparison was made between predicted achievement and actual achievement of veteran and nonveteran students in their first year of college. In four institutions a prediction of the freshman grades was made from scores on an aptitude test, using the American Council on Education Psychological Examination (ACE) in three instances and the College Board Scholastic Aptitude Test (SAT) in the fourth. Within each group, veteran and nonveteran, a division was then made on the basis of background variables, for the purpose of discovering whether or not they were associated with a tendency to accomplish more in college than the test scores predicted. If the aptitude tests were assigning improperly low scores to students of lower socioeconomic status, one would expect such students to overachieve (in relation to predictive test score) on the criterion variable, whatever it might be. Such was not the case for these four institutions. Background data were available on income of family head, formal education of father, and size of community. No clear trends emerged to show that the student's position relative to these variables was related to his tendency to overachieve, whether veteran or nonveteran students were considered.

In the study of the Army-Navy College Qualifying Test, the results of which I have reported, no criterion data were obtained. Such data were, however, gathered in an unpublished study by Conrad and Robbins, who used the same qualifying test to predict achievement after two semesters of the Navy V-12 College Training Program. They then attempted to account for the errors in prediction on the basis of educational handicap in high school, using as the measure of educational handicap the average teacher's salary in the school system from which the individual came. The hypothesis tested was that teacher's salary should correlate negatively with overachievement: the lower the salary, the greater the excess of achievement over prediction.

Out of seventeen colleges studied, negative correlations were found in six, a zero correlation in one, and positive correlations in ten, showing that whatever educational handicap was reflected in the aptitude scores was reflected to at least as great a degree in first-year college achievement.

These findings suggest that intergroup differences on scholastic aptitude tests, when the grouping is based on factors usually associated with cultural or educational handicap, are valid for the prediction of college freshman grades. Admittedly, this is a limited criterion, but the nature of validation demands that we investigate our criteria one by one.

The findings based on freshman grades were corroborated in a further eight-college study reported by Conrad and Robbins (1) at the 1947 meeting of the American Educational Research Association. In that study, the authors found that errors in prediction of *fifth-term* college work from aptitude test scores were not related either to average teacher's salary or to size of community from which the student came: that is, whatever handicap the factors of teacher's salary or community size may reflect manifested itself as strongly in achievement through the fifth college term as it did in the aptitude scores obtained before entrance to college.

I wish I could report findings of similar studies aimed at longer-range criteria of greater social significance. Unfortunately, however, I know of no existing data that will help us answer the question of the validity, for such criteria, of the intergroup differences under consideration.

To summarize, the study of intergroup differences on the Army-Navy College Qualifying Test, reported earlier in this paper, illustrates the magnitude of the score differences obtained when one administers a typical scholastic aptitude test to groups of high school graduates in various geographical regions and from communities of different sizes. The analysis of differences on individual test questions points to the causal influence of cultural differences in producing score differences. Other investigations have uncovered evidence that such score differences have some predictive utility, i.e., that when college grades through the fifth term are accepted as a criterion, the test scores reflect accurately the performance of the various subgroups. What we need in order to provide a more generally useful answer to the question of predictive utility are studies in which test scores are used to forecast long-term life success. Only studies of this kind can tell us how great should be the intergroup differences on predictive tests.

REFERENCES

1. Conrad, H. S., & Robbins, I. The measurement of educational handicap. (Address delivered at the 1947 meeting of the American Educational Research Association, March 3, 1947.)
2. Frederiksen, N., & Schrader, W. B. *Adjustment to college: a study of 10,000 veteran and nonveteran students in sixteen American colleges.* Princeton, N.J.: Educational Testing Service, 1951.
3. Lewis, W. D. A comparative study of the personalities, interests, and home backgrounds of gifted children of superior and inferior educational achievement. *Journal of Genetic Psychology,* 1941, 39, 208–218.
4. Stroud, J. B. Predictive value of obtained intelligence quotients of groups favored and unfavored in socio-economic status. *Elementary School Journal,* 1942, 43, 97–104.

Difference or Bias in Tests of Intelligence

IRVING LORGE

1952

From time to time, scientists need to reappraise the concepts of their science, their methods of measurement, and the application of their knowledges for the general good. Psychologists, during the nature-nurture controversy, have had to re-evaluate not only the concept of intelligence but also that of environment. For more than fifty years, they have been revising the *meaning* of intelligence, the various tests and procedures for its estimation, and, more especially, the implications of the evidence from tests for the understanding of children and their achievements. And, of course, they have critically reviewed the applicability of general and special intelligence tests for the selection, classification, and guidance of individuals.

Psychologists, as well as educators, in the fullness of time may feel obligated to Eells and his associates for *Intelligence and Cultural Differences* (1). For again, these authors have asked them to reconsider the meaning of test-intelligence. As contemplated, this book has motivated anew serious re-examination of intelligence and of intelligence tests. Perhaps the authors, too, intended that some psychologists should become emotionally disturbed by the use of "differences" in the title in contrast to the use of "bias" within the text. Such feelings of disturbance may arise when such psychologists think of *bias* as some procedure by which some person "with malice aforethought" consciously prejudices a method of measurement to support an unfavorable (or favorable) opinion about persons, things, or ideas. Few objective psychologists report "differences" for the purpose of proving a bias or a disparity. Most studies of individual or of trait differences, beginning with Galton and including Eells, have provided the evidence that measurable differences between groups exist. In test-intelligence, in particular, whether general or specific, *differences* have been found between groups classified by sex, age, education, geographic origin, occupation of father, cultural background, and socioeconomic status. Indeed, differences have been found in test-intelligence between groups classified by body type, physical health, personality structure, nutritional status, and family unity. Such reported differences from tests of intelligence have made test makers as well as test users increasingly aware of the multiplicity and intricacies of factors related to test performances of individuals and of groups. Not only are differences affiliated with groups, but they are affected by environment. Inadequate stimulation, within deprivational environments, may affect performance negatively. Indeed, we do now recognize the interactions of heredity as endowment and environment as opportunity for each maturing individual. Children who during their early years are deprived of linguistic and of social stimulation, as a group, do poorly in test-intelligence, and indeed, often are inadequate to cope with the range of adjustments the environment demands. The fact of "differences" is well established: test performance reflects the specifics of environmental opportunities, training, experience, and stored achievement.

Test users have been instructed, over and over again, that an individual's test score must be interpreted always in the light of an understanding of the variety of factors and conditions that are related to measures of intellect. Psychologists have provided normative data for a variety of groups because they know that differences in test performance are related to sex, age, grade-placement, and socioeconomic status. Furthermore, they have cautioned that a child's motivations and physical well-being do influence test performances.

Inevitably some users of tests neglected to profit from the tutelage. They willfully treated test scores as absolute determinations about individuals or, even, groups. Others, of course, failed to appreciate fully the range and interaction of circumstances that affect test performance. To overcome such perversity and such ignorance, some psychometricians tried to be quit of the *bias* of the test user by attempting to eliminate the *differences* from the tests.

Usually, the attempt to make an *unbiased* test of intelligence is an attempt to reduce some kind of group *difference* to zero. For instance, it is well known that boys and girls (and men and women) perform differently on tests of verbal and of numerical content and process. For the fear that the *biased opinion* that women are superior to men should predominate, psychometricians, for upwards of a half century, have reduced "differences" by addition. All of us are fully aware that to overcome the obtained verbal superiority of women, the test maker adds a sufficiency of numerical reasoning items to make the average total score of men equal that of women. *No difference, ergo, no bias.* Fortunately, there still are differences between the sexes.

Partial justification, indeed, does exist for such a procedure. In general, a test score that is based on a composite of many kinds of intellectual processes and contents does give valid (and reliable) estimates about most persons' potentialities for success with the kinds of ideas and skills taught in schools. The emphasis should be on "most"; many, however, may be misappraised because a score from many different tasks will fail to reveal the facts about differences within the individual's mental organization, and hence, by extension, fail to give information about differences in the mental organization of different groups. Of course, to apply Galton's suggestion of sinking many "shafts" does require more time than most test users are willing to expend. For practical purposes, then, psychometricians have accepted either Binet's theory about the unitary character of intelligence, or Spearman's demonstration of the pervasiveness of *g*. The consequent acceptance of the single index of mental age, or intelligence quotient, or an intelligence score led to expectations that these scores were the absolutes about a person. They are not. The results of factor analysis have proved the need for the measurement of different aspects of intelligent functioning. Basically, differential aptitude tests attempt to measure "differences" as differences.

The measurement of "differences," however, is both costly in test construction and expensive in testing time, so that the *single-index* score will exist for some time to come. It must be recognized that most, if not all, so-called unbiased tests of intelligence are such *single-index* appraisals.

Another method for attempting to produce an unbiased test score is to try to reduce group *difference* by subtraction. Essentially, instead of adding items to conceal a difference, this method removes the items that produce the difference. The research reported in *Intelligence and Cultural Differences* deals with a technique for discovering the kinds of items in some current tests of intelligence that differentiate between some socioeconomic groups. Eells, as a matter of fact, has found a significant relationship between measures of social and economic status and measures of intelligence. He realized, as careful workers had before him, that, on the average, the test-intelligence of groups with lower socioeconomic status scores was lower than that of those whose status was higher. The fact of socioeconomic differences in test-intelligence is reconfirmed. The implications of those facts, too, had led to the development of social inventions to reduce the environmental differentials that may affect the test performance of the socially and economically less privileged. Indeed, the full history of American educational legislation and practice, from the "Old Deluder" Act to the contemporary requirement of compulsory schooling for all, illustrates the dynamics of democratic social engineering. Eells and his co-workers, however, took a different view of the facts.

They, apparently, assumed that the individuals in the various socioeconomic stratifications were *equal* in intelligence. Hence, if any differences were found, it must be the test or some kinds of test items that produce the differences. Thus was created the logical dilemma: *difference, ergo, bias.* In avoiding the one horn, psychologists must inevitably be embarrassed by the other. In facing the alternatives, however, educators and psychologists must be aware of the general nature of the procedure. Eells, having established that differences obtain in test-intelligence between groups that they assigned to socioeconomic strata, proceeded to select two samples at either extreme of the status score range, namely, children of old American stock who were either classified as of very high or very low status by the credits on the "Composite Index of Status Characteristics." He then made an item analysis of a large portion of the tasks in the several intelligence tests that the individuals in each extreme had taken. Since the median percentage of correct responses for the High Status group was about 81, and that for the Low Status group was about 70, it must follow that a plurality of the items will favor the High Status group. This, indeed, was established by the analysis. The interesting finding, however, is that the differences in item performance between the two extreme status groups have "a direct relation to the form of symbolism in which the item is expressed." The High Status group is favored most on verbal items, but the gradient of difference becomes less and less for items "based on meaningless number combinations" and approaches zero for items involving pictures, geometric designs, and stylized drawings. Apparently, the discovery of such a symbolism difference *suggests* that a culture-fair test could be made of those tasks that minimize verbal processes and that favor those that require the manipulation of numbers, geometric designs, and pictures. Such a test of such tasks, of course, can be made. But, if it were, what would it measure? It seems excessively trustful to put reliance only on those items that fail to distinguish between demonstrably different status groups. Some criterion about intellectual functioning, other than the one that the items make for no diversity, seems, at least, a psychological prerequisite. Certainly, within each extreme, variation in test performance must have been symptomatic of intelligent behavior that, to a very large degree, was a consequent of differences in ability or aptitude.

If such an unbiased test were produced by subtraction, it neither would be a test of intelligence nor would it give any evidence about the impact of status or culture on test performance. Certainly, Eells and his co-authors had methods available for item selection that would have maintained some relation to a criterion for intelligent functioning while minimizing the impact of status or culture. At least, partial correlation would have led to the making of a culture-fair test without losing the appraisal of intelligent behavior. At best, Eells's method could produce a test—but it would be a matter of conjecture as to what such a test measures. Clearly, the evidence from the many so-called nonverbal and nonlanguage tests suggests that what they measure is different from what is measured by the so-called verbal tests.

Of course, the administration of the same verbal test to groups maturing under different language experiences would favor the group for whom the test language was their own vernacular. Test scores from a verbal intelligence test designed for Chinese would certainly put some Americans at a disadvantage. Indeed, not only will groups perform differently if they are separated widely by their languages, but also if they have developed different cultural attitudes and values. Many psychometricians have endeavored to produce tests that are culture-free. From the days of Army Beta, attempts to remove the differences attributable to culture have been ingenious although not fully successful. To the long line of such tests, including Dodd's International Group Mental Test, Cattell's Culture-Free Intelligence Test, Spearman's Visual Perception Test, and the Multi-Mental Non-Language Test, should be added Rulon's Semantic Test of Intelligence.[1] Each of these tries to achieve an unbiased test by substitution. Since the fact of different cultural and linguistic background prohibits the use of the language of any one group or a language common to all groups, the test maker attempts to appraise intellectual performance by the manipulation of objects, or of pictures, or of designs, or of numbers. The tasks set by the psychologist require intelligent behaviors of perception, selection, generalization, and organization. In cross-cultural comparisons, however, differential experience with pictorial representation, for example, may significantly influence the way the tasks are perceived, the specifics selected, and the aspects restructured. Some of you, indeed, may remember the nonlanguage item in the Army Non-Language Test, in which the task was to cross out the picture that did not belong with the other four. Chinese inductees, invariably, viciously and erroneously crossed out the illustration of a rising sun because of its symbolism for them.

Rulon's new semantic test should prove ultimately to be a fruitful lead. In essence, it sets the task of "learning" to associate a geometric symbol for a concept generalized from a number of drawings of worldly events. The process involves the acquisition of a symbolic glossary which is tested by

---

[1] See paper by P. J. Rulon, immediately following this paper—Ed.

requiring the subject to show his mastery of the glossary not only as individual signs, but also in combined semantic and syntactic organization. Involved in the task of learning the glossary and in demonstrating mastery over it is the additional one for the subject to infer what he is to do. Basically, the kind of learning is somewhat like associating a Chinese ideograph with a concept generalized from several pictures. In contrast with the more extensive spoken or visual vocabulary, the Rulon glossary approach involves very few signs, meanings, and syntactical patterns. Under such limitation, the process differs in complexity from the more usual tests of verbal intelligence. Rulon, indeed, finds that the correlation between Stanford-Binet mental ages and the score on the Semantic Test of Intelligence is very low for a constrained sample of feebleminded children. One reason, but not the only one, may be that the processes tapped by the Semantic Test are quite different from those appraised by the Stanford-Binet. The added evidence contrasting the relation of school achievement with the Semantic Test and with the Stanford-Binet supports the belief that the two tests are not measures of the same functions.

Test makers apparently have tried to eliminate bias from the appraisal of intelligence by covering up group differences, by eliminating tasks that make for group differences, or by substituting different processes in evaluating groups. Do such procedures really remove the bias from the measurement of intelligence? My answer is no. They do reduce, of a certainty, the amounts and kinds of information about test performance of separable groups. Scientifically, however, ignorance of difference is a costly way to produce unbiased tests of intelligence.

The objective psychologist cannot fail to see the *reductio ad absurdum* of making unbiased tests of intelligence. For instance, following the implications of Eells's procedure and findings, a test involving manipulation of numbers, geometric designs, and stylized drawings will probably favor men and boys. Will it then be necessary to select from such items the few on which women and girls will be equal to men? And if this be accomplished, should only those items on which endomorphs make performances equivalent to ectomorphs be retained?

There can be little doubt that among some kinds of groups differences do exist. As a matter of fact, the wide range of general and specific tests of intelligence has made it possible to establish much of the available knowledge of differential psychology. Not only has the awareness of such differences led to the emergence of a more adequate understanding of the relative advantages and limitations of intelligence tests, but it also has increased our appreciation of the significance of difference in the understanding of children as individuals, and in groups. In a democracy, such as ours, respect for difference as difference is necessary. There is no virtue in developing instruments so blunted that they decrease the amount of information. Perhaps the best method for reducing bias in tests of intelligence is to use them with the full knowledge that endowment interacting with opportunity produces a wide range of differences. Appraisal of the variation of different kinds of intellectual functioning requires many kinds of tests so that the differences can be utilized for the benefit of the individual and for the good of society. Intellectual functioning certainly does involve the ability to learn to adjust to the environment or to adapt the environment to individual needs and capacities by the process of solving problems either directly or incidentally. Such a concept recognizes a variety of different aptitudes for success with different kinds of problems. The full appreciation of the variety of aptitudes and the development of adequate methods for appraising them should ultimately lead to the production of enough information to eliminate bias.

As the psychologist develops tests to measure mastery of different contents and processes, he will obtain the evidence about the inequalities of opportunity for maximum development. With such information, the psychologist, in cooperation with educators and others interested in social amelioration, will try to make those social inventions which will allow all in our democracy to have an equal opportunity for maximum development of their potentialities. The full utilization of such social inventions and social engineering will not eliminate the established fact that there will be differences among individuals and between groups. When differences are reduced by the advantages of opportunity, the credit will be to the tests that showed their existence. Difference as difference is not bias, but the information about it will lead to the gradual disappearance of some kinds of bias.

REFERENCE

1. Eells, K., *et al. Intelligence and cultural differences.* Chicago: Univer. of Chicago Press, 1951.

A Semantic Test of Intelligence

PHILLIP J. RULON

1952

Nonverbal tests of intelligence have never been satisfactory. They have not correlated well with verbal tests of intelligence nor with success in intellectual or academic endeavors. In the case of many nonverbal tests, the intellectual operation called for does not seem to be the same as that called for in academic or intellectual pursuits.

The distinction between the usual verbal test and the usual nonverbal test is not so clear when easy items are considered as when more subtle or difficult items are examined. The strictly nonverbal tests of the past have by and large retreated from the function they were trying to get at whenever they were made difficult enough to be useful in selecting a few of the more able members of the population tested.

The problem we undertook was to develop a testing technique that would be free from the more or less glaring shortcomings of the usual nonverbal test, and at the same time be free from some of the commoner defects of verbal tests.

The following defects in the typical nonverbal tests were regarded as worthy of avoidance:

1) In the administration of some nonverbal tests, verbal instructions are employed to tell the examinee what is required of him.

2) The examinee is presented with novel material that deprives him of the opportunity to exhibit any use he may have made of opportunities to make ordinary observations of the surroundings in which he has lived.

3) A time limit is sometimes imposed which renders the nonverbal test a speed test rather than a power test.

4) Some nonverbal tests require the manipulation of concrete objects, such as blocks, marbles, or other simple familiar things. It is hard to contrive items making use of these materials such that the items are difficult in the sense ordinarily understood by *intellectual* difficulty.

472

5) Some nonverbal tests require the reading of symbols (such as Arabic digits) that may be nonlanguage strictly speaking, but that are nevertheless associated with the use of language in our culture.

6) Some nonverbal tests require a verbal response from the examinee.

7) Some nonverbal tests, such as form-comparison tests, put a premium upon visual perception almost to the extent of rewarding visual acuity: the difference which the subject is required to detect between two geometrical figures may be so minute as to present essentially a problem of visual acuity.

The deficiencies in certain verbal tests that were regarded as particularly to be avoided include the following:

1) Some verbal tests give an advantage to persons from certain cultural backgrounds, regardless of the language employed. That is, the content is more familiar to persons from one culture than to those from another.

2) Some verbal tests require an exhibition of previously acquired knowledge, rather than testing a skill necessary for accomplishing a new task.

3) Some verbal tests are essentially speed tests.

4) Some verbal tests allow a free response that causes scoring difficulties.

5) Some verbal tests put a premium upon the examinee's facility with his native language.

It was the purpose of our work to derive a nonverbal test technique that would be acceptable on general grounds and be free from as many as possible of these undesirable characteristics.

The work was conducted in the Harvard Graduate School of Education under a contract between the President and Fellows of Harvard College and the United States Government, represented by the Personnel Research Section of the Personnel Research and Procedures Branch of the Personnel Bureau of the Adjutant General's Office, Department of the Army.

The manner in which we have attacked this problem can be seen best, I think, by turning to the sample test booklet [reproduced on pp. 477–480]. The left-hand inside page of this booklet [p. 478] pretty closely parallels the first page of our 42-page test booklet as it is now arranged. In giving the test, we make motions indicating that the symbol at the top goes with the five pictures. Motions then indicate to the examinee that the first symbol in the exercises is identical to that in the definition above. This is done without saying anything. Searching motions among the five options in the first exercise terminate in locating the COW WALKING in the third option. Motions of comparison between this picture and the fourth picture above and also motions of comparison between the symbol at the left and the symbol above terminate in the examiner's drawing a circle around the third octagon in the first exercise. I suggest that, like the examinees, you now draw a circle around the third octagon in the first exercise.

Similar motions of comparison terminate in the examiner's circling the fourth option in the second exercise. Suppose you now circle the JUMPING COW at that place. The motions are again repeated, still without saying anything, and the first octagon is circled in the third exercise. I suggest that you circle that STANDING COW and then go on with the rest of the page as our examinees are encouraged to do.

On the adjacent right-hand page [p. 479] you will find a layout very much like page 13 of our 42-page test booklet. You will see that the symbols at the left alternate between COW and JUMPING. For the first exercise we make motions indicating the similarity between the symbol in the exercise and the right-hand symbol above, and then make searching motions among the five options which terminate in the second option. Motions of comparison between this picture and the WOMAN JUMPING in the glossary above terminate in the examiner's drawing a large circle around the second option in the first exercise. In the second exercise motions of comparison are made between the symbol and the COW symbol above, and searching motions among the options terminate in the fifth option. Motions of comparison between this option and the WALKING COW above terminate in the examiner's drawing a large circle around the last option in item 2. Similarly, in the next item, the fourth option is circled by the examiner, after which the examinee is encouraged to circle the appropriate options on the rest of the page. Suppose you go ahead and do that at this time.

So far we have been engaged in a relatively simple intellectual operation that may be identified as a digit-symbol substitution exercise, except—you may have noticed—that in the second exercise on this page the WALKING COW was a mirror image of the one in the definition. Furthermore, in the third exercise, the JUMPING CAT was not the same JUMPING CAT as in the glossary at the top. In the next exercise—that is, the fourth one—you circled a jumping animal that was not shown at all in the glossary for JUMPING. In marking that exercise you must have abstracted the concept of JUMPING from the actions shown in the glossary at the top. You couldn't have marked that answer by a simple digit-symbol substitution.

On the back page of the sample booklet [p. 480], I have shown you what happens on page 24 of our 42-page booklet. In dealing with the first item, the examiner must here make two sets of motions of comparison. By such motions he shows that the first symbol agrees with the COW symbol above, and the second symbol agrees with the JUMPING symbol above. The searching motions among the options terminate with option 4. Then motions of comparison are used between this option and the JUMPING COW at the top left, and other motions of comparison between this picture and the JUMPING COW at the upper right. These motions terminate in the examiner's circling the JUMPING COW in the fourth option. In the next exercise, similar motions of comparison terminate in the examiner's circling the first option. If you will circle this option, and in the next item circle the second option after comparing the symbols, you may then proceed on your own to complete the page.

As you may well suppose, the next step is to introduce three-symbol sentences such as MAN BEATS HORSE or HORSE DRAGS BOY or BOY BEATS MAN. The highest level to which we are now going is to the four-symbol sentence, such as WOMAN KICKS DOG LYING DOWN or MAN BEATS WOMAN RUNNING, and the like.

I am sure you must have got the idea by this time why we called it the Semantic Test of Intelligence. What we have done is to imitate in a non-verbal test the semantic relationships presented in the typical low-level verbal intelligence test; that is, to require the subject to associate an arbitrary symbol with a worldly referent, to indicate his mastery of this association, and then to combine these symbols into groups in which the relationships between the symbols in each group are semantic or syntactical relationships.

In order to avoid putting a premium upon urban culture or amount of schooling, it was decided to use as wordly referents only the actors, verbs, and objects familiar in all Western cultures, even the most primitive. These were felt to be sex differentiation, the young of the species, and domesticated animals, as far as the nominatives were concerned, and simple objects like bowls, stools, trees, etc.—in addition to men, women, children, and common animals—for the objects of transitives. For intransitive verbs, the most universal actions were used: standing, walking, running, jumping, sitting, and the like. For transitive verbs, again the most primitive operations upon objectives were employed: pushing, dragging, lifting, beating, chasing, leading, etc.

The test is nonverbal to the extent of being administered without any word in any language being spoken by anyone.

The appearance of validity of the material is not merely superficial, since the operations required of the examinee are the simpler linguistic or semantic operations, not just operations thought up for the purpose of constructing a test. These operations are undoubtedly related to the operations of reading in any language.

It has been found possible to construct a test of substantial difficulty which does not seem to offer any reward for visual acuity or pure visual perception.

Also it seems possible now to produce such a test using such materials so as not to give any advantage whatever to the Northern child over the Southern, the white over the colored, or the time-server in school over the bright youngster with less schooling.

STI

SEMANTIC TEST OF INTELLIGENCE

by

Phillip J. Rulon

Harvard Graduate School of Education

Form 00

Special Edition for ETS Invitational Conference on Testing Problems

Saturday 1 November 1952

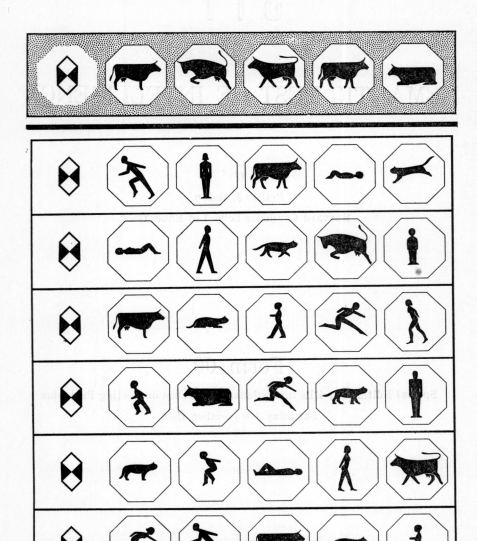

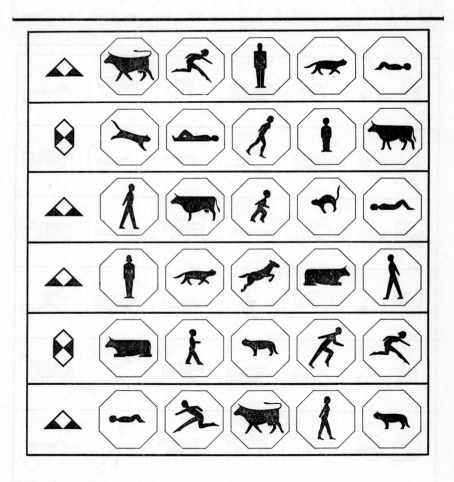

479

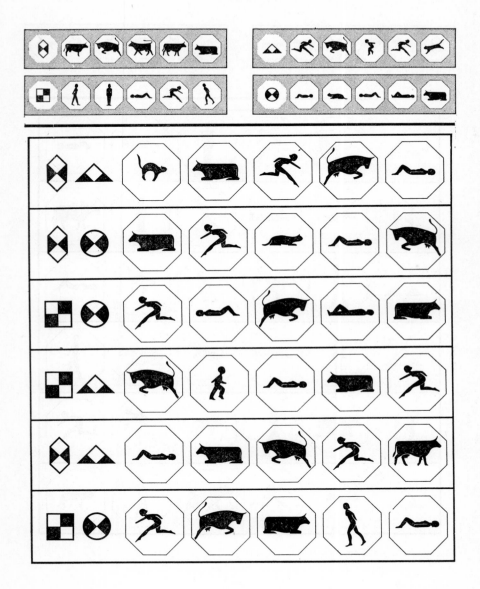

480

Social Class and Cultural Group Differences in Diverse Mental Abilities[1]

GORDON FIFER

1964

The problems of differentiated mental abilities and of their relationships to class and cultural group composition challenge us directly in the urban centers. The provision of suitable educational programs for all the children in our schools presupposes our knowledge of what these children are like (12).

Despite the considerable amount of work by psychologists to create so-called culture-free or culture-fair tests, little has been shown to yield consistent and valid results. The problem still remains as to how to evaluate the intellectual potential of children whose backgrounds necessarily handicap them seriously on the usual tests of mental ability (1, 2, 3, 4, 7).

This study focused on two major aspects of the problem: first, to devise tests that would be as free as possible of any direct class or cultural bias but also would still be acceptable measures of intellectual traits. (It should be noted that no attempt was made to devise any remarkably new or unique tests.) The second goal was to structure a testing situation that would enable each child to be evaluated under optimal conditions.

HYPOTHESES

The specific goal of this study was to examine the patterns among various mental abilities in first-grade children from different social-class and cultural backgrounds. We accepted a definition of intelligence that postulates diverse mental abilities; hence, intelligent behavior can be manifested in a wide variety of forms. This provided the premise for the hypotheses tested in the study: that class and cultural influences differ not only in degree

[1] This study was made possible by a Cooperative Research Grant from the Office of Education, United States Department of Health, Education, and Welfare. A full report of the study is given in Lesser, Fifer, and Clark (10).

but in kind, with the consequence that different kinds of intellectual skills are fostered in various environments.

The specific hypotheses tested were that:

1) significant differences exist among groups of children from different social-class and cultural backgrounds in each of the mental ability areas specified below;

2) significant differences exist among groups of children from different social-class and cultural backgrounds in the pattern or configuration of scores from these diverse areas of mental ability;

3) significant interactions exist between the variables of social class and cultural background in determining the level of each mental ability and the nature of the patterns among them.

THE SAMPLING

The four ethnic groups selected for the study were Chinese, Jews, Negroes, and Puerto Ricans. The design provided for 20 boys and 20 girls at both the middle-class and lower-class levels in each of the ethnic groups. The total number of subjects was, therefore, 320. The age level selected was from 6 years to 7 years of age. The actual, ultimate sample ranged in age from 6 years 3 months to 7 years 5 months. The sample was obtained with a few exceptions entirely in urban, congested New York City. In brief, the sampling procedure consisted of a rather detailed study of census-tract information on ethnic group distributions and income-level distributions in the city. Additional data were obtained from a variety of agencies including charitable institutions, government bureaus, and market research companies. After careful plotting of the location of our population, the relevant public schools were spotted and the school authorities were contacted with regard to sampling children in the first grade. Once classes were identified, our examiners sampled as randomly as possible the children at these various locations. Children with physical handicaps or emotional disorders, as well as those who became ill for more than a week, were excluded. Also, the results of children whose testing was "requested" were omitted. Approximately 500 children were either completely or partially tested in order to try to maintain a fairly random selection within our stratified sample.

THE SCALES

The scales used in this study are rather extensive modifications of scales previously developed under a U.S. Office of Education grant conducted at

Hunter College from 1957 to 1960 (8). The four scales are: Verbal, Reasoning, Numerical, and Space. The Verbal scale consists of a 30-item picture vocabulary test and two 15-item word definition tests, yielding two part-scores (a Picture Vocabulary score and a Word Vocabulary score) plus a total score. Both of these subtests are scored on the basis of two points for each correct or completely acceptable response, and one point for partially correct responses. The scoring keys were carefully developed by the group of psychologists participating in the study.

The Reasoning scale consists of three tests: Picture Analogies, Picture Arrangements, and Jump Peg. The first two tests are relatively well-known types, and no major deviation from the usual format is employed. The Jump Peg test, however, is quite novel in that the task required of the subject is unlike that of any of the children's games available on the market, although somewhat similar. The administration of this subtest is planned to enable each child to start from the same point of knowledge about the task. It is felt that the test is a good measure of reasoning whenever perceptual variance can be neutralized.

The Numerical scale consists of five subtests: Enumeration (6 items), Addition (10 items), Subtraction (10 items), Multiplication (10 items), Division (10 items). Knowledge of neither numbers nor operational symbols is required on any of these tests. All material is presented pictorially and with the exception of the Enumeration test, in which the subject is permitted to count with his finger touching the picture, all of the numerical operations have to be done in the child's head. It is recognized that this scale is quite unlike the usual number factor tests.

The Space scale consists of four subtests: Object Completion, Jig Saws, Estimating Path, and Perspective. The Object Completion subtest is more a perceptual-visualization measure than a pure space measure, but this type of test has been shown to correlate fairly well with three-dimensional measures. The Jig Saws consist of puzzles quite unlike those available in children's games. They require the subject to perceive spatial relationships in order to complete them successfully, but require little motor proficiency and contain none of the usual reasoning cues found in popular jig-saw puzzles. The Estimating Path test was adapted from spatial tests used in the Air Force, and probably is the weakest test in our battery owing to its susceptibility to chance. The task of the test is to estimate visually projected paths of airplanes. The Perspective subtest consists of identifying the field of vision of several persons at various points in a scene. Although it is felt that the hypothetical construct underlying this test is primarily spatial, it is admitted that the method used to evaluate the construct possibly introduces verbal and reasoning variance at the age level studied.

Some general considerations about the construction of the tests should be noted:

1) No reading was required of the subject on any test.

2) All pictorial materials were clearly presented on large cards for easy viewing.

3) All persons were drawn as neutral as possible with a careful avoidance of the precious, pretty pictures of the usual children's picture books.

4) No items required the naming of an object by the subject except on the Verbal scale. The additional exception to this was the Object Completion test; however, the subject could obtain full credit without naming an object if he could indicate his recognition in some other way.

5) An attempt was made to include only elements that appear commonly in all cultural and class groups in New York City.

Table 1 contains the characteristics of the tests and the results obtained with the total group. It can be noted that the reliabilities of the four total scales are: Verbal, .93; Reasoning, .92; Numerical, .96; and Space, .85. Reasonably high reliability coefficients were obtained for all of the fourteen subtests with the exception of Estimating Path, Perspective, and the 6-item Enumeration subtest. The intercorrelations of the four main scales are as follows: Verbal—Reasoning, .58; Verbal—Numerical, .54; Verbal—

TABLE 1

Characteristics of the Tests and the Results Obtained with the Total Group
(N = 320)

Scale	Subtest	No. of Items	Total Possible Score	Mean	SD	Reliability Coefficient
Verbal	Picture Vocabulary	30	60	43.4	8.8	.84
	Word Vocabulary	30	60	31.0	11.0	.90
	Total	60	120	74.4	18.3	.93
Reasoning	Picture Analogies	18	18	9.8	3.4	.80
	Picture Arrangements	16	16	7.1	4.5	.91
	Jump Peg	12	12	5.7	3.3	.89
	Total	46	46	22.6	8.6	.92
Numerical	Enumeration	6	6	5.0	1.2	.68
	Addition	10	10	5.1	3.0	.88
	Subtraction	10	10	6.0	3.1	.82
	Multiplication	10	10	3.5	3.3	.90
	Division	10	10	3.8	2.9	.88
	Total	46	46	23.4	10.9	.96
Space	Object Completion	16	32	17.0	6.8	.80
	Estimating Path	12	12	8.1	1.9	.29
	Jig Saws	16	16	7.7	3.6	.89
	Perspective	10	10	5.2	2.2	.57
	Total	54	70	38.0	10.7	.85

Space, .44; Reasoning—Numerical, .73; Reasoning—Space, .62; and Numerical—Space, .54. As you can see, these are higher than one would like them to be. Fortunately, the high reliabilities enable us to assume sufficient unique variance to justify utilizing these scales to differentiate these four areas of mental ability.

TESTING PROCEDURES

Four psychologists helped with the revision of the scales and administered the tests. One was Jewish, one Negro, one Puerto Rican, and one Chinese. Each had been trained beyond the master's degree level and each had ample experience administering psychological tests, including the standard tests of intelligence. Each of the 320 children in our study was tested by a psychometrician who shared his cultural identity (6). While the length of the testing period varied and was determined primarily by the examiner's judgment regarding degree of rapport and fatigue, most commonly a child was seen for one session on each of three separate days for thirty to forty-five minutes.

The test required neither reading nor writing ability, and directions were kept extremely simple. The test could be administered in English or in the child's primary language, or in a combination of the two; children were permitted to respond in any combination of languages. Ample practice material was provided prior to each subtest, and examiners were instructed to proceed with scored items only when certain that the child was familiar with the material and understood the task.

There were no formal steps of test administration left to the discretion of the examiner; each step was specified in detail to assure standard procedure. Each examiner saw every other examiner and himself administer the test to a child (during the pretest phase) on video tape. Each examiner also tested a child before a one-way vision screen while the other three took careful notes of the most minute deviation from standard procedure.

With four exceptions, each child was tested in his own school, in a room alone with the examiner. Examiners presented the tasks with a "game" orientation, but were instructed to change the orientation to a serious one if the child seemed more comfortable and productive when dealing with "work."

CLASS AND ETHNIC GROUP DESIGNATION

The designation of socioeconomic class provided one of the major problems in the study. To make a very long story short, the ultimate technique employed was an adaptation of the Hollingshead and Redlich scale (9).

The three factors of father's (that is, head of the household's) occupation, father's education, and dwelling unit were rated. A composite was then computed resulting in a five-class scale. Classes I, II, and III were designated middle class; Classes IV and V lower class.

A major limitation of our study is the differential level of the class designations of the subjects in the four ethnic groups and the differential separation of the class designations within the various groups. For example, approximately two-thirds of the Jewish middle-class subjects were in Class I on our scale. The Chinese and Negro middle-class subjects were predominantly Class II. The Puerto Rican middle-class subjects were in Classes II and III. The Jewish lower-class subjects were equally divided between Classes IV and V, whereas the other three lower-class groups were almost entirely in Class V. Hence, although we achieved good class separation— that is, at least one class position in our scale was skipped by each ethnic group—the separations did not occur at equivalent points on the scale. However, this situation is the reality in New York City, and we would have distorted our population by sampling to obtain equated groups.

The ethnic designation was somewhat simpler on paper. The parents of each subject had to be known to be of the particular ethnic group. The only problem was the actual determination of the facts for some of the subjects. Cases were discarded, however, if verification of the parentage could not be obtained.

Results

The analyses (5, 11) of the data are too extensive to be presented here in any detail, but certain highlights should prove of interest. The support or lack of support for our three hypotheses can be seen in Table 2 and the graphic representation of them in Figure 1.

Our first hypothesis, that significant differences exist among groups of children from different social-class and cultural backgrounds in each of the four mental ability areas, was supported.

Our second hypothesis, that significant differences exist among groups of children from different social-class and cultural backgrounds in pattern or configuration of scores from these diverse areas of mental ability, was partially supported.

Our third hypothesis, that significant interactions exist between the variables of social class and cultural background in determining the level of each mental ability and nature of the patterns among them, was partially supported.

TABLE 2

Means of Normalized Standard Scores on the Four Scales
Listed by Ethnic and Social Class Group

Group	Verbal	Reasoning	Numerical	Space
Jewish: Middle Class	62.6	56.7	59.2	56.5
Lower Class	54.7	48.5	50.2	47.0
Total	58.7	52.6	54.7	51.8
Chinese: Middle Class	51.2	56.0	56.0	56.8
Lower Class	45.2	51.8	51.8	52.0
Total	48.2	53.9	53.9	54.4
Negro: Middle Class	55.8	53.9	51.2	53.0
Lower Class	44.0	41.5	39.6	40.1
Total	49.9	47.7	45.4	46.5
Puerto Rican: Middle Class	47.4	48.7	49.2	49.4
Lower Class	39.3	42.5	43.0	45.3
Total	43.3	45.6	46.1	47.4
Total: Middle Class	54.2	53.8	53.9	53.9
Lower Class	45.8	46.1	46.1	46.1

One can see from the graphic representation of the means that social class seems to influence *level* of functioning, and cultural identity seems to influence the *pattern,* or relative high and low ability areas. We have no evidence that these two factors interact in any way that creates significant differences in functioning.

One or two points should be emphasized. Note that the lowest mean group score is earned by the lower-class Puerto Ricans on the verbal tasks. Yet this same group does quite well, compared with the lower-class Negroes, on spatial tasks.

There is a clear and almost uniform difference within each cultural group that is imposed by social class and runs across the four mental ability areas. Yet, notice the difference in degree of separation between the two social classes of Chinese and the two social classes of Negroes. To be sure, this may be partly due to factors built into our study, but it still suggests the strong possibility that social-class difference will more strongly affect one's identity and intellectual performance if he is a Negro than if he is Chinese.

If may be wise to point out that these data refer to differences in the performance of *groups* and not the performance of *individuals.* They do not indicate how an individual will perform, but if he belongs to one of these eight groups, they suggest how he is *likely* to perform. His individual deviation, be it high or low, on one score or another, thereby becomes more useful information in understanding his individual abilities.

One approach to utilizing test data such as these for identifying particular patterns for individuals is a classification technique suggested by Tatsuoka (13). This technique compares the pattern of scores for each individ-

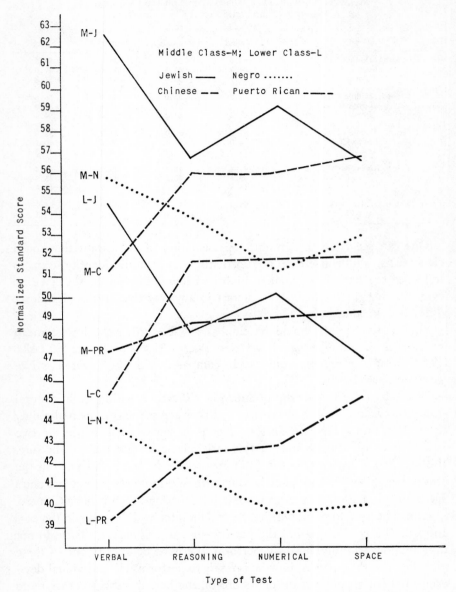

FIG. 1. *Test performance in relation to ethnic and socioeconomic classification.*

ual subject with the pattern profiles of his group and other groups. It yields data concerning the degree to which a subject's profile resembles the profile of his or the other groups. Table 3 illustrates the application of the method to our data. Note that the middle-class Jewish children and the lower-class Negro children were most accurately classified and the lower-class Puerto Rican children slightly less so. Note, however, that in addition to the 20 Puerto Rican lower-class children typical of their class and ethnic group pattern, an additional 15 had patterns like other lower-class patterns (that is, Chinese and Negro). It is apparent that the middle-class Puerto Rican children were the most heterogeneous of any of the eight groups.

TABLE 3

Group Profile Analysis (For each group, N = 40)

Group	Group Patterns							
	M Ch	L Ch	M J	L J	M N	L N	M PR	L PR
Middle Chinese	13[a]	10	6	1	5	1	2	2
Lower Chinese	6	14	2	4	3	1	1	9
Middle Jewish	4	0	32	4	0	0	0	0
Lower Jewish	0	1	9	18	7	4	0	1
Middle Negro	5	1	11	10	11	0	0	2
Lower Negro	1	3	0	3	0	28	0	5
Middle Puerto Rican	6	6	3	6	4	0	3	12
Lower Puerto Rican	0	7	1	1	0	8	3	20

[a] Figures to be read across as follows: The scores of 13 middle-class Chinese subjects fit the middle-class Chinese pattern and level on the four mental ability scales; 10 middle-class Chinese look more like lower-class Chinese; 6 look more like middle-class Jews, 1 more like a lower-class Jew, etc.

CONCLUSIONS

It is apparent that our study has raised more questions than it has produced neat answers. Our tests need revision and refinement. Additional analyses currently being completed of the factorial composition of the battery and of the unique nonchance variance of each subtest will be useful in further interpretation of our data. It is believed that we have strong evidence of differential patterns of mental abilities among four New York City ethnic groups. The data reveal sharp test-performance differences between middle- and lower-class groups regardless of ethnic group and that the differences differ among the ethnic groups. Replications of the study on the same and additional ethnic groups using psychometricians of like and unlike background would be valuable. There is some evidence of differences in patterns among the groups that may be of considerable value in educational planning. The value of the study will be finally realized in the follow-up studies we hope it will stimulate.

REFERENCES

1. Anastasi, Anne. Cultural differences. In C. W. Harris (Ed.), *Encyclopedia of educational research.* (3rd ed.) New York: Macmillan, 1960. Pp. 350–358.
2. Anastasi, Anne, & Cordova, F. A. Some effects of bilingualism upon the intelligence test performance of Puerto Rican children in New York City. *Journal of Educational Psychology,* 1953, 44, 1–19.
3. Anastasi, Anne, & D'Angelo, Rita Y. A comparison of Negro and white preschool children in language development and Goodenough Draw-a-Man IQ. *Journal of Genetic Psychology,* 1952, 81, 147–165.
4. Anastasi, Anne, & deJesús, C. Language development and nonverbal IQ of Puerto Rican preschool children in New York City. *Journal of Abnormal and Social Psychology,* 1953, 48, 357–366.
5. Block, J., Levine, L., & McNemar, Q. Testing for the existence of psychometric patterns. *Journal of Abnormal and Social Psychology,* 1951, 46, 356–359.
6. Canady, H. G. The effect of "rapport" on the IQ: a new approach to the problem of racial psychology. *Journal of Negro Education,* 1936, 5, 209–219.
7. Carson, A. S., & Rabin, A. I. Verbal comprehension and communication in Negro and white children. *Journal of Educational Psychology,* 1960, 51, 47–51.
8. Davis, F. B., Lesser, G. S., French, Elizabeth, *et al.* Identification and classroom behavior of gifted elementary-school children. *Cooperative Research Monographs,* 1960, No. 2, 19032. In *The Gifted Student,* OE–35016, Monograph No. 2, Office of Education, U.S. Department of Health, Education, and Welfare.
9. Hollingshead, A. B., & Redlich, F. C. *Social class and mental illness: a community study.* New York: Wiley, 1958.
10. Lesser, G. S., Fifer, G., & Clark, D. H. Mental abilities of children in different social and cultural groups. Cooperative Research Project No. 1635, Office of Education, U.S. Department of Health, Education, and Welfare, 1964. (Spiral Bound—copies available through Laboratory for Human Development, Harvard Univer.)
11. McNemar, Q. *Psychological statistics.* (3rd ed.) New York: Wiley, 1962.
12. Passow, A. H. (Ed.) *Education in depressed areas.* New York: Teachers College Bureau of Publications, 1963.
13. Tatsuoka, M. M. *Joint probability of membership and success in a group.* Cambridge, Mass.: Harvard Graduate School of Education, Harvard Studies in Career Development, No. 6, 1957.

The Measurement of Environments

RICHARD WOLF

1964

There is abundant evidence that many of the behavioral differences we find in test performance are largely the result of differences in the environments in which individuals have lived rather than of inherent differences in individuals themselves. This finding has been demonstrated rather spectacularly in studies by Lee (12) and Kirk (11), and most recently in the work of J. W. B. Douglas in England (5). Hunt (8) and Bloom (3) have each summarized the results of a number of such studies. However, despite this accumulation of evidence, we have persisted in our view of testing in essentially individualistic terms. That is, the individual is still considered an "X" to be solved, and the environment in which the individual has lived is considered as but one source of error which can be handled by appropriate weighting of test results or some other procedure. This view of testing is reflected in Buros' *Mental Measurements Yearbook,* which contains descriptions and reviews of thousands of instruments for the measurement of individual characteristics, but very few for the measurement of environments.

This is indeed an unfortunate state of affairs. All theories of learning and behavior make provision for the influence of the environment on the development of human characteristics, but, as noted above, we have not had a corresponding emphasis in our measurement procedures. I would also submit that we have rarely attempted to systematically relate individual test data to environmental data in ways that are designed to increase our understanding of the interactive process between the individual and the environment.

To be sure, we do have some environmental measures. However, the number of instruments designed to measure characteristics of the environment is quite small when compared with the number of instruments designed to measure characteristics of the individual. Also, those environmental measures that are available are usually limited to general measures of social status or economic well-being. However, it would seem that just as a

491

general measure of intelligence or IQ has obscured many important differences among individuals, so a general index of social status or economic well-being has obscured many very important differences among environments. The work of Kahl (9), for example, has been quite revealing in its findings of some of the differences that are to be found *within* a given social class. There is, however, an even more basic difficulty in the use of a general index of social status or economic well-being to characterize an environment. Such indices usually represent a summation of a number of symptoms or surface characteristics of an environment and, as such, give little information about the specific ways in which environmental factors might affect the development of specific behavioral characteristics. This point was emphasized by Bayley (2) in her 1956 address, and was one of the central themes in Anastasi's paper, "Heredity, Environment, and the Question 'How?' " (1).

In our work, we have attempted to follow some of the guidelines for environmental research suggested by Anastasi, Bayley, Bloom, and others. In doing so, we have utilized a conception of the environment that is different from that used in the development of previous environmental measures in four ways:

1) Instead of viewing an environment as a single entity, we have postulated that a single physical environment may be made up of a number of sub-environments, with each sub-environment operating to influence the development of a specific characteristic. For purposes of measurement, we would conceive of an environment for the development of stature, another environment for the development of general intelligence, another for the development of independence, and so forth. Thus, for us, the problem of measuring an environment was reduced to the identification and measurement of those aspects of the total environment that were likely to be related to the development of selected specific characteristics.

2) Rather than measuring some of the more surface manifestations or symptoms of an environment, we have been interested in measuring environmental variables that we have hypothesized would be likely to *directly* influence the development of specific characteristics. This departure from some of the more conventional approaches has, in the case of measuring the home environment, for example, resulted in our investigating what parents *do* in their interactions with their children rather than what parents are in terms of status level of father's occupation, type of dwelling, source of income, and so forth.

3) We have attempted to summarize and treat environmental data through the use of psychometric procedures. Instead of isolating any particular environmental variable that might be related to a particular characteristic, we have attempted to sample a variety of the processes and conditions in an environment that were hypothesized to be related to a characteristic, and to summarize these in describing an environment. This is essentially the same procedure we follow in testing. That is, we would no sooner describe a student's performance in a certain subject by his response to a single test item than we would describe an environment on the basis of a single feature of that environment. We have felt, in other words, that a summarization of a number of variables is as important in describing an environment as a number of test items is in describing a student's competence in a subject.

4) We have attempted to systematically relate measurements of the environment to measurements of the individual. This has been an extremely important feature of our work. A number of investigators have developed environmental instruments that attempt to measure selected aspects of an environment, but have not related environmental data to individual test data. In our work, the importance of systematically relating the two kinds of data can be indicated by noting that one of the criteria for the validation of our environmental measures has been individual measures of the characteristic under study.

To summarize briefly, our approach to the measurement of environments has been characterized by conceiving of specific environments for the development of particular characteristics, attempting to measure environmental variables that were hypothesized to be directly related to the development of particular characteristics, summarizing and treating environmental data through the use of psychometric procedures, and relating environmental measurements to individual measurements. The remainder of this paper will be devoted to describing the development of two environmental measures based on the above ideas and presenting some of the results we have obtained.

While environmental influences may range from the most immediate social interaction to the most remote cultural forces, we chose the home as the physical environment for our study. The reason for this was our assumption that the home produces the first, and perhaps most insistent, influences on the development of the characteristics we were concerned with—general intelligence and academic achievement.

The first step in developing our environmental measures was to compile a list of the conditions and processes in the environment that theory and previous research indicated were likely to influence the development of general intelligence and/or academic achievement. The areas from which such variables were drawn included child development, learning theory, motivation, and psychometry. Special efforts were made to select variables that were as close as possible to being environmental counterparts of the components of the individual characteristics. The environmental variables that were identified as likely to be related to academic achievement were: the climate created for achievement motivation; the opportunities provided for verbal development; the nature and amount of assistance provided in overcoming academic difficulties; the activity level of the significant individuals in the environment; the level of intellectuality in the environment; and the kinds of work habits that are expected of the individual. Environmental variables identified as likely to be related to general intelligence were: the stimulation provided for intellectual growth; the opportunities provided for, and emphasis on, verbal development; and the provision for general types of learning in a variety of situations.

No claim is made that these two lists of variables exhaust the range of conditions in the home that can influence the development of academic achievement and general intelligence. Rather, they are viewed as a sample of environmental conditions that were hypothesized to be related to the development of these characteristics.

There are two notable features about these two lists of environmental variables. First, there is a considerable overlap between the two lists, which is largely a reflection of the overlap between the two characteristics, as has been pointed out by Kelley (10) and Coleman and Cureton (4). Second, the variables were stated in quite general terms. This lack of specificity made it necessary to define each environmental variable in an operational form for purposes of measurement. Thus, for each variable, we developed a list of process characteristics consisting of specific behaviors of parents and others in the home that were likely to be related to general intelligence, academic achievement, or both.

An illustration or two is perhaps in order. One of the variables hypothesized to influence the development of academic achievement was the climate in the home for achievement motivation. The specific process characteristics that were defined as comprising this variable were: the parental aspirations for the child's education; the parents' own aspirations; parental concern for academic achievement; the social press in the home for academic achievement; the rewards accorded academic accomplishments; parental knowledge of the educational progress of the child; and the preparations made for the attainment of educational goals. The breakdown of each environmental variable into specific measurable characteristics was, in each case, based on relevant theory and previous research. In a similar way, the variable termed "opportunities provided for verbal development"—one of the three variables hypothesized as comprising the environment for the development of general intelligence—was analyzed into the following process characteristics: the emphasis on use of language in a variety of situations; the opportunities provided for enlarging vocabulary; parental emphasis on correctness of usage; and the quality of language models available.

Once the process characteristics comprising each environmental variable were specified, it was necessary to develop a set of procedures for gathering evidence about the strength of each characteristic. The procedure finally settled upon involved the use of an extended interview with the mother (and sometimes both parents) in the home without the child being present, and the use of a set of rating scales. Questions were developed to elicit information about the presence and strength of each process characteristic. These questions were then organized into an interview schedule. At the same time, a series of rating scales was constructed. These scales were used to obtain ratings for each of the process characteristics.

Once the interview schedule was developed, it was pilot-tested in a small sample of homes. On the basis of preliminary findings, the interview schedule was revised and retested. This time it was found that enough information could be obtained in an interview lasting about an hour and a half and consisting of 63 questions. The information that was obtained was used in rating the 13 process characteristics comprising the instrument measuring the environment for general intelligence, and the 21 process characteristics that comprised the instrument measuring the environment for academic achievement.

It was noted earlier that the focus of our investigation was what parents did rather than what parents were in terms of status, economic well-being, or some other demographic variable. The questions in the interview schedule were carefully designed to elicit information about what parents actually did insofar as general intelligence and academic achievement were concerned.

One process characteristic which was measured, for example, was the parents' educational aspirations for the child. In the course of the interview, the parents were asked how much education they wished their child to have, how much education they actually expected their child to receive, and the minimum amount of education they felt their child must have. In response to these questions, a number of parents indicated that they hoped their child would receive a college education. Later in the interview, the topic was brought up again, and parents who had indicated that they hoped their child would go on to college were queried as to what plans had been made to finance a college education. The answers to this latter question were most illuminating in differentiating a seemingly homogeneous group —parents who hoped that their child would have a college education. The responses ranged from the total absence of any plan for financing a college education to the most elaborate of plans. At the high end of the scale were several parents who had already established trust funds earmarked for their children's college expenses. It may be noted that parents who rated high on the planning for the attainment of educational goals were also the ones who indicated that education was frequently discussed in the home, and that the child was aware of the educational plans that had been made.

In the main study we selected a sample of 60 homes from a medium-sized Midwestern community comprised of urban, suburban, and rural areas. Preliminary information was collected on all 1,062 fifth-grade students in the school system. On the basis of student descriptions of the father's occupation, social class ratings were obtained and a stratified random sample of homes was selected for study. The number of cases drawn from each social class grouping was proportional to the number of male adults in each grouping in the United States population according to Department of Labor data.

Contact was made with each of the selected homes and an interview with the mother was requested. In those cases in which the mother was unwilling or unable to participate, an alternate home was selected. The interviews were conducted in the home with the mother when the child was not present. To establish rapport, the mothers were assured at the outset of the interview that all information would be treated confidentially and that the school would receive only group results and not individual reports.

On the basis of the information collected during the course of the interviews, each home was rated on each of the process characteristics comprising the two instruments. For each environmental measure, all homes were rated on one process characteristic, then on another, and so forth. The process characteristics in each instrument were averaged to obtain the environmental variable ratings. These ratings were, in turn, combined to obtain the two total environmental ratings—one for the environment for academic achievement and one for the environment for intelligence. Thus, it was possible to conduct two separate investigations based on the same interview material.

At a later time, achievement test scores on the Metropolitan Achievement Tests and intelligence test scores on the Henmon-Nelson Test of Mental Ability were obtained from school files for the 60 fifth-graders in the homes selected for study. The environmental data and the test data were then systematically related.

A full discussion of the results of our work is unfortunately beyond the bounds of this paper. However, the major findings can be presented and some implications for further research as well as educational practice can be tentatively drawn. The first major finding concerns the relationship between the total rating for the intellectual environment and measured general intelligence. The correlation between these two variables was +.69. This can be contrasted with the correlation between social status and measured general intelligence which has been found to lie between +.20 and +.40. Accepting the correlation of +.40 as the correct estimate of the relationship between social status and intelligence, it would seem that the newer approach to the measurement of the environment accounts for about three times as much of the variance in general intelligence as a measure of social status.

The second major finding in our work concerns the relationship between the total rating of the environment for the development of academic achievement and achievement test data. The correlation between the total environmental rating and the total achievement battery score was +.80. Again, this may be contrasted with the correlation between social status and academic achievement which has been found to be of the order of +.50. In terms of the proportion of variance accounted for, the newer approach to the measurement of the environment would seem to account for at least two and one-half times as much of the variance in total academic achievement as a measure of social status. Taken together, the two correlations between the new environmental measures and intelligence and academic achievement reflect a new level of relationship between measures of the environment and measures of individual characteristics.

This new order of relationship can have a number of important implications for theory, research, and practice. The findings would suggest that the conception of a single physical environment as consisting of a number of sub-environments for the development and maintenance of specific characteristics is a powerful one indeed and, if fully developed, could greatly enhance our understanding of the interactive process between the individual and the environment.

The correlations between the over-all environmental rating and specific achievement subtest scores ranged from +.55 for arithmetic computation to +.77 for word knowledge. The six subtests ranked in decreasing order of their correlation with the over-all environmental rating were: word knowledge; reading; language; arithmetic problem solving and concepts;

word discrimination; and arithmetic computation. This ordering of the various subtest score correlations with the total environmental rating might well have been anticipated. The influence of the environment on academic achievement could be expected to be greatest in the language area because much of the basic socialization of the child is usually accomplished through the medium of language and, in our culture, this responsibility rests pretty clearly in the home. Thus, the fact that the three highest correlations with the total environmental rating were word knowledge, reading, and language might well have been expected. Similarly, the one individual characteristic in which the responsibility for development rests most clearly with the school is arithmetic computation. Again, the fact that arithmetic computation had the lowest correlation with the over-all environmental rating might also have been anticipated. It should be noted that this ordering of the correlations between the achievement subtest scores and the total environmental rating helps to establish the construct validity of the two instruments as much as do the correlations with over-all academic achievement and with general intelligence.

It was mentioned earlier that the correlation between the over-all rating for the environment for the development of academic achievement and the total achievement battery score was $+.80$. This represents a high level of relationship and can be considered to be quite sufficient for purposes of prediction. That is, a measure of what parents *do* in the home can be used to predict school achievement with a fairly high degree of accuracy. In actual practice, however, the results of intelligence tests are often used as the basis for making decisions about the placement and educational treatment of students. This fact prompted us to find out what happened when intelligence and environmental data were combined to predict academic achievement. This involved the computation of the multiple correlation between IQ and the over-all environmental rating for academic achievement with the total achievement battery score. The multiple correlation thus obtained was $+.87$. This represents an extremely high level of relationship. In fact, this is almost the upper limit for such a correlation when one takes into consideration the reliability of the various instruments. Statistically speaking, the amount of variance in academic achievement accounted for by intelligence test scores alone was 58 per cent ($r = +.76$). When a measure of the environment is added, the amount of variance in academic achievement accounted for rises to 76 per cent. Thus, the addition of a measure of the environment greatly enhances the estimation of academic achievement.

Since the studies described here represent the application of a psychometric approach to the measurement of environments, it is customary to report some technical data about the instruments. The reliabilities of the two instruments were estimated through an analysis of variance procedure suggested by Hoyt (7). The reliability estimates obtained through use of this procedure were .89 for the measure of the environment for the development of intelligence, and .95 for the measure of the environment for the development of academic achievement.

Validity data about the two environmental measures inhere largely in the correlations with the measured individual characteristics—general intelligence and academic achievement. Additional evidence about the validity of the measure of the intellectual environment was obtained through a double cross-validation. This procedure was proposed by Mosier (13) and is designed to furnish evidence about the stability of results based on a single testing. It involves the random division of the total sample into two subsamples, computation of regression weights for each subsample separately, and the application of each set of regression weights to the other subsample for prediction of the criterion. In our study, the resulting correlations for the two subsamples were +.663 and +.664. These are extremely close to the correlation of +.690 for the total sample and, as such, tend to fortify the original findings.

There are a number of additional findings but, unfortunately, these will have to wait until a fuller report of our work is prepared. However, with even the sketchy outline presented, some generalizations and implications can be drawn. The first generalization we would offer is that the conception of the environment upon which the present instruments were based does indeed seem to be a fruitful one for measuring and analyzing environments. The high correlations between the environmental measures and the specific characteristics selected for study furnish direct support for this generalization. However, we do not regard our list of environmental variables as by any means complete. It is hoped that further research will result in the identification of other environmental variables, which can be added to, or even replace, some of our variables. This will have to be determined at some future date. The point that we would emphasize is that research on the measurement of environments be directed towards the identification and measurement of ongoing environmental processes in relation to specific human characteristics. It would seem to us that environments for the development and maintenance of such characteristics as dependence, aggression, dogmatism, and others could be delineated and measured and systematically related to measures of the particular characteristic. Such research endeavors could greatly enhance our understanding of the development of many human characteristics.

A second generalization which emerges from our work concerns the relationship between the environment and intelligence and academic achievement. Much of our work gives quantitative support to the ideas of the effect of experience on intelligence and achievement put forth by Hebb (6), Hunt (8), and others. The levels of relationship between the measures of the environment and of intelligence and achievement are significantly higher than those found in previous studies that used social status or some other general index as a measure of the nature and quality of the environment. Moreover, these new levels of relationship seem to be quite in line with the expectations of the theoreticians. It is again hoped that further research will be undertaken to test these findings.

If additional research does confirm these findings, then it would seem that there are a number of implications for educational practice. One obvious implication would involve the development of new curricula designed to help overcome identified environmental deficiencies among students. Useful information about the ingredients for programs of compensatory education could be obtained from careful examination of the environmental measures. The reason for this is that the environmental process variables identified for study are, by and large, educationally malleable ones. That is, the variables represent environmental processes that can be manipulated in an educational situation. For example, one of the process characteristics in the measure of the intellectual environment was the opportunity provided for learning outside the home (excluding the school). If the homes students come from are found to rate low in this characteristic, it would seem that the school might well undertake to furnish a number of experiences in this area. An extensive program of field trips, for example, could be undertaken to overcome this deficiency. Similarly, if the homes students come from are found to be deficient in according rewards for academic achievement, the school could undertake to develop a greater system of rewards for such accomplishments and, perhaps, begin to work in concert with the home in insuring that academic achievement is acknowledged and rewarded. The point here is that the measure of environmental processes rather than status characteristics can furnish information that can be of direct service in the planning and conduct of educational programs.

It is rather fortunate that the framework for educational programs designed to overcome environmental deficiencies already exists at the elementary school level. The existence of self-contained classrooms and the recent development of an ungraded primary system could greatly facilitate compensatory educational programs. Even the traditional parent-teacher conference can be of great assistance in educational programs designed to overcome environmental deficiencies. As currently used, the parent-teacher conference serves mainly to inform parents of the child's progress in school. It seems possible that this function could be easily expanded to include the collection of certain standard information about the home environment. Thus, environmental data could be easily gathered and serve as a basis for planning programs of instruction.

There are a number of other practical uses for environmental data which could be suggested. However, the most tantalizing problems are probably the theoretical ones. For example, how stable is the environment or, more importantly, what are the conditions that make for stability in an environment? Also, how can one assess the variety of environments affecting the child as he grows older? What are the points when environmental intervention will have the greatest likelihood for success? These are thorny problems, and we do not have the answers. However, we do believe we have a methodology that can be of service in attacking these questions. Essentially, this methodology involves the application of our measurement procedures to the study of the environment and consists of four steps.

The first step entails the definition of an environment for the development of a specific characteristic. This construct is drawn largely from the relevant theory concerning the development of a particular characteristic. The second step involves the identification of the specific environmental conditions and processes that are likely to directly affect the development of the characteristic. Again, this step involves the extensive use of theory coupled with previous research concerning the development of the characteristic under study. The third step consists of the collection of evidence about the various environmental processes. In our work, we made use of an interview and a series of rating scales. However, there are a number of additional ways to gather such evidence. The work of Pace and Stern (14) suggests that the use of participant observers can furnish important information about an environment. Observational procedures can also be utilized. It would seem that many of the procedures that have been developed to measure individual characteristics can be adapted and applied to the measurement of environments. The fourth step in measuring an environment consists of treating environmental data through the use of psychometric procedures, and systematically relating data about the individual to data about the environment. This is an extremely important step since it is only through this process that environmental information can give full meaning to data about individual characteristics.

In addition to the four steps listed above, the same technical considerations about reliability and validity that we are concerned with in the development of tests of individual characteristics must be dealt with. Again, our psychometric procedures can be utilized to gain answers to these technical questions.

It is not necessary to follow the four steps in the order listed above and study the environment in relation to one characteristic, then another, and so forth. A number of environments and individual characteristics can, and perhaps should, be studied simultaneously. It would seem that factor analysis, which has proven so powerful in the identification of the major dimensions on which individuals differ, may prove to be as powerful in defining the dimensions on which environments differ.

In closing, I invite you to give consideration to the prospects for environmental research. I would submit that as we make use of the conception that a single physical environment may consist of a number of sub-environments and seek to develop measurement procedures that capture the operant social and psychological conditions and processes in an environment, we should be able to greatly increase our understanding of the process of how individual characteristics are developed and maintained. Only when we have such understanding can we develop more adequate theories of behavior, and only then can we determine how particular characteristics can be maintained or altered.

REFERENCES

1. Anastasi, Anne. Heredity, environment, and the question "how?" *Psychological Review,* 1958, 65, 197–208.
2. Bayley, Nancy. Changing concepts of intelligence: a new look at the curve of intelligence. *Proceedings of the 1956 Invitational Conference on Testing Problems.* Princeton, N.J.: Educational Testing Service, 1957. Pp. 11–25.
3. Bloom, B. *Stability and change in human characteristics.* New York: Wiley, 1964.
4. Coleman, W., & Cureton, E. E. Intelligence and achievement: the "jangle fallacy" again. *Educational and Psychological Measurement,* 1954, 14, 347–351.
5. Douglas, J. W. B. *The home and the school.* London: MacGibbon & Kee, 1964.
6. Hebb, D. O. *The organization of behavior: a neuropsychological theory.* New York: Wiley, 1949.

7. Hoyt, C. Test reliability estimated by analysis of variance. *Psychometrika*, 1941, 6, 153–160.
8. Hunt, J. McV. *Intelligence and experience*. New York: Ronald Press, 1961.
9. Kahl, J. A. Educational and occupational aspirations of "common man" boys. *Harvard Educational Review*, 1953, 23, 186–203.
10. Kelley, T. L. *Interpretation of educational measurements*. Yonkers, N.Y.: World Book, 1927.
11. Kirk, S. A. *Early education of the mentally retarded*. Urbana, Ill.: Univer. of Illinois Press, 1958.
12. Lee, E. S. Negro intelligence and selective migration: a Philadelphia test of the Klineberg hypothesis. *American Sociological Review*, 1951, 16, 227–233.
13. Mosier, C. I. The need and means of cross-validation. I. Problems and designs of cross-validation. *Educational and Psychological Measurement*, 1951, 11, 5–11.
14. Pace, C. R. Psychological differences between college students. Paper read before the Annual Meeting of the Western Personnel Institute, Pasadena, Calif., November 1959.

11 · PERSONALITY TESTING

THE REASON for grouping papers on personality testing into a single chapter in Part III, which covers special problems in the assessment of individual differences, is twofold. First, the measurement of personality traits has received relatively little attention in the Invitational Conference. Because of the primary focus on the educational use of tests, achievement tests and group tests of academic aptitude have clearly predominated in the papers presented over the 25-year period. Individual intelligence tests, tests of organic impairment, and tests that detect personality disorders are of more interest to the clinical than to the educational psychologist; and measures of attitudes and of interpersonal traits are of more interest to the social psychologist and the personality theorist. Thus it is only as the scope of the Invitational Conference has expanded to cover the measurement of individual differences in all contexts that discussions of personality testing have been introduced. A second reason for their present location is that the specific papers included in this chapter deal chiefly with special problems encountered in testing personality characteristics, over and above the general problems of test construction and use presented by all types of tests. Finally, it should be noted that additional papers on the assessment of personality have been included in Chapter 12, since they pertain to nontest techniques.

One of the innovations introduced at the 1947 Invitational Conference was the scheduling of a session on projective techniques. This was the first time the Invitational Conference had included a session dealing with personality tests of any kind. Hanfmann's paper, presented at that session, describes two of the tests employed in the assessment program of the Office of Strategic Services (OSS) during World War II. These tests, "sentence completion" and "improvisations," illustrate a relatively subjective, clinical application of projective techniques. Although both are cited by Hanfmann as projective tests, the improvisations test may also be classified with the situational tests that played such a large part in the OSS testing program. In such tests, the behavior sample obtained is somewhat more elaborate and resembles criterion situations more closely than is true of projective tests.

In his 1951 paper, MacKinnon gives a brief account of the beginnings of the Institute of Personality Assessment and Research (IPAR), established at the University of California, Berkeley, along the lines of the OSS assessment program. MacKinnon describes several of the instruments developed in the IPAR program and discusses their application to the prediction of academic achievement and personal effectiveness of graduate students. Many of these instruments have subsequently been utilized in IPAR research on creative persons in a number of fields.

In a special invited address, McClelland provides an informal and lively discussion of the measurement of achievement motivation. Following a quick look at the types of procedures psychologists have used to assess individual differences in human motivation, he describes the technique developed in his own research, namely, the content analysis of fantasy behavior, as evoked by an adaptation of the Thematic Apperception Test. The scoring system was empirically derived through a comparison of the responses obtained under experimentally aroused achievement motivation with those obtained under neutral, control conditions. Results are cited on the relation between achievement motivation as measured by this technique and a number of other behavioral variables. McClelland gave this talk in 1952, when the ideas and procedures that later developed into his long-term research program on achievement motivation were beginning to take shape.

Crutchfield describes a technique for measuring individual differences in conformity to group judgment. His procedure may be characterized as an objective and controlled adaptation of a situational type of test. In any test involving the interaction of the examinee with a group, an uncontrolled source of variation is the behavior of the other members of the group. Through simulated group responses, conveyed to each subject on a response panel, Crutchfield exposes each subject to identical, pre-established group pressure. The extent to which the individual yields to such group pressure in his perceptual, logical, and attitudinal responses can thus be measured under standardized conditions. After describing the procedure, Crutchfield reports the results of studies in which it was employed to investigate the nature and correlates of conformity behavior.

Loevinger offers a novel and provocative interpretation of scores on self-report inventories. She proposes a developmental hypothesis of self conceptualization that unifies and gives meaning to previously unrelated findings from several studies. Reflecting the increasing tendency to regard responses on self-report personality inventories as indicators of the individual's self concept, Loevinger outlines three stages in the development of a mature self concept: the individual begins with no capacity to conceptualize himself, progresses through a stereotyped and socially acceptable self concept, and eventually attains a differentiated and realistic self concept.

Messick's paper is a comprehensive and critical survey of personality measurement. While specifically oriented toward the use of personality tests in the prediction of college performance, its principal points apply to other contexts as well. Messick first presents an evaluation of available personality tests in terms of psychometric standards. He identifies three major approaches to personality measurement—self-report questionnaires, behavior ratings, and objective performance tests—and evaluates each in terms of reliability, construct validity, predictive validity, and controls for faking and response styles. Messick then turns to certain questions of values raised when personality measures are used for practical decisions. In this connection, he considers the intrinsic validity of criterion measures, the reduction of diversity resulting from selection procedures, and other questions pertaining to the ultimate goals of the selection process. Taken together with the other papers in this chapter, Messick's survey gives some idea of the wide variety of techniques that have been developed in the attempt to test personality traits. It also suggests that, despite many ingenious and promising approaches, few techniques are ready for operational use.

Projective Techniques in the Assessment Program of the Office of Strategic Services

EUGENIA HANFMANN

1947

Before attempting to describe and evaluate the use of projective techniques in the wartime assessment program of the Office of Strategic Services, it may be well to say a few words about the nature and goals of this program. The assessment, which, from a certain date on, was undergone by all candidates for service overseas, was designed to give as complete a picture of the candidate's personality as could be obtained in the course of three days of intensive testing and observation in the maximally revealing situation of group life and group work. The goal of obtaining a picture of *total personality*, rather than merely of any of its particular aspects, was determined by both theoretical and practical considerations. Even when the nature of the performance required of the given candidate in his assignment was well known, we felt that no reliable estimate of his chances for success could be made merely on the basis of his performance in a number of pertinent tests, without a knowledge of the underlying patterns of his personal attitudes and strivings. Actually, however, the nature of the performances required by many of the OSS assignments was very imperfectly known to us, or for that matter to anybody. Moreover, the candidates, once overseas, were only too frequently given duties totally different from those for which they had been recruited. This situation limited the usefulness of our tests of special abilities and made it particularly important to evaluate the candidate's general effectiveness in situations involving novelty, frustration, and stress, and necessitating interactions with a wide variety of people. For such an evaluation, a conception of the candidate's personality as a whole was indispensable. It must be emphasized, however, that in the assessment program, as in any practically oriented program, the understanding of the individual personality was not a goal in itself, but merely a means for making broader and more reliable predictions of his performance.

These goals of assessment were implemented through a variety of techniques which cannot be described in detail at this time. I may say only that an extensive and varied use of situational, lifelike tests was an outstanding feature of the program, and that the information and impressions obtained in a clinical interview were given a central position in the interpretation of the rest of the data. Here we are concerned with the questions: how did the projective techniques fit into this program, and how much did they contribute to the realization of the goals of assessment? In attempting to answer these questions I cannot, unfortunately, draw on any results of systematic investigations concerning the diagnostic and predictive value of the various methods used in assessment. The program was first and foremost a service program, and although some research was carried on in the assessment centers, the limited time allotted to it prevented us from doing all that we would have wanted to do. Yet the remarks that follow represent more than mere expression of individual opinion. Rather, they are based on a fairly general consensus of the assessment staff members which resulted from their accumulated experience with various techniques. The relative contributions of these techniques were discussed by the group at intervals, and changes, omissions, and additions were decided upon. The opinions presented here are based on the experiences on *one* of the OSS assessment centers. The staffs of the other centers, working under different conditions and with different programs, may have arrived at different conclusions.

At the assessment center with which I was connected, various projective techniques were tried out, including variations of the Thematic Apperception Test and of the Rorschach, but many of them were abandoned because the gains obtained from them were felt not to be in proportion to the time expended. Their use was subsequently limited to cases in which the evaluation of personality presented particular difficulties. The main reason for this limited usefulness of the projective techniques aiming at a revelation of the deeper personality levels lies in the practical nature of the goals of the assessment. The material obtained through these techniques was often so far removed from the level of manifest behavior with which we were ultimately concerned in our predictions that the two kinds of data could not always be meaningfully synthesized without a much more prolonged and intensive study. Such synthesis would have been our ideal, since without it one could hardly expect to obtain a completely adequate picture of the total personality. However, when this synthesis could not be achieved and we were faced with a discrepancy between the trends uncovered by the projective methods and the trends consistently revealed in the person's past and present behavior, we considered the behavioral evidence as more pertinent for a prediction of his future behavior and performance. This situation points up not so much a weakness of the projective techniques as such, as our deficient knowledge of the laws of interaction of the different personality levels. Given data from various levels, we may be able to synthesize them through a complex and laborious interpretative process. We have, however, no simple methods at our disposal enabling us to conclude without fail from manifest behavior to underlying trends, and are perhaps even less able to "predict" from a knowledge of a person's hidden motives and conflicts the specific ways in which he expresses these tendencies or resolves these conflicts on the level of manifest behavior. An explicit formulation of interrelationships that exist between processes on different levels that would permit such "predictions" from one level to another is a timely task for research.

We did not, however, abandon *all* projective techniques as a source of information. Two of the simpler and less time-consuming ones not only survived, but were valued increasingly highly by the staff. These two were *sentence completion* and *improvisations* (a name that we used for a variation of psychodrama). A brief description of these techniques and an evaluation of their contributions may serve to point out the features which make some projective techniques well adapted for the practical purposes of assessment.

In the sentence-completion test, the subject is asked to complete, in writing, a number of incomplete sentences—a task that may be advantageously presented as a speed test. Some of the sentences we used were in the third person, such as "Charlie was happiest when. . . ."; others in the first person, e.g., "I admire. . . ." In some sentences the situation was set, and a reaction to it was required: "When Dick failed the course, he. . . ."; in another type, the emotional reaction was stated and the situation producing it had to be supplied: "Nothing made Harry more furious than. . . ." The combination of these devices permits one to structure the situation for the subject to a considerable extent and practically to ask him questions of any degree of specificity the examiner may desire. In the assessment program, the sentences were selected with a view to providing information about the subject's attitudes toward his past and his future, toward his family and other people (equals, superiors, and inferiors), as well as information about his main motives and goals, his response to frustration, his energy level, and the nature of his prevalent emotions and feelings and of the situations that aroused them.

In going over the completed sentences, the interpreter sorted out items pertaining to the same topic and, after inspecting them as well as the total record, wrote a brief interpretative personality sketch of the subject. This sketch (in conjunction with other material) served as a preview of the candidate for the staff member who was later to interview him; and it proved extremely useful in helping the interviewer to select for investigation crucial areas productive of important material. Data obtained in the interview could be then compared and synthesized with those obtained in the sentence completions; this process might be considered as an informal and unsystematic validation of the projective technique against the data of the interview.

The results of this impressionistic "validation" may be summarized as follows. While the particular content of the single sentence completions was by no means always duplicated or confirmed in the interview, by and large the personality sketch based on sentence completion showed a remarkable congruence with the picture obtained by the interviewer. Radical discrepancy of the two was the exception rather than the rule. It is true that some of the tendencies apparent in the sentence completion were either denied by the subject in the interview, or appeared in a different form, and that some of his manifest modes of adjustment did not come to the fore in the projective material. But in many essential points the pictures were often practically identical, and the disparate data frequently complemented each other and could be brought together into a meaningful whole with a minimum amount of interpretation. Thus, the material of the sentence completions served both to verify and to enrich the conclusions drawn from the more direct expressions of attitudes with much greater ease and plausibility than did the results of some other projective techniques.

The explanation that suggests itself for this greater immediate effectiveness of the sentence-completion test is the intermediate level of depth on which it seems to operate. Possibly because of the verbal nature of the material and of its greater degree of structuredness, the test seems to elicit expressions of attitudes readily available to consciousness (which, presupposing complete frankness, might be obtained in an interview) along with some less easily accessible material. The use of the first person in the formulation of part of the sentences may have enhanced this "questionnaire" effect. This interpretation is to some extent borne out by the fact that many subjects easily saw through the disguise of the test; others, while not explicitly aware of its nature, responded quite naturally to the interviewer's introducing some of their completions as evidence of their own attitudes and frequently accepted this evidence. If the sentence-completion test can be considered as a cross between a questionnaire and a projective technique, it is understandable that its results can be easily integrated with the manifest picture of personality.

The second technique that proved extremely valuable in assessment can also be considered as partaking of the nature both of projective and of expressive tests. Even to a greater extent than the sentence completion, the modified form of psychodrama came to be considered by the staff as a unique and indispensable feature of the assessment program. While the sentence completion, given at the very beginning of the assessment period, provided a preliminary orientation about the candidate and helped to formulate questions to be asked in the interview, the "improvisations" were scheduled late in the program and served to answer questions that still remained unanswered; they helped to clarify, confirm, and, if necessary, modify the conceptions of the candidate's personality that had been developed up to that point. In this way the improvisations often proved crucial in arriving at a final decision about the candidate.

The improvisations consisted of having two candidates enact an interpersonal situation the nature of which was briefly indicated to them. The performance was witnessed by the rest of the candidates and the staff. The situation as described to the subjects might involve competition, or an urgent problem to be solved together, or attempts to obtain something from the partner, or the problem of assigning blame, and so on. The roles into which the actors were cast might imply equality (two business partners) or difference of status (officer and private). In general, the nature of most of the situations contained some potentiality for producing a conflict of interests.

The improvisations did not assume their final shape and their role in the program until after some experimentation had taken place. Our experience has shown that a number of conditions have to be observed if this procedure is to give the maximum diagnostic yield. These conditions pertain to the attitude of the participants, to the choice and presentation of the situation, and to the utilization of the audience participation.

The task of "acting out" a certain situation is apt to be taken by the subjects as an invitation to *act,* to portray either realistically, or dramatically, or amusingly, the character (for example, a businessman, an artist) whom they feel they are supposed to "represent." For the procedure to be maximally revealing, it is absolutely essential to counteract this interpretation of the task as "acting" and to highlight in the performance, not the "role," but the actor himself. This we found can be best done by placing emphasis on the situation as such, and by introducing it as a *problem to be solved* by the subject in his own way, without any consideration of the likelihood that a "businessman" or an "artist" would behave in this way We had to tell the subjects again and again that we did not care how well they acted, that we did not want them to act, but merely to solve the problem presented by this particular interpersonal situation. The best results are achieved if the participants throw themselves into the situation and try to handle it to the best of their ability, much as they would in real life. This is the first condition essential for the success of improvisations.

The second set of conditions pertains to the selection of the situation to be enacted and to the way of presenting it to the subjects.

The improvisations are most productive of insights if the situation is pertinent to the personal patterns and problems of each individual subject. In our program, improvisations came at a time when we had already collected a large amount of data on the candidates and had tentatively located their assets and their weak areas, particularly in reference to their projected assignments. For example, one person might have excellent ideas, but might not be able to stand up to authority and to put his suggestions across; another one might appear too abrupt and authoritarian, which made us suspect that he might not be tactful enough to handle the natives of other countries successfully; a third one seemed prone to irritation, or to exaggerated guilt feelings; about a fourth one we had a hunch that he might be excellent in getting information from people, but we were not entirely certain of it.

With these questions and hypotheses in mind, we constructed situations for each candidate that were likely to give us pertinent evidence on the points involved. Since two (occasionally three) candidates were actors in each situation, we could also combine personalities in such a way that their interaction would be maximally significant and revealing, bringing together, say, a timid man and a bully. (Usually each candidate took part in two scenes, with two different partners.) The fact that the scenarios were made to order for the individual candidates gave improvisations a unique position among the other assessment techniques and was probably the main determinant of their great value in arriving at the final conclusions about the subjects.

In constructing the scenarios or "plots," we had also to consider whether the situation as initially depicted would be acceptable to the subject. Since we wanted his wholehearted participation, we had to refrain from placing him in a situation in which, he might feel, a person of his kind would never find himself. One could not, say, tell anybody who was basically honest, or at least assumed that he was, that he had committed a theft and was now being accused of it. This would only result in either overt or covert refusal to deal with the situation in earnest. It might, however, be possible to have the accusation sprung on the subject by the partner and to see whether his behavior would imply assumption of own guilt or of innocence. But no assumptions must be initially made about the subject that would prevent him from entering the situation.

This rule does not mean that one cannot place the subject into situations far removed from his sphere of life and from his social role; they may be entirely acceptable to him. However, in order to enable the subject to handle the situation with some resourcefulness, we felt that he should have some ammunition, some knowledge of objective factors, of the technicalities involved in the situation. We knew the professional backgrounds of our candidates, their hobbies, and their plans for the future, and in devising scenarios, we frequently chose situations from fields of activities fairly close to their own, if not identical with them. A student of social science might find himself in the role of a public-opinion expert whose conclusions are found to contradict those of another survey; a journalist in real life would be promoted to a novelist and find himself involved in an argument with a vituperative critic, and so on. Many of the situations used required no special knowledge and could be used to advantage with candidates of any background.

Fully as important as the choice of the situation is the way in which it is presented to the participants. The presentation must leave the situation completely unstructured with regard to the feelings of the participants and to the line of action they are going to take. When we started working with improvisations, we did not always follow this rule strictly. Let us take, for example, the story involving the high school teacher who had assigned to his students an essay on their "most unhappy experience" with their families. The scene enacted is the teacher's subsequent encounter with the school principal who had received numerous complaints from the students' parents. If, in instructing the principal, we tell him, "You are very upset about the situation and now you call the teacher to give him a talking-to," we overstructure the situation and make it not very productive. It is best presented in terms like the following: "This and that happened, this is the situation. You are going to see Mr. B about it. . . . Now, I do not know how you feel about this whole thing, but you just decided to talk to him about it." This leaves the person free to set any goal for himself and to use any line of approach: he may attack or accuse the teacher, be sympathetic with him, or require an explanation; he may solve the situation by firing the teacher, by making him promise to be more circumspect in the future, or by deciding to back him up in the conflict with the parents. All these variations should be left entirely to him.

A very good device both for leaving the situation unstructured and for making it realistic is to give separate instructions to the two participants. Each of them in turn would be sent out of the room, and the other given his part of the story. Then when they met, they would not at first know what was on the other person's mind. The two parts of the story would be brought together in the course of this encounter, and some surprises might be sprung on one or on both partners.

One of our favorite plots may help to illustrate the point. A person has left a car at his garage for a thorough check-up, with the understanding that he will pick it up next day at a quarter past twelve. The garageman is told (in absence of the customer) that he had everything done, except putting in oil, and that he went out for lunch planning to be back before 12:15 to finish the job. He came back at 12:10 and found the car gone. He had left the keys in the car. That is all he knows of the story. We had some subjects who at this point became really panicky about the possibility of the car having been stolen.

The owner of the car, in turn, is told that he arrived at the garage a little before the time, saw the car sitting there with the keys in the car, and, assuming that everything had been done, drove it away. Before long, the bearings were burnt out, and after getting the car to the nearest garage, he returns to talk to his garageman.

When the two meet, each one knows only part of the story, as would be true in real life; each one is eager to find out from the other what happened, and we have a chance to observe their response to this information. Their common task is to solve this situation in one way or another within the limited time of five to ten minutes, but their respective goals and techniques are in no way prejudiced by the instructions.

The last important aspect of our use of improvisations was the participation of the audience. The audience included the rest of the candidates, each of whom in the course of the session was also called upon to participate in the playlets. This naturally increased the amount of interest and involvement in the performance of others, and we utilized this interest for obtaining the reactions of the candidates to one another's performance. After each "act," the staff member in charge asked the audience what they thought about it, whether they felt that a given actor's behavior was natural to him, consistent with his behavior as they had observed it in the course of the three days they had spent with him. These questions usually elicited a vivid response. The acting, the "hamming," was immediately detected and criticized, and many relevant observations about the candidate's everyday behavior were made by the audience. The audience was also asked to appraise the solution of the problem: How would they themselves handle it? What were the weaknesses? Did this man give the other fellow a fair chance? Did he stand up for his own rights or opinions adequately? Did the two of them succeed in working out a real solution together? The actors themselves were drawn into the discussion and were given a chance to explain or defend their performance. Frequently their comments would make clear how they interpreted the originally ambiguous situation, what assumptions they made about the other person's motives, how they themselves felt about the situation, and what they were driving at in their attempted solutions. This lively exchange between the momentary actors and audience threw light on the personal characteristics and patterns of interactions of all the members of the assessed group and greatly amplified and enriched the material obtained in the improvisations.

A word of warning, however, is in order with regard to discussion. Its success depends almost entirely on the competence of the discussion leader; with incompetent guidance, discussion by audience may do more damage than good. Even though introducing improvisations as problems to be solved permits centering the discussion on the effectiveness of the performance rather than on the personality of the actor, still very central personal problems of the subjects may come up in the course of discussion. It requires a fine and quick judgment on the part of the leader to decide how far to go, or to let others go, with questions and comments, where to leave off, when to terminate the situation quickly with a joke in order to obtain the most information and at the same time keep up the group spirit of cheerfulness and spontaneity which is essential for improvisations. The leader who combines a serious purposive interest in understanding the psychological basis of the performance with a sense of balance, of timing, and with a "light touch" in handling the "dangerous" themes, can bring forth an extremely frank and productive discussion. In the assessment center, the improvisations were one of the highlights of the program. Most groups of candidates not merely enjoyed them as entertainment, but became seriously involved in the problems of human interaction that were brought up and frequently continued the discussion among themselves long after the end of the session.

A review of the conditions under which we found improvisations to be most revealing shows that they were calculated to keep the "role-playing" away from the sphere of purely imaginative productions and to make it reflect the person's everyday practical behavior in interpersonal situations. However, the improvisations yielded deeper insights into the personalities of our subjects than an observation of an equally brief episode in real life might be expected to give. This is due to the selection of the situations and partners with a view to highlighting the personal problems and interpersonal difficulties, and to the additional information provided by the discussion. The aspect of the personality that is brought into clear relief through improvisations is the individual style of interpersonal relationships, with more than a suggestion as to the mechanisms operative in producing this style.

In summary, both of the projective procedures that proved particularly valuable in the assessment aim at eliciting material that is closer to the level of manifest attitudes or behavior than is the material obtained with such methods as the Rorschach or the Thematic Apperception Test. They are similar to these more elaborate techniques in that they also demand an interpretative, dynamically oriented synthesis of the separate data and depend for their success on the acuity of the interpreter. While they do not exclude imaginative productions altogether, they do not seem to unearth materials from very deep strata of personality which are difficult of access. Within the limitations of the program this is an asset rather than a liability. Our experience seems to indicate that, for the purposes of assessment, it is better to describe the personality in terms of relatively manifest, well-stabilized patterns than to attempt to trace *all* the suppressed trends, of which these patterns are the ultimate synthesis and outcome.

Tests for the Measurement of
Personal Effectiveness

Donald W. MacKinnon

1951

By way of introduction, I should like to say a few words about the setting in which and the purposes for which the tests that I am about to describe were developed. I feel the necessity, however, of pointing out at the very beginning that these tests are still far from fully developed and, in most cases, to call them useful is more an expression of hope than a statement of fact.

In 1949, through a grant from the Rockefeller Foundation, the Institute of Personality Assessment and Research (IPAR) was established on the Berkeley campus of the University of California. The research of the Institute is directed to the discovery of the determinants and characteristics of personal effectiveness in our society, with special emphasis upon the effectiveness of persons in the arts, sciences, and professions. The subjects of our first two years' investigations have been male University graduate students about to receive their advanced degrees either in the natural or social sciences, or in medicine. Most intensively studied have been 80 graduate students drawn from 14 teaching departments. In the spring of 1950, 40 of these students were assessed, 10 at a time in weekend assessment programs running from Friday afternoon to Sunday after lunch. The other 40 were similarly assessed over weekends of the following fall and winter.

Criterion data have consisted of ratings given each subject by at least three of his instructors on the following variables: P, the candidate's Potential Success in his chosen field; O, his Originality as scholar or scientist; and S, his Soundness as a person. These ratings were given prior to assessment, but were not made known to the Institute's staff until after the last assessment had been completed and each staff member had rated each subject on 40 variables, including the criterion variables.

In addition to several tests of intellectual functions, our program of as-

518

sessment has included a variety of procedures that are germane to the topic of this panel.

Increasingly in recent years has the individual's perception of himself been urged as *the* key to an understanding of his behavior. To tap this dimension of personality, Harrison G. Gough has prepared an Adjective Check List, which, in use, has proved to be as ingenious as it is simple. Presented with a list of 284 adjectives arranged alphabetically, the subject is instructed to check those that he considers descriptive of himself. He checks as many or as few as he wishes.

The method of analysis has involved determination of those adjectives that *both* in the first (spring) sample *and* in the second (fall) sample have shown a significant differentiation between high and low subjects with respect to any rated or measured variable, e.g., Potential Success, Originality, Soundness, Spatial Aptitude, Likeableness, etc.

At the end of every assessment period, each member of the staff has checked an Adjective Check List for each of the assessees. Thus we have for each of our subjects not only a picture adjectively expressed of that aspect of his self-perception that he is willing to make public, but also a picture of his stimulus value. Applying the same sort of analysis to the adjectives checked by the staff we can discover our common perception of subjects who, in fact, are high or low on any measured or rated variable.

In addition, it is possible to derive a large number of rational scores from the adjectives checked either by the subjects for themselves, or by the staff for them, or from some combination of self- and staff-checks. For example, if the adjectives are classified as favorable, unfavorable, or neutral, a subject's checks can be analyzed to determine the relative favorableness or unfavorableness of his self-percept. Or an index of a subject's likeableness, as judged by the staff, can be derived from the ratio of the number of favorable adjectives to the number of both favorable and unfavorable adjectives checked on the staff's composite list for the subject, and so on.

It is not the findings we have obtained through the use of the Adjective Check List that I wish to stress, but rather its simplicity as a personality test and the promise which it holds.

In the attempt to develop tests of significant, nonintellectual functions, attention has long been given to measures of opinions, attitudes, sentiments, and beliefs. Working in this tradition we, too, collected a large pool of statements, to be answered by the subjects as true or false for themselves, which on empirical, intuitive, or theoretical grounds were considered to hold promise for the prediction of graduate achievement. The predictive efficiency of these face-relevant items was determined by comparing the responses of the more highly and less highly rated students in our first sample and repeating this procedure with our second sample.

An examination of the surviving items on the IPAR scale and the differentiating responses of the more highly and less highly rated subjects to them conveys the impression that the two groups differ with respect to at least the four following dimensions:

Tempo. The high-ranked subjects seem to lead a more consistent, stabilized existence. The tempo itself may be fast or slow, but it tends to show less variation. The tempo seems to be "internally determined." The low-ranked subjects show more variability. They are more influenced by group demands; they are more concerned with problems of pacing; and the tempo seems to be more "externally determined."

Self-confidence. The high-ranked subjects are more self-confident. They seem to have a more stable sense of trust in the world, and are basically more optimistic. Some of this may be reaction to their present success, but it appears to run deeper than this alone. The low-ranked subjects are more influenced by the vicissitudes of the day. Their mood depends on current achievements; they feel that luck plays a large part in success, and that good effort alone deserves to be rewarded. They are less secure, and seek assurance in fate, endeavor, etc. They are more easily swayed by others' opinions.

Time-perspective. The high-ranked subjects tend to project their goals into the future; they look ahead; they are concerned with the future use of present training. The low-ranked subjects are more concerned with immediate issues; their "learning set" is more for a present examination than for some application ten years hence.

Criticality. Both high- and low-ranked subjects criticize their graduate training, but on different grounds. The Highs feel that departmental standards are often too lax, that training is not thorough enough, etc. They tend to be problem-centered. The Lows, on the other hand, complain of disagreement among faculty members, of poor teaching, etc. They tend to be more personality-centered.

Promising as this scale appears, let me add the caution that in its present stage it can be considered as little more than a set of guides and suggestions for further, more systematic research.

In planning our researches it seemed not unlikely that differences in personal effectiveness might be related to differences in esthetic judgment and preference. Specifically, we wondered whether the esthetic preferences of our Highs were different from those of our Lows, and whether such differences bore any systematic relationship to expert artistic judgment. What was needed was a test consisting of stimulus material about which esthetic judgments could be made, and on which experts in art would differ from nonexperts in their preferences. The Welsh Figure Preference Test (5) seemed suitable for this purpose, and Frank Barron, using some of Welsh's original standardization data plus two new samples of artists, developed an Art Scale. The 400 figures of the test (ruled and freehand figures drawn on 3″ × 5″ cards) were given to 37 artists and art students with instructions to sort them into two groups, those "Liked" and those "Disliked." Their judgments of each figure were then compared with the judgments of 150 nonartists (75 women and 75 men) differing widely in age, education, occupation, and geographical location.

In this manner the 65-item Barron-Welsh Art Scale (2) was derived, consisting of 40 items disliked by artists significantly more often than by people in general (P less than .01), and 25 items liked significantly more often by artists (P less than .05). It is worthy of note that the figures *disliked* significantly more often by artists were generally simple, symmetrical, and rather obviously balanced, while the figures *liked* significantly more often by artists were highly complex, asymmetrical, and rather restless and moving in their general effect. The items were made to constitute a scale, a high score on which indicates artistic preferences.[1]

When the 65 items of the Art Scale, abstracted now from the total Figure Preference Test, were administered to the assessees in our first sample, scores on it were found to be bimodally distributed; so much so, in fact, that it was clear that two distinct groups were thus defined. When the 4 middle-most cases of the distribution were discarded, there was an interval of 20 points on the 65-unit scale which was not occupied by any case, 18 of the cases falling on each side of this interval.

That the figure preferences are not unrelated to other aspects of person-

---

[1] "When applied back to the original standardization groups, this 65-item scale separated the artists from the non-artists quite effectively. The mean score of the non-artists was 16.9, that of the artists 40.25. The critical ratio was 8.46, P less than .0001. Four of the 37 artists scored below the mean of the non-artists, while four of the 150 non-artists scored above the mean of the artists.

"The scale was then tested on two new groups, 30 artists and 30 non-artists, and again discriminated the groups effectively. The means of the cross-validation samples were 18.37 for the non-artists, and 39.07 for the artists. These values do not differ significantly from the comparable values in the original standardization groups. They do, however, differ significantly from one another (C.R. of 3.97, P less than .001). Four of the 30 artists scored below the mean of the 30 non-artists, while five of the non-artists scored above the mean of the artists. Eight artists and 22 non-artists scored below the mean of the total distribution. In a new sample of 80 non-artists, the reliability of the scale, as determined by correlating the odd-numbered items with the even-numbered, proved to be .96" (2).

ality is revealed by an analysis of the adjectives checked by the subjects in these two groups as descriptive of themselves. These are the adjectives differentiating, at the .05 level of significance, those who prefer simple, symmetrical figures from those who prefer complex and asymmetrical drawings.

Simple, Symmetrical	*Complex, Asymmetrical*
contented	gloomy
gentle	loud
conservative	unstable
unaffected	bitter
patient	cool
peaceable	dissatisfied
	pessimistic
	emotional
	irritable
	pleasure-seeking

A further difference between those who prefer the simple-symmetrical and those who favor the complex-asymmetrical was revealed in a Preferences for Paintings test, also developed and administered by Frank Barron (1).

In this test the subject is presented with 105 postcard-size reproductions in color of paintings by a large number of European artists. The paintings differ widely with respect to time and place of origin, style, and subject matter. The subject is shown the pictures one at a time and is asked to indicate the degree of his liking for each by placing it in one of four categories ranging from "Like Very Much" to "Like Least of All." The subject is asked to place twice as many pictures in each of the middle categories as in each of the extremes, thus approximating a normal distribution.

An item analysis of the Preferences for Paintings reveals that those who like the simple and symmetrical figures like best of all portraits, religious scenes, and landscapes, and like least of all abstractions, the radically experimental, the "unnatural," and the frankly sensual in paintings.

It is the other way around for those who on the Art Scale choose the complex and asymmetrical. Among paintings they prefer the products of various modern movements in art—Primitivism, Expressionism, Impressionism, Cubism—the radically experimental, the abstract, the primitive, and pictures that portray the commonplace and the sensual. They dislike religious themes in paintings, portraits of lords and ladies, and the simple representational.

Considering the striking congruences thus demonstrated to exist between figure preferences, preferences in painting, and the self-percept as revealed in self-checked adjectives, it looks as though the Art Scale is something more than a device for the measurement of artistic discrimination. It would appear to be an instrument capable of revealing the type of perceptual preferences that characterizes an individual, the one type preferring "what is stable, regular, balanced, predictable, clear-cut, traditional and following some general abstract principle, which in human affairs is personified as authority" (1), the other type favoring in perception "what is unstable, asymmetrical, unbalanced, whimsical, rebellious against tradition, and at times seemingly irrational, disordered and chaotic" (1).

Though the possession of one or the other of these types of perceptual preference would certainly have many consequences, it is interesting and reassuring to note that, in our investigation, the two types were observed about equally frequently among those rated high and those rated low on potential success. There is reason to believe, as Barron has pointed out, that, "Either of these alternative perceptual decisions may be associated with a high degree of personal effectiveness. It is as though there is an effective and an ineffective aspect of each alternative" (2). It is worthy of note, however, that a preference for complexity and asymmetry is related to originality, the correlation of Art Scale scores with departmental ratings of Originality being +.30 in the spring sample, +.44 in the fall sample.

Special attention has been given in our assessment program to the possible development of relatively simple and quickly administered tests of perceptual and cognitive abilities. Previous work in this area has suggested that simple tests of this sort may turn out to be surprisingly good measures of more complex aspects of personality. It is our hope that some of them may prove to be easily obtained and precise measures of certain aspects of what the psychoanalysts have called "reality testing." If these simpler measures can be shown to be systematically related to the more complex functions of personality revealed by more molar assessment procedures, a significant extension of quantitative method to personality testing will have been achieved.

For this part of our program, Richard S. Crutchfield adapted or developed a series of 14 perceptual, cognitive, and intellective tasks, performances on which have been so scored as to yield 52 measures.

Briefly noted, these tasks are:

1) *Insight puzzles*—nine problems that can be solved through sudden insight.

2) *Gottschaldt Figures*—each of which requires the subject to perceive a simple geometrical figure imbedded in a more complex figure.

3) *Masked figure*—a single drawing constructed of a word and its mirror image from below, so joined that the word tends to be masked by the larger symmetrical figure. The task is to perceive the word.

4) *Tilted square*—a procedure which requires the subject to locate the vertical position of a luminous rod in a completely dark room, the only visual cue being a luminous tilted square, which provides a distorting frame of reference (from Asch and Witkin).

5) *Autokinetic movement*—with measurements of the extent, direction, and character of the perceived movement.

6) *Visual-motor organization*—which requires the subject to trace a luminous outline square exposed in an otherwise dark room.

7) *Line movement*—in which a pattern of 45° angle lines, drawn on a roll of paper moving downward at a constant rate, is exposed behind a square aperture. The elapsed time before the perception of vertical movement gives way to horizontal movement is measured, after which fluctuations of vertical and horizontal movement are recorded.

8) *Weight-judgment*—which measures the character of shift in "adaption level" of a series of lifted weights as a function of systematic changes introduced, without the subject's knowledge, into the range of weights being judged.

9) *Kinesthetic after-effect*—a test that measures distortions in kinesthetic perception under several conditions as a consequence of previous kinesthetic stimulation, and the persistence of such distortions.

10) *Tapping*—which consists simply in determining the tempo of tapping under instructions to tap at a "natural" or "neutral" rate.

11) *Retinal rivalry*—the determination of the rate of alternation when rivaling retinal stimuli are exposed in a stereoscope.

12) *Size constancy*—requiring judgments of equality of a variable distant triangle with a nearby standard one.

13) *Multiple choice*—employing a modified Yerkes multiple-choice apparatus on which after three problems solvable by the same general method have been presented, a fourth problem, requiring a new type of solution, is presented.

14) *Street Gestalt Test*—in which the subject is presented with 25 incomplete pictures of objects, his task being to infer, in each case, the correct identity of the object.

It is too early to say which, if any, of these perceptual-cognitive (p-c) tests either individually or in a brief battery will prove to be effective predictors of the criteria of personal effectiveness that we have been studying.

In our first sample, the scores of the two criterion groups—Highs and Lows in average departmental ratings of P O S—on each of the 52-p-c measures were inspected for significant differences. Sixteen were chosen as most differentiating. Each assessee was then scored on this battery of 16 p-c measures by averaging his *T* scores. As would be expected, the summary scores thus obtained correlated quite highly in our first sample (+.80 with P), but the correlation showed considerable shrinkage on cross-validation. But that these tests are measuring significant aspects of personality is suggested by an item analysis of the adjectives checked by the staff for those subjects scoring high vs. those subjects scoring low on these tests.

Adjectives checked significantly more often as descriptive of the high scorers on the p-c measures were:

1. adaptable	13. helpful	24. realistic
2. appreciative	14. honest	25. reliable
3. calm	15. interests wide	26. responsible
4. capable	16. mature	27. resourceful
5. clear-thinking	17. moderate	28. self-confident
6. conscientious	18. organized	29. serious
7. cooperative	19. persistent	30. sincere
8. curious	20. poised	31. sympathetic
9. fair-minded	21. progressive	32. thoughtful
10. foresighted	22. quick	33. tolerant
11. frank	23. rational	34. unassuming
12. friendly		

In striking contrast to these are the adjectives checked significantly more often for those poor on the p-c tests:

1. affected	7. fearful	13. self-centered
2. confused	8. fussy	14. self-punishing
3. dependent	9. immature	15. submissive
4. dissatisfied	10. meek	16. talkative
5. dominant	11. natural	17. unstable
6. emotional	12. resentful	18. weak

In his factorial studies of perception and visual thinking, Thurstone (3, 4) has identified two closure factors. The Street Gestalt is a test of the first closure factor, the Gottschaldt Figures a test of the second closure factor. Both of these factors, Thurstone reports, seem to transcend to some extent the visual modality. It has been his impression that those who are high on the first closure factor (Street Gestalt) tend to be outgoing and extroverted, while those who are high on the second closure factor (Gottschaldt Figures) tend to turn inward in a more introverted manner.

We find some confirmation of this in the adjectives checked significantly more often by us for high scorers on the Street Gestalt vs. high scorers on the Gottschaldt Figures.

Closure Factor I—Street Gestalt

Highs	Lows
adaptable	aloof
assertive	awkward
cheerful	effeminate
energetic	hostile
enthusiastic	idealistic
frank	sarcastic
good-natured	sentimental
mature	shy
natural	thoughtful
practical	
responsible	
sincere	
sociable	

Closure Factor II—Gottschaldt Figures

Highs	Lows
clear-thinking	anxious
enterprising	awkward
foresighted	submissive
honest	
organized	
rational	
thorough	

The tests that I have described for you, as well as many others which there has not been time to discuss, are, of course, fairly crude. Our work with them is still rather preliminary and our findings to date are highly tentative. It is, however, I feel confident, along such lines as we are exploring that eventually useful tests for the measurement of nonintellectual functions will be developed.

REFERENCES

1. Barron, F. Personality style and perceptual choice. *Journal of Personality,* 1952, 20, 385–401.
2. Barron, F., & Welsh, G. S. Artistic perception as a possible factor in personality style: its measurement by a figure preference test. *Journal of Personality,* 1952, 33, 199–203.
3. Thurstone, L. L. *A factorial study of perception.* Chicago: Univer. of Chicago Press, 1944.
4. Thurstone, L. L. *Some primary abilities in visual thinking.* The Psychometric Laboratory, Univer. of Chicago, No. 59, August 1950.
5. Welsh, G. S. A projective figure-preference test for diagnosis of psychopathology: 1. A preliminary investigation. Unpublished doctoral dissertation, Univer. of Minnesota, 1949.

The Measurement of Human Motivation:
An Experimental Approach[1]

DAVID C. McCLELLAND

1952

What I have to say this morning will be somewhat of a change of pace from what you have been listening to, since I approach the measurement problem from an experimental point of view rather than from the traditional testing point of view.

I should like first to review the different ways in which psychologists have attempted to measure motivation in the past. In the first place, the simplest way, apparently, to measure human motivation is to ask a subject how motivated he is for something or other. The psychologist always starts with the simplest approach: just ask the subject. Of course, we psychologists did this and we did it elaborately. We did it by setting up self-rating scales; we drew graphs to show the normal distribution, and we urged the subject to follow the normal distribution or put his check marks in some kind of a pattern; but fundamentally the method involves simply asking the subject how motivated he is.

I do not need to tell you, I think, what the difficulties are with this approach. One of the major ones is, of course, that subjects have different subjective standards, and if you ask them how motivated they are for achievement, each one will have a different idea of what intense achievement motivation is, so that when you try to compare their self-judgments, you get "hash."

The second approach is, if you can't ask the subject, then ask somebody else how motivated he is. Of course, you choose somebody that knows him fairly well, presumably, like a teacher, and you get the teacher to rate the pupil on how motivated the pupil is. If you don't think teachers are capable of doing this correctly or validly, you can ask a clinical psychologist, who may study the person for several weeks, or even several years if he is a psy-

---

[1] A more recent discussion of this topic by the author can be found in Atkinson (1, Ch. 1)—Ed.

choanalyst, and then get him to make a rating as to how motivated the person is for achievement. And I suppose if the clinical psychologist does not feel he is capable of doing it, you can always ask a psychiatrist, whose judgment may be even better.

But again I do not need to tell you the difficulties with this methodological approach. One difficulty is circumvented: if you ask the same judge to judge several people, he can more or less keep his standards the same, so that you do not have the problem of shifting norms quite so badly as you do if you ask the subjects to rate themselves. But other difficulties arise. For example, it is not exactly clear what the judge is judging, just what his definition of the motive is. His definition isn't always communicable.

The chief objection to this approach is partly practical and partly theoretical. Practically, I do not think that judgments of motivation have proven extremely fruitful in predicting performance, and I suspect that the reason is that the judgments are not pure enough. Too many factors are taken into account in a clinical judgment so that it is difficult to tease out precise relationships with performance. This difficulty ties in with the theoretical objection that I have—an objection that can be highlighted by comparing the process to asking a group of physicists to measure temperature by pooling their judgments as to how hot it is or how cold it is. You can undoubtedly get a reliable estimate; that is, you can get agreement this way, but it isn't exactly measurement. I have always been interested in pushing our measurement of motivation more in the objective direction.

A third way of measuring motivation, at least achievement motivation, which I am chiefly concerned with here this morning, is to look at behavior —this darling of American psychology, behavior. It is what the person does that counts. It is not what he thinks, feels, or believes; it is what he does, and if he works hard, he has a high achievement motive. Why not use that as a simple method of measuring motivation: how hard does the pupil work? Well, again there are difficulties here. Theoretical psychologists tell us that performance is determined by more factors than just motivation, so that if you use performance as an index of motivation, you get a lot of other things mixed in there, too, such as past learning, intelligence, etc. Another difficulty, even more serious for motivational theory, is this: a person may work hard for several different reasons. He may work hard because he is anxious or worried, not because he has a high achievement motive. So performance can never prove a very adequate method of measuring achievement motivation per se.

With this background, I want to introduce the method of measuring motivation that we have adopted, I think more or less by accident. I must tell you that a lot of things become clearer in the cold clear light of hindsight than they are at the time. I assure you that five years ago, when we began our research on the achievement motive, we did not go through this step-by-step analysis of other measurement methods, reject them, and then choose the one I am going to describe to you. It happened much more accidentally than that, but now that we have done it this way, our line of reasoning looks sensible to me.

What we did was to do *content analyses of imaginative behavior or fantasy*. Why did we choose fantasy or imaginative behavior? I use "fantasy" for my clinical friends, and "imaginative behavior" as a kind of bow to my Yale background. They mean the same thing.

I think our primary reason for choosing fantasy was that it has so obviously worked. Psychologists have had a long history in the clinical field in which free association, fantasy, and dream analysis in the hands of the psychoanalysts have led to very fruitful and productive motivational analyses. If you stand off and look at the whole psychoanalytic tradition, beginning with Freud, you can oversimplify it by saying that it really deals primarily with motivation. Freud was not particularly interested in learning or problem solving in the great American tradition; he was much more interested in motivation, and I think the reason is partly methodological. What Freud studied was not problem solving, not learning, not how you get a pencil through a maze; instead, he studied fantasy—free association—and because he studied this type of behavior, I think he arrived at a motivational type of theory.

So we took this as a lead and, of course, we had the support of the long Murray tradition at Harvard, which had shown some very fruitful motivational analyses based on fantasy.

One might discuss here why fantasy should provide a good index of motivation, but I will not try to do it; it would lead me too far afield. The sort of argument you make is that fantasy is not influenced much by factual statements, by knowledge. It is not much influenced by values, what a person ought to say in a test, as he doesn't have a very clear idea of what he ought to write in a Thematic Apperception Test (TAT). So, the reasoning runs, the only thing that is left to determine his responses is motivation, by a process of exclusion. At any rate, we use fantasy for whatever reason.

Why content analysis? Well, content analysis, in my opinion, is just a more systematic way of making a judgment. The usual way of treating a TAT record is to have a judge read the whole record and synthesize his impression of it into a rating. From my comments earlier about the complexities of such ratings and what goes into them, you can see that I would want to move in the direction of a more objective nose-counting operation. A good analogy, which I have often had clearly in mind, is the process of making blood counts such as a medical technician makes: you get a sample of blood under standard conditions, you put it under a microscope with a grid over it, you count the number of red corpuscles and white corpuscles, etc.

Our approach is somewhat similar: you get a series of thought samples, or samples of imaginative behavior, and then develop a categorizing or classifying system. Then you count the number of times that a certain imaginative element appears. The operation is a simple yes-no dichotomous type of thing—presence, absence—the imagery is either there or isn't there, like the white corpuscle.

So much for backgound; now a little more detail about the procedure. We need three things: first, we need a method of collecting thought samples. Here we modified the Murray TAT technique by obtaining brief written stories from subjects under group testing conditions. In this way, we can test as many people at once as you can get into a room in clear view of the screen on which we project the pictures, in response to which the subjects write their stories. So it is a group testing procedure. We put a short time limit on the story, because we didn't want to give people extra credit for verbal fluency. Since some people obviously can write long stories and others can write only very short stories, we limit the amount of time to around five minutes. In this time we obtain a kind of standardized thought sample averaging around 90 words in length.

Second, we need a method of scoring for the achievement motive. I will refer to the achievement motive in the Murray tradition as the need for achievement, or more briefly, n Achievement. We need several things as prerequisites for a scoring system. First of all, we need a criterion of achievement imagery; we have to recognize the white blood corpuscle when we see it, so to speak; we have to recognize the achievement imagery when it is there. We developed, by a method which I will describe a little later, a scoring criterion that can be briefly summarized in this phrase, a kind of catch phrase that we use: "competition with a standard of excellence." Examples of it can, of course, be multiplied. A person wants to do a good job; he wants to beat somebody else. These are the two types of standards of excellence that you find, the same standards that golfers use in medal and match play. In medal play, you try to beat par; in match play, you try to beat the other player. Both these types of standards are included under our scoring criterion of "competition with a standard of excellence."

Next, we need a set of related categories. Having got the imagery criterion, we must be able to identify other thought elements relating to this central category. Here we tried very hard to get a *related* set of categories that had some theoretical sense, that hung together. To do this we simply followed the standard description of the problem-solving behavior sequence that you find in any elementary textbook, for example, the process of adjustment. It is usually represented with an arrow for the motive, with a rectangle for the obstacle which the person goes around to get to the goal (represented again by a "detour" arrow), etc. We defined subcategories for each part of this behavior sequence. I will not go into more detail here, because I assume that you are not interested in the detailed definition of these subcategories.

Third, we wanted a method of scoring that was, as I said earlier, as operational as possible, as simple as possible, so that it could be readily communicated and readily used by scorers. Here, of course, the ultimate test is scorer reliability, the ease with which you get high agreement coefficients between two trained scorers. We succeeded pretty well. Our agreement coefficients ran around .90–.95 for scorers judging on different occasions if they were well trained. Training, incidentally, takes a week for some people, longer for others. There seems to be an ability factor involved in ease of learning to score such records. If somebody can tell me what it is, I would appreciate it.

Fourth, we need a scoring system that is as economical and simple to apply as possible. You may ask at this point why we didn't use a multiple-choice system so that a machine could do the scoring instead of a human being. It is obviously much more expensive to use a human being and much more tedious, when you have hundreds and hundreds of records to score. The answer is, of course, that we would like to use a multiple-choice test, but it doesn't work; and if any of you want to go out and try it, all I can say is, more power to you. We have tried it and it has just never worked. The same seems to be true of the multiple-choice Rorschach. Some day we will know why multiple-choice projective tests don't work. Now there is just plenty of practical evidence that they don't. It may be because multiple-choice introduces a reality factor which tends to minimize the importance of motivational determinants of perception.[2]

In any case, our scoring system is not so terribly inefficient and uneconomical. It turns out that a trained scorer, if you can keep him at it (which is another problem) can score fifty to sixty records a day without straining himself, and this means that if you have ten scorers, you can score five hundred

---

[2] See a recent experiment by Postman and Crutchfield (3) on the effects of hunger on perception.

a day. It is practical, in other words. It takes about a minute to score a story, or five minutes to score an individual record, which isn't excessive.

So far, we had a method of collecting the thought samples, a method of scoring them, and next we needed a method of arousing the achievement motive experimentally. Here is where we took a new step in the testing field, I believe. That is, we argued that we did not want to have an a priori scoring system. We wanted one that reflected sensitively experimentally-induced changes in achievement motivation.

So we began with two groups of subjects: roughly, a control group, and a group in which the achievement motive was aroused. Our method was to compare the imagery in the stories written under neutral conditions with the imagery in the stories written under aroused conditions. We found shifts in achievement imagery. Students wrote different kinds of stories under these two conditions, and we used these differences to arrive at the definition of achievement imagery which I gave you earlier. Note the importance of the experimental variable in arriving at our scoring system. We used only those imagery categories that increased in frequency when the motive was aroused. In fact, we redefined our categories so as to capture as best we could the differences in stories written under "control" and "arousal" conditions.

Now for the payoff, if any. You may well ask: all right, you have demonstrated that imagery in stories changes when you arouse achievement motivation; how can you use this to measure individual differences in achievement motivation?

We took several steps here to see whether we were able to measure individual differences. First, we did a very simple and elementary thing. Having decided on our scoring system based on the categories that increased when the motive was aroused, we simply summed these characteristics in a given person's record. Suppose a person wrote eight stories: we went through and scored each story separately, according to the achievement-motive scoring system, and then counted the different types of achievement imagery that appeared in his eight stories and got his total score. People varied enough in this total score to give us a reasonable spread and we could begin to relate individual differences as measured in this way to other types of behavior. The basic assumption is that if a person shows a lot of the kind of achievement imagery that appears when the motive is aroused, he must have a strong achievement motive.

To what other types of behavior did we relate our achievement score? First and foremost, as you might expect, we were interested in knowing whether the achievement motive, if measured in this way, was related to performance. That I suppose would be the first question any of you would ask: do the students with high achievement motivation work any harder? It seems logical that they should. Our first experiments in this field were done with laboratory tests. If you take a simple test like adding two-place numbers and give college students a ten-minute repetitive test of this sort, you find that there is a very significant difference between subjects with high achievement motivation and those with low achievement motivation. That is, we found that the ones with high motivation had a higher output of arithmetic problems; they completed more of them in the time allowed.

Second, if you take a more complex task, like unscrambling words, which is a relatively unfamiliar task as compared with adding two-place numbers, you find that while the people with high and low achievement motivation start out at about the same output level, the ones with low motivation do not improve during a 20-minute test period. Those with high motivation do improve, so that at the end of the test period they are turning out more work per unit time than they did at the beginning. In other words, they are sufficiently motivated to learn new and better ways of unscrambling words.

I suspect that some of you will be interested in whether or not this measure of motivation is related to grades. I am going to leave that until last— because it is a complex question—and treat it separately.

Let me go on first to other types of behavior in the laboratory to which this measure of motivation is related. Take memory, for example. For years the problem of the better memory of incompleted tasks, the so-called Zeigarnik effect, has been something of a puzzle, at least to some psychologists. Why are incompleted tasks remembered better? There have been, as you know, some conflicting results. Sometimes you find this effect and sometimes you don't. We found that one of the variables correlated with better memory for incompleted tasks is achievement motivation. Subjects with high achievement motivation have a better memory for incompleted tasks. Subjects with low achievement motivation generally have a better memory for completed tasks. They remember their successes, as it were. They are a little bit defensive about this. The ones with high motivation, on the other hand, apparently regard the incompleted task as a challenge. They want to recall it so that they can complete it. They think to themselves, so to speak, "If I had only had time to finish that. If that guy hadn't interrupted me, I would have finished it."

Or take level of aspiration—something that you would think motivation should be related to. Here again we found a relationship, if you rule out reality factors. That is, level of aspiration, as most of us have assumed from the beginning, is partly determined by wish factors and partly determined by reality factors. If you ask a person what kind of a grade he expects to get in a course, his reply will be determined partly by his past performance, by his previous grades in this course, and also presumably partly by his need for achievement.

We found if you just correlate the achievement motive score with level of aspiration, you don't get any correlation, but if you do it when the reality factors are minimized, or are in conflict, when the subject doesn't really have any basis for saying in reality what he will do on a certain test, then you get a very significant correlation with achievement motivation. This, of course, is exactly what you would expect.

Take perception. We have done experiments on the recognition of words with the tachistoscope, and we find, as one would expect, a certain selective sensitivity. The ones with high achievement motivation recognize words relating to achievement more rapidly.

Let me just mention two other examples. A very popular test nowadays is the *F* scale, a measure of Authoritarianism. Roger Brown (2) at Michigan tested to see whether achievement motivation was related to the *F* scale. I must say I did not expect any relationship. To my surprise, he found one, but it was inverse. That is, students with lower achievement motivation are generally higher on the Authoritarianism scale. I think you will see why this may be so in just a minute.

Some of you are familiar with the Asch judgment experiments. Typically he presents three comparison lines and a standard line to six "stooges" and one "non-stooge." The six stooges all say in succession that one of the comparison lines is the same length as the standard, when it is obvious that it is really longer. So this places the non-stooge in a conflict situation. He has just heard six other students say that these two things are objectively equal, and it is perfectly plain that they are *not* equal. So what does he do? Well, under these pressure conditions, about a third of the subjects, e.g. college students, "fold": they yield to social pressure and call out the wrong line.

Asch has wondered why some students yield and some do not. We found, quite surprisingly, that the non-yielders, the people who refuse to yield under this pressure, are the ones with high achievement motivation. There is almost no overlap in n Achievement scores of the yielders and non-yielders.

A reason for this can be found in our research on the origins of achievement motivation. What kind of home background, what kind of childhood training is characteristic of the people with high and low achievement motivation? A very nice thesis has just been completed by Marian Winterbottom (4) at the University of Michigan on this problem. It begins to explain how some of these things hang together. She was interested in the number of demands and restrictions that parents placed on their children, and at what age. She chose sons aged eight to ten, and she interviewed their mothers and gave them questionnaire schedules to fill out.

What she found, to make a long story very short, is that the mothers of children with high achievement motivation made many more demands for independent decisions earlier than those with low achievement motivation. For example, consider an item she actually used, "Do you expect your child to learn his way around town by himself?" This is one aspect of independence training. All the mothers said they did require this of their sons. But the mothers of children with high achievement motivation said that they expected the child to know how to do this before the age of eight, which happened to be the median age at which the distribution of expected ages could be split. These mothers required more independence earlier; in other words, there was great pressure from these mothers for independent activity of various sorts—crossing the street by oneself, making friends, doing well in school, etc. All of these independence-training needs seemed to be required earlier by the mothers of sons with high achievement motivation. So I think you can begin to understand why the products of this kind of parental background would stand out against the pressure of the group in the Asch experiment, why they would be more at the democratic end of the Authoritarianism scale. And vice versa: you can see why the ones with low achievement motivation, coming from a more protected background, would tend to be more dependent on other people of authority; why they would be willing to follow the crowd, even when it is wrong, and so forth. I need not elaborate.

Now, to turn to my last point, namely, the problem of predicting judgments of performance. This is a long way of saying "predicting grades," and I chose the long way on purpose. Predicting judgments of performance is no mean trick, as most of you know. I do not regard it as especially difficult in this case to predict performance, but to predict *judgments* of performance is quite a different matter; it is the criterion problem with which you are all familiar.

Actually, we have done a number of studies of the relationship between n Achievement scores and grades in high schools and colleges of all sorts, and our correlations are sometimes high and sometimes low. I remember when we first ran this correlation for a college sample; it came to .51. We were so elated that we nearly sat down and sent a telegram to Professor Terman saying "Forget about your intelligence test; we can predict grades better with a 20-minute projective test." Well, it is a good thing we didn't, because we ran the correlation on another sample and the next time the correlation was zero. A healthy corrective for enthusiasm, the repeated experiment!

To summarize this research as it now stands: there is a median correlation of n Achievement with grades in the .20's with intelligence partialled out —significant, but nothing to get terribly excited about.

Let me mention what I think are two of the main problems in getting such predictions of grades. In the first place, how much does the criterion —namely, grades—depend on motivation in a particular case? We have found a case—and I am sure you know of such cases—where the correlation of Otis IQ with high school grades is .70. Can you expect any correlation of grades with motivation if this is so? You may find one, but you certainly aren't going to add anything to the prediction of grades that you get from the Otis IQ alone. Maybe the teacher just looked up the intelligence test scores and graded accordingly.

How much does the grade criterion depend on motivation? And how much on the teacher's idiosyncrasies? Langlie and others showed twenty-five years ago that grades—in high school, at any rate, and I suppose in college—are correlated with teacher judgments of other personality characteristics, e.g., attractiveness, physical maturity, and other characteristics of that sort. So there is certainly impurity in the criterion—i.e., judgment of performance as compared with performance itself.

The other problem that has been very puzzling to me is whether or not it is really legitimate to partial out intelligence. The normal way of proceeding is to correlate n Achievement with grades, intelligence with grades, and then partial out the correlation of intelligence with n Achievement. There is always a positive correlation between achievement motivation and intelligence, and there ought to be, it seems to me. Take the extreme case. Whatever the native ability of a person, if he has no motivation to learn, he is not going to get a high intelligence test score. So it seems to me there ought to be some correlation between achievement motivation and intelligence test score.

There are two places where motivation enters into an intelligence test score: one in the accumulation of knowledge that the subject shows on the intelligence test or achievement test, and the other in the attention he gives at the time he takes the test. We know that people who have high achievement motivation will actually do better in the testing situation. So there is an intertwining here of achievement motivation and the intelligence measure. Is it fair then to partial out IQ in relating motivation to grades, if we know motivation also determined the IQ to some extent? If we do, we are eliminating part of the effect that motivation has on performance. If we don't, we can be accused of simply finding a correlate of IQ, which therefore ought to predict grades to some extent. It is a difficult problem to think through—the relation of motivation to performance and intelligence; but these are our contributions to it to date. At least we think we have a method of measuring motivation that should provide plenty of food for thought.

REFERENCES

1. Atkinson, J. W. (Ed.) *Motives in fantasy, action, and society: a method of assessment and study.* Princeton, N.J.: Van Nostrand, 1958.
2. Brown, R. W. Some determinants of the relationship between rigidity and authoritarianism. Unpublished doctoral dissertation, Univer. of Michigan, 1952.
3. Postman, L., & Crutchfield, R. S. The interaction of need, set, and stimulus-structure in a cognitive task. *American Journal of Psychology,* 1952, 55, 196–217.
4. Winterbottom, Marian R. The relation of childhood training in independence to achievement motivation. Unpublished doctoral dissertation, Univer. of Michigan, 1953.

A New Technique for Measuring Individual Differences in Conformity to Group Judgment

RICHARD S. CRUTCHFIELD

1954

Central to research both in personality and in group dynamics are methods for the measurement of the individual's behavior in situations of group interaction, for example, conformity behavior to group pressure.

Such measurement is made difficult by certain demanding requirements: 1) ideally, the behavior should be measured *directly* in actual group situations, rather than indirectly by questionnaires about group situations; 2) the group situations should be psychologically *relevant* for the individual; 3) there should be *standardization* of the group situation so that measurements of different individuals may properly be compared; and 4) there should be adequate *economy* of the test method, so that substantial numbers of persons may be tested without unreasonable cost in time and money.

The standardization problem is the most acute. In genuine groups involving face-to-face interaction of several subjects, the stimulus situation confronting each person is *unique*, being dependent in part upon what the others in the group do. This leads to an undesirable confounding of personal and situational factors in the measurement of the individual's group behavior, and there is no simple way to disentangle the two.

One fruitful attack on this problem is what in previous research applications I have called the "quasi group-interaction method." Its essence is simple. Subjects to be measured are placed together in a group situation which, though perceived as genuine by them, is actually so contrived by the experimenter that he wholly controls and manipulates the conditions of group interaction. This serves to standardize the situation for each subject in an identical fashion, so that observed individual differences in behavior may properly be ascribed to differences among the persons rather than to situational differences.

The quasi group methodology is by no means new. Earlier variants are found throughout the field of experimental social psychology. Little, however, has been made of it in personality measurement, and in general, the method has not been widely exploited.

In recent work, I have applied it to what gives promise of being a powerful new technique for measuring individual differences in conformity to group judgment. Five persons are tested simultaneously. They are seated in a row in front of an electrical switchboard apparatus, consisting of five identical panels. Each panel is shielded from the other four and contains 11 numbered switches by which the person may signal his response. It also contains five rows of signal lights which can display the responses being made by the other four group members. In short, there is a simple electrical communication system among the five persons. No *direct* communication is permitted.

The task for each person is to make judgments pertaining to a large number of slides which are projected on a wall facing the group. Each slide offers a set of numbered alternative answers among which he is to choose. He records his choice by closing the appropriately numbered switch and this causes his response to be displayed on the panels of the other four members. He is also instructed to respond in a specified serial *order* within the group, person A going first, then B, and so on, E being last. The designation of his letter position—A, B, C, D, or E—is indicated to him by the experimenter. Such letter designations are rotated from time to time, permitting each person to respond in each of the five serial positions. The experimenter offers no further explanation of the purpose of this procedure.

The slides offer a mixture of materials—simple *perceptual* comparisons, such as of relative length of lines; *logical* problems, such as the completion of a number series of the kind found in standard mental tests; expression of one's own *opinions* and *attitudes* on various issues, etc.

On the first set of slides, the person finds the judgments fairly easy to make, and he observes that there is a sensible agreement between his judgments and those of the other four members. But when later in the series he is for the first time designated as E, so that he must respond in last position, he experiences something new and disturbing. On the slide presented this time, calling for a simple judgment of relative length of lines, he sees the other four members unanimously agree on a choice which clearly contradicts his own. This throws him into a severe conflict between the clear evidence of his own senses and the unanimous contradictory consensus of the rest of the group. How he chooses to resolve this conflict, either by yielding to the group pressure and conforming to its judgment or by remaining independent of it, is the basic measure of conformity behavior in our procedure.

There is, of course, more than one such critical slide. While responding in position E, he is presented with more than twenty other critical slides—pertaining variously to matters of perception, of logic, of opinion, and of attitude—on each of which he is confronted with a serious disagreement between his own judgment and that of the rest of the group.

As you will doubtless have surmised, the situation is not really what the persons have been led to understand. They have been grossly deceived. The five panels are not connected to one another at all, but to a control board operated by the experimenter. It is he who signals the responses which allegedly come from the other group members. The wiring is in parallel so that the pattern of signals he chooses to simulate appears simultaneously and identically on all five panels. Moreover, the designations of serial order of responding—A through E—are likewise identical for all five persons at every moment.

By this deception, therefore, a quasi group-interaction situation has been contrived, permitting each person to be exposed to a standardized set of simulated group judgments and to be confronted at predetermined points with identical external pressures toward conformity.

Since the spring of 1953, when this technique was first developed, three studies have been made using different populations of subjects. The first study was of 50 men, averaging 34 years of age, all members of a profession in which leadership is one of the most important qualifications. They were tested at the Institute of Personality Assessment and Research as part of a larger assessment program. The second study was of 59 college students, mostly sophomores. The third was of 50 women, all college alumnae, in their early forties being studied under the auspices of the Mary Conover Mellon Foundation.

The results of these studies, which attest to the technical success of the method and throw light on the nature and determinants of conformity behavior are summarized with great brevity in the following eight points:

1) *The general amount of conformity behavior exhibited is large.* A single fairly representative item will serve to illustrate this finding. A circle and a star are exposed side by side, the circle being about one-third larger in area than the star. The false group consensus is on *star* as the larger, and as a consequence, 46 per cent of the men give this same false judgment.

2) *The degree of conformity shown depends in part on the kind of material being judged.* Although some amount of conformity can be elicited on every one of the critical items, the range in effectiveness among them is extremely wide. At the lower end, a simple expression of *personal preference* for one of two line-drawings is very little susceptible to a contradictory group consensus, the degree of conformity varying from zero to 10 per cent in the several studies. At the upper end, the most effective item is one which has been deliberately maximized for ambiguity. The subjects are asked to complete a number series, for which there is actually no logical solution. When the simulated group judgment agrees unanimously on an obviously illogical completion, 79 per cent of the men express agreement with this answer.

3) *Substantial conformity is elicited on socially important judgments as well as on more abstract judgments.* A critical methodological issue is whether the conformity effects so far mentioned merely represent rather superficial readinesses of the person to agree with the group on matters of little real importance to him, or whether instead they do reflect more basic conformity tendencies in the person. Support for the latter interpretation is found by the introduction of new critical items in the studies of college students and mature women. These items called for expression of the person's attitudes on matters of civil liberties, subversion, ethics, crime and punishment, etc. Pronounced conformity effects are found on these socially and psychologically relevant items. Take a single example from the study of college students. The question was asked, "Which one of the following do you feel is the most important problem facing our country today?" These five alternatives were offered: economic recession, educational facilities, subversive activities, mental health, crime and corruption. Among control subjects tested alone, only 12 per cent chose "subversive activities" as the most important. But when exposed to a spurious group consensus unanimously making this choice, 48 per cent of the subjects gave this answer.

4) *There are pronounced individual differences in amount of conformity shown.* A total conformity score for each person may be readily computed by summing the number of the critical items on which he exhibits conformity to the false group consensus. Virtually the entire possible range of such scores is found in all three studies. Among the men, for instance, at the lower end, several subjects showed practically no conformity, being influenced on one or two items at the most. At the upper end, one man was influenced on 17 of 21 critical items. The scores are

well distributed between these extremes, with a mean score of about 8 items and a tendency for greater concentration of scores toward the lower conformity end. As estimated from the correlation of subscores on two matched halves of the critical items, the reliability of the total score for the sample of men is .90.

5) *There are both generality and specificity in the conformity tendencies among individuals.* Although there is a generally positive matrix of intercorrelations of degree of conformity effect for the various items, there are also some useful differentiations to be made among the items. A cluster analysis yields one principal set pertaining to highly structured items, i.e., those involving clear judgments and unambiguous stimuli. A second main cluster consists of poorly structured items, i.e., those involving uncertain judgments and ambiguous stimuli. The individuals can be scored separately on these clusters. There is evidence that these cluster scores as well as individual performance on single items must be taken into account in the analysis of conformity behavior.

6) *The degree of conformity behavior relates significantly to relevant dimensions of personality.* Validity of the conformity measure is attested to by its substantial relationships with numerous ratings, objective test scores, and other personality determinations in assessment of the sample of men. Those low in conformity, that is, those who successfully resist the group pressure, can be clearly characterized as having intellectual effectiveness, ego-strength, self-acceptance, leadership ability, and maturity of social relations. The high conformists, on the contrary, reveal inferiority feelings, rigid and excessive self-control, intolerance of own impulses and lack of self-insight, authoritarian outlook, emphasis on external and socially approved values, and disturbed attitudes toward other people. This general picture coincides well with prior theoretical and empirical studies of the personal traits associated with conformity, but, of course, it represents a gross oversimplification of the complex relationships yet to be explored.

7) *There are significant differences in average amount of conformity exhibited by the several populations of subjects.* The college student sample was made up of both males and females. The male students exhibited just about the same average level of conformity as previously found in the adult, professional men. But the female students exhibited significantly *more* conformity than these male groups. On the other hand, the sample of mature women—college alumnae in their early

forties—showed significantly *less* conformity on the average than that found in all the other groups.

8) *Experimental variations in the testing situation can change the amount of conformity shown.* We have seen that there are differences in degree of conformity relating to personality determinants, to the nature of the populations of subjects, and to the kind of items being judged. We can also show differences resulting from certain experimental changes in the situation itself. As one example, when a group of student subjects were exposed to additional pressure, namely, that given by having the experimenter later confirm the "correctness" of the false group consensus, conformity effects were markedly increased.

To revert now to our initial statement of requirements for proper measures of individual behavior in situations of group interaction, namely, directness, relevance, standardization, and economy, it would appear that the present method fulfills all these requirements. The very essence of the method is such as to guarantee standardization of conditions. It is clearly economical, providing for the testing of five persons at once in a period of approximately one hour. It is direct, in that the persons perform in a situation which is for them one of real group interaction. On this point, it should be emphasized that the genuineness of the situation is virtually never challenged by the subjects. Of the total of 159 persons already tested in the procedure, only a small handful, when questioned immediately afterwards, expressed doubts of its genuineness; of these, only two or three seemed to have felt such doubts while actually in the situation.

Finally, with regard to psychological relevance, we may judge from both the manifest behavior and the retrospective reports by the subjects that the situation was deeply involving and that the group pressure created anxiety, often acute. A substantial number of persons freely admitted on later questioning that they had violated their own inner convictions in order to give responses in accord with those of the group.

The findings attest to a rich potential use of this measurement technique when applied to a variety of problems—personality assessment, group dynamics research, sociological and cross-cultural comparisons of groups, experimental and theoretical study of the psychological conditions of conformity. A number of such studies are contemplated and several are now in progress.

A Theory of Test Response[1]

Jane Loevinger
1958

In recent months, working in collaboration with Abel Ossorio and Kitty LaPerriere, I found taking shape a conceptualization of a trait that I currently believe to be the major source of variance in structured personality tests, regardless of their intent. Manifestations of the trait have been called façade, test-taking defensiveness, response set, "social desirability," acquiescence, and so on. The term "response bias" can serve as generic for these phenomena, though Jackson and Messick (13) prefer to emphasize that they are components of personal style. The fact that response bias is a manifestation of the trait by no means implies that the trait is inconsequential outside of the testing situation. On the contrary, its importance in the test situation reflects its importance in many other aspects of life.

The trait may be defined metaphorically as the ability to assume distance from oneself, or more exactly, as capacity to conceptualize oneself. It is one cognitive aspect of ego development. That it should greatly influence the kind of self-report that most personality tests call for is obvious; not quite so obvious is that capacity to conceptualize oneself varies as a function of age, of education, and of one's station in life. Note that the trait does not refer so much to the content of one's self concept as to one's ability to form a self concept. At least three points are needed to bring the dimension into focus. At the lowest point, there is no capacity to conceptualize oneself; at the midpoint, there is a stereotyped, usually conventional and socially acceptable self conception; and at the highest point, a differentiated and more or less realistic self concept.

Let us look first at how this trait normally develops with age. We are all familiar with the baby's wonder as he discovers his own body. But at stake here is the conception of one's psychological rather than one's physical person. The moment of discovery may be perhaps the time the child first says

[1] Preparation of this paper was supported by a research grant, M-1213, from the National Institute of Mental Health, Public Health Service.

545

"Bad" to himself as he does or refrains from doing something his parents have proscribed. At that moment, the child has conceptualized himself as having impulses that are sometimes bad and are not necessarily acted on. That he has achieved a rudimentary idea of good and bad is no more important than that he has a rudimentary idea of impulse and control. Extension and elaboration of the pair of constructs, impulse and control, are major tasks all through childhood. At this point the argument is reminiscent of Kelly's (15) psychology of personal constructs: to have the construct of impulse is to have its opposite, control, and thus to achieve a degree of choice. What Kelly does not seem to recognize clearly is that in just this instance, not having the construct of impulse does not eliminate impulses from one's repertory, but rather leaves one completely at their mercy.

By early adolescence, the ability to conceptualize one's impulses and the concomitant degree of control is fairly well established. But the typical adolescent is in many respects an "authoritarian personality" (1). He is prone to think in stereotypes, to be punitive, disciplinarian, conventional, antipsychological, and intolerant of those who are different (8, 19). In terms of the aspect of ego development here being described, he has achieved distance from his impulses, but not from his ego. He has some ability to think about himself as a psychological person, but his self-characterization tends to follow a conventional, socially approved stereotype. The strongly derogatory self-portrait which is also common in adolescence is equally stereotyped. Everyday observation leads to suspicion that the derogatory and flattering stereotypes may alternate in some children in short time span.

During the college years, there is in favorable instances a change from the typically authoritarian to an intellectually sophisticated point of view. There is usually, or at least often, a marked increase in capacity to view oneself with some detachment, to see oneself as having a style of life, to report feelings without taking refuge in conventional stereotypes. The changes that take place during the college years in personality in general and test behavior in particular have been documented in the Vassar study of Sanford, Freedman, and Webster (22). That response stereotypy on tests is somewhat characteristic of college freshmen but not of advanced undergraduates has been noted by Christie, Havel, and Seidenberg (4).

Thus, the capacity to attain distance from oneself grows with age, from infancy, where there is no distance from impulse, through adolescence, where there is distance from impulse but not ego, to the college years, where there is distance from ego as well as impulse. Were the sole purpose of this discussion to present a picture of the normal course of ego development, this would be a pale and one-dimensional version of Erik Erikson's (8) vivid and dynamic portrait, "Growth and Crises of the Healthy Personality," prepared for the Midcentury White House Conference. My purpose is not to describe personality development, but to make a contribution to personality measurement. Erikson's brilliant paper does not, by itself, lead to measurement. The elision of some of the stages Erikson describes results from using available psychometric research as a sieve for his intuitive observations.

The usefulness of the concept of ego development as a psychometric dimension depends on whether one can convincingly describe some individuals in terms of levels of ego development not characteristic of their age. When we speak of an adult as having a mental age of 2 or 8 or 10, we of course do not mean that his behavior is identical with that of the average child of the given age. Rather, there is an abstract characteristic of his behavior which can be so measured. Similarly, some children and a few adults have as little control and as little capacity to conceptualize their impulses as infants or small children. Redl and Wineman (18) have depicted preadolescent children of this type in a book that contributes much to our understanding of ego development. Many, perhaps most, adults have a self conception hardly less stereotyped than that characteristic of adolescence. If we take a slice of the population of constant age, we will find ego development as measured on this hypothetical scale correlated with intelligence, with educational level, and with some measures of social class. Since intelligence, social class, and educational level are themselves intercorrelated, this represents a single additional datum in support of the conceptualization. But while it is a single argument, it is supported by a large amount of research. Several recent summaries of research with the California F scale, which is as much a measure of ego level as of anything, have confirmed these relationships (3, 5, 24).

There have been now presented three lines of argument in support of the construct of ego development. It is a constantly increasing function of age, at least through the early adult years. It tends to increase constantly as a function of intelligence, educational level, and social status. And it can be conceptualized as increase in a single function, to wit, capacity to assume distance from oneself. There is a fourth argument: ego development tends to increase constantly with psychotherapy.

All forms of psychotherapy push the patient upward on this dimension. In the case of delinquent or disorganized persons who remain at the low end of the scale beyond the appropriate age, increase in conventionality and control is an aim. In the case of conventional people, increase in sophistication, in capacity to conceptualize themselves, is not necessarily an aim but is the means of therapy. Rogers (21), in describing the therapeutic process, has postulated essentially the same dimension. An apparent paradox is that Rogers describes the later stages of therapy in terms of *decreased* distance from one's feelings. This paradox is explained in psychoanalytic writings in terms of a temporary splitting of the ego (7). To achieve distance from oneself is the condition for achieving immediate grasp of feelings as feelings. The patient must talk about himself and his feelings in the therapeutic transaction, which surely implies a capacity to attain distance from them.

Let us look at characteristic manifestations of different levels of ego development in personality tests. The most striking fact, of course, is the tendency of most people to answer in terms of response stereotypes, most notably, a defensive or favorable self-portrayal. The tendency to describe oneself favorably has been shown to increase between the ages of 8 and 13 (10), and to decrease during the college years (22). This nonmonotonic relation between "socially desirable" self-portrayal and age corresponds exactly to the nonmonotonic relation between conventionality and ego development. That is, conventionality tends to increase as we go from lowest to middle level, and to decrease between middle and highest level. The nonmonotonic relation between the most obvious phenotypic test manifestation and the genotypic trait is surely a major obstacle to personality measurement.

In measuring maladjustment, neuroticism, and the like, one must set up a set of responses as "normal." Psychologists in recent years have tended to use a statistical definition of normality. So doing, however, does not alter the normal key very much from what would have been chosen a priori by psychologists of a more naive era, for the socially acceptable responses are just the ones chosen most frequently by the numerous middle group. Middle-class children and adults tend to appear a little better adjusted on personality tests than their lower-class contemporaries (2). On the other hand, Vassar seniors tend to test more maladjusted than Vassar freshmen (22). While personality changes undoubtedly take place during the college years, they are probably predominantly in the direction of greater ego development and intellectual maturity. It seems unlikely that basically the seniors are a lot more maladjusted than they had been as freshmen. Rather, they are more self-critical, less conventional and stereotyped in their thinking. They are capable of admitting to consciousness and to their test responses problems that had been there all along, but were concealed beneath a façade of normality. Just this sort of phenomenon has made measurement of adjustment enormously difficult. For psychotherapy itself tends to move the patient up the scale of ego development. And, other things equal, greater ego maturity at the upper extreme leads to a decrease in stereotyped favorable self-portrayal. No doubt there are many exceptions to the latter generalization. Some sick people give a stereotyped unfavorable self-portrayal, and therapy could be expected to brighten their self-portrait. Moreover, symptoms that actually disappear could be expected to be so reported. All in all, however, evidence indicates that response to structured personality tests is more clearly related to ego development than to adjustment.

What the test behavior is of those lowest on ego development is not known in detail. These people include small children, as well as older children and adults in whom impulsivity is unduly predominant. Anyone who has tried to obtain tests from individuals of low social status, where the lowest level of ego development is overrepresented, has discovered that refusals to cooperate and sabotage of various sorts are more frequent than at higher social levels. The suspicion of, and resistance to, such small authority as a research psychologist represents is itself a fact worth recording, and strikingly similar to the negativism of preschool children in testing situations.

These individuals do become accessible to psychological observation through more or less involuntary referral to guidance clinics, alcoholic treatment centers, and so on. Their inability to put their troubles, however overwhelming, into words is only partly a matter of opposition to the authority of the clinic. Skillful, sympathetic clinicians report that it appears to represent a genuine inability to conceptualize themselves. Diffuse physical complaints seem to represent a kind of "body English"; i.e., their physical complaints may represent in part psychological malaise for which they have no concepts.

Resistance to authority, impulsivity, and lack of ability for self conceptualization: surely this is a coherent syndrome, and one different from the identification with authority that characterizes the midpoint of our variable. Documentation of this syndrome can be found in the description of the lowest social class by Hollingshead and Redlich (11, Ch. 4), though I do not maintain that all individuals in the lowest class are at the lowest level of ego development.

The ideas presented here are meant to apply chiefly to objective personality tests. There is, however, one problem of long standing in projective testing, especially the Thematic Apperception Test (TAT), which has some relation to these concepts. The puzzle is, when do aggressive responses on the TAT indicate aggression in overt behavior, and, alternatively, when do aggressive fantasies substitute for aggressive behavior? Probably no one has a complete and clear-cut answer to this question. There are indications that in youths from low social classes there is a positive relation between overt and fantasy aggression; in higher social classes, a negative relation. The psychoanalytic concept of "primary process" helps to bridge the gap between this finding and the concept of ego development. Predominance of primary process is a translation of the impulsivity that characterizes the lowest level of ego development. For individuals at this level, words and fantasies serve to trigger the kinds of behavior they symbolize. Since there is minimal control of impulse expression in behavior, the impulses expressed in fantasy are the same as those expressed in behavior. In the two higher levels of ego development, on the contrary, secondary process is well established, which is to say, words and fantasies serve to delay, control, and substitute for expression of impulses in behavior. Therefore, it is not surprising to find a slight negative relation between fantasy aggression and overt aggression in middle- and upper-class groups.

Lyle and Gilchrist (16) compared TAT protocols of delinquent boys with those of a matched control group; there was no difference in the number of aggressive or antisocial themes expressed, but the nondelinquents used various devices to indicate greater distance from antisocial impulses, such as denial of the reality of the situation, inhibition of the impulse by guilt, and rationalization of the antisocial act. Note that Lyle and Gilchrist use the same metaphor, distance, to indicate the means by which control over impulses is maintained, and that they find representation of the control devices in the TAT protocol. Purcell (17) found similar results studying psychiatric referrals in an Army training camp. He divided his cases into three groups according to case history evidence of antisocial conduct. Best differentiation of the groups was in terms of fantasy themes of internal punishment and ratings of the aggressive fantasies as to "remoteness," which referred to time, place, degree of reality, and so on. The antisocial group showed few themes of internal punishment and little remoteness from their aggressive fantasies. While Purcell interpreted the absence of themes of internal punishment in the antisocial group in superego terms, note that it is also evidence of lack of ability to conceptualize inner life.

Kenneth Isaacs has just sent me a manuscript in which he develops a construct very similar to what I call ego development (12). He calls it "relatability," stressing the capacity to perceive other people and capacity for differentiated interpersonal relations. His studies also show that level of relatability can be judged from TAT protocols, but specific criteria are not listed.

In sketching ego development as a major dimension of personality, I am using Binet's work as my model. His breakthrough in the field of ability measurement, which has not been matched in the following fifty years, succeeded, I believe, because he found a *process* that corresponded to an intuitively perceived *dimension*. There have been attempts to define personality traits after Binet's model. But if we imitate him too closely, we end up measuring almost the same trait that he did, rather than a personality trait. In fact, correlation of a personality test with age or intelligence is often interpreted as that much evidence for invalidity. Yet it is absurd to assert that personality does not change with age, and both gratuitous and contrary to everyday observation to assume that personality trends will be uncorrelated with IQ or social status. We cannot lift ourselves out of this problem by our correlational bootstraps; we need to mind the psychological content of our measurements.

The dimension of ego development I have sketched is a kind of common denominator in Erikson's description of the normal process of ego development; Rogers' description of the process of therapy; Sullivan, Grant, and Grant's (23) description of the growth of capacity for interpersonal relations; and results with objective personality tests pertaining to authoritarianism and response stereotypy. The three papers describing process all refer to seven stages, whether by coincidence or not. From the psychometric point of view, each involves a forbidding array of details. On the other hand, the psychometric approach has been to assume that everyone can be classified as having more or less of some one thing, like dominance or adjustment, or lies somewhere between a pair of poles, like authoritarian-democratic. The idea that if you can name it, you can measure it dies hard. The journals are full of studies using little *ad hoc* tests of traits that struck that research worker's fancy.

I have, then, followed Binet in using process as touchstone of dimension; but I have tried to avoid the circumstantial details of particular processes, as well as the nominalistic fallacy that still vitiates many psychometric approaches to personality.

The authors of *The Authoritarian Personality* (1) considered and rejected the idea that the authoritarian was an immature version of the liberal person. However, the meaning of authoritarianism shifted in the course of their research. At its inception, they were concerned with a harsh and pathological extreme of anti-Semitism and fascism, which they found only in a few individuals in their San Quentin sample, who fit the description of the lowest level of ego development. The core of the trait that emerged from their studies was very much like what I have described as the middle stage of ego development, much less vicious than what they looked for at first. The reason the California group was diverted away from political aspects of authoritarianism and in the direction of ego development is that the latter aspects are far more pervasive in personality and are just the aspects of personality most accessible to measurement and interview.

The California disclaimer that authoritarianism and liberalism are stages in a developmental process has not stood up. Evidence that adolescence is typically a more authoritarian period than later maturity has come from many independent sources, including clinical observation (8), opinion polls (19), and studies with the *F* scale. The thinking of the California group evolved from that of looking for a few wicked authoritarians to recognizing the authoritarian tendencies in large groups of ordinary people. They never quite admitted that the conventional authoritarian represents the norm in our society. To see authoritarian tendencies in a developmental framework, as I have tried to do today, is to carry the evolution of the concept one painful step further: the struggle against authoritarian tendencies is one each of us must make within himself, and it is a battle never wholly won.

That the fight against authoritarianism takes place in each of us was the theme of Erich Fromm's (9) 1941 book, *Escape from Freedom*. But Fromm, seeing the similarity in the child's spontaneity and the spontaneity that can be recaptured by a truly mature adult, wrote as if people knew their real selves and then deliberately surrendered that knowledge to slip into a conformist or authoritarian stereotype. The dialectics of growth seem more accurately represented by the sequence: impulsivity, rigid control enforced by intellectual stereotypes, and flexible controls enforced by genuine insight. Riesman (20), though much influenced by Fromm, has drawn a picture essentially the same as that sketched here. His term for the lowest level of ego development is anomic; for the middle level, conformist or, most often, adjusted; for the highest level, autonomous. Riesman has enriched our understanding of different patterns of conforming by his description of the tradition-directed, the inner-directed, and the other-directed man. These types of conformity characterize the middle level of ego development in different societies and in different groups within a given society. So far no one has traced the differential manifestations on tests of the inner-directed and the other-directed man, though there has been at least one attempt. But Allen Edwards' (6) finding, that the number of people claiming that an item describes them is a high rectilinear function of the independently judged "social desirability" of the item, is remarkable evidence for our other-directedness.

Proponents of factor analysis, cluster analysis, and multidimensional scaling set up artificial problems with boxes or random numbers and demonstrate that their preferred method will indeed capture the dimensions built into the problem. I have begun instead with a real trait of central importance in test behavior, and would now emphasize that factor analysis or cluster analysis or multidimensional scaling could not possibly reconstruct such a trait. Impulsivity is a distinguishing mark of the lowest level of ego development, but the flexible controls of mature life are phenotypically closer to the impulsive stage than are the rigid controls of the intermediate stage. The nonmonotonic relation between conventionality and ego development has already been noted. The complex of ego development leaves many traces, and with respect to each of them there are individual differences. Factor analysts make much of getting from phenotypic variables to genotypic traits. But only such genotypic variables as are linearly, or at least monotonically, related to phenotypic ones will be revealed by factor analysis. By themselves, statistical techniques can yield only partial insights. I trust, however, that no one will carry away the message that I don't think it worthwhile to master or use difficult statistics. The psychological research worker who does not understand statistical principles is as handicapped as the psychometrician who does not permit himself to develop a feeling for the traits he studies. Factor analysis is an important technique in the hands of a responsible psychologist with insight into the psychological content of his variables.

Suppose you answer that you prefer to stick with whatever factor analysis reveals, that you find nothing compelling about the construct I have sketched. This raises an interesting and profound question, one that will be answered neither in short time nor by the self-elected. Since personality is complicated enough to encourage many alternative constructions, what are the criteria for the validity of alternative ways of construing it? Ego development as here sketched provides a framework within which one can view such major researches as *The Authoritarian Personality* and subsequent related studies (1, 3, 24); Redl and Wineman's (18) *The Aggressive Child;* Riesman's (20) studies of American character; Erikson's (8) work on growth and crises of the normal personality; studies of personality development in the college years by Sanford and others (22); Edwards' (6) work on the social desirability variable in personality tests; work on the relation between content and style or response bias (13); Rogers' (21) study of the process of therapy; and Kelly's (15) psychology of personal constructs. Dozens of smaller or less familiar studies contribute also to the over-all picture. The line of research that originally gave rise to these speculations, work which I have been doing with Blanche Sweet, Abel Ossorio, Kitty LaPerriere, and others on patterns of child rearing, I have not even mentioned. Work now in progress is testing the hypothesis that different patterns of child rearing characterize different levels of ego development; here is another far-reaching application.

If memory serves, factor analysis originally aimed to give an economical account of much data with few concepts. I am claiming that the single construct I have proposed accounts for much data. By contrast, application of factor analysis to personality tests has too often taken small amounts of data and developed a confusingly large number of constructs. Has factor analysis of personality tests given rise to any powerful constructs—any constructs of sufficient utility, for example, that clinicians have made use of them?

A problem of concern to Educational Testing Service has been measuring the behavioral outcomes of higher education. I would like finally to show how this problem is related to the discussion. In regard to education at the nursery school and kindergarten level, no doubt specific behaviors can be used to measure the success of the educational endeavor. The child is taught to lay his coat on the floor, slip his arms into it, and flip it on by raising his arms. He must learn to conform to bells, commands, and classroom routines. The aim of university education is emphatically not to inculcate such stereotyped behavior patterns, but to free the graduate from conformity to cultural and behavioral stereotypes. I do not have any pat suggestions as to how to measure the outcomes of higher education, but it seems safe to say that the search for specific behavioral outcomes is doomed to failure. It represents, moreover, a spurious and misguided objectivity. William James made the point in his essay on Harvard: "The day when Harvard shall stamp a single hard and fast type of character upon her children will be that of her downfall. Our undisciplinables are our proudest product" (14, p. 355).

SUMMARY

A cognitive aspect of ego development, ability to conceptualize oneself, is postulated as accounting for a major portion of the variance in structured personality tests. At least three points are needed to define the dimension. At the lowest point there is no capacity to conceptualize oneself as a psychological person; at the midpoint, a stereotyped self conception; at the highest point, a differentiated, realistic self conception. More or less synonymously, at the lowest point there is no distance from impulses; at the midpoint, distance from impulse but not from ego; at the highest point, ability to assume distance from ego as well as from impulse. This trait increases constantly with age; for constant age, it tends to increase with intelligence, education, and social status; and it tends to increase with psychotherapy. However, ego development has no conspicuous constantly increasing manifestations. Its most conspicuous manifestation in personality tests, tendency to answer in a stereotyped, usually a socially approved style, is not monotonically related to the trait, tending to decrease in the upper range and probably tending to increase in the lower range. A further difficulty in measuring favorable outcome of higher education, and incidentally, favorable outcome of psychotherapy, is that the highest level of ego development is characterized precisely by the absence of stereotyped, objectively specifiable behaviors and attitudes. I have followed Binet in using process as touchstone for dimension, but not imitated him too closely for fear of returning exactly to general ability.

Many methodologists, until recently including myself, believe that our job is to perfect a method for discovering traits, and the right method will lead us straightaway to a complete catalogue of important traits. Purely for its shock value I wish to record a contrary hypothesis, that every major human trait will be discovered and established by a unique method. Whether that hypothesis is true or not, methodological sophistication in the absence of psychological acumen will lead only to fragmentary dimensions and insights.

REFERENCES

1. Adorno, T. W., Frenkel-Brunswik, Else, Levinson, D. J., & Sanford, R. N. *The authoritarian personality.* New York: Harper, 1950.
2. Auld, F., Jr. Influence of social class on personality test responses. *Psychological Bulletin,* 1952, 49, 318–332.
3. Christie, R., & Cook, Peggy. A guide to the published literature relating to the authoritarian personality through 1956. *Journal of Psychology,* 1958, 45, 171–199.
4. Christie, R., Havel, Joan, & Seidenberg, B. Is the *F* scale irreversible? *Journal of Abnormal and Social Psychology,* 1958, 56, 143–159.

5. Cohn, T. S. The relation of the *F* scale to intelligence. *Journal of Social Psychology,* 1957, 46, 207–217.
6. Edwards, A. L. *The social desirability variable in personality assessment and research.* New York: Dryden Press, 1957.
7. Ekstein, R. Psychoanalytic techniques. In D. Brower & L. E. Abt (Eds.), *Progress in clinical psychology.* Vol. 2. New York: Grune & Stratton, 1956. Pp. 79–97.
8. Erikson, E. H. Growth and crises of the healthy personality. In M. J. E. Senn (Ed.), *Symposium on the healthy personality.* New York: Josiah Macy, Jr. Foundation, 1950.
9. Fromm, E. *Escape from freedom.* New York: Farrar & Rinehart, 1941.
10. Getzels, J. W., & Walsh, J. J. The method of paired direct and projective questionnaires in the study of attitude structure and socialization. *Psychological Monographs,* 1958, 72, No. 1 (Whole No. 454).
11. Hollingshead, A. B., & Redlich, F. C. *Social class and mental illness: a community study.* New York: Wiley, 1958.
12. Isaacs, K. S. Relatability, a proposed construct and an approach to its validation. Unpublished doctoral dissertation, Univer. of Chicago, 1956.
13. Jackson, D. N., & Messick, S. Content and style in personality assessment. *Psychological Bulletin,* 1958, 55, 243–252.
14. James, W. The true Harvard. As reprinted in W. James, *Memories and studies.* New York: Longmans Green & Co., 1911. Pp. 348–355.
15. Kelly, G. A. *The psychology of personal constructs.* Vol. 1. *A theory of personality.* New York: Norton, 1955.
16. Lyle, J. G., & Gilchrist, A. A. Problems of TAT interpretation and the diagnosis of delinquent trends. *British Journal of Medical Psychology,* 1958, 31, 51–59.
17. Purcell, K. The TAT and antisocial behavior. *Journal of Consulting Psychology,* 1956, 20, 449–456.
18. Redl, F., & Wineman, D. *The aggressive child.* Glencoe, Ill.: Free Press, 1957.
19. Remmers, H. H., & Radler, D. H. *The American teenager.* Indianapolis: Bobbs-Merrill, 1957.
20. Riesman, D., Denny, R., & Glazer, N. *The lonely crowd: a study of the changing American character.* New Haven: Yale Univer. Press, 1950.
21. Rogers, C. R. A process conception of psychotherapy. *American Psychologist,* 1958, 13, 142–149.
22. Sanford, N. (Ed.) Personality development during the college years. *Journal of Social Issues,* 1956, 12(4), 3–70.
23. Sullivan, C., Grant, Marguerite Q., & Grant, J. D. The development of interpersonal maturity: applications to delinquency. *Psychiatry,* 1957, 20, 373–385.
24. Titus, H. E., & Hollander, E. P. The California *F* scale in psychological research: 1950–1955. *Psychological Bulletin,* 1957, 54, 47–64.

Personality Measurement and
College Performance[1]

SAMUEL MESSICK

1963

In this paper I will discuss personality measurement primarily in terms of its potential contributions to the prediction of college performance. In this context, two major questions arise: 1) Are personality tests any good as measures of the purported personality characteristics? 2) What should these tests be used for? The first question is a scientific one and may be answered by an evaluation of available personality instruments against scientific standards of psychometric adequacy. The second question is at least in part an ethical one and may be answered by a justification of proposed uses for a test in terms of ethical standards and social or educational values. I will first discuss the scientific standards for appraising personality measures and will then consider how well these standards are typically met by instruments developed by each of three major approaches to personality measurement. The final section of the paper will discuss some of the ethical problems raised when personality measures are used for practical decisions.

PSYCHOMETRIC STANDARDS FOR
PERSONALITY MEASUREMENT

The major measurement requirements in personality, as in psychology generally, involve 1) the demonstration, through substantial consistency of response to a set of items, that *something* is being measured; and 2) the accumulation of evidence about the nature and meaning of this "something," in terms of the network of the measure's relations with theoretically relevant variables and its lack of relation with theoretically unrelated variables

[1] A preliminary version of some portions of this paper was prepared for the Committee of Examiners in Aptitude Testing of the College Entrance Examination Board. The author wishes to thank Salvatore Maddi for his many suggestions about the nature of the problems and the organization of the material. Grateful acknowledgment is also due Sydell Carlton, Norman Frederiksen, John French, Nathan Kogan, and Lawrence Stricker for their helpful comments on the manuscript.

(2, 10, 11, 19, 23, 49). In psychometric terms, these two critical properties for the evaluation of a purported personality measure are the measure's *reliability* and its *construct validity*.

An investigation of the measure's relations with other well-known variables may also provide a basis for determining whether the thing measured represents a relatively separate dimension with important specific properties or whether its major variance is predictable from a combination of other, possibly more basic, characteristics. Such information bears upon the status of the construct as a separate variable and upon the structure of its relations with other variables.

Whether the measure reflects a separate trait or a combination of characteristics or, indeed, whether the proposed construct is a valid integration of observed response consistencies or merely a gratuitous label, there is still another important property of the measure that can be independently evaluated—namely, its usefulness in predicting concurrent and future nontest behaviors as a possible basis for decision making and social action. For such purposes, which primarily include classification and selection situations, it is necessary that the measure display *predictive validity* in the form of substantial correlations with the criterion measures chosen to reflect relevant performances in the nontest domain. Although some psychologists would argue that such predictive validity is all that is necessary to warrant the use of a measure in making practical decisions, it will be maintained here that predictive validity is not sufficient and that it may be unwise to ignore construct validity even in practical prediction problems (28, 29, 37). This point will be discussed more fully later.

Just as a test has as many empirical validities as there are criterion measures to which it has been related, so too may a test display different proportions of reliable variance or reflect different construct interpretations, primarily because the motivations and defenses of the subjects are implicated in different ways under different testing conditions. Thus, instead of talking about the reliability and construct validity (or even the empirical validity) of the *test* per se, it might be better to talk about the reliability and construct validity of the *responses* to the test, as summarized in a particular score, thereby emphasizing that these test properties are relative to the processes used by the subjects in responding (47). These processes, in turn, may differ under different circumstances, particularly those affecting the conceptions and intentions of the subjects. Thus, the same test, for example, might measure one set of things if administered in the context of diagnostic guidance in a clinical setting, a radically different set of things if administered in the context of anonymous inquiry in a research laboratory, and yet another set if administered as a personal evaluation for industrial or academic selection. Furthermore, these different testing settings impose different ethical constraints upon the manner and conditions of eliciting personal, and what the subject may consider private, information (1, 18).

This point that personality tests, and even personality testers, may operate differently under different circumstances was one of the main reasons I initially chose to limit the present discussion to a particular context—namely, personality measurement in relation to college performance. Various contexts differ somewhat in the types of problems posed for personality measurement, but the timely context of assessment for college contains nearly all the problems at once. Of major concern in considering this context, however, is the inherently evaluative atmosphere of the testing settings. This means that we must take into account not only the ubiquitous response distortions due to defense mechanisms of self-deception and personal biases in self-regard (cf. 30), but also the distortions in performance and self-report that are at least partially deliberate attempts at faking and impression management (cf. 34).

The extent to which attempts are made to handle the problems of both deliberate misrepresentation and unintentional distortion becomes an important criterion for evaluating personality instruments, particularly for use in evaluative settings. Many personality measures have been developed in research contexts where deliberate misrepresentation may have been minimal; little is known of their psychometric properties under conditions of real or presumed personal evaluation. Some personality tests include specific devices for detecting faking, such as validity or malingering keys, which would enable students with excessive "lie" responses to be spotted and would also permit the use of the control scores as suppressor variables in correcting other scales (51). Other personality instruments rely on test formats that attempt to make faking difficult, such as the use of forced-choice techniques on questionnaires or of objective performance measures where the direction of faking is not obvious. Still other procedures use indirect items and disguised façades to circumvent the subject's defensive posture (8, 9, 48).

PSYCHOMETRIC PROBLEMS IN SOME TYPICAL APPROACHES TO PERSONALITY MEASUREMENT

We have considered several psychometric criteria for evaluating personality measures: reliability, empirical validity in predicting criteria or nontest behaviors, the structure of relations with other known variables, the adequacy of controls for faking and distortion, and—more basic because it subsumes aspects of the preceding properties—construct validity. We will now inquire how well these standards are typically met by instruments developed by three major approaches to personality measurement: self-report questionnaires, behavior ratings, and objective performance tests.

Self-Report Inventories

Before various types of self-report questionnaires are discussed, the general problem of stylistic consistencies or response sets on such instruments should be broached (16, 41). A major portion of the response variance on many personality inventories, particularly those with "True-False" or "Agree-Disagree" item formats, has been shown to reflect consistent stylistic tendencies that have a cumulative effect on presumed content scores (e.g., 24, 25, 42, 44). The major response styles emphasized thus far are the tendency to agree or acquiesce (15, 55), the tendency to respond desirably (24, 52), the tendency to respond deviantly (6, 63), and, to a lesser extent, the tendency to respond extremely in self-rating (60). These response styles have been conceptualized and studied as personality variables in their own right (41), but their massive influence on some personality inventories can seriously interfere with the measurement of other content traits (43). The problem becomes one of measuring response styles as potentially useful personality variables and at the same time controlling their influence on content scores (53, 78). The extent to which controls for response styles have been effective in reducing overwhelming stylistic variance becomes an important criterion in evaluating the measurement characteristics of self-report instruments.

We will consider three kinds of self-report or questionnaire measure of personality: 1) a type that I will call a *factorial inventory,* in which factor analysis or some other criterion of internal consistency is used to select items reflecting homogeneous dimensions (12, 13); 2) *empirically derived inventories,* in which significant differentiation among criterion groups is the basis of item selection; and 3) *rational inventories,* in which items are chosen on logical grounds to reflect theoretical properties of specified dimensions.

Factorial inventory scales are developed through the use of factor analysis or other methods of homogeneous keying (39, 50, 74) to isolate dimensions of consistency in response to self-descriptive items. The pool of items collected for analysis usually consists of a conglomeration of characteristics possibly relevant to some domain and sometimes includes items specifically written to represent the variables under study.

The most widely known of the current factored inventories are the Cattell 16 Personality Factor Questionnaire and the Guilford-Zimmerman Temperament Survey. Becker's (4) recent empirical comparison of the Cattell questionnaire with an earlier form of the Guilford scales has revealed an equivalence between four factors from the two inventories and substantial similarity for two other factors. Although considerable factor-analytic evidence at the item level generally supports the nature of the scales (12, 36), when two subscale scores were used to represent each factor supposedly measured by these inventories, Becker (4) found only eight distinguishable factors within the 16 PF and only five within 13 Guilford scales.

These factorial inventories were developed primarily in research settings, so that attention must be given to possible defensive distortions induced by their use in evaluative situations. Although procedures for detecting faking have been suggested, their systematic use has not been emphasized, nor has their effectiveness been clearly demonstrated. Further, empirical controls for response styles have usually not been included, although their operation has recently been noted on some of the factor scales (4, 5).

In the construction of *empirically derived inventory* scales, items are selected that significantly discriminate among criterion groups. The most widely known examples are scales from the Minnesota Multiphasic Personality Inventory (MMPI) and from the California Psychological Inventory (CPI). The justification of these scales is in terms of their empirical validity and their usefulness in classifying subjects as similar or dissimilar to criterion groups. Scale homogeneity, reliability, and construct validity are seldom emphasized. The difficulty arises when these scales are used not to predict criterion categories but rather to make inferences about the personality of the respondent. This latter use has become the typical one (cf. 73), but such application cannot be justified by empirical validity alone—homogeneity and construct validity become crucial under such circumstances (17, 41, 43).

Because of the widespread use of these inventories in clinical settings, considerable attention has been given to the problem of faking, particularly on the MMPI. Several scales are available for detecting lying and malingering (L, Mp, Sd, etc.), along with a validity scale (F) for uncovering excessive deviant responses (20). A measure of "defensiveness" (K) is also used both as a means of detecting this tendency and as a suppressor variable for controlling test-taking attitudes (51). Several studies of the effectiveness of these scales have indicated a somewhat variable, and usually only moderate, level of success (cf. 73, 77).

A major problem on the MMPI and CPI is the predominant role of the response styles of acquiescence and desirability, which in the former instrument define the first two major factors and together account for roughly half the total variance (25, 40, 42, 44). Presumably, these response styles are correlated with the criterion distinction utilized in the empirical scale construction (cf. 72), but their massive influence on these inventories drastically interferes with the attempted measurement of other content traits and limits their possible discriminant validity (43).

Rational inventories comprise items that have been written on theoretical or logical grounds to reflect specified traits. That such scales measure something is demonstrated subsequently by high internal consistency coefficients; that they measure distinguishable characteristics is shown by relatively low scale intercorrelations. Factor analysis is also sometimes used subsequently to investigate scale interrelations (65). On some of these inventories, such as Stern's Activities Index, little attention has been given initially to the role of response styles, while on others, such as the Edwards Personal Preference Schedule (EPPS), the major attraction has been the attempt to limit stylistic variance.

The EPPS employs a forced-choice item format: statements are presented to the subject in pairs, the members of each pair having been previously selected to be as equal as possible in average judged desirability. The respondent is required to select from each pair the statement that better describes his personality. Such forced-choice items do not offer an opportunity for the response style of acquiescence to operate. Further, since the paired statements are also approximately matched in desirability, a consistent tendency to respond desirably should in principle have relatively little effect upon item choices (14, 24, 26). Even though desirability variance is not eliminated thereby, primarily because of the existence of consistent personal viewpoints about desirability that cannot be simultaneously equated (7, 38, 46, 52, 62), the forced-choice approach offers considerable promise for reducing the overwhelming influence of response styles on questionnaires (58). Unfortunately, the EPPS still cannot be recommended for other than research purposes because insufficient evidence exists concerning its empirical and construct validity (66).

The different approaches to scale construction that distinguish factorial, empirically derived, and rational inventories might well be combined into a single measurement enterprise, wherein scale homogeneity, construct validity, and the theoretical basis of item content, as well as empirical differentiation, would be successively refined in an iterative cycle (49, 58). In this way, the differences among the approaches, depending as they would upon the particular point in the cycle that one chose to start with, would become trivial, and scales would be systematically developed in terms of joint criteria of homogeneity, theoretical relevance, construct validity, and empirical utility.

Behavior Ratings

Behavior ratings represent a second major approach to personality measurement. Direct ratings of behavior, both of job performance and of personality characteristics have been frequently employed in educational and industrial evaluation (75). Personality ratings, however, have seldom been formally or systematically used in the typical selection situation for many reasons, one of them being the difficulty of obtaining reliable or comparable ratings for candidates coming from different sources. However, if teacher- and peer-ratings of personality made in college, for example, were to prove valid in predicting behavioral criteria of college success (cf. 69) and if these ratings could, in turn, be predicted by other measures (such as self-report inventories), then the predicted ratings might be useful in pre-college decisions. Behavior ratings that correlate with college success could thus serve as intermediate criteria for validating self-report measures of the same dimensions.

Cattell (12) has isolated approximately fifteen dimensions from behavior ratings, reflecting such qualities as ego strength, excitability, dominance, and surgency. Tupes and Christal (71), on the other hand, in analyzing the same rating scales and in a few cases the same data, provided evidence for only five strong and recurrent factors, which were labeled extroversion, agreeableness, conscientiousness, emotional stability, and culture (see also 59). Cattell (12) has also claimed a congruence between most of his behavior rating factors and their questionnaire counterparts, which suggests that questionnaire scales can indeed predict rating dimensions. Cattell's claim of a one-to-one matching of behavior rating and questionnaire factors has been challenged by Becker (3), however, who concluded that available evidence did not support the alleged relation.

Norman (58), on the other hand, has clearly demonstrated that questionnaire scales can be developed that will correlate substantially with behavior rating factors. In his particular study, he attempted to predict the five rating factors obtained by Tupes and Christal (70, 71) from peer nominations. Since these ratings had previously exhibited substantial validity in predicting officer effectiveness criteria at the USAF Officer Candidate School (OCS) (69), the subsequent prediction of these ratings by questionnaire scales has direct implications for selection.

Incidentally, Norman's (58) scale construction procedure involved an extremely promising technique for handling faking in evaluative settings. Items in a forced-choice format equated for "admission-to-OCS desirability" were administered under normal and faking instructions. In the construction of the scales, the items were balanced between those showing a mean shift under faking instructions in the direction of the keyed response and those showing a mean shift away from the keyed response. Mean scores for the resulting scales were thus equated under normal and faking conditions, and, in addition, powerful detection scales were developed to isolate extreme dissemblers.

Objective Performance Tests

The third major approach to personality measurement considered here is the objective performance test. According to Campbell (9), an objective measure of personality, like an objective measure of ability or achievement, is a test in which the examinee believes that he should respond accurately because correct answers exist as a basis for evaluating his performance. Cattell (12), on the other hand, considers a test objective if the subject is unaware of the manner in which his behavior affects the scoring and interpretation, a property that Campbell (9) prefers to use in the definition of indirect measurement.

Cattell's (12) analyses of objective performance measures of personality have uncovered approximately eighteen dimensions, with such labels as "harric assertiveness," "inhibition," "anxiety," and "critical practicality." Thurstone (68) and Guilford (e.g., 35) have also developed measures of several perceptual and cognitive dimensions that represent objective tests of personality. Measures of speed and flexibility of closure (68), for example, and of ideational fluency appear more congenial in a personality framework than in the traditional ability formulation (cf. 12, 35, 80). Some of Guilford's (35) work on divergent thinking also deals with stylistic restrictions in the generation and manipulation of ideas, which appear as much like personality consistencies as measures of "maximum performance" abilities (18).

In many cases, the objective nature of these tests makes it difficult to decide how to fake, since some look very much like ability tests and appear to have clear adaptive requirements that subjects should strive to achieve. Test properties, however, have been studied primarily in research contexts, where deliberate faking may have been minimal. Certain characteristics may change under other conditions. Available objective tests also tend to be unreliable, primarily because they have been deliberately kept short for use in large test batteries. Because of practice and order effects on some of the procedures, however, there is no guarantee that high reliabilities can be obtained simply by lengthening the tests.

Considerable attention has been given in recent years to certain stylistic dimensions in the performance of cognitive tasks (31, 32, 79, 80). These personality dimensions have been conceptualized as cognitive styles, which represent a person's typical modes of perceiving, remembering, thinking, and problem solving. Approaches to the measurement of these variables have routinely included objective procedures. Some examples of these dimensions are 1) *field-dependence-independence*—"an analytical, in contrast to a global, way of perceiving [which] entails a tendency to experience items as discrete from their backgrounds and reflects ability to overcome the influence of an embedding context" (80; see also 45, 54); 2) *leveling-sharpening*—a dimension where subjects at the leveling extreme tend to assimilate new material to an established framework, whereas sharpeners, at the other extreme, tend to contrast new material with the old and to maintain distinctions (31); and 3) *category-width preferences*—a dimension of individual consistencies in modes of categorizing perceived similarities and differences, reflected in consistent preferences for broad or narrow categories in conceptualizing (31, 33, 56, 61, 64).

Both the cognitive nature and the stylistic nature of these variables make them appear particularly relevant to the kinds of cognitive tasks performed in academic settings. Certain types of subject matter and certain problems or problem formulations might favor broad categorizers over narrow categorizers, for example, or levelers over sharpeners, and vice versa. This "vice versa" is extremely important: since it is unlikely that one end of such stylistic dimensions would prove uniformly more adaptive than the other, the relativity of their value should be recognized. (Incidentally, the possibility of such relativity of value might well be extended to other personality variables where the desirability of one end of the trait has usually been prejudged. What conceptions would change, for example, if "flexibility vs. rigidity" had been called "confusion vs. control"?)

It is quite possible that we have already unwittingly included such stylistic variance in some measure of intellectual aptitude, such as the Scholastic Aptitude Test (SAT), but if this is the case, the nature and direction of its operation should be specified and controlled. It is possible, for example, that the five-alternative multiple-choice form of quantitative aptitude items might favor subjects who prefer broad categories on category-width measures. Quick, rough approximations to the quantitative items might appropriately be judged by these subjects to be "close enough" to a given alternative, whereas "narrow range" subjects may require more time-consuming exact solutions before answering. Significant correlations between category preferences and quantitative aptitude tests have indeed been obtained and have been found to vary widely as a function of the spacing of alternatives on multiple-choice forms of the quantitative aptitude tests (57).

THE ETHICS OF SELECTION

In considering personality measures of potential utility in the evaluative context of college performance, I have tried to give the impression that many measures are available, but none is adequate when systematically evaluated against psychometric standards. In addition, I have tried to give some indication of the rapidly advancing technology that is evolving in personality measurement to support research efforts. In the relatively near future, this technology may produce personality measures that are acceptable by measurement and prediction standards, so that the question may soon arise in earnest as to the scope of their practical application. We have considered some of the scientific standards for deciding their appropriateness, but what about the ethical ones?

The choice of any particular personality measure for use, say, in college admission involves an implicit value judgment, which, at the least, should be made explicit in an educational policy that attempts to justify its use. One compelling justification for using personality measures in college selection would be to screen out extreme deviants. Colleges would be well advised, for example, to consider rejecting assaultive or suicidal psychotics, and some schools might wish to eliminate overt homosexuals. The use of personality measures for differentiating among normal subjects might also be justified in terms of empirical validity. After all, as long as there are many more candidates for admission than can be accepted, it seems better to make selections on the basis of valid measures than on the basis of chance. But is empirical validity enough? Validity for what? Certainly the role of the criterion in such an argument must be clearly specified.

The relevant domain of criterion performances should be outlined and attempts should be made to develop appropriate criterion measures. Since different criterion domains can be defined for different aspects of college success, selection might be oriented toward several of them simultaneously or toward only a few. Consider some of the possibilities: In *selection for academic performance,* criterion measures might include global grade point averages, separate grades for different subject-matter fields, or standardized curriculum achievement examinations. In *selection for college environment,* criterion measures could be set up in terms of desired contributions to extracurricular college life (such as football playing and newspaper editing) or in terms of balancing geographic, social class, sex, and, perhaps, temperament distributions in the student body. If the demands and pressures of the college environment and social structure have been studied, criterion standards might also be specified for selecting students with congenial needs that will fit well with (and hopefully have a higher probability of being satisfied by) the college enivronment (cf. 65). We could also talk in terms of *selection for ultimate career satisfaction* and *selection for desirable personal characteristics* (cf. 21)—or for desirable attitudes.

In each of these cases, it should be emphasized that potential predictor measures are not evaluated in terms of their empirical validity for *criterion behaviors,* but, rather, in terms of their prediction of *criterion measures,* which, in turn, are presumed to reflect the criterion behaviors of interest. And these criterion measures should be evaluated against the same psychometric standards as any other measures. Not only should they be reliable, but also the nature of the attributes measured should be elucidated in a construct validity framework (22). Since each of these criterion measures may also contain some specific variance that is not particularly related to the criterion behaviors, one should also be concerned that an obtained validity coefficient reflects a correlation with relevant domain characteristics and not with irrelevant variance incidentally reflected in the putative criterion measure. Thus, the question of the *intrinsic validity* of the predictor and of the criterion measures should be broached, even if in practice many of the answers may seem presumptive ones (37). In the last analysis, ultimate criteria are determined on rational grounds in any event (67). Should a reading comprehension test predict grades in gunner's mates school (28)? Should a college that found docile, submissive students receiving higher grades in freshman courses select on this basis, or should they consider revising their grading system? Such decisions might become more difficult if the personality characteristics involved had more socially desirable labels.

Just as we have been concerned about predicting grades not as they are but as they should be (27, 29), so too should we be concerned not only with predicting personality characteristics that are presently considered desirable for college students but also with deciding which characteristics, if any, should be considered desirable. It is possible, for example, that certain prepotent values, such as the desire for diversity, would override decisions to select students in terms of particular personal qualities. The very initiation of selection on any given personality variables might lead to conformity pressures toward the stereotype implied by the selected characteristics. Apart from the effects of the selection itself, such pressures to simulate desired personal qualities would probably decrease diversity in the college environment and in the personalities of the students. Wolfle (81) and others have emphasized the value of diversity and even the value of uneven acquisition of skills within individuals as important contributors to the optimal development of talent. Restrictions upon diversity, however subtle, should therefore be undertaken cautiously.

I should like to close metaphorically with a story of the lineage of King Arthur. At the end of the second book of *The Once and Future King,* T. H. White (76) points out that Arthur's half-sister bore him a son, Modred, who was his ultimate downfall; that on the eve of the conception Arthur was a very young man drunk with the spoils of recent victory; that his half-sister was much older than he and active in the seduction; and that Arthur did not know that the woman was his sister. But it seems that "in tragedy, innocence is not enough." And in the use of personality measures in college admission, empirical validity is not enough.

REFERENCES

1. American Psychological Association. Ethical standards of psychologists. *American Psychologist,* 1963, 18, 56–60.
2. Bechtoldt, H. P. Construct validity: a critique. *American Psychologist,* 1959, 14, 619–629.
3. Becker, W. C. The matching of behavior rating and questionnaire personality factors. *Psychological Bulletin,* 1960, 57, 201–212.
4. Becker, W. C. A comparison of the factor structure and other properties of the 16 PF and the Guilford-Martin Personality Inventories. *Educational and Psychological Measurement,* 1961, 21, 393–404.
5. Bendig, A. W. "Social desirability" and "anxiety" variables in the IPAT Anxiety Scale. *Journal of Consulting Psychology,* 1959, 23, 377.
6. Berg, I. A. Response bias and personality: the deviation hypothesis. *Journal of Psychology,* 1955, 40, 61–72.
7. Borislow, B. The Edwards Personal Preference Schedule (EPPS) and fakability. *Journal of Applied Psychology,* 1958, 42, 22–27.
8. Campbell, D. T. The indirect assessment of social attitudes. *Psychological Bulletin,* 1950, 47, 15–38.
9. Campbell, D. T. A typology of tests, projective and otherwise. *Journal of Consulting Psychology,* 1957, 21, 207–210.

10. Campbell, D. T. Recommendations for APA test standards regarding construct, trait, or discriminant validity. *American Psychologist,* 1960, 15, 546–553.

11. Campbell, D. T., & Fiske, D. W. Convergent and discriminant validation by the multitrait-multimethod matrix. *Psychological Bulletin,* 1959, 56, 81–105.

12. Cattell, R. B. *Personality and motivation structure and measurement.* New York: Harcourt, Brace & World, 1957.

13. Comrey, A. Factored homogeneous item dimensions: a strategy for personality research. In S. Messick & J. Ross (Eds.), *Measurement in personality and cognition.* New York: Wiley, 1962. Pp. 11–26.

14. Corah, N. L., *et al.* Social desirability as a variable in the Edwards Personal Preference Schedule. *Journal of Consulting Psychology,* 1958, 22, 70–72.

15. Couch, A., & Keniston, K. Yeasayers and naysayers: agreeing response set as a personality variable. *Journal of Abnormal and Social Psychology,* 1960, 60, 151–174.

16. Cronbach, L. J. Further evidence on response sets and test design. *Educational and Psychological Measurement,* 1950, 10, 3–31.

17. Cronbach, L. J. Review of basic readings on the MMPI in psychology and medicine (G. S. Welsh & W. G. Dahlstrom, Eds.). *Psychometrika,* 1958, 23, 385–386.

18. Cronbach, L. J. *Essentials of psychological testing.* (2nd ed.) New York: Harper, 1960.

19. Cronbach, L. J., & Meehl, P. E. Construct validity in psychological tests. *Psychological Bulletin,* 1955, 52, 281–302.

20. Dahlstrom, W. G., & Welsh, G. S. *An MMPI handbook.* Minneapolis: Univer. of Minnesota Press, 1960.

21. Davis, J. A. Desirable characteristics of college students: the criterion problem. Paper read at American Psychological Association, Philadelphia, September 1963.

22. Dunnette, M. D. A note on *the* criterion. *Journal of Applied Psychology,* 1963, 47, 251–254.

23. Ebel, R. L. Must all tests be valid? *American Psychologist,* 1961, 16, 640–647.

24. Edwards, A. L. *The social desirability variable in personality assessment and research.* New York: Dryden, 1957.

25. Edwards, A. L., Diers, Carol J., & Walker, J. N. Response sets and factor loadings on 61 personality scales. *Journal of Applied Psychology,* 1962, 46, 220–225.

26. Edwards, A. L., Wright, C. E., & Lunneborg, C. E. A note on "Social Desirability as a Variable in the Edwards Personal Preference Schedule." *Journal of Consulting Psychology,* 1959, 23, 558.

27. Fishman, J. A. Unsolved criterion problems in the selection of college students. *Harvard Educational Review,* 1958, 28, 340–349.

28. Frederiksen, N. Statistical study of the achievement testing program in gunner's mates schools. (Navpers 18079), 1948.

29. Frederiksen, N. The evaluation of personal and social qualities. In *College Admissions, No. 1.* New York: College Entrance Examination Board, 1954. Pp. 93–105.

30. Frenkel-Brunswik, Else. Mechanisms of self deception. *Journal of Social Psychology,* 1939, 10, 409–420.

31. Gardner, R. W., *et al.* Cognitive control. *Psychological Issues,* 1959, 1, Monograph 4.

32. Gardner, R. W., Jackson, D. N., & Messick, S. Personality organization in cognitive controls and intellectual abilities. *Psychological Issues,* 1960, 2, Monograph 8.

33. Gardner, R. W., & Schoen, R. A. Differentiation and abstraction in concept formation. *Psychological Monographs,* 1962, 76, No. 41 (Whole No. 560).

34. Goffman, E. *The presentation of self in everyday life.* New York: Doubleday Anchor Books, 1959.

35. Guilford, J. P. *Personality.* New York: McGraw-Hill, 1959.

36. Guilford, J. P., & Zimmerman, W. S. Fourteen dimensions of temperament. *Psychological Monographs,* 1956, 70, No. 10 (Whole No. 417).

37. Gulliksen, H. Intrinsic validity. *American Psychologist,* 1950, 5, 511–517.

38. Heilbrun, A. B., & Goodstein, L. D. Relationships between personal and social desirability sets and performance on the Edwards Personal Preference Schedule. *Journal of Applied Psychology,* 1959, 43, 302–305.

39. Henrysson, S. The relation between factor loadings and biserial correlations in item analysis. *Psychometrika,* 1962, 27, 419–424.

40. Jackson, D. N. Stylistic response determinants in the California Psychological Inventory. *Educational and Psychological Measurement,* 1960, 20, 339–346.

41. Jackson, D. N., & Messick, S. Content and style in personality assessment. *Psychological Bulletin,* 1958, 55, 243–252.

42. Jackson, D. N., & Messick, S. Acquiescence and desirability as response-determinants on the MMPI. *Educational and Psychological Measurement,* 1961, 21, 771–790.

43. Jackson, D. N., & Messick, S. Response styles and the assessment of psychopathology. In S. Messick & J. Ross (Eds.), *Measurement in personality and cognition.* New York: Wiley, 1962. Pp. 129–155.

44. Jackson, D. N., & Messick, S. Response styles on the MMPI: comparison of clinical and normal samples. *Journal of Abnormal and Social Psychology,* 1962, 65, 285–299.

45. Kagan, J., Moss, H. A., & Sigel, I. E. The psychological significance of styles of conceptualization. In J. C. Wright & J. Kagan (Eds.), Basic cognitive processes in children. *Monographs of the Society for Research in Child Development,* 1963, 28, No. 2, 73–112.

46. Lapointe, R. E., & Auclair, G. A. The use of social desirability in forced-choice methodology. *American Psychologist,* 1961, 16, 446. (Abstract)

47. Lennon, R. Assumptions underlying the use of content validity. *Educational and Psychological Measurement,* 1956, 16, 294–304.

48. Loevinger, Jane. Some principles of personality measurement. *Educational and Psychological Measurement,* 1955, 15, 3–17.
49. Loevinger, Jane. Objective tests as instruments of psychological theory. *Psychological Reports,* 1957, 3, 635–694.
50. Loevinger, Jane, Gleser, Goldine, & DuBois, P. H. Maximizing the discriminating power of a multiple-score test. *Psychometrika,* 1953, 18, 309–317.
51. Meehl, P. E., & Hathaway, S. R. The K factor as a suppressor variable in the MMPI. *Journal of Applied Psychology,* 1946, 30, 525–564.
52. Messick, S. Dimensions of social desirability. *Journal of Consulting Psychology,* 1960, 24, 279–287.
53. Messick, S. Response style and content measures from personality inventories. *Educational and Psychological Measurement,* 1962, 22, 41–56.
54. Messick, S., & Fritzky, F. J. Dimensions of analytic attitude in cognition and personality. *Journal of Personality,* 1963, 31, 346–370.
55. Messick, S., & Jackson, D. N. Acquiescence and the factorial interpretation of the MMPI. *Psychological Bulletin,* 1961, 58, 299–304.
56. Messick, S., & Kogan, N. Differentiation and compartmentalization in object-sorting measures of categorizing style. *Perceptual and Motor Skills,* 1963, 16, 47–51.
57. Messick, S., & Kogan, N. Category width and quantitative aptitude. *Perceptual and Motor Skills,* 1965, 20, 493–497.
58. Norman, W. T. Personality measurement, faking, and detection: an assessment method for use in personnel selection. *Journal of Applied Psychology,* 1963, 47, 225–241.
59. Norman, W. T. Toward an adequate taxonomy of personality attributes: replicated factor structure in peer nomination personality ratings. *Journal of Abnormal and Social Psychology,* 1963, 66, 574–583.
60. Peabody, D. Two components in bipolar scales: direction and extremeness. *Psychological Review,* 1962, 69, 65–73.
61. Pettigrew, T. F. The measurement and correlates of category width as a cognitive variable. *Journal of Personality,* 1958, 26, 532–544.
62. Rosen, E. Self-appraisal, personal desirability, and perceived social desirability of personality traits. *Journal of Abnormal and Social Psychology,* 1956, 52, 151–158.
63. Sechrest, L., & Jackson, D. N. Deviant response tendencies: their measurement and interpretation. *Educational and Psychological Measurement,* 1963, 23, 33–53.
64. Sloane, H. N., Gorlow, L., & Jackson, D. N. Cognitive styles in equivalence range. *Perceptual and Motor Skills,* 1963, 16, 389–404.
65. Stern, G. G. The measurement of psychological characteristics of students and learning environments. In S. Messick & J. Ross (Eds.), *Measurement in personality and cognition.* New York: Wiley, 1962. Pp. 27–68.
66. Stricker, L. J. A review of the Edwards Personal Preference Schedule. In O. K. Buros (Ed.), *The sixth mental measurements yearbook.* Highland Park, N.J.: Gryphon Press, 1965.

67. Thorndike, R. L. *Personnel selection: test and measurement techniques.* New York: Wiley, 1949.
68. Thurstone, L. L. A factorial study of perception. *Psychometric Monograph* No. 4, 1944.
69. Tupes, E. C. Relationships between behavior trait ratings by peers and later officer performance of USAF Officer Candidate School graduates. USAF PTRC tech. Note, 1957, No. 57–125.
70. Tupes, E. C., & Christal, R. E. Stability of personality trait rating factors obtained under diverse conditions. USAF WADC tech. Note, 1958, No. 58–61.
71. Tupes, E. C., & Christal, R. E. Recurrent personality factors based on trait ratings. USAF ASD tech. Rep., 1961, No. 61–97.
72. Wahler, H. J. Response styles in clinical and nonclinical groups. *Journal of Consulting Psychology,* 1961, 25, 533–539.
73. Welsh, G. S., & Dahlstrom, W. G. (Eds.) *Basic readings on the MMPI in psychology and medicine.* Minneapolis: Univer. of Minnesota Press, 1956.
74. Wherry, R. J., & Winer, B. J. A method for factoring large numbers of items. *Psychometrika,* 1953, 18, 161–179.
75. Whisler, T. L., & Harper, Shirley F. (Eds.) *Performance appraisal.* New York: Holt, Rinehart, & Winston, 1962.
76. White, T. H. *The once and future king.* New York: Putnam, 1958.
77. Wiggins, J. S. Interrelations among MMPI measures of dissimulation under standard and social desirability instructions. *Journal of Consulting Psychology,* 1959, 23, 419–427.
78. Wiggins, J. S. Strategic, method, and stylistic variance in the MMPI. *Psychological Bulletin,* 1962, 59, 224–242.
79. Witkin, H. A., *et al. Personality through perception.* New York: Harper, 1954.
80. Witkin, H. A., *et al. Psychological differentiation.* New York: Wiley, 1962.
81. Wolfle, D. Diversity of talent. *American Psychologist,* 1960, 15, 535–545.

12 · JUDGMENTAL ASSESSMENT PROCEDURES

PSYCHOMETRICS REQUIRES judgmental evaluations for a variety of purposes. Ratings by supervisors, teachers, co-workers, and other observers are often incorporated into the criterion measures against which tests are validated. Personal judgments by subject-matter experts play a major part in the content validation of achievement test items. Judgments are needed in scoring performance on certain types of tests not amenable to objective scoring—such as tests of literary or artistic composition or situational tests. Judgmental assessment procedures, such as interviewing techniques, are also widely employed to elicit information not available from tests, as well as to supplement test data. Finally, the integration of data from different test and nontest sources and their interpretation with reference to specific decisions usually involve the judgment of a clinician, counselor, personnel psychologist, or other professional specialist.

Several of these applications of the judgment process are illustrated in the papers reproduced in this chapter. Tucker's paper concerns the content validation of achievement tests. Particularly within a controversial area, subject-matter experts often disagree as to the relevance of individual items to the objectives of the test. Tucker reports an investigation of the relevance ratings assigned to 225 social studies items by 17 teachers of social studies. An obverse factor analysis of the intercorrelations among the 17 judges yielded a "type" factor revealing two contrasting schools of thought among subgroups of judges. One subgroup favored "information" items, the other favored "self-contained" items calling for reasoning and interpretation.

Obverse factor analysis was again employed in French's study, this time to identify schools of thought among the scorers of English compositions. A group of 53 judges, including not only teachers of English but also social scientists, natural scientists, writers, editors, lawyers, and business executives, rated 300 short essays written by college freshmen. The intercorrelations among the 53 judges were factor analyzed. By identifying the qualities that influence judges' evaluations of such writing samples, the results of this study suggest possible ways of rescuing essay writing tests from psychometric oblivion and of improving their grading by trained judges.

In another effort to systematize the evaluation of writing ability, Lorge proposes a novel approach. He begins by considering the various techniques developed for assessing the readability or comprehensability of books, and notes that no available readability formula takes into account the structure, organization, or coherence of the writing. It is to the assessment of structure in student writing the Lorge addresses himself. On the basis of two factor-analytic studies of the rated qualities of compositions and other written passages, he concludes that structure is not independently evaluated by judges but tends to be included under the "general goodness" of writing. Nor do the definitions of structure given in handbooks of writing suggest useful operational measures. On the other hand, a rearrangement test, using scrambled texts, showed promise of providing an independent measure of structure. This technique could be employed either by examinees in an objective test of writing structure or by raters in judging the coherence of written prose.

While the first three papers consider applications of judgment to the construction and scoring of tests, the last three pertain to the use of judgmental techniques in gathering or interpretating data about individuals. Sanford's paper was presented at a 1953 symposium on the interview as an evaluative technique. In it, Sanford concentrates on the functions of the interview as a data-gathering technique in personality research. After showing how the research interview differs from other types of interview, he describes specific ways of improving its effectiveness and notes precautions to be observed in this context. Among others, he discusses procedures for reducing halo effect and needed controls for the influence that participation in the study may have upon the subject's psychological development.

Following the publication in 1954 of Meehl's book, *Clinical vs. Statistical Prediction,* widespread interest was aroused in the clinician's role in synthesizing and interpreting personnel data. The ensuing controversy stimulated the publication of both theoretical analyses and empirical studies of the nature of "clinical judgment." The specific question raised by Meehl was: given the same quantitative data on a group of individuals, how do predictions based on clinical judgment compare with those derived from a regression equation? The studies Meehl surveyed favored the latter, especially when the vastly greater cost of the clinical prediction was taken into account.

At the Invitational Conference held in 1955, a session was devoted to "Clinical versus Actuarial Prediction," in which Meehl participated as the invited discussant. The last two papers in this chapter were selected from this session. McArthur argues that available investigations do not provide a proper comparison of the two methods, and proceeds to outline the requirements of an ideal experiment for this purpose. The clinician and the actuary, he maintains, should not be compared under constant conditions, but under conditions maximally favorable to the application of their respective methods. He then describes the optimum conditions for the use of the clinical method, with regard to kinds of data, type of analysis, and nature of predictions to be made. Essentially, McArthur argues that the clinician is qualified to perform a *different* task from that of the actuary. In his discussion of McArthur's paper, Meehl[1] agrees with this point, but insists that in actual practice clinicians spend too much of their time performing actuarial predictions, from which they should be freed so that they might have more time to devote to distinctly clinical functions.

Zubin, too, argues that *both* clinical and statistical predictions are needed, but he goes further in maintaining that they cannot be separated and that their comparison poses a pseudo-problem. His examples of the specific ways in which the two approaches interact are taken largely from clinical research rather than from clinical practice, a fact emphasized by Meehl in his discussion of the paper. Meehl insists that in clinical practice these two methods for making predictions can be clearly differentiated. On the other hand, Zubin points out that the clinician uses predictions, stated in terms of probabilities, to reach a decision about the individual; and this decision involves a clinical judgment. Zubin goes on to discuss the need for fuller development of statistical techniques suitable for the analysis of the individual case and of homogeneous or "like-minded" subgroups, or types. He illustrates his discussion by citing two investigations: one dealing with subjects' reactions to drugs, the other with the response patterns of schizophrenics and normals to a personality inventory.

With Zubin's plea for the development of clinical statistics, this chapter comes full circle. Having started with a consideration of how judgmental ("clinical") procedures could serve the goals of the psychometrician, we have ended with a consideration of how psychometric ("actuarial") methods may be modified and adapted to meet the needs of the clinician. From still another angle, the experimental psychologist is predominantly concerned with the general effects of systematically controlled variables. The

---

[1] See *Proceedings* of the 1955 Conference, pp. 136–141, and especially pp. 138–139.

subgroup or typological analyses proposed by Zubin are designed essentially to identify interactions between individual variables (of primary concern to psychometrician and clinician) and experimental variables. A joint consideration of the clinical, statistical, *and* experimental approaches may suggest ways to effect a productive synthesis of all three.

Factor Analysis of Relevance Judgments: An Approach to Content Validity[1]

LEDYARD R TUCKER

1961

Content validity seems to be an almost universally accepted requisite of tests used to evaluate achievement and performance. For example, *Technical Recommendations for Psychological Tests and Diagnostic Techniques* states: "Content validity is especially important in the case of achievement and proficiency measures" (2, p. 13). Similar sentiment is expressed in *Technical Recommendations for Achievement Tests* (1). Texts and manuals on the construction of achievement tests emphasize the importance of consulting subject-matter experts so as to achieve not only accuracy in the questions included in a test but also a proper coverage of material in the area to be examined.

Problems exist, however, in the precise definition of content validity. A frequent definition is in terms of the sampling of a specified universe of content. While a coefficient of content validity could be developed theoretically, relating performance on a test to performance over the universe of content, the Achilles Heel in this definition is the specification of the universe of content. Some universes of content are easy to specify. A universe for spelling proficiency, for example, might contain all the words in some accepted dictionary. Other universes, such as the composition of business letters, are less easily specified. A unit task in this case may be taken as the composition of a letter in a given business situation and the universe of content can be defined in terms of the universe of business situations. But this universe may be infinitely varied with a large number of common situations and a variety of increasingly rare situations. Complete enumeration of the spelling proficiency universe is quite possible while for the business letter such an enumeration is quite impossible.

[1] This paper is based, in part, on research conducted by William E. Coffman of Educational Testing Service and the author, jointly supported by Educational Testing Service and the College Entrance Examination Board.

Fortunately in the case of the business letter, a universe of business situations does exist in the real world, and a survey of these situations is possible. Such a survey could yield a sample of situations to be used in a test.

There exist in education, however, many cases for which the specifications of universes of content are much more difficult. Often a general field of knowledge or skill is defined in general terms which correspond to no existing universe of situations. These terms of definition may be such that qualified people could judge whether a given situation lies within the universe or does not. Frequently, however, the general terms of definition are open to different interpretation by qualified people. This leads to proper controversy as to the nature of the universe of content for each such field of knowledge or skill and compounds the problem. There is neither a universe in actual existence nor agreement whether particular situations lie in the universe or not. Consider, for example, a general science course for ninth graders. Suppose that this course is described as presenting an introduction to scientific method and knowledge in the fields of physical and biological sciences. Insofar as the totality of existing scientific knowledge and procedures is growing, there is considerable question whether a universe of these situations is in actual existence. To guarantee complete existence of a universe of content, the general terms should be qualified with a statement as to present knowledge. Even with this statement, the universe for a general science course is not completely delineated. What material is introductory and what is not? Answers to this question depend on the judgments of the person answering the question.

A commonly stated proposition is that the objectives of instruction should be described in concrete terms rather than in vague, abstract terms. In many aspects, this description in concrete terms is equivalent to enumeration of the universe of content. Once a complete description of the objectives of a course is made in concrete terms, a considerable part of the problem of content validity of a measuring instrument for evaluation of the achievement of students has been solved. A close inspection of this procedure of translating the abstract terms of a concept into concrete terms reveals again the possibility of differences of opinion among individuals, even among individuals commonly accepted as qualified in some particular field. Strong controversy exists, for example, as to whether in citizenship training students should be trained toward political conservatism or toward political progressivism. There would not be agreement between individuals advocating one or the other of these views as to the concrete content of a course in citizenship, although they might agree that such a course under the general description would be worthwhile.

From the foregoing, we may conclude that the content validity of a test not only depends on the material included in the test and a general definition of an area of knowledge and skills when this definition is couched in abstract terms, but also depends on the point of view of the person interpreting the general definition of the area. A test having content validity for one interpretation may lack content validity for another interpretation. Herein lies a major problem in the construction of standardized achievement tests. When such divergent interpretations occur, no single test yielding a single score can have content validity for all interpretations, and several tests are indicated, one for each interpretation. Thus, it is of vital importance that systematic knowledge exist as to the extent and kind of different interpretations of accepted general concepts of areas of knowledge.

In some cases, the divergent interpretations are well known, especially when each view has been vigorously advocated by some individuals. In other cases, the divergent interpretations may not be well known, especially when there has not been active debate. The divergent interpretations may not be solidified into distinct points of view; rather, there may be flexible discussions and disagreements couched in polite tolerance. Experimental methods for investigating these cases which yield indications of the latent controversies and divergent interpretations should add materially to our ability to construct tests with content validity. One such procedure is involved in the factor analysis of relevance judgments of items. I shall discuss this procedure as studied in research by William E. Coffman and the author, supported by the College Entrance Examination Board and Educational Testing Service.

As part of its continuing program of test research and development, the College Entrance Examination Board, a few years ago, appointed committees to work with the Test Development Division of Educational Testing Service in the preparation of experimental tests in three broad content areas: science, humanities, and social studies. These tests were termed "The Tests of Developed Abilities" and were to examine college applicants on the broad knowledge and skills that might be expected to grow out of experiences in a sound program of secondary education. Each committee, including the Social Studies Committee, was responsible for defining "developed abilities" in its field and for constructing test questions to measure the abilities thus defined. The Social Studies Committee defined its field through an outline naming the general abilities which the student should have mastered and the content through which the abilities should be applied. The concrete definition consisted of 225 test questions. A majority of the questions were of a "composite" type, requiring the simultaneous use of both knowledge and skill, but two other types were included. One of these types, termed "information items," focused primarily on knowledge while the other, termed "self-contained items," required only that the student do something with content presented explicitly in the item.

But would a test score derived from the 225 items be valid as a measure of developed abilities in social studies as judged by a sample of experts more representative of social studies teachers than the five-member committee? To answer this question, the College Board appointed a panel of critics to review the proposed test material. Data for our study were collected from 17 members of this panel. We wished to investigate for systematic differences in value opinions regarding the proper content of such a test.

Each judge was requested to review each item in the sample of 225 and to rate it on a scale from 0 to 5 as to importance in evaluating the developed abilities of the examinees. The panel members were further warned to discount the effect of difficulty of an item in making the judgment as to importance. They were asked to judge difficulty separately and then to remember that while one might attach great importance to a right answer to a difficult item, a similar importance could not be attached to a wrong answer. Likewise, while one might attach great importance to a wrong answer to an easy item, a similar importance could not be attached to a right answer. And finally, both right and wrong answers might be considered important when items were of middle difficulty.

The task, then, was to evaluate the relevance of each item for measuring the developed abilities in social studies. A rating of 0 was defined to indicate that the item was irrelevant, and a rating of 5 was defined to indicate that the item was extremely relevant.

A sample of the ratings is given in Table 1. The order of the judges and of the items is related to results obtained in the study and will be discussed later as will the last two columns of this table. Note that each of the rating values from 0 to 5 is used, especially from 1 to 5 with an occasional 0. In fact, the ratings for many of the items extend over the 1 to 5 range. Some of the items are rated a bit lower on the average than the other items, but the major feature is the variety of ratings for each item. Having an array of ratings such as this, one may inquire whether the differences are random over the raters or whether there may be systematic agreement for groups of raters. To answer this kind of inquiry, we performed a type of obverse factor analysis using each judge as a variable.

The first step in the factor analysis was to compute the sum of squares of ratings for each judge and the sum of products between each pair of judges.

TABLE 1
Ratings of Judges on a Sample of Items

Item No.	5	14	3	4	7	6	9	1	16	2	8	10	12	13	15	17	11	Group A (5, 14, 3)	Group B (12, 13, 15, 17, 11)
3	2	1	2	3	2	1	5	2	3	3	1	3	4	3	3	3	4	1.7	3.4
46	1	3	3	5	2	3	4	2	4	3	4	4	4	4	3	3	5	2.3	3.8
10	1	1	2	4	2	3	2	2	3	2	1	3	4	2	2	2	3	1.3	2.6
5	2	3	1	3	2	2	3	2	3	4	1	3	4	2	2	2	4	2.0	2.8
2	3	2	2	3	2	1	5	4	3	3	2	3	4	3	3	3	4	2.3	3.4
26	2	4	4	5	3	4	3	4	4	4	3	4	4	4	5	3	5	3.3	4.2
4	3	3	2	5	3	1	3	3	2	2	1	3	4	3	2	3	3	2.7	3.0
36	2	3	2	5	2	4	3	3	4	4	4	2	3	2	4	2	4	2.3	3.0
40	3	3	4	3	2	3	3	4	3	4	4	3	3	2	4	3	5	3.3	3.4
43	2	3	4	3	2	2	2	4	4	3	4	3	3	3	4	3	5	3.0	3.6
39	4	4	4	4	2	5	3	2	3	5	4	4	5	3	5	3	5	4.0	4.2
16	3	2	3	4	2	2	3	3	2	4	1	2	3	2	1	0	5	2.7	2.2
32	3	4	4	5	2	4	2	4	4	4	3	3	5	3	5	1	4	3.7	3.6
50	3	4	4	3	3	2	4	4	4	4	3	4	4	0	4	4	5	3.7	3.4
51	3	4	5	4	1	3	4	4	4	4	3	1	4	3	0	4	5	4.0	3.2
81	4	3	5	4	3	2	4	2	4	3	1	3	3	3	2	1	5	4.0	2.8
65	2	3	4	4	2	1	3	3	3	3	4	3	3	3	1	1	1	3.0	1.8
80	4	3	5	3	3	3	4	3	3	3	5	3	3	2	1	2	5	4.0	2.6
52	3	5	5	4	3	4	4	5	3	3	2	1	4	0	4	3	5	4.3	3.2
85	4	4	5	2	3	0	4	3	2	3	4	3	4	3	1	1	2	4.3	2.2
110	5	5	5	5	3	2	3	4	4	3	3	3	4	1	2	3	5	5.0	3.0
104	4	4	5	5	2	1	3	3	2	3	3	3	3	3	1	0	3	4.3	2.0
95	4	4	5	5	2	4	3	2	3	3	3	2	3	1	2	0	1	4.3	1.4
199	5	5	5	5	3	4	3	3	4	3	2	3	3	1	2	1	1	5.0	1.6
200	5	5	5	5	3	3	3	3	4	3	2	2	1	1	1	1	1	5.0	1.0

TABLE 2
Matrix of Intercorrelations[a]

Judges	5	14	3	4	7	6	9	1	16	2	8	10	12	13	15	17	11	Mean Rating	SD
5		66	69	21	42	20	32	25	19	15	18	03	-12	-26	-15	-28	-45	3.09	1.31
14	66		55	15	41	28	12	41	27	07	20	02	-20	-27	-02	-23	-35	3.17	1.12
3	69	55		17	37	19	27	33	27	14	31	-06	-08	00	-10	-14	-33	4.14	1.04
4	21	15	17		18	17	-20	00	11	09	04	05	01	-08	04	04	-14	4.45	1.01
7	42	41	37	18		18	25	17	46	20	16	11	-04	-02	24	25	-07	2.74	.57
6	20	28	19	17	18		06	24	08	06	24	05	10	05	28	11	-02	2.36	1.25
9	32	12	27	-20	25	06		19	15	11	08	07	21	10	08	06	-07	3.15	.66
1	25	41	33	00	17	24	19		22	14	39	13	10	01	29	11	09	3.14	.81
16	19	27	27	11	46	08	15	22		06	29	08	-03	-14	32	20	11	3.52	.77
2	15	07	14	09	20	06	11	14	06		12	08	24	08	18	21	05	3.12	.66
8	18	20	31	04	16	24	08	39	29	12		-03	17	04	29	19	30	2.48	1.07
10	03	02	-06	05	11	05	07	13	08	08	-03		21	22	23	22	08	2.68	.89
12	-12	-20	-08	01	-04	10	21	10	-03	24	17	21		29	39	35	33	3.47	.89
13	-26	-27	00	-08	-02	05	10	01	-14	08	04	22	29		19	24	24	2.58	1.17
15	-15	-02	-10	04	24	28	08	29	32	18	29	23	39	19		37	45	2.52	1.14
17	-28	-23	-14	04	25	11	06	11	20	21	19	22	35	24	37		53	2.39	1.38
11	-45	-35	-33	-14	-07	-02	-07	09	11	05	30	08	33	24	45	53		3.68	1.51

[a] Decimal points are omitted.

Mean square and mean cross-product values were obtained by dividing the sums by the number of items, 225.

Before considering the factor analysis, it will be of interest to consider the matrix of intercorrelations between the judges in Table 2. Note that the judges 5, 14, and 3 have high intercorrelations. Note also that the ratings of these judges correlate negatively with the last five judges, 12, 13, 15, 17, and 11, while these five judges intercorrelate positively within their group. The judges in the middle group have only moderate correlations,

TABLE 3
Principal-Axes Factor Matrix

Judges	Factor I	Factor II
5	3.13	.99
14	3.20	.74
3	4.17	.64
4	4.44	.17
7	2.76	.12
6	2.40	.11
9	3.15	.08
1	3.17	.08
16	3.54	.03
2	3.13	− .03
8	2.54	− .06
10	2.68	− .14
12	3.48	− .37
13	2.58	− .43
15	2.58	− .48
17	2.44	− .79
11	3.69	−1.06

with no distinctive patterning. This inspection tends to indicate the existence of two schools of thought as to what kinds of items are most relevant for the evaluation of social studies abilities at the end of secondary school. The factor analysis to be discussed will bring this observation out in more precise form.

Returning to the main thread of our analysis, the factor analysis of the matrix of mean cross-products, communality estimates were inserted in the diagonal cells of the matrix. The characteristic roots and vectors of the corrected matrix were found in order to obtain principal-axes factors. There seemed to be two significant factors. The loadings of these two factors are presented in Table 3. Loadings on Factor I are approximately equal to the mean ratings for the judges. Loadings on Factor II range from .99 to −1.06 with the first three judges having positive loadings and the last five judges having negative loadings. The middle nine judges have near zero loadings on Factor II. Note that the judges have been listed in descending order of their loadings on Factor II.

Interpretation of the results is now to be considered. A rotation of axes could have been performed in the two-dimensional space defined by the two principal-axes factors, but there did not seem to be any preferable location of the axes over the original ones. Remember that the loadings on this first factor approximated closely the mean ratings of the judges; conse-

TABLE 4
Scatterplot of Group Ratings

Ratings: Group B (Judges 12, 13, 15, 17, 11)	Ratings: Group A (Judges 5, 14, 3)						Total Frequency
	0.0–0.9	1.0–1.9	2.0–2.9	3.0–3.9	4.0–4.9	5.0	
5.0							
4.0–4.9			4	14	5		23
3.0–3.9		5	35	41	27	3	111
2.0–2.9		7	12	5	27	8	59
1.0–1.9		1	3	4	11	13	32
0.0–0.9							
Total Frequency		13	54	64	70	24	225

Mean Ratings: Group A (Judges 5, 14, 3)   3.5
            Group B (Judges 12, 13, 15, 17, 11) 2.9

quently, we may interpret the first factor as a measure of general approval of the sample items. The magnitude of the loadings for this factor in relation to those for the second may be interpreted as indicating considerable agreement among the judges concerning the appropriateness of the items.

The second factor indicates a difference of opinion between two groups of judges. In order to interpret this difference in opinion, mean group ratings were found for each item as illustrated by the last two columns in Table 1. Inspection of these two columns reveals a distinct trend from top to bottom of the table for the ratings to increase for Group A (judges 5, 14, and 3) while the ratings for the other group tend to decrease. A scatterplot was made between these two sets of group ratings and is presented in Table 4. The correlation appears to be very low and is, in fact, negative. Most striking is the array of items rated 5 by all three judges in Group A. The other group of judges tended to rate these items down.

The item types and content that are rated high by one group and low by the other group are of interest. Those items rated high by Group B and low by the other group were the "information" items, calling for recognition of terms used in the social studies and the recall of fairly specific information. In comparison, the items rated high by Group A and low by Group B were the "self-contained" items, involving reasoning and interpretation from given material, such as reading comprehension of passages or interpretation of data in the social studies area. The items classified as "composite," requiring both knowledge and skill, which were actually most numerous in the sample, tended to show no such sharp differentiation between the groups.

As a further aid to interpretation of the opinions and factors, general comments and criticisms by the judges were collected.

From the item rating and comments, it seemed clear that Group A emphasized, for both secondary school instruction and examining, the gaining of problem-solving abilities. Group B, on the other hand, emphasized at this level the development of a facility to organize material and to express generalized conclusions effectively. This second group tends to feel that, if there is any value in the objective test, it is in measuring the knowledge which is a prerequisite to organizing and presenting thought.

The results of this study, we feel, tend to demonstrate that basic differences in value patterns can exist between groups of specialists in a content field, and that the application of factor analysis to ratings of test questions can identify the groups and clarify the nature of the differences. The collecting of general comments can serve to insure that ideas not included implicitly in the sample of items are brought to the attention of the investigator. In some cases, points raised in the comments may indicate the necessity for augmenting the pool with additional kinds of questions and repeating the analysis. The analysis can also provide an index of the magnitude of the differences thus identified. We may suggest that, in order for a generally acceptable test to be constructed, it may be necessary to provide part scores so that groups with differing points of view may utilize different weights reflecting their special value patterns when evaluating examinees. Thus, the methodology outlined is adequate to indicate those cases when high general content validity is possible as well as to indicate the existence and nature of ambiguity and controversy relevant to the content validity of a test.

REFERENCES

1. American Educational Research Association and National Council on Measurements Used in Education. *Technical recommendations for achievement tests.* Washington, D.C.: American Educational Research Association, 1955.
2. American Psychological Association. *Technical recommendations for psychological tests and diagnostic techniques.* Washington, D.C.: American Psychological Association, 1954.

[Ed. Note—both references have been superseded by: *Standards for educational and psychological tests and manuals.* Washington, D.C.: American Psychological Association, 1966.]

Schools of Thought in Judging
Excellence of English Themes

JOHN W. FRENCH

1961

A perennial bone of contention between English teachers and psychometricians has been the effectiveness of essay tests of writing ability. The testing program of the College Entrance Examination Board has reflected the crazy ups and downs of this controversy. Fifteen years ago, a written composition was an integral part of the Board's achievement test in English. The psychometricians then proved that a verbal aptitude test could predict English grades or ratings on writing ability better than a test which actually required the students to write.

The College Board then dropped the English composition from its program. Shouts of horror arose, and a committee was formed. This resulted in a new, ingeniously garnished two-hour essay test called the General Composition Test. The College Board, with some misgivings, put this test into its program. The psychometricians, of course, swung into action and came up with lots of data to show that even this new test, when compared with the verbal aptitude test, had low reliability, low validity, high cost, and no important effect, during at least a five-month period, on either what the English teachers taught or what the students studied.

The College Board then dropped the General Composition Test from its program. Shouts of horror arose, and a committee was formed. At the present time, the College Board again has an English Composition Test, called the "Writing Sample," in its program, but this one doesn't get scored at all. We just send carbon copies to the colleges, and wonder what the colleges are going to do with them and how much longer they are going to want to receive all those almost unreadable handwritten papers.

Well, enough about the controversy. Let's consider the sources of error in the scores on a composition test. It is possible to divide the error into four parts:

1) Student Error. A student can do well one day and poorly another day on the very same task. This is, of course, true of both composition and objective tests, but can be greatly aggravated for the composition test, because the student may guess sometimes correctly and sometimes incorrectly about what style of writing or what kind of content his particular examiner will want to find.

2) Test Error. A test calls for a sample of the student's behavior. A long objective test calls for many small samples or items; the items that happen to favor one group of students are usually balanced by items that are especially difficult for the same group. The composition test is almost like a one-item test. Some students may happen to enjoy the topic assigned, while others may find it difficult and unstimulating; this results in error.

3) Scale Error. The reader of a composition can be an easy marker or a tough marker. Therein hangs much of a student's fate. To get all readers for an examination to grade papers on the same scale is no easy matter. It may be largely a matter of administrative persuasion.

4) Reader Disagreement. Even if readers could be persuaded to use the same scale, that is, to give the same proportions of A's, B's, C's, etc., their grades would still not look alike, because there is disagreement on what kind of writing is best.

To recapitulate, an essay test is subject to student error, test error, scale error, and reader disagreement. The experiment I am about to discuss is an exploration of this fourth kind of error: Reader Disagreement, or, in more elegant terms, the dimensionality in the grading behavior of the readers. The study was carried out by Paul B. Diederich, Sydell T. Carlton, and the speaker with the support of the Carnegie Corporation.

The stimuli for the readers were 300 short essays written as homework by college freshmen. These were written on two rather general essay topics: "Who Should Go to College?" and, "When Should Teen-agers Be Treated as Adults?" The papers were selected from a larger number of available papers so as to include those written by a larger percentage of low-ability and very high-ability students than is usually found in a freshman English course. This was done to make discrimination among the papers easier, so that the different kinds of discrimination made by the readers would stand out as clearly as possible.

We considered our interest in the evaluation of writing to extend beyond teachers of English. We had in mind all kinds of persons who have reason to savor or suffer from the quality of writing achieved by graduates of our colleges. Consequently, we sought and were able to secure the participation of ten English teachers, nine social scientists, eight natural scientists, ten writers or editors, nine lawyers, and seven business executives—all highly competent people in their respective fields. All of these—bless them—read and graded 300 student essays for what can only be considered nominal compensation.

The instructions for the grading that were given to the readers were probably quite important to this study. In the past, when the College Board had readers grade an essay test, every effort was made to bring about high agreement on the grades that were assigned. The readers would be assembled; they would discuss and agree to certain rules for grading students' responses to the particular essay topic; they would grade sample papers, discuss the results, and revise the rules to cover all contingencies. After three days of this, they would start doing the grading that counted. The average correlation of one reader's grades with those of another would be about .70. That would not be bad, if we could be sure that the things the readers were able to agree on were just as important as the things they must ignore in order to achieve this high level of agreement. In the present study, the readers were not assembled to discuss their ideas about reading. They worked at home. They were told merely to "Use your own judgment as to what constitutes 'writing ability.' Do not assume that we want you to do this or that." Nothing was said about style or grammar or quality of ideas. They were merely asked to "sort the papers into nine piles in order of merit," with at least 6 out of the 150 papers on each topic in each pile. In addition, they were asked to write on the papers comments as to why they liked or disliked them.

The next step in our procedure was to compute the correlations between every possible pair of readers. In spite of the fact that discrimination was aided by the wider-than-normal range of ability among the students, the average correlation was only .31. You can understand just how low this is when I tell you that, out of the 300 papers, 101 received all nine different grades, and no paper received less than five different grades.

It was the objective of this research to analyze the agreement, such as it is, and to find out whether schools of thought exist among the readers. One hypothesis was easy to check by looking at the correlations. Do English teachers represent one school of thought, social scientists another, and so on? If such is the case, the average correlation among the English teachers would be higher than .31. Since the College Board readers are all English teachers, this might account for part of the success in achieving an average correlation of .70 in the Board program. We then computed the average of our correlations between English teachers and found it to be .41. Since this is appreciably above the average for the whole group, there seemed at first to be some evidence for an English-teacher school of thought. However, we computed similar averages for the other occupational groups, and these were all very low. It turns out that members of all the other occupational groups agreed better on the average with the English teachers than they agreed with members of their own group. This means that the English teachers do not represent a school of thought but are able to grade papers with less random error than that which prevailed in the other groups.

In order to find out what schools of thought do exist among readers, the matrix of intercorrelations among the readers was submitted to a factor analysis. Since it is possible to consider the grades of each reader as an evaluation of the student writing the essay, we thought it reasonable to include in the factor analysis other available evaluations of the students: their College Board Scholastic Aptitude Test (SAT) Verbal scores, SAT-Mathematical scores, and English Composition Test scores. These scores were included just as if there had been three extra readers.

Six principal-component factors were extracted, the first being very large in comparison to the others. This indicates that there are six sources of variation or schools of thought explaining the relationships among the readers and the tests. However, the large size of the first factor indicates that such agreement among readers as exists is represented by a set of values having importance for all readers. This set of values could have been defined by a general factor, which would be supplemented by the five other group factors, representing differences of opinion beyond the central core of agreement. However, in order to obtain the clearest possible picture of the different opinions of the readers, the six factors were rotated to oblique simple structure, the position of each rotation being determined graphically.

It became apparent immediately that one factor was a test factor. The three objective College Board tests appeared close together and quite remote in the six-dimensional factorial space from any of the readers. There was nothing in this particular factorial space to separate the mathematical test, SAT-M, from the verbal tests, SAT-V and the English Composition Test.

Each of the other five factors was represented by a small group of readers having high loadings on it. Here commenced the most challenging phase of this research. Since, in this study, the factors are groups of readers, it might be possible to find something in their backgrounds or experiences that was responsible for the groupings. This would lead to a very different kind of analysis from the one we carried out. Our concern was directly with the behavior in grading papers that caused the factors to emerge. Nevertheless, it was sensible first to check two obvious characteristics of the readers: occupation and sex.

Table 1 gives the occupational fields of the readers having factor loadings of .25 and above. The mixture of occupations on every factor leads us to reject the hypothesis that schools of thought in grading papers are mediated by occupational affiliations. It can be considered noteworthy, however,

TABLE 1

The Fields of Readers Having Factor Loadings of .25 and Above[a]

Factor I		Factor IV	
English	.33, .33, .30, .27	English	.47, .36, .35, .32, .31, .30, .30
Soc. Sci.	.58, .53, .25	Soc. Sci.	.26
Nat. Sci.	.47, .34	Nat. Sci.	.38
Writers	.40, .37, .31, .27	Writers	.29
Lawyers	.41	Lawyers	.33, .26
Business	.44, .43	Business	.40
Factor II		Factor V	
Nat. Sci.	.42, .31	Soc. Sci.	.35, .29
Writers	.35, .35	Nat. Sci.	.29, .25
Lawyers	.37	Writers	.26
Business	.37, .32, .29, .29	Lawyers	.30, .25
		Business	.31, .27
Factor III			
Soc. Sci.	.26	Factor VI	
Nat. Sci.	.27	SAT-V	.67
Writers	.41, .34, .33, .28	ECT	.65
Lawyers	.26	SAT-M	.58

[a] The three highest loadings for each factor are underlined.

that the three highest loadings on Factor III are all from the one group of writers and editors, and more than half of the readers listed for Factor IV are English teachers.

Four of the 53 readers were women. Three of them had their highest loadings on Factor V, but none of these loadings was high enough to seem convincing; they were .30, .22, and .20. The fourth woman reader did have a high loading, .40, but it was on Factor I. Thus, we were able to identify no sex factor.

Another approach to the interpretation of the factors was to observe various objective characteristics of the papers and correlate these with the grades assigned to the papers by readers representing each factor. This was done by Paul Jacobs. Among the objective characteristics tried were length in inches, proportion of unusual words as defined by the Lorge magazine list (1), and number of mechanical errors—not errors on which readers happened to comment, but a complete listing of all identifiable errors compiled by independent specialists. The only one of these that worked was *length*. Average grades of the five readers with highest loadings on Factor I correlated about .8 with length. Average grades of readers with the lowest loadings on Factor I correlated about −.3 with length. This fitted well with some preconceptions many of us had about some readers of English essays, but we were later to change this interpretation, and possibly, this preconception.

A third and more thorough approach to the interpretation of factors was through the comments that were written on the papers by the readers. This is a study with a lot of data. There were 53 readers, 300 papers each, and an average of about 11 words commenting on each paper: some 50,000 comments totalling 175,000 words. Therefore, we limited the analysis to papers bearing the three highest or three lowest grades by the readers who had the three highest or three lowest loadings on each factor. This called for the analysis of 11,018 comments written on 3,557 papers.

After a prolonged study of the comments without reference to the factor loadings of the readers, 55 categories of comments were adopted and listed on scoring sheets for a systematic tallying of the kind of comment made by each reader in the analysis group. All classifying and tallying of comments was done by a single person who knew nothing of the factor loadings of the readers. For each comment, the length of the comment was recorded, and a tally mark was entered for all categories covered by the comment. For example, if a reader said of a paper, "Good ideas and organization but several spelling errors," tallies were entered opposite "Quality of Ideas," "Organization," and "Spelling." If the reader went on to encircle two spelling errors, he was given two additional tallies opposite "Spelling."

It was now possible to compute the percentage of a reader's comments that were devoted to comments in each of the 55 categories. This percentage was computed separately for each of the two essay topics, and the readers were found to be consistent in the nature of their comments from topic to topic. Now, by summing the percentages for each topic for each of the three readers who were highest on a factor, we arrived at a figure we called the *index of emphasis* for the factor. For comparison, an *index of emphasis* was also computed for the three readers who were lowest on each factor.

These *indices of emphases* for 33 of the 55 categories are shown in Table 2. Each category is listed with the factor for which the three readers with highest loadings had the greatest *index of emphasis*. For example, in the first row of the table, Relevance is listed for Factor I, because the three

TABLE 2

Index of Emphasis for the Highest and Lowest Readers on Each Factor

Categories of Comments	Three highest readers					Three lowest readers				
	I	II	III	IV	V	I	II	III	IV	V
I. IDEAS *										
Relevance	44	26	29	15	34	16	40	23	20	29
Concise—wordy	20	15	03	17	18	22	13	19	24	09
Clarity of ideas	18	10	16	09	15	07	35	11	06	16
Quantity of ideas	28	09	01	20	08	09	30	13	08	14
Development	19	18	04	12	09	13	11	12	03	05
Too brief or long	21	13	02	10	14	06	07	01	06	02
Persuasiveness	16	00	07	03	06	06	20	03	06	06
Ending	13	04	03	03	09	07	10	06	03	09
Generality	09	08	00	03	03	00	03	11	00	05
II. FORM *										
Spelling	58	105	06	73	72	96	11	48	07	31
Clarity of expression	39	65	57	62	25	85	58	17	12	33
Organization	24	44	35	09	26	15	19	52	23	15
Coherence of ideas	21	34	19	17	29	22	32	31	21	17
Reader agreement	10	39	05	23	08	24	25	07	16	10
Analysis	13	35	03	04	17	01	08	42	19	10
Maturity	07	09	01	08	07	06	08	12	05	06
III. FLAVOR *										
Quality of ideas	72	51	89	30	43	51	64	51	26	25
Style (general)	19	05	77	08	19	32	14	13	31	09
Mechanics (general)	19	01	57	19	00	01	26	14	01	07
Originality	15	08	39	13	16	07	24	33	05	04
Interest	08	02	32	10	15	04	11	06	04	02
Beginning	03	03	20	01	12	01	01	05	07	01
Sincerity	05	06	12	00	09	04	06	04	02	04
Information & Illustration	06	01	08	01	06	05	01	10	05	00
IV. MECHANICS *										
Punctuation	10	02	00	69	29	17	06	23	15	17
Grammar	17	17	02	39	22	34	08	14	17	23
Sentence structure	01	04	00	21	21	11	06	03	14	02
Phrasing, idiom	10	03	00	14	05	18	04	10	08	18
V. WORDING *										
General	20	35	45	20	49	10	52	49	33	04
Word choices	18	07	04	32	34	43	13	26	88	44
Logic	10	10	09	05	11	03	10	14	01	06
Clichés	06	03	10	04	10	06	11	01	02	08
Jargon-slang	03	02	00	03	03	04	03	00	00	05

* The column in which the highest readers on each factor stood first is marked by an asterisk. Ties for first place in any category within a factor are underlined.

readers with highest loadings on Factor I used this category a higher percentage of times than did the readers who were highest on any other factor. The lowest readers on each factor did not affect the listing. Within each factor, the categories are listed in order of diminishing sums of the indices over all five factors. Twenty-two categories have been omitted from the list entirely because their indices were so low that their placement would not be reliable.

The factors, or schools of thought among the readers, may now be interpreted by considering the categories listed for each factor and by referring judiciously to the relative sizes of the various indices. Our interpretations are given in capital letters as names for each factor. They are IDEAS, FORM, FLAVOR, MECHANICS, and WORDING. It is now of interest to recall the close association, mentioned earlier, between grades of readers representing Factor I and the length of the essays in inches. A reasonable explanation seems to be that ideas, particularly quantity of ideas, require room on the page.

Now, in this analysis, in order to achieve the clearest, truest picture of the factors, we rotated the factor axes obliquely. This means that the factors are not independent of each other. The intercorrelations among them are given in Table 3. You will see that the MECHANICS and WORDING factors are rather closely associated with each other and also have some high correlations with the other factors. Perhaps the most interesting finding in Table 3 is the row of correlations for the test factor. The test factor is unrelated to IDEAS and essentially unrelated to FORM and FLAVOR. On the other hand, there is a substantial relationship to MECHANICS and WORDING. This tells us something about the tests, something that all of us may not be happy to learn. The test scores are somewhat like the essay grades given by readers of the MECHANICS and WORDING schools of thought, and they appear to be completely unrelated to the grades assigned by readers who grade on ideas.

TABLE 3
Factor Intercorrelations

Factors	I	II	III	IV	V	VI
I. IDEAS		.03	.27	.25	.55	−.02
II. FORM	.03		−.03	.33	.10	.16
III. FLAVOR	.27	−.03		.45	.34	.07
IV. MECHANICS	.25	.33	.45		.63	.50
V. WORDING	.55	.10	.34	.63		.45
VI. TESTS	−.02	.16	.07	.50	.45	

Isn't this what the English teachers have been telling us psychometricians all along—that essay tests of writing ability measure something that the objective tests do not measure? They seem to be right. Form, flavor, and, particularly, ideas are missed by the tests. But, then, of course, they are also pretty much missed by the readers. The low correlations among the readers, as well as the 101 papers receiving all nine grades, can only mean that nothing at all is being measured very well by the essays. It could be pointed out that readers trained to grade a particular essay can achieve a figure of .70 for correlations among themselves. But are they still grading on ideas, form, flavor, or whatever they want? Of course, they are not. The training forces them to grade in ways which they would not ordinarily grade. In fact, the *well-trained* reader may simply be measuring verbal aptitude—poorly.

What, then, can be done about these interesting things that essays can rather foggily measure? A first step will be to decide what we *want* to measure. Let's say it is ideas, form, and flavor, *not* mechanics, wording, or scholastic aptitude. The present study points to certain individuals who chose without special direction to pay particular attention to ideas, form, and flavor. Right here there is an advance in the reliability of measurement. The average intercorrelation among the seven readers whose loading was above .40 on IDEAS, for example, was .46, as compared with .31 reported earlier for the whole group of 53 readers. Now let's increase agreement still further by finding a group of readers who at least espouse the importance of reading for ideas, form, and flavor. Let's have these readers choose the essay topic for sensitivity to these particular qualities, come to an agreement on how to grade the chosen topic, and train themselves to grade it in a consistent way. There can still be no guarantee that agreement will go as high as .70, because the qualities being graded may be harder to grade consistently than something like mechanics. However, the readers, at least, would be allowed to grade in more nearly the way they like best and that should help reliability.

In addition, a clear perspective of what is being looked for by the readers might have a diminishing effect on student error. With some teachers stressing one quality and others harping on another, a student may very reasonably respond to a test essay by stressing his own teacher's favorite essay characteristic, or he may allow the essay topic to suggest one thing or another to stress. Only if he is lucky will he even try to impart to his essay the characteristic that his particular reader is going to inspect most closely. On the other hand, if the readers were determined to grade on, say, an equal weighting of ideas, form, and flavor, and if they communicated this intention to the students through test directions, it is likely that the students would respond by a more uniform effort to stress these things in their writing. The test would now measure the students on something they have done more nearly to the limit of their capacity, and so would benefit by reduced student error.

So, if we psychometricians can encourage testing and further clarification of those aspects of writing that objective tests cannot measure, encourage the use of readers who favor grading those particular qualities that are desirable to grade, and see to it that the students are aware of what they are being graded on, we can enlighten rather than merely disparage the polemic art of essay testing.

REFERENCE

1. Thorndike, E. L., & Lorge, I. *The teacher's word book of 30,000 words.* New York: Bureau of Publications, Teachers College, 1944.

Estimating Structure in Prose[1]

IRVING LORGE

1960

Since the turn of the century, schoolmen have been trying to obtain or to develop a valid, reliable, and impartial method of appraising the comprehensibility of textbooks and related teaching materials. These attempts have considered the responses of pupils on examinations based on the texts they have read; on ratings and judgments of the understandability for children by teachers, librarians, and professors; and on the expressed reactions of children to books. E. L. Thorndike's *Teacher's Word Book* (15), published in 1921, provided a more objective basis for estimating the difficulty of texts in terms of relative frequency (or rarity) of the words used.

READABILITY FORMULAS

The concept of readability, however, received its primary impetus from the researches of Vogel and Washburne (16). They were asked to assign books for supplementary reading to appropriate grades. Instead of judging the difficulty of the books, they based the classification of each book on the tested reading ability of children who had read and *liked* the book. About 37,000 children, who had also taken the paragraph-meaning section of the Stanford Achievement Test, indicated on a ballot each book read and liked in the year's supplementary reading. For each of the 700 titles that had received at least 25 favorable votes, the book's score was the median of the reading grade scores of the children who had read and liked the book. Thus, the Winnetka list (18) provided an empirically graded list of 700 supplementary books.

[1] It is a pleasure for me to express my appreciation to the staff members of the Institute of Psychological Research, Teachers College, Columbia University, who made most of the tortuous analyses, Mabel Wilcox, Dorothy Heft, and Luciana Visentini Steinzor; to my former graduate students, Joshua Fishman and Walter MacGinitie; to the College Entrance Examination Board and Educational Testing Service for supplying the candidates' General Compositions; to John Carroll for supplying the 150 passages from his Subtreasury with their factor scores; and to the hundreds of students in Freshman English in the School of General Studies, Columbia University, for their cooperation.

But what of new books? Or of books that had been read by fewer than 25 children? Vogel and Washburne tried to identify factors within the book that would predict its grade placement. They were the first to develop a multiple-regression formula predicting grade placement from four factors internal to the book, namely, the number of different words per thousand words, the number of uncommon words per thousand words, the number of simple sentences in 75 successive sentences, and the number of prepositions per thousand words. The Vogel and Washburne Grade Placement Formula (17) became the prototype for a series of multiple-regression equations that predicted a criterion from the internal aspects of the book— e.g., vocabulary load, sentence complexity, idea density, and human interest.

No other internal element of a text added significantly to *estimated grade placement or difficulty.* In general, in most available multiple-regression equations, such as those of Lorge (11), Flesch (6), or Dale-Chall (5), grade placement is estimated from the weighted contribution of at least two of the four elements. It should not be surprising, therefore, that grade placement estimated from vocabulary load, sentence complexity, idea density, and human interest of a text *is invariant for any rearrangement* of the sentences in a text. The Lorge Reading Grade Index for the Gettysburg Address, for example, would be the same no matter in what order the sentences are presented to the unwary reader.

No readability formula credits structure, or organization, or coherence, or sequence, or unity. While it may be assumed that nearly all published books have some structure or organization or unity, few teachers of English composition would grant that structure is an inevitable ingredient of student essays.

FACTOR ANALYSES OF RATED QUALITIES OF COMPOSITIONS

In the search for some valid and equitable basis for evaluating candidates' compositions and essays, the College Entrance Examination Board and Educational Testing Service, indeed, have devoted considerable research endeavor. For example, in May 1956, candidates for the CEEB Achievement Test in General Composition were asked to write on the topic, "Pressures of Modern Society that Tend to Direct the Lives of Young People." As a basis for their essays, they were asked first to read a relatively easy passage of about 1,900 words relevant to the assigned broad topic. The candidate was instructed to spend 5 minutes in giving the theme in one or two concise sentences, another 20 minutes in preparing an outline, and 75 minutes in writing and revising the essay. The candidates were informed that the essay was to be judged for five qualities: Mechanics, Style, Organization, Reasoning, and Content.

Since two of the qualities to be considered in evaluating the candidates' compositions were related to structure, I asked Educational Testing Service to send me a sample of the compositions. The purpose was to ascertain whether structure or style, as rated by the expert readers of the compositions, might be related to the Lorge Readability Indexes for the compositions. ETS sent the 194 compositions which had been used in estimating the reliabilities of the readers who had evaluated the General Composition (14). From these, a random sample of 69 compositions was selected. For each of these, a Lorge Readability Index was computed. The Lorge Readability Index is based on a count of the number of words written, the number of sentences, the number of prepositions, and the number of different hard words. These four counts are the basis for the values: average sentence length, the proportion of prepositional phrases, and the proportion of different hard words. The readers' ratings for each composition for Mechanics, Style, Organization, Reasoning, and Content, as well as the candidates' Verbal and Mathematical scores on the Scholastic Aptitude Test (SAT), were supplied by ETS.

Since an IBM 650 was available, the complete matrix of intercorrelations among the 24 variables was computed, followed by a factor analysis and rotation by Kaiser's varimax (9) of the five qualities rated by two readers, the average sentence length, ratio of prepositional phrases, the ratio of hard words, and the SAT-V and SAT-M scores.

The two qualities of major interest for the estimation of structure were the ratings for organization and style. According to the directions to the readers, "*Organization* had to do with the extent to which the writer has formulated a clear intention which lent order to his essay and had, as a consequence, arranged the blocks of material in a reasonable and effective way." Transition between paragraphs (or blocks of material) was considered under organization, but transition within paragraphs was considered a matter of style (12). *Style* was to include "choice of words, construction of sentences, and the internal organization of paragraphs . . . ," that is, ". . . internal construction of the transition of the paragraph had to do with transition between sentence elements and the general flow of language within a paragraph unit. . . ."

The first orthogonal factor was identified as general academic ability; the second, as a factor common to the first reader's ratings on organization, reasoning, and content; and the third, as a factor common to the idea density (in terms of prepositional phrases) and word choice (in terms of different hard words) in the composition.

On the first orthogonal factor, academic ability, the loadings for Mechanics, Style, Organization, Reasoning, and Content by the first reader were .80, .83, .78, .72, and .70 respectively; for the second reader, the loadings respectively were .83, .86, .81, .81, and .80. On the same first factor, the loading on the SAT-Verbal score was .77 and on the SAT-Mathematical score, .72. On the elements of the Lorge Readability Index, the loadings on the first factor were .04 for average sentence length, .34 for ratio of prepositional phrases, and .32 for ratio of hard words.

Apparently, the readers cannot evaluate organization independently of the "halo" either of the general goodness of the object (i.e., the composition) or of the person (i.e., the candidate). The elements in the Lorge Readability Index, however, seem to be measuring aspects of the composition that are related more to the composition than to the person. Moreover, the Lorge Readability Index, as may have been expected on logical grounds, is related in a minor way to ratings for either organization or style. A sort of "haloed" general evaluative judgment is subsumed in the readers' ratings for the five qualities.

Another opportunity to attempt to evaluate structure and unity was afforded through John Carroll's massive and significant study of literary style (4). Carroll collected a sample of 150 passages from various sources to represent a very wide range of content and style. Each of these passages was judged in terms of "semantic differential" adjectival scales and independently appraised in terms of objective measures. The average of the ratings given by eight expert judges for each composition on each of 29 semantic differential adjectival scales and the actual counts for each passage in terms of 39 objective measures—e.g., number of paragraphs, of sentences, of unmodified nouns—provided 68 scores for the matrix of intercorrelations.

On factor analysis, the matrix was resolved as six orthogonal factors (or at least nearly orthogonal). These factors were identified as good-bad, personal-impersonal, ornamented-plain, abstract-concrete, serious-humorous, and descriptive-narrative. As must be recognized, this represents an important resolution of the 68 scores of literary performance into six independent components.

For my interest in appraising structure, attention was directed to three of the "semantic differential" adjectival scales: namely, those for rating the passage on a seven-point scale for meaningless-meaningful, hazy-clear, and chaotic-ordered. Of all the experts' judgments for each passage, these three seemed to me to be related most nearly to what intuitively may be considered structure.

These three adjectival judgment scales have loadings on Carroll's first factor, *good-bad,* of .61 for meaningful, of .63 for clear, and of .58 for ordered, but apparently are independent of any of the five other orthogonal factors identified by Carroll. None of the objective scores (which are similar to those used as elements in readability formulas) had any significant loading on the first factor. Apparently, expert judges using "semantic differential" adjectival scales utilized a sort of "general goodness" as an internalized referent for judging the passages for most of the 29 aspects.

It seemed useful to ascertain the extent to which the Carroll orthogonal factors may be related to the Lorge Readability Index. Carroll generously provided the 150 passages and the six factor scores for each passage. For each of these 150 passages, except the one that was an incomplete 300-word sentence from a will, the Lorge Readability Index was computed.

A Kaiser varimax rotation yielded at least two orthogonal factors: the first, defined by Carroll's *ornamented-plain,* had loadings on average sentence length of .62, on ratio of prepositional phrases of .44, and on ratio of hard words of .41; suggesting that Carroll's ornamented-plain summarizes whatever elements are measured in the Lorge Readability Index. The second factor, identified by Carroll's *personal-impersonal* factor, is negatively related to Lorge's ratio of prepositional phrases with a loading of −.65 and the ratio of hard words with a loading of −.40. Apparently, structure or unity was not identified in Carroll's factors nor in the elements of the Lorge Readability Index.

DEFINITIONS OF STRUCTURE

Is structure or organization, then, so integral a part of a written passage that it cannot be evaluated or measured? Is it always subsumed in a halo of "general goodness" or general evaluative set? Perhaps structure or organization of a text is taken so much for granted that only exceptional deviations in organization are recognized. Some of you may remember your first difficulties with the structure of Dos Passos, or Gertrude Stein, or James Joyce. Perhaps some of you may remember Bartlett's (2) *Remembering,* in which he asked subjects to reproduce the Indian tale called the "War of the Ghosts." Undoubtedly, some of the memorial inadequacies in reproducing the original text are related to the Indian folk tale's unusual structure for British or American subjects who have internalized a "more logical" structure. Sequence, unity, and coherence may be so well learned that experts accept most written material as structured. Of course, handbooks on writing refer to the necessity for "good" structure in English prose. Textbook discussions about good structure imply that "structure," "coherence," and "good organization" are practically synonymous. Words such as "unity," "order," "lucidity," and "sequence," if not used synonymously, suggest at least a close association with the concept of "good" structure.

None of these terms, as yet, has been defined adequately. Some understanding of the range of concepts implied by structure can be had from the contexts in which the words are used.

Handbooks about writing usually do define "coherence," "organization," "unity," and "sequence." In defining *coherence,* for example, Greever and Jones (8) indicate that "coherence implies a close and natural sequence of parts where every part of a sentence must have a clear and natural connection with the adjoining part. A sentence is coherent when one idea is completed at a time, and when the idea which naturally comes first in thought or sequence is placed first in the sentence." For Goodwin and Guill (7), coherence "is the natural and logical order of development of a sentence, paragraph, or composition, through a single idea. To be coherent, words, phrases, and clauses must stand as near as possible to the words they modify. The development of the main theme should follow a natural and logical order. Succeeding paragraphs should be an amplification of the topic paragraph." Baldwin (1) considers coherence to be synonymous with order; that is, "a composition is coherent when the people that listen to it follow it readily, and when each part prepares for the next. To be coherent, a composition must take hold of both subject matter and audience. It should be arranged according to a plan, since natural thought sequences are not orderly." Perry (13) indicates that coherence occurs when parts that belong together are placed together. Writing is incoherent when instead of saying all that one has to on one topic in one place, one writes a little, changes the subject, remembers something that might have been said on the first topic, says it, and after saying it, resumes the second topic. Perry emphasizes that coherence demands unity in the sense of orderly connection of thought rather than mere consecutiveness.

Organization for Burrows, Fereber, Jackson, and Saunders (3) is "clarification from the verbalization of ideas," although they state that "the power of organization is not learned but follows 'need' in a concrete setting. It develops with the clearness of purpose for which specific material is being gathered and presented. Organization involves choosing relevant levels in terms of a specific problem. A feeling for organization is an innate part of everyone."

As defined by Greever and Jones, *unity* is "a combination of related ideas where each sentence contains only one thought." Baldwin calls unity "a principle of clearness involving expansion of an idea and the fixing of interest," and Goodwin and Guill state that "unity is present when a theme presents a complete whole and holds firmly to a point of view. To secure a well-organized whole, a definite plan must be used. The point of view should not shift within a sentence, and the beginning of a paragraph should bear strongly upon the central idea."

Burrows, Fereber, Jackson, and Saunders indicate that *sequence* "is the proper 'bundling of material,' " and that "the ability to use sequential writing develops in children maturationally with the dawning of a 'sense of order.' "

These definitions, however, do not give the principle of structure nor suggestions for many procedures needed to achieve proper unity, coherence, or sequence in prose.

THE ARRANGEMENT TEST

The basic problem, then, was to discover some operational demonstration of unity of prose. If unity means that sentences follow each other in an orderly fashion, then if any passage were to be fragmented into portions and put into random order, educated subjects should be able to to reconstitute the portions into a useful order. If this random portion procedure were adopted, then two kinds of questions may be asked: 1) are people agreed as to the structuring of prose passages, and 2) if such agreement is found, is the reordering an aspect of unity, coherence, and structure?

For investigation of the operational approach, three stories from *Reader's Digest* of October 1954 and four passages from *Encore* of July 1944 were selected. Each of the three stories from *Reader's Digest* was divided into twelve or thirteen portions of approximately 150 words each. The passage entitled "Nature Man" was chosen because it presented several short themes (marsh birds, Captain Frank's life, Louisiana iris) loosely connected with each other, without any logical or chronological order. The passage on "World Bank" was selected as presenting two major themes (Eugene Black's efforts for the World Bank, and the character of the bank itself) in a spiraling order—i.e., topic A leading to topic B, back to topic A, then again to topic B, etc. The piece called "Russian Story" was chosen because it presented one consecutive theme (Lt. Colonel Grigori Burlutski's activities in the Russian Army).

The four passages from *Encore* were each divided into their ten to thirteen constituent sentences. "Some Old Families" presented two major themes (description of Catamount, West Virginia, and "Bill"); "The Assassination of President Garfield" presented several aspects of Garfield's life (freemasonry, scrapbook hobby, mastery of language and science); "On W. S. Gilbert" presented two major themes (people in Gilbert's serious plays versus those in Gilbert's fairyland); "The Last of R. S." presented one continuous theme (the last illness of R. S.)

The portions of each story and the sentences of each passage were randomized and numbered. A disarranged story of dissected portions, and a disarranged passage of sentences were collated in each of the possible combinations of two at a time. The sets were distributed as a homework assignment to students in freshman English classes in the School of General Studies at Columbia University. Each student, thus, was given a set of scrambled portions which he was to rearrange into a complete story, and a set of scrambled sentences for arrangement into a paragraph. Students were asked to do the assignment independently and to record what they judged to be the correct order by writing the numbers of the portions and of the sentences on a special answer sheet.

From the returned responses, a random sample was selected. For each of the three stories and four passages, the first 48 papers from the randomized pile were analyzed.

The objectives were: first, to ascertain whether these subjects would agree with one another in the ordering of the disarranged texts; and second, to ascertain how many breaks in sequence there would be. For estimating agreement in order, Kendall's coefficient of concordance (10) was used. For estimating recognition of sequence, the number of breaks from published sequence was obtained.

Intuitively, for the passages with disarranged portions the expected order from most structured to least was expected to be: "Russian Story," "Nature Man," and "World Bank." The intersubject agreement in the ranks given the disarranged portions, in terms of Kendall's coefficient of concordance, was .70, .86, and .51. These results put the passage considered least structured in the last position, but did not put the other two passages in the "expected" order. But on the average number of departures from sequence, the expected order was found—i.e., 2.4, 2.7, and 6.5, or in percentage terms about 16 per cent, 20 per cent, and 43 per cent departure from sequence.

For the disarranged sentences, the intuitively judged order for structure was expected to be: "Some Old Families," "The Last of R. S.," "President Garfield," and "W. S. Gilbert." The agreement in assigned ranks did not follow the "expected" order: the coefficients of concordance were .72, .37, .52, and .37. The average departures from sequence, however, were more nearly in line with expectations. The averages were 3.4, 5.6, 5.4, and 9.3, and in percentage terms, 21 per cent, 36 per cent, 46 per cent, and 62 per cent. If these two leads are suggestive, some departure from sequence may be used as a measure of structure.

Joshua Fishman and I used still another approach for estimating structure. For the same disarranged portions of the stories, graduate students at Teachers College were asked to find for each portion the other portion that would go best with it either forward or backward. The results placed the three stories correctly in the intuitive order of structuredness—i.e., "Russian Story," "Nature Man," and "World Bank."

On the bases of these several explorations, it seems that structure can be evaluated independently of "general goodness" or "evaluative" estimations. The arrangement test, which is so useful for establishing the structure in a set of pictures or cartoons, seems to have utility in getting at the structure in prose. The departures from published sequence, or the departures from an order accepted by consensus may serve as the basis of a new approach for judging structure—although I doubt that it is an approach that will be relished by either teachers of composition or by expert readers.

In general, subjects found it easier to put portions into proper order than to rearrange sentences into proper sequence. This undoubtedly reflects the redundancy of more information given within a portion. Conversely, it is more difficult to put sentences into structural sequence because of the lack of enough redundancy.

The methods, though not new, may be applied to measure the connectedness of the text materials. Indeed, the measure may be an addition to the ratings by expert judgment of coherence and organization in written prose.

Perhaps a partial solution for the problems of rating or evaluating printed materials and candidates' compositions is to get rid of the excess in synonymy by restricting the evaluative words to two: 1) *coherence,* for sequence from sentence to sentence and from paragraph to paragraph; and 2) *organization,* for clarity in the development and expansion of an idea.

REFERENCES

1. Baldwin, C. S. *Composition oral and written.* New York: Longmans Green, 1922.
2. Bartlett, F. C. *Remembering: a study in experimental and social psychology.* New York: Macmillan, 1932.

3. Burrows, Alvina T., *et al. They all want to write.* Indianapolis: Bobbs-Merrill, 1939.
4. Carroll, J. B. Vectors of prose style. In T. A. Sebeok (Ed.), *Style in language.* New York: Wiley, 1960. Pp. 283–292.
5. Dale, E., & Chall, Jeanne S. A formula for predicting readability. *Educational Research Bulletin,* 1948, 27, 11–20.
6. Flesch, R. F. Marks of readable style: a study in adult education. *Teachers College Contributions to Education,* 1943, No. 897.
7. Goodwin, Mary L., & Guill, K. G. *Students handbook of composition.* New York: Macmillan, 1918.
8. Greever, G., & Jones, E. S. *The Century handbook of writing.* (3rd ed.) New York: Century, 1933.
9. Kaiser, H. F. Varimax solution for primary mental abilities. *Psychometrika,* 1960, 25, 153–158.
10. Kendall, M. G. *Rank correlation methods.* London: C. Griffin, 1948.
11. Lorge, I. *The Lorge Formula for estimating difficulty of reading materials.* New York: Teachers College, Bureau of Publications, 1959.
12. Olsen, Marjorie. Summary of main findings on the validity of the 1955 College Board General Composition Test. Statistical Report No. 56–9. Princeton, N.J.: Educational Testing Service, 1956.
13. Perry, Frances M. *Progressive composition.* Yonkers, N.Y.: World Book, 1925.
14. Swineford, Frances. College Entrance Examination Board General Composition Test L. Statistical Report No. 56–45. Princeton, N.J.: Educational Testing Service, 1956.
15. Thorndike, E. L. *The teacher's word book.* New York: Teachers College, Bureau of Publications, 1921.
16. Vogel, Mabel, & Washburne, C. An objective method of determining grade placement of children's reading material. *Elementary School Journal,* 1938, 38, 373–381.
17. Washburne, C., & Morphett, Mabel V. Grade placement of children's books. *Elementary School Journal,* 1938, 38, 355–364.
18. Washburne, C., & Vogel, Mabel. *Winnetka graded book list.* Chicago: American Library Association, 1926.

The Interview in Personality Appraisal

NEVITT SANFORD

1953

Even within the relatively limited area of personality appraisal, the conduct of the interview and the handling of the data it yields will depend upon the aims pursued and conditions under which the work is undertaken. The present paper is concerned with the use of the interview in a fairly comprehensive, longitudinal study of personality development in normal late adolescents or young adults, the interviewers being trained at a fairly high level in clinical psychology, and the subjects being volunteers. My intention is to describe a procedure that promises to be useful despite the numerous problems and difficulties to be anticipated. From time to time, the contrast with what might better be done under different conditions will be pointed up.

PURPOSES OF THE INTERVIEW

Fifteen or twenty years ago, the inclusion of the interview among the techniques to be used in such a study would have been taken for granted. Today, one must seriously question whether it is wise to use the interview at all. There seems to be general awareness of the filing cabinets about the country, bulging with unanalyzed interview material. Knowledge of research methodology has become so widespread that the interview is often perceived as a vast tenderloin of sin and error. The young investigator, trained to conceive of Heaven in quantitative terms, shrewdly induces other unsuspecting souls—teachers, psychiatrists, employers, supervisors, and the like—to provide the unreliable criterion measures while he with unassailable innocence provides the predictor measures. Actually, this approach has been so successful, the objective standardized tests, empirically validated, have so far outstripped the projective techniques and other more global clinical devices as predictors of external criteria, as to give rise to the hope that a new day of righteousness might be at hand. Still, there are sinners among us, those who believe that something has been hidden from our view and who exhibit an insatiable curiosity about the inner workings of things. They are apt to regard the interview as an effective probe. But today, they must face the question: are there any scientific purposes to be achieved by the interview that cannot more efficiently be achieved by other methods? (Discussion is limited to the type of research undertaking outlined above. It seems obvious that where certain immediately practical aims are involved, the interview is indispensable. If one has to decide whether to undertake extended psychotherapy with a given individual, or which of a number of applicants to accept as members of a small research team or to take along on an extended cruise, he will do well to interview them no matter what the battery of tests they have taken.)

It seems safe to say, in the first place, that in the field of personality there is still place for the *exploratory* interview. In many areas, the need is still to *find* the important variables, to give them preliminary definitions, and to gain some notion of the signs by which they are to be known.

The exploratory interview also offers a means for seeing relations among variables, and thus for setting up hypotheses for future testing. One of the great difficulties in personality research springs from the fact that in order to understand a given phenomenon it is necessary to take simultaneous account of numerous factors. It is because the interview, or the series of interviews, makes this to some extent possible that it has been the major source of fruitful hypotheses in the field of personality.

In the second place, it seems at the present time that the interview may provide estimates of variables for which no objective tests are as yet available. Although efficient objective instruments are produced at an increasingly rapid rate, it cannot be claimed that they have so far embraced more than a small section of the total sphere of personality variables, or that they even keep pace with the finding and definition of new variables. There is a fairly new scale for measuring rigidity; but we now know that there are several different kinds of rigidity and of nonrigidity for which objective measures are needed. A study of personality with any pretentions of comprehensiveness cannot wait for the development of these tests.

Again, if one wishes to perform case studies, to exemplify in detail the common patterns found in his data, to add to our understanding of the organization of personality, or to seek for new relationships of the kind which appear only when numerous variables are considered together, he is almost bound to make use of interview material. Even after the most comprehensive testing program, with the fullest use of projective techniques and situational tests, it will be found that in order to make the case "come alive" or "hang together," interview material will be needed. This is not merely because the use of the case study involves some commitment to an idiographic approach, that is, to the assumption that in each individual the organization of variables is in some sense unique; the number of common traits that will enter the picture will undoubtedly exceed the number of available objective tests, and the use of available ones will involve more testing than is ordinarily feasible. More than this, the study of an individual personality, properly carried out, will require attention to sequences and continuities in time; the interview is well designed for getting the life story, and in lieu of the most comprehensive longitudinal study, it will have to be used.

Finally, there is an area that may be approached either by means of the interview or by means of the questionnaire, a decision in favor of the one or the other depending on circumstances and a variety of rather subtle factors. The life-history—matters of fact about childhood, education, work, and the like—has long been the special province of the interview. But the questionnaire has made enormous inroads in this area; and this, very probably, is why Professor Kinsey must be at such pain to show that the questionnaire would not have been suitable for his purposes. One argument for the interview is that certain significant facts of the life-history are, for most people, sufficiently embarrassing or otherwise painful so that we should not expect an accurate account except under very favorable conditions. The anonymous questionnaire can go quite a long way toward establishing these conditions; it is by no means to be scorned by those who desire such facts as are contained in the Kinsey Report. If, however, one is undertaking a longitudinal study, or any study of personality that requires repeated contacts with the same subject, that subject is bound to become known to the investigators, and account must be taken of his sensibilities. In these circumstances it would be foolish to go on asking, by means of the questionnaire, highly personal questions about past events and current practices without obtaining information about how these questions were understood and reacted to. With respect to certain significant matters, we should expect a certain amount of conscious withholding of information, and a great deal of unconscious resistance or distortion. There is no guarantee that even the most careful interview will overcome these obstacles, but it would appear to be at the present time the best instrument we have for the purpose. It must be emphasized that the concern here is with matters of fact, with what actually happened or what is going on now; where one is interested only in the subject's thoughts and attitudes, his conception of his childhood, his imagery of his parents, and the like, there is no question that questionnaire and projective techniques may even now go a long way, particularly when there is knowledgeable use of indirection.

The Role of Theory

Probably the main reason why so much interview material is collected without its ever being analyzed is that the interviewing was undertaken without thought being given to what was significant, and in what way. We have commonly proceeded on the notion that if one asks about education, jobs, hobbies, relations of parents, expectations for the future, and the like, he will get material of which something can be made later on. We shall probably have to admit that what can be made of it in the end is directly proportional to what was put in at the beginning, in the way of theory and hypotheses. The chances are that no one is going to theorize about one's interview material except oneself; I should argue that this theorizing were better done before the actual work of interviewing rather than after. Every question, or at least every line of questioning, should have its theoretical rationale; one should even have thought about the kinds of answers likely to be elicited and about how these were going to be categorized in the analysis. It might be objected that this procedure would interfere with the exploratory function of the interview. The answer is that, at this stage of our knowledge, more will be discovered by conceiving hypotheses and following them through in the interview or by the study of material systematically gathered, than by floating about in a sea of undifferentiated verbal material.

It might also be objected that the direction of interviewing and of interview analysis by theory, by conceptual schemes and hypotheses, opens wide the door through which the investigator's biases will intrude. The answer would be that, while bias has always to be contended with in interviewing as elsewhere in personality research, it is no more of a problem in theory-directed interviewing than in any other kind, and that in any case, bias is not to be controlled by the avoidance of hypotheses but rather by meeting certain methodological standards in the conduct of the interview, and in the analysis of the material it elicits.

The Conditions of the Interview

The fact that an interview is undertaken with normal volunteers, the subjects being sought by the interviewer rather than vice versa, has immediate implications for the conduct of the interview. It here becomes necessary to act in such a way as to maintain the subject's motivation on as high a level as possible, to encourage positive attitudes toward the research both before and after the interview. It has, I believe, been sufficiently demonstrated that a wish to take part in an investigation that promises to make a contribution to science is sufficient motivation for most subjects, provided the demands upon their time are kept within reasonable limits. (Allowances may have to be made for "volunteer error," however; and nonvolunteers will have to be offered additional inducements.) This being so, it is ordinarily a mistake to promise that the subjects "will get something out of it too," meaning counseling of one sort or another. (But this does not mean that counseling may not in fact have to be given, a matter to be gone into later.)

The necessity for maintaining positive attitudes toward the research calls into serious question the use of nondirective interviewing techniques. Since the subject has not sought the interview, it is of course out of the question for the interviewer to signify that he is ready to listen while the subject tells "what's the trouble" or "what's on his mind." And even though the subject may be brought to accept the task of telling about himself in his own way, we may expect difficulty and resistance to mount as time goes on. The situation is well calculated to arouse anxiety and hostility even in the healthiest individual. Intelligent, educated subjects will, to be sure, go to work on some such question as "What influences have had most to do with your becoming the kind of person you are?", but an interviewer should have very good reasons for imposing so difficult a task—and, of course, some extraordinarily efficacious way of exploiting the material he collects. There is no denying that much can be learned by permitting a subject to bring up whatever topics he likes, in whatever order he likes, but it is difficult to justify the investment of time, either that of the subject or that of the researcher. And this is assuming that some way has been found to analyze the material.

Nondirective interviewing, or that kind of directed interviewing that begins with the most innocuous topic and proceeds warily in the direction of the touchy ones, usually assumes that the subject will be seen a number of times, perhaps over an extended period. But in a longitudinal study, the need is for an appraisal of the personality *now*—this month or this fall—at the time that other tests or diagnostic procedures are being administered. Although several interviews may be considered to belong to the "now," one must be careful not to mistake "on better acquaintance" for an actual change in the personality. The need is for reliable estimates of the present state of affairs, something with which later states of affairs may be compared. Let us accept this requirement then, and ask how we might proceed when the task is a fairly comprehensive appraisal of the personality *now,* when not more than two or three interviews can be given and these within the space of a few days, and where there is the necessity of maintaining sufficiently good relations with the subject so that he will come again six months, or a year, hence and after that. Interviewing under these conditions requires a schedule based upon theory; it seems better carried forward according to some procedures rather than others; and it must yield material that can be handled in an objective or quantitative fashion.

THE TECHNIQUE OF THE INTERVIEW

Let it be assumed, then, that the interviewer begins his conversations with his subject with a well-conceived interview schedule on his desk. And let it also be assumed that he intends to cover the ground within the time allotted. Covering the ground here means getting enough material bearing on a given topic so that judges, independently examining that material later on, can make an appraisal of the variables which were supposedly brought into focus by the discussion of that topic. The interview schedule is not, however, a list of the questions which will scrupulously be put to every subject. If this were the case, one might as well have used a questionnaire in the first place. No, the schedule will be made up of the questions which the interviewer is asking himself; ideally, the area in question has been sufficiently differentiated in advance, well enough mapped out conceptually, so that he knows just what he wants to find out. The matter of how to draw the subject out on the points in question will have to be left to the interviewer's judgment. It is just here, of course, that art or skill or experience will enter the picture. The task is to get the subject to go far enough into the significant matter at hand without arousing too much anxiety or hostility or causing him to regret it later. This calls for some ability to be aware of the subject's feelings, considerable knowledge of how anxiety and hostility are expressed, and particularly, perhaps, the ability to judge what the traffic will bear. If one knows about these matters, he can persist in his purpose despite some discomfort on the subject's part, because he knows that this discomfort is within reasonable limits and that he can dispel it later on. By and large, we should expect from the less skillful or less experienced interviewer errors of two kinds: that through over-cautiousness he has failed to bring out enough significant material, or that he has elicited the material at the cost of our having disgruntled subjects on our hands.

The experienced interviewer may demand a completely free hand in the matter of how he is going to draw out the subject and manage the emotion that is generated, but he will rarely refuse to discuss with his colleagues the way he proposes to proceed in approaching the particular topics of the interview schedule. A result of such discussion might very well be that a number of suggestions about questions to put to the subject will be included in the interview schedule.

It should be emphasized that having accepted the general procedure being described here, the interviewer, whatever his gifts, must accept the discipline of the interview schedule. Although he need not maintain any particular order in taking up the topics, he must hold himself to the task of covering them and not be led off in directions which might seem to him more important in some particular case. The point is emphasized because, in other types of situations, the interviewer is more than willing to be led in directions that seem significant at the moment. If one has to make a practical decision based on a thoroughgoing understanding of a subject—for example, when the question concerns psychotherapy (when, and what kind), or when one is responsible for a tentative formulation of the central dynamic structure of a case, as in certain types of assessment work—the best procedure is quite different from that indicated above. In these latter instances, the interviewer must formulate hypotheses as he goes along, find the means for rejecting quickly the unpromising ones, and spend the bulk of his time following up leads that point to the centrally important. Of all types of interviewing, this is the kind that calls for the greatest skill and knowledge. There will probably always be a place for this kind of interviewing, but the research setting with which we are concerned is not one of them.

Contrary to what appears to be a common opinion, the interview schedule is, in the research interview, an actual aid to the management of anxiety and the maintenance of morale. It helps to lend an air of impersonality to the proceedings, and it may serve as a convenient scapegoat. It is not that the interviewer wants to pry into personal affairs; the schedule is the taskmaster; the interviewer and the subject have no choice but to do its bidding. With an interview schedule clearly in the picture, the interviewer may put the touchy questions in the same even tone, in the same routine manner, that he employs with other questions; and he may, if he notices signs of embarrassment, relieve the situation by passing on to the next question. (In the questionnaire or inventory that touches on affect-laden topics, this control is lacking. An item may start a chain of free associations which leads to the subject, amid mounting anxiety, deep into fantasy. These are the subjects who seek out the investigator to protest the whole proceeding.) In the systematic interview, the subject may be spared this kind of painful rumination. Thus, there is something to be said for the famous "rapid-fire" questioning of the Kinsey interview. However much the psychologist might object to the neglect of the psychology of sex in the Kinsey researches, it probably must be admitted that the data on tumescence-detumescence were fairly accurate and collected without undue hardship on the subjects.

There is, of course, a question about the after-effects of this kind of interviewing. I have conducted, in different settings, quite a large number of rather probing "one-shot" interviews with volunteers and with paid subjects without becoming aware of any undue repercussions, and one may well believe that this was true of the Kinsey investigations. The trouble is, one may never know. It is my impression that we are safe in conducting research interviews of this kind provided certain precautions are taken. Obviously, we must, in the beginning, establish confidence in the whole investigation and particularly in those who do the interviewing; and obviously, the conduct of the interview must be such as to keep any painful emotions within bounds. Beyond this, there are steps that may be taken to leave "good feeling all 'round" at the end. For example, a lapse into a nondirective approach, or an indication that the formal part of the interview was over and that what was now said was off the record, might enable the subject to bring out his doubts or misgivings or unresolved tensions so that they might be dealt with constructively. Finally, the door should be left open for another conference at some future time. Although, as stated above, it is a poor policy to "sell" a research interview by suggesting that the subject will get something out of it, it is wise to provide the possibility of counseling, or of telling something of the results, for those subjects who make this request. This is not only wise, it is a minimum requirement of a human approach. It is not our wish to regard the subject's problems and private thoughts and deeply felt sentiments as nothing more than grist for our statistical mill. He has the right to expect human reactions to these human expressions. Experience shows, however, that few volunteers avail themselves of opportunities for counseling, and that those who do are not very demanding.

In a longitudinal study, the matter of counseling the research subject assumes very considerable importance. When a subject is seen from time to time over long periods, some kind of relationship between him and the investigator, or investigators, develops inevitably. Thus, the subject of study changes as a result of being studied. (This consideration makes it all the more essential, in a longitudinal study, that all possible effort be directed to achieving a formulation of the case at the time the study begins.) The investigator has no choice but to assume responsibility for these changes, and to act in a way that is in the best interests of his subject. A developing relationship between subject and investigator has serious implications for experimental design. If, for example, one is studying psychological changes accompanying physical growth, or changes resulting from education, the effects of repeated contacts with the investigator may be very considerable.

Such effects are probably minimal when techniques are limited to objective tests, even though these be administered individually, but the repeated use of the interview would seem to be quite another matter. We cannot solve the problem by avoiding all counseling or by striving to keep everything on an impersonal basis. The wisest course, it seems to me, is to make a virtue of a necessity, to hypothesize that subjects interviewed over a period of months or years will as a result of that experience be somewhat different in the end from similar subjects who did not have the experience, to test the hypothesis through the use of the control group, and to keep close watch upon the whole interaction process, trying to observe which aspects of this interpersonal process have which effects with which subjects.

A device that would seem to offer several advantages for research is that of having the same subject interviewed, within a relatively narrow space of time, by two or more investigators. It is interesting to note here that in the Tavistock Institute of Human Relations, which carries on in the spirit of the War Office Selection Board (the British "Assessment Center"), assessment in selection work has been boiled down to just two procedures: the group discussion (in which the performances of 10 or 12 candidates are evaluated by the staff) and the interview (in which a given candidate is interviewed by four people in the course of an afternoon). Thus, a high premium is placed upon judgment, that of the assessment experts and that of the executive with whom the successful candidate will be working. It would seem that if the ability to judge people counts for anything in personality research—and I believe that it does—the interview offers the best means for enabling us to take advantage of it. Why not avail ourselves of the judgments of the most experienced people we have, and let them serve as checks upon one another? Let us divide the task of covering the interview schedule among several interviewers, and let them, after covering the topics assigned, offer their judgments concerning some of those pervasive aspects of personality that would be subtly manifested as well in a discussion of future plans as in a discussion of childhood.

The Exploitation of Interview Material

The whole conception of the research interview, as set forth here, has been worked out with an eye firmly fixed on the problem of how to handle the interview material. The device just mentioned, that of having several interviews for each subject, is an obvious attempt to avoid throwing out the expert altogether and yet to meet the minimum requirements of sound methodology. A check list of several hundred adjectives, to be filled out for each subject by each of, say, four interviewers should provide ample opportunity for setting forth the uniqueness of each subject even while it afforded data for quantitative treatment. Ratings on some of the so-called generalized traits of personality can still be very useful; as a matter of fact, for many common traits of personality they are still the best measures we have. Moreover, if we are going to have experts, and if they are going to undertake to penetrate the outer layers of the personality, then we should have the benefits of their judgments concerning the more central, or the more subtle, aspects of the personality. These judgments, too, may be rendered by means of a rating scale, the interviewers having agreed in advance upon the form and content of this device.

But the general procedure of interviewing that has been described here has been designed with particular attention to the objective, quantitative analysis of the subject's own reports. It is a part of the interviewer's task to record, under appropriate headings, what the subject has to say about the topic in question. During the interview and during the recording, the interviewer bears in mind that judges other than himself are going to be required to classify the material bearing on a given topic, and that they are going to do this without reference to other parts of the record. The proposal here is that the interview protocol be divided into a number of sections corresponding to the topics of the schedule; that the productions of all the subjects, on a given topic, be then assembled and handed, without names or identifying data being attached, to two or more judges; and that the judges, working on one topic at a time, categorize the material or make estimates of variables in accordance with the conceptual scheme upon which the interview was based. This procedure should eliminate halo effect and insure that judgments on particular issues are not contaminated by any other kinds of information about the subject; it should yield data that are ready for quantitative treatment. Measures obtained in this way, like the measures based on ratings by the interviewers themselves, may be used either as predictors of external criteria or as measures against which tests can be validated.

Clinical Versus Actuarial Prediction

CHARLES C. McARTHUR

1955

Our question is, "Which predict better, clinical or actuarial methods?" The correct answer is, "We don't know; no one has done the experiment." The moral is, "Somebody ought to!"

I know there have been experiments purporting to answer this question. They just seem for the most part so poorly designed that they are irrelevant.

How should a relevant experiment be designed? The general rule is that both clinician and actuary should be given every opportunity to show their wares. That's the only possible way to match them. If, with apparent scientific sophistication, you hold the conditions under which the actuary and the clinician must predict "constant," one or both men will be handicapped by the conditions you prescribe. How can you say "how much" of a handicap each man suffers, or how to make his opponent's handicap "equal"?

Years ago, we had a similar problem in intelligence testing. In the early days of the testing movement, it was thought that the way to be "fair" to all the children tested was to repeat precisely the same external ritual, with the examiner working in the same office, with the same lighting, introducing himself and the test in the same way and giving instructions verbatim. The IQ's so derived were presumed to be directly comparable. Alas, they were not. What was soon learned about intelligence testing was that true comparability could be had only when the examiner varied his behavior appropriately from child to child, so as to obtain for each child the maximally favorable conditions. When each child was "given all the breaks," the resulting IQ's could be justly compared.

So it is with our question. If we really want to know how the clinician and the actuary compare, we have to let each man

1) use the data of his choice,
2) make the analysis of his choice, and
3) make the predictions of his choice.

617

Now, I'm not an actuary and I'm speaking to actuaries, so I'd better let them make their own choice of data, analyses, and predictions. It is about the clinical half of this contest that I feel entitled to speak, if only because, at the Harvard Study of Adult Development, we have recently gathered some experimental observations on the way people gather good and bad clinical predictions. I would like therefore to review the proper choices of data, analysis, and predictions for the clinical half of a good clinical versus actuarial experiment.

CLINICAL DATA

If we want to make good clinical predictions, what kinds of data[1] will be the data of our choice?

We want plentiful data. Plentiful enough to make us feel that we may have an adequate sample of all kinds of our subject's behavior. Those of us who earn a living as working clinicians go day after day, year after year, jumping to premature conclusions on inadequate evidence. That's what we're paid to do. All the same, when we do experiments for the advancement of knowledge, we are forced to accept the stern reminder of Robert White (7) that "An attempt to cut the testing schedule below ten to fifteen hours with each subject is merely a proposal to sabotage the research." A more usual battery for experimental purposes would run to thirty or forty hours.

We want various data. It is almost indispensable to watch one subject interacting with at least half a dozen examiners. It *is* indispensable to sample his behavior at all psychic "levels." Projective devices are a must, but so are observations of S performing workaday acts in his everyday setting.

We want overlapping data. We had best see our man tackling comparable problems under very different conditions, with different examiners, different degrees of stress, in different contexts.

We want open-ended data. The ratio of the subject's talk to the examiner's talk should be at least ten to one.

We want fully recorded data. That is another lesson from intelligence testing. More and more, the by-products of a test situation turn out to be more useful than the measurement that was the historical purpose of the

---

[1] Quite typical of the problems of communication across the two frames of reference, clinical and actuarial, is the fact that this talk was prepared with no awareness that the word "data" contained any ambiguity. In an informal conversation before the panel discussion, the writer became aware that when he says "data" he means "contents of verbal or behavioral acts," and that when actuaries say "data" they mean "scores." Neither usage is perfectly exclusive, but the difference is gross enough to tangle communication badly.

test. A Wechsler-Bellevue recorded verbatim, the irrelevant remarks being recorded most scrupulously of all, tells us many times as much as the IQ or even the subtest profile of scores. White (7) has made this point well, at the same time explaining why we insist on obtaining overlapping data. "Our problem-solving test," he points out, "will perhaps also be a test of frustration tolerance, a test of control over anxiety, a test of level of aspiration, or a situation that happens to mobilize an infant traumata, *and our report on its results must include as much of this information as can be observed.*" The rhetorical italics are mine.

CLINICAL ANALYSIS

If we have now collected the right kind of data, we may be in a position to take our second step and ask what should be the clinical analysis of our choice. And there *is* one best analysis. I, too, have heard the rumor that each clinician uses the method that is his personal favorite. The rumor may even be true; tastes vary, though science be constant. Nonetheless, both logic and empirical validation identify *one* best technique of clinical analysis. This technique is neither intuitive, as rumor so often has it, nor a Mystery, nor is it unavailable to actuaries. You see, the clinical analysis of choice is nothing but the application of the Scientific Method!

I am not the only clinician who has this idea. "The diagnosis of each personality is," according to White (7), "a miniature scientific experiment." Meehl (2) would also, although with some caution, accept the idea that the good clinician makes " 'little special theories' the applicability of which is to one person."

Nor am I without evidence. At the Study of Adult Development, we recently asked a series of clinicians to formulate rich case data that were ten years old, and then to make postdictions of the subject's behavior during the ten years since the last recorded entry. We knew what the subject had been doing these last ten years; and, while our clinical prophet tried to guess what had happened, we all smugly sat around in a circle, "holding the book on him."

What all our clinical prophets did under these very trying validation conditions seemed to be to build from the data a clinical construct, a conceptual device, a "special theory applicable to one person," a *model* of that person, that made this statement on page 17 of the record consistent with that remarkable quotation back on page 14. Each datum became grist from which was ground a formulation of the premises governing *all* of S's behavior, the lifelong premises, the treasured self-consistencies with which the person being studied had learned to face the world. Each batch of data lent itself to hypotheses about the person, hypotheses that could be checked out against new data as the record progressed, and could be revised with each successive cross-validation provided by turning another page. After conning all the data, the clinician possessed a fuzzy, but gradually sharpening, conceptualization of the man under study. "He seems to be the sort of a person who. . . ." Then the clinician could make his predictions by doing imaginary experiments with the model. There would be paths down which the conceptualized person could effortlessly stroll, while there were alleys into which he simply could not be made to turn. And that was how good predictions got generated.

Tomkins (6) has rigidly formulated this technique. Perhaps his most important statement is that we have to derive from the data themselves *the very categories in which those data will be cast.* "In general," he warns us, "we do not know exactly what to look for. If we prejudge the categories of analysis, we may commit serious errors. What check, then," he asks, "have we on the adequacy of our selection of categories of analysis? It is our conviction that the logic of the individual's fantasy itself must be our ultimate criterion." I would agree unreservedly. That facility at induction which enables him to derive for each new person studied a fresh set of categories that maximize the patterning of this particular set of data is the very hallmark of the good clinician.

Tomkins goes on, in a chapter that should be required reading for all graduate students, to specify how one can deduce from the data what categories were implicit in the mind of the subject himself (6, Ch. IV). Nor are Tomkins' instructions vague or dependent upon intuition; he uses as his tool John Stuart Mill's canons of logic! Mill sets down rules like, "If two or more instances of the phenomenon under investigation have only one circumstance in common, the circumstance in which alone all the instances agree is the cause, or effect of the given phenomenon." Or else, "If an instance in which the phenomenon under investigation occurs, and an instance in which it does not occur, have every circumstance in common, save one, that one occurring only in the former, the circumstance in which alone the two instances differ is the effect, or cause, or an indispensable part of the cause of the phenomenon." And so forth, down through the Joint Method of Agreement and Difference, the Method of Concomitant Variation, Necessary Causes, Sufficient Causes, etc.

Furiously pedantic as they may sound, Mill's canons work. Suppose, for instance, that on the Thematic Apperception Test (TAT) your man tells one story in which the boy's mother wants him to practice the violin, but the boy rebels, afterward feeling very guilty. Suppose in another story the mother wants the son to go to school, but the boy quits school, again feeling guilty. Suppose a third story tells of another rebellious son who is now, however, being reconciled to his mother and doing as she wishes, and consequently this son becomes a great success and feels very happy. Mill and Tomkins would have us infer that, for this narrator, only a hero who does as his mother wishes may be permitted a happy ending. The category "obedient sons" will therefore play a dynamic part in our formulation of this man's personality, and hence in what we can predict about his reactions to future events. For some other man whom we might study, this category could have absolutely no meaning.

I realize that clinicians don't usually think that systematically. The best empirical evidence about how clinicians actually think in practice is provided by Shneidman (5). After reviewing fifteen shockingly different systems for interpreting the same TAT protocol, each system being offered by an "authority," Shneidman is able to discern a common set of steps in the clinical analyses. For most workers, the initial step is Charcot's: to look and look and look. They read and reread the data. The next stage seems to be "semi-organized notes" on repetitive or logically consistent patterns in the data. Then the criterion of internal consistency is applied and reapplied to trial hypotheses about the structure of the person's motives. Only in the end, when a diagnostic label is sought or if some one datum sticks out as incongruent with the rest, is any general psychological theory invoked. That was also true of our Study of Adult Development clinicians; theory came last. The one discussant we had who was embarrassingly inaccurate tried to deduce the behavior of the man he was discussing directly from the postulates of a general psychological theory. The successful prophets were those who remained inductive. None seemed to be as systematic as Tomkins would have them; but that only proves that the methods of analysis we use in everyday practice are less than ideal. It is probably true that we all could profit from more seminars entitled "The Diagnosis of Personality as a Hypothetico-Deductive Process."

CLINICAL PREDICTIONS

Coming to the third portion of our clinical versus actuarial experiment, Tomkins' logic calls our attention to what sort of predictions clinicians should choose to make. If the categories in which we cast our data were those that logically arose from the data themselves, then we have already decided what aspects of a particular case we can categorize, and hence we have unintentionally decided which aspects of the case we can predict. The clinical analysis has both this virtue and this liability: that it predicts what will be predictable . . . and what won't. An allied technique, usually called "thematic" analysis, has this same property. There are certain themes in which S is very emotionally involved and it is these matters that we have most data on and can best predict. We have no basis for trying to predict any and all aspects of S's behavior.

Tomkins' formulation also gives us a second rule about our predictions: they must be contingent predictions. What we know is what Tomkins calls "the conditions for . . ." a certain behavior's appearing. "If S perceives his boss as a nurturant elder, he will react by being ungrateful." If not, something else will happen. "If S sees a woman as a sexual object, he will assume her to be evil, but if he perceives her as a supportive mother figure, he will assume her to be good." Always our predictions have the form "If . . . then . . . ."

It follows that the usual experimental demand that the clinician predict multiple-choice criteria, which look nicely objective but never state contingencies, almost certainly dooms the clinician to failure. It just isn't possible to say, in general, that "S will be very aggressive." It *is* possible to say, "If S sees the situation in this or that way, he'll be very aggressive." It is absurd to say, "S will get well." It makes sense to say, "If his therapist can play this or that role toward S, S will respond beautifully." Indeed, I wonder if it isn't more important to make these contingent predictions, not only because they turn out to be right more often, but also because they have more practical value.

Clinicians themselves don't seem to be aware of what predictions they can and can't make. Time after time, an excellent clinical analysis gets reported in terms of a rating scale, and so dooms itself to being invalidated on follow-up. When are we going to learn that we can't say, "Mr. A will be more aggressive than Mr. B," without specifying the conditions? Not only do our available methods of analysis prevent this, but it is quite likely that people just aren't made that way. Some of the most famous and recent and spectacular failures of really good clinical studies to stand up under cross-validation have arisen because of this one error.

I would insist, then, that any valid estimate of the accuracy of clinical prediction must permit the clinician to make contingent predictions and to limit himself to predictions about topics of his choice. I would hasten to add, however, that giving the clinician this liberty will not result in trivial, superficial, or safe and sure generalizations. The predictions the clinician can make relate to those very behaviors that have most importance of all, because they are the behaviors that matter to the subject himself.

AVAILABLE STUDIES

So now we have reviewed three sets of conditions: the proper data, the proper analysis, and the proper predictions that must be had if we are to learn whether the clinician be a prophet or a charlatan. Perhaps you see why I feel that none of the studies done till now are very relevant.

There are two sets of such studies.

Meehl (2) has judiciously reviewed a set of studies that hold data and predictions constant while comparing two forms of analysis, one actuarial, one what the experimenters call "clinical." Perhaps the best known of these experiments is Sarbin's (2, pp. 90–92), though Meehl has located a dozen and a half more. The nature of the analysis is always insufficiently specified, but the piecemeal data supplied as a basis for prophecy always seem to preclude the use of a truly clinical analysis. Sarbin, who did better than some of the others, provided his prophets only with high school rank in class, aptitude test scores, a preliminary interviewer's notes, and a paper-and-pencil personality inventory. Apparently no one, save the "preliminary interviewer," who left only "notes," had looked at the person in action. From such straws the clinician was asked to make bricks! That the clinicians in this study did as well as the actuaries is irrelevant; what they had to be doing, with such nonclinical data, was what Sarbin accuses them of doing: they were managing somehow to function as a human substitute for an IBM machine. Almost all the other studies supply nonclinical data; all demand multiple-choice, noncontingent predictions.

A second group of studies includes recent large-scale follow-ups on assessment batteries, such as Murray's OSS program (3, 4), the Kelly and Fiske studies at Michigan on predicting the success of clinical psychologists (1), and the California studies of personality that are beginning to be published.[2] None of these has suggested any great validity for the clinical method. We have to take these failures of the clinical method more seriously; they were designed by good clinicians and used excellent clinical data. One presumes that proper clinical analysis got applied, though this is not always clear from the published accounts. What vitiates all these studies, however, is their failure, in two senses, to make clinical predictions. First, there seems to be little or no contingent prediction. Worse, nearly all the predictions take the form of rating scales. That decision in designing these studies determined the nature of the findings.

[2] See MacKinnon paper, reproduced in Chapter 11—Ed.

CONCLUSION

So we still don't know the answer to the main question before us.

Only a study under proper conditions will be conclusive. If clinical predictions under ideal conditions fail to come true, running the actuarial half of the experiment will hardly be required! I happen to believe, however, that clinical predictions, as operationally defined in this paper, will turn out to be 100 per cent true; 100 per cent, that is, less only the sampling error that is inevitable because we see 40 hours and not 40 years of our subject's behavior, and less the error arising from unreliability of those who observe both the independent variables and the criterion variable.

That's my null hypothesis. I, like all my fellow clinicians, am eager to see the hypothesis tested.

REFERENCES

1. Kelly, E. L., & Fiske, D. W. *The prediction of performance in clinical psychology.* Ann Arbor, Mich.: Univer. of Michigan Press, 1951.
2. Meehl, P. E. *Clinical vs. statistical prediction: a theoretical analysis and a review of the evidence.* Minneapolis: Univer. of Minnesota Press, 1954.
3. Murray, H. A., & MacKinnon, D. W. Assessment of OSS personnel. *Journal of Consulting Psychology,* 1946, 10, 76–80.
4. Office of Strategic Services, Assessment Staff. *Assessment of men: selection of personnel for the Office of Strategic Services.* New York: Holt, Rinehart & Winston, 1948.
5. Shneidman, E. S., *et al.* (Eds.) *Thematic test analysis.* New York: Grune & Stratton, 1951.
6. Tomkins, S. S. *The Thematic Apperception Test: the theory and technique of interpretation.* New York: Grune & Stratton, 1947.
7. White, R. W. What is tested by psychological tests? In P. H. Hoch and J. Zubin (Eds.), *Relation of psychological tests to psychiatry.* New York: Grune & Stratton, 1951. Pp. 3–14.

Clinical Versus Actuarial Prediction: A Pseudo-Problem

JOSEPH ZUBIN

1955

There are three possible ways of dealing with the problem presented by the title of this paper: 1) adopt the clinical point of view, 2) adopt the actuarial point of view, or 3) declare the dilemma to be nonexistent. The third course is the one I have chosen and as a result I expect to get the brickbats from both sides. Clinicians may accuse me of "leaving the field" because of my inability to cope with the dilemma, while actuarians may regard my approach as merely probing the null hypothesis. I feel, however, that the dilemma is in reality a pseudo-dilemma created by the hopefully temporary gap that now separates the clinician from the research worker.

The reason for my position becomes quite clear in retrospect. I began my career in psychology with a statistical net to bag the elusive differences that may exist between abnormals and normals. Disappointment in this undertaking turned me to the study of the individual case. As a result, I began to realize that both sides of the coin—the actuarial and the clinical—belong to each other in an inextricable manner. It was not, however, until I began to study the philosophy of science that I could logically resolve the opposition between the two approaches.[1]

INTERACTION OF CLINICAL AND ACTUARIAL METHODS

Scientific method is characterized by a continued interaction between observation and schematization (2). Which came first is difficult to determine. Primitive man's observation of nature soon led him to notice certain regularities which he schematized into expectation or hypothesis as we now call it. These hunches, hypotheses, or discoveries, if you will, constitute the first step—the context of discovery according to Reichenbach (11). This step might be likened to the storming of a beachhead in the continuing war

---

[1] I owe much of this insight to Eugene I. Burdock and to Raymond J. McCall, former students who guided my reluctant steps.

between science and ignorance. The second step is to verify the hypothesis. This leads us to the context of justification which might be likened to the establishing of law and order in the territory which the beachhead opened up. No amount of beach-storming, however, can conquer a territory, and no amount of empty drill can lead to victory. It is the sequential interaction between the two contexts that leads to success. The clinician, on the one hand, often becomes lost in the land of discovery, narcissistically enjoying every new idea, smelling every new hunch, and titillated by every new possibility, but only too rarely, if ever, leaving the context of discovery for the context of verification. The actuarian, on the other hand, often becomes lost among his equations, gadgets, and techniques—sharpening and polishing under the assumption that the sharper the tool, the better the eventual results. But for much of our work, our tools are already too fine. Most of the concepts that we deal with clinically are too open, too crude to warrant even the .01 level of significance on the score of either type of inference error (Type I or Type II). But psychology is not alone in this fix. Even biology, a science supposedly higher in the hierarchy of exactness, suffers from loosely defined concepts which nevertheless do not prevent scientific progress. Julian Huxley (6, p. 11), in defining the concept of species, says:

However, we must remember that species and other taxonomic categories may be of very different type and significance in different groups; and also that there is no single criterion of species. Morphological difference; failure to interbreed; infertility of offspring; ecological, geographical, or genetical distinctness—all those must be taken into account, but none of them singly is decisive. Failure to interbreed or to produce fertile offspring is the nearest approach to a positive criterion. It is, however, meaningless in apogamous forms, and as a negative criterion it is not applicable, many obviously distinct species, especially of plants, yielding fertile offspring, often with free Mendelian recombination on crossing. A combination of criteria is needed, together with some sort of flair. With the aid of these, it is remarkable how the variety of organic life falls apart into biologically discontinuous groups. In the great majority of cases species can be readily delimited, and appear as natural entities, not merely convenient fictions of the human intellect. Whenever intensive analysis has been applied, it on the whole, confirms the judgments of classical taxonomy.

It is thus not the precision of the concept, but its power in explaining behavior that differentiates the good from the poor concepts (7). The clinician who enchants himself with the brilliance of his discoveries and hunches as well as the actuary who spends his time putting a keener edge on his tools and proudly contemplates their sheen are fanatics who have "redoubled their energies when they lost their goal." For the goal, after all, is the verifiable understanding and prediction of human behavior, and to achieve this goal, the observations of the clinician and his hunches as well as the verification of these hunches by the actuary are essential.

From this point of view, the question of whether the actuarial approach is superior to the clinical is tantamount to asking whether the sperm is more important than the ovum. Both are equally important and no progress can be made with one alone. In fact, exercising one alone in isolation from the other is a rather unproductive form of activity despite the satisfaction it may afford.

The better the hunches, the more effective will be the actuarial prediction, once the hunches are verified. To compare clinical impressionistic prognosis with the actuarial prognosis derived from a previously formulated clinical hunch is a travesty! How could a new, untried clinical impression ever equal the statistically verified residue of earlier clinical impressions? We should have been so certain of our actuarial techniques that nothing but a complete victory in every precinct should have satisfied. Why did the results of the 24 studies surveyed by Meehl (10) fail to show an advantage in each instance? The answer lies in the relative rigor or looseness of the criteria. When rigorous, specific, and specified criteria are available, one can always build tests that will prognosticate successfully. As the criteria become looser and less explicit, it is debatable whether either method, actuarial or clinical, can accomplish much. Prognoses of mental illness, for example, should be based on a specified follow-up period, since outcome varies with period of follow-up. If the actuarial formula is based on immediate outcome as a criterion, while the clinical prognosis is based on eventual outcome, it is no wonder that the actuarial method is superior when the results are evaluated against immediate outcome.

Despite Meehl's very thoughtful book (10), the distinction between actuarial and clinical prediction is heuristic rather than basic. The process of prediction for a group is quite different from prediction for an individual. The former can be completely actuarial, as in life expectancy tables; the latter by its very nature must be clinical if it is to result in action. A distinction needs to be made between a *prediction* and a *decision* based on that prediction. The prediction might be that there is a .70 probability of success. What one does on the basis of such a probability in the case of a single individual is best exemplified by what one does for *himself* when faced with such a prediction. In the last analysis, decision is a "clinical" act, not an "actuarial" one. To have one standard in mind when one makes decisions about his own fate, and another standard when one makes decisions for a patient is the "double standard" at its worst. No one would select a secretary or a wife on test scores alone, even if the multiple R were as high as

.80 (which it rarely is in any prediction studies I have seen). Why should one be willing to decide on a patient's therapy on actuarial grounds alone? Mind you, I am not arguing against utilizing regression equations for prediction; but I am concerned with what you do as a consequence of the prediction. When actuarial predictions succeed in encompassing 90 per cent of the variance in the behavior under observation, we can safely leave prediction to a statistical clerk and save the clinician's time for the more arduous task of therapy. Since most actuarial predictions account for less than half of the variance in the observed behavior, actions based on such predictions need the integrating act of the clinical decision.

When the clinician makes a prediction, looks up tables of dosages of drugs, contemplates syndromes of symptoms, he is engaged in statistical or actuarial activity. What he does with this information—his volitional decision—is a "clinical" act. When the statistician chooses an experimental design, selects a technique, or decides on the relative weights to be assigned to certain factors, he is acting clinically. His subsequent analysis and the predictions derived from probability considerations are, of course, actuarial.

The complete process by which a decision is reached, with or without the help of Wald's decision functions, is a volitional act that has been described introspectively by Ach[2] (1). According to Ach, man is never closer to his inner self than when he makes a volitional decision. Freedom of the will, apparent or real, underlies this decision-making process, and is the very essence of mental life. To maintain that, in our present state of ignorance, we can substitute a regression equation for the volitional act would be flying in the face of reality. Decision belongs to the context of discovery, a land whose rules and regulations are as yet unknown.

CLINICAL STATISTICS

Nevertheless, it is important to call the attention of clinicians to the fact that they have spent too much time in "hunch-land" and not enough in the land of verification. By the same token, it is important to indicate to the statistician that the assumptions of normality, linearity, continuity, homoscedasticity, etc. that underlie many of his techniques, including the multiple regression equation, discriminant functions, and factor analysis, are not suitable for the nonlinear, discontinuous, unit-less type of observation the clinician deals with. Between the land of discovery and the land of verification a bridge must be built, consisting of the proper techniques to meet the clinical needs. Clinical psychology today is in about the same posi-

---

[2] The author translated this book into English some ten years ago and carbon copies are available at the Psychology Library of Columbia University.

tion that agriculture was before Fisher or physics was before Newton. Just as Fisher had to develop techniques for dealing with the hunches emanating from the practical agronomist, so a new Fisher is required to develop techniques for testing the hunches emanating from the clinic. This new Fisher will have to convert our present group-centered techniques into individual-centered tools, will have to deal with syndromes and patterns and profiles emanating not from data that satisfy the requirements of factor analysis, but from the crude, amorphous qualitative data that defy factor-analytic methods, or that are verily disemboweled by such high-powered techniques.

A good case in point is a recent study on the effects of drugs on psycho-

TABLE 1

The Critical Flicker-Fusion (CFF) Threshold
in Cycles per Second for the Various
Chemical Agents (N = 24)

Chemical Agent	Day	Mean
Placebo	1	30.8
Stimulant	2	31.1
Antihistamine (low)	3	30.7
Soporific (low)	4	31.1
Antihistamine (high)	5	30.7
Soporific (high)	6	31.4
Hypnotic	7	31.7
Placebo	8	31.3

logical test function (9). In order to determine the effect of a new antihistamine on psychological test performance, the effect of the new drug was contrasted with the effect of a placebo, a stimulant, and a hypnotic drug. The psychological techniques consisted of a group of conceptual, perceptual, and psychomotor tasks, and an interview. The results of one of the tests, the critical flicker-fusion (CFF) test, will be sufficient to clarify the point at issue (5). The means of the group of 24 patients who participated in this experiment are shown in Table 1.

The data were subjected to an analysis of variance, the results of which are shown in Table 2. It will be noted that the between-agent variance was not significant when compared with its largest interaction term, but the between-individual variance and its interactions were statistically significant, as shown by the F ratios.

Because of the significance of the interindividual variance and its interactions, each individual subject was treated separately as an independent universe. Since each measure used in the total analysis of variance (Table 2)

TABLE 2

Summary of the Results of the Total Analysis of Variance for
Three Threshold Determinations of CFF at Three Levels of
Apparent Brightness at Each of the Two Light-Dark Ratios
for 22 Subjects over Eight Days

Source of Variation	Sums of Squares	df	Mean Square	F	P
1 Chemical agent (Days)	278.97	7	39.85	1.83	—
2 Brightness levels	38572.66	2	19286.33	118.42	.01
3 Light-dark ratios	2190.67	1	2190.67	13.45	—
4 Individuals	7202.85	21	342.99	15.78	.01
1×2	115.64	14	8.26	2.12	—
1×3	110.24	7	15.75	2.08	.05
1×4	3193.69	147	21.73	2.87	.01
2×3	325.73	2	162.87	30.44	.01
2×4	370.03	42	8.81	1.65	.05
3×4	379.38	21	18.07	2.39	.05
1×2×3	54.43	14	3.89	1.69	—
1×2×4	979.70	294	3.33	1.45	.01
2×3×4	224.75	42	5.35	2.33	.01
1×3×4	1111.29	147	7.56	3.29	.01
1×2×3×4	675.71	294	2.30		
Within cells	387.47	2112	0.18		
Total	56173.21	3167			

was the average of ten CFF determinations on each individual, an analysis
of variance for the single individual could be performed. The results indicated that the group treatment of the data had hidden more than it revealed. The individual treatment of the data indicated that half of the group
(11 cases) had remained unaffected by the chemical agents. In those who
showed significant effects, the low soporific dosage showed a significantly
improved performance in 6 subjects and a significantly poorer performance
in 2 subjects. The higher dosage of the soporific agent improved the performance of 8 subjects and reduced the performance of 3, leaving the other
11 subjects unaffected. The relevant data are shown in Table 3.

It is clear that the group of subjects was quite heterogeneous with respect
to the effect of the various chemical agents. For this reason, group statistics
should always be examined in conjunction with individual statistics wherever possible.

Just how a heterogeneous group can be subdivided into more homogeneous subgroups becomes an important question for the clinical-actuarial
controversy. If we could find a technique for subdividing a group into homogeneous subgroups, we could then apply group statistics to the
subgroups and avoid the impasse that occurred in the previous example.

An example of the application of individual-centered techniques which

TABLE 3

Number of Subjects Showing Significant Improvement or
Worsening for Each Chemical Agent on the
Critical Flicker-Fusion Test (N = 22)

Chemical Agent	Improved	Worse	Unaffected
Stimulant	4	5	13
Antihistamine (low)	5	4	13
Soporific (low)	6	2	14
Antihistamine (high)	3	8	11
Soporific (high)	8	3	11
Hypnotic	6	4	12
Total	32	26	74
Mean	5.4	4.3	12.3

keeps the sights of the experimenter focused on the individual instead of on the group is the technique of like-mindedness (12). Some twenty years ago, we faced the problem of developing a personality inventory that would be of help in classifying mental patients. This study was reported in part in 1937, but because of an error in computation lay uncompleted until recently, when the error was discovered and the analysis completed. While we have since given up the use of inventory items as the sole basis for classification, and have (we believe) found more pertinent indicators, the method is general enough to be applicable to most of the data in the clinical field.

The Personal Inquiry Form (8), which consisted of a distillate of 70 items from a matrix of 1,000 found in other inventories and in case histories, was administered to some 1,000 patients of varying types of illness and to 1,000 normal controls. In the process of selecting the 70 items, only those items were retained that differentiated the patients from the normals in all the age groupings, the two sex groups, and all illness categories, since we wished to get a screening test that would separate the ill from the well. In retrospect, this seems to have been a mistake. In picking out only the items that differentiated, we selected the liabilities of the patient group, and eliminated their assets. Perhaps the patterning of the assets and liabilities is a more useful basis for screening than the total number of liabilities alone.

A sample of 68 male schizophrenic patients and 68 normal controls matched for age, sex, and education was then obtained, and by the use of IBM scoring machines it was possible to obtain the agreement scores of each patient with each of his 67 colleagues and each of the normal controls. Similarly the agreement scores for the normals were also obtained. The cu-

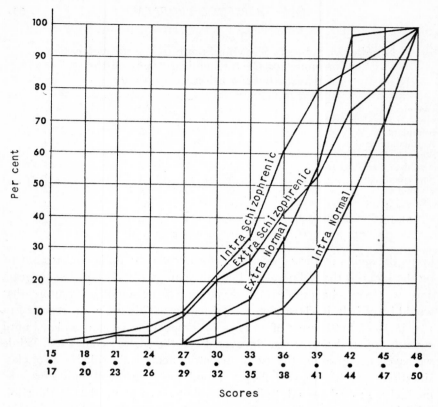

FIG. 1. *Cumulative percentage distribution of intragroup agreement scores of 68 schizophrenics and 68 matched normal controls and of extragroup agreement scores of 34 schizophrenics and 34 matched normal controls.*

TABLE 4

Means and SD's of Intragroup Agreement Scores of 68 Schizophrenics and 68 Matched Normal Controls and of Extragroup Agreement Scores of 34 Schizophrenics and 34 Matched Controls

Group	Agreement Scores					
	Intragroup			Extragroup		
	N	M	σ	N	M	σ
Normal Controls	68	44.6	4.69	34	40.2	3.94
Schizophrenics	68	37.0	5.44	34	40.2	7.31
Difference		7.6			—	3.37
t		8.5				3.34
P		< .01				< .01

mulative percentage distributions of these agreement scores are given in Figure 1; their means and SD's are in Table 4.[3]

The agreement scores for each of 17 individuals in each group were then correlated and the intercorrelations of these agreement scores were subjected to a factor analysis. Table 5 shows the intercorrelations. The factor analyses of the two groups were done separately. Three factors were extracted for normals and four for schizophrenics. These were rotated to simple structure by R. J. Williams. The factor loadings are shown in Table 6.[4]

Since these factors are merely for the purpose of classifying the schizophrenics into homogeneous subgroups, their nature and identity are of no consequence and, as soon as we have established the subtypes in our two samples of normals and abnormals, the factors can be discarded. Thirteen of the patients showed a significant loading on only one factor—ten of them on Factor I', two on Factor II', and one on Factor IV'. One patient showed significant loadings on Factors I' and III', and three individuals were mavericks, showing no significant loadings on any of the factors. In the normal group, fourteen individuals showed a significant loading on one factor—eleven on Factor I, two on Factor II (one with a positive and the other with a negative loading), and one on Factor III; the remaining two had significant loadings on Factors I and III. It is not profitable to pursue this analysis further except to indicate that this technique permits us to subdivide a large group into like-minded or like-structured subgroups, regardless of the number of variables involved and regardless of the types of distributions that characterize them. It is a type of distribution-free factor analysis. I prefer to regard it as a method for typological analysis. The next step is to find out what the various subtypes have in common, and this can be done by studying the common properties of each of the subgroups either with reference to their response pattern or other characteristics such as vital statistics, socioeconomic background, genetic factors, etc.

SUMMARY

I have tried to point out three major issues. First, the contrast between actuarial and clinical prediction is an unwarranted one. Instead, the two types of prediction supplement each other and the discrepancies between the two should be studied for improving each other reciprocally. Meehl has pointed out that behind the clinician looms the shadow of the actuary and

---

[3] In some of the analyses, the number of cases was cut to 34 and in some to 17, in order to reduce computational labor.

[4] I have since been told by Ledyard R Tucker that computing the correlations was an unnecessary step, since the agreement scores themselves, after correction for chance, were a better basis for the subsequent factor analysis.

TABLE 5
Intercorrelations of Agreement Scores for 17 Normals and 17 Schizophrenics[a]

	1	2	3	4	5	6	7	8	9	10	11	12	13	14	15	16	17	
A		-.011	-.211	-.387	.180	.052	.267	.086	-.008	-.053	.067	-.141	-.512	-.141	-.077	-.220	-.012	1
B	.504		.728	.631	.607	.518	.372	.741	.822	.748	.846	.554	.280	.840	.895	.840	.782	2
C	.414	.856		.478	.387	.277	.034	.673	.731	.683	.682	.605	.506	.836	.743	.783	.654	3
D	.701	.863	.839		.322	.190	.055	.389	.467	.571	.482	.409	.553	.537	.588	.580	.518	4
E	.647	.864	.839	.920		.571	.570	.570	.759	.421	.653	.383	-.066	.491	.609	.544	.485	5
F	.704	.846	.841	.956	.912		.563		.609	.556	.405	.297	-.057	.389	.476	.614	.427	6
G	.229	.516	.517	.447	.442	.356		.345	.347	.284	.399	.096	-.241	.198	.407	.286	.376	7
H	.396	-.034	.030	.172	.179	.234	.032		.732	.610	.801	.436	.123	.701	.938	.665	.686	8
I	.544	-.654	.652	.791	.787	.777	.241	.283		.664	.872	.625	.271	.119	.820	.845	.723	9
J	.128	-.404	-.366	-.250	-.161	-.174	-.325	.417	.095		.677	-.359	.301	.773	.820	.832	.763	10
K	.524	.832	.846	.863	.876	.900	.384	.200	.750	-.209		.553	.195	.785	.872	.771	.759	11
L	.175	.474	.442	.624	.596	.626	.272	.504	.514	-.100	.526		.448	.621	.577	.645	.497	12
M	.115	-.120	-.170	-.119	.003	-.110	-.091	.164	.012	.343	-.065	-.201		.433	.341	.399	.401	13
N	.169	-.197	-.171	-.017	.052	-.067	-.271	.276	.345	.568	-.102	.576	.349		.905	.852	.670	14
O	.610	.775	.658	.825	.786	.832	.258	.170	.743	-.086	.773	.627	-.127	.019		.845	.800	15
P	.325	.014	-.065	.122	.165	.217	-.118	.413	.198	.277	.153	.330	.144	.116	.244		.751	16
Q	.349	.539	.633	.643	.625	.641	.328	.046	.592	-.199	.645	.181	.221	-.377	.446	.129		17
	A	B	C	D	E	F	G	H	I	J	K	L	M	N	O	P	Q	

[a] The correlations above the diagonal are for normals (1–17); those below are for schizophrenics (A–Q).

TABLE 6
Loadings on Rotated Factors Underlying Agreement Scores of 17 Schizophrenics and 17 Normal Controls on the Personal Inquiry Form

Rotated Factor Loadings[a]

		Normals[b]						Schizophrenics				
Type	Subj.	I	II	III	h²	Type	Subj.	I'	II'	III'	IV'	h'²
I	25	.97	.06	.18	.97	I'	D	.98	-.07	.03	.03	.97
I	19	.92	.00	-.36	.98	I'	F	.97	.07	.05	.15	.97
I	12	.91	.09	.10	.86	I'	E	.96	.06	.05	-.05	.92
I	21	.90	-.07	.19	.85	I'	K	.91	-.07	.10	-.01	.84
I	26	.89	.35	-.01	.92	I'	B	.88	-.21	.05	-.27	.90
I	27	.84	.11	.04	.71	I'	C	.86	-.20	.07	-.30	.89
I	18	.83	-.12	.20	.74	I'	O	.84	.03	.17	.11	.74
I	13	.74	.43	.15	.75	I'	I	.84	.41	.09	-.02	.87
I	15	.73	-.27	.05	.61	I'	A	.68	.17	-.20	.24	.59
I	16	.62	-.13	.14	.42	I'	Q	.67	.08	-.37	.19	.63
I	14	.55	.46	.04	.53	II'	M	-.01	.83	.11	.05	.71
+II	23	.25	.74	.06	.62	II'	J	-.16	.69	-.03	.29	.59
-II	17	.45	-.52	-.01	.47	IV'	P	.17	.16	.10	.60	.42
+III	22	.48	.32	.68	.79	I'+III'	L	.54	.02	.69	.22	.81
+I+III	24	.75	.29	.58	.98	—	G	.44	.32	.11	-.21	.35
+I-III	20	.82	.12	-.56	1.00	—	H	.21	-.48	.45	.10	.49
						—	M	-.01	.41	-.38	.09	.32

[a] The significant loadings are underscored.
[b] One case was omitted from this analysis.

that the latter like the undertaker will have the last word. I doubt this. For behind this actuary is another clinician looking over his shoulder to see just where the formula fails and behind him is a new actuary to see whether the corrections introduced by the clinician hold, etc. I would like to make a plea for the clinician to leave "hunch-space" long enough to see how his hunches hold up and for the actuarian to leave hyperspace long enough to see whether his canonical formulas are applicable and what modifications they need for meeting the demands of the clinic.

Second, there is a need for more attention to the statistical problem of the evaluation of the individual case. The next breakthrough in our field is clinical statistics—the gearing of our powerful methods to the consideration of the individual case.

Third, there are signs on the horizon that some type of breakthrough has already taken place. The emergence of interest in pattern analyses or typological analysis is beginning to make a dent in the interaction between clinician and psychometrician. By providing like-minded or like-structured subgroups, it becomes possible to apply present-day statistics to homogeneous groups in our clinical population. This is the first step in the rediscovery of the individual. Our second most important problem today is to find the pertinent variables for classifying the groups into homogeneous subgroups. Here a reorientation in psychology is called for. But what are the pertinent variables for the description of man? Factor-analytic methods have attempted to answer this question. Factor analysis, however, has been applied largely to the conceptual responses of man. The psychomotor, sensory, and physiological levels of response have hardly been tapped in factorial studies. But the perceptual and conceptual functions are largely dependent upon man's past experience and to a lesser extent on the immediate "here and now" effects of brain function.

As long as we limit ourselves to the perceptual and conceptual levels, we could regard man as an empty organism. When we begin to examine the behavior of patients we often find that the conceptual area is relatively intact. The functions which have been ingrained in the individual are generally unaltered by shock therapy, psychosurgery, and by the disease process itself. The physiological, sensory, and psychomotor levels, and the stimulus-bound perceptual level, reflecting as they do immediate brain functioning, are more pertinent for detecting the deviations of the mind.[5] When we develop better techniques for tapping these functions, and apply suitable in-

[5] Further discussion of this point and a proposed schema for classifying behavior categories and stimulus classes can be found in Burdock, Sutton, and Zubin (3).

dividual-centered statistical techniques, we may resolve much of the conflict that now exists between the clinic and the laboratory.

REFERENCES

1. Ach, N. *Analyse des Willens. Handbuch der biologischen Arbeitsmethoden.* Abt. VI, Teil E. Berlin: Urban & Schwarzenberg, 1935.
2. Bronowski, J. *The common sense of science.* Cambridge, Mass.: Harvard Univer. Press, 1953.
3. Burdock, E. I., Sutton, S., & Zubin, J. Personality and psychopathology. *Journal of Abnormal and Social Psychology,* 1958, 56, 18–30.
4. Burdock, E. I., & Zubin, J. A rationale for the classification of experimental techniques in abnormal psychology. *Journal of Genetic Psychology,* 1956, 55, 35–49.
5. Davis, R. J. A comparison of the stability of the measures of critical flicker-fusion made at two different light-dark ratios as provided by the episoco-tister and the strobotac. M.A. dissertation, Columbia Univer., 1952.
6. Huxley, J. S. Introductory: towards the new systematics. In J. S. Huxley (Ed.), *The new systematics.* Oxford, 1940. Pp. 1–46.
7. Kaplan, A. Definition and specification of meaning. *Journal of Philosophy,* 1946, 43, 281–288.
8. Landis, C., & Zubin, J. Personal Inquiry Form. New York: New York Psychiatric Institute, 1934. (For experimental use only.)
9. Landis, C., & Zubin, J. The effect of thonzylamine hydrochloride and phenobarbital sodium on certain psychological functions. *Journal of Psychology,* 1951, 31, 181–200.
10. Meehl, P. E. *Clinical vs. statistical prediction: a theoretical analysis and a review of the evidence.* Minneapolis: Univer. of Minnesota Press, 1954.
11. Reichenbach, H. *Experience and prediction.* Chicago: Univer. of Chicago Press, 1938.
12. Zubin, J. Sociobiological types and methods for their isolation. *Psychiatry,* 1938, 1, 237–247.
13. Zubin, J. A technique for measuring like-mindedness. *Journal of Abnormal and Social Psychology,* 1938, 33, 508–516.

APPENDIX

APPENDIX

Past chairmen of the Invitational Conference on Testing Problems, photographed at the 25th Conference in New York, October 1964. Left to right, *front row:* Ralph F. Berdie, Roger T. Lennon, John B. Carroll, Eric F. Gardner, Alexander G. Wesman, Chester W. Harris. *Second row:* Dorothy Adkins, Ben D. Wood, H. H. Remmers, E. F. Lindquist, John M. Stalnaker, Herschel T. Manuel, Henry Chauncey. *Third row:* John C. Flanagan, Oscar K. Buros, Robert L. Thorndike, Arthur E. Traxler, Henry S. Dyer, Walter N. Durost, George K. Bennett, Edward E. Cureton. *Not shown:* Paul L. Dressel (unable to attend); H. E. Hawkes, Irving Lorge, and George F. Zook (deceased).

COMPLETE LIST OF CONFERENCE PAPERS

Because of the criteria employed in the selection of papers—described in the Preface—many excellent papers could not be included in this volume. Moreover, the very nature of the Invitational Conference, in which papers are given by invitation only, insures a high level of quality throughout. For these reasons, the complete list of papers presented at each conference is given below.

During the first two meetings, in 1936 and 1937, there were no formal papers. While prepared papers by individual speakers were presented from 1938 on, no *Proceedings* were published prior to 1946. The papers presented at the 1946 and 1947 conferences were published in the *American Council on Education Studies* (Series I—Reports of Committees and Conferences, Vol. 11, No. 28, August 1947 and Vol. 12, No. 32, October 1948). Beginning with the 1948 conference, all papers have appeared in the annual *Proceedings of the Invitational Conference on Testing Problems*, published and distributed by Educational Testing Service.

1936 Chairman: H. E. Hawkes
Discussion of Common Problems
Role of a Central Agency

1937 Chairmen: George F. Zook and H. E. Hawkes
Reports on Status of State Testing Programs
Machine Scoring Techniques, Costs, and Possible Improvements
Outline of Program of Cooperation on Common Problems

1938 Chairmen: George F. Zook, Ben D. Wood, and H. H. Remmers
Growth of State Testing Programs—*George F. Zook*
A National Perspective on Testing and Guidance—*Walter V. Bingham*
The Use of Test Results—*Herschel T. Manuel*
Bibliography of Tests and Reviews—*Oscar K. Buros*
Theoretical and Technical Aspects of Measurement and Standardization—*Herbert A. Toops*
The Interchange of Test Materials—*E. F. Lindquist*
Scaled Scores—*John C. Flanagan*
The Use and Costs of Machine Scoring—*E. C. Schroedel*

1939 Chairman: H. H. Remmers
Limitations of Statewide and Regional Testing Programs—*Joseph U. Yarborough*

Possibilities and Limitations of Regional and National Testing Programs—*Herschel T. Manuel*

A Proposal for a "Standard Million" for Compiling Norms—*Herbert A. Toops*

Possibilities and Limitations of Interchange of Test Materials—*Eleroy L. Stromberg* and *E. F. Lindquist*

The Testing Programs of the Joint Committee of the National Office Managers Association and the Business Council of the Business Education Association—*William J. E. Crissy*

Factor Analysis from the Point of View of the Practical Test Man (with special reference to L. L. Thurstone's Tests for Primary Mental Abilities)—*John M. Stalnaker*

Some Implications of Scaled Scores—*John C. Flanagan*

The Present Status of Machine Scoring and Machine Item Analysis—*E. C. Schroedel* (read by W. J. McNamara)

1940 Chairman: E. F. Lindquist

Establishing and Reporting Norms—*Edward E. Cureton*

Report on the American Council Study of Educational Evaluation—*Phillip J. Rulon*

The Classification of Military Personnel—*Walter V. Bingham*

Guidance as a Means of Restoring Quality to Present-Day Education—*Joseph U. Yarborough*

The Calculation and Reporting of Test Reliability Coefficients—*M. W. Richardson*

Efficient Procedures in Collating and Reporting Results in Educational Testing Programs—*John M. Stalnaker*

1941 Chairman: John M. Stalnaker

The Objectives and Procedures of a Statewide Testing Program—*D. D. Feder*

The Validity of Army Classification Tests—*T. W. Harrell and Lt. H. W. Bues, Jr.*

The Influence of Tests on Teaching—*Ralph W. Tyler*

Some Problems Associated with the Critical Evaluation of Tests—*Oscar K. Buros*

The Concept of Reliability—*Paul Horst*

Problems in the Measurement of Reading—*Arthur E. Traxler*

1942– 1945 War years—no meetings

1946 Chairman: Herschel T. Manuel

The Measurement Book Project of the American Council on Education—*E. F. Lindquist*

Units and Norms in Educational Measurement—*John C. Flanagan*

Validity of Educational Tests—*Phillip J. Rulon*

Logical Dilemmas in the Estimation of Reliability—*Robert L. Thorndike*

The Projects of the Graduate Record Office—*Kenneth W. Vaughn*

Norms and the Individual Pupil—*Lee J. Cronbach*
Norms and the Individual Community—*Robert L. Thorndike*
Norms for Scholastic Aptitude and Achievement Tests of Independent
  Secondary School Pupils—*Arthur E. Traxler*
Norms of Achievement by Schools—*E. F. Lindquist*
Some Basic Problems Concerning Achievement Test Norms at the Ele-
  mentary and Intermediate Grades—*Walter N. Durost*

1949   Chairman: Oscar K. Buros

Panel I: Influence of Cultural Background on Test Performance
Some Implications of Cultural Factors for Test Construction—*Anne
  Anastasi*
Influence of Cultural Background on Test Performance—*Ernest A.
  Haggard*
Influence of Cultural Background on Test Performance—*William
  Stephenson*
Influence of Cultural Background on Predictive Test Scores—*William W.
  Turnbull*

Panel II: Uses and Limitations of Factor Analysis in Psychological Research—*George K. Bennett, H. J. Eysenck,* and *Paul Horst*

Panel III: Information Which Should Be Provided by Test Publishers and
  Testing Agencies on the Validity and Use of Their Tests
Aptitude and Intelligence Tests—*Herbert S. Conrad*
Achievement Tests—*Paul L. Dressel*
Personality Tests—*Laurance F. Shaffer*

1950   Chairman: Robert L. Thorndike

Panel I: Validation of Professional Aptitude Batteries
Tests for Accounting—*Arthur E. Traxler* and *Robert Jacobs*
Tests for Law—*A. Pemberton Johnson*
Tests for Dentistry—*Shailer Peterson*
Tests for Medicine—*John M. Stalnaker*

Address: Creative Talent—*L. L. Thurstone*

Panel II: Criteria for the Evaluation of Achievement Tests
From the Point of View of the Test Editor—*Frederick B. Davis*
From the Point of View of the Subject Matter Specialist—*Joseph J.
  Schwab*
From the Point of View of Their Internal Statistics—*John B. Carroll*
From the Point of View of Their External Statistical Relationships—
  Harold Gulliksen

1951   Chairman: Henry S. Dyer

Panel I: The Supply and Identification of High Level Talent
The Supply and Identification of High Level Talent: Three Basic Prob-
  lems—*Toby Oxtoby*
Stretching the Supply of High Level Talent—*John T. Dailey*

Psychological and Sociological Factors Affecting the Supply of Talent—
  Robert J. Havighurst
A Look Ahead—*Robert L. Thorndike*

Address: Problems of Evaluation in General Education—*Paul L. Dressel*

Luncheon address: Military Manpower Problems—*Major General Lewis B. Hershey*

Panel II: The Development of Useful Tests for the Measurement of Non-
  intellectual Functions
Tests for the Measurement of Personal Effectiveness—*Donald W. MacKinnon*
Personality Structure and Personality Measurement—*Raymond B. Cattell*
Discussion of MacKinnon Paper—*John Dollard*
Discussion of Cattell Paper—*Silvan S. Tomkins*

1952 Chairman: George K. Bennett

Panel I: Selecting Appropriate Score Scales for Tests
The Importance of Reference Groups in Scaling Procedure—*Eric F. Gardner*
Scales Minimizing the Importance of Reference Groups—*Ledyard R Tucker*
Discussion—*John C. Flanagan*
Discussion—*E. F. Lindquist*

Address: The Measurement of Human Motivation: An Experimental Approach—*David C. McClelland*

Luncheon Symposium: Trends in Public Opinion Polling Since 1948 and
  Their Probable Effect on 1952 Election Predictions
What About the Sampling? A Bit of Pseudohistory—*Frederick F. Stephan*
Interviewing—*Herbert Hyman*
Analysis—*Samuel Stouffer*

Panel II: Techniques for the Development of Unbiased Tests
Difference or Bias in Tests of Intelligence—*Irving Lorge*
A Semantic Test of Intelligence—*Phillip J. Rulon*
Techniques for the Development of Unbiased Tests—*Ernest A. Haggard*
Discussion of Papers—*Quinn McNemar*
Reply to McNemar—*Ernest A. Haggard*

1953 Chairman: Walter N. Durost

General Meeting: Improving Evaluation of Educational Outcomes at the
  College Level
How an Examination Service Helps College Teachers to Give Better
  Tests—*Robert L. Ebel*
The Evaluation Dividend for the Individual Student—*Lily Detchen*
Evaluation as Instruction—*Paul L. Dressel*

Section I: Individual Versus Group Decision Making—*Irving Lorge*

Section II: Problems and Procedures in Profile Analysis
An Application of Profile Similarity Techniques to Rorschach Data on
2,161 Marine Corps Officer Candidates—*O. F. Anderhalter*
A Geometric Model for the Profile Problem—*David V. Tiedeman*

Section III: Making Test Results Meaningful
Bringing National and Regional Testing Programs into Local Schools—
Ralph F. Berdie
Making Testing Meaningful to Teachers Through Local Test Construc-
tion and Analysis of Test Data—*Max D. Engelhart*
The Test Manual as a Medium of Communication—*Roger T. Lennon*

Section IV: The Teaching of Educational Measurement
The Introductory Course in Educational Measurement—*Victor H. Noll*
In-Service Training in Measurement by Means of University Extension
Courses—*William C. Kvaraceus*
Training for Research in Psychological Measurement—*Harold Gulliksen*

Section V: The Interview as an Evaluation Technique
An Evaluation of the Interview as a Selective Technique—*E. Lowell Kelly*
Inter-Personal Aspects of the Interview—Procedural Techniques and Re-
search Practice—*William J. E. Crissy*
The Interview in Personality Appraisal—*Nevitt Sanford*

Luncheon Address: Measurement for the Joint Betterment of Individual
and Society—*Truman L. Kelley*

General Meeting: Impact of Machines and Devices on Developments in
Testing and Related Fields
The IBM Test Scoring Machine: An Evaluation—*Arthur E. Traxler*
The University Service Bureau—*John E. Alman*
Use of Electronic Computing Machines for Testing Problems—*Ledyard
R Tucker*
AGO Machines for Test Analysis—*Harry H. Harman* and *Bertha P.
Harper*
New Developments in Test Scoring Machines—*Elmer J. Hankes*
The Iowa Electronic Test Processing Equipment—*E. F. Lindquist*
Speaking for International Business Machines—*Philip H. Bradley*

1954 Chairman: Edward E. Cureton

General Meeting: Application of Information Theory to Testing
Multiple Assignments of Persons to Jobs—*Paul S. Dwyer*
New Light on Test Strategy from Decision Theory—*Lee J. Cronbach*
The Relation Between Uncertainty and Variance—*William J. McGill*

Section I: Recent Advances in Psychometric Methods
Some Recent Results in Latent Structure Analysis—*T. W. Anderson*
The "Moderator Variable" as a Useful Tool in Prediction—*David R.
Saunders*
A Method of Factoring without Communalities—*L. L. Thurstone*

Section II: Evaluating Group Interaction

A New Technique for Measuring Individual Differences in Conformity to Group Judgment—*Richard S. Crutchfield*

The Russell Sage Social Relations Test: A Measure of Group Problem-Solving Skills in Elementary School Children—*Dora E. Damrin*

Description of Group Characteristics—*John K. Hemphill*

Luncheon Address: ". . . And Have Not Wisdom"—*Daniel Starch*

General Meeting: New Developments in the Education of Abler Students
Acceleration: Basic Principles and Recent Research—*Sidney L. Pressey*
College Admission with Advanced Standing—*William H. Cornog*
Special Treatment for Abler Students and Its Relation to National Man-power—*Dael L. Wolfle*

1955 Chairman: Ralph F. Berdie

General Meeting: Multifactor Ability Test Batteries in Counseling and Guidance
The Use of Multifactor Aptitude Tests in School Counseling—*Robert D. North*
The Use of the General Aptitude Test Battery in the Employment Service—*Pauline K. Anderson*
Service Tests of Multiple Aptitudes—*Edward E. Cureton*
The Logic of and Assumptions Underlying Differential Testing—*John W. French*

General Meeting: Communication of Test Information
Helping Students Understand Test Information—*John W. Gustad*
The Obligations of the Test User—*Alexander G. Wesman*
How Basic Organization Influences Testing—*David H. Dingilian*

Luncheon Address: The Psychologist and Society—*Morris S. Viteles*

Panel Discussion: Clinical Versus Actuarial Prediction
Clinical and Actuarial Prediction in a Setting of Action Research—*Nevitt Sanford*
Clinical Versus Actuarial Prediction—*Charles C. McArthur*
Clinical Versus Actuarial Prediction: A Pseudo-Problem—*Joseph Zubin*
Clinical Versus Actuarial Prediction—*Lloyd G. Humphreys*
Discussion of Papers—*Paul E. Meehl*

1956 Chairman: Irving Lorge
Theme: Testing—Then and Now

General Meeting: Changing Concepts of Intelligence
A New Look at the Curve of Intelligence—*Nancy Bayley*
Implications for Test Construction—*Thelma G. Thurstone*

General Meeting: Changing Concepts of Personality
Concepts of Personality—Then and Now—*Gardner Murphy*
Changing Methods of Appraising Personality—*Morris Krugman*

Luncheon Address: Testing—Then and Now—*Ben D. Wood*

General Meeting: The Changing Curriculum and Testing

The Curriculum—Then and Now—*Ralph W. Tyler*
New Kinds of Students and New Ways of Testing Achievement—*Louis M. Hacker*
Measuring Achievement in a Changing Curriculum—*John E. Dobbin*

1957 Chairman: Arthur E. Traxler
Theme: Improving the Quality and Scope of Measurement

Session I: Improving Criteria for Educational and Psychological Measurement
Improving Criteria for Complex Mental Processes—*Robert C. Wilson*
Criteria of Nonintellectual Aspects of Personality—*Morris I. Stein*

Session II: Improving Measurement Through Better Exercise Writing
Exercise Writing in the Field of the Humanities—*Paul B. Diederich*
Exercise Writing in the Natural Sciences—*Leo Nedelsky*
Exercise Writing in the Social Sciences—*Max D. Engelhart*

Luncheon Address: Prediction of Educational and Vocational Success Through Interest Measurement—*Edward K. Strong, Jr.*

Session III: Test Users' Problems as Guides to Better Measurement
The School Administrator's Problems for Testers—*Paul T. Rankin*
Discussion of the School Administrator's Problems—*Roger T. Lennon*
The Guidance Director's Problems and Suggestions for the Test Specialist—*Edward Landy*
The Consumer and the Producer—*Donald E. Super*

1958 Chairman: Roger T. Lennon

Session I
Measurement of Cognitive Abilities at the Preschool and Early Childhood Level—*Dorothea A. McCarthy*
Prediction of Maladjustive Behavior—*William C. Kvaraceus*

Session II
A Theory of Test Response—*Jane Loevinger*
Discussion—*David V. Tiedeman*
Measurement and Prediction of Teacher Effectiveness—*David G. Ryans*
Discussion—*Harry B. Gilbert*

Luncheon Address: Some Observations on Soviet Education—*Henry Chauncey*

Session III
What Kinds of Tests for College Admission and Scholarship Programs?—*Robert L. Ebel*
Criteria for Selecting Tests for College Admissions and Scholarship Programs—*John C. Flanagan*
The Nature of the Problem of Improving Scholarship and College Entrance Examinations—*E. F. Lindquist*
What Kinds of Tests for College Admission and Scholarship Programs?—*Alexander G. Wesman*

1959 Chairman: Dorothy Adkins
Theme: The Impact of Testing on the Educational Process

Session I
What Testing Does to Teachers and Students—*Ralph W. Tyler*
Some Lessons from High School Physics—*Walter C. Michels*
Education 1975—*Paul Woodring*

Luncheon Address: The 1959 Salzburg Seminar for American Studies;
Various Aspects of Comparative Education—*James B. Conant*

Session II
Intrinsically Programmed Teaching Devices—*Norman A. Crowder*
Teaching Machines: An Application of Principles from the Laboratory
—*James G. Holland*
Self-Correcting Homework in English—*Paul B. Diederich*

1960 Chairman: John B. Carroll

Session I: Research in Testing and the Cooperative Research Program
The Support of Measurement Projects by the Cooperative Research Pro-
gram—*Roy M. Hall, Howard F. Hjelm, Herbert S. Conrad*
In-Basket Tests and Factors in Administrative Performance—*Norman
Frederiksen*
Models of Teacher Behavior in the Classroom—*Robert M. W. Travers*
The Prediction of Talented Behavior in the Junior High School—*Carson
McGuire*

Luncheon Address: The Pace of Change—*Arthur S. Adams*

Session II: Testing in the Language Arts
Testing for Elegance—*Harold C. Martin*
Competency First: New Tests in Foreign Languages—*Wilmarth H. Starr*
Estimating Structure in Prose—*Irving Lorge*

1961 Chairman: Paul L. Dressel

Session I: Implications of Factor Analysis for Achievement Testing
Factors of Verbal Achievement—*John B. Carroll*
Schools of Thought in Judging Excellence of English Themes—*John W.
French*
Factor Analysis of Relevance Judgments: An Approach to Content
Validity—*Ledyard R Tucker*

Session II: Use of Achievement Tests in Award of Course Credit
Credit and the Advanced Placement Program—*Jack N. Arbolino*
The Examining Program at Antioch College—*Ruth D. Churchill*
Examinations and Instruction by Television—*Clifford G. Erickson*
Credit and Waiver Examinations at Michigan State University—*Willard
G. Warrington*

Luncheon Address: Management of the Learning Environment—*John E.
Ivey, Jr.*

In Memoriam: Irving Lorge—*Robert L. Thorndike*

Session III: Extended Conceptions of Evaluation in Higher Education
Measuring the Quality of a College or University—*Dewey B. Stuit*
The Nature and Use of Institutional Research—*James I. Doi*

1962 Chairman: Eric F. Gardner

Session I: Creativity
Knowledge and Creativity—*Theodore C. Denise* and *Hobert W. Burns*
Potentiality for Creativity and Its Measurement—*J. P. Guilford*
Some Methodological Issues in the Study of Creativity—*Robert L. Thorndike*

Session II: Comparability of Scores
Can Useful General-Purpose Equivalency Tables Be Prepared for Different College Admissions Tests?—*William H. Angoff*

Luncheon Address: Approaches to the Measurement of Intellectual Disposition—*T. R. McConnell*

Session III: Processing Educational Data
Information Systems in the Educational Environment—*Charles R. DeCarlo*
The Role of Machines in Educational Decision-Making—*Ralph W. Tyler*

1963 Chairman: Alexander G. Wesman

Session I: Basic Concepts in Measurement—1963
Norms—*Roger T. Lennon*
Reliability—*Robert L. Thorndike*
Some Current Developments in the Measurement and Interpretation of Test Validity—*Anne Anastasi*

Session II: Testing and the Medical Profession
Programmed Testing in the Examinations of the National Board of Medical Examiners—*John P. Hubbard*
Alternate Criteria in Medical Education and Their Correlates—*E. Lowell Kelly*

Luncheon Address: Growing—*Jerome S. Bruner*

Session III: Implications and Consequences of Measurement
Ability and Performance—*Warren G. Findley*
Personality Measurement and College Performance—*Samuel Messick*
The Social Consequences of Educational Testing—*Robert L. Ebel*

1964 Chairman: Chester W. Harris

Session I: Effects of Testing
A Test-Dominated Society: China, 1115 B.C.–1905 A.D.—*Philip H. DuBois*
The Subject Looks at Psychological Tests—*Donald W. Fiske*

Session II: Technical Advances
The Structure of Interrelations among Intelligence Tests—*Louis Guttman*
Psychometric Approaches to Factor Analysis—*Henry F. Kaiser*
Experiments in Multimode Factor Analysis—*Ledyard R Tucker*

INDEXES

INDEXES

SUBJECT INDEX

AUTHOR INDEX

Pages of selections are shown in boldface type. All authors are indexed, not only when cited by name, but also when cited by reference number.